Traditions & Encounters

CONNECT WITH THE
Stories
OF HISTORY

Students will readily engage with the past when they see that history is the work of real people. Bentley and Ziegler enliven world history through the vivid tales of merchants, missionaries, monarchs, explorers, conquerors, and commoners across cultures:

> I n 629 . . . in defiance of the [Chinese] emperor [Tang Taizong], a young Buddhist monk slipped past imperial watchtowers under cover of darkness and made his way west. His name was Xuanzang, and his destination was India, homeland of Buddhism . . . [where he would] visit the holy sites of Buddhism, and . . . learn about Buddhism from the purest sources. Xuanzang could not have imagined the difficulties he would face. Immediately after his departure from China, his guide abandoned him in the Gobi desert. After losing his water bag and collapsing in the heat, Xuanzang made his way to the oasis town of Turpan on the silk roads . . . [Then] Xuanzang crossed three of the world's highest mountain ranges—the Tian Shan, Hindu Kush, and Pamir ranges—and lost one-third of his party. . . . Yet Xuanzang persisted and arrived in India in 630. By the time of his return [to Chang'an] in 645, Xuanzang had logged more than 16,000 kilometers (10,000 miles) on the road.

MAP 12.1

The silk roads, 200 B.C.E.–300 C.E.
Note the extent of the land and sea routes known collectively as the silk roads.

Consider the political and economic conditions that would be necessary for regular travel and trade across the silk roads.

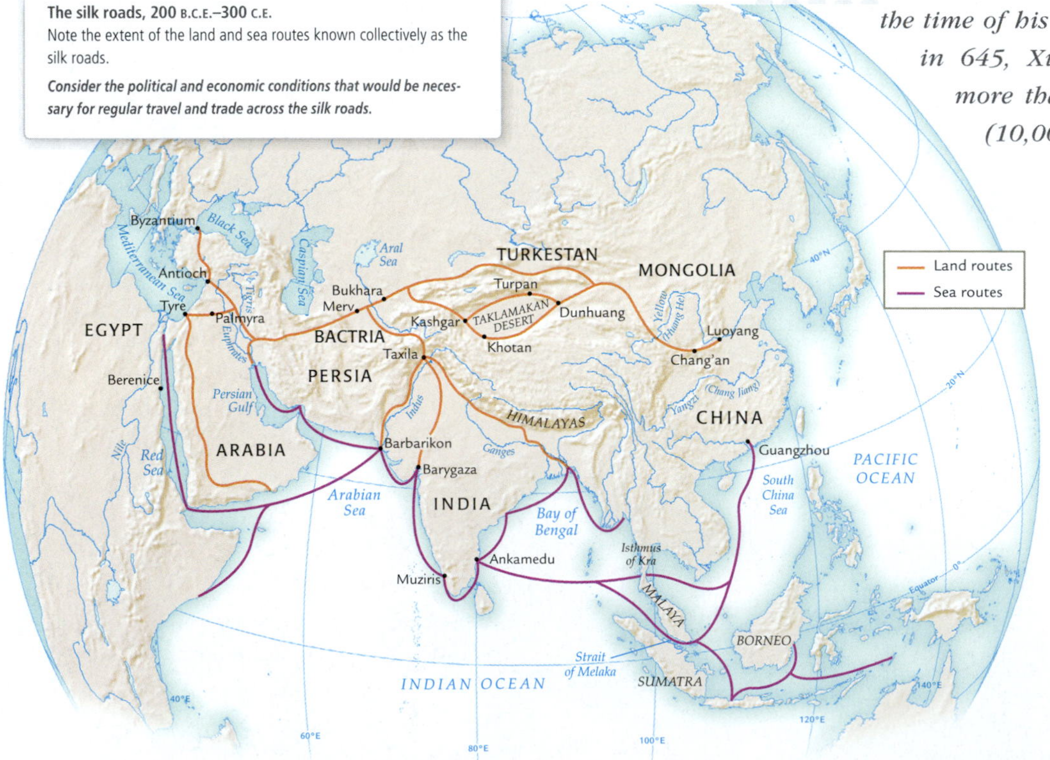

- Vivid stories keep students involved and help them to get the most from their study of world history.

- Clear, vibrant, precise maps with extended captions—entirely redesigned for this edition—help students put the experiences of individual historical actors in geographical context.

CONNECT TO THE
Experience
OF HISTORY

Students will experience history interactively:

- With *Connect History*—a visual, auditory, and interactive online experience—students no longer skim a text passively for facts and dates to memorize. They engage with what they read through hands-on activities, and they expand upon and apply what they learn in the process.

- Through its features, *Traditions & Encounters* emphasizes the point that history is not just a collection of facts. It is rather a creative effort based on detective work of historians examining evidence from the past and the analysis of themes that cross cultural boundary lines.

- New "Thinking About Traditions" and "Thinking About Encounters" boxes pose critical-thinking questions about the ways these twin themes play out across cultures and time periods.

- Images—paintings, mosaics, photos, posters, sculptures, architecture, and the like—draw students into the related narrative, and extended captions help them learn how to analyze visual clues to the past.

thinking about TRADITIONS

Competing Christianities
The Byzantine empire and western Europe inherited the same Christianity from the late Roman empire. How did Christianity develop along distinct lines in the two regions? What influences contributed to the development of such different understandings of Christianity?

CONNECT TO
Success
IN HISTORY

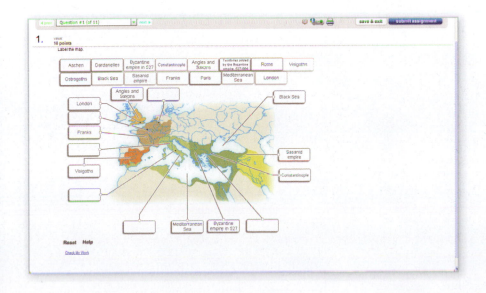

Connect History paves a path to student success:

- *Connect History*, a groundbreaking digital learning solution, helps students study more effectively—confirming what they know and pushing their learning further through engaging activities.

- *Connect History* works in tandem with questions accompanying image captions and primary sources in each chapter and builds a personalized study plan for each student.

- *Connect History* builds critical-thinking skills by placing students in a historical "critical mission" scenario and asking them to examine, evaluate, and analyze relevant data to support a recommended action.

- *Connect History* includes tools for understanding maps and geography, analyzing primary source documents, and writing a research paper (including documenting sources and avoiding plagiarism).

EDITION 5

Traditions & Encounters

A Global Perspective on the Past

Volume II: From 1500 to the Present

Jerry H. Bentley
University of Hawai`i

Herbert F. Ziegler
University of Hawai`i

McGraw Hill

Connect
Learn
Succeed™

Published by McGraw-Hill, an imprint of The McGraw-Hill Companies, Inc., 1221 Avenue of the
Americas, New York, NY 10020. Copyright © 2011, 2008, 2006, 2003, 2000. All rights reserved.
No part of this publication may be reproduced or distributed in any form or by any means, or
stored in a database or retrieval system, without the prior written consent of The McGraw-Hill
Companies, Inc., including, but not limited to, in any network or other electronic storage or
transmission, or broadcast for distance learning.

This book is printed on acid-free paper.

1 2 3 4 5 6 7 8 9 0 DOW/DOW 9 8 7 6 5 4 3 2 1 0

ISBN: 978-0-07736803-6
MHID: 0-07-736803-7

Vice President Editorial: *Michael Ryan*
Publisher: *Christopher Freitag*
Sponsoring Editor: *Matthew Busbridge*
Executive Marketing Manager: *Stacy Best Ruel*
Executive Director of Development: *Lisa Pinto*
Senior Developmental Editor: *Mikola De Roo*
Editorial Coordinators: *Elena Mackawgy, Jaclyn Mautone*
Senior Production Editor: *Carey Eisner*
Art Editor: *Robin Mouat*
Cartography: *Mapping Specialists and Mary Swab*
Design Manager: *Jeanne Schreiber*
Interior Designer: *Amanda Kavanagh*
Cover Designer: *Kirk DouPonce, DogEared Design*
Manager, Photo Research: *Brian J. Pecko*
Buyer II: *Tandra Jorgensen*
Composition: *9/12 Garamond Book by Thompson Type*
Printing: *45# New Era Matte Thin, R.R. Donnelley & Sons*

Cover: Poster: East African Transport: © HIP/Art Resource, NY; Equestrian portrait of Shah Jahan:
© Francis G. Mayer/Corbis; image of Gandhi: © Bettmann/Corbis; Global warming, a digital image
of earth afire: © William Radcliffe/Science Faction/Corbis; Illustration of Dona Marina translating
for Hernan Cortez entering an alliance with Tlaxcala ruler: Benson Latin American Collection,
General Libraries, University of Texas at Austin; Maris Pacifici, detail of Magellan's ship Victory
by Abraham Ortelius, 1589: © Royalty-Free/Corbis; Earth: © istockphoto.com/7nuit

Library of Congress Cataloging-in-Publication Data

Bentley, Jerry H., 1949–
  Traditions & encounters : a global perspective on the past / Jerry Bentley, Herbert
Ziegler. — 5th ed.
      v. cm.
  Includes bibliographical references and index.
  ISBN-13: 978-0-07-736803-6 (v. 2 : softcover : alk. paper)
  ISBN-10: 0-07-736803-7 (v. 2 : softcover : alk. paper)

  1. World history. 2. Intercultural communication—History. I. Ziegler, Herbert F., 1949–
II. Title. III. Title: Traditions and encounters.
  D20.B42 2011
  909—dc22

                                            2010036144

www.mhhe.com

briefcontents

part 5

The Origins of Global Interdependence, 1500 to 1800   462

part 6

An Age of Revolution, Industry, and Empire, 1750 to 1914   618

part 7

Contemporary Global Realignments, 1914 to the Present   760

contents

part 5

The Origins of Global Interdependence, 1500 to 1800 462

part6

An Age of Revolution, Industry, and Empire, 1750 to 1914   618

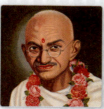

part 7
Contemporary Global Realignments, 1914 to the Present   760

maps

sources from the past

preface

Since its first edition, *Traditions & Encounters* has broken new ground. It has explored the grand scheme of world history as a product of real-life human beings pursuing their individual and collective interests. It has also offered a global perspective on the past by focusing on both the distinctive characteristics of individual societies and the connections that have linked the fortunes of different societies. It has combined a clear chronological framework with the twin themes of tradition and encounter, which help to make the unwieldy story of world history both more manageable and more engaging. From the beginning, *Traditions & Encounters* has offered an inclusive vision of the global past—one that is meaningful and appropriate for the interdependent world of contemporary times.

With this fifth edition, *Traditions & Encounters* takes another bold step and becomes the first truly interactive world history program by integrating an engaging text narrative with an innovative online learning platform, *Connect History.** The narrative and analysis of world history presented in *Traditions & Encounters* are now married to *Connect History*'s hands-on online activities, an adaptive diagnostic, and additional pedagogy, primers, and resources. The result is a unique learning environment that promotes active student learning, student success, and better course results.

(*A fully integrated e-book is included in *Connect Plus History*.)

How does *Traditions & Encounters* help students comprehend what they read?

Traditions & Encounters connects students to the story of world history.

A Cohesive Organization that Frames Global History into Seven Eras.
How is it possible to make sense of the entire human past? Given the diversity of human societies, gathering and organizing the sheer mass of information in a meaningful way is a daunting challenge for any world history survey course. *Traditions & Encounters* addresses this challenge through its seven-part chronological organization, which enables students to understand the development of the world through time while also exploring broader, big-picture thematic issues in world history.

Captivating Stories of World History, in Geographical Context.
Chapter-opening "Eyewitness" vignettes and an engaging narrative of the people and processes that have shaped world history work together with a highly praised map program to lend a strong framework to historical knowledge—clearly connecting the *who* and the *what* of world history (individual human actors, networks of communication and exchange, significant events, and global processes) to the *when* and the *where* (the chronological and geographical context).

Online Activities in *Connect History* Turn Reading about World History into a Hands-On, Sensory Learning Experience. The activities in *Connect History,* a new Web-based assignment and assessment platform, are based on the narrative content of *Traditions & Encounters,* so they build on what students learn from reading the text and push them to explore that knowledge at greater depth. Making full use of the Web's flexibility as a learning platform, the activities in *Connect History* take a range of forms—textual, audio, and visual—and address multiple learning styles. Some exercises require students to interact with and analyze images and primary sources; others prompt students to compare and contrast the political structures or religious beliefs of different cultures they've been reading about; still others assess students' knowledge of chronology or geography. Across the board, these activities prompt active dialogue between student and text. As a result, students go beyond reading to engagement and interaction with the tools of world history.

How does *Traditions & Encounters* guide students from seeing history as an assortment of facts to a hands-on, interactive engagement with the past?

Traditions & Encounters connects students to the experience of world history.

A Pair of Themes Organize the Complexity of Global Human Experience. Since its first edition, *Traditions & Encounters* has used its title's twin themes to bring focus to the vastness of world history. The "tradition" theme draws attention to the distinctive political, social, economic, and cultural traditions that the world's peoples have devised to organize their societies and guide their affairs:

> *What forms of political leadership have different peoples devised?* • *How have the world's peoples exploited natural resources to provide themselves with food, shelter, and other necessities?* • *What forms of social organization have different peoples developed, on the basis of birth, class, wealth, gender, ethnicity, or other criteria?* • *What kinds of religious beliefs have the world's peoples espoused, which scientific and philosophical ideas have they explored, and what artistic and cultural practices have they pursued?*

The "encounter" theme directs attention to the networks of transportation, communication, and exchange that have linked individual societies to one another through processes of cross-cultural interaction:

> *Why have individuals left their own societies to explore the larger world?* • *What kinds of relationships did they establish with their counterparts in other societies?* • *What networks of transportation, communication, and exchange did they construct to sustain interactions among different societies?* • *What effects did these exchanges have on the societies that engaged in dealings with one another?*

Through new chapter-level and part-level features, the hallmark twin themes of *Traditions & Encounters* emerge in greater clarity than ever before in this fifth edition. As a result, students have resources that enable them to move beyond the facts of history and examine the past critically, analyze causes and effects, and recognize similarities and differences across world regions and time periods. By digging deeper into the implications of world history's stories—not just the *who,* the *what,* and the *where,* but also the *why* and the *how*—students can make sense of the human past.

Connect History Activities, Learning Scenarios, and Intellectual Tools that Hone Students' Analytical Skills. *Connect History* offers a range of online resources and assignments designed to cultivate the skills that enable students to think like historians—from geography diagnostics and primary source tutorials to exercises in the critical analysis of historical images, artifacts, and primary sources. These tools help students read maps, understand geography, question primary sources and other historical evidence, and develop the skills of analysis and synthesis.

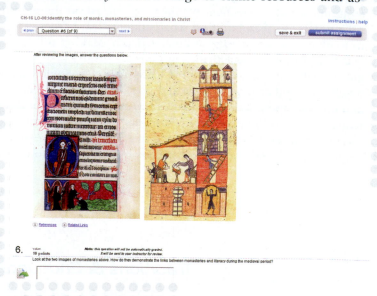

How does **Traditions & Encounters** enable students to comprehend reading assignments, think critically about important issues, and prepare for essays and exams?

Traditions & Encounters connects students to success in your world history course.

Comprehensive Chapter-Ending Pedagogy and Current Scholarship. Chronology boxes outline each chapter's most important dates and events. "In Perspective" sections, chapter-ending summaries, offer brief overviews of significant developments. "For Further Reading" sections, fully updated for the fifth edition, mention the most important works available about the chapter's topics and serve as a resource for further study or research projects. A running pronunciation guide appearing at the bottom of pages and an end-of-book glossary help students with unfamiliar names and terms.

Digital Assignments that Assess and Improve Students' Knowledge Base. The groundbreaking digital tools in *Connect History* enable students reading *Traditions & Encounters* to create a personalized study plan tailored to their own learning styles. By using the online diagnostics, exercises, and activities that *Connect History* provides for every chapter of *Traditions & Encounters,* students can clearly identify what they know well and what they need to study more carefully. The interactivity and assessment feedback of *Connect History* reinforces what students read, ensuring that they genuinely understand events and their sequence, key historical developments in chronological and geographical context, important concepts, and cause-and-effect relationships. As a result, students not only read more, but they also devote their studying time and energy to the most useful issues, and they are able to think and write critically about what they read.

CHANGES FOR THE FIFTH EDITION

PART 1: The Early Complex Societies, 3500 to 500 B.C.E.

CHAPTER 1: Before History

Revised discussions of early Homo sapiens *and* Homo erectus *use of language and communication, and expanded discussion on origins of agriculture*

CHAPTER 5: Early Society in East Asia

Expanded discussion of iron weapons in the Zhou dynasty

CHAPTER 6: Early Societies in the Americas and Oceania

Expanded discussion of migrations to the Americas and Oceania and revised discussion of Olmec influence in Mesoamerica

PART 2: The Formation of Classical Societies, 500 B.C.E. to 500 C.E.

CHAPTER 7: The Empires of Persia

Revised discussion of Xerxes' Persian rule in Mesopotamia and Egypt

CHAPTER 8: The Unification of China

Revised and expanded discussion of the Qin and Han emperors' bureaucracy and Ban Zhao's treatise

CHAPTER 9: State, Society, and the Quest for Salvation in India

New discussion of Ghandara-style art

CHAPTER 10: Mediterranean Society: The Greek Phase

Revised discussion of Socrates and new discussion of Greek contributions to the sciences and mathematics

CHAPTER 11: Mediterranean Society: The Roman Phase

New discussion of sea lanes and expanded discussion of Mediterranean trade

CHAPTER 12: Cross-Cultural Exchanges on the Silk Roads

Expanded discussion of the monsoon system and the spread of disease caused by maritime travel

PART 3: The Postclassical Era, 500 to 1000 C.E.

CHAPTER 13: The Expansive Realm of Islam

Revised and expanded discussion of Abbasid capital Baghdad and cultural adaptation

A brand-new "Sources from the Past," Al-Muqaddasi on Iraq in the late tenth century

CHAPTER 14: The Resurgence of Empire in East Asia

New discussion of Wu Zhao and the spread of Buddhism in China

CHAPTER 16: The Two Worlds of Christendom

A "Sources from the Past" included in Chapter 13 in the previous edition, Benjamin of Tudela on the Caliph's Court at Baghdad, now appears in this new chapter.

PART 4: The Acceleration of Cross-Cultural Interaction, 1000 to 1500 C.E.

CHAPTER 17: Nomadic Empires and Eurasian Integration

New discussion of nomadic pastoralists in Central Asia

A brand-new "Sources from the Past," William of Rubruck on Gender Relations among the Mongols

CHAPTER 18: States and Societies of Sub-Saharan Africa

New discussion of Jenne-jeno and revised discussion of the effects of the slave trade in sub-Saharan Africa

CHAPTER 19: The Increasing Influence of Europe

New discussion of the decline of the Byzantine empire and revised discussion of Christian influence during the High Middle Ages, the Bogomils and Cathars heresies, and the Crusades of 1095

PART 5: The Origins of Global Interdependence, 1500 to 1800

CHAPTER 22: Transoceanic Encounters and Global Connections

Revised discussion of the effects of the Columbian exchange of food crops, goods and animals, and world population growth

CHAPTER 23: The Transformation of Europe

New discussion of notable female scientists, including Émilie du Châtelet, and their contributions to the sciences during the sixteenth and seventeenth centuries

A brand-new "Sources from the Past," an excerpt from John Locke's An Essay Concerning Human Understanding

CHAPTER 24: New Worlds: The Americas and Oceania

New discussion of the effects of race and ethnicity on social hierarchy in colonial society

CHAPTER 27: The Islamic Empires

Revised discussion of the Ottoman Empire of early modern times and the three Islamic ruling empires

PART 6: An Age of Revolution, Industry, and Empire, 1750 to 1914

CHAPTER 28: Revolutions and National States in the Atlantic World

Revised and expanded discussion of revolutionary wars in America, France, and Haiti

NEW FEATURES AND CHANGES THROUGHOUT THE TEXT

"Thinking About" features. New "Thinking About Traditions" and "Thinking About Encounters" boxes focus on historical elements that highlight how the twin themes of traditions and encounters play out across cultures and time periods. Each box ends with related critical-thinking questions around these two forces that have shaped world history.

New primary sources. Eight brand-new "Sources from the Past," along with a wealth of resources in *Connect History* provide students with plenty of opportunities for critical analyses of primary sources. The primary sources new to this edition: Al-Muqaddasi, on Iraq in the Late Tenth Century; William of Rubruck on Gender Relations among the Mongols; an excerpt from John Locke's *An Essay Concerning Human Understanding;* The Royal Niger Company Mass-Produces Imperial Control in Africa; Memorandum from the General Syrian Congress; Joseph Stalin on the First Five-Year Plan; an excerpt on climate change from Al Gore's *An Inconvenient Truth,* and Aung San Suu Kyi's "Politics and Family: The Hope of and for Girl Children."

New part-ending features. "State of the World" assesses the global themes covered during the preceding chapters, giving students a thematic big-picture snapshot—both textually and visually using a combined global map and timeline—of the world during a particular period.

New map program. An entirely redesigned map program offers superior clarity, better topographical information, and greater global geographical precision and context with more vivid and distinct use of color and new globe locator icons within regional maps to better orient students. Extended captions with critical-thinking questions enrich students' understanding of the relationship between geography and history.

Fresh, inviting design for visual engagement and ease of use. An engaging, modern, and vivid design with new images and extended captions draws students into the narrative, provides visual cues for remembering content, and makes content easier to parse and digest.

Streamlined organization. Reorganization of content reduces the total number of chapters in the text, making the individual volumes more manageable to teach in one semester.

A new Chapter 16, "The Two Worlds of Christendom," combines elements of former Chapters 13 and 17 and places Europe in a more global perspective.

Elimination of the prior edition's Chapter 38 ("The Bipolar World") integrates the events of the cold war more seamlessly and clearly into coverage of World War II (Chapter 36, "New Conflagrations: World War II") and post–World War II decline of imperialist empires (Chapter 37, "The End of Empire").

Traditions & Encounters

FIFTH EDITION:

more emphasis on critical thinking and analysis

thinking about ENCOUNTERS

Trading-Post Empires

Trading-post empires provided the most prominent spaces for cross-cultural interactions between Europeans, Africans, and Asians. Trading posts also limited European intrusion into Africa and Asia, especially in contrast to the settlement empires of the Americas. What characterized the relations between, for example, the Portuguese and the inhabitants of the Indian Ocean basin? Why were Europeans confined to such posts?

thinking about TRADITIONS

Empires and Their Roads

All the classical empires invested resources in the building of roads and transportation networks that helped them to integrate their vast territories into manageable societies. Compare the road system of the Roman empire with those of the Persian, Han, and Mauryan empires. How did Roman roads complement Mediterranean sea lanes to link regions of the empire?

NEW

"Thinking About Traditions" and "Thinking About Encounters" boxes

These brief boxes—one of each in every chapter—spotlight instances in which the traditions and encounters themes arise in specific historical contexts. Each box ends with critical-thinking questions that prompt reflection about the roles of traditions and encounters in shaping the global past.

NEW

"Sources From the Past"

Every chapter showcases primary source documents—letters, journal entries, political tracts, philosophical reflections, religious writings, and other relevant primary sources. Each source concludes with a critical-thinking question that prompts students to explore the issues raised in the document. The fifth edition includes eight brand-new "Sources from the Past"—including Stalin's thoughts about his First Five-Year Plan and an excerpt from Al Gore's *An Inconvenient Truth*. Together with a wealth of resources in *Connect History*, students have numerous opportunities for critical analyses of primary sources.

sources from the past

The Royal Niger Company Mass-Produces Imperial Control in Africa

The 1880s proved a crucial time for sub-Saharan African societies and European imperial adventurers. European nations at the Berlin Conference set forth the rules by which they would partition and rule African states, and then those nations—such as Great Britain—commissioned companies like the Royal Niger Company to assert imperial prerogatives. To fend off French competitors in the Niger River delta, the British-controlled Royal Niger Company had local rulers sign its "standard treaty," a mass-produced, fill-in-the-blank treaty that essentially ceded trade and political control to the company, and thus to Britain, in what became the British colony of Nigeria.

We, the undersigned Chiefs of _____, with the view to the bettering of the condition of our country and our people, do this day cede to the Royal Niger Company, for ever, the whole of our territory from _____.

We also give to the said Royal Niger Company full power to settle all native disputes arising from any cause whatever, and we pledge ourselves not to enter into any war with other tribes without the sanction of the said Royal Niger Company.

We understand that the said Royal Niger Company have full power to mine, farm, and build in any portion of our country.

We bind ourselves not to have any intercourse with any strangers or foreigners except through the said Royal Niger Company.

In consideration of the foregoing, the said Royal Niger Company (Chartered and Limited) bind themselves not to interfere with any of the native laws or customs of the country, consistently with the maintenance of order and good government.

The said Royal Niger Company agree to pay native owners of land a reasonable amount for any portion they may require.

The said Royal Niger Company bind themselves to protect the said Chiefs from the attacks of any neighboring aggressive tribes.

The said Royal Niger Company also agree to pay the said Chiefs _____ measures native value.

We, the undersigned witnesses, do hereby solemnly declare that the _____ Chiefs whose names are placed opposite their respective crosses have in our presence affixed their crosses of their own free will and consent, and that the said _____ has in our presence affixed his signature.

Done in triplicate at _____, this _____ day of _____, 188__.

Declaration by interpreter I, _____, of _____, do hereby solemnly declare that I am well acquainted with the language of the country, and that on the _____ day of _____, 188__, I truly and faithfully explained the above Agreement to all the Chiefs present, and that they understood its meaning.

For Further Reflection

- What did this "standard treaty" promise to Nigerian leaders, and what was expected in return? Given language barriers and imperial greed, do you believe Nigerians received true and faithful explanations of the treaty's meaning?

Source: Alfred J. Andrea and James H. Overfield, eds. *The Human Record: Sources of Global History*, 3rd ed., vol. 2. Boston: Wadsworth, 1998, pp. 299–300.

stronger support for the main themes discussed in each era

part4
THE ACCELERATION OF CROSS-CULTURAL INTERACTION, 1000 TO 1500 C.E.

The half millennium from 1000 to 1500 C.E. differed markedly from earlier eras. During classical and postclassical times, large, regional societies situated in China, India, southwest Asia, and the Mediterranean basin dominated the eastern hemisphere. Peoples of these lands built extensive networks of trade and communication that spanned the eastern hemisphere and influenced the development of all its societies. From 1000 to 1500 C.E., however, nomadic Turkish and Mongol peoples overran settled societies and established vast transregional empires from China to eastern Europe.

Nomadic peoples toppled several postclassical states, most notably the Song empire in China and the Abbasid realm in southwest Asia. By building empires that transcended the boundaries of postclassical states, however, nomadic Turks and Mongols laid a political foundation for sharply increased trade and communication between peoples of different societies and cultural regions. Indeed, their empires prompted the peoples of the eastern hemisphere to forge closer links than ever before in history. By the mid-fourteenth century, merchants, diplomats, and missionaries traveled frequently between lands as far removed as Italy and China.

Increased trade in the Indian Ocean basin also promoted more intense cross-cultural communications. Maritime trade built on the political stability, economic expansion, and demographic growth of the postclassical era. By the fourteenth century, mariners called at ports throughout the Indian Ocean basin from southeast Asia to India, Ceylon, Arabia, and east Africa, while sea lanes through the South China Sea offered access to ports in the islands of southeast Asia, China, Japan, and Korea. Commercial goods traveled over the Indian Ocean in larger quantities than ever before. From the eleventh century forward, cargoes increasingly consisted of bulky commodities such as timber, coral, steel, building materials, grains, dates, and other foodstuffs. This trade in bulk goods indicated a movement toward economic integration as societies of the Indian Ocean basin concentrated increasingly on cultivating crops or producing goods for export while importing foods or goods that they could not produce very well themselves.

Demographic growth, increased agricultural production, and economic expansion helped to underwrite rapid political development in sub-Saharan Africa and western Europe. Powerful regional states and centralized empires

350

Part Openers

Seven brief part openers—newly designed for this edition—explain the coherence of each major era in human history by introducing the themes that run through all the chapters in each part. Taken together, the seven part openers provide a brief, highly analytical summary of the book's seven-era periodization of the global past.

NEW
"State of the World" Part Closers

Each of the seven parts now ends with a "State of the World" essay, which reassesses the global themes that emerged in the preceding chapters. Each "State of the World" essay is accompanied by a global map and timeline, which offer students a big-picture snapshot of the world that is both textual and visual.

State of the World
A World on the Point of Global Integration

When Christopher Columbus and his crew sailed across the Atlantic Ocean in 1492, the world's peoples were no strangers to long-distance travels and meetings, nor were cross-cultural interactions and exchanges foreign experiences for them. Peoples of the world's three major geographical zones—the eastern hemisphere, the western hemisphere, and Oceania—had been dealing for thousands of years with counterparts from different societies. Even as they built their own distinctive political, social, economic, and cultural traditions, the world's peoples also engaged the larger world beyond their own societies. Their interactions were often hostile or unpleasant, taking the form of raids, wars, campaigns of imperial expansion, or transmissions of epidemic diseases. Yet their engagements frequently took more peaceful and beneficial forms, as trade, missionary activity, technological diffusion, and the spread of agricultural crops linked peoples of different societies.

Until 1492, however, long-distance travels and cross-cultural interactions took place mostly within the world's three broad regions. With rare and fleeting exceptions, peoples of the eastern hemisphere, the western hemisphere, and Oceania kept to their own parts of the world. They rarely possessed nautical technologies that would have enabled them to cross the earth's oceans regularly and carry on sustained relationships with peoples across the waters. Even when sufficient nautical technologies were available, the costs, dangers, and uncertain prospects of transoceanic voyaging mostly discouraged mariners from making efforts to venture beyond their own zones.

Developments of the era 1000 to 1500 were the immediate context for efforts to cross the world's largest bodies of water. Even as they carried out brutal campaigns of conquest, peoples of nomadic pastoral societies forged links between settled agricultural societies throughout Eurasia and created a demand for continuing relationships, particularly commercial relationships. While Turkish and Mongol peoples wielded more influence than any of their nomadic ancestors in Eurasia, Muslim Arab and Persian merchants drew the societies of sub-Saharan Africa increasingly into interaction with others of the eastern hemisphere. The region of the eastern hemisphere with the most to gain from transoceanic voyaging was western Europe, which otherwise had few good routes providing access to lands to the south and east. Thus, even though mariners from China, India, Persia, the Pacific islands, and other lands also possessed effective nautical technologies, it is not surprising that western European peoples most energetically and most systematically explored opportunities to establish maritime networks of travel, transport, trade, communication, and exchange.

In the year 1500 the world stood on the brink of a new era in the experience of humankind. Peoples of the world's three major geographical zones—the eastern hemisphere, the western hemisphere, and Oceania—were poised to enter into permanent and sustained interaction. The results of their engagements were profitable or beneficial for some peoples but difficult or disastrous for others. It is impossible to comprehend them except in context of the acceleration of cross-cultural interaction in the era 1000 to 1500.

460

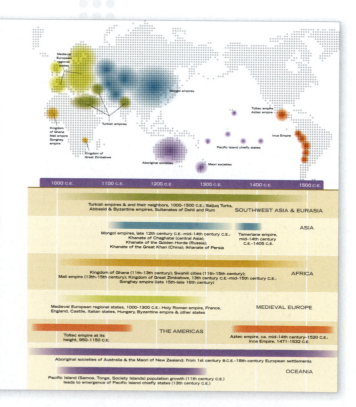

a visual program that deepens the understanding of world history

NEW
Maps Program

The entire map program has been redesigned to make topographical features clearer and boundaries more distinct. Regional maps include new globe locator icons that place individual regions in global context.

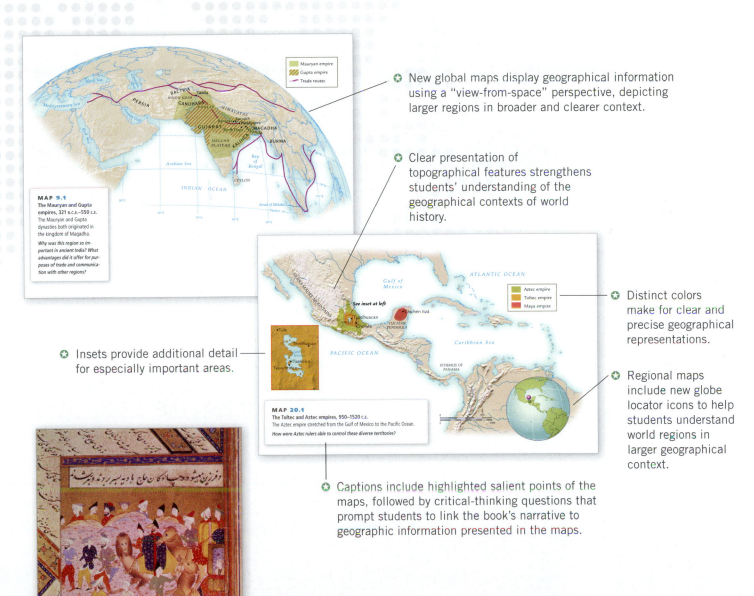

✪ New global maps display geographical information using a "view-from-space" perspective, depicting larger regions in broader and clearer context.

✪ Clear presentation of topographical features strengthens students' understanding of the geographical contexts of world history.

MAP 9.1
The Mauryan and Gupta empires, 321 B.C.E.–550 C.E.
The Mauryan and Gupta dynasties both originated in the kingdom of Magadha.
Why was this region so important in ancient India? What advantages did it offer for purposes of trade and communication with other regions?

✪ Distinct colors make for clear and precise geographical representations.

✪ Insets provide additional detail for especially important areas.

MAP 20.1
The Toltec and Aztec empires, 950–1520 C.E.
The Aztec empire stretched from the Gulf of Mexico to the Pacific Ocean.
How were Aztec rulers able to control these diverse territories?

✪ Regional maps include new globe locator icons to help students understand world regions in larger geographical context.

✪ Captions include highlighted salient points of the maps, followed by critical-thinking questions that prompt students to link the book's narrative to geographic information presented in the maps.

Integrated Illustrations Program

Images that personalize the past by depicting everyday individuals at work and play are well integrated with the larger narrative, enhancing and supporting the themes of traditions and encounters.

A watercolor painting from sixteenth-century Iran depicts a caravan of pilgrims traveling to Mecca while making the hajj. In what ways did the hajj facilitate social and business relationships?

✪ Critical-thinking questions enable students to analyze Illustrations in the historical and cultural contexts discussed in the text.

a brief note on usage

This book qualifies dates as B.C.E. ("Before the Common Era") or C.E. ("Common Era"). In practice, B.C.E. refers to the same epoch as B.C. ("Before Christ"), and C.E. refers to the same epoch as A.D. (*Anno Domini,* a Latin term meaning "in the year of the Lord"). As historical study becomes a global, multicultural enterprise, however, scholars increasingly prefer terminology that does not apply the standards of one society to all the others. Thus reference in this book to B.C.E. and C.E. reflects emerging scholarly convention concerning the qualification of historical dates.

Measurements of length and distance appear here according to the metric system, followed by their English-system equivalents in parentheses.

The book transliterates Chinese names and terms into English according to the *pinyin* system, which has largely displaced the more cumbersome Wade-Giles system. Transliteration of names and terms from other languages follows contemporary scholarly conventions.

supplements

PRIMARY SOURCE INVESTIGATOR

McGraw-Hill's Primary Source Investigator is available online at www.mhhe.com/psi and gives students and instructors access to more than 650 primary and secondary sources, including documents, images, maps, and videos.

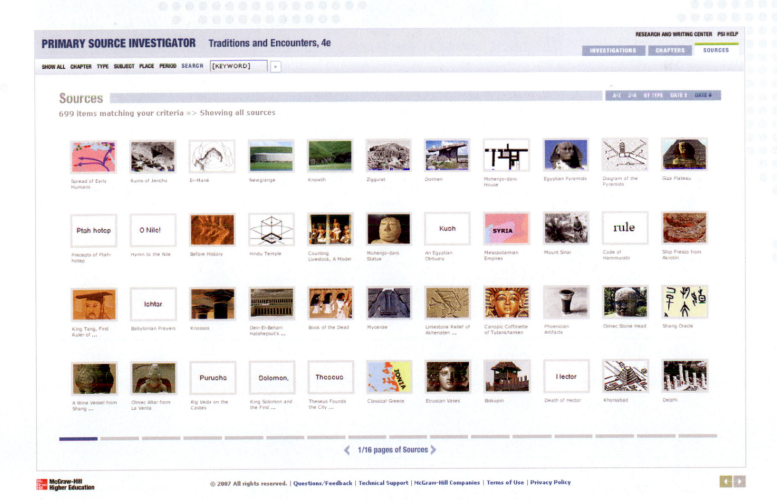

ONLINE LEARNING CENTER

The book's Online Learning Center located at http://onlinelearning.mhhe.com includes a computerized test bank, PowerPoint slides, and an instructor's manual to aid the instructor. On the student side of the OLC are self-testing quizzes.

Welcome To Online Learning

Always at the forefront of learning innovation, McGraw-Hill Online Learning offers a complete range of online solutions, including the most comprehensive, engaging, thought-provoking online courses available in the market. Get ready to change course...

➤ See Our Story
➤ Examine our rigorous course development process

Featured Course

Introduction to Criminal Justice

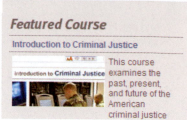

This course examines the past, present, and future of the American criminal justice

ADDITIONAL RESOURCES FOR STUDENTS

- Two "After the Fact Interactive" units are available for use with *Traditions & Encounters*: "After the Fact Interactive: Tracing the Silk Roads" for Volume I (ISBN 0-07-281843-3) and "After the Fact Interactive: Envisioning the Atlantic World" for Volume II (ISBN 0-07-281844-1). These rich, visually appealing modules on CD-ROM allow students to be apprentice historians, examining a variety of multimedia primary source material and constructing arguments based on their research.

- Titles in the Exploration in World History Series: This McGraw-Hill series conveys the results of recent research in world history in a form wholly accessible to beginning students. It also provides a pedagogical alternative to, or supplement for, the large and inclusive core textbooks. Each volume in the series focuses briefly on a particular theme, set in a global and comparative context. Each book in this series is "open-ended," raising questions and drawing students into the larger issues which animate world history.

- Rainer Buschmann, *Oceans in World History,* ISBN 0-07-301903-8

- Carl J. Guarneri, *America in the World: United States History in Global Context,* ISBN 0-07-254115-6

- Donald Johnson & Jean Elliot Johnson, *Universal Religions in World History: Buddhism, Christianity, and Islam,* ISBN 0-07-295428-0

- Xinru Liu & Lynda Shaffer, *Connections Across Eurasia: Transportation, Communication, and Cultural Exchange on the Silk Roads,* ISBN 0-07-284351-9

- Lauren Ristvet, *In the Beginning: World History from Human Evolution to First Civilizations,* ISBN 0-07-284803-0

- Robert Strayer, *Communist Experiment: Revolution, Socialism, and Global Conflict in the Twentieth Century,* ISBN 0-07-249744-0

- Catherine Clay, Christine Senecal & Chandrika Paul, *Envisioning Women in World History: 1500–Present, Volume 2,* ISBN 0-07-351322-9

- Pamela McVay, *Envisioning Women in World History: 1500–Present, Volume 2,* ISBN 0-07-353465-X

about the authors

Jerry H. Bentley is professor of history at the University of Hawai`i and editor of the *Journal of World History.* He has written extensively on the cultural history of early modern Europe and on cross-cultural interactions in world history. His research on the religious, moral, and political writings of the Renaissance led to the publication of *Humanists and Holy Writ: New Testament Scholarship in the Renaissance* (1983) and *Politics and Culture in Renaissance Naples* (1987). His more recent research has concentrated on global history and particularly on processes of cross-cultural interaction. His book *Old World Encounters: Cross-Cultural Contacts and Exchanges in Pre-Modern Times* (1993) studies processes of cultural exchange and religious conversion before modern times, and his pamphlet *Shapes of World History in Twentieth-Century Scholarship* (1996) discusses the historiography of world history. His current interests include processes of cross-cultural interaction and cultural exchange in modern times.

Herbert F. Ziegler is an associate professor of history at the University of Hawai`i. He has taught world history since 1980 and currently serves as director of the world history program at the University of Hawai`i. He also serves as book review editor of the *Journal of World History.* His interest in twentieth-century European social and political history led to the publication of *Nazi Germany's New Aristocracy* (1990). He is at present working on a study that explores from a global point of view the demographic trends of the past ten thousand years, along with their concomitant technological, economic, and social developments. His other current research project focuses on the application of complexity theory to a comparative study of societies and their internal dynamics.

acknowledgments

Many individuals have contributed to this book, and the authors take pleasure in recording deep thanks for all the comments, criticism, advice, and suggestions that helped to improve the work. The editorial team at McGraw-Hill did an outstanding job of keeping the authors focused on the project. Special thanks go to Chris Freitag, Lisa Pinto, Matthew Busbridge, Mika De Roo, Arthur Pomponio, Carey Eisner, Stacy Best Ruel, Elena Mackawgy, Jaclyn Mautone, Sarah Remington, Robin Mouat, Jeanne Schreiber, and Brian J. Pecko, who provided crucial support by helping the authors work through difficult issues and solve the innumerable problems of content, style, and organization that arise in any project to produce a history of the world. Many colleagues at the University of Hawai`i and elsewhere aided and advised the authors on matters of organization and composition. Finally, we would like to express our appreciation for the advice of the following individuals, who read and commented on the fifth edition, as well as previous editions of *Traditions & Encounters*.

Manuscript Reviewers

Heather J. Abdelnur
Blackburn College

Henry Abramson
Florida Atlantic University

Wayne Ackerson
Salisbury University

Roger Adelson
Arizona State University

Sanjam Ahluwalia
Northern Arizona University

William Alexander
Norfolk State University

Alfred Andrea
University of Vermont

Ed Anson
University of Arkansas at Little Rock

Henry Antkiewicz
East Tennessee State University

Maria Arbelaez
University of Nebraska at Omaha

Peter Arnade
University of California, San Marcos

Karl Bahm
University of Wisconsin, Superior

Vaughan Baker
University of Louisiana at Lafayette

Gene Barnett
Calhoun Community College

Beth Allison Barr
Baylor University

Ian Barrow
Middlebury College

Dixee Bartholomew-Feis
Buena Vista University

Mike Balyo
Chemeketa Community College

Guy Beckwith
Auburn University

Lynda Bell
University of California, Riverside

Norman Bennett
Boston University

Houri Berberian
California State University, Long Beach

Robert Blackey
California State University, San Bernardino

David Blaylock
Eastern Kentucky University

Wayne Bodle
Indiana University of Pennsylvania

Beau Bowers
Central Piedmont Community College

Connie Brand
Meridian Community College

Michael Brescia
State University of New York, Fredonia

Brian T. Brownson
Murray State University

Samuel Brunk
University of Texas, El Paso

Deborah Buffton
University of Wisconsin, La Crosse

Maureen Burgess
Colorado State University

Rainer Buschmann
Hawai`i Pacific University

Sharon L. Bush
LeMoyne-Owen College

Antonio Calabria
University of Texas, San Antonio

Lewis Call
California Polytechnic State University, San Luis Obispo

Thomas Callahan, Jr.
Rider University

Alice-Catherine Carls
University of Tennessee at Martin

Kay Carr
Southern Illinois University

James Carroll
Iona College

Carol Carter
University of Central Arkansas

Tom Carty
Springfield College

Bruce Castleman
San Diego State University

Douglas Catterall
Cameron University

Douglas Chambers
University of Southern Mississippi, Hattiesburg

Choi Chatterjee
California State University, Los Angeles

Orazio Ciccarelli
University of Southern Mississippi

Andrew Clark
University of North Carolina at Wilmington

Hugh R. Clark
Ursinus College

Harold Cline
Middle Georgia College

Tim Coates
College of Charleston

Joan Coffey
Sam Houston State University

Daniel Connerton
North Adams State

Keith Cox
California State University

Bruce Cruikshank
Hastings College

Graciella Cruz-Tara
Florida Atlantic University

Lynn Curtright
Tallahassee Community College

Richard Cusimano
University of Louisiana at Lafayette

Ken Czech
St. Cloud State University

Francis K. Danquah
Southern University

Touraj Daryaee
California State University, Fullerton

Jon Davidann
Hawai`i Pacific University

Allen Davidson
Georgia Southern University

Denise Z. Davidson
Georgia State University

Brian Davies
University of Texas, San Antonio

John Davis
Radford University

Thomas Davis
Virginia Military Institute

Elisa Denlinger
University of Wisconsin, La Crosse

Stewart Dippel
University of the Ozarks

Kevin Dougherty
University of Southern Mississippi

Ross Doughty
Ursinus College

Cathi Dunkle
Mid-Michigan Community College

Ross Dunn
San Diego State University

Peter Dykema
Arkansas Tech University

Lane Earns
University of Wisconsin, Oshkosh

Christopher Ehret
University of California, Los Angeles

Laura Endicott
Southwestern Oklahoma State

Nancy Erickson
Erskine College

James Evans
Southeastern Community College

David Fahey
Miami University

Edward Farmer
University of Minnesota

James David Farthing
Oklahoma Baptist University

Lanny Fields
California State University, San Bernardino

Allan Fisher
Michigan State University

Robert Frankle
University of Memphis

Bonnie Frederick
Washington State University

Karl Friday
University of Georgia

Amy Froide
University of Tennessee, Chattanooga

James Fuller
University of Indianapolis

Jessie Ruth Gaston
California State University, Sacramento

Kurt Gingrich
Radford University

Robert Gomez
San Antonio College

Paul Goodwin
University of Connecticut, Storrs

Matthew Gordon
Miami University of Ohio

Steve Gosch
University of Wisconsin, Eau Claire

Andrew Goss
University of New Orleans

Joseph Gowaskie
Rider University

Sherry Sanders Gray
Mid-South Community College

Brian Gurian
Harrisburg Area Community College

John Haag
University of Georgia

Dr. John Haas
Cerritos College

Raymond J. Haberski, Jr.
Marian College

Jeffrey Hamilton
Baylor University

Michael Hamm
Centre College

Travis Hanes III
University of North Carolina—Wilmington

Eric J. Hanne
Florida Atlantic University

Preston Hardy, Jr.
University of Tennessee, Martin

Stephen Harmon
Pittsburg State University

Alice K. Harris
University of California, Davis

Russell Hart
Hawai`i Pacific University

John Hayden
Southwestern Oklahoma State

Randolph Head
University of California, Riverside

Mary Hedberg
Saginaw Valley State University

Gerald Herman
Northeastern University

David Hertzel
Southwestern Oklahoma State

Udo Heyn
California State University, Los Angeles

Kathryn Hodgkinson
The Hockaday School

Caroline Hoefferle
Wingate University

Peter Hoffenberg
University of Hawai`i, Manoa

Blair Holmes
Brigham Young University

Mary Hovanec
Cuyahoga Community College

Scott Howlett
Saddleback Community College

Kailai Huang
Massachusetts College of Liberal Arts

J. Sanders Huguenin
University of Science and Arts of Oklahoma

Richard Hume
Washington State University

Carol Sue Humphrey
Oklahoma Baptist University

Alfred Hunt
State University of New York

Rebecca C. Huskey
Georgia State University

Raymond Hylton
J. Sergeant Reynolds Community College

W. Scott Jessee
Appalachian State University

Phyllis Jestice
University of Southern Mississippi, Hattiesburg

Eric F. Johnson
Kutztown University of Pennsylvania

Cheryl Johnson-Odim
Loyola University

Kimberley Jones-de Oliveira
Long Island University

Jonathan Judaken
University of Memphis

Theodore Kallman
Delta College

Alan Karras
University of California, Berkeley

Thomas Kay
Wheaton College

Charles Keller
Pittsburgh State University

David L. Kenley
Elizabethtown College

Winston Kinsey
Appalachian State University

Cengiz Kirli
Purdue University

Mark Klobas
Scottsdale Community College

Paul Knoll
University of Southern California

Keith Knuuti
University of Hawai`i, Hilo

Kenneth Koons
Virginia Military Institute

Cheryl Koos
California State University, Los Angeles

Cynthia Kosso
Northern Arizona University

Zoltan Kramer
Central Washington University

James Krokar
DePaul University

Glenn Lamar
University of Louisiana at Lafayette

Lisa Lane
Miracosta College

George Lankevich
Bronx Community College

Dennis Laumann
University of Memphis

Donald Layton
Indiana State University

Loyd Lee
SUNY-New Paltz

Jess LeVine
Brookdale Community College

Keith Lewinstein
Bridgewater State University

Richard Lewis
St. Cloud State University

Yi Li
Tacoma Community College

Tony Litherland
Oklahoma Baptist University

Paul Lococo, Jr.
Leeward Community College

James Long
Colorado State University

David Longfellow
Baylor University

Christine E. Lovasz-Kaiser
University of Southern Indiana

Ben Lowe
Florida Atlantic University

Jared Ludlow
Brigham Young University, Hawai`i

Herbert Luft
Pepperdine Univeristy

Lu Lui
University of Tennessee—Knoxville

Paul Madden
Hardin-Simmons University

Moira Maguire
University of Arkansas, Little Rock

Farid Mahdavi
San Diego State University

Dorothea A. L. Martin
Appalachian State University

Tracey Martin
Benedictine University

Ken Mason
Santa Monica College

Robert Mathews
Northshore Community College

Laura E. Mayhall
The Catholic University of America

William Maynard
Arkansas State University

Robert McCormick
University of South Carolina—Spartanburg

Jeff McEwen
Chattanooga State Technical College

Randall McGowen
University of Oregon

Adam McKeown
Columbia University

John McNeill
Georgetown University

James McSwain
Tuskegee University

Pamela McVay
Ursuline College

John Mears
Southern Methodist University

Daniel Miller
Calvin College

Monserrat Miller
Marshall University

Laura Mitchell
University of Texas, San Antonio

David Montgomery
Brigham Young University

Garth Montgomery
Radford University

George Moore
San Jose State University

Gloria Morrow
Morgan State University

David Mungello
Baylor University

Jeffrey Myers
Avila College

Peter Nayenga
St. Cloud State University

Ruth Necheles-Jansyn
Long Island University

Virginia Carolyn Neel
(aka Carolyn Neel)
Arkansas Tech University

Eric Nelson
Missouri State University

Marian Nelson
University of Nebraska

Wing Chung Ng
University of Texas at San Antonio

C. Brid Nicholson
Kean University

Janise Nuckols
Windward Community College

Deanne Nuwer
*University of Southern Mississippi,
Hattiesburg*

Greg O'Brien
*University of Southern Mississippi,
Hattiesburg*

Thomas F. O'Brien
University of Houston

Agnes A. Odinga
Minnesota State University, Mankato

Veena Talwar Oldenburg
Baruch College

Brian O'Neil
University of Southern Mississippi

Patricia O'Niell
Central Oregon Community College

Samuel Oppenheim
California State University, Stanislaus

John Oriji
*California Polytechnic State University,
San Luis Obispo*

Anne Osborne
Rider University

James Overfield
University of Vermont

Keith Pacholl
State University of West Georgia

Melvin Page
East Tennessee State University

Loretta Pang
Kapiolani Community College

Jean Paquette
Lander University

Jotham Parsons
University of Delaware

Denis Paz
University of North Texas

Patrick Peebles
University of Missouri—Kansas City

Peter W. Petschauer
Appalachian State University

Phyllis Pobst
Arkansas State University

Elizabeth Pollard
San Diego State University

Jon Porter
Franklin College

Carl J. Post
Essex County College

Clifton Potter
Lynchburg College

David Price
Santa Fe Community College

Rebecca Pulju
Kent State University

Alfonso Quiroz
Bernard M. Baruch College, CUNY

Julie Rancilio
Kapi`olani Community College

Stephen Rapp
Georgia State University

Vera Reber
Shippensburg University

John Reid
Georgia Southern University

Thomas Renna
Saginaw Valley State University

Diana Reynolds
Point Loma Nazarene University

Douglas Reynolds
Georgia State University

Ira Rice
Ball State University

Cheryl Riggs
*California State University,
San Bernardino*

John Ritter
Chemeketa Community College

Leonard R. Ronaldson
Robert Morris University

Lynn Rose
Truman State University

Aviel Roshwald
Georgetown University

Chad Ross
East Carolina University

Dan Russell
Springfield College

Eric Rust
Baylor University

John Ryan
Kansas City Kansas Community College

Pamela G. Sayre
Henry Ford Community College

Cristofer Scarboro
King's College

William Schell
Murray State University

Daryl Schuster
University of Central Florida

Jane Scimeca
Brookdale Community College

Gary Scudder
Georgia Perimeter College

Kimberly Sebold
University of Maine, Presque Isle

Michael J. Seth
James Madison University

Tara Sethia
California State University, Pomona

Howard Shealy
Kennesaw State College

Nancy Shoemaker
University of Connecticut, Storrs

MaryAnn Sison
University of Southern Mississippi, Hattiesburg

Jonathan Skaff
Shippensburg University

David Smith
California State Polytechnic University, Pomona

Michael Smith
Purdue University

Roland Spickerman
University of Detroit—Mercy

Wendy St. Jean
Springfield College

Michelle Staley
East Mississippi Community College

Tracy Steele
Sam Houston State University

Richard Steigmann-Gall
Kent State University, Kent

John Steinberg
Georgia Southern University

Heather Streets
Washington State University

Laichen Sun
California State University, Fullerton

Roshanna Sylvester
California State University, Fullerton

Stephen Tallackson
Purdue University, Calumet

Lenette S. Taylor
Kent State University

John Thornton
Millersville University

Robert Tignor
Princeton University

Elisaveta B. Todorova
University of Cincinnati

James Tueller
Brigham Young University, Hawai`i

Kirk Tyvela
Ohio University

Michael G. Vann
California State University, Sacramento

Tom Velek
Mississippi University for Women

Deborah Vess
Georgia College and State University

John Voll
Georgetown University

Sandra Wagner-Wright
University of Hawai`i, Hilo

Mark Wasserman
Rutgers University

Jeff Wasserstrom
Indiana University—Bloomington

Mary Watrous-Schlesinger
Washington State University, Pullman

Theodore Weeks
Southern Illinois University

Guy Wells
Kent State University

Robert Wenke
University of Washington

Sally West
Truman State University

Sherri West
Brookdale Community College

Michael J. Whaley
Lindenwood University

Scott Wheeler
West Point

Joe Whitehorne
Lord Fairfax Community College

S. Jonathan Wiesen
Southern Illinois University, Carbondale

Anne Will
Skagit Valley Community College

Richard Williams
Washington State University

Allen Wittenborn
San Diego State University

David Wittner
Utica College

William Wood
Point Loma Nazarene University

John Woods
University of Chicago

Anand Yang
University of Utah

Ping Yao
California State University, Los Angeles

C. K. Yoon
James Madison University

Herb Zettl
Springfield College

Design Reviewers

Wayne Ackerson
Salisbury University

Hussein A. Amery
Colorado School of Mines

Michael Balyo
Chemeketa Community College

Carolyn Neel
Arkansas Tech University

C. Brid Nicholson
Kean University

Carl J. Post
Essex County College

Julie Rancilio
Kapi`olani Community College

Leah Renold
Texas State University

Pamela G. Sayre
Henry Ford Community College

Linda Bregstein Scherr
Mercer County Community College

Michael J. Seth
James Madison University

Elisaveta B. Todorova
University of Cincinnati

Michael G. Vann
California State University, Sacramento

Michael J. Whaley
Lindenwood University

Carlton Wilson
North Carolina Central University

Marc Zayac
Georgia Perimeter College

Connect History Board of Advisors

Clare Balawajder
Thomas Nelson Community College

Brett Berliner
Morgan State University

Jeff Bowersox
University of Southern Mississippi

Sue Gronewold
Kean University

Andrew P. Haley
University of Southern Mississippi

Linda Bregstein Sherr
Mercer County Community College

Brian Ulrich
Shippensburg University

Connect History Reviewers

Jennifer Foray
Purdue University

Aimee Harris-Johnson
El Paso Community College

Andrew Lewis
American University

Christine E. Lovasz-Kaiser
University of Southern Indiana

David Mock
Tallahassee Community College

Stuart Smith III
Germanna Community College

part 5

THE ORIGINS OF GLOBAL INTERDEPENDENCE, 1500 TO 1800

By 1500 C.E., peoples throughout the world had built well-organized societies with distinctive cultural traditions. Powerful agricultural societies dominated most of Asia, the Mediterranean basin, Europe, much of sub-Saharan Africa, Mexico, and the central Andean region. Pastoral nomads thrived in the dry grassy regions of central Asia and Africa, and hunting and gathering societies with small populations survived in lands where cultivation and herding were not practical possibilities. The vast majority of the world's peoples, however, lived in agricultural societies that observed distinctive political, social, and cultural traditions.

By 1500, peoples of the world had also established intricate transportation networks that supported travel, communication, and exchange between their societies. For more than a millennium, merchants had traveled the silk roads that linked lands from China to the Mediterranean basin, and mariners had plied the Indian Ocean and neighboring waters in connecting lands from Japan to east Africa. Caravan routes across the Sahara desert brought sub-Saharan west Africa into the larger economy of the eastern hemisphere. Although pioneered by merchants in the interests of trade, these transpor-

tation networks also supported cultural and biological exchanges. Several religious traditions—most notably Buddhism, Christianity, and Islam—traveled along the trade routes and attracted followers in distant lands. Similarly, food crops, animal stocks, and disease pathogens spread throughout much of the eastern hemisphere in premodern times. Transportation networks in the Americas and Oceania were not as extensive as those in the eastern hemisphere, but they also supported communication and exchange over long distances. Trade linked societies throughout North America, and seafarers routinely sailed between island groups in the central and western Pacific Ocean.

Commercial, cultural, and biological exchanges of premodern times prefigured much more intense cross-cultural interactions after 1500. These later interactions followed the establishment of new transportation networks in the form of sea lanes linking the lands of the Indian, Atlantic, and Pacific Ocean basins. Beginning in the fifteenth century, European mariners sought new, all-sea routes to the markets of Asia. As a result of their exploratory voyages, they established trade routes throughout the world's oceans and entered into dealings with many of the world's peoples. The new sea lanes not only fostered direct contact between Europeans and the peoples of sub-Saharan Africa and Asia but also facilitated interaction among the peoples of the eastern hemisphere, the western hemisphere, and Oceania. In short, European mariners created globe-girdling networks of transportation, communication, and exchange that supported cross-cultural interactions much more

systematic and intense than those of earlier times.

The establishment of links among all the world's regions and peoples gave rise to the early modern era of world history, approximately 1500 to 1800 C.E. The early modern era differed from the period from 1000 to 1500, when there were only sporadic contacts among peoples of the eastern hemisphere, the western hemisphere, and Oceania. It also differed from the modern era from 1800 to the present, when national states, heavy industry, powerful weapons, and efficient technologies of transportation and communication enabled peoples of European ancestry to achieve political and economic dominance in the world.

During the early modern era, several global processes touched peoples in all parts of the world and influenced the development of their societies. One involved biological exchange: plants, animals, diseases, and human communities crossed the world's oceans and established themselves in new lands where they dramatically affected both the natural environment and established societies. Another involved commercial exchange: merchants took advantage of newly established sea lanes to inaugurate a genuinely global economy in which agricultural products, manufactured goods, and other

commodities reached markets in distant lands. Yet another process involved the diffusion of technologies and cultural traditions: printing and gunpowder spread throughout the world, and Christianity and Islam attracted increasing numbers of converts in widely spread regions of the world.

These global processes had different effects for different peoples. The indigenous peoples of the Americas and Oceania experienced turmoil and disruption: diseases introduced from the eastern hemisphere ravaged their populations and sometimes led to the collapse of their societies. Europeans in contrast largely flourished during the early modern era: they traded profitably throughout the world and claimed vast stretches of land in the Americas, where they founded colonies and cultivated crops for sale on the open market. Africans benefited from the introduction of new food crops and the opportunity to obtain trade goods from abroad, but those benefits came at a terrible cost: millions of enslaved individuals from sub-Saharan Africa underwent a forced migration to the western hemisphere, where they performed hard labor, lived in poverty, and suffered both physical and psychological abuse. East Asian and Islamic peoples sought to limit the influence of global processes in their lands: they prospered from increased trade but restricted the introduction of foreign ideas and technologies into their societies.

European peoples drew the most benefit from global processes of the period 1500 to 1800, but by no means did they dominate world affairs in early modern times. They established empires and settler colonies in the Americas, but most of the western hemisphere lay beyond their control until the nineteenth century. They established a series of fortified trading posts and the colony of Angola in Africa, but they traded in Africa at the sufferance of local authorities and rarely wielded direct influence beyond the coastlines. They conquered the Philippines and many Indonesian islands but posed no threat at all to the powerful states that ruled China, India, southwest Asia, and Anatolia, or even to the island state of Japan. Although they did not achieve global hegemony in early modern times, European peoples nevertheless played a more prominent role in world affairs than any of their ancestors, and their efforts fostered the development of an increasingly interdependent world.

Transoceanic Encounters and Global Connections

chapter22

An unknown artist created a seventeenth-century portrait of Vasco da Gama, who established a sea route between Portugal and India.

PART 5

EYEWITNESS:

Vasco da Gama's Spicy Voyage

On 8 July 1497 the Portuguese mariner Vasco da Gama led a small fleet of four armed merchant vessels with 170 crewmen out of the harbor at Lisbon. His destination was India, which he planned to reach by sailing around the continent of Africa and through the Indian Ocean. He carried letters of introduction from the king of Portugal as well as cargoes of gold, pearls, wool textiles, bronzeware, iron tools, and other goods that he hoped to exchange for pepper and spices in India.

Before there would be an opportunity to trade, however, da Gama and his crew had a prolonged voyage through two oceans. They sailed south from Portugal to the Cape Verde Islands off the west coast of Africa, where they took on water and fresh provisions. On 3 August they headed south into the Atlantic Ocean to take advantage of the prevailing winds. For the next ninety-five days, the fleet saw no land as it sailed through some six thousand nautical miles of open ocean. By October, da Gama had found westerly winds in the southern Atlantic, rounded the Cape of Good Hope, and entered the Indian Ocean. The fleet slowly worked its way up the east coast of Africa, engaging in hostilities with local authorities at Mozambique and Mombasa, as far as Malindi, where da Gama secured the services of an Indian Muslim pilot to guide his ships across the Arabian Sea. On 20 May 1498—more than ten months after its departure from Lisbon—the fleet anchored at Calicut in southern India.

In India the Portuguese fleet found a wealthy, cosmopolitan society. Upon its arrival local authorities in Calicut dispatched a pair of Tunisian merchants who spoke Spanish and Italian to serve as translators for the newly arrived party. The markets of Calicut offered not only pepper, ginger, cinnamon, and spices but also rubies, emeralds, gold jewelry, and fine cotton textiles. Alas, apart from gold and some striped cloth, the goods that da Gama had brought attracted little interest among merchants at Calicut. Nevertheless, da Gama managed to exchange gold for a cargo of pepper and cinnamon that turned a handsome profit when the fleet returned to Portugal in August 1499. Da Gama's expedition opened the door to direct maritime trade between European and Asian peoples and helped to establish permanent links between the world's various regions.

Cross-cultural interactions have been a persistent feature of historical development. Even in ancient times mass migration, campaigns of imperial expansion, and long-distance trade deeply influenced societies throughout the world. As a result of those interactions, Buddhism, Islam, and Christianity spread from their places of birth to the distant corners of the eastern hemisphere. Long before modern times, arteries of long-distance trade served also as the principal conduits for exchanges of plants, animals, and diseases.

After 1500 C.E., cross-cultural interactions took place on a much larger geographic scale, and encounters were often more disruptive than in earlier centuries. Equipped with advanced technologies and a powerful military arsenal, western European peoples began to cross the world's oceans in large numbers during the early modern era. At the same time, Russian adventurers built an enormous Eurasian empire and ventured tentatively into the Pacific Ocean.

Europeans were not the only peoples who actively explored the larger world during the early modern era. In the early fifteenth century the Ming emperors of China sponsored a series of seven massive maritime expeditions that visited all parts of the Indian Ocean basin. Although state-sponsored expeditions came to an end after 1435, Chinese merchants and mariners were prominent figures in east Asian and southeast Asian lands throughout the early modern era. In the sixteenth century Ottoman mariners also ventured into the Indian Ocean. Following the Ottoman conquest of Egypt in 1517, both merchant and military vessels established an Ottoman presence throughout the Indian Ocean basin. Ottoman subjects traveled as far as China, but they were most active in Muslim lands from east Africa and Arabia to India and southeast Asia, where they enjoyed especially warm receptions.

Although other peoples also made their way into the larger world, Europeans linked the lands and peoples of the eastern hemisphere, the western hemisphere, and Oceania. Because they traveled regularly between the world's major geographic regions, European peoples benefited from unparalleled opportunities to increase their power, wealth, and influence. The projection of European influence brought about a decisive shift in the global balance of power. During the millennium 500 to 1500 C.E., the world's most powerful societies were those organized by imperial states such as the Tang dynasty of China, the Abbasid dynasty in southwest Asia, the Byzantine empire in the eastern Mediterranean region, and the Mongol empires that embraced much of Eurasia. After 1500, however, European peoples became much more prominent than before in the larger world, and they began to establish vast empires that by the nineteenth century dominated much of the world.

The expansion of European influence also resulted in the establishment of global networks of transportation, communication, and exchange. A worldwide diffusion of plants, animals, diseases, and human communities followed European ventures across the oceans, and intricate trade networks gave birth to a global economy. Although epidemic diseases killed millions of people, the spread of food crops and domesticated animals contributed to a dramatic surge in global population. The establishment of global trade networks ensured that interactions between the world's peoples would continue and intensify.

THE EXPLORATION OF THE WORLD'S OCEANS

Between 1400 and 1800, European mariners launched a remarkable series of exploratory voyages that took them to all the earth's waters, with the exception of those in extreme polar regions. These voyages were very expensive affairs. Yet private investors and government authorities had strong motives to underwrite the expeditions and outfit them with advanced nautical technology. The voyages of exploration paid large dividends: they enabled European mariners to chart the world's ocean basins and develop an accurate understanding of world geography. On the basis of that knowledge, European merchants and mariners established global networks of communication, transportation, and exchange—and profited handsomely from their efforts.

Motives for Exploration

A complex combination of motives prompted Europeans to explore the world's oceans. Most important of these motives were the search for basic resources and lands suitable for the cultivation of cash crops, the desire to establish new trade routes to Asian markets, and the aspiration to expand the influence of Christianity.

Portuguese Exploration Mariners from the relatively poor and hardscrabble kingdom of Portugal were most prominent in the search for fresh resources to exploit and lands to cultivate. Beginning in the thirteenth century, Portuguese seamen ventured away from the coasts and into the open Atlantic Ocean. They originally sought fish, seals, whales, timber, and lands where they could grow wheat to supplement the meager resources of Portugal. By the early fourteenth century, they had discovered the uninhabited Azores and Madeiras Islands. They called frequently at the Canary Islands, inhabited by the indigenous Guanche people, which Italian and Iberian mariners had visited since the early fourteenth century. Because European demand for sugar was strong and increasing, the prospect of establishing sugar plantations on the Atlantic islands was very tempting. Italian entrepreneurs had organized sugar plantations in Palestine and the Mediterranean islands since the twelfth century, and in the fifteenth century Italian investors worked with Portuguese mariners to establish planta-

tions in the Atlantic islands. Continuing Portuguese voyages also led to the establishment of plantations on more southerly Atlantic islands, including the Cape Verde Islands, São Tomé, Principe, and Fernando Po.

The Lure of Trade Even more alluring than the exploitation of fresh lands and resources was the goal of establishing maritime trade routes to the markets of Asia. During the era of the Mongol empires, European merchants often traveled overland as far as China to trade in silk, spices, porcelain, and other Asian goods. In the fourteenth century, however, with the collapse of the Mongol empires and the spread of bubonic plague, travel on the silk roads became much less safe than before. Muslim mariners continued to bring Asian goods through the Indian Ocean and the Red Sea to Cairo, where Italian merchants purchased them for distribution in western Europe. But prices at Cairo were high, and Europeans sought ever-larger quantities of Asian goods, particularly spices.

By the fourteenth century the wealthy classes of Europe regarded Indian pepper and Chinese ginger as expensive necessities, and they especially prized cloves and nutmeg from the spice islands of Maluku. Merchants and monarchs alike realized that by offering direct access to Asian markets

A detail from the Catalan Atlas, a magnificent illustrated representation of the known world produced about 1375, depicts a camel caravan traveling from China to Europe across the silk roads.

and eliminating Muslim intermediaries, new maritime trade routes would increase the quantities of spices and other Asian goods available in Europe—and would also yield enormous profits.

African trade also beckoned to Europeans and called them to the sea. Since the twelfth century, Europeans had purchased west African gold, ivory, and slaves delivered by the trans-Saharan camel caravans of Muslim merchants to north African ports. Gold was an especially important commodity because the precious metal from west Africa was Europeans' principal form of payment for Asian luxury goods. As in the case of Asian trade, maritime routes that eliminated Muslim intermediaries and offered more direct access to African markets would benefit European merchants.

Missionary Efforts Alongside material incentives, the goal of expanding the boundaries of Christianity also drove Europeans into the larger world. Like Buddhism and Islam, Christianity is a missionary religion. The New Testament specifically urged Christians to spread their faith throughout the world. Efforts to spread the faith often took peaceful forms. During the era of the Mongol empires, Franciscan and Dominican missionaries had traveled as far as India, central Asia, and China in search of converts. Yet the expansion of Christianity was by no means always a peaceful affair. Beginning in the eleventh century, western Europeans had launched a series of crusades and holy wars against Muslims in Palestine, the Mediterranean islands, and Iberia. Crusading zeal remained especially strong in Iberia, where the *reconquista* came to an end in 1492: the Muslim kingdom of Granada fell to Spanish Christian forces just weeks

before Christopher Columbus set sail on his famous first voyage to the western hemisphere. Whether through persuasion or violence, overseas voyages offered fresh opportunities for western Europeans to spread their faith.

In practice, the various motives for exploration combined and reinforced each other. Dom Henrique of Portugal, often called Prince Henry the Navigator, promoted voyages of exploration in west Africa specifically to enter the gold trade, discover profitable new trade routes, gain intelligence about the extent of Muslim power, win converts to Christianity, and make alliances against the Muslims with any Christian rulers he might find. When the Portuguese mariner Vasco da Gama reached the Indian port of Calicut in 1498, local authorities asked him what he wanted there. His reply: "Christians and spices." The goal of spreading Christianity thus became a powerful justification and reinforcement for the more material motives for the voyages of exploration.

The Technology of Exploration

Without advanced nautical technology and navigational skills, even the strongest motives would not have enabled European mariners to reconnoiter the world's oceans. Embarking on voyages that would keep them out of the sight of land for weeks at a time, mariners needed sturdy ships, navigational equipment, and sailing techniques that would permit them to make their way across the seas and back again. They inherited much of their nautical technology from Mediterranean and northern European maritime traditions and combined it imaginatively with elements of Chinese or Arabic origin.

Ships and Sails From their experiences in the coastal waters of the Atlantic, European sailors learned to construct ships strong enough to survive most adverse conditions. Beginning about the twelfth century, they increased the maneuverability of their craft by building a rudder onto the stern. (The sternpost rudder was a Chinese invention that had diffused across the Indian Ocean and probably became known to Europeans through Arab ships in the Mediterranean.) They outfitted their vessels with two main types of sail, both of which Mediterranean mariners had used since classical times. Square sails enabled them to take full advantage of a following wind (a wind blowing from behind), although these sails did not work well in crosswinds. Triangular lateen sails, on the other hand, were very maneuverable and could catch winds from the side as well as from behind. With a combination of square and lateen sails, European ships were able to use whatever winds arose. Their ability to tack—to advance against the wind by sailing across it—was crucial for the exploration of regions with uncooperative winds.

Navigational Instruments The most important navigational equipment on board these vessels were magnetic compasses and astrolabes (soon replaced by cross staffs and back staffs). The compass was a Chinese invention of the

By using cross staffs to measure the angle of the sun or the pole star above the horizon, mariners could determine latitude.

Tang or Song dynasty that had diffused throughout the Indian Ocean basin in the eleventh century. By the mid-twelfth century, European mariners used compasses to determine their heading in Mediterranean and Atlantic waters. The astrolabe was a simplified version of an instrument used by Greek and Persian astronomers to determine latitude by measuring the angle of the sun or the pole star above the horizon. Portuguese mariners visiting the Indian Ocean in the late fifteenth century encountered Arab sailors using simpler and more serviceable instruments for determining latitude, which the Portuguese then used as models for the construction of cross staffs and back staffs.

European mariners' ability to determine direction and latitude enabled them to assemble a vast body of data about the earth's geography and to find their way around the world's oceans with tolerable accuracy and efficiency. (The measurement of longitude requires the ability to measure time precisely and so had to wait until the late eighteenth century, when dependable, spring-driven clocks became available.)

Knowledge of Winds and Currents

Equipped with advanced technological hardware, European mariners ventured into the oceans and gradually compiled a body of practical knowledge about the winds and currents that determined navigational possibilities in the age of sail. In both the Atlantic and the Pacific Oceans, strong winds blow regularly to create giant "wind wheels" both north and south of the equator, and ocean currents follow a similar pattern. Between about five and twenty-five degrees of latitude north and south of the equator, trade winds blow from the east. Between about thirty and sixty degrees north and south, westerly winds prevail. Winds and currents in the Indian Ocean follow a different, but still regular and reliable, pattern. During the summer months, generally between April and October, monsoon winds blow from the southwest throughout the Indian Ocean basin, whereas during the winter they blow from the northeast. Once mariners understood these patterns, they were able to take advantage of prevailing winds and currents to sail to almost any part of the earth.

The *volta do mar* Prevailing winds and currents often forced mariners to take indirect routes to their destinations. European vessels sailed easily from the Mediterra-

nean to the Canary Islands, for example, since regular trade winds blew from the northeast. But those same trade winds complicated the return trip. By the mid-fifteenth century, Portuguese mariners had developed a strategy called the *volta do mar* ("return through the sea") that enabled them to sail from the Canaries to Portugal. Instead of trying to force their way against the trade winds—a slow and perilous business—they sailed northwest into the open ocean until they found westerly winds and then turned east for the last leg of the homeward journey.

Although the *volta do mar* took mariners well out of their way, experience soon taught that sailing around contrary winds was much faster, safer, and more reliable than butting up against them. Portuguese and other European mariners began to rely on the principle of the *volta do mar* in sailing to destinations other than the Canary Islands. When Vasco da Gama departed for India, for example, he sailed south to the Cape Verde Islands and then allowed the trade winds to carry him southwest into the Atlantic Ocean until he approached the coast of Brazil. There da Gama caught the prevailing westerlies that enabled him to sail east, round the Cape of Good Hope, and enter the Indian Ocean. As they became familiar with the wind systems of the world's oceans, European mariners developed variations on the *volta do mar* that enabled them to travel reliably to coastlines throughout the world.

Voyages of Exploration: from the Mediterranean to the Atlantic

Exploratory voyaging began as early as the thirteenth century. In 1291 the Vivaldi brothers departed from Genoa in two ships with the intention of sailing around Africa to India. They did not succeed, but the idea of exploring the Atlantic and establishing a maritime trade route from the Mediterranean to India persisted. During the fourteenth century Genoese, Portuguese, and Spanish mariners sailed frequently into the Atlantic Ocean and rediscovered the Canary Islands. The Guanche people had settled the Canaries from their original home in Morocco, but there had been no contact between the Guanches and other peoples since the time of the Roman empire. Iberian mariners began to visit the Canaries regularly, and in the fifteenth century Castilian forces conquered the islands and made them an outpost for further exploration.

The earliest surviving world globe, produced in 1492 by the German cartographer Martin Behaim, depicts the eastern hemisphere quite accurately but shows almost no land west of Iberia except for east Asia.

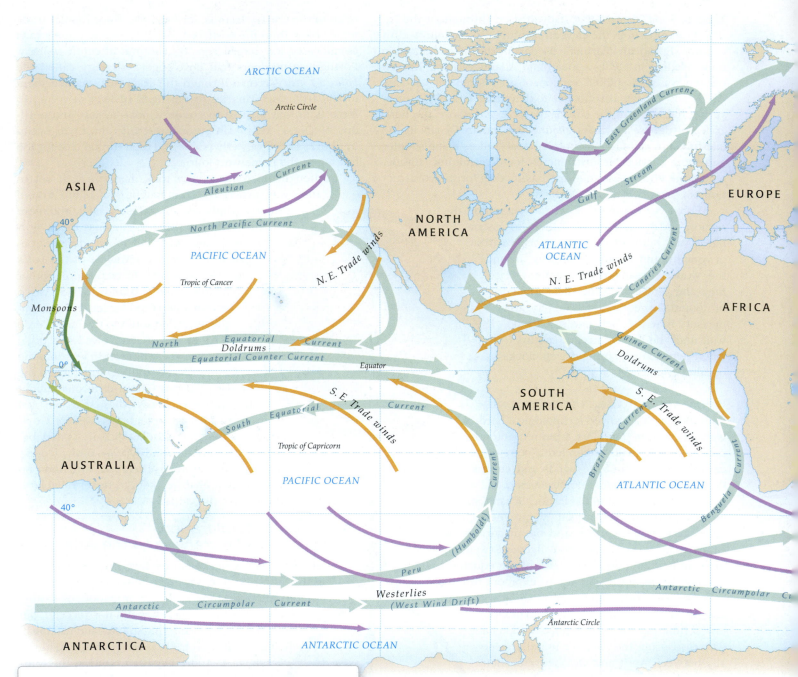

MAP 22.1

Wind and current patterns in the world's oceans.

Note how the winds of the Atlantic and Pacific resemble wind wheels, revolving clockwise north of the equator and counterclockwise south of the equator.

How crucial was an understanding of the world's wind patterns to the success of European overseas expansion?

Prince Henry of Portugal The pace of European exploration quickened after 1415 when Prince Henry of Portugal (1394–1460) conquered the Moroccan port of Ceuta and sponsored a series of voyages down the west African coast. Portuguese merchants soon established fortified trading posts at São Jorge da Mina (in modern Ghana) and other strategic locations. There they exchanged European horses, leather, textiles, and metalwares for gold and slaves. Portuguese explorations continued after Henry's death, and in 1488 Bartolomeu Dias rounded the Cape of Good Hope and entered the Indian Ocean. He did not proceed farther because of storms and a restless crew, but the route to India, China, and the spice-bearing islands of southeast Asia lay open. The sea route to the Indian Ocean offered European

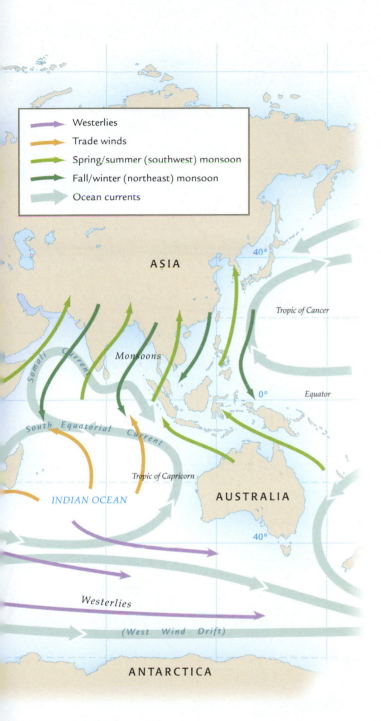

Legend:
- Westerlies
- Trade winds
- Spring/summer (southwest) monsoon
- Fall/winter (northeast) monsoon
- Ocean currents

ASIA

Tropic of Cancer

Somali Current

Monsoons

Equator

South Equatorial Current

Tropic of Capricorn

INDIAN OCEAN

AUSTRALIA

Westerlies

(West Wind Drift)

ANTARCTICA

40°

0°

40°

than three months without seeing land, and his cargoes excited little interest in Indian markets. His return voyage was especially difficult, and less than half of his crew made it safely back to Portugal. Yet his cargo of pepper and cinnamon was hugely profitable, and Portuguese merchants began immediately to organize further expeditions. By 1500 they had built a trading post at Calicut, and Portuguese mariners soon called at ports throughout India and the Indian Ocean basin. By the late sixteenth century, English and Dutch mariners had followed the Portuguese into the Indian Ocean basin.

Christopher Columbus While Portuguese navigators plied the sea route to India, the Genoese mariner Cristoforo Colombo, known in English as Christopher Columbus (1451–1506), proposed sailing to the markets of Asia by a western route. On the basis of wide reading of literature on geography, Columbus believed that the Eurasian landmass covered 270 degrees of longitude and that the earth was a relatively small sphere with a circumference of about 17,000 nautical miles. (In fact, the Eurasian landmass from Portugal to Korea covers only 140 degrees of longitude, and the earth's circumference is almost 25,000 nautical miles.) By Columbus's calculations, Japan should be less than 2,500 nautical miles west of the Canary Islands. (The actual distance between the Canaries and Japan is more than 10,000 nautical miles.) This geography suggested that sailing west from Europe to Asian markets would be profitable, and Columbus sought royal sponsorship for a voyage to prove his ideas. The Portuguese court declined his proposal, partly out of skepticism about his geography and partly because Dias's voyage of 1488 already pointed the way toward India.

Although Fernando and Isabel of Spain eventually agreed to sponsor Columbus's expedition, Italian bankers actually financed the voyage. In August 1492 his fleet of three ships departed Palos in southern Spain. He sailed south to the Canaries, picked up supplies, and then turned west with the trade winds. On the morning of 12 October 1492, he made landfall at an island in the Bahamas that the native **Taíno** inhabitants called Guanahaní and that Columbus rechristened San Salvador (also known as Watling Island). Thinking that he had arrived in the spice islands known familiarly as the Indies, Columbus called the Taíno "Indians." In search of gold he sailed around the Caribbean for almost three months, and at the large island of Cuba he sent a delegation to seek the court of the emperor of China. When Columbus returned to Spain, he reported to his royal sponsors that he had reached islands just off the coast of Asia.

Hemispheric Links Columbus never reached the riches of Asia, and despite three additional voyages across the Atlantic Ocean, he obtained very little gold in the Caribbean.

merchants the opportunity to buy silk, spices, and pepper at the source, rather than through Muslim intermediaries, and to take part in the flourishing trade of Asia described by Marco Polo.

Vasco da Gama Portuguese mariners did not immediately follow up Dias's voyage, because domestic and foreign problems distracted royal attention from voyages to Asia. In 1497, however, Vasco da Gama departed Lisbon with a fleet of four armed merchant ships bound for India. His experience was not altogether pleasant. His fleet went more

Taíno (TEYE-noh)

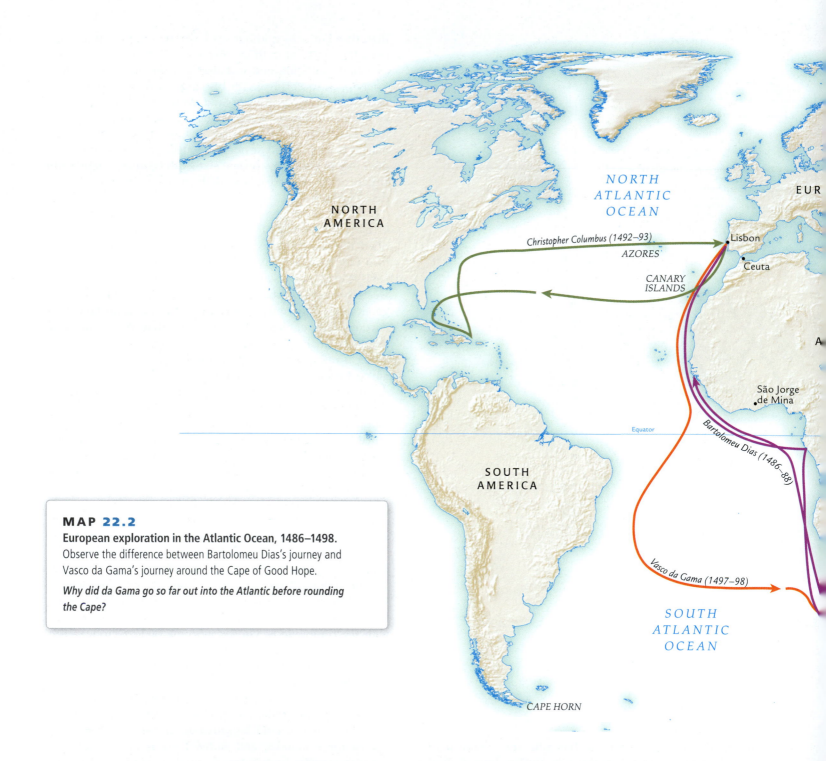

MAP 22.2

European exploration in the Atlantic Ocean, 1486–1498.
Observe the difference between Bartolomeu Dias's journey and
Vasco da Gama's journey around the Cape of Good Hope.

*Why did da Gama go so far out into the Atlantic before rounding
the Cape?*

Yet news of his voyage spread rapidly throughout Europe,
and hundreds of Spanish, English, French, and Dutch mariners soon followed in his wake. Particularly in the early sixteenth century, many of them continued to seek the passage
to Asian waters that Columbus himself had pursued. Over a
longer term, however, it became clear that the American continents and the Caribbean islands themselves held abundant
opportunities for entrepreneurs. Thus Columbus's voyages
to the western hemisphere had unintended but momentous

consequences, since they established links between the eastern and western hemispheres and paved the way for the
conquest, settlement, and exploitation of the Americas by
European peoples.

Voyages of Exploration: from the Atlantic to the Pacific

While some Europeans sought opportunities in the Americas, others continued to seek a western route to Asian mar-

Bartolomeu Dias (1486–88)
Christopher Columbus (1492–93)
Vasco da Gama (1497–98)

ASIA

Calicut

Equator

Mombasa

INDIAN
OCEAN

AUSTRALIA

APE OF GOOD HOPE

kets. The Spanish military commander Vasco Nuñez de Balboa sighted the Pacific Ocean in 1513 while searching for gold in Panama, but in the early sixteenth century no one knew how much ocean lay between the Americas and Asia. Indeed, no one even suspected the vast size of the Pacific Ocean, which covers one-third of the earth's surface.

Ferdinand Magellan The reconnaissance of the Pacific Ocean basin began with the Portuguese navigator Fernão de Magalhães (1480–1521), better known as Ferdinand Magellan.

While sailing in the service of Portugal, Magellan had visited ports throughout the Indian Ocean basin and had traveled east as far as the spice islands of Maluku. He believed that the spice islands and Asian markets lay fairly close to the western coast of the Americas, and he decided to pursue Christopher Columbus's goal of establishing a western route to Asian waters. Because Portuguese mariners had already reached Asian markets through the Indian Ocean, they had little interest in Magellan's proposed western route. Thus, on his Pacific expedition Magellan sailed in the service of Spain.

sources from the past

Christopher Columbus's First Impressions of American Peoples

Christopher Columbus kept journals of his experiences during his voyages to the western hemisphere. The journal of his first voyage survives mostly in summary, but it clearly communicates Columbus's first impressions of the peoples he met in the Caribbean islands. The following excerpts show that Columbus, like other European mariners, had both Christianity and commerce in mind when exploring distant lands.

Thursday, 11 October [1492]. . . .

I . . . in order that they would be friendly to us—because I recognized that they were people who would be better freed [from error] and converted to our Holy Faith by love than by force—to some of them I gave red caps, and glass beads which they put on their chests, and many other things of small value, in which they took so much pleasure and became so much our friends that it was a marvel. Later they came swimming to the ships' launches where we were and brought us parrots and cotton thread in balls and javelins and many other things, and they traded them to us for other things which we gave them, such as small glass beads and bells. In sum, they took everything and gave of what they had willingly.

But it seemed to me that they were a people very poor in everything. All of them go as naked as their mothers bore them; and the women also, although I did not see more than one quite young girl. And all those that I saw were young people, for none did I see of more than 30 years of age. They are very well formed, with handsome bodies and good faces. Their hair [is] coarse—almost like the tail of a horse—and short. They wear their hair down over their eyebrows except for a little in the back which they wear long and never cut. . . .

They do not carry arms nor are they acquainted with them, because I showed them swords and they took them by the edge and through ignorance cut themselves. They have no iron. Their javelins are shafts without iron and some of them have at the end a fish tooth and others of other things. All of them alike are of good-sized stature and carry themselves well. I saw some who had marks of wounds on their bodies and I made signs to them asking what they were; and they showed me how people from other islands nearby came there and tried to take them, and how they defended themselves and I believed and believe that they come here from *tierra firme* [the continent] to take them captive. They should be good and intelligent servants, for I see that they say very quickly everything that is said to them; and I believe that they would become Christians very easily, for it seemed to me that they had no religion. . . .

Monday, 12 November. . . .

They are very gentle and do not know what evil is; nor do they kill others, nor steal; and they are without weapons and so timid that a hundred of them flee from one of our men even if our men are teasing them. And they are credulous and aware that there is a God in heaven and convinced that we come from the heavens; and they say very quickly any prayer that we tell them to say, and they make the sign of the cross. So that Your Highnesses ought to resolve to make them Christians: for I believe that if you begin, in a short time you will end up having converted to our Holy Faith a multitude of peoples and acquiring large dominions and great riches and all of their peoples for Spain. Because without doubt there is in these lands a very great quantity of gold; for not without cause do these Indians that I bring with me say that there are in these islands places where they dig gold and wear it on their chests, on their ears, and on their arms, and on their legs; and they are very thick bracelets. And also there are stones, and there are precious pearls and infinite spicery. . . . And also here there is probably a great quantity of cotton; and I think that it would sell very well here without taking it to Spain but to the big cities belonging to the Grand [Mongol] Khan.

For Further Reflection

■ On the basis of Columbus's account, what inferences can you draw about his plans for American lands and peoples?

Source: Christopher Columbus. *The Diario of Christopher Columbus's First Voyage to America.* Trans. by Oliver Dunn and James E. Kelley Jr. Norman: University of Oklahoma Press, 1989, pp. 65–69, 143–45.

The Circumnavigation Magellan's voyage was an exercise in endurance. He left Spain in September 1519, and then began probing the eastern coast of South America in search of a strait leading to the Pacific. Eventually, he found and sailed through the tricky and treacherous strait, later to bear his name, near the southern tip of South America. After exiting the strait, his fleet sailed almost four months before taking on fresh provisions at Guam. During that period crewmen survived on worm-ridden biscuits, leather that they had softened in the ocean, and water gone foul. Ship's rats that were unfortunate enough to fall into the hands of famished sailors quickly became the centerpiece of a meal. A survivor reported in his account of the voyage that crewmen even ate ox hides, which they softened by dragging them through the sea for four or five days and then grilled on coals. Lacking fresh fruits and vegetables in their diet, many of the crew fell victim to the dreaded disease of scurvy, which caused painful rotting of the gums, loss of teeth, abscesses, hemorrhaging, weakness, loss of spirit, and in most cases death. Scurvy killed twenty-nine members of Magellan's crew during the Pacific crossing.

Conditions improved after the fleet called at Guam in March 1521, but its ordeal had not come to an end. From Guam, Magellan proceeded to the Philippine Islands, where he became involved in a local political dispute that took the lives of Magellan himself and 40 of his crew. The survivors continued on to the spice islands of Maluku, where they took on a cargo of cloves. Rather than brave the Pacific Ocean once again, they sailed home through the familiar waters of the Indian Ocean—and thus completed the first circumnavigation of the world—returning to Spain after a voyage of almost exactly three years. Of Magellan's five ships and 280 men, a single spice-laden ship with 18 of the original crew returned.

This color engraving features an idealized portrait of mariner Ferdinand Magellan.

Exploration of the Pacific
The Pacific Ocean is so vast that it took European explorers almost three centuries to chart its features. Spanish merchants built on information gleaned from Magellan's expedition and established a trade route between the Philippines and Mexico, but they did not continue to explore the ocean basin itself. English navigators, however, ventured into the Pacific in search of an elusive northwest passage from Europe to Asia. In fact, a northwest passage exists, but most of its route lies within the Arctic Circle. It is so far north that ice clogs its waters for much of the year, and it was only in the twentieth century that the Norwegian explorer Roald Amundsen traveled from the Atlantic to the Pacific by way of the northwest passage. Nevertheless, while searching for a passage, English mariners established many of the details of Pacific geography. In the sixteenth century, for example, Sir Francis Drake scouted the west coast of North America as far north as Vancouver Island. By the mid-eighteenth century, French mariners had joined English seafarers in exploring the Pacific Ocean in search of a northwest passage.

Russian expansion was mostly a land-based affair in early modern times, but by the eighteenth century Russians also were exploring the Pacific Ocean. Russian officials commissioned the Danish navigator Vitus Bering to undertake two maritime expeditions (1725–1730 and 1733–1742) in search of a northeast passage to Asian ports. Bering sailed through the icy Arctic Ocean and the Bering Strait, which separates Siberia from Alaska, and reconnoitered northern Asia as far as the Kamchatka peninsula. Other Russian explorers made their way from Alaska down the western Canadian coast to northern California. By 1800, Russian mariners were scouting the Pacific Ocean as far south as the Hawaiian Islands. Indeed, they built a small fort on the island of Kaua`i and engaged in trade there for a few years in the early nineteenth century.

Captain James Cook Along with the Russian explorers and Magellan, one of the most important of the Pacific explorers was Captain James Cook (1728–1779), who led three expeditions to the Pacific and died in a scuffle with the indigenous people of Hawai`i. Cook charted eastern Australia and New Zealand, and he added New Caledonia, Vanuatu, and Hawai`i to European maps of the Pacific. He probed the frigid waters of the Arctic Ocean and spent months at a time in the tropical islands of Tahiti, Tonga, and Hawai`i, where he showed deep interest in the manners, customs, and languages of Polynesian peoples. By the time Cook's voyages had come to an end, European geographers had compiled a reasonably accurate understanding of the world's ocean basins, their lands, and their peoples.

TRADE AND CONFLICT IN EARLY MODERN ASIA

The voyages of exploration taught European mariners how to sail to almost any coastline in the world and return safely. Once they arrived at their destinations, they sought commercial opportunities. In the eastern hemisphere they built a series of fortified trading posts that offered footholds in regions where established commercial networks had held sway for centuries. They even attempted to control the spice trade in the Indian Ocean but with limited success. They mostly did not have the human numbers or military power to impose their rule in the eastern hemisphere, although Spanish and Dutch forces established small island empires in the Philippines and Indonesia, respectively. In a parallel effort involving expansion across land rather than the sea, Russian explorers and adventurers established a presence in central Asian regions formerly ruled by the Mongols and in the tundra and forests of Siberia, thus laying the foundations for a vast Eurasian empire. Commercial and political competition in both the eastern and the western hemispheres led to conflict between European peoples, and by the end of the Seven Years' War in 1763, English military and merchant forces had gained an initiative over their rivals that enabled

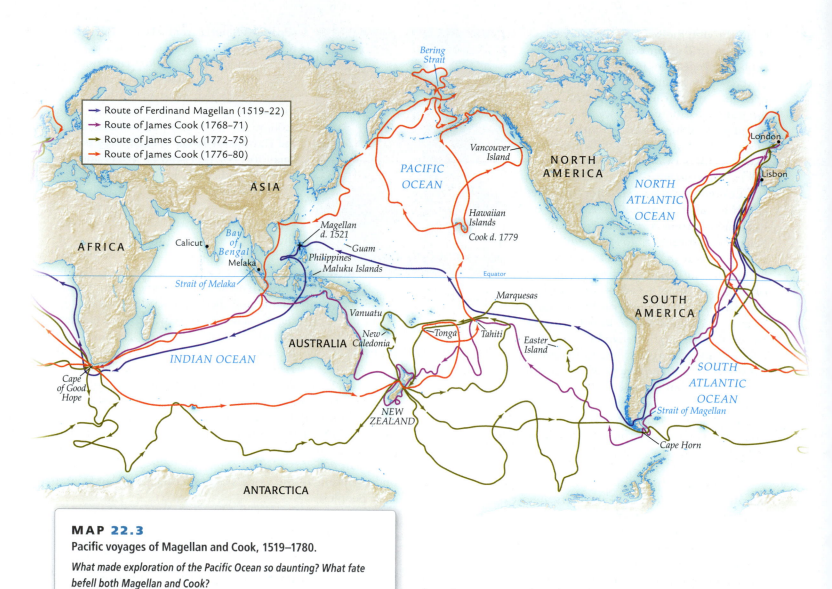

MAP 22.3

Pacific voyages of Magellan and Cook, 1519–1780.

What made exploration of the Pacific Ocean so daunting? What fate befell both Magellan and Cook?

them to dominate world trade and build the vast British empire of the nineteenth century.

Trading-Post Empires

Portuguese Trading Posts
Portuguese mariners built the earliest trading-post empire. Their goal was not to conquer territories but, rather, to control trade routes by forcing merchant vessels to call at fortified trading sites and pay duties there. Vasco da Gama obtained permission from local authorities to establish a trading post at Calicut when he arrived there in 1498. By the mid-sixteenth century, Portuguese merchants had built more than fifty trading posts between west Africa and east Asia. At São Jorge da Mina, they traded in west African slaves, and at Mozambique they attempted to control the south African gold trade. From Hormuz they controlled access to the Persian Gulf, and from

Goa they organized trade in Indian pepper. At Melaka they oversaw shipping between the South China Sea and the Indian Ocean, and they channeled trade in cloves and nutmeg through Ternate in the spice islands of Maluku. Posts at Macau and Nagasaki offered access to the markets of China and Japan.

Afonso d'Alboquerque
Equipped with heavy artillery, Portuguese vessels were able to overpower most other craft that they encountered, and they sometimes trained their cannon effectively onshore. The architect of their aggressive policy was Afonso d'Alboquerque, commander of Portuguese forces in the Indian Ocean during the early sixteenth century. Alboquerque's fleets seized Hormuz in 1508, Goa in 1510, and Melaka in 1511. From these strategic sites, Alboquerque sought to control Indian Ocean trade by forcing merchant ships to purchase safe-conduct passes and present them at Portuguese trading posts. Ships without passes were subject to confiscation, along with their cargoes. Alboquerque's forces punished violators of his policy by executing

them or cutting off their hands. Alboquerque was confident of Portuguese naval superiority and its ability to control trade in the Indian Ocean. After taking Melaka, he boasted that the arrival of Portuguese ships sent other vessels scurrying and that even the birds left the skies and sought cover.

Alboquerque's boast was an exaggeration. Although heavily armed, Portuguese forces did not have enough vessels to enforce the commander's orders. Arab, Indian, and Malay merchants continued to play prominent roles in Indian Ocean commerce, usually without taking the precaution of securing a safe-conduct pass. Portuguese ships transported perhaps half the pepper and spices that Europeans consumed during the early and middle decades of the sixteenth century, but Arab vessels delivered shipments through the Red Sea, which Portuguese forces never managed to control, to Cairo and Mediterranean trade routes.

By the late sixteenth century, Portuguese influence in the Indian Ocean weakened. Portugal was a small country with a small population—about one million in 1500—and was unable to sustain a large seaborne trading empire for very long. The crews of Portuguese ships often included Spanish, English, and Dutch sailors, who became familiar with Asian waters while in Portuguese service. By the late

This European drawing from Captain James Cook's first voyage focuses on the exotic features of a Maori chief's son.

A portrait of Captain James Cook painted by William Hodges about 1775 depicts a serious and determined man.

sixteenth century, investors in other lands began to organize their own expeditions to Asian markets. Most prominent of those who followed the Portuguese into the Indian Ocean were English and Dutch mariners.

English and Dutch Trading Posts Like their predecessors, English and Dutch merchants built trading posts on Asian coasts and sought to channel trade through them, but they did not attempt to control shipping on the high seas. They occasionally seized Portuguese sites, most notably when a Dutch fleet conquered Melaka in 1641. Yet Portuguese authorities held many of their trading posts into the twentieth century: Goa remained the official capital of Portuguese colonies in Asia until Indian forces reclaimed it in 1961. Meanwhile, English and Dutch entrepreneurs established parallel networks. English merchants concentrated on India and built trading posts at Bombay, Madras, and Calcutta, while the Dutch operated more broadly from Cape Town, Colombo, and Batavia (modern Jakarta on the island of Java).

sources from the past

Afonso D'Alboquerque Seizes Hormuz

Afonso d'Alboquerque the mariner had a son of the same name who in 1557 published a long set of historical Commentaries on his father's deeds. His account of the battle for Hormuz vividly illustrates the effectiveness of Portuguese artillery as well as the chaos and confusion of sea battles in early modern times.

As some time had passed since the king [of Hormuz] had received information about the [Portuguese] fleet and the destruction that the great Afonso d'Alboquerque had wrought along the [Arabian] coast, he began to prepare himself to fight with him. For this end he gave orders to detain all the ships that came into the port of Hormuz and added a force of sixty great vessels into which he draughted off many soldiers and much artillery with everything that was required for the undertaking. And among these great vessels there was one belonging to the king of Cambay [in India] . . . and another of the prince of Cambay. . . . And besides these ships there were in the harbor about 200 galleys, which are long ships with many oars. . . . There were also many barks full of small guns and men wearing sword-proof dress and armed from head to foot, most of them being archers. All this fleet was rigged out with flags and standards and colored ensigns, and made a very beautiful appearance. . . .

When Afonso d'Alboquerque perceived the gleaming of the swords and waving of the bucklers and other doings of the Moors [Muslims] on shore, . . . he understood by these signs that the king was determined to give him battle. . . . When morning broke, . . . he ordered a broadside to be fired. The bombardiers took aim so that with the first two shots they fired they sent two large ships which were in front of them, with all their men, to the bottom—one being the prince of Cambay's ship. . . . Afonso Lopez da Costa, who was stationed on the land side, vanquished and sent to the bottom some portion of the galleys and guard boats that his artillery could reach. Manuel Telez, after having caused great slaughter upon some vessels, . . . ran into a large vessel that lay close to him and killed a part of the men in it, while the rest threw themselves into the sea, and those who were heavy-armed went down at once. João da Nova too with his artillery did great execution among the ships that lay along the piles, as did also Antonio do Campo and Francisco de Tavora among the galleys that had surrounded them, and all night long they kept on hooking their anchors together in order to catch the galleys in the middle of them. And although the Moors endeavored to avenge themselves with their artillery, our men were so well fortified with their defenses that they did them no harm, except on the upper deck, and with their arrows they wounded some people.

The fight was so confused on this side and on that, both with artillery and arrows, that it lasted some time without either party seeing each other by reason of the smoke. As soon as this cleared off, . . . and when Afonso saw the discomfiture of the king's fleet and the unexpected victory that Our Lord had sent him and the Moors throwing themselves into the sea from fear of our artillery, thinking that they could escape in that way by swimming, . . . [Afonso] called out to the captains to take to their boats and follow up the victory.

For Further Reflection

■ How might a Muslim commentator have described the battle for Hormuz?

Source: Afonso d'Alboquerque. *Commentaries of the Great Afonso Dalboquerque*, 4 vols. Trans. by Walter de Gray Birch. London: Hakluyt Society, 1875–84, 1:105, 112–14. (Translation slightly modified.)

English and Dutch merchants enjoyed two main advantages over their Portuguese predecessors. They sailed faster, cheaper, and more powerful ships, which offered both an economic and a military edge over their competitors. Furthermore, they conducted trade through an efficient form of commercial organization—the joint-stock company—which enabled investors to realize handsome profits while limiting the risk to their investments.

The Trading Companies English and Dutch merchants formed two especially powerful joint-stock companies: the English East India Company, founded in 1600, and its Dutch counterpart, the United East India Company, known from its initials as the VOC (Vereenigde Oost-Indische Compagnie), established in 1602. Private merchants advanced funds to launch these companies, outfit them with ships and crews, and provide them with commodities and money to trade. Although they enjoyed government support, the companies were privately owned enterprises. Unhampered by political oversight, company agents concentrated strictly on profitable trade. Their charters granted them the right to buy, sell, build trading posts, and even make war in the companies' interests.

The English and Dutch companies experienced immediate financial success. In 1601, for example, five English ships set sail from London with cargoes mostly of gold and silver

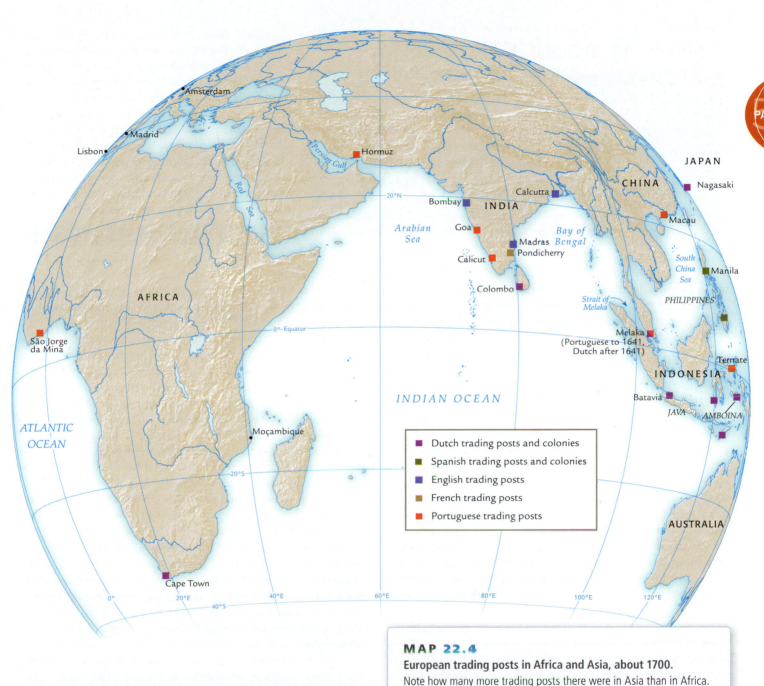

MAP 22.4

European trading posts in Africa and Asia, about 1700.

Note how many more trading posts there were in Asia than in Africa.

What accounts for the difference?

coins valued at thirty thousand pounds sterling. When they returned in 1603, the spices that they carried were worth more than one million pounds sterling. The first Dutch expedition did not realize such fantastic profits, but it more than doubled the investments of its underwriters. Because of their advanced nautical technology, powerful military arsenal, efficient organization, and relentless pursuit of profit, the English East India Company and the VOC contributed to the early formation of a global network of trade.

European Conquests in Southeast Asia

Following voyages of exploration to the western hemisphere, Europeans conquered indigenous peoples, built territorial empires, and established colonies settled by Eu-

ropean migrants. In the eastern hemisphere, however, they were mostly unable to force their will on large Asian populations and powerful centralized states. With the decline of the Portuguese effort to control shipping in the Indian Ocean, Europeans mostly traded peacefully in Asian waters alongside Arab, Indian, Malay, and Chinese merchants.

Yet in two island regions of southeast Asia—the Philippines and Indonesia—Europeans conquered existing authorities and imposed their rule. Though densely populated,

thinking about ENCOUNTERS

Trading-Post Empires

Trading-post empires provided the most prominent spaces for cross-cultural interactions between Europeans, Africans, and Asians. Trading posts also limited European intrusion into Africa and Asia, especially in contrast to the settlement empires of the Americas. What characterized the relations between, for example, the Portuguese and the inhabitants of the Indian Ocean basin? Why were Europeans confined to such posts?

neither the Philippines nor Indonesia had a powerful state when Europeans arrived there in the sixteenth century. Nor did imperial authorities in China or India lay claim to the island regions. Heavily armed ships enabled Europeans to bring considerable force to bear and to establish imperial regimes that favored the interests of European merchants.

Conquest of the Philippines

Spanish forces approached the Philippines in 1565 under the command of Miguel López de Legazpi, who named the islands after King Philip II of Spain. Legazpi overcame local authorities in Cebu and Manila in almost bloodless contests. Because the Philippines had no central government, there was no organized resistance to the intrusion. Spanish forces faced a series of small, disunited chiefdoms, most of which soon fell before Spanish ships and guns. By 1575 Spanish forces controlled the coastal regions of the central and northern islands, and during the seventeenth century they extended their authority to most parts of the archipelago. The main region outside their control was the southern island of Mindanao, where a large Muslim community stoutly resisted Spanish expansion.

Manila

Spanish policy in the Philippines revolved around trade and Christianity. Manila soon emerged as a bustling, multicultural port city—an entrepôt for trade particularly in silk—and it quickly became the hub of Spanish commercial activity in Asia. Chinese merchants were especially prominent in Manila. They occupied a specially designated commercial district of the city, and they accounted for about one-quarter of Manila's forty-two thousand residents in the mid-seventeenth century. They supplied the silk goods that Spanish traders shipped to Mexico in the so-called Manila galleons. Their commercial success brought suspicion on their community, and resentful Spanish and Filipino residents massacred Chinese merchants by the thousands in at least six major eruptions of violence in 1603, 1639, 1662, 1686, 1762, and 1819. Nevertheless, Spanish authorities continued to rely heavily on the wealth that Chinese merchants brought to Manila.

Apart from promoting trade, Spanish authorities in the Philippines also sought to spread Roman Catholicism throughout the archipelago. Spanish rulers and missionaries pressured prominent Filipinos to convert to Christianity in hopes of persuading others to follow their example. They opened schools to teach the fundamentals of Christian doctrine, along with basic literacy, in densely populated regions throughout the islands. The missionaries encountered stiff resistance in highland regions, where Spanish authority was not as strong as on the coasts, and resistance drew support from opponents of Spanish domination as well as from resentment of the newly arrived faith. Over the long term, however, Filipinos turned increasingly to Christianity, and by the nineteenth century the Philippines had become one of the most fervent Roman Catholic lands in the world.

Conquest of Java

Dutch mariners, who imposed their rule on the islands of Indonesia, did not worry about seeking converts to Christianity, but concentrated instead on the trade in spices, particularly cloves, nutmeg, and mace. The architect of Dutch policy was Jan Pieterszoon Coen, who in 1619 founded Batavia on the island of Java to serve as an entrepôt for the VOC. Batavia occupied a strategic site near the Sunda Strait, and its market attracted both Chinese and Malay vessels. Coen's plan was to establish a VOC monopoly over spice production and trade, thus enabling Dutch merchants to reap enormous profits in European markets. Coen brought his naval power to bear on the small Indonesian islands and forced them to deliver spices only to VOC merchants. On larger islands such as Java, he took advantage of tensions between local princes and authorities and extracted concessions from many in return for providing them with aid against the others. By the late seventeenth century, the VOC controlled all the ports of Java as well as most of the important spice-bearing islands throughout the Indonesian archipelago.

Dutch numbers were too few for them to rule directly over their whole southeast Asian empire. They made alliances with local authorities to maintain order in most regions, reserving for direct Dutch rule only Batavia and the most important spice-bearing islands such as clove-producing Amboina and the Banda Islands. They sought less to rule than to control the production of spices. The Dutch did not embark on campaigns of conquest for purposes of adding to their holdings, but they uprooted spice-bearing plants on islands they did not control and mercilessly attacked peoples who sold their spices to merchants not associated with the VOC. Monopoly profits from the spice trade not only enriched the VOC but also made the Netherlands the most prosperous land in Europe throughout most of the seventeenth century.

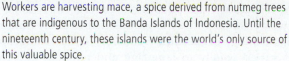
Workers are harvesting mace, a spice derived from nutmeg trees that are indigenous to the Banda Islands of Indonesia. Until the nineteenth century, these islands were the world's only source of this valuable spice.

Foundations of the Russian Empire in Asia

While western European peoples were building maritime empires, Russians were laying the foundations for a vast land empire that embraced most of northern Eurasia. This round of expansion began in the mid-sixteenth century, as Russian forces took over several Mongol khanates in central Asia. These acquisitions resulted in Russian control over the Volga River and offered opportunities for trade with the Ottoman empire, Iran, and even India through the Caspian Sea. Because of its strategic location on the Volga delta where the river flows into the Caspian Sea, the city of Astrakhan became a bustling commercial center, home to a community

A woodcut illustration depicts indigenous peoples of Siberia delivering fur tribute to Russian merchants in a walled, riverside fort.

of several hundred foreign merchants from as far away as northern India. During the seventeenth and eighteenth centuries, some of the Indian merchants regularly made their way up the Volga River to trade in Moscow and the Russian interior, while others devised plans (which they never realized) to extend their activities to the Baltic Sea and take their business to western Europe. In the eighteenth century, Russian forces extended their presence in the Caspian Sea region by absorbing much of the Caucasus, a vibrant multiethnic region embracing the modern-day states of Georgia, Armenia, and Azerbaijan.

Encounters in Siberia Far more extensive were Russian acquisitions in northeastern Eurasia. The frozen tundras and dense forests of Siberia posed formidable challenges, but explorers and merchants made their way into the region in a quest for fur. Throughout the early modern era, fur was a lucrative commodity that lured Russians eastward, just as North American fur attracted the interest of English, French, and Dutch merchants. Russian expansion in northeastern

Eurasia began in 1581 when the wealthy Stroganov family hired a freebooting adventurer named Yermak to capture the khanate of Sibir in the Ural Mountains. In the following decades, Russian explorers pushed into the interior regions of Siberia by way of the region's great rivers. By 1639 they had made their way across the Eurasian landmass and reached the Pacific Ocean.

Native Peoples of Siberia Siberia was home to about twenty-six major ethnic groups that lived by hunting, trapping, fishing, or herding reindeer. These indigenous peoples varied widely in language and religion, and they responded in different ways to the arrival of Russian adventurers who sought to exact tribute from them by coercing them to supply pelts on a regular basis. Some groups readily accepted iron tools, woven cloth, flour, tea, and liquor for the skins of fur-bearing animals such as otter, lynx, marten, arctic fox, and especially the sleek sable. Others resented the ever-increasing demands for tribute and resisted Russian encroachment on their lands. Russian forces then

resorted to punishing raids and hostage taking to induce Siberian peoples to deliver furs. The Yakut people of the Lena and Aldan River valleys in central Siberia mounted a revolt against Russian oppression in 1642 and experienced a brutal retribution that continued for forty years, forcing many Yakut out of their settlements and reducing their population by an estimated 70 percent. Quite apart from military violence, the peoples of Siberia also reeled from epidemic diseases that reduced many populations by more than half.

As violence and disease sharply diminished the delivery of furs, the Russian government recognized that its interests lay in protection of the "small peoples," as state officials called the indigenous inhabitants of Siberia. Government-sponsored missionaries sought to convert Siberian peoples to Orthodox Christianity and bring them into Russian society, but they had little success. Few Siberians expressed an interest in Christianity, and those few came mostly from the ranks of criminals, abandoned hostages, slaves, and others who had little status in their own societies. Furthermore, once indigenous peoples converted to Christianity, they were exempt from obligations to provide fur tributes, so the Russian government demonstrated less zeal in its religious mission than did the Spanish monarchs, who made the spread of Roman Catholic Christianity a prime goal of imperial expansion. Although they managed to attract a few Siberian converts, Orthodox missionaries mostly served the needs of Russian merchants, adventurers, and explorers in Siberia. For their part, the indigenous peoples of Siberia continued to practice their inherited religions guided by native shamans.

The Russian Occupation of Siberia

The settlers who established a Russian presence in Siberia included social misfits, convicted criminals, and even prisoners of war. Despite the region's harsh terrain, Russian migrants gradually filtered into Siberia and thoroughly altered its demographic complexion. Small agricultural settlements grew up near many trading posts, particularly in the fertile Amur River valley. Siberian landowners offered working conditions that were much lighter than those of Russia proper, so disgruntled peasants sometimes fled to settlements east of the Ural Mountains. Over time, Siberian trading posts with their garrisons developed into Russian towns with Russian-speaking populations attending Russian Orthodox churches. By 1763 some 420,000 Russians lived in Siberia, nearly double the number of indigenous inhabitants. In the nineteenth century, large numbers of additional migrants moved east to mine Siberian gold, silver, copper, and iron, and the Russian state was well on the way toward consolidating its control over the region.

Commercial Rivalries and the Seven Years' War

Exploration and imperial expansion led to conflicts not only between Europeans and Asians but also among Europeans themselves. Mariners competed vigorously for trade in Asia

and the Americas, and their efforts to establish markets—and sometimes monopolies as well—led frequently to clashes with their counterparts from different lands.

Competition and Conflict Indeed, throughout the seventeenth and early eighteenth centuries, commercial and political rivalries led to running wars between ships flying different flags. Dutch vessels were most numerous in the Indian Ocean, and they enabled the VOC to dominate the spice trade. Dutch forces expelled most Portuguese merchants from southeast Asia and prevented English mariners from establishing secure footholds there. By the early eighteenth century, trade in Indian cotton and tea from Ceylon had begun to overshadow the spice trade, and English and French merchants working from trading posts in India became the dominant carriers in the Indian Ocean. Fierce competition again generated violence: in 1746 French forces seized the English trading post at Madras, one of the three principal centers of British operations in India.

Commercial competition led to conflict also in the Caribbean and the Americas. English pirates and privateers preyed on Spanish shipping from Mexico, often seizing vessels carrying cargoes of silver. English and French forces constantly skirmished and fought over sugar islands in the Caribbean while also contesting territorial claims in North America. Almost all conflicts between European states in the eighteenth century spilled over into the Caribbean and the Americas.

The Seven Years' War Commercial rivalries combined with political differences and came to a head in the Seven Years' War (1756–1763). The Seven Years' War was a global conflict in that it took place in several distinct geographic theaters—Europe, India, the Caribbean, and North America—and involved Asian and indigenous American peoples as well as Europeans. Sometimes called "the great war for empire," the Seven Years' War had deep implications for global affairs, since it laid the foundation for 150 years of British imperial hegemony in the world.

In Europe the war pitted Britain and Prussia against France, Austria, and Russia. In India, British and French forces each allied with local rulers and engaged in a contest for hegemony in the Indian Ocean. In the Caribbean, Spanish forces joined with the French in an effort to limit British expansion in the western hemisphere. In North America—where the Seven Years' War merged with a conflict already under way known as the French and Indian War (1754–1763)—British and French armies made separate alliances with indigenous peoples in an effort to outmaneuver each other.

British Hegemony British forces fought little in Europe, where their Prussian allies held off massive armies seeking to surround and crush the expansive Prussian state. Elsewhere, however, British armies and navies handily overcame their enemies. They ousted French merchants from

ATLANTIC
OCEAN

North
Pole

ARCTIC OC

45°W   90°

0°

45°E

45°E

90°E

Baltic Sea

Warsaw
POLAND

LITHUANIA
LATVIA
ESTONIA

Murmansk

Barents
Sea

Novgorod

Archangel

Danube

Kiev
UKRAINE   Moscow

THE
CRIMEA

Black Sea

Volga

URAL MOUNTAINS

Ob

SIBERIA

Lena

CAUCASUS
MOUNTAINS

Astrakhan

Ob

Yenisey

Caspian Sea

Aral
Sea

Lena

Irkutsk

GOBI
DESERT

HIMALAYAS

INDIA

CHINA

MAP 22.5

Russian expansion, 1462–1795.
Observe how vast the empire became after it added the territory of Siberia.

How did Russians exert their control over such a huge and unforgiving territory?

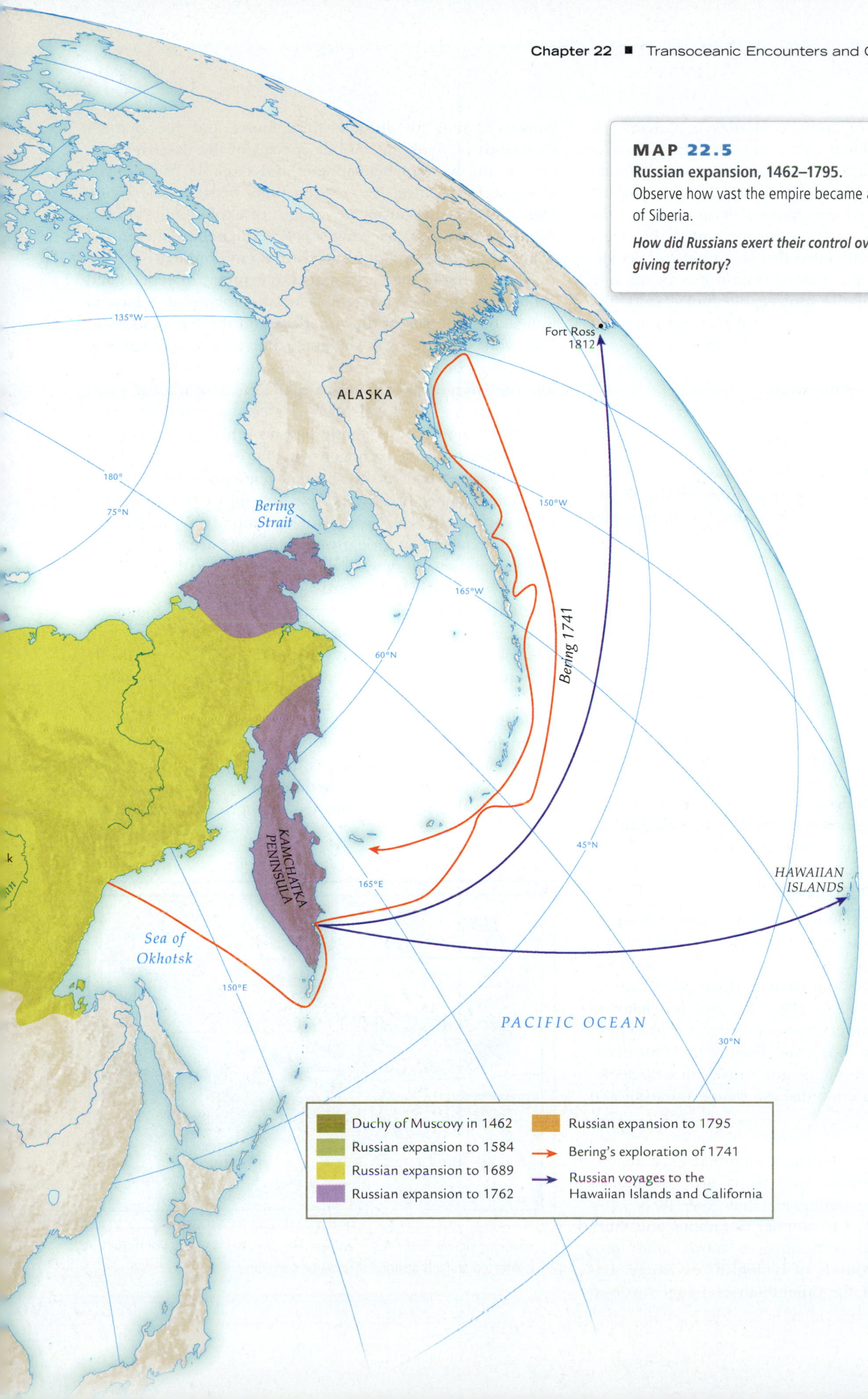

PART 5

135°W

ALASKA

Fort Ross
1812

Bering
Strait

180°

75°N

150°W

165°W

60°N

Bering 1741

KAMCHATKA
PENINSULA

45°N

HAWAIIAN
ISLANDS

165°E

Sea of
Okhotsk

150°E

PACIFIC OCEAN

30°N

Duchy of Muscovy in 1462	Russian expansion to 1795
Russian expansion to 1584	Bering's exploration of 1741
Russian expansion to 1689	Russian voyages to the Hawaiian Islands and California
Russian expansion to 1762	

India and took control of French colonies in Canada, although they allowed French authorities to retain most of their Caribbean possessions. They allowed Spanish forces to retain Cuba but took Florida from the Spanish empire. By no means did these victories make Britain master of the world, or even of Europe: both in Europe and in the larger world, powerful states challenged British ambitions. Yet victory in the Seven Years' War placed Britain in a position to dominate world trade for the foreseeable future, and "the great war for empire" paved the way for the establishment of the British empire in the nineteenth century. The war also suggested how close together earlier global exchanges had brought the peoples of the world.

ECOLOGICAL EXCHANGES

European explorers and those who followed them established links between all lands and peoples of the world. Interaction between peoples in turn resulted in an unprecedented volume of exchange across the boundary lines of societies and cultural regions. Some of that exchange involved biological species: plants, food crops, animals, human populations, and disease pathogens all spread to regions they had not previously visited. These biological exchanges had differing and dramatic effects on human populations, destroying some of them through epidemic diseases while enlarging others through increased food supplies and richer diets. Commercial exchange also flourished in the wake of the voyages of exploration as European merchants traveled to ports throughout the world in search of trade. By the late sixteenth century, they had built fortified trading posts at strategic sites in the Indian, Atlantic, and Pacific Ocean basins. By the mid-eighteenth century, they had established global networks of trade and communication.

The Columbian Exchange

Processes of biological exchange were prominent features of world history well before modern times. The early expansion of Islam had facilitated the diffusion of plants and food crops throughout much of the eastern hemisphere during the period from about 700 to 1100 C.E., and transplanted species helped spark demographic and economic growth in all the lands where they took root. During the fourteenth century the spread of bubonic plague caused drastic demographic losses when epidemic disease struck Eurasian and north African lands.

Biological Exchanges Yet the "Columbian exchange"—the global diffusion of plants, food crops, animals, human populations, and disease pathogens that took place after voyages of exploration by Christopher Columbus and other European mariners—had consequences much more profound than did earlier rounds of biological exchange. Unlike the earlier processes, the Columbian exchange involved lands with radically different flora, fauna, and diseases. For thousands of years the various species of the eastern hemisphere, the western hemisphere, and Oceania had evolved along separate lines. By creating links between these biological zones, the European voyages of exploration set off a round of biological exchange that permanently altered the world's human geography and natural environment.

Beginning in the early sixteenth century, infectious and contagious diseases brought sharp demographic losses to indigenous peoples of the Americas and the Pacific islands. The worst scourge was smallpox, but measles, diphtheria, whooping cough, and influenza also took heavy tolls. Before the voyages of exploration, none of these maladies had reached the western hemisphere or Oceania, and the peoples of those regions consequently had no inherited or acquired immunities to those pathogens. In the eastern hemisphere, these diseases had mostly become endemic: they claimed a certain number of victims from the ranks of infants and small children, but survivors gained immunity to the diseases through exposure at an early age. In some areas of Europe, for example, smallpox was responsible for 10 to 15 percent of deaths, but most victims were age ten or younger. Although its effects were tragic for individual families and communities, smallpox did not pose a threat to European society as a whole because it did not carry away adults, who were mostly responsible for economic production and social organization.

Epidemic Diseases and Population Decline
When infectious and contagious diseases traveled to previously unexposed populations, however, they touched off ferocious epidemics that sometimes destroyed entire societies. Beginning in 1519, epidemic smallpox ravaged the Az-

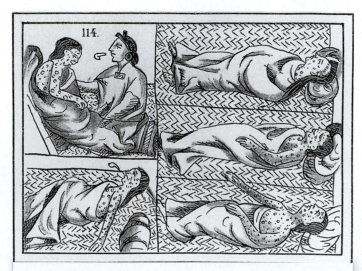

Smallpox victims in the Aztec empire. The disease killed most of those it infected and left disfiguring scars on survivors.

tec empire, often in combination with other diseases, and within a century the indigenous population of Mexico had declined by as much as 90 percent, from about 17 million to 1.3 million. By that time Spanish conquerors had imposed their rule on Mexico, and the political, social, and cultural traditions of the indigenous peoples had either disappeared or fallen under Spanish domination.

Imported diseases took their worst tolls in densely populated areas such as the Aztec and Inca empires, but they did not spare other regions. Smallpox and other diseases were so easily transmissible that they raced to remote areas of North and South America and sparked epidemics even before the first European explorers arrived in those regions. By the 1530s smallpox may have spread as far from Mexico as the Great Lakes in the north and the pampas of Argentina in the south.

When introduced to the Pacific islands, infectious and contagious diseases struck vulnerable populations with the same horrifying effects as in the Americas, albeit on a smaller scale. All told, disease epidemics sparked by the Columbian exchange probably caused the worst demographic calamity in all of world history. Between 1500 and 1800, upwards of 100 million people may have died of diseases imported into the Americas and the Pacific islands.

Food Crops and Animals Over the long term, however, the Columbian exchange increased rather than diminished human population because of the global spread of food crops and animals that it sponsored. In the long term, a better-nourished world was an important contributing factor in the growth of the world's population, which began in the eighteenth century and has continued to the present. Out of Eurasia to the western hemisphere traveled wheat, rice, sugar, bananas, apples, cherries, peaches, peas, and citrus fruits. Wheat in particular grew well on the plains of North America and on the pampas of Argentina, regions either too dry or too cold for the cultivation of indigenous maize (corn). Africa contributed yams, okra, collard greens, and coffee. Dairy and meat-yielding animals—horses, cattle, pigs, sheep, goats, and chickens—went from Europe to the Americas, where they sharply increased supplies of food and animal energy.

American Crops Food crops native to the Americas also played prominent roles in the Columbian exchange. American crops that took root in Africa, Asia, and Europe include maize, potatoes, beans, tomatoes, peppers, peanuts, manioc, papayas, guavas, avocados, pineapples, and cacao, to name only the most important. (A less nutritious transplant was tobacco.) Residents of the eastern hemisphere only gradually developed a taste for American crops, but by the eighteenth century maize and potatoes had contributed to a sharply increased number of calories in Eurasian diets. Maize became especially important in China because it grew in eco-niches unsuitable for rice and millet produc-

tion. With the exception of Bengal (India), Asian lands proved less welcoming to the potato. It did eventually conquer most of northern Europe, from Ireland to Russia, because of its impressive nutritional qualities. American bean varieties added protein, and tomatoes and peppers provided vitamins and zesty flavors in lands from western Europe to China. Peanuts and manioc flourished in tropical southeast Asian and west African soils that otherwise would not produce large yields or support large populations. The Americas also supplied medicinal plants. Derived from the bark of the Peruvian cinchona tree, bitter-tasting quinine was the first effective treatment for malaria and proved vital to Europeans trying to survive mosquito-ridden tropics.

Population Growth The Columbian exchange of plants and animals fueled a surge in world population. In 1500, as Eurasian peoples were recovering from epidemic bubonic plague, world population stood at about 425 million. By 1600 it had increased more than 25 percent to 545 million. Human numbers increased less rapidly during the next century,

Tabacum latifolium.

Tobacco was long used for religious and spiritual purposes in the Americas. After their arrival in the Americas, Europeans quickly popularized tobacco as a trade item and as a recreational drug to be smoked, snuffed, or chewed.

thinking about TRADITIONS

Local Foodways

For millennia, humans had generally relied on locally tended crops and foraged foods for their sustenance. How did the Columbian exchange alter those traditional foodways? What new crops and animals traveled between the eastern and western hemispheres—and what were the consequences?

reaching 610 million in 1700. But thereafter they increased at a faster rate than ever before in world history. By 1750 human population stood at 720 million, and by 1800 it had surged to 900 million, having grown by almost 50 percent during the previous century. Much of the rise was due to the increased nutritional value of diets enriched by the global exchange of food crops and animals.

Migration Alongside disease pathogens and plant and animal species, the Columbian exchange also involved the spread of human populations through transoceanic migration, whether voluntary or forced. During the period from 1500 to 1800, the largest contingent of migrants consisted of enslaved Africans transported involuntarily to South American, North American, and Caribbean destinations. A smaller but still sizable migration involved Europeans who traveled to the Americas and settled in lands depopulated by infectious and contagious diseases. During the nineteenth century, European peoples traveled in massive numbers mostly to the western hemisphere but also to south Africa, Australia, and Pacific islands where diseases had diminished indigenous populations, and Asian peoples migrated to tropical and subtropical destinations throughout much of the world. In combination, those migrations have profoundly influenced modern world history.

The Origins of Global Trade

The trading-post empires established by Portuguese, Dutch, and English merchants linked Asian markets with European consumers and offered opportunities for European mariners to participate in the carrying trade within Asia. European vessels transported Persian carpets to India, Indian cottons to southeast Asia, southeast Asian spices to India and China, Chinese silks to Japan, and Japanese silver and copper to China and India. By the late sixteenth century, European merchants were as prominent as Arabs in the trading world of the Indian Ocean basin.

Transoceanic Trade Besides stimulating commerce in the eastern hemisphere, the voyages of European merchant mariners encouraged the emergence of a genuinely global trading system. As Europeans established colonies in the Caribbean and the Americas, for example, trade networks extended to all areas of the Atlantic Ocean basin. European manufactured goods traveled west across the Atlantic in exchange for silver from Mexican and Peruvian mines and agricultural products such as sugar and tobacco, both of which were in high demand among European consumers. Trade in human beings also figured in Atlantic commerce. European textiles, guns, and other manufactured goods went south to west Africa, where merchants exchanged them for African slaves, who then went to the tropical and subtropical regions of the western hemisphere to work on plantations.

The Manila Galleons The experience of the Manila galleons illustrates the early workings of the global economy in the Pacific Ocean basin. For 250 years, from 1565 to 1815, Spanish galleons—sleek, fast, heavily armed ships capable of carrying large cargoes—regularly plied the waters of the Pacific Ocean between Manila in the Philippines and Acapulco on the west coast of Mexico. From Manila they took Asian luxury goods to Mexico and exchanged them for silver. Most of the precious metal made its way to China, where a thriving domestic economy demanded increasing quantities of silver, the basis of Chinese currency. In fact, the demand for silver was so high in China that European merchants exchanged it for Chinese gold, which they later traded profitably for more silver as well as luxury goods in Japan. Meanwhile, some of the Asian luxury goods from Manila remained in Mexico or went to Peru, where they contributed to a comfortable way of life for Spanish ruling elites. Most, however, went overland across Mexico and then traveled by ship across the Atlantic to Spain and European markets.

Environmental Effects of Global Trade As silver lubricated growing volumes of global trade, pressures fell on several animal species that had the misfortune to become prominent commodities on the world market. Fur-bearing animals came under particularly intense pressure, as hunters sought their pelts for sale to consumers in China, Europe, and North America. During the seventeenth century, an estimated two hundred to three hundred thousand sable pelts flowed annually from Siberia to the global market, and during the eighteenth century, more than sixteen million North American beaver pelts fed consumers' demands for fur hats and cloaks. Wanton hunting of fur-bearing animals soon drove many species into extinction or near-extinction, permanently altering the environments they had formerly inhabited. Quite apart from fur-bearing animals, early modern hunters harvested enormous numbers of deer, codfish, whales, walruses, seals, and other species as merchants

This is an artist's rendering of a Spanish galleon. Galleons were large, multidecked, highly stable and maneuverable sailing ships used by Europeans for war or commerce. The Spanish and the Portuguese built the largest types for their profitable overseas trade.

sought to supply skins, food, oil, ivory, and other animal products to global consumers.

By the late sixteenth century, conditions favored the relentless human exploitation of the world's natural and agricultural resources, as European mariners had permanently linked the world's port cities and created global trading networks. During the next two centuries, the volume of global trade expanded, as English, Dutch, French, and other merchants contributed to the development of global markets. During the seventeenth century, for example, Dutch merchants imported, among other commodities, wheat from south Africa, cowry shells from India, and sugar from Brazil. The wheat fed domestic consumers, who increasingly worked as merchants, bankers, or manufacturers rather than as cultivators. English, Dutch, and other merchants eagerly purchased the cowry shells—which served as currency in much of sub-Saharan Africa—and exchanged them for slaves destined for plantations in the western hemisphere. The sugar went on the market at Amsterdam and found its way to consumers throughout Europe. During the eighteenth century, world trade became even more intricate as mass markets emerged for commodities such as coffee, tea, sugar, and tobacco. By 1750 all parts of the world except Australia participated in global networks of commercial relations in which European merchant mariners played prominent roles.

in perspective

Global commercial and biological exchanges arose from the efforts of European mariners to explore the world's waters and establish sea lanes that would support long-distance trade. Their search for sea routes to Asia led them to the western hemisphere and the vast expanse of the Pacific Ocean. The geographic knowledge that they accumulated enabled them to link the world's regions into a finely articulated network of trade. But commercial exchange was not the only result of this global network. Food crops, animal stocks, disease pathogens, and human migrants also traveled the sea lanes and dramatically influenced societies throughout the world. Transplanted crops and animal species led to improved nutrition and increasing populations throughout the eastern hemisphere. Epidemics sparked by unfamiliar disease pathogens ravaged indigenous populations in the Americas and the Pacific islands. Massive migrations of human communities transformed the social and cultural landscape of the Americas and encouraged increased mingling of the world's peoples. The European voyages of exploration, transoceanic trade networks, and the Columbian exchange pushed the world's regions toward interdependence and global integration. ●

CHRONOLOGY	
1394–1460	Life of Prince Henry the Navigator of Portugal
1488	Bartolomeu Dias's voyage around the Cape of Good Hope into the Indian Ocean
1492	Christopher Columbus's first voyage to the western hemisphere
1497–1499	Vasco da Gama's first voyage to India
1500	Establishment of Portuguese trading post in Calicut, India
1519–1522	Ferdinand Magellan's circumnavigation of the world
1565–1575	Spanish conquest of the Philippines
1619	Establishment of Batavia by the Dutch on the island of Java
1756–1763	Seven Years' War
1768–1780	Captain James Cook's voyages in the Pacific Ocean

For Further Reading

David R. Abernathy. *The Dynamics of Global Dominance: European Overseas Empires, 1415–1980.* New Haven, 2000. A survey of the rise and decline of European overseas empires during a period of more than five hundred years.

Rene J. Barendse. *The Arabian Seas.* Eastgate, N.Y., 2002. A path-breaking and complex work that emphasizes the long predominance of Asia in the world economy.

Francisco Bethencourt and Diogo Curto, eds. *Portuguese Overseas Expansion.* New York, 2007. A collection of essays provides an overview of Portuguese maritime expansion between 1400 and 1800.

K. N. Chaudhuri. *Trade and Civilisation in the Indian Ocean: An Economic History from the Rise of Islam to 1750.* Cambridge, 1985. A brilliant analysis that places the European presence in the Indian Ocean in a larger historical context.

———. *The Trading World of Asia and the English East India Company, 1660–1760.* Cambridge, 1978. The best study of the English East India Company and its role in world trade.

Carlo Cipolla. *Guns, Sails, and Empires: Technological Innovation and the Early Phases of European Expansion, 1400–1700.* New York, 1965. A well-written study of the naval and military technology available to European mariners.

Christopher Columbus. *The Diario of Christopher Columbus's First Voyage to America.* Trans. by Oliver Dunn and James E. Kelley Jr. Norman, Okla., 1989. A careful translation.

Alfred W. Crosby. *The Columbian Exchange: Biological and Cultural Consequences of 1492.* Westport, Conn., 1972. Focuses on early exchanges of plants, animals, and diseases between Europe and America.

———. *Ecological Imperialism: The Biological Expansion of Europe, 900–1900.* Cambridge, 1986. An important study that examines the establishment of European biological species in the larger world.

Philip D. Curtin. *Cross-Cultural Trade in World History.* New York, 1984. Focuses on the roles of cross-cultural brokers in facilitating trade between different societies.

Stephen Frederic Dale. *Indian Merchants and Eurasian Trade, 1600–1750.* Cambridge, 1994. Scholarly analysis of Indian merchant communities trading in Russia, Persia, and central Asia in early modern times.

Andre Gunder Frank. *ReORIENT: Global Economy in the Asian Age.* Berkeley, 1998. Important and challenging analysis of global economic integration in the early modern world.

Jonathan L. Israel. *Dutch Primacy in World Trade, 1585–1740.* Oxford, 1989. A thorough examination of the Dutch seaborne empire at its height.

Michael Khodarkovsky. *Where Two Worlds Meet: The Russian State and the Kalmyk Nomads, 1600–1771.* Ithaca, 1992. One of the first major studies to look at Russian imperial expansion in Siberia through the eyes of colonized peoples.

Pablo E. Perez-Mallaina. *Spain's Men of the Sea: Daily Life on the Indies Fleet in the Sixteenth Century.* Trans. by Carla Rahn Phillips. Baltimore, 1988. Recounts shipboard life in vivid detail.

William H. McNeill. *Plagues and Peoples.* Garden City, N.Y., 1976. Examines the effects of infectious and contagious diseases in world history.

David Ormrod. *The Rise of Commercial Empires: England and the Netherlands in the Age of Mercantilism, 1650–1770*. New York, 2003. An important contribution to an understanding of European imperialism and colonialism that focuses on the issues surrounding Dutch decline and British ascendancy.

Anthony Pagden. *European Encounters with the New World: From Renaissance to Romanticism*. New Haven, 1993. Scholarly examination of early European responses to the peoples, societies, and environments they encountered in the Americas.

John H. Parry. *The Age of Reconnaissance*. Berkeley, 1982. Reliable and readable survey of European expansion.

M. N. Pearson. *The Portuguese in India*. Cambridge, 1987. A brief, lively discussion of the early Portuguese empire in India.

William D. Phillips Jr. and Carla Rahn Phillips. *The Worlds of Christopher Columbus*. Cambridge, 1992. The best general study of Christopher Columbus.

Antonio Pigafetta. *Magellan's Voyage: A Narrative Account of the First Circumnavigation*. 2 vols. Trans. by R. A. Skelton. New Haven, 1969. Valuable account by a crewman on Magellan's circumnavigation of the world.

Kenneth Pomeranz. *The Great Divergence: China, Europe, and the Making of the Modern World Economy*. Princeton, 2000. Pathbreaking scholarly study that illuminates the economic history of the early modern world through comparison of economic development in Asian and European lands.

————— and Steven Topik. *The World That Trade Created: Society, Culture, and the World Economy, 1400 to the Present*. Armonk, N.Y., 1999. Informative articles arguing the fundamental importance of trade and commerce in world history, both as a precursor to globalization and as a historically transformative force.

John F. Richards. *The Unending Frontier: An Environmental History of the Early Modern World*. Berkeley, 2003. Thoroughly explores the environmental effects of the global historical processes that shaped the early modern world.

Stuart B. Schwartz, ed. *Implicit Understandings: Observing, Reporting, and Reflecting on the Encounters between Europeans and Other Peoples in the Early Modern Era*. Cambridge, 1994. Fascinating collection of essays by specialists on cross-cultural perceptions in early modern times.

Yuri Slezkine. *Arctic Mirrors: Russia and the Small Peoples of the North*. Ithaca, 1994. Thoughtful analysis of Russian relations with the hunting, fishing, and herding peoples of Siberia.

Sanjay Subrahmanyam. *The Career and Legend of Vasco da Gama*. Cambridge, 1997. The best critical study of the famous Portuguese mariner.

—————. *The Portuguese Empire in Asia, 1500–1700: A Political and Economic History*. London, 1993. A sophisticated analysis of the Portuguese trading-post empire.

Hugh Thomas. *Rivers of Gold: The Rise of the Spanish Empire, from Columbus to Magellan*. New York, 2003. Detailed narrative of a brief period in Spain's imperial outreach.

James D. Tracy, ed. *The Political Economy of Merchant Empires: State Power and World Trade, 1350–1750*. Cambridge, 1991. Essays on the interconnections between political, military, and commercial relationships in early modern times.

—————. *The Rise of Merchant Empires: Long-Distance Trade in the Early Modern World, 1350–1750*. Cambridge, 1990. Essays by specialists on global trade in early modern times.

Immanuel Wallerstein. *The Modern World-System*. 3 vols. New York, 1974. A controversial but influential interpretation of global political and economic development in modern times.

Merry E. Wiesner-Hanks. *Christianity and Sexuality in the Early Modern World: Regulating Desire, Reforming Practice*. London, 2000. Pioneering comparative study of Christian sexuality in global context.

The Transformation of Europe

chapter 23

In SILENCIO ET SPE ERIT   M · L   FORTITVDO VESTRA

Martin Luther at age forty-two, depicted as a conscientious and determined man by the German painter Lucas Cranach in 1525.

EYEWITNESS:
Martin Luther Challenges the Church

In 1517 an obscure German monk posed a challenge to the Roman Catholic church. Martin Luther of Wittenberg denounced the church's sale of indulgences, a type of pardon that excused individuals from doing penance for their sins and thus facilitated their entry into heaven. Indulgences had been available since the eleventh century, but to raise funds for the reconstruction of St. Peter's basilica in Rome, church authorities began to market indulgences aggressively in the early sixteenth century. From their point of view, indulgences were splendid devices: they encouraged individuals to reflect piously on their behavior while also bringing large sums of money into the church's treasury.

To Martin Luther, however, indulgences were signs of greed, hypocrisy, and moral rot in the Roman Catholic church. Luther despised the pretentiousness of church authorities who arrogated to themselves powers that belonged properly to God alone: no human being had the power to absolve individuals of their sins and grant them admission to heaven, Luther believed, so the sale of indulgences constituted a huge fraud perpetrated on an unsuspecting public. In October 1517, following academic custom of the day, he offered to debate publicly with anyone who wished to dispute his views, and he denounced the sale of indulgences in a document called the *Ninety-Five Theses.*

Luther did not nail his work to the church door in Wittenberg, although a popular legend credited him with that heroic gesture, but news of the *Ninety-Five Theses* spread instantly: within a few weeks, printed copies were available throughout Europe. Luther's challenge galvanized opinion among many who resented the power of the Roman church. It also drew severe criticism from religious and political authorities seeking to maintain the established order. Church officials subjected Luther's views to examination and judged them erroneous, and in 1520 Pope Leo X excommunicated the unrepentant monk. In 1521 the Holy Roman emperor Charles V, a devout Roman Catholic, summoned Luther to an assembly of imperial authorities and demanded that he recant his views. Luther's response: "I cannot and will not recant anything, for it is neither safe nor right to act against one's conscience. Here I stand. I can do no other. God help me. Amen."

Martin Luther's challenge held enormous religious and political implications. Though expelled from the church, Luther still considered himself Christian—indeed, he considered his own faith true Christianity—and he held religious services for a community of devoted followers. Wittenberg became a center of religious dissent, which by the late 1520s had spread through much of Germany and Switzerland. During the 1530s dissidents known as Protestants—because of their protest against the established order—organized movements also in France, England, the Low Countries, and even Italy and Spain. By mid-century Luther's act of individual rebellion had mushroomed into the Protestant Reformation, which shattered the religious unity of western Christendom.

For all its unsettling effects, the Protestant Reformation was only one of several powerful movements that transformed European society during the early modern era. Another was the consolidation of strong centralized states, which took shape partly because of the Reformation. Between the sixteenth and the eighteenth centuries, monarchs in western Europe took advantage of religious quarrels to tighten control over their societies. By curbing the power of the nobility, expanding royal authority, and increasing control over their subjects, they built states much more powerful than the regional monarchies of the middle ages. By the mid-eighteenth century, some rulers had concentrated so much power in their own hands that historians refer to them as absolute monarchs.

Alongside religious conflict and the building of powerful states, capitalism and early modern science also profoundly influenced western European society in early modern times. Early capitalism pushed European merchants and manufacturers into unrelenting competition with one another and encouraged them to reorganize their businesses in search of maximum efficiency. Early modern science challenged traditional ways of understanding the world and the universe. Under the influence of scientific discoveries, European intellectuals sought an entirely rational understanding of human society as well as the natural world, and some sought to base European moral, ethical, and social thought on science and reason rather than Christianity.

Thus between 1500 and 1800, western Europe underwent a thorough transformation. Although the combination of religious, political, social, economic, intellectual, and cultural change was unsettling and often disruptive, it also strengthened European society. The states of early modern Europe competed vigorously and mobilized their human and natural resources in effective fashion. By 1800 several of them had become especially powerful, wealthy, and dynamic. They stood poised to play major roles in world affairs during the nineteenth and twentieth centuries.

THE FRAGMENTATION OF WESTERN CHRISTENDOM

In the third century C.E., Christian missionaries began to spread their faith from the Mediterranean basin throughout Europe, and by 1000 C.E. Christianity had established a foothold as far north as Scandinavia and Iceland. Although the peoples of western Europe spoke different languages, ate different foods, and observed different customs, the church of Rome provided them with a common religious and cultural heritage. During the sixteenth and seventeenth centuries, however, revolts against the Roman Catholic church shattered the religious unity of western Europe. Followers of Martin Luther and other Protestant reformers established a series of churches independent of Rome, and Roman Catholic leaders strengthened their own church against the challengers. Throughout early modern times, religious controversies fueled social tensions.

The Protestant Reformation

Roots of Reform The Protestant Reformation dates from the early sixteenth century, but many of the underlying conditions that prompted reformers to challenge the authority of the Roman Catholic church had existed for hundreds of years. Over the course of centuries, the church and its top officials had become deeply embroiled in the political affairs of western Europe. But political intrigues, combined with the church's growing wealth and power, also fostered greed and corruption, which undermined the church's spiritual authority and made it vulnerable to criticism. The blatant hedonism and crass materialism of church officials only further emphasized the perceived betrayal of Christian ideals. Although the church continued to enjoy the loyalty of most Christians, it faced a disapproval of its abuses that became increasingly strident in the decades before 1517. Alongside such criticism came a growing demand for a more personal involvement with the divine. Efforts by

church authorities to eliminate pre-Christian traditions and alternative kinds of spirituality only intensified the desire among laypeople for forms of devotion that would connect them more directly with God than the church allowed. Martin Luther coalesced these expressions of religious discontent into a powerful revolt against the church.

Martin Luther Martin Luther (1483–1546) attacked the sale of indulgences as an individual, but he soon attracted enthusiastic support from others who resented the policies of the Roman church. Luther was a prolific and talented writer, and he published scores of works condemning the Roman church. His cause benefited enormously from the printing press, which had first appeared in Europe in the mid-fifteenth century. A sizable literate public inhabited European cities and towns, and readers eagerly consumed printed works on religious as well as secular themes. Printed editions of Luther's writings appeared throughout Europe and sparked spirited debates on indulgences and theological issues. His supporters and critics took their own works to the printers, and religious controversies kept the presses busy churning out pamphlets and treatises for a century and more.

Luther soon moved beyond the issue of indulgences: he attacked the Roman church for a wide range of abuses and called for thorough reform of Christendom. He advocated the closure of monasteries, translation of the Bible from Latin into vernacular languages, and an end to priestly authority, including the authority of the pope himself. When opponents pointed out that his reform program ran counter to church policy, he rejected the authority of the church hierarchy and proclaimed that the Bible was the only source of Christian religious authority.

Luther's works drew an enthusiastic popular response, and in Germany they fueled a movement to reform the church along the lines of Luther's teachings. Lay Christians flocked to hear Luther preach in Wittenberg, and several princes of the Holy Roman Empire warmed to Luther's views—partly because of personal conviction but partly also because religious controversy offered opportunities for them to build their own power bases. During the 1520s and 1530s, many of the most important German cities—Strasbourg, Nuremberg, and Augsburg, among others—passed laws prohibiting Roman Catholic observances and requiring all religious services to follow Protestant doctrine and procedures.

Reform outside Germany By the mid-sixteenth century, about half the German population had adopted Lutheran Christianity, and reformers had launched Protestant movements and established alternative churches in other lands as well. By the late 1520s the prosperous cities of Switzerland—Zurich, Basel, and Geneva—had fledgling Protestant churches. The heavily urbanized Low Countries also responded enthusiastically to Protestant appeals. Protestants appeared even in Italy and Spain, although authorities in those lands handily suppressed their challenge to the Roman church.

In England a Reformation took place for frankly political as well as religious reasons. Lutherans and other Protestants worked to build a following in England from the 1520s, but they faced stout government resistance until King Henry VIII (reigned 1509–1547) came into conflict with the pope. Henry wanted to divorce his wife, who had not borne a male heir, but the pope refused to allow him to do so. Henry's response was to sever relations with the Roman church and make himself Supreme Head of the Anglican church—an English pope, as it were. While Henry reigned, the theology of the English church changed little, but under pressure of reformers, his successors replaced Roman Catholic with Protestant doctrines and rituals. By 1560 England had permanently left the Roman Catholic community.

John Calvin Meanwhile, an even more influential Reformation was taking shape in France and the French-speaking parts of Switzerland. The initiator was a French lawyer, John Calvin (1509–1564), who in the 1530s converted to Protestant Christianity. Because the French monarchy sought to suppress Protestants, Calvin slipped across the border to French-speaking Geneva in Switzerland. There he organized a Protestant community and worked with local officials to impose a strict code of morality and discipline on the city. Calvin also composed an influential treatise, *Institutes of the Christian Religion* (first published in 1536 and frequently reprinted with revisions), that codified Protestant teachings and presented them as a coherent and organized package.

Calvin's Geneva was not only a model Protestant community but also a missionary center. Calvinist missionaries were most active in France, where they attracted strong interest in the cities, but they ventured also to Germany, the Low Countries, England, Scotland, and even distant Hungary. They established churches in all these lands and worked for reform along Protestant lines. They were most successful in the Netherlands and Scotland. By the late sixteenth century, Lutherans, Anglicans, and Calvinists together had built communities large enough that a return to religious unity in western Christendom was inconceivable.

The Catholic Reformation

Partly in response to the Protestant Reformation, Roman Catholic authorities undertook an enormous reform effort within their own church. To some extent their efforts represented a reaction to Protestant success. Yet Roman Catholic authorities also sought to define points of doctrine so as to clarify differences between Roman and Protestant churches, to persuade Protestants to return to the Roman church, and to deepen the sense of spirituality and religious commitment in their own community. Taken together, their efforts constituted the Catholic Reformation.

The Council of Trent Two institutions were especially important for defining the Catholic Reformation and advancing its goals—the Council of Trent and the Society of Jesus.

The Council of Trent was an assembly of bishops, cardinals, and other high church officials who met intermittently between 1545 and 1563 to address matters of doctrine and reform. Drawing heavily on the works of the thirteenth-century scholastic theologian St. Thomas Aquinas, the council defined the elements of Roman Catholic theology in detail. The council acknowledged that abuses had alienated many people from the Roman church, and it took steps to reform the church. The council demanded that church authorities observe strict standards of morality, and it required them to establish schools and seminaries in their districts to prepare priests properly for their roles.

St. Ignatius Loyola

While the Council of Trent dealt with doctrine and reform, the Society of Jesus went on the offensive and sought to extend the boundaries of the reformed Roman church. The society's founder was St. Ignatius Loyola (1491–1556), a Basque nobleman and soldier who in 1521 suffered a devastating leg wound that ended his military career. While recuperating he read spiritual works and popular accounts of saints' lives, and he resolved to put his energy into religious work. In 1540, together with a small band of disciples, he founded the Society of Jesus.

The Society of Jesus

Ignatius required that members of the society, known as Jesuits, complete a rigorous and advanced education. They received instruction not only in theology and philosophy but also in classical languages, literature, history, and science. As a result of that preparation—and their unswerving dedication to the Roman Catholic church—the Jesuits made extraordinarily effective missionaries. They were able to outargue most of their opponents and acquired a reputation for discipline and determination. They often served as counselors to kings and rulers and used their influence to promote policies that benefited the Roman church. They also were the most prominent of the early Christian missionaries outside Europe: in the wake of the European reconnaissance of the world's oceans, Jesuits at-

Under inspiration of the Catholic Reformation, many devout individuals sought mystic union with God. One of the most famous of the mystics was St. Teresa of Avila (in Spain), who founded a strict order of nuns and often experienced religious visions. A famous sculpture by the Italian artist Gianlorenzo Bernini depicts St. Teresa in an ecstatic trance accompanied by an angel.

tracted converts in India, China, Japan, the Philippines, and the Americas, thus making Christianity a genuinely global religion.

Witch-Hunts and Religious Wars

Europeans took religion seriously in the sixteenth century, and religious divisions helped to fuel social and political conflict. Apart from wars, the most destructive violence that afflicted early modern Europe was the hunt for witches, which was especially prominent in regions such as the Rhineland where tensions between Protestants and Roman Catholics ran high.

Like many other peoples, Europeans had long believed that certain individuals possessed unusual powers to influence human affairs or discover secret information such as the identity of a thief. During the late fifteenth century, theologians developed a theory that witches derived their powers from the devil. According to that theory, witches made agreements to worship the devil in exchange for supernatural powers, including the ability to fly through the night on brooms, pitchforks, or animals. Theorists believed that the witches regularly flew off to distant places to attend the "witches' sabbath," a gathering that featured devil worship, lewd behavior, and the concoction of secret potions, culminating in sexual relations with the devil himself.

Witch-Hunting

Although the witches' sabbath was sheer fantasy, fears that individuals were making alliances with the devil sparked an intensive hunt for witches. Witchcraft became a convenient explanation for any unpleasant turn of events—failure of a crop, outbreak of a fire, an unexpected death, or inability to conceive a child. About 110,000 individuals underwent trial as suspected witches during the sixteenth and seventeenth centuries, and about 45,000 of them died either by hanging or by burning at the stake. As a rule, church courts tried large numbers of witches, but they usually imposed nonlethal penalties such as excommunication or imprisonment. It was secular courts that condemned and executed the vast majority of witches.

Witches and Gender Gender played an important role in the witch-hunts. Men were among the victims, and in places such as Finland they actually exceeded the number of women accused of witchcraft. Most convicted witches were women, however. Indeed, women may have accounted for 85 percent or more of the condemned. Many of the women were poor, old, single, or widowed—individuals who lived on the margins of their societies and were easy targets for accusers, since they had few protectors. Witch-hunting was mostly a European affair, but it also spread to European colonies in the Americas. The most intense witch-hunt in the Americas took place in seventeenth-century New England, where a population of about 100,000 colonists tried 234 individuals for witchcraft and executed 36 of them by hanging.

By 1700 the fear of witches had largely diminished. Accusations, trials, and executions occurred only sporadically thereafter. The last legal execution for witchcraft in Europe took place in Switzerland in 1782. For the better part of two centuries, however, the intermittent pursuit of witches revealed clearly the stresses and strains that afflicted European society during early modern times.

Religious Wars Religious tensions even led to outright war between Protestant and Roman Catholic communities. Religious wars racked France for thirty-six years (1562–1598), for example, and they also complicated relations between Protestant and Roman Catholic states. In 1588 King Philip II of Spain (reigned 1556–1598) attempted to force England to return to the Roman Catholic church by sending the Spanish Armada—a huge flotilla consisting of 130 ships and 30,000 men—to dethrone the Protestant Queen Eliza-beth. The effort collapsed, however, when English forces disrupted the Spanish fleet by sending blazing, unmanned ships into its midst. Then a ferocious gale scattered Spanish vessels throughout the North Sea.

Religious convictions also aggravated relations between the Netherlands and Spain by fueling the revolt of the Dutch provinces from their overlord, the king of Spain. In 1567 Philip sent an army to tighten his control over the provinces and to suppress the Calvinist movement there. Resistance escalated into a full-scale rebellion. By 1610 the seven northern provinces (the modern Netherlands) had won their independence and formed a republic known as the United Provinces, leaving ten southern provinces (modern Belgium) under Spanish and later Austrian rule until the late eighteenth century.

The Thirty Years' War The religious wars culminated in a massive continental conflict known as the Thirty Years' War (1618–1648). The war opened after the Holy Roman emperor attempted to force his Bohemian subjects to return to the Roman Catholic church, and the main battleground was the emperor's territory in Germany. Other parties soon entered the fray, however, and by the time the war ended, Spanish, French, Dutch, German, Swedish, Danish, Polish, Bohemian, and Russian forces had taken part in the conflict.

The motives that prompted these states to enter the war were sometimes political or economic, but religious differences complicated the other issues and made them more difficult to resolve. Regardless of the motives, the Thirty Years' War was the most destructive European conflict before the twentieth century. Quite apart from violence and brutalities committed by undisciplined soldiers, the war damaged

Henry Fuseli's 1783 painting offers a dramatic depiction of three witches. The painter based his image on the three witches who appear in William Shakespeare's play *Macbeth*. He titled his painting "The Weird Sisters" or "The Three Witches." Which physical features identify these women as "weird" witches?

A la fin ces Voleurs infames et perdus ,
Comme fruits malheureux a cet arbre pendus

Monstrent bien que le crime (horrible et noire engeance)
Est luy mesme instrument de honte et de vengeance ,

Et que cest le Destin des hommes vicieux
Desprouuer tost ou tard la iustice des Cieux . 1)

The Thirty Years' War offered abundant opportunity for undisciplined mercenary soldiers to prey on civilian populations. Only rarely, as in the mass hanging depicted in this engraving of 1633, did soldiers receive punishment for their criminal acts.

economies and societies throughout Europe and led to the deaths of about one-third of the German population. The destructiveness of the Thirty Years' War raised questions about the viability of Europe as a region of strong, independent, well-armed, and intensely competitive states.

THE CONSOLIDATION OF SOVEREIGN STATES

Although fundamentally a religious movement, the Reformation had strong political implications, and centralizing monarchs readily made use of religious issues in their efforts to strengthen their states and enhance their authority. Ruling elites had their own religious preferences, and they often promoted a Protestant or Roman Catholic cause out of personal conviction. Religious controversies also offered splendid opportunities for ambitious subordinates who built power bases by appealing to particular religious communities. Over the long run, centralizing monarchs profited most from religious controversy generated by the Reformation. While the Holy Roman Empire fell into disarray because of political and religious quarrels, monarchs in other lands augmented their revenues, enhanced their authority, and created powerful sovereign states. After the devastation of the Thirty Years' War, rulers of these states devised a diplomatic system that sought to maintain order among the many independent and competitive European states.

The Attempted Revival of Empire

After the dissolution of the Carolingian empire in the ninth century C.E., there was no effective imperial government in western Europe. The so-called Holy Roman Empire emerged in the tenth century, but its authority extended only to Germany and northern Italy, and even there the emperors encountered stiff opposition from powerful princes and thriving cities. During the early sixteenth century, it seemed that Emperor Charles V (reigned 1519–1556) might establish the Holy Roman Empire as the preeminent political authority in Europe, but by midcentury it was clear that there would be no revival of empire. Thus, unlike China, India, and Ottoman lands in southwest Asia and north Africa, early modern Europe developed as a region of independent states.

Charles V After 1438 the Habsburg family, with extensive dynastic holdings in Austria, dominated the Holy Roman Empire. Through marriage alliances with princely and royal families, the Habsburgs accumulated rights and titles to lands throughout Europe and beyond. Charles V inherited authority over the Habsburgs' Austrian domains as well as the duchy of Burgundy (including the wealthy provinces of the Low Countries) and the kingdom of Spain (including its possessions in Italy and the Americas). When he became emperor in 1519, he acquired authority over Germany, Bohemia, Switzerland, and parts of northern Italy. His empire stretched from Vienna in Austria to Cuzco in Peru.

Imperial Fragmentation In spite of his far-flung holdings, Charles did not extend his authority throughout Europe or even establish a lasting imperial legacy. Throughout his reign Charles had to devote much of his attention and energy to the Lutheran movement and to imperial princes who took advantage of religious controversy to assert their independence. Moreover, Charles did not build an administrative structure for his empire but, instead, ruled each of his lands according to its own laws and customs. He was able to draw on the financial resources of wealthy lands such as the Low Countries and Spain to maintain a powerful army. Yet Charles did not have the ambition to extend his authority by military force, but used his army mostly to put down rebellions.

Foreign Challenges Foreign difficulties also prevented Charles from establishing his empire as the arbiter of Europe. The prospect of a powerful Holy Roman Empire struck fear in the kings of France, and it caused concern among the sultans of the Ottoman empire as well. Charles's holdings surrounded France, and the French kings suspected that the emperor wanted to absorb their realm and extend his authority throughout Europe. To forestall that possibility, the French kings created every obstacle they could for Charles. Even though they were staunch Roman Catholics, they aided German Lutherans and encouraged them to rebel. The French kings even allied with the Muslim Ottoman Turks against the emperor.

MAP 23.1

Sixteenth-century Europe.

Note the extent of Habsburg territories and the wide boundaries of the Holy Roman Empire.

With such powerful territories, what prevented the Habsburgs from imposing imperial rule on most of Europe?

Spanish Habsburg possessions

Austrian Habsburg possessions

Holy Roman Empire

For their part, the Ottoman sultans did not want to see a powerful Christian empire threaten their holdings in eastern Europe and their position in the Mediterranean basin. With the encouragement of the French king, Turkish forces conquered Hungary in 1526, and three years later they even laid siege briefly to Vienna. Moreover, during the early sixteenth century Ottoman forces imposed their rule beyond Egypt and embraced almost all of north Africa. By midcentury, Turkish holdings posed a serious threat to Italian and Spanish shipping in the Mediterranean.

Thus numerous domestic and foreign problems prevented Charles V from establishing his vast empire as the supreme political authority in Europe. His inability to suppress the Lutherans was especially disappointing to Charles, and in 1556, after agreeing that imperial princes and cities could determine the religious faith observed in their jurisdictions, the emperor abdicated his throne and retired to a monastery in Spain. His empire did not survive intact. Charles bestowed his holdings in Spain, Italy, the Low Countries, and the Americas on his son, King Philip II of Spain, while his brother Ferdinand inherited the Habsburg family lands in Austria and the imperial throne.

The New Monarchs

In the absence of effective imperial power, guidance of public affairs fell to the various regional states that had emerged during the middle ages. The city-states of Italy were prominent because of their economic power: since the eleventh century they had been Europe's most important centers of trade, manufacturing, and finance. The most powerful European states, however, were the kingdoms of England, France, and Spain. During the late fifteenth and sixteenth centuries, rulers of these lands, known as the "new monarchs," marshaled their resources, curbed the nobility, and built strong centralized regimes.

Finance The new monarchs included Henry VIII of England, Louis XI and Francis I of France, and Fernando and Isabel of Spain. All the new monarchs sought to enhance their treasuries by developing new sources of finance. The French kings levied direct taxes on sales, households, and the salt trade. A new sales tax dramatically boosted Spanish royal income in the sixteenth century. For fear of provoking rebellion, the English kings did not introduce new taxes, but they increased revenues by raising fines and fees for royal services. Moreover, after Henry VIII severed ties between the English and Roman churches, he dissolved the monasteries and confiscated church wealth in England. This financial windfall enabled Henry to enhance royal power by increasing the size of the state and adding to its responsibilities. After the English Reformation, for example, the state provided poor relief and support for orphans, which previously had been responsibilities of churches and monasteries.

State Power With their increased income the new monarchs enlarged their administrative staffs, which enabled them to collect taxes and implement royal policies more reliably than before. The French and Spanish monarchs also maintained standing armies that vastly increased their power with respect to the nobility. Their armies with thousands of infantrymen were too large for individual nobles to match, and they equipped their forces with cannons that were too expensive for nobles to purchase. The English kings did not need a standing army to put down the occasional rebellion that flared in their island realm and so did not go to the expense of supporting one. Yet they too increased their power with respect to the nobles by subjecting them to royal justice and forcing them to comply with royal policy.

The debates and disputes launched by the Protestant Reformation helped monarchs increase their power. In lands that adopted Protestant faiths—including England, much of Germany, Denmark, and Sweden—rulers expropriated the monasteries and used church wealth to expand their powers. That option was not open to Roman Catholic kings, but Protestant movements provided them with a justification to mobilize resources, which they used against political as well as religious adversaries.

The Spanish Inquisition The Spanish Inquisition was the most distinctive institution that relied on religious justifications to advance state ends. Fernando and Isabel founded the Spanish Inquisition in 1478, and they obtained papal license to operate the institution as a royal agency. Its original task was to ferret out those who secretly practiced Judaism or Islam, but Charles V charged it with responsibility also for detecting Protestant heresy in Spain. Throughout the late fifteenth and sixteenth centuries, however, the Spanish Inquisition served political as well as religious purposes. Moreover, its reach extended well beyond the Iberian peninsula. Just as the fear of witchcraft crossed the Atlantic Ocean and inspired witch-hunts in England's North American colonies, concerns about heresy also made their way to the western hemisphere, where inquisitors worked to protect Spanish colonies from heretical teachings.

Inquisitors had broad powers to investigate suspected cases of heresy. Popular legends have created an erroneous impression of the Spanish Inquisition as an institution running amok, framing innocent victims and routinely subjecting them to torture. In fact, inquisitors usually observed rules of evidence, and they released many suspects after investigations turned up no sign of heresy. Yet, when they detected the scent of heresy, inquisitors could be ruthless. They sentenced hundreds of victims to hang from the gallows or burn at the stake and imprisoned many others in dank cells for extended periods of time. Fear of the inquisition intimidated many into silence, and a strict Roman Catholic orthodoxy prevailed in Spain. The inquisition deterred nobles from adopting Protestant views out of political ambition, and it used its influence on behalf of the Span-

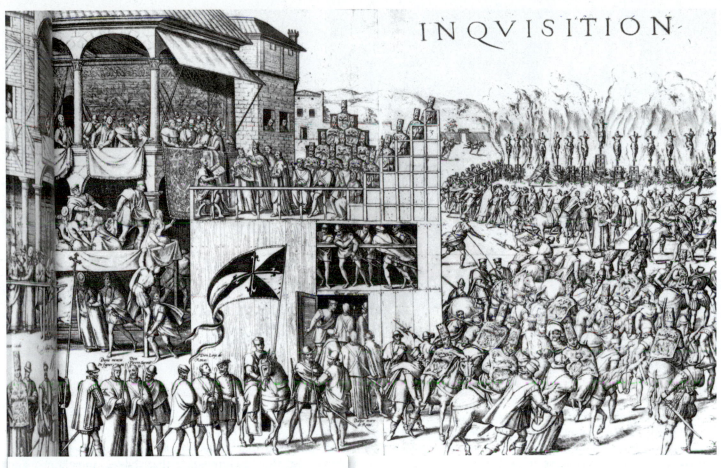

INQVISITION

When the Spanish Inquisition detected traces of Protestant heresy, the punishment could be swift and brutal. In this engraving of about 1560, a large crowd observes the execution of heretics (top right) by burning at the stake.

ish monarchy. From 1559 to 1576, for example, inquisitors imprisoned the archbishop of Toledo—the highest Roman Catholic church official in all of Spain—because of his political independence.

Constitutional States

During the seventeenth and eighteenth centuries, as they sought to restore order after the Thirty Years' War, European states developed along two lines. Rulers in England and the Netherlands shared authority with representative institutions and created constitutional states, whereas monarchs in France, Spain, Austria, Prussia, and Russia concentrated power in their own hands and created a form of state known as absolute monarchy.

Constitutional States

The island kingdom of England and the maritime Dutch republic did not have written constitutions specifying the powers of the state, but during the seventeenth century they evolved governments that claimed limited powers and recognized rights pertaining to individuals and representative institutions. Their constitutional states took different forms: in England a constitutional monarchy emerged, whereas the Netherlands produced a republic based on representative government. In neither land did constitutional government come easily into being: in England it followed a civil war, and in the Netherlands it emerged after a long struggle for independence. In both lands, however, constitutional government strengthened the state and provided a political framework that enabled merchants to flourish as never before in European experience.

The English Civil War

Constitutional government came to England after political and religious disputes led to the English civil war (1642–1649). From the early seventeenth century, the English kings had tried to institute new taxes without approval of the parliament, which for more than three centuries had traditionally approved new levies. While royal financial policies generated political tensions, religious disagreements aggravated matters further. As Anglicans, the kings supported a church with relatively ornate ceremonies and a hierarchy of bishops working under authority of the monarchs themselves. Meanwhile, however, many of the boldest and most insistent voices within parliament belonged

In this contemporary painting, the executioner holds up the just-severed head of King Charles I of England. The spectacle of a royal execution overcomes one woman, who faints (at bottom). How does the image of a beheaded king reflect the ongoing political changes in Europe?

to zealous Calvinists known as Puritans because they sought to purify the English church of any lingering elements, such as ornate ceremonies and a hierarchy of bishops, suggestive of Roman Catholic Christianity. By 1641, King Charles I and parliament were at loggerheads, unable to cooperate or even communicate effectively with each other. Both sides raised armies. In the conflicts that followed, parliamentary forces under the leadership of Oliver Cromwell (1599–1658) captured Charles, tried him for tyranny, and in an act that shocked all of Europe, marched him up on a platform and beheaded him in 1649.

The Glorious Revolution

In the absence of a king, Cromwell's Puritan regime took power but soon degenerated into a disagreeable dictatorship, prompting parliament to restore the monarchy in 1660. King and parliament, however, soon resumed their conflicts. The issue came to a head in a bloodless change of power known as the Glorious Revolution (1688–1689), when parliament deposed King James II and invited his daughter Mary and her Dutch husband, William of Orange, to assume the throne. The resulting arrangement provided that kings would rule in cooperation with parliament, thus guaranteeing that nobles, merchants, and other constituencies would enjoy representation in government affairs.

The Dutch Republic

As in England, a potent combination of political and religious tensions led to conflict from which constitutional government emerged in the Netherlands. In the mid-sixteenth century, authority over the Low Countries, including modern-day Belgium as well as the Netherlands, rested with King Philip II of Spain. In 1567 Philip, a devout Roman Catholic, moved to suppress an increasingly popular Calvinist movement in the Netherlands—a measure that provoked large-scale rebellion against Spanish rule. In 1579 a group of Dutch provinces formed an anti-Spanish alliance, and in 1581 they proclaimed themselves the independent United Provinces. Representative assemblies organized local affairs in each of the provinces, and on this foundation political leaders built a Dutch republic. Spain did not officially recognize the independence of the United Provinces until the end of the Thirty Years' War in 1648, but the Dutch republic was effectively organizing affairs in the northern Low Countries by the early seventeenth century.

In many ways, the constitutional governments of England and the Dutch republic represented historical experiments. Apart from the Roman republic in classical times and a few Italian city-states of the medieval and Renaissance eras, European peoples had little experience with representative government. In their responses to political crises, popular leaders in both England and the Netherlands found it possible to mobilize support by appealing to the political and religious interests of broad constituencies and making a place for them in the government. The result was a pair of states that effectively harnessed popular support and used it to magnify state power.

In both England and the Dutch republic, merchants were especially prominent in political affairs, and state policy in both lands favored maritime trade and the building of commercial empires overseas. The constitutional states allowed entrepreneurs to pursue their economic interests with minimal interference from public authorities, and during the late seventeenth and eighteenth centuries, both states experienced extraordinary prosperity as a result of those policies. Indeed, in many ways the English and Dutch states represented an alliance between merchants and rulers that worked to the benefit of both. Merchants supported the state with the wealth that they generated through trade—especially overseas trade—while rulers followed policies that looked after the interests of their merchants.

Absolute Monarchies

Whereas constitutional states devised ways to share power and authority, absolute monarchies found other ways to increase state power. Absolutism stood on a theoretical foundation known as the divine right of kings. This theory held that kings derived their authority from God and served as "God's lieutenants upon earth." There was no role in divine-right theory for common subjects or even nobles in public affairs: the king made law and determined policy. Noncompliance or disobedience merited punishment, and rebellion was a despicable act tantamount to blasphemy. In fact, absolute monarchs always relied on support from nobles and other social groups as well, but the claims of divine-right theory clearly reflected efforts at royal centralization.

The most conspicuous absolutist state was the French monarchy. The architect of French absolutism was a prominent church official, Cardinal Richelieu, who served as chief minister to King Louis XIII from 1624 to 1642. Richelieu worked systematically to undermine the power of the nobility and enhance the authority of the king. He destroyed nobles' castles and ruthlessly crushed aristocratic conspiracies. As a counterweight to the nobility, Richelieu built a large bureaucracy staffed by commoners loyal to the king. He also appointed officials to supervise the implementation of royal policy in the provinces. Finally, Richelieu attacked French Calvinists, who often allied with independent nobles, and destroyed their political and military power, although he allowed them to continue observing their faith. By midcentury France was under control of a tightly centralized absolute monarchy.

The Sun King The ruler who best epitomized royal absolutism was King Louis XIV (reigned 1643–1715), who once reportedly declared that he was himself the state: "*l'état, c'est moi.*" Known as *le roi soleil* ("the sun king"), Louis surrounded himself with splendor befitting one who ruled by divine right. During the 1670s he built a magnificent residence at **Versailles,** a royal hunting lodge near Paris, and in the 1680s he moved his court there. Louis's palace at Versailles was the largest building in Europe, with 230 acres of formal gardens and 1,400 fountains. Because Louis did not want to wait years for saplings to grow, he ordered laborers to dig up 25,000 fully grown trees and haul them to Versailles for transplanting.

The sun king was the center of attention at Versailles. Court officials hovered around him and tended to his every need. All prominent nobles established residences at Versailles for their families and entourages. Louis strongly encouraged them to live at court, where he and his staff

Although best known as Louis XIII's "first minister," Cardinal Richelieu also gained fame for his patronage of the arts. Most notably, he founded the Académie Française, the learned society responsible for matters pertaining to the French language.

Versailles (vehr-SEYE)

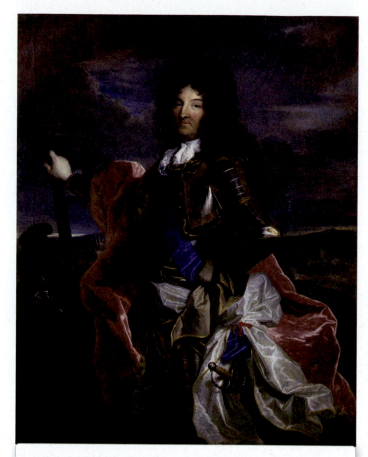

The French painter Hyacinthe Rigaud, renowned for his portrait paintings of the royalty and nobility of Europe, created this vision of Louis XIV. Louis' reign, from 1643 to his death in 1715, lasted seventy-two years, three months, and eighteen days, and is the longest documented reign of any European monarch.

Absolutism in Russia

Louis XIV was not the only absolute monarch of early modern Europe: Spanish, Austrian, and Prussian rulers embraced similar policies. The potential of absolutism to increase state power was particularly conspicuous in the case of Russia, where tsars of the Romanov dynasty (1613–1917) tightly centralized government functions. (*Tsar,* sometimes spelled *czar,* is a Russianized form of the term *caesar,* which Russian rulers borrowed from Byzantine emperors, who in turn had borrowed it from the classical Roman empire to signify their imperial status.) The Romanovs inherited a state that had rapidly expanded its boundaries since the mid-fourteenth century. Building on the foundation of a small principality around the trading city of Moscow, by 1600 Russia had become a vast empire extending from the Arctic seas in the north to the Caspian Sea in the south, with an increasing presence in the tundra and forests of Siberia as well.

Peter I

Most important of the Romanov tsars was Peter I (reigned 1682–1725), widely known as Peter the Great, who inaugurated a thoroughgoing process of state transformation. Peter had a burning desire to make Russia, a huge but underpopulated land, into a great military power like those that had recently emerged in western Europe. In pursuit of that goal, he worked to transform Russia on the model of western European lands. In 1697–1698 he led a large party of Russian observers on a tour of Germany, the Netherlands, and England to learn about western European administrative methods and military technology. His traveling companions often behaved crudely by western European standards: they consumed beer, wine, and brandy in quantities that astonished their hosts, and King William III sent Peter a bill for damages done by his entourage at the country house where they lodged in England. (Among other things, Peter had ruined the gardens by having his men march through them in military formation.)

Upon return to Moscow, Peter set Russia spinning. He reformed the army by offering better pay and drafting peasants who served for life as professional soldiers. He provided his forces with extensive training and equipped them with modern weapons. He ordered aristocrats to study mathematics and geometry so that they could calculate how to aim cannons accurately, and he began the construction of a navy with an eye toward domination of the Baltic and other northern seas. He also overhauled the government bureaucracy to facilitate tax collection and improve administrative efficiency. His transformation of Russia even involved a cosmetic makeover, as he commanded his aristocratic subjects to wear western European fashions and ordered men to shave their traditional beards. These measures, which were extremely unpopular among conservative Russians, provoked spirited protest among those who resented the influence of western European ways. Yet Peter insisted on observance of his policies—to the point that he reportedly went into the streets and personally hacked the beards off

could keep an eye on them, and ambitious nobles gravitated there anyway in hopes of winning influence with the king. Louis himself was the arbiter of taste and style at Versailles, where he lavishly patronized painters, sculptors, architects, and writers whose creations met with his approval.

While nobles living at Versailles mastered the intricacies of court ritual and attended banquets, concerts, operas, balls, and theatrical performances, Louis and his ministers ran the state. In effect, Louis provided the nobility with luxurious accommodations and endless entertainment in exchange for absolute rule. From Versailles, Louis and his advisors promulgated laws and controlled a large standing army that kept order throughout the land. They also promoted economic development by supporting the establishment of new industries, building roads and canals, abolishing internal tariffs, and encouraging exports. Finally, they waged a series of wars designed to enlarge French boundaries and establish France as the preeminent power in Europe.

Tsar Peter the Great, with a pair of shears, readies himself to remove the beard of a conservative noble. Peter had traveled widely in Europe, and he wanted to impose newer European customs on his subjects. That included being more cleanly shaved. Nobles wishing to keep their beloved beards had to pay a yearly tax to do so.

recalcitrants' faces. Perhaps the best symbol of his policies was St. Petersburg, a newly built seaport that Peter opened in 1703 to serve as a magnificent capital city and haven for Russia's fledgling navy.

Catherine II and the Limits of Reform
The most able of Peter's successors was Catherine II (reigned 1762–1796), also known as Catherine the Great. Like Peter, Catherine sought to make Russia a great power. She worked to improve governmental efficiency by dividing her vast empire into fifty administrative provinces, and she promoted economic development in Russia's towns. For a while, she even worked to improve the conditions of Russia's oppressed peasantry by restricting the punishments that noble landowners could inflict on the serfs who worked their lands. She sought to eliminate common penalties such as torture, beating, and the mutilation of individuals by cutting off their noses, ears, or tongues.

Yet her interest in social reform cooled rapidly when it seemed to inspire challenges to her rule. She faced a particularly unsettling trial in 1773 and 1774, when a disgruntled former soldier named Yemelian Pugachev mounted a rebellion

This is a regal Russian portrait of the German-born empress of Russia, Catherine II. Although admired by many Russians as a source of national pride, she is also remembered as a ruthless ruler who affirmed autocracy and extended serfdom on a large scale.

in the steppe lands north of the Caspian Sea. Pugachev raised a motley army of adventurers, exiles, peasants, and serfs who killed thousands of noble landowners and government officials before imperial forces crushed the uprising. Government authorities took the captured Pugachev to Moscow in chains, beheaded him, quartered his body, and displayed his parts throughout the city as a warning against rebellion. Thereafter, Catherine's first concern was the preservation of autocratic rule rather than the transformation of Russia according to western European models.

Thus, in Russia as in other European lands, absolutist policies resulted in tight centralization and considerable strengthening of the state. The enhanced power that flowed from absolutism became dramatically clear in the period 1772 to 1797, when Austria, Prussia, and Catherine II's Russia picked the weak kingdom of Poland apart. In a series of three "partitions," the predatory absolutist states seized Polish territory and absorbed it into their own realms, ultimately wiping Poland entirely off the map. The lesson of the partitions was clear: any European state that hoped to

survive needed to construct an effective government that could respond promptly to challenges and opportunities.

The European States System

Whether they relied on absolutist or constitutional principles, European governments of early modern times built states much more powerful than those of their medieval predecessors. This round of state development led to difficulties within Europe, since conflicting interests fueled interstate competition and war. In the absence of an imperial authority capable of imposing and maintaining order in Europe, sovereign states had to find ways to resolve conflicts by themselves.

The Peace of Westphalia
The Thirty Years' War demonstrated the chaos and devastation that conflict could bring. In an effort to avoid tearing their society apart, European states ended the Thirty Years' War with the Peace of Westphalia (1648), which laid the foundations for a system of independent, competing states. Almost all the European states participated in drafting the Peace of Westphalia, and by the treaty's terms they regarded one another as sovereign and equal. They also mutually recognized their rights to organize their own domestic affairs, including religious affairs. Rather than envisioning imperial or papal or some other sort of supreme authority, the Peace of Westphalia entrusted political and diplomatic affairs to states acting in their own interests. European religious unity had disappeared, and the era of the sovereign state had arrived.

The Peace of Westphalia did not bring an end to war. Indeed, war was almost constant in early modern Europe. Most conflicts were minor affairs inaugurated by monarchs seeking to extend their authority to new lands or to reclaim territories seized by others, but they nevertheless disrupted local economies and drained resources. A few wars, however, grew to sizable proportions. Most notable among them were the wars of Louis XIV and the Seven Years' War. Between 1668 and 1713, the sun king sought to expand his borders east into Germany and to absorb Spain and the Spanish Netherlands into his kingdom. That prospect prompted England, the United Provinces, and Austria to mount a coalition against Louis. Later, the Seven Years' War (1756–1763) pitted France, Austria, and Russia against Britain and Prussia, and it merged with conflicts between France and Britain in India and North America to become a global war for imperial supremacy.

The Balance of Power
These shifting alliances illustrate the principal foundation of European diplomacy in early modern times—the balance of power. No ruler wanted to see another state dominate all the others. Thus, when any particular state began to wax strong, others formed coalitions against it. Balance-of-power diplomacy was risky business: it was always possible that a coalition might repress one strong state only to open the door for another. Yet, in playing balance-of-power politics, statesmen prevented the

building of empires and ensured that Europe would be a land of independent, sovereign, competing states.

Military Development Frequent wars and balance-of-power diplomacy drained the resources of individual states but strengthened European society as a whole. European states competed vigorously and sought to develop the most expert military leadership and the most effective weapons for their arsenals. States organized military academies where officers received advanced education in strategy and tactics and learned how to maintain disciplined forces. Demand for powerful weapons stimulated the development of a sophisticated armaments industry that turned out ever more lethal products. Gun foundries manufactured cannons of increasing size, range, power, and accuracy as well as small arms that allowed infantry to unleash withering volleys against their enemies.

In China, India, and Islamic lands, imperial states had little or no incentive to encourage similar technological innovation in the armaments industry. These states possessed the forces and weapons they needed to maintain order within their boundaries, and they rarely encountered foreign threats backed up with superior armaments. In Europe, however, failure to keep up with the latest improvements in arms technology could lead to defeat on the battlefield and decline in state power. Thus Europeans continuously sought to improve

---

MAP 23.2

Europe after the Peace of Westphalia, 1648.
Compare this map with Map 23.1.

How have the boundaries of the Holy Roman Empire changed, and why?

Spanish Habsburg possessions
Austrian Habsburg possessions
Holy Roman Empire

their military arsenals, and as a result, by the eighteenth century European armaments outperformed all others.

EARLY CAPITALIST SOCIETY

While the Protestant Reformation and the emergence of sovereign states brought religious and political change, a rapidly expanding population and economy encouraged the development of capitalism, which in turn led to a restructuring of European economy and society. Technologies of communication and transportation enabled businessmen to profit from distant markets, and merchants and manufacturers increasingly organized their affairs with the market rather than local communities in mind.

Capitalism generated considerable wealth, but its effects were uneven and sometimes unsettling. Economic development and increasing prosperity were noticeable in western Europe, particularly England, France, Germany, and the Netherlands. Yet eastern Europe experienced much less economic ferment, as Poland and Russia increasingly became suppliers of grain and raw materials rather than centers of trade or production. Even in western Europe, early capitalism encouraged social change that sometimes required painful adjustments to new conditions.

Population Growth and Urbanization

American Food Crops The foundation of European economic expansion in early modern times was a rapidly growing population, which reflected improved nutrition and decreasing mortality. The Columbian exchange enriched European diets by introducing new food crops to European fields and tables. Most notable of the introductions was the potato, which during the sixteenth and seventeenth centuries enjoyed the reputation of being an aphrodisiac. Although potatoes probably did not inspire much romantic ardor, they provided a welcome source of carbohydrates for peasants and laborers who were having trouble keeping up with the rising price of bread. From Ireland to Russia and from Scandinavia to the Mediterranean, cultivators planted potatoes and harvested crops that added calories to European diets. American maize also made its way to Europe. Maize, however, served mostly as feed for livestock rather than as food for human consumption, although peasants sometimes used cornmeal to make bread or porridges like polenta. Other American crops, such as tomatoes and peppers, added vitamins and tangy flavor to European diets.

While recently introduced American crops improved European diets, old diseases lost some of their ferocity. Smallpox continued to carry off about 10 percent of Europe's infants, and dysentery, influenza, tuberculosis, and typhus claimed victims among young and old, rich and poor alike. Yet better-nourished populations were better able to resist those maladies. Bubonic plague, a virulent epidemic killer during the fourteenth and fifteenth centuries, receded from European society. After its initial onslaught in the mid-fourteenth century, plague made periodic appearances throughout the early modern era. After the mid-seventeenth century, however, epidemics were rare and isolated events. The last major outbreaks of plague in Europe occurred in London in 1660 and Marseilles in 1720. By the mid-seventeenth century, epidemic disease was almost negligible as an influence on European population.

Population Growth Although European birthrates did not rise dramatically in early modern times, decreasing mortality resulted in rapid population growth. In 1500 the population of Europe, including Russia, was about 81 million. During the sixteenth century, as Europe recovered from epidemic plague, the population rose to 100 million. The Thirty Years' War—along with the famine and disease that the war touched off—led to population decline from about 1620 to 1650, but by 1700 European population had rallied and risen to 120 million. During the next century it grew by an additional 50 percent to 180 million.

Urbanization Rapid population growth drove a process of equally rapid urbanization. Some cities grew because rulers chose them as sites of government. Madrid, for example, was a minor town with a few thousand inhabitants until 1561 when King Philip II decided to locate his capital there. By 1600 the population of Madrid had risen to 65,000, and by 1630 it had reached 170,000. Other cities were commercial and industrial as well as government centers, and their numbers expanded along with the European economy. In the mid-sixteenth century, for example, the population of Paris was about 130,000, and London had about 60,000 inhabitants. A century later the population of both cities had risen to 500,000. Other European cities also experienced growth, even if it was not so dramatic as in Madrid, Paris, and London: Amsterdam, Berlin, Copenhagen, Dublin, Stockholm, Vienna, and others became prominent European cities during the early modern era.

Early Capitalism and Protoindustrialization

The Nature of Capitalism Population growth and rapid urbanization helped spur a round of remarkable economic development. This economic growth coincided with the emergence of capitalism—an economic system in which private parties make their goods and services available on a free market and seek to take advantage of market conditions to profit from their activities. Whether they are single individuals or large companies, private parties own the land, machinery, tools, equipment, buildings, workshops, and raw materials needed for production. Private parties pursuing their own economic interests hire workers and decide for themselves what to produce: economic decisions are the prerogative of capitalist businessmen, not governments or social superiors. The center of a capitalist system is the market in which businessmen compete with one another, and the

forces of supply and demand determine the prices received for goods and services. If businessmen organize their affairs efficiently, they realize handsome profits when they place their goods and services on the market. Otherwise, they incur losses and perhaps even lose their businesses.

The desire to accumulate wealth and realize profits was by no means new. Ever since the introduction of agriculture and the production of surplus crops, some individuals and groups had accumulated great wealth. Indeed, for several thousand years before the early modern era, merchants in China, southeast Asia, India, southwest Asia, the Mediterranean basin, and sub-Saharan Africa had pursued commercial ventures in hopes of realizing profits. Banks, investors, and insurance underwriters had supported privately organized commercial ventures throughout much of the eastern hemisphere since the postclassical era (500–1500 C.E.).

Supply and Demand During early modern times, however, European merchants and entrepreneurs transformed their society in a way that none of their predecessors had done. The capitalist economic order developed as businessmen learned to take advantage of market conditions by building efficient networks of transportation and communication. Dutch merchants might purchase cheap grain from Baltic lands such as Poland or Russia, for example, store it in Amsterdam until they learned about a famine in

The Old Stock Exchange of Amsterdam, depicted here in a painting of the mid-seventeenth century, attracted merchants, investors, entrepreneurs, and businessmen from all over Europe. There they bought and sold shares in joint-stock companies such as the VOC and dealt in all manner of commodities traded in Amsterdam.

the Mediterranean, and then transport it and sell it in southern France or Spain. Their enormous profits fueled suspicions that they took advantage of those in difficulty, but their activities also supplied hungry communities with the necessities of life, even if the price was high.

Private parties organized an array of institutions and services to support early capitalism. Banks, for example, appeared in all the major commercial cities of Europe: they held funds on account for safekeeping and granted loans to merchants or entrepreneurs launching new business ventures. Banks also published business newsletters—forerunners of the *Wall Street Journal* and *Fortune* magazine—that provided readers with reports on prices, information about demand for commodities in distant markets, and political news that could have an impact on business. Insurance companies mitigated financial losses from risky undertakings such as transoceanic voyages. Stock exchanges arose in the major European cities and provided markets where investors could buy and sell shares in joint-stock companies and trade in other commodities as well.

Joint-Stock Companies

Joint-stock companies were especially important institutions in early capitalist society. Large trading companies such as the English East India Company and its Dutch counterpart, the Vereenigde Oost-Indische Compagnie (VOC), spread the risks attached to expensive business enterprises and also took advantage of extensive communications and transportation networks. The trading companies organized commercial ventures on a larger scale than ever before. They were the principal foundations of the global economy that emerged in early modern times, and they were the direct ancestors of contemporary multinational corporations.

Politics and Empire

Capitalism did not develop in a political vacuum. To the contrary, it emerged with the active support of government authorities who saw a capitalist order as the one best suited to their individual and collective interests. Merchants were especially influential in the affairs of the English and Dutch states, so it is not surprising that these lands adopted policies that were most favorable to capitalist enterprises throughout the early modern era. The English and Dutch states recognized individuals' rights to possess private property, enforced their contracts, protected their financial interests, and settled disputes between parties to business transactions. They also chartered joint-stock companies and authorized some of them to explore, conquer, and colonize distant lands in search of commercial opportunities. Thus early capitalism developed in the context of imperialism, as European peoples established fortified

An anonymous engraver depicts activity in a Dutch shipyard where workers build a massive, oceangoing sailing ship. In the seventeenth century, Dutch ships were inexpensive to operate, yet they accommodated abundant cargoes. What kinds of cargoes were Dutch ships likely to carry in this period?

trading posts in Asia and colonial regimes in both southeast Asia and the Americas. Indeed, imperial expansion and colonial rule were crucial for the development of capitalism, since they enabled European merchants to gain access to the natural resources and commodities that they distributed so effectively through their transportation networks.

Quite apart from its influence on trade and the distribution of goods, capitalism encouraged European entrepreneurs to organize new ways to manufacture goods. For centuries, craft guilds had monopolized the production of goods such as textiles and metalwares in European towns and cities. Guilds fixed prices and wages, and they regulated standards of quality. They did not seek to realize profits so much as to protect markets and preserve their members' places in society. As a result, they actively discouraged competition and sometimes resisted technological innovation.

Putting-out System Capitalist entrepreneurs seeking profits found the guilds cumbersome and inflexible, so they sidestepped them and moved production into the countryside. Instead of relying on urban artisans to produce cloth, for example, they organized a "putting-out system" by which they delivered unfinished materials such as raw wool to rural households. Men and women in the countryside would then spin the wool into yarn, weave the yarn into cloth, cut the cloth according to patterns, and assemble the pieces into garments. The entrepreneur paid workers for their services, picked up the finished goods, and sold them on the market. During the seventeenth and eighteenth centuries, entrepreneurs moved the production of cloth, nails, pins, pots, and many other goods into the countryside through the putting-out system.

Because rural labor was usually plentiful, entrepreneurs spent relatively little on wages and realized handsome profits on their ventures. The putting-out system represented an early effort to organize efficient industrial production. Indeed, some historians refer to the seventeenth and eighteenth centuries as an age of "protoindustrialization." The putting-out system remained a prominent feature of European society until the rise of industrial factories in the nineteenth century.

Social Change in Early Modern Europe

Capitalist economic development brought unsettling change to European lands. The putting-out system, for example, introduced considerable sums of money into the countryside. Increased wealth brought material benefits, but it also undermined long-established patterns of rural life. The material standards of rural life rose dramatically: peasant households acquired more cabinets, furnishings, and tableware, and rural residents wore better clothes, ate better food, and drank better wine. Individuals suddenly acquired incomes that enabled them to pursue their own economic interests and to become financially independent of their families and neighbors. When young adults and women began to earn their own incomes, however, many feared that they might slip out of the control of their families and abandon their kin who continued to work at agricultural tasks.

The putting-out system did not become a prominent feature of production in eastern Europe, but early capitalism prompted deep social change there as well as in lands to the west. Eastern Europe had few cities in early modern times, so in expansive agrarian states such as Poland, Bohemia, and Russia, most people had no alternative to working in the countryside. Landlords took advantage of this situation by forcing peasants to work under extremely harsh conditions.

Serfdom in Russia Russia in particular was a vast but sparsely populated empire with little trade or manufacturing. Out of a concern to retain the allegiance of the powerful nobles who owned most of Russia's land, the Romanov tsars restricted the freedoms of most Russian peasants and tied them to the land as serfs. The institution of serfdom had emerged in the early middle ages as a labor system that required peasants to provide labor services for landowners and prevented them from marrying or moving away without their landlords' permission. After the fifteenth century, serfdom gradually came to an end in western Europe. In eastern Europe, however, landowners and rulers tightened restrictions on peasants during the sixteenth century, and in Russia the institution of serfdom survived until the nineteenth century. In effect, the Romanovs won the support of the Russian nobles by ensuring that laborers would be available to work their estates, which otherwise would have been worthless. In 1649 the government promulgated a law code that provided for tight state control over the Russian labor force by establishing a rigid, castelike social order that sharply restricted both occupational and geographic mobility. The law of 1649 did not turn serfs into chattel slaves, but during the late seventeenth and eighteenth centuries, landlords commonly sold serfs to one another as if they were indeed private property. Under those conditions, landlords operated estates with inexpensive labor and derived enormous incomes from the sale of agricultural products on the market.

thinking about ENCOUNTERS

Capitalism and Overseas Expansion

In the early modern era, Europeans consolidated previous economic developments into a new and profitable system of capitalism, where the central organizing form became the market. Capitalism provided the key tools for more efficient forms of overseas expansion. What were the signal capitalist institutions that underpinned overseas endeavors? How in turn did imperial expansion promote the further growth of capitalism?

These arrangements played crucial roles in the emergence of capitalism. In the larger economy of early modern Europe, eastern European lands relied on serfs to cultivate grains and provide raw materials such as timber for export to western Europe, where merchants and manufacturers were able to employ free wage labor in building a capitalist economy. Already by the early sixteenth century, consumers in the Netherlands depended for their survival on grains imported from Poland and Russia through the Baltic Sea. Thus it was possible for capitalism to flourish in western Europe only because the peasants and semifree serfs of eastern Europe provided inexpensive foods and raw materials that fueled economic development. From its earliest days, capitalist economic organization had implications for peoples and lands far removed from the centers of capitalism itself.

Profits and Ethics Capitalism also posed moral challenges. Medieval theologians had regarded profit-making activity as morally dangerous, since profiteers looked to their own advantage rather than the welfare of the larger community. Church officials even attempted to forbid the collection of interest on loans, since they considered interest an unearned and immoral profit. But profit was the lifeblood of capitalism, and bankers were not willing to risk large sums of money on business ventures without realizing returns on their investments in the form of interest. Even as it transformed the European economy, capitalism found advocates who sought to explain its principles and portray it as a socially beneficial form of economic organization. Most important of the early apostles of capitalism was the Scottish philosopher Adam Smith (1723–1790), who held that society would prosper when individuals pursued their own economic interests.

Nevertheless, the transition to capitalist society was long and painful. When individuals abandoned the practices of their ancestors and declined to help those who had fallen on hard times, their neighbors readily interpreted their actions as expressions of selfishness rather than economic prudence. Thus capitalist economic practices generated deep social strains, which often manifested themselves in violence. Bandits plagued the countryside of early modern Europe, and muggers turned whole sections of large cities into danger zones. Some historians believe that witch-hunting activities reflected social tensions generated by early capitalism and that accusations of witchcraft represented hostility toward women who were becoming economically independent of their husbands and families.

The Nuclear Family In some ways, capitalism favored the nuclear family as the principal unit of society. For centuries European couples had mostly married late—in their mid-twenties—and set up independent households. Early capitalism offered opportunities for these independent families to increase their wealth by cultivating agricultural crops or producing goods for sale on the market. As nuclear families became more important economically, they also became more socially and emotionally independent. Love between a man and a woman became a more important consideration in the making of marriages than the interests of the larger extended families, and affection between parents and their children became a more important ingredient of family life. Capitalism did not necessarily cause these changes in family life, but it may have encouraged developments that helped to define the nature and role of the family in modern European society.

SCIENCE AND ENLIGHTENMENT

While experiencing religious, political, economic, and social change, western Europe also underwent intellectual and cultural transformation. Astronomers and physicists rejected classical Greek and Roman authorities, whose theories had dominated scientific thought during the middle ages, and based their understanding of the natural world on direct observation and mathematical reasoning. During the seventeenth and eighteenth centuries, they elaborated a new vision of the earth and the larger universe. Scholars relied on observation and mathematics to transform the natural sciences in a process known as the scientific revolution. The results of early modern science were so powerful that some European intellectuals sought to overhaul moral, social, and political thought by adapting scientific methods and relying on reason rather than traditional cultural authorities. Their efforts weakened the influence of churches in western Europe and encouraged the development of secular values.

The Reconception of the Universe

The Ptolemaic Universe Until the seventeenth century, European astronomers based their understanding of the universe on the work of the Greek scholar Claudius Ptolemy of Alexandria. About the middle of the second century C.E., Ptolemy composed a work known as the *Almagest* that synthesized theories about the universe. Ptolemy envisioned a motionless earth surrounded by a series of nine hollow, concentric spheres that revolved around it. Each of the first seven spheres had one of the observable heavenly bodies—the sun, the moon, Mercury, Venus, Mars, Jupiter, and Saturn—embedded in its shell. The eighth sphere held the stars, and an empty ninth sphere surrounded the whole cosmos and provided the spin that kept all the others moving. Beyond the spheres Christian astronomers located heaven, the realm of God.

Following Ptolemy, astronomers believed that the heavens consisted of matter unlike any found on earth. Glowing like perfect jewels in the night skies, heavenly bodies were composed of a pure substance that did not experience change or corruption, and they were not subject to the physical laws that governed the world below the moon. They followed perfect circular paths in making their revolutions around the earth.

sources from the past

Adam Smith on the Capitalist Market

Adam Smith devoted special thought to the nature of early capitalist society and the principles that made it work. In 1776 he published a lengthy book entitled An Inquiry into the Nature and Causes of the Wealth of Nations, *a vastly influential work that championed free, unregulated markets and capitalist enterprise as the principal ingredients of prosperity. Smith's optimism about capitalism sprang from his conviction that society as a whole benefits when individuals pursue their own economic interests and trade on a free market.*

Every individual is continually exerting himself to find out the most advantageous employment for whatever capital he can command. It is his own advantage, indeed, and not that of the society, which he has in view. . . .

As every individual, therefore, endeavours as much as he can both to employ his capital in the support of domestic industry, and so to direct that industry that its produce may be of the greatest value, every individual necessarily labours to render the annual revenue of the society as great as he can. He generally, indeed, neither intends to promote the public interest, nor knows how much he is promoting it. By preferring the support of domestic to that of foreign industry, he intends only his own security; and by directing that industry in such a manner as its produce may be of the greatest value, he intends only his own gain, and he is in this, as in many other cases, led by an invisible hand to promote an end which was no part of his intention. Nor is it always the worse for the society that it was no part of it. By pursuing his own interest he frequently promotes that of the society more effectually than when he really intends to promote it. I have never known much good done by those who affected to trade for the public good. It is an affectation, indeed, not very common among merchants, and very few words need be employed in dissuading them from it.

What is the species of domestic industry which his capital can employ, and of which the produce is likely to be of the greatest value, every individual, it is evident, can, in his local situation, judge much better than any statesman or lawgiver can do for him. The statesman, who should attempt to direct private people in what manner they ought to employ their capitals, would not only load himself with a most unnecessary attention, but assume an authority which could safely be trusted, not only to no single person, but to no council or senate whatever, and which would nowhere be so dangerous as in the hands of a man who had folly and presumption enough to fancy himself fit to exercise it.

To give the monopoly of the home market to the produce of domestic industry, in any particular art or manufacture, is in some measure to direct private people in what manner they ought to employ their capitals, and must, in almost all cases, be either a useless or a hurtful regulation. If the produce of domestic industry can be brought there as cheap as that of foreign industry, the regulation is evidently useless. If it cannot, it must generally be hurtful. It is the maxim of every prudent master of a family, never to attempt to make at home what it will cost him more to make than to buy. The tailor does not attempt to make his own shoes, but buys them of the shoemaker. The shoemaker does not attempt to make his own clothes, but employs a tailor. The farmer attempts to make neither the one nor the other, but employs those different artificers. All of them find it for their interest to employ their whole industry in a way in which they have some advantage over their neighbours, and to purchase with a part of its produce, or, what is the same thing, with the price of a part of it, whatever else they have occasion for.

For Further Reflection

- To what extent do you think Adam Smith's analysis reflected the experiences of his own times, and to what extent did they represent universally valid observations?

Source: Adam Smith. *An Inquiry into the Nature and Causes of the Wealth of Nations.* Edinburgh: 1863, pp. 198–200.

Planetary Movement Although theoretically attractive, this earth-centered, or geocentric, cosmology did not mesh readily with the erratic movements of the planets—a term that comes from the Greek word *planetes,* meaning "wanderer." From the vantage point of the earth, the planets often followed regular courses through the skies, but they sometimes slowed down, stopped, or even turned back on their courses—motions that would be difficult to explain if the planetary spheres revolved regularly around the earth. Astronomers went to great lengths to explain planetary behavior as the result of perfect circular movements. The result was an awkward series of adjustments known as epicycles—small circular revolutions that planets made around a point in their spheres, even while the spheres themselves revolved around the earth.

The Copernican Universe As astronomers accumulated data on planetary movements, most of them sought to reconcile their observations with Ptolemaic theory by adding increasing numbers of epicycles to their cosmic maps.

In 1543, however, the Polish astronomer Nicolaus Copernicus published a treatise, *On the Revolutions of the Heavenly Spheres,* that broke with Ptolemaic theory and pointed European science in a new direction. Copernicus argued that the sun rather than the earth stood at the center of the universe and that the planets, including the earth, revolved around the sun.

Compared with Ptolemy's earth-centered universe, this new sun-centered, or heliocentric, theory harmonized much better with observational data, but it did not receive a warm welcome. Copernicus's ideas not only challenged prevailing scientific theories but also threatened cherished religious beliefs. His theory implied that the earth was just another planet and that human beings did not occupy the central position in the universe. To some it also suggested the unsettling possibility that there might be other populated worlds in the universe—a notion that would be difficult to reconcile with Christian teachings, which held that the earth and humanity were unique creations of God.

The Scientific Revolution

Although it was unpopular in many quarters, Copernicus's theory inspired some astronomers to examine the heavens in fresh ways. As evidence accumulated, it became clear that the Ptolemaic universe simply did not correspond with reality. Astronomers based their theories on increasingly precise observational data, and they relied on mathematical reasoning to organize the data. Gradually, they abandoned the Ptolemaic in favor of the Copernican model of the universe. Moreover, some of them began to apply their analytical methods to mechanics—the branch of science that deals with moving bodies—and by the mid-seventeenth century accurate observation and mathematical reasoning dominated both mechanics and astronomy. Indeed, reliance on

In this seventeenth-century engraving, Galileo Galilei faces the Inquisition, a Roman Catholic institution that prosecuted individuals accused of a wide variety of crimes related to heresy. At a trial in 1633, the Inquisition found Galileo "vehemently suspect of heresy," forced him to recant Copernicanism, and placed him under house arrest for the remainder of his life.

observation and mathematics transformed the study of the natural world and brought about the scientific revolution.

Galileo Galilei The works of two scientists—Johannes Kepler of Germany and Galileo Galilei of Italy—rang the death knell for the Ptolemaic universe. Kepler (1571–1630) demonstrated that planetary orbits are elliptical, not circular as in Ptolemaic theory. Galileo (1564–1642) showed that the heavens were not the perfect, unblemished realm that Ptolemaic astronomers assumed but, rather, a world of change, flux, and many previously unsuspected sights. Galileo took a recently invented instrument—the telescope—turned it skyward, and reported observations that astonished his contemporaries. With his telescope he could see spots on the sun and mountains on the moon—observations that discredited the notion that heavenly bodies were smooth, immaculate, unchanging, and perfectly spherical. He also noticed four of the moons that orbit the planet Jupiter—bodies that no human being had ever before observed—and he caught sight of previously unknown distant stars, which implied that the universe was much larger than anyone had previously suspected.

In addition to his astronomical discoveries, Galileo contributed to the understanding of terrestrial motion. He designed ingenious experiments to show that the velocity of falling bodies depends not on their weight but, rather, on the height from which they fall. This claim brought him scorn from scientists who subscribed to scientific beliefs deriving from Aristotle. But it offered a better explanation of how moving bodies behave under the influence of the earth's gravitational pull. Galileo also anticipated the modern law of inertia, which holds that a moving body will continue to move in a straight line until some force intervenes to check or alter its motion.

Isaac Newton The new approach to science culminated in the work of the English mathematician Isaac Newton (1642–1727), who depended on accurate observation and mathematical reasoning to construct a powerful synthesis of astronomy and mechanics. Newton outlined his views on the natural world in an epoch-making volume of 1687 entitled *Mathematical Principles of Natural Philosophy.* Newton's work united the heavens and the earth in a vast, cosmic system. He argued that a law of universal gravitation regulates the motions of bodies throughout the universe, and he offered precise mathematical explanations of the laws that govern movements of bodies on the earth. Newton's laws of universal gravitation and motion enabled him to synthesize the sciences of astronomy and mechanics. They also allowed him to explain a vast range of seemingly unrelated phenomena, such as the ebb and flow of the tides, which move according to the gravitational pull of the moon, and the eccentric orbits of planets and comets, which reflect the gravi-

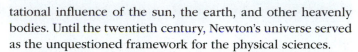

thinking about TRADITIONS

Science and the Enlightenment
Inspired by the advances in science, European intellectuals questioned long-standing beliefs concerning the nature and functioning of human society. What specific traditions did scientists and intellectuals challenge? How did religious tenets fare under such scrutiny?

tational influence of the sun, the earth, and other heavenly bodies. Until the twentieth century, Newton's universe served as the unquestioned framework for the physical sciences.

Newton's work symbolized the scientific revolution, but it by no means marked the end of the process by which observation and mathematical reasoning transformed European science. Inspired by the dramatic discoveries of astronomers and physicists, other scientists began to turn away from classical authorities and to construct fresh approaches to the understanding of the natural world. During the seventeenth and eighteenth centuries, anatomy, physiology, microbiology, chemistry, and botany underwent a thorough overhaul, as scientists tested their theories against direct observation of natural phenomena and explained them in rigorous mathematical terms.

Women and Science

In the sixteenth and seventeenth centuries, Europe's learned men challenged some of the most hallowed traditions concerning the nature of the physical universe and supplanted them with new scientific principles. Yet, when male scientists studied female anatomy, female physiology, and women's reproductive organs, they were commonly guided not by scientific observation but by tradition, prejudice, and fanciful imagination. William Harvey (1578–1657), the English physician who discovered the principles of the circulation of human blood, also applied his considerable talents to the study of human reproduction. After careful dissection and observation of female deer, chickens, and roosters, he hypothesized that women, like hens, served as mere receptacles for the "vivifying" male fluid. According to him, it was the male semen—endowed with generative powers so potent that it did not even have to reach the uterus to work its magic—from which the unfertilized egg received life and form. Anatomy, physiology, and limited reproductive function seemed to confirm the innate inferiority of women, adding a "scientific" veneer to the traditionally limited images, roles, and functions of women. With the arrival of printing, men were able to disseminate more widely those negative conclusions about women.

Émilie du Châtelet Despite prevailing critical attitudes, some women found themselves drawn to the new intellectual currents of the time. Women formulated their own

Émilie du Châtelet was perhaps the most exceptional female scientist of the Enlightenment. Although she had to contend with the conventional demands on women, she remained committed to her study of Newton and science.

theories about the natural world and published their findings. One of the most notable female scientists of her age was Émilie du Châtelet (1706–1749), a French mathematician and physicist. Long famous for being the mistress of the celebrated French intellectual Voltaire, she was in fact a talented intellectual and scientist in her own right. A precocious child, du Châtelet was apparently fluent in six languages at the age of twelve, and she benefited from having an unusually enlightened father who provided his rebellious daughter with an education more typical for boys. Her obvious intellectual abilities made her mother despair over her daughter's future, and her mother complained about a daughter who "flaunts her mind, and frightens away the suitors her other excesses have not driven off." Émilie du Châtelet nonetheless did marry, as was custom, and she had three children with her husband, the Marquis du Châtelet. She did this while also engaged in affairs of the intellect.

Du Châtelet established her reputation as a scientist with her three-volume work on the German mathematician Gottfried Leibniz (1646–1716) in 1740. Her crowning achievement, however, was her translation of Isaac Newton's monumental work *Principia Mathematica,* which has remained the standard French translation of the work. She did not simply render Newton's words into another language, however; rather, she explained his complex mathematics in graceful prose, transformed his geometry into calculus, and assessed the current state of Newtonian physics. She finished her work in the year of her death, at age forty-three, six days after giving birth to a child. Underscoring the difficulty of reconciling a woman's reproductive duties with her intellectual aspirations was her lover Voltaire's commentary. He declared in a letter to his friend Frederick II, King of Prussia (reigned 1740–1786), that du Châtelet was "a great man whose only fault was being a woman."

The Enlightenment

Newton's vision of the universe was so powerful and persuasive that its influence extended well beyond science. His work suggested that rational analysis of human behavior and institutions could lead to fresh insights about the human as well as the natural world. From Scotland to Sicily and from Philadelphia to Moscow, European and Euro-American thinkers launched an ambitious project to transform human thought and to use reason to transform the world. Like the early modern scientists, they abandoned Aristotelian philosophy, Christian theology, and other traditionally recognized authorities, and they sought to subject the human world to purely rational analysis. The result of their work was a movement known as the Enlightenment.

Science and Society Enlightenment thinkers sought to discover natural laws that governed human society in the same way that Newton's laws of universal gravitation and motion regulated the universe. Their search took different forms. The English philosopher John Locke (1632–1704) worked to discover natural laws of politics. He attacked divine-right theories that served as a foundation for absolute monarchy and advocated constitutional government on the grounds that sovereignty resides in the people rather than the state or its rulers. Indeed, he provided much of the theoretical justification for the Glorious Revolution and the establishment of constitutional monarchy in England. The Scottish philosopher Adam Smith turned his attention to economic affairs and held that laws of supply and demand determine what happens in the marketplace. The French nobleman Charles Louis de Secondat, better known as the Baron de Montesquieu (1689–1755), sought to establish a science of politics and discover principles that would foster political liberty in a prosperous and stable state.

The center of Enlightenment thought was France, where prominent intellectuals known collectively as *philosophes* ("philosophers") advanced the cause of reason. The philo-

Joseph Wright of Derby's painting entitled "A philosopher gives a lecture on the orrery" centers on a three-dimensional image of the cosmos (the orrery); his use of light offers a metaphor for the Enlightenment and natural philosophy.

sophes were not philosophers in the traditional sense of the term so much as public intellectuals. They addressed their works more to the educated public than to scholars: instead of formal philosophical treatises, they mostly composed histories, novels, dramas, satires, and pamphlets on religious, moral, and political issues.

Voltaire More than any other philosophe, François-Marie Arouet (1694–1778) epitomized the spirit of the Enlightenment. Writing under the pen name Voltaire, he published his first book at age seventeen. By the time of his death at age eighty-four, his published writings included some ten thousand letters and filled seventy volumes. With stinging wit and sometimes bitter irony, Voltaire championed individual freedom and attacked any institution sponsoring intolerant or oppressive policies. Targets of his caustic wit included

the French monarchy and the Roman Catholic church. When the king of France sought to save money by reducing the number of horses kept in royal stables, for example, Voltaire suggested that it would be more effective to get rid of the asses who rode the horses. Voltaire also waged a long literary campaign against the Roman Catholic church, which he held responsible for fanaticism, intolerance, and incalculable human suffering. Voltaire's battle cry was *écrasez l'infame* ("crush the damned thing"), meaning the church that he considered an agent of oppression.

Deism Some philosophes were conventional Christians, and a few turned to atheism. Like Voltaire, however, most of them were deists who believed in the existence of a god but denied the supernatural teachings of Christianity, such as Jesus' virgin birth and his resurrection. To the deists the universe was an orderly realm. Deists held that a powerful god set the universe in motion and established natural laws that govern it, but did not take a personal interest in its development or intervene in its affairs. In a favorite simile of the deists, this god was like a watchmaker who did not need

sources from the past

John Locke Claims People Are the Products of Their Environment

John Locke (1632–1704) was one of the leading intellectuals of his age. Although commonly recognized as an influential political theorist, he was also intensely curious about how humans acquired knowledge. In his seminal An Essay Concerning Human Understanding *(1690), Locke repudiates the prevailing view that knowledge—knowledge of certain moral truths or knowledge of the existence of God, for example—is innate, that is, imprinted on the human mind at birth. He argues instead that the foundation of all knowledge is sense experience (sensation), like the color of a flower, and awareness that one is thinking (reflection). These "ideas" provide the mind with knowledge.*

The way shown how we come by any knowledge, sufficient to prove it not innate. It is an established opinion amongst some men, that there are in the understanding certain innate principles; some primary notions, characters, as it were stamped upon the mind of man; which the soul receives in its very first being, and brings into the world with it. It would be sufficient to convince unprejudiced readers of the falseness of this supposition, if I should only show (as I hope I shall in the following parts of this Discourse) how men, barely by the use of their natural faculties, may attain to all the knowledge they have, without the help of any innate impressions; and may arrive at certainty, without any such original notions or principles. . . .

All ideas come from sensation or reflection. Let us then suppose the mind to be, as we say, white paper, void of all characters, without any ideas:—How comes it to be furnished? Whence comes it by that vast store which the busy and boundless fancy of man has painted on it with an almost endless variety? Whence has it all the materials of reason and knowledge? To this I answer, in one word, from Experience. In that all our knowledge is founded; and from that it ultimately derives itself. Our observation employed either, about external sensible objects, or about the internal operations of our minds perceived and reflected on by ourselves, is that which supplies our understandings with all the materials of thinking. These two are the fountains of knowledge, from whence all the ideas we have, or can naturally have, do spring.

The objects of sensation one source of ideas. First, our Senses, conversant about particular sensible objects, do con- vey into the mind several distinct perceptions of things, according to those various ways wherein those objects do affect them. And thus we come by those ideas we have of yellow, white, heat, cold, soft, hard, bitter, sweet, and all those which we call sensible qualities; which when I say the senses convey into the mind, I mean, they from external objects convey into the mind what produces there those perceptions. This great source of most of the ideas we have, depending wholly upon our senses, and derived by them to the understanding, I call Sensation.

The operations of our minds, the other source of them. Secondly, the other fountain from which experience furnisheth the understanding with ideas is,—the perception of the operations of our own mind within us, as it is employed about the ideas it has got;—which operations, when the soul comes to reflect on and consider, do furnish the understanding with another set of ideas, which could not be had from things without. And such are perception, thinking, doubting, believing, reasoning, knowing, willing, and all the different actings of our own minds;—which we being conscious of, and observing in ourselves, do from these receive into our understandings as distinct ideas as we do from bodies affecting our senses. This source of ideas every man has wholly in himself; and though it be not sense, as having nothing to do with external objects, yet it is very like it, and might properly enough be called internal sense. But as I call the other Sensation, so I Call this Reflection, the ideas it affords being such only as the mind gets by reflecting on its own operations within itself.

For Further Reflection

■ What are the implications of Locke's claim for the development of human society that people are solely the products of their environment? How are those implications bound up with criticism of existing social structures?

Source: John Locke. *An Essay Concerning Human Understanding.* Kitchener, Ontario, Canada: Batoche Books, 1690, pp. 24, 73, 74. http://site.ebrary.com/lib/uhmanoa/Doc?id=2001993&ppg=24, 73, 74.

to interfere constantly in the workings of his creation, since it operated by itself according to rational and natural laws.

The Theory of Progress Most philosophes were optimistic about the future of the world and humanity. They expected knowledge of human affairs to advance as fast as modern science, and they believed that rational understanding of human and natural affairs would bring about a new era of constant progress. In fact, progress became almost an ideology of the philosophes, who believed that natural science would lead to greater human control over the world while rational sciences of human affairs would lead to indi-

Socially prominent women deeply influenced the development of Enlightenment thought by organizing and maintaining salons—gatherings where philosophes, scientists, and intellectuals discussed the leading ideas of the day. Though produced in 1814, this painting depicts the Parisian salon of Mme. Geoffrin (center left), a leading patron of the French philosophes, about 1775. In the background is a bust of Voltaire, who lived in Switzerland at the time.

vidual freedom and the construction of a prosperous, just, and equitable society.

The philosophes' fond wishes for progress, prosperity, and social harmony did not come to pass. Yet the Enlightenment helped to bring about a thorough cultural transformation of European society. It weakened the influence of organized religion, although it by no means destroyed institutional churches. Enlightenment thought encouraged the replacement of Christian values, which had guided European thought on religious and moral affairs for more than a millennium, with a new set of secular values arising from reason rather than revelation. Furthermore, the Enlightenment encouraged political and cultural leaders to subject society to rational analysis and intervene actively in its affairs in the interests of promoting progress and prosperity. In many ways, the Enlightenment legacy continues to influence European and Euro-American societies.

in**perspective**

During the early modern era, European society experienced a series of profound and sometimes unsettling changes. The Protestant Reformation ended the religious unity of western Christendom, and intermittent religious conflict disrupted European society for a century and more. Centralizing monarchs strengthened their realms and built a society of sovereign, autonomous, and intensely competitive states. Capitalist entrepreneurs reorganized the production and distribution of manufactured goods, and although their methods led to increased wealth, their quest for efficiency and profits clashed with traditional values. Modern science based on direct observation and mathematical explanations emerged as a powerful tool for the investigation of the natural world, and its influence extended even to thought about human affairs. Some people rejected traditional religious beliefs altogether and worked toward the construction of a new moral thought based strictly on science and reason. At just the time that European merchants, colonists, and adventurers were seeking opportunities in the larger world, European society was becoming more powerful, more experimental, and more competitive than ever before. ●

CHRONOLOGY

1473–1543	Life of Nicolaus Copernicus
1478	Foundation of the Spanish Inquisition
1483–1546	Life of Martin Luther
1491–1556	Life of Ignatius Loyola
1509–1547	Reign of King Henry VIII
1509–1564	Life of John Calvin
1517	Publication of the *Ninety-Five Theses*
1519–1556	Reign of Emperor Charles V
1540	Foundation of the Society of Jesus
1545–1563	Council of Trent
1556–1598	Reign of King Philip II
1564–1642	Life of Galileo Galilei
1571–1630	Life of Johannes Kepler
1588	Spanish Armada
1618–1648	Thirty Years' War
1632–1704	Life of John Locke
1642–1727	Life of Isaac Newton
1643–1715	Reign of King Louis XIV
1648	Peace of Westphalia
1689–1755	Life of the Baron de Montesquieu
1694–1778	Life of Voltaire
1706–1749	Life of Émilie du Châtelet
1723–1790	Life of Adam Smith

For Further Reading

Philip Benedict. *Christ's Churches Purely Reformed: A Social History of Calvinism.* New Haven, 2002. Impressive and very readable synthesis of the history of Calvinism and the general impact of the Protestant Reformation in Europe.

William J. Bouwsma. *John Calvin: A Sixteenth-Century Portrait.* New York, 1989. A penetrating examination of one of the principal Protestant reformers.

Fernand Braudel. *Civilization and Capitalism, 15th to 18th Century.* 3 vols. Trans. by S. Reynolds. New York, 1981–84. A rich analysis of early capitalist society by one of the greatest historians of the twentieth century.

Paul Dukes. *The Making of Russian Absolutism, 1613–1801.* 2nd ed. London, 1990. A succinct study of two disparate centuries, the seventeenth and eighteenth, and two influential tsars, Peter and Catherine.

Robert S. Duplessis. *Transitions to Capitalism in Early Modern Europe.* Cambridge, 1997. A valuable synthesis of research on early capitalism and protoindustrialization.

Elizabeth L. Eisenstein. *The Printing Press as an Agent of Change.* 2 vols. Cambridge, 1979. An insightful study that examines the significance of printing for the Protestant Reformation and the scientific revolution.

Patricia Fara. *Pandora's Breeches: Women, Science, and Power in the Enlightenment.* London, 2004. An engaging account of the contributions women made to science in the seventeenth and eighteenth centuries.

Peter Gay. *The Enlightenment: An Interpretation.* 2 vols. New York, 1966–69. A classic study making the case for the Enlightenment as a turning point in European cultural history.

Philip S. Gorski. *The Disciplinary Revolution: Calvinism and the Rise of the Early Modern State.* Chicago, 2003. Argues that the formation of strong European states was a result of religious and social control policies initiated by the Protestant Reformation.

Margaret Jacob. *The Cultural Meaning of the Scientific Revolution.* New York, 1989. Explores the larger cultural and social implications of early modern science.

Lisa Jardine. *Ingenious Pursuits: Building the Scientific Revolution.* New York, 1999. A close study of the messy context of the scientific revolution and of the ambiguous boundary between what have come to be thought of as the natural and the human sciences.

E. L. Jones. *The European Miracle: Environments, Economies, and Geopolitics in the History of Europe and Asia.* 2nd ed. Cambridge, 1987. Examines European politics and economic growth in comparative perspective.

———. *Growth Recurring: Economic Change in World History.* Oxford, 1988. Compares processes of economic growth in China, Europe, and Japan.

Leonard Krieger. *Kings and Philosophers, 1689–1789.* New York, 1970. A thoughtful analysis of European history during an age of absolutism and Enlightenment.

Thomas S. Kuhn. *The Structure of Scientific Revolutions.* 3rd ed. Chicago, 1997. An influential theoretical work that views scientific thought in larger social and cultural contexts.

Brian P. Levack. *The Witch-Hunt in Early Modern Europe.* New York, 1987. A compact but comprehensive survey of European witchcraft beliefs and pursuit of witches in the sixteenth and seventeenth centuries.

William H. McNeill. *The Pursuit of Power: Technology, Armed Force, and Society since A.D. 1000.* Chicago, 1982. Insightful analysis exploring the influence of sovereign states and early capitalism on military technology and organization.

Jerry Z. Muller. *The Mind and the Market: Capitalism in Modern European Thought.* New York, 2002. Broad history of the development of capitalism through the eyes of major European thinkers, including Adam Smith, Joseph Schumpeter, and Karl Marx.

Heiko A. Oberman. *Luther: Man between God and the Devil.* Trans. by E. Walliser-Schwartzbart. New Haven, 1989. A perceptive study of the first Protestant reformer by a foremost scholar.

Geoffrey Parker. *The Military Revolution: Military Innovation and the Rise of the West, 1500–1800.* Cambridge, 1988. A thoughtful essay on European military affairs in early modern times.

Kenneth Pomeranz. *The Great Divergence: China, Europe, and the Making of the Modern World Economy.* Princeton, 2000. Pathbreaking scholarly study that illuminates the economic history of the early modern world through comparison of economic development in Asian and European lands.

Roy Porter. *The Creation of the Modern World: The Untold Story of the British Enlightenment.* New York, 2000. An important work that returns the Enlightenment to Britain.

Eugene F. Rice Jr. and Anthony Grafton. *The Foundations of Early Modern Europe, 1460–1559.* 2nd ed. New York, 1994. Excellent introduction to political, social, economic, and cultural developments.

Jessica Riskin. *Science in the Age of Sensibility: The Sentimental Empiricists of the French Enlightenment.* Chicago, 2002. Study of the development of modern science not simply as a result of empiricism but also of sentimental, humanist sensibility.

Daniel Roche. *France in the Enlightenment.* Trans. by Arthur Goldhammer. Cambridge, Mass., 1998. Comprehensive account of the French Enlightenment and some of its most significant cultural, social, and political contexts.

Paolo Rossi. *The Birth of Modern Science.* Malden, Mass., 2001. Explores specific seventeenth-century value systems and traditions that were central to the rise of modern science.

Simon Schama. *The Embarrassment of Riches: An Interpretation of Dutch Culture in the Seventeenth Century.* New York, 1987. A marvelous popular study of the wealthy Dutch republic at its height.

Keith Thomas. *Religion and the Decline of Magic.* New York, 1971. A riveting analysis of popular culture in early modern times, especially strong on the explanation of magic and witchcraft.

James Van Horn Melton. *The Rise of the Public in Enlightenment Europe.* Cambridge, 2001. Work on the cultural aspects of the Enlightenment and the emergence of a public sphere in Britain, France, and German-speaking territories.

New Worlds:
The Americas and Oceania

chapter24

A mural by Tlaxala artist Desiderio Hernández Xochitiotzin depicts the central place of Doña Marina in facilitating encounters between Hernán Cortés (on the right) and the indigenous peoples of Mexico.

EYEWITNESS:

The Mysterious Identity of Doña Marina

A remarkable young woman played a pivotal role in the Spanish conquest of Mexico. Originally called Malintzin, over the years she has come to be better known as Doña Marina, the name bestowed on her by Spanish forces. Doña Marina was born about 1500 to a noble family in central Mexico. Her mother tongue was Nahuatl, the principal language of the Aztec empire. When she was a girl, Doña Marina's family sent her to the Mexican coast as a slave, and her new family later passed her on to their neighbors in the Yucatan peninsula. During her travels she became fluent in Maya as well as her native Nahuatl language.

When Hernán Cortés arrived on the Mexican coast in 1519, his small army included a Spanish soldier who had learned the Maya language during a period of captivity in the Yucatan. But he had no way to communicate with the Nahuatl-speaking peoples of central Mexico until a Maya chieftain presented him with twelve young women, including Doña Marina, when he entered into an alliance with the foreigner. Doña Marina's linguistic talents enabled Cortés to communicate through an improbable chain of languages—from Spanish to Maya to Nahuatl and then back again—while making his way to the Aztec capital of Tenochtitlan. (Doña Marina soon learned Spanish and thus eliminated the Maya link in the linguistic chain.)

Doña Marina provided Cortés with intelligence and diplomatic as well as linguistic services. On several occasions she learned of plans by native peoples to overwhelm and destroy the tiny Spanish army, and she alerted Cortés to the danger in time for him to forestall an attack. Once, she was able to report the precise details of a planned ambush because she played along with an effort to bring her into the scheme. She also helped Cortés negotiate with emissaries from Tenochtitlan and other major cities of central Mexico. Indeed, in the absence of Doña Marina's services, it is difficult to see how Cortés's small band could have survived to see the Aztec capital.

Precisely because of her pivotal role in aiding Cortés and forwarding his invasion of the Aztec empire, Doña Marina earned another name commonly bestowed on her in Mexican history: La Malinche, or the traitor. The belief that she betrayed her people by collaborating with the Spanish underscored how native Americans faced many challenges and conflicts in their encounters with Europeans. Other subjects of the Aztec empire also chose to ally themselves with the Spanish given their disaffection from Aztec imperial rule, so Doña Marina represented the existing divisions within Mesoamerican society as well as the demonstrated bravery, intelligence, and survival skills of a woman often harshly treated. Because of her symbolic richness, she has likewise attained the status of mother of the Mexican peoples.

Apart from facilitating the Spanish conquest of the Aztec empire, Doña Marina played a role in the formation of a new society in Mexico. In 1522, one year after the fall of Tenochtitlan, she gave birth to a son fathered by Cortés, and in 1526 she bore a daughter to a Spanish captain whom she had married. Her offspring were not the first children born in the western hemisphere of indigenous and Spanish parentage, but they symbolize the early emergence of a mestizo population in Mexico. Doña Marina died soon after the birth of her daughter, probably in 1527, but during her short life she contributed to the thorough transformation of Mexican society.

Until 1492 the peoples of the eastern and western hemispheres had few dealings with one another. About 1000 C.E. Norse explorers established a short-lived colony in modern Newfoundland, and sporadic encounters between European fishermen and indigenous peoples of North America probably occurred before Christopher Columbus undertook his first voyage across the Atlantic Ocean. It is likely, too, that an occasional Asian or Austronesian mariner reached the Pacific coast of North or South America before 1492. Yet travel between the eastern hemisphere, the western hemisphere, and Oceania was too irregular and infrequent to generate interaction between peoples of different societies until the fifteenth century.

After 1492, however, the voyages of European mariners led to permanent and sustained contact between the peoples of the eastern hemisphere, the western hemisphere, and Oceania. The resulting encounters brought profound and often violent change to both American and Pacific lands. European peoples possessed powerful military weapons, horses, and sailing ships that provided them with technological advantages over the peoples they encountered in the Americas and the Pacific islands. Moreover, most Europeans also enjoyed complete or partial immunity to diseases that caused demographic disasters when introduced to the western hemisphere and Oceania. Because of their technological advantages and the wholesale depopulation that followed from epidemic diseases, European peoples were able to establish a presence throughout the Americas and much of the Pacific Ocean basin.

The European presence did not lead to immediate change in Australia and the Pacific islands, although it laid a foundation for dramatic and often traumatic change in the nineteenth and twentieth centuries. In the western hemisphere, however, large numbers of European migrants helped to bring about a profound transformation of American societies in early modern times. In Mexico and Peru, Spanish conquerors established territorial empires that were ruled from Spain. In Brazil, Portuguese entrepreneurs founded sugar plantations and imported African slaves to perform the heavy labor required for their operation. In North America, French, English, and Dutch fur traders allied with indigenous peoples who provided them with animal skins, and their more sedentary compatriots founded settler societies concentrating on the production of cash crops for export. Throughout the western hemisphere, peoples of European, African, and American ancestry interacted to fashion new worlds.

COLLIDING WORLDS

When European peoples first sought to establish their presence in the Americas, they brought a range of technology unavailable to the peoples they encountered in the western hemisphere. Even more important than European technology, however, were the divisions between indigenous peoples that Europeans were able to exploit and the effects of epidemic diseases that devastated native societies. Soon after their arrival in the western hemisphere, Spanish conquerors toppled the Aztec and Inca empires and imposed their own rule in Mexico and Peru. In later decades Portuguese planters built sugar plantations on the Brazilian coastline. French, English, and Dutch migrants displaced indigenous peoples in North America and established settler colonies under the rule of European peoples.

Die figur anzaigt uns das volck und insel die gefunden ist durch den christenlichen künig zu Portigal oder von seinen underthonen. Die leüt sind also nacket hübsch, braun wolgestalt von leib, ir hei halß, arm, scham, füß, frawen und mann ain wenig mit federn bedeckt. Auch haben die mann in iren angesichten und brust vil edel gestain. Es hat auch nyemann nichts sunder sind alle ding ge Unnd die mann haben die weyber welche in gefallen, es sey müter, schwester oder freündt haben sy kain underschayd. Sy streyten auch mit einander. Sy essen auch ainander selbs die ersch werden, und hencken das selbig fleisch in den rauch. Sy werden alt hundert und fünfzig iar. Und haben kain regiment.

One of the earliest European depictions of Native Americans was this engraving of 1505. The caption informed readers that American peoples lived in communal society, where men took several wives but none had private possessions, and that they routinely smoked and consumed the bodies of slain enemies. How might such representations have shaped European ideas about native Americans?

The Spanish Caribbean

The Taíno The first site of interaction between European and American peoples was the Caribbean. When Spanish mariners arrived there, the Taíno (also known as Arawaks) were the most prominent people in the region. During the late centuries B.C.E., the ancestors of the Taíno had sailed in canoes from the Orinoco River valley in South America to the Caribbean islands, and by about 900 C.E. they had settled throughout the region. The Taíno cultivated manioc and other crops, and they lived in small villages under the authority of chiefs who allocated land to families and super-vised community affairs. They showed interest in the glass, beads, and metal tools that Spanish mariners brought as trade goods and offered little initial resistance to the visitors.

Spanish Arrival Christopher Columbus and his immediate followers made the island of Hispaniola (which embraces modern Haiti and the Dominican Republic) the base of Spanish operations in the Caribbean. There, Spanish settlers established the fort of Santo Domingo, and the city, officially founded in 1498, became the capital of the Spanish Caribbean. Columbus's original plan was to build forts and trading posts where merchants could trade with local peoples for products desired by European consumers. Within a few years of Spanish arrival, however, it became clear that the Caribbean region offered no silks or spices for the European market. If Spanish settlers wanted to maintain their presence in the Caribbean, they would need to find some way to make a living.

The settlers first attempted to support their society by mining gold. Spanish settlers were too few in number to mine

sources from the past

First Impressions of Spanish Forces

As the Spanish army made its way to Tenochtitlan, Motecuzoma dispatched a series of emissaries to communicate with Cortés and learn his intentions. The following document, based on indigenous accounts but filtered through imperial Spanish sensibilities, suggested that Motecuzoma reacted with fright when presented with reports that were less than reassuring, since they focused on fearsome weapons and animals of the Spanish. Given the martial response of the Aztecs to the Spanish invasion, it seems highly unlikely that Motecuzoma or the Aztecs would have expressed terror in such a humiliating fashion.

And when [Motecuzoma] had heard what the messengers reported, he was terrified, he was astounded. . . .

Especially did it cause him to faint away when he heard how the gun, at [the Spaniards'] command, discharged [the shot]; how it resounded as if it thundered when it went off. It indeed bereft one of strength; it shut off one's ears. And when it discharged, something like a round pebble came forth from within. Fire went showering forth; sparks went blazing forth. And its smoke smelled very foul; it had a fetid odor which verily wounded the head. And when [the shot] struck a mountain, it was as if it were destroyed, dissolved. And a tree was pulverized; it was as if it vanished; it was as if someone blew it away.

All iron was their war array. In iron they clothed themselves. With iron they covered their heads. Iron were their swords. Iron were their crossbows. Iron were their shields. Iron were their lances.

And those which bore them upon their backs, their deer [that is, horses], were as tall as roof terraces.

And their bodies were everywhere covered; only their faces appeared. They were very white; they had chalky faces; they had yellow hair, though the hair of some was black. Long were their beards; they also were yellow. They were yellow-headed. [The black men's hair] was kinky, it was curly.

And their food was like fasting food—very large, white, not heavy like [tortillas]; like maize stalks, good-tasting as if of maize stalk flour; a little sweet, a little honeyed. It was honeyed to eat; it was sweet to eat.

And their dogs were very large. They had ears folded over; great dragging jowls. They had fiery eyes—blazing eyes; they had yellow eyes—fiery yellow eyes. They had thin flanks—flanks with ribs showing. They had gaunt stomachs. They were very tall. They were nervous; they went about panting, with tongues hanging out. They were spotted like ocelots; they were varicolored.

And when Motecuzoma heard all this, he was much terrified. It was as if he fainted away. His heart saddened; his heart failed him.

For Further Reflection

■ What did the Spanish and their indigenous allies hope to gain by presenting this image of Motecuzoma?

Source: Bernardino de Sahagún. *Florentine Codex: General History of the Things of New Spain,* 13 vols. Trans. by Arthur J. O. Anderson and Charles E. Dibble. Salt Lake City: University of Utah Press, 1950–82, 13:19–20. (Translation slightly modified.)

---

gold—and in any case they were not inclined to perform heavy physical labor—so the miners came largely from the ranks of the Taíno. Recruitment of labor came through an institution known as the **encomienda,** which gave Spanish *encomenderos* ("settlers") the right to compel the Taíno to work in their mines or fields. In return for labor, *encomenderos* assumed responsibility to look after their workers' health and welfare and to encourage their conversion to Christianity.

Conscription of Taíno labor was a brutal business. *Encomenderos* worked their charges hard and punished them severely when they did not deliver the expected quantities of gold or work sufficiently hard in the fields. The Taíno occasionally organized rebellions, but their bows, arrows, and slings had little effect against horse-mounted Spanish forces

wielding steel swords and firearms. By about 1515, social disruption and physical abuse had brought decline to Taíno populations on the large Caribbean islands—Hispaniola, Jamaica, Puerto Rico, and Cuba—favored by Spanish settlers.

Smallpox Serious demographic decline set in only after 1518, however, when smallpox reached the Caribbean region and touched off devastating epidemics among the peoples of the western hemisphere. To replace laborers lost to disease, *encomenderos* launched raiding parties to kidnap and enslave the Taíno and other peoples. This tactic exposed additional victims to introduced diseases and hastened the decline of indigenous populations.

Under pressure of epidemic disease, the native population of the Caribbean plummeted from about four million in 1492 to a few thousand in the 1540s. Native societies

encomienda (ehn-KOH-mee-ehn-dah)

themselves also passed out of existence. Only a few Taíno cultural elements survived: *canoe, hammock, hurricane, barbecue, maize,* and *tobacco* all derive from Taíno words, but the society that generated them had largely disappeared by the middle of the sixteenth century.

From Mining to Plantation Agriculture Deposits of gold were thin in the Caribbean, but optimistic Spanish adventurers continued to seek treasure there for a century and more. After the mid-sixteenth century, however, when Spanish explorers located exceptionally rich sources of silver in Mexico and Peru, the Caribbean became a sleepy backwater of the Spanish empire. English pirates lurked in Caribbean waters hoping to intercept imperial fleets carrying American silver to Spain, but the region was not a center of production. Then, about the 1640s, French, English, and Dutch settlers began to flock to the Caribbean with the intention of establishing plantations. It became clear that even if the Caribbean islands lacked precious metals, they offered ideal conditions for the cultivation of cash crops, particularly sugar, which would fetch high prices in European markets. Later, tobacco also became a prime cash crop of the region. Meanwhile, because indigenous populations were extinct, planters lacked the labor they needed to operate their estates, so they imported several million slaves. By 1700 Caribbean society consisted of a small class of European administrators and large masses of African slaves.

The Conquest of Mexico and Peru

Spanish interest soon shifted from the Caribbean to the American mainland, where settlers hoped to find more resources to exploit. During the early sixteenth century, Spanish *conquistadores* ("conquerors") pressed beyond the Caribbean islands, moving west into Mexico and south into Panama and Peru. Between 1519 and 1521 Hernán Cortés and a small band of men brought down the Aztec empire in Mexico, and between 1532 and 1533 Francisco Pizarro and his followers toppled the Inca empire in Peru. Those conquests laid the foundations for colonial regimes that would transform the Americas.

In Mexico and Peru, Spanish explorers found societies quite different from those of the Caribbean islands. Both Mexico and Peru had been sites of agricultural societies, cities, and large states for more than a millennium. In the early fifteenth century, both lands fell under the sway of powerful imperial states: the Mexica people and their allies founded the Aztec empire that expanded to embrace most of Mesoamerica, while the Incas imposed their rule on a vast realm extending from modern Ecuador in the north to modern Chile in the south—the largest state South America had ever seen. The Aztec and Inca empires both had clear lines of political authority, and both had the means to mobilize massive populations, collect taxes or tribute to maintain their societies, and recruit labor for public works projects. (See chapter 20.)

Hernán Cortés The conquest of Mexico began with an expedition to search for gold on the American mainland. In 1519 Cortés led about 450 soldiers to Mexico and made his way from Veracruz on the Gulf coast to the island city of Tenochtitlan, the stunningly beautiful Aztec capital situated in Lake Texcoco. They seized the emperor Motecuzoma II, who died in 1520 during a skirmish between Spanish forces and residents of Tenochtitlan. Aztec forces soon drove the conquistadores from the capital, and Cuauhtémoc (ca. 1502–1525)—the nephew and son-in-law of Motecuzoma—emerged as the last Aztec emperor. Cortés built a small fleet of ships, placed Tenochtitlan under siege, and in 1521 starved the city into surrender. Cuauhtémoc stood up to the torture Cortés inflicted upon him in an attempt to uncover the whereabouts of Aztec gold and treasures, but he did not escape the execution ordered by Cortés in 1525.

Steel swords, muskets, cannons, and horses offered Cortés and his soldiers some advantage over the forces they met and help to account for the Spanish conquest of the Aztec empire. Yet weaponry alone clearly would not enable Cortés's tiny force to overcome a large, densely populated society. Quite apart from military technology, Cortés's expedition benefited from divisions among the indigenous peoples of Mexico. With the aid of Doña Marina, the conquistadores forged alliances with peoples who resented domination by the Mexica, the leaders of the Aztec empire, and who reinforced the small Spanish army with thousands of veteran warriors. Native allies also provided Spanish forces with logistical support and secure bases in friendly territory.

Epidemic Disease On the mainland, as in the Caribbean, epidemic disease aided Spanish efforts. During the siege of Tenochtitlan, smallpox raged through the city, killing inhabitants by the tens of thousands and fatally sapping the strength of defensive forces. Smallpox rapidly spread beyond the capital, raced through Mexico, and carried off so many people that Aztec society was unable to function. Only in the context of this drastic depopulation is it possible to understand the Spanish conquest of Mexico.

thinking about ENCOUNTERS

Conquest

Spaniards Hernán Cortés and Francisco Pizarro initiated the contacts with Mexico and Peru that resulted in the collapse of those previously strong imperial states. What was the nature of the initial relations between these Spaniards, the Aztecs, and the Incas? What factors altered the balance of power in these encounters?

This late-sixteenth-century painting idealized the Spanish conquest of the Aztec empire. Shown on the wall is Motecuzoma, captured by the Spaniards attacking his palace, and he is pleading with the Aztecs to surrender.

Francisco Pizarro Francisco Pizarro experienced similar results when he led a Spanish expedition from Central America to Peru. Pizarro set out in 1530 with 180 soldiers, later joined by reinforcements to make a force of about 600. The conquistadores arrived in Peru just after a bitter dispute between Huascar (1503–1532) and Atahualpa (ca. 1502–1533), two brothers within the Inca ruling house, and Pizarro's forces exploited the differences between those factions. Already by 1533 they had taken the Inca capital at Cuzco. Under pretext of holding a conference, they called the Inca ruling elites together, seized them, and killed most of them. They spared the Inca ruler Atahualpa until he had delivered a large quantity of gold to Pizarro. Then they strangled him and decapitated his body. The search for treasure continued after the end of Inca rule. Pizarro and his conquistadores looted gold and silver plaques from Cuzco's temples and public buildings, melted down statuettes fashioned from precious metals, and even filched jewelry and ornaments from the embalmed bodies of deceased Inca rulers.

Several considerations help to explain how Pizarro's tiny force was able to topple the Inca empire. Many subjects of the empire despised the Incas as overlords and tax collectors and put up little resistance to Pizarro's forces. Indeed, many allied with the Spanish invaders. Epidemic disease also discouraged resistance: smallpox had spread from Mexico and Central America to Peru in the 1520s, long before Pizarro's arrival, and had already taken a heavy toll among Andean populations. Pizarro and his army actually faced more threats from fresh Spanish interlopers than from native peoples. The conquest of Peru took longer than the conquest of Mexico, but by 1540 Spanish forces had established themselves securely as lords of the land.

Iberian Empires in the Americas

During the early days after the conquests, Cortés and Pizarro allocated lands and labor rights to their troops on their own authority. Gradually, however, the Spanish monarchy extended its control over the growing American empire, and

In this illustration from Peru-native Felipe Guaman Poma de Ayala's letter of complaint to the Spanish king—a record of grievances against Spanish overlords—conquistadores decapitate Atahualpa after executing him by strangulation in 1533.

by about 1570 the semiprivate regime of the conquistadores had given way to formal rule under the Spanish crown. Bureaucrats charged with the implementation of royal policy and the administration of royal justice replaced the soldiers of fortune who had conquered Mexico and Peru. The conquistadores did not welcome the arrival of the bureaucrats, but with the aid of Spanish lawyers, tax collectors, and military forces, royal officials had their way.

Spanish Colonial Administration

Spanish administrators established two main centers of authority in the Americas—Mexico (which they called New Spain) and Peru (known as New Castile)—each governed by a viceroy who was responsible to the king of Spain. In Mexico they built a new capital, Mexico City, on top of Tenochtitlan. In Peru they originally hoped to rule from the Inca capital of Cuzco, but they considered the high altitude unpleasant and also found the Andean city too inaccessible for their purposes. In 1535 they founded Lima and transferred the government to the coast where it was accessible to Spanish shipping.

The viceroys were the king's representatives in the Americas, and they wielded considerable power. The kings of Spain, attempting to ensure that their viceroys would not build personal power bases and become independent, subjected them to the review of courts known as *audiencias* staffed by university-educated lawyers. The *audiencias* heard appeals against the viceroys' decisions and policies and had the right to address their concerns directly to the Spanish king. Furthermore, the *audiencias* conducted reviews of viceroys' performance at the end of their terms, and negative reviews could lead to severe punishment.

In many ways, Spanish administration in the Americas was a ragged affair. Transportation and communication difficulties limited the ability of viceroys to supervise their territories. In many regions, local administration fell to *audiencias* or town councils. Meanwhile, the Spanish monarchy exercised even less influence on American affairs than the viceroys. It often took two years for the central government in Spain to respond to a query from Mexico or Peru, and many replies simply asked for further information rather than providing firm directives. When viceroys received clear orders that they did not like, they found ways to procrastinate: they often responded to the king that "I obey, but I do not enforce," implying that with additional information the king would alter his decision.

New Cities

Spanish rule in the Americas led to the rapid establishment of cities throughout the viceroyalties. Like their compatriots in Spain, colonists preferred to live in cities even when they derived their income from the agricultural production of their landed estates. As the numbers of migrants increased, they expanded the territory under Spanish imperial authority and built a dense network of bureaucratic control based in recently founded cities. The jurisdiction of the viceroyalty of New Spain reached from Mexico City as far as St. Augustine in Florida (founded in 1565). Administrators in Lima oversaw affairs from Panama (founded in 1519) to Concepción (founded in 1550) and Buenos Aires (founded in 1536).

Portuguese Brazil

While Spanish conquistadores and administrators built a territorial empire in Mexico and Peru, Portuguese forces established an imperial presence in Brazil. The Portuguese presence came about by an odd twist of diplomatic convention. In 1494 Spain and Portugal signed the Treaty of Tordesillas, which divided the world along an imaginary north-south line 370 leagues west of the Azores and Cape Verde Islands. According to this agreement, Spain could claim any land west of that line, so long as it was not already under Christian rule, and Portugal gained the same rights for lands east of the line. Thus Portugal gained territory along the northeastern part of the South American continent, a region known as Brazil from the many brazilwood trees that grew along the coast, and the remainder of the western hemisphere fell under Spanish control.

The Portuguese mariner Pedro Alvares de Cabral stopped in Brazil briefly in 1500 while making a tack through the Atlantic Ocean en route to India. His compatriots did not

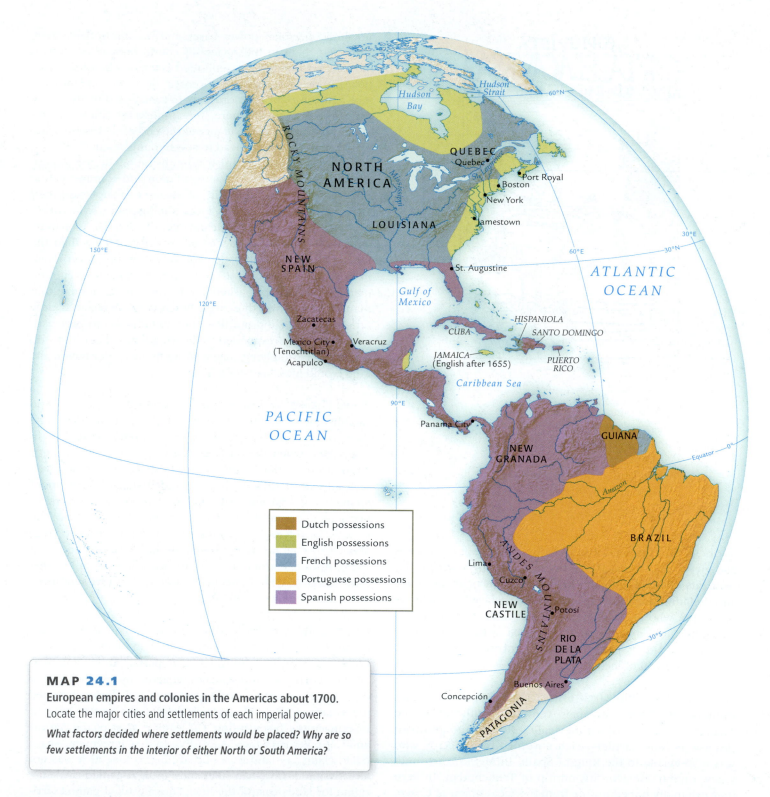

MAP 24.1

European empires and colonies in the Americas about 1700.
Locate the major cities and settlements of each imperial power.

What factors decided where settlements would be placed? Why are so few settlements in the interior of either North or South America?

display much immediate interest in the land. When French and Dutch mariners began to visit Brazilian shores, however, the Portuguese king decided to consolidate his claim to the land. He made vast land grants to Portuguese nobles in the expectation that they would develop and colonize their holdings, and later he dispatched a governor to oversee affairs and implement royal policy. Portuguese interest in Brazil rose dramatically after mid-century when entrepreneurs established profitable sugar plantations on the coast.

Colonial American Society   The cities of the Spanish and Portuguese empires became centers of European-style society in the Americas: the spires of churches and cathedrals defined their skylines, and Spanish and Portuguese

were the languages of government, business, and society. Beyond the urban districts, however, indigenous ways of life persisted. In the Amazon basin and Paraguay, for example, native peoples produced little agricultural surplus, and there were no mineral deposits to attract European migrants. The few Spanish and Portuguese colonists who ventured to those regions learned to adapt to indigenous societies and customs: they ate bread made of manioc flour, made use of native hammocks and canoes, and communicated in the Guaraní and Tupí languages. Indeed, indigenous languages flourish even today throughout much of Latin America: among the more prominent are Nahuatl in Mexico, K'iché in Guatemala, Guaraní in Paraguay, and Quechua in the Andean highlands of Peru, Ecuador, and Bolivia.

Spanish and Portuguese peoples saw the western hemisphere more as a land to exploit and administer than as a place to settle and colonize. Nevertheless, sizable contingents of migrants settled permanently in the Americas. Between 1500 and 1800, upwards of five hundred thousand Spanish migrants crossed the Atlantic, alongside one hundred thousand Portuguese. Their presence contributed to the making of a new world—a world characterized by intense interaction between the peoples of Europe, Africa, and the Americas—in the western hemisphere.

Settler Colonies in North America

Throughout the sixteenth century, Spanish explorers sought opportunities north of Mexico and the Caribbean. They established towns, forts, and missions from modern Florida as far north as Virginia on the east coast of North America, and they scouted shorelines off Maine and Newfoundland. On the west coast they ventured into modern Canada and established a fort on Vancouver Island. By mid-century, French, English, and Dutch mariners sailed the North Atlantic in search of fish and a northwest passage to Asia, and by the early seventeenth century they were dislodging Spanish colonists north of Florida. Their search for a northwest passage proved fruitless, but they harvested immense quantities of fish from the cod-filled banks off Labrador, Newfoundland, Nova Scotia, and New England.

Foundation of Colonies More important, in the early seventeenth century explorers began to plant permanent colonies on the North American mainland. French settlers established colonies at Port Royal (Nova Scotia) in 1604 and Quebec in 1608, and English migrants founded Jamestown in 1607 and the Massachusetts Bay Colony in 1630. Dutch entrepreneurs built a settlement at New Amsterdam in 1623, but the colony did not remain long in Dutch hands: an English fleet seized it in 1664, rechristened it New York, and absorbed it into English colonial holdings. During the seventeenth and eighteenth centuries, French migrants settled in eastern Canada, and French explorers and traders scouted the St. Lawrence, Ohio, and Mississippi Rivers, building forts all the way to the Gulf of Mexico. Meanwhile, English settlers established colonies along the east coast of the present-day United States of America.

Life in those early settlements was extremely difficult. Most of the settlers did not expect to cultivate food crops but, rather, hoped to sustain their communities by producing valuable commodities such as fur, pitch, tar, or lumber, if not silver and gold. They relied heavily on provisions sent from Europe, and when supply ships did not arrive as expected, they sometimes avoided starvation only because indigenous peoples provided them with food. In Jamestown, food shortages and disease became so severe that only sixty of the colony's five hundred inhabitants survived the winter of 1609–1610. Some settlers went so far as to disinter corpses and consume the flesh of their departed neighbors. One man even slaughtered and ate his wife.

Colonial Government The French and English colonies in North America differed in several ways from Spanish and Portuguese territories to the south. Whereas Iberian explorations had royal backing, private investors played larger roles in French and English colonial efforts. Individuals put up the money to finance expeditions to America, and they retained much more control over their colonies' affairs than did their Iberian counterparts. Although English colonies were always subject to royal authority, for example, they also maintained their own assemblies and influenced the choice of royal governors: there were no viceroys or *audiencias* in the North American colonies. At the conclusion of the Seven Years' War (1763), the French colony in Canada fell under British control, and it, too, soon acquired institutions of self-government.

Relations with Indigenous Peoples French and English colonies differed from Iberian territories also in their relationships with indigenous peoples. French and English migrants did not find large, centralized states like the Aztec and Inca empires. Nor did they encounter agricultural peoples living in densely settled societies. Although most of them spoke Algonquian, Iroquois, or Lakota languages, the peoples of eastern North America had formed dozens of distinct societies. Many of them practiced agriculture, but most also relied on hunting and consequently moved their villages frequently in pursuit of game. They did not claim ownership of precisely bounded territories, but they regularly migrated between well-defined regions.

When European settlers saw forested lands not bearing crops, they staked out farms and excluded the indigenous peoples who had frequently visited the lands during the course of their migrations. The availability of fertile farmland soon attracted large numbers of European migrants. Upwards of 150,000 English migrants moved to North America during the seventeenth century alone, and sizable French, German, Dutch, and Irish contingents joined them in the search for land.

European migrants took pains to justify their claims to American lands. English settlers in particular sought to

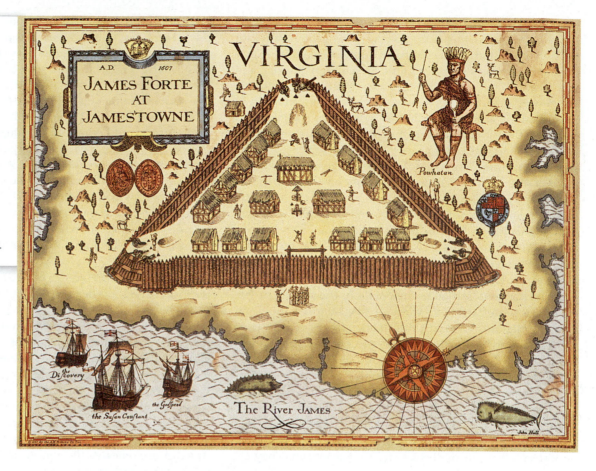

A painting of the English settlement at Jamestown in the early seventeenth century illustrates the precarious relations between European settlers and indigenous peoples. Note the heavy palisades and numerous cannons deployed within the fort, as well as the imposing figure of the native chief Powhatan depicted outside the settlement's walls.

provide legal cover for their expanding communities by negotiating treaties with the peoples whose lands they colonized. Quite apart from legal niceties, migrants also justified their occupation on the grounds that they made productive use of the land, whereas native peoples merely used it as a hunting park. In Europe, hunting was a pastime that only aristocratic and privileged classes could enjoy. Settlers did not recognize that hunting was a way of life, not a sport or a hobby, for the peoples of North America.

Conflict French and English settlers frequently clashed with native peoples who resented intrusions on their hunting grounds, but the conflicts differed from the campaigns of conquest carried out by the conquistadores in Mexico and Peru. English settlers negotiated rights to American lands by treaty, but native peoples did not appreciate the fine points of English law and frequently mounted raids on farms and villages. During an assault of 1622, for example, they massacred almost one-third of the English settlers in the Chesapeake region. Attacks on their communities brought reprisals from settlers, who ruthlessly destroyed the fields and villages of native peoples. Edward Waterhouse, who survived the raid of 1622, went so far as to advocate annihilation of the indigenous population: "Victorie may bee gained many waies: by force, by surprize, by [causing] famine [through]

burning their Corne, by destroying and burning their Boats, Canoes, and Houses, by breaking their fishing Weares [nets], by assailing them in their huntings, whereby they get the greatest part of their sustenance in Winter, by pursuing and chasing them with our horses, and blood-Hounds to draw after them, and Mastives [mastiffs] to teare them."

Indeed, a combination of epidemic disease and violent conflict dramatically reduced the indigenous population of North America in early modern times. In 1492 the native population of the territory now embraced by the United States was greater than five million, perhaps as high as ten million. By the mid-sixteenth century, however, smallpox and other diseases had begun to spread north from Mexico and ravage native societies in the plains and eastern woodlands of North America. Between 1600 and 1800 about one million English, French, German, Dutch, Irish, and Scottish migrants crossed the Atlantic and sought to displace native peoples as they pursued economic opportunities in North America. By 1800, indigenous peoples in the territory of the present-day United States numbered only six hundred thousand, as against almost five million settlers of European ancestry and about one million slaves of African ancestry. Although the settler colonies of North America differed markedly from the Iberian territorial empires to the south, they too contributed greatly to the transformation of the western hemisphere.

COLONIAL SOCIETY IN THE AMERICAS

The European migrants who flooded into the western hemisphere interacted both with the native inhabitants and with African peoples whom they imported as enslaved laborers. Throughout the Americas, relations between individuals of American, European, and African ancestry soon led to the emergence of mestizo populations. Yet European peoples and their Euro-American offspring increasingly dominated political and economic affairs in the Americas. They mined precious metals, cultivated cash crops such as sugar and tobacco, and trapped fur-bearing animals to supply capitalist markets that met the voracious demands of European and Asian consumers. Over time they also established their Christian religion as the dominant faith of the western hemisphere.

The Formation of Multicultural Societies

Mestizo Societies Although their influence reached the American interior only gradually, European migrants radically transformed the social order in the regions where they estab-

Indigenous Zapotec painter Miguel Mateo Maldonado y Cabrera (1695–1768) created this domestic portrait of a multicultural family in the viceroyalty of New Spain, today's Mexico. A Spanish man gazes at his Mexican Indian wife and their mestizo daughter.

lished imperial states or settler colonies. All European territories became multicultural societies where peoples of varied ancestry lived together under European or Euro-American dominance. Spanish and Portuguese territories soon became not only multicultural but ethnically mixed as well, largely because of migration patterns. Migrants to the Iberian colonies were overwhelmingly men: about 85 percent of the Spanish migrants were men, and the Portuguese migration was even more male-dominated than the Spanish. Because of the small numbers of European women, Spanish and Portuguese migrants entered into relationships with indigenous women, which soon gave rise to an increasingly *mestizo* ("mixed") society.

Most Spanish migrants went to Mexico, where there was soon a growing population of mestizos—those of Spanish and native parentage, like the children of Doña Marina. Women were more prominent among the migrants to Peru than to Mexico, and Spanish colonists there lived mostly in cities, where they maintained a more distinct community than did their counterparts in Mexico. In the colonial cities, Spanish migrants married among themselves and re-created a European-style society. In less settled regions, however, Spanish men associated with indigenous women and gave rise to mestizo society.

With few European women available in Brazil, Portuguese men readily entered into relations both with indigenous women and with African slave women. Brazil soon had large populations not only of mestizos but also of mulattoes born of Portuguese and African parents, *zambos* born of indigenous and African parents, and other combinations arising from these groups. Indeed, marriages between members of different racial and ethnic communities became common in colonial Brazil and generated a society even more thoroughly mixed than that of mestizo Mexico.

The Social Hierarchy In both Spanish and Portuguese colonies, migrants born in Europe known as **peninsulares,** those who came from the Iberian peninsula, stood at the top of the social hierarchy, followed by *criollos*, or *creoles*, those born in the Americas of Iberian parents. In the early days of the colonies, mestizos lived on the fringes of society. As time went on, however, the numbers of mestizos grew, and they became essential contributors to their societies, especially in Mexico and Brazil. Meanwhile, mulattoes, *zambos*, and others of mixed parentage became prominent groups in Brazilian society, although they were usually subordinate to European migrants, Euro-American creoles, and even mestizos. In all the Iberian colonies, imported slaves and conquered peoples stood at the bottom of the social hierarchy.

Sexual Hierarchies Race and ethnicity were crucial in shaping a person's position and role in colonial society. But

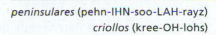

peninsulares (pehn-IHN-soo-LAH-rayz)
criollos (kree-OH-lohs)

the defining factor in both Spanish and Portuguese America was the existence of a clear sexual hierarchy that privileged men. Women lived in a patriarchal world, where men occupied positions of power and delineated the boundaries of acceptable female behavior. Only when it came to punishing disobedient slaves did society ignore gender—both male and female slaves could count on the same harsh punishment, which usually took the form of flogging. To the extent that women did exercise power, most of it was informal and limited to the confines of the home.

Gender alone, however, did not explain the diverse experiences of women in colonial society. Commonly, the ratio of men to women in a given community either enhanced or limited women's choices. Women's experiences also varied with the degree of prosperity and the nature of the local economy. As women moved from childhood through marriage and motherhood, to being widows or "spinsters," their experiences and roles in society likewise underwent change. Race and class usually figured as powerful forces shaping women's lives. Women of European descent, though under strict patriarchal control and under pressure to conform to the stereotype of female dependence and passivity, sometimes used their elite position to their advantage. By necessity, women of color and low class became part of the colonial labor force, performing tasks closely tied to the commercialization of traditional female work such as food preparation, laundering, and weaving. Although poor, these women were freer to move about in public and to interact with others than were their elite counterparts. The most disadvantaged women were black, mulatta, and zamba slaves, who were required to perform hard physical tasks such as planting and cutting cane or working as laundresses.

North American Societies The social structure of the French and English colonies in North America differed markedly from that of the Iberian colonies. Women were more numerous among the French and especially the English migrants than in Spanish and Portuguese communities, and settlers mostly married within their own groups. French fur traders often associated with native women and generated *métis* (French for "mixed") in regions around forts and trading posts. In French colonial cities such as Port Royal and Quebec, however, liaisons between French and native peoples were less common.

Mingling between peoples of different ancestry was least common in the English colonies of North America. Colonists disdained the native peoples they encountered and regarded them as lazy heathens who did not recognize private property and did not exert themselves to cultivate the land. Later, they also scorned imported African slaves as inferior beings. Those attitudes fueled a virulent racism, as English settlers attempted to maintain sharp boundaries between themselves and peoples of American and African ancestry.

Yet even English settlers interacted with American and African peoples, and they readily borrowed useful cultural elements from other communities. They learned about American plants and animals, for example, and they used native terms to refer to unfamiliar animals such as raccoons and opossums or trees such as hickory and pecan. They adapted moccasins and deerskin clothes, and they gave up European military customs of marching in massed ranks and announcing their presence with drums and flying colors. From their slaves they borrowed African food crops and techniques for the cultivation of rice. Yet, unlike their Iberian neighbors to the south, the English settlers strongly discouraged relationships between individuals of different ancestry and mostly refused to accept or even acknowledge offspring of mixed parentage.

Mining and Agriculture in the Spanish Empire

From the Spanish perspective the greatest attractions of the Americas were precious metals, which drew thousands of migrants from all levels of Spanish society. The conquistadores thoroughly looted the easily accessible treasures of the Aztec and Inca empires. Ignoring the artistic or cultural value of artifacts, the conquerors simply melted down silver and gold treasures and fashioned them into ingots. Their followers opened mines to extract the mineral wealth of the Americas in more systematic fashion.

Silver Mining Gold was not the most abundant American treasure. Silver far outweighed gold in quantity and value, and much of Spain's American enterprise focused on its extraction. Silver production concentrated on two areas: the thinly populated Mexican north, particularly the region around Zacatecas, and the high, cold central Andes, particularly the stunningly rich mines of Potosí (present-day Bolivia). Both sites employed large numbers of indigenous laborers. Many laborers went to Zacatecas voluntarily as their home villages experienced the pressures of conquest and disease. Over time they became professional miners, spoke Spanish, and lost touch with the communities of their birth.

Meanwhile, Spanish prospectors discovered a large vein of silver near Potosí in 1545 and began large-scale mining there in the 1580s. By 1600 Potosí was a boomtown with a population of 150,000. Rapid growth created an explosive demand for labor. As in the Mexican mines, Spanish administrators relied mostly on voluntary labor, but they also adapted the Inca practice of requisitioning draft labor, known as the *mita* system, to recruit workers for particularly difficult and dangerous chores that free laborers would not accept. Under the *mita* system, Spanish authorities annually required each native village to send one-seventh of its male population to work for four months in the mines at Potosí. Draft laborers received payment for their work, but wages were very low, and the conditions of work were extremely harsh. Some *mita* laborers hauled heavy baskets of silver ore up steep mine shafts, while others worked with toxic mercury, which miners used to separate the silver from

Mining operations at Potosí in South America gave rise to a large settlement that housed miners and others who supplied food, made charcoal, fashioned tools, and supported the enterprise. In this illustration from the mid-1580s, llamas laden with silver ore descend the mountain (background) while laborers work in the foreground to crush the ore and extract pure silver from it.

its ore. Death rates of draft laborers were high, and many native men sought to evade *mita* obligations by fleeing to cities or hiding in distant villages. Thus, even though at any given moment draft laborers represented only about 10 percent of the workforce at Potosí, the *mita* system touched a large portion of the indigenous population and influenced settlement patterns throughout the Andean region.

The Global Significance of Silver

The mining industries of Mexico and Peru powered the Spanish economy in the Americas and even stimulated the world economy of early modern times. Silver produced profits for private investors and revenues for the crown. The Spanish government reserved a fifth of the silver production for itself. This share, known as the *quinto,* represented the principal revenue that the crown derived from its American possessions. American silver helped Spanish kings finance a powerful army and bureaucracy, but much of it also went well beyond Spain to lubricate the European and the larger world economies.

Most American silver made its way across the Atlantic to Spain and markets throughout Europe, and from there European merchants traded it for silk, spices, and porcelain in the markets of Asia. Some silver went from Acapulco on the west coast of Mexico across the Pacific to the Philippines in the Manila galleons, and from Manila it also made its way to Asian markets. No matter which direction it went or which oceans it crossed, American silver quickly traveled throughout the world and powerfully stimulated global trade.

The Hacienda

Apart from mining, the principal occupations in Spanish America were farming, stock raising, and craft production. The organization of mining industries created opportunities for cultivators, herders, and artisans to provision mining towns with food, wine, textiles, tools, furniture, and craft items. By the seventeenth century the most prominent site of agricultural and craft production in Spanish America was the estate, or hacienda, which produced foodstuffs for its own use as well as for sale to local markets in nearby mining districts, towns, and cities. The products of the hacienda were mostly of European origin: wheat, grapes, and meat from pigs and cattle were the most prominent agricultural products. Bordering the large estates were smaller properties owned by Spanish migrants or creoles as well as sizable tracts of land held by indigenous peoples who lived in native villages and practiced subsistence agriculture.

Labor Systems

The major source of labor for the haciendas was the indigenous population. Spanish conquerors first organized native workforces under the *encomienda* system. As originally developed in Spain during the era of the *reconquista* (see chapter 19), the *encomienda* system rewarded Spanish conquerors by allowing them to exact both labor and tribute from defeated Moorish populations, while requiring the *encomenderos* to look after the physical and spiritual welfare of their workers. Later, Spanish conquerors transferred the system to the Caribbean, Mexico, Central America, and Andean South America. From the 1520s to the 1540s, the *encomienda* system led to rampant abuse of indigenous peoples, as Spanish landowners overworked their laborers and skimped on their maintenance. After mid-century, *encomenderos* in agriculturally productive regions increasingly required their subject populations to provide tribute but not labor. Populations living under native leadership owned much of the land that they cultivated in villages. In some ways, their payments to Spanish colonists resembled the tributes their ancestors had provided to Aztec rulers.

As the *encomienda* system gradually went out of use, Spanish landowners resorted to a system of debt peonage to recruit labor for their haciendas. Under this system, landowners advanced loans to native peoples so that they could buy seeds, tools, and supplies. The debtors then repaid the loans with labor, but wages were so low that they were never able to pay off their debts. Because legal restrictions often prevented debtors from fleeing and escaping their obligations, landowners had in effect a captive labor force to work their estates.

Resistance to Spanish Rule The Spanish regimes in the Americas met considerable resistance from indigenous peoples. Resistance took various forms: rebellion, half-hearted work, and retreat into the mountains and forests where Spanish power did not reach. In 1680, for example, after experiencing nearly a century of forced labor on Spanish estates, several native groups in northern Mexico (the modern-day American state of New Mexico) mounted a large uprising known as the Pueblo revolt. Led by a native shaman named Popé, the rebels attacked missions, killed priests and colonists, and drove Spanish settlers out of the region for twelve years. Spanish forces in Peru faced an even larger rebellion in 1780, when a force of about sixty thousand native peoples revolted in the name of Túpac Amaru, the last of the Inca rulers, whom Spanish conquistadores had beheaded in 1572. This Túpac Amaru rebellion raged for almost two years before Spanish forces suppressed it and executed thousands of its participants.

On some occasions, indigenous peoples turned also to Spanish law and administrators in search of aid against oppressive colonists. In 1615, for example, Felipe Guaman Poma de Ayala, a native of Peru, fired off a 1,200-page letter—accompanied by some four hundred hand-drawn illustrations—to King Philip III of Spain asking for protection for native peoples against rapacious colonists. Guaman Poma's letter went astray: the king never saw it. The missive somehow made its way to Denmark, where it remained unknown in a library until 1908.

Nevertheless, Guaman Poma's complaint serves as a record of grievances against Spanish overlords. The author

Felipe Guaman Poma de Ayala depicted himself several times in his letter of complaint. Here, kneeling, he presents a copy of his work to the king of Spain. In fact, Guaman Poma never traveled to Spain, and his letter never reached the king. Nevertheless, Guaman Poma's illustrations offer remarkable images of early colonial Peru.

wrote passionately of men ruined by overtaxation and women driven to prostitution, of Spanish colonists who grabbed the lands of native peoples and Spanish priests who seduced the wives of native men. Guaman Poma warned the king that the peoples of Peru were dying fast because of disease and abuse and that if Philip wanted anything to remain of his Andean empire, he should intervene and protect the indigenous peoples of the land.

Sugar and Slavery in Portuguese Brazil

Whereas the Spanish American empire concentrated on the extraction of silver, the Portuguese empire in Brazil depended on the production and export of sugar. The different economic and social foundations of the Spanish and Portuguese empires led to different patterns of labor recruitment. Spanish conquistadores subjugated sedentary peoples with effective administrative systems and compelled them to pro-

vide labor in the mines and estates of Mexico and Peru. Portuguese nobles and entrepreneurs established sugar plantations in regions without the administrative machinery to recruit workers and relied instead on imported African slaves as laborers. Indeed, Africans and their descendants became the majority of the population in Brazil, not simply an auxiliary labor force as in Spanish America.

The *Engenho*

Colonial Brazilian life revolved around the sugar mill, or *engenho*. Strictly speaking, the term *engenho* (related to the English word *engine*) referred only to the mill itself, but it came to represent a complex of land, labor, buildings, animals, capital, and technical skills related to the production of sugar. Unlike other crops, sugarcane required extensive processing to yield molasses or refined sugar as a profitable export. Thus *engenhos* always combined agricultural and industrial enterprises. They depended both on heavy labor for the planting and harvesting of cane and on the specialized skills of individuals who understood the intricacies of the sugar-making process. As a result, *engenhos* were among the most complex business enterprises in the Americas.

In a colonial economy where sugar figured as the most important export, the Portuguese planters and owners of sugar mills were a privileged class, exercising political, social, and economic power. As long as they contributed to the government's revenues, they could usually count on strong royal support. The planters acted like landed nobility, but the nature of their enterprises required them to pay attention to affairs like businessmen. They operated on very small profit margins. Their exalted social position often disguised difficult financial predicaments, and turnover in the business was always high.

The Search for Labor

Like their Spanish counterparts, Portuguese colonists first tried to enlist local populations as laborers. Unlike the inhabitants of Mexico and Peru, however, the peoples of Brazil were not sedentary cultivators. They resisted efforts to commandeer their labor, evaded Portuguese forces by retreating to interior lands, and took every opportunity to escape captors who managed to force them into servitude. From the Portuguese perspective, relying on native peoples as laborers had an additional drawback. In Brazil, as elsewhere in the Americas, epidemic diseases devastated indigenous populations. During the 1560s, smallpox and measles ravaged the whole Brazilian coast, making it difficult for Portuguese settlers even to find potential laborers, let alone force them to work.

Slavery

Faced with those difficulties, the colonists turned to another labor source: the African slave. Portuguese plantation managers imported slaves as early as the 1530s, but they began to rely on African labor on a large scale only in the 1580s. The labor demands of cane cultivation and sugar production exacted a heavy toll from slave communities. Arduous working conditions, mistreatment, tropical heat, poor nutrition, and inadequate housing combined to produce high rates of disease and mortality: *engenhos* typically lost 5 to 10 percent of their slaves annually. In Brazil, as in most other plantation societies, the number of deaths in the slave population usually exceeded the number of births, so there was a constant demand for more slaves.

The system had its critics, but government officials mostly left matters of labor management to slave owners. To them the balance sheet of sugar production dictated practices that paid scant heed to the preservation of slaves' lives, as long as the owners realized profits. Indeed, if a slave lived five to six years, the investment of the average owner doubled and permitted him to purchase a new and healthy slave without taking a monetary loss. Hence owners had little economic incentive to improve conditions for slaves or to increase their birthrates. Children required financial outlays for at least twelve years, which from the perspective of the owner represented a financial loss. All told, the business of producing Brazilian sugar was so brutal that every ton of the sweet substance cost one human life.

Fur Traders and Settlers in North America

The Fur Trade

European mariners first frequented North American shores in search of fish. Although fishing was a profitable enterprise, trade in furs became far more lucrative. The North American fur trade began when fishermen bartered for fur with local peoples. After explorers found a convenient entrance to rich fur-producing regions through the Hudson Strait and Hudson Bay, they began the systematic exploitation of the northern lands. Royal agents, adventurers, businessmen, and settlers began to connect large parts of the North American interior by a chain of forts and trading posts. Indigenous peoples trapped animals for Europeans and exchanged the pelts for manufactured goods such as wool blankets, iron pots, firearms, and distilled spirits. The hides went mostly to Europe, where capitalist markets experienced burgeoning demand for beaver skin hats and fur clothing.

Effects of the Fur Trade

The fur trade generated tremendous conflict. American beaver populations, which were the chief targets of the trade, declined so rapidly that trappers constantly had to push farther inland in search of untapped beaver grounds. When hunting grounds became depleted, native peoples poached or invaded others' territories, which frequently led to war. Among the most brutal of those conflicts were the Beaver Wars of the seventeenth century, which pitted Iroquois against Hurons. The Iroquois sought to expand their hunting grounds at the expense of the Hurons and others, and thus monopolize the fur trade with Europeans.

The fur trade also took place in the context of competition between European states. This competitive atmosphere contributed to further conflict, as indigenous peoples became embroiled in their patrons' rivalries. During the mid-seventeenth century, for example, Iroquois peoples who were allies of Dutch fur traders in New Amsterdam launched a war against Hurons living north of the Great Lakes, who had allied themselves with the French. Equipped with firearms supplied by their Dutch allies, the Iroquois sought to exterminate the Hurons and extend their trapping to the northern lands. Hurons survived the war, although in greatly diminished numbers, but the Iroquois vastly increased their strength and destroyed Huron power.

Settler Society European settler-cultivators posed an even more serious challenge to native ways of life than did the fur traders, since they displaced indigenous peoples from the land and turned hunting grounds into plantations. The earliest colonists experienced difficult times, since European crops such as wheat did not grow well in their settlements. Indeed, many of the early colonies would have perished except for maize, game, and fish supplied by native peoples. Over time, however, French and especially English migrants stabilized their societies and distinguished them sharply from those of indigenous peoples.

Tobacco and Other Cash Crops As colonists' numbers increased, they sought to integrate their American holdings into the larger capitalist economy of the Atlantic Ocean basin by producing cash crops that they could market in Europe. In the English colonies of Virginia and Carolina, settlers concentrated on the cultivation of tobacco, a plant integral to the indigenous societies of the Americas. Christopher Columbus had observed the native Taíno smoking the leaves of a local plant through a pipe called a *tobago*— the origin of the word *tobacco*. Later, European visitors frequently observed tobacco consumption among indigenous peoples, who had used the plant as early as two thousand years ago for ritual, medicinal, and social purposes. Maya worshipers blew tobacco smoke from their mouths as offerings to the gods. Priests of the Aztec empire both smoked tobacco and took it in the form of snuff as an accompaniment to religious sacrifices.

The widespread popularity of this plant was due to the addictive nature of nicotine, an oily, toxic substance present in tobacco leaves and named after the French diplomat, Jean Nicot, who introduced tobacco use to Paris in 1560. Spanish and English promoters first touted the health benefits of tobacco to European consumers. Many physicians ascribed miraculous healing powers to tobacco, which they referred to as "the herb panacea," "divine tobacco," or the "holy herb nicotine." Merchants and mariners soon spread the use of tobacco throughout Europe and beyond to all parts of the world that European ships visited.

In 1612, English settlers cultivated the first commercial crop of tobacco in Virginia. By 1616, Virginia colonists exported 2,300 pounds of tobacco. European demand for the addictive weed resulted in skyrocketing exports amounting to 200,000 pounds in 1624 and three million pounds in

European moralists often denounced tobacco as a noxious weed, and they associated its use with vices such as drunkenness, gambling, and prostitution. Nevertheless, its popularity surged in Europe, and later in Africa and Asia as well, after its introduction from the Americas.

1638, and by the late seventeenth century, most consumers used tobacco socially and for pleasure, since tobacco's alleged health benefits never quite lived up to expectations. By the eighteenth century settlers in the southern colonies had established plantation complexes that produced rice and indigo as well as tobacco, and by the nineteenth century cotton also had become a prominent plantation crop.

Indentured Labor The plantations created high demand for cheap labor. Colonists in North America displaced indigenous peoples but could not subjugate them or induce them to labor in their fields. Planters initially met the demand for cheap labor by recruiting indentured servants from Europe. People who had little future in Europe—the chronically unemployed, orphans, political prisoners, and criminals—were often willing to sell a portion of their working lives in exchange for passage across the Atlantic and a new start in life. Throughout the seventeenth and

eighteenth centuries, indentured servants streamed into the American colonies in hopes that after they had satisfied their obligation to provide four to seven years of labor they might become independent artisans or planters themselves. (The indentured labor trade in the Americas continued on a smaller scale even into the early twentieth century.) Some indentured servants went on to become prominent figures in colonial society, but many died of disease or overwork before completing their terms of labor, and others found only marginal employment.

Slavery in North America Most indentured servants eventually gained their freedom, but other suppliers of cheap labor remained in bondage all their lives. Like settlers in the Iberian colonies, English settlers in North America found uses for slave labor from Africa. In 1619 a group of about twenty Africans reached Virginia, where they worked alongside European laborers as indentured servants. Over time, some individual blacks fell into permanent servitude, others continued to work as indentured laborers, and some gained their freedom. In 1661, however, Virginia law recognized all blacks as slaves, and after 1680, planters increasingly replaced indentured servants with African slaves. By 1750 about 120,000 black slaves tilled Chesapeake tobacco, and 180,000 more cultivated Carolina rice.

Slave labor was not prominent in the northern colonies, principally because the land and the climate were not suitable for the cultivation of labor-intensive cash crops. Nevertheless, the economies of these colonies also profited handsomely from slavery. Many New England merchants traded in slaves destined for the West Indies: by the mid-eighteenth century, half the merchant fleet of Newport carried human cargo. The economies of New York and Philadelphia benefited from the building and outfitting of slave vessels, and the seaports of New England became profitable centers for the distillation of rum. The chief ingredient of this rum was slave-produced sugar from the West Indies, and merchants traded much of the distilled spirits for slaves on the African coast. Thus, although the southern plantation societies became most directly identified with a system that exploited African labor, all the North American colonies participated in and profited from the slave trade.

Christianity and Native Religions in the Americas

Like Buddhists and Muslims in earlier centuries, European explorers, conquerors, merchants, and settlers took their religious traditions with them when they traveled overseas. The desire to spread Christianity was a prominent motive behind European ventures overseas, and missionaries soon made their way to the Americas as well as other lands where Europeans established a presence.

Spanish Missionaries From the beginning of Spanish colonization in Mexico and Peru, Roman Catholic priests served as representatives of the crown and reinforced civil administrators. Franciscan, Dominican, Jesuit, and other missionaries campaigned to Christianize indigenous peoples. In Mexico, for example, a group of twelve Franciscan missionaries arrived in 1524. They founded a school in Tlatelolco, the bustling market district of the Aztec capital of Tenochtitlan, where they educated the sons of prominent noble families in Latin, Spanish, and Christian doctrine. The missionaries themselves learned native languages and

An eighteenth-century engraving depicts work on a plantation: Several African slaves prepare flour and bread from manioc (left) while others hang tobacco leaves to dry in a shed (right). A male turkey—a fowl native to the Americas—ignores the bustle and displays his feathers (right foreground).

Famed Mexican painter Miguel Cabrera crafted this eighteenth-century depiction of the Virgin of Guadalupe. Recognized as the greatest painter in New Spain, he featured in this work one of Mexico's most powerful religious icons.

to eliminate the worship of pagan deities. Native peoples honored idols in caves and inaccessible mountain sites, and they may have occasionally even continued to sacrifice human victims to their traditional gods.

Yet Christianity won adherents in Spanish America. In the wake of conquest and epidemic disease, many native leaders in Mexico concluded that their gods had abandoned them and looked to the missionaries for spiritual guidance. When native peoples adopted Christianity, however, they blended their own interests and traditions with the faith taught by Spanish missionaries. When they learned about Roman Catholic saints, for example, they revered saints with qualities like those of their inherited gods or those whose feast days coincided with traditional celebrations.

The Virgin of Guadalupe

In Mexico, Roman Catholicism became especially popular after the mid-seventeenth century, as an increasingly mestizo society embraced the Virgin of Guadalupe almost as a national symbol. According to legends, the Virgin Mary appeared before the devout peasant Juan Diego on a hill near Mexico City in 1531. The site of the apparition soon became a popular local shrine visited mostly by Spanish settlers. By the 1640s the shrine attracted pilgrims from all parts of Mexico, and the Virgin of Guadalupe gained a reputation for working miracles on behalf of individuals who visited her shrine. The Virgin of Guadalupe, with her darker indigenous complexion, came to symbolize a distinctly Mexican faith and promise of salvation, and she became transformed as a result into a powerful symbol of Mexican nationalism. The popularity of the Virgin of Guadalupe helped to ensure not only that Roman Catholic Christianity would dominate cultural and religious matters in Mexico but also that Mexican religious faith would retain strong indigenous influences.

French and English Missions

French and English missionaries did not attract nearly as many converts to Christianity in North America as their Spanish counterparts did in Mexico and Peru, partly because French and English colonists did not rule over conquered populations of sedentary cultivators: it was much more difficult to conduct missions among peoples who frequently moved about the countryside than among those who lived permanently in villages,

sought to explain Christianity in terms understandable to their audiences. They also compiled a vast amount of information about native societies in hopes of learning how best to communicate their message. The work of the Franciscan Bernardino de Sahagún was especially important. Sahagún preserved volumes of information about the language, customs, beliefs, literature, and history of Mexico before the arrival of Spanish forces there. His work remained largely unstudied until the twentieth century, but in recent times it has shed enormous light both on Aztec society and on the methods of early missionaries in Mexico.

Survival of Native Religions

Christian missionaries encountered considerable resistance in the Americas. In both Mexico and Peru, indigenous peoples continued to observe their inherited faiths into the seventeenth century and beyond, even though Spanish authorities sponsored the Roman Catholic faith and tried

thinking about TRADITIONS

Women and Religion
Indigenous Mexican women and indigenous religious beliefs faced real challenges upon the arrival of the conquistadores and their Christian faith. How did European men and Christianity alter the fate of indigenous women and religion? How does the Virgin of Guadalupe speak to the survival of both?

towns, or cities. In addition, English colonists displayed little interest in converting indigenous peoples to Protestantism. The colonists did not discourage converts, but they made little effort to seek them, nor did they welcome native converts into their agricultural and commercial society. In contrast, Catholic French missionaries worked actively among native communities in the St. Lawrence, Mississippi, and Ohio River valleys and experienced modest success in spreading Christianity. Even though native peoples did not embrace Christianity, the burgeoning settlements of French and especially English colonists guaranteed that European religious traditions would figure prominently in North American society.

EUROPEANS IN THE PACIFIC

Though geographically distant from the Americas, Australia and the Pacific islands underwent experiences similar to those that transformed the western hemisphere in early modern times. Like their American counterparts, the peoples of Oceania had no inherited or acquired immunities to diseases that were common to peoples throughout the eastern hemisphere, and their numbers plunged when epidemic disease struck their populations. For the most part, however, Australia and the Pacific islands experienced epidemic disease and the arrival of European migrants later than did the Americas. European mariners thoroughly explored the Pacific basin between the sixteenth and eighteenth centuries, but only in Guam and the Mariana Islands did they establish permanent settlements before the late eighteenth century. Nevertheless, their scouting of the region laid a foundation for much more intense interactions between European, Euro-American, Asian, and Oceanic peoples during the nineteenth and twentieth centuries.

Australia and the Larger World

At least from the second century C.E., European geographers had speculated about *terra australis incognita* ("unknown southern land") that they thought must exist in the world's southern hemisphere to balance the huge landmasses north of the equator. As European mariners reconnoitered the Atlantic and Pacific Oceans during early modern times, they watched expectantly for a southern continent. Yet their principal interest was trade, and they rarely abandoned the pursuit of profit to sail out of their way in search of an unknown land.

Dutch Exploration When they visited the islands of southeast Asia in the quest for spices, however, they approached Australia from the west. Portuguese mariners most likely charted much of the western and northern coast of Australia as early as the 1520s, but Dutch sailors made the first recorded European sighting of the southern continent in 1606. The Dutch VOC authorized exploratory voyages, but mariners found little to encourage further efforts. In 1623, after surveying the dry landscapes of western Austra-

lia, the Dutch mariner Jan Carstenzs reported that his party had not seen "one fruit-bearing tree, nor anything that man could make use of: there are no mountains or even hills, so that it may be safely concluded that the land contains no metals, nor yields any precious woods," and he described the land as "the most arid and barren region that could be found anywhere on earth."

Nevertheless, Dutch mariners continued to visit Australia. By the mid-seventeenth century, they had scouted the continent's northern, western, and southern coasts, and they had ascertained that New Guinea and Tasmania were islands separate from Australia itself. Dutch explorers were so active in the reconnaissance of Australia that Europeans referred to the southern continent as "New Holland" throughout the seventeenth century. Yet neither Dutch nor any other European seamen visited the eastern coast until James Cook approached Australia from the southeast and charted the region in 1770, barely escaping destruction on the Great Barrier Reef.

Although European mariners explored Australian coastlines in the seventeenth and eighteenth centuries, they made only brief landfalls and had only fleeting encounters with indigenous peoples. The aboriginal peoples of Australia had formed many distinct foraging and fishing societies, but European visitors did not linger long enough to become familiar with either the peoples or their societies. Because they were nomadic foragers rather than sedentary cultivators, Europeans mostly considered them wretched savages. In the absence of tempting opportunities to trade, European mariners made no effort to establish permanent settlements in Australia.

British Colonists Only after Cook's charting of the eastern coast in 1770 did European peoples become seriously interested in Australia. Cook dropped anchor for a week at Botany Bay (near modern Sydney) and reported that the region was suitable for settlement. In 1788 a British fleet arrived at Sydney carrying about one thousand passengers, eight hundred of them convicts, who established the first European settlement in Australia as a penal colony. For half a century Europeans in Australia numbered only a few thousand, most of them convicts who herded sheep. Free settlers did not outnumber convicted criminal migrants until the 1830s. Thus exploratory voyages of the seventeenth and eighteenth centuries led to fleeting encounters between European and aboriginal Australian peoples, but only in the nineteenth and twentieth centuries did a continuing stream of European migrants and settlers link Australia more directly to the larger world.

The Pacific Islands and the Larger World

The entry of European mariners into the Pacific Ocean basin did not bring immediate change to most of the Pacific islands. In these islands, as in Australia, European merchants and settlers did not arrive in large numbers until the late eighteenth century. Guam and the Mariana Islands

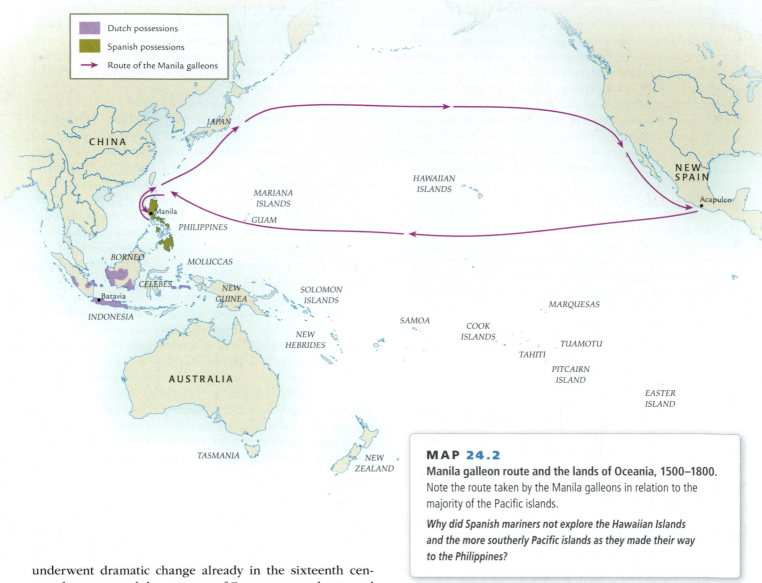

MAP 24.2

Manila galleon route and the lands of Oceania, 1500–1800.
Note the route taken by the Manila galleons in relation to the majority of the Pacific islands.

Why did Spanish mariners not explore the Hawaiian Islands and the more southerly Pacific islands as they made their way to the Philippines?

underwent dramatic change already in the sixteenth century, however, and the ventures of European merchants and explorers in the Pacific basin set the stage for profound upheavals in other island societies during the nineteenth and twentieth centuries.

Spanish Voyages in the Pacific In 1521 Ferdinand Magellan and his crew became the first Europeans to cross the Pacific Ocean. Before reaching the Philippines, they encountered only one inhabited island group—the Marianas, dominated by Guam. In 1565 Spanish mariners inaugurated the Manila galleon trade between Manila and Acapulco. Because their primary goal was to link New Spain to Asian markets, they rarely went out of their way to explore the Pacific Ocean or to search for other islands. Spanish vessels visited the Marquesas, Tuamotu, Cook, Solomon, and New Hebrides islands in the sixteenth century, and it is likely that one or more stray ships fetched up in Hawai`i. Yet Spanish

mariners found little to interest them in most of the Pacific islands and did not establish regular communications with island peoples. They usually sailed before the trade winds from Acapulco to Manila on a route that took them south of Hawai`i and north of other Polynesian islands. On the return trip they sailed before the westerlies on a route that took them well north of all the Pacific islands.

Guam The only Pacific islands that attracted substantial Spanish interest in the sixteenth century were Guam and the northern Mariana Islands. Manila galleons called regularly at Guam, which lay directly on the route from Acapulco to Manila. For more than a century, they took on fresh provisions and engaged in mostly peaceful trade with the indigenous Chamorro people. During the 1670s and 1680s,

As depicted in 1816 by artist Ludwig Choris, the port of Honolulu in the Hawaiian Islands was home to European ships, horses, cattle, and warehouses as well as Hawaiians inhabiting traditional dwellings and keeping native pigs.

Spanish authorities decided to consolidate their position in Guam and bring the Mariana Islands under the control of the viceroy of New Spain in Mexico. They dispatched military forces to the islands to impose Spanish rule and subject the Chamorro to the spiritual authority of the Roman Catholic church. The Chamorro stoutly opposed those efforts, but a smallpox epidemic in 1688 severely reduced their numbers and crippled their resistance. By 1695 the Chamorro population had declined from about fifty thousand at mid-century to five thousand, partly because of Spanish campaigns but mostly because of smallpox. By the end of the seventeenth century, Spanish forces had established garrisons throughout the Mariana Islands and relocated surviving Chamorro into communities supervised by Spanish authorities.

Visitors and Trade Like the aboriginal peoples of Australia, the indigenous peoples of the Pacific islands had mostly fleeting encounters with European visitors during early modern times. By the late eighteenth century, however, growing European and Euro-American interest in the Pacific Ocean basin led to sharply increased interactions between islanders and mariners. English and French mariners explored the Pacific basin in search of commercial opportunities and the elusive northwest passage from Europe to Asia. They frequently visited Tahiti after 1767, and they soon began to trade with the islanders: European mariners received provisions and engaged in sexual relations with Tahitian women in exchange for nails, knives, iron tools, and textiles. Although trade was mostly peaceful, misunderstandings often led to minor skirmishes, and European captains occasionally trained their cannons on fleets of war canoes or villages in the Pacific islands.

**Captain Cook and Hawai`i** The experiences of Captain James Cook in Hawai`i illustrate a common pattern. In 1778, while sailing north from Tahiti in search of the northwest passage, Cook happened across the Hawaiian Islands. He immediately recognized Hawaiians as a people related to Tahitians and other Polynesians whose lands he had visited during his explorations of the Pacific Ocean since 1768, and he was able to communicate with Hawaiians on the basis of familiarity with Polynesian languages. Apart from some early concerns about thievery, Cook and his crew mostly got along well with Hawaiians, who readily traded pigs and provisions for iron wares. Sailors and island women avidly consorted with one another, resulting in the transmission of venereal diseases to Hawai`i, even though Cook had ordered infected crewmen to remain aboard ship. After a few weeks' stay in the islands, Cook resumed his northern course to seek the northwest passage. When he revisited Hawai`i late in 1779, he faced a very different climate, one in which islanders were less accommodating than before. Indeed, he lost his life when disputes over petty thefts escalated into a bitter conflict between his crew and islanders of Hawai`i.

Nevertheless, in the wake of Cook, whose reports soon became known throughout Europe, whalers began to venture into Pacific waters in large numbers, followed by missionaries, merchants, and planters. By the early nineteenth century, European and Euro-American peoples had become prominent figures in all the major Pacific islands groups. During the nineteenth and twentieth centuries, interactions among islanders, visitors, and migrants brought rapid and often unsettling change to Pacific islands societies.

sources from the past

Captain James Cook on the Hawaiians

Spanish mariners may well have been the first Europeans to visit the Hawaiian Islands, but Captain James Cook made the earliest surviving record of a European visit. His journal entries for the first few days of his visit depict a thriving society closely related to those of Tahiti and other Polynesian islands.

[Monday, 19 January 1778] There were three and four men in each [canoe] and we were agreeably surprised to find them of the same nation as the people of Otahiete [Tahiti] and the other [Polynesian] islands we had lately visited. It required but very little address to get them to come along side, but we could not prevail upon any one to come on board; they exchanged a few fish they had in the Canoes for any thing we offered them, but valued nails, or iron above every other thing; the only weapons they had were a few stones in some of the Canoes and these they threw overboard when they found they were not [needed]. . . . As soon as we made sail the Canoes left us, but others came off from the shore and brought with them roasting pigs and some very fine [sweet] Potatoes, which they exchanged, as the others had done, for whatever was offered them; several small pigs were got for a sixpenny nail or two apiece, so that we again found our selves in the land of plenty. . . .

[Tuesday, 20 January 1778] The next morning we stood in for the land and were met by several Canoes filled with people, some of them took courage and ventured on board. I never saw Indians so much astonished at the entering a ship before, their eyes were continually flying from object to object, the wildness of their looks and actions fully expressed their surprise and astonishment at the several new objects before them and evinced that they never had been on board of a ship before. However the first man that came on board did not with all his surprise forget his own interest, the first moveable thing that came in his way was the lead and line, which he without asking any questions took to put into his Canoe and when we stopped him said "I am only going to put it into my boat" nor would he quit it till some of his countrymen spoke to him. . . .

As there were some venereal complaints on board both the Ships, in order to prevent its being communicated to these people, I gave orders that no Women, on any account whatever were to be admitted on board the Ships, I also forbid all manner of connection with them, and ordered that none who had the venereal upon them should go out of the ships. But whether these regulations had the desired effect or not time can only discover. . . .

[Wednesday, 21 January 1778] As soon as every thing was settled to my satisfaction, I . . . took a walk up the Valley, accompanied by Dr. Anderson and Mr. Webber, conducted by one of the Natives and attended by a tolerable train. Our guide proclaimed our approach and every one whom we met fell on their faces and remained in that position till we passed. This, as I afterwards understood, is done to their great chiefs. Our road lay in among the Plantations, which were chiefly of Taro, and sunk a little below the common level so as to contain the water necessary to nourish the roots. . . .

At the beach I found a great crowd and a brisk trade for pigs, fowls and roots which was carried on with the greatest good order, though I did not see a man that appeared of more consequence than another if there was they did not show themselves to us. . . . No people could trade with more honesty than these people, never once attempting to cheat us, either ashore or along side the ships. Some indeed at first betrayed a thievish disposition, or rather they thought they had a right to any thing they could lay their hand upon but this conduct they soon laid aside.

For Further Reflection

■ How does Cook's record of his first meeting with the Hawaiians compare and contrast with Christopher Columbus's account, presented earlier (in chapter 22), of his first encounter with indigenous American peoples?

SOURCE: James Cook. *The Journals of Captain Cook.* Ed. by Philip Edwards. London: Penguin, 1999, pp. 530–34. (Translation slightly modified.)

in perspective

The Americas underwent thorough transformation in early modern times. Smallpox and other diseases sparked ferocious epidemics that devastated indigenous populations and undermined their societies. In the wake of severe depopulation, European peoples toppled imperial states, established mining and agricultural enterprises, imported enslaved Afri-

can laborers, and founded colonies throughout much of the western hemisphere. Some indigenous peoples disappeared entirely as distinct groups. Others maintained their communities, identities, and cultural traditions but fell increasingly under the influence of European migrants and their Euro-American offspring. In Oceania only Guam and the Mariana

Islands felt the full effects of epidemic disease and migration in the early modern era. By the late eighteenth century, however, European and Euro-American peoples with advanced technologies had thoroughly explored the Pacific Ocean basin, and epidemic diseases traveled with them to Australia and the Pacific islands. As a result, during the nineteenth and twentieth centuries, Oceania underwent a social transformation similar to the one experienced earlier by the Americas. ●

CHRONOLOGY

1492	First voyage of Christopher Columbus to the western hemisphere
1494	Treaty of Tordesillas
1500	Brazil claimed for Portugal by Pedro Alvarez de Cabral
1518	Smallpox epidemic in the Caribbean
1519–1521	Spanish conquest of Mexico
1525	Execution of Cuauhtémoc
1532–1540	Spanish conquest of Peru
1545	Spanish discovery of silver near Potosí
1604	Foundation of Port Royal (Nova Scotia)
1607	Foundation of Jamestown
1608	Foundation of Quebec
1623	Foundation of New Amsterdam
1630	Foundation of the Massachusetts Bay Colony
1688	Smallpox epidemic on Guam
1754–1763	French and Indian war in North America
1763	Transfer of French Canadian possessions to British rule
1768–1779	Captain James Cook's exploration of the Pacific Ocean
1788	Establishment of first European colony in Australia

For Further Reading

Rolena Adorno. *Guaman Poma: Writing and Resistance in Colonial Peru.* Austin, 2000. A native Andean, who came of age after the fall of the Inca empire, tells Philip III of Spain of the evils of colonialism and the need for reform.

Alvar Nuñez Cabeza de Vaca. *Castaways.* Trans. by F. M. López-Morillas. Berkeley, 1993. Translation of Cabeza de Vaca's account of his shipwreck and travels through what is now the southwestern United States to Mexico.

Colin G. Callaway. *New Worlds for All: Indians, Europeans, and the Remaking of Early America.* Baltimore, 1997. Scholarly synthesis examining interactions and cultural exchanges between European and indigenous American peoples.

William Cronon. *Changes in the Land: Indians, Colonists, and the Ecology of New England.* New York, 1983. Brilliant study concentrating on the different ways English colonists and native peoples in colonial New England used the environment.

Philip D. Curtin. *The Rise and Fall of the Plantation Complex: Essays in Atlantic History.* 2nd ed. Cambridge, 1998. Examines plantation societies and slavery as institutions linking lands throughout the Atlantic Ocean basin.

Bernal Díaz del Castillo. *The Conquest of New Spain.* Trans. by J. M. Cohen. Harmondsworth, 1963. A conveniently available translation of Bernal Díaz's account of the conquest of Mexico from the viewpoint of a soldier.

John H. Elliot. *Empires of the Atlantic World: Britain and Spain in America 1492–1830.* New Haven, 2006. Excellent comparative study of Spanish and English colonies in the Americas.

K. R. Howe. *Where the Waves Fall: A New South Sea Island History from First Settlement to Colonial Rule.* Honolulu, 1984. A thoughtful survey of Pacific islands history emphasizing interactions between islanders and visitors.

Frances A. Karttunen. *Between Worlds: Interpreters, Guides, and Survivors.* New Brunswick, N.J., 1994. Reflective essays on Doña Marina and others who served as translators or interpreters between their society and the larger world.

John E. Kicza. *Resilient Cultures: America's Native Peoples Confront European Colonization, 1500–1800.* Upper Saddle River, N.J., 2002. A comprehensive comparative study assessing the impact of colonization on indigenous American peoples as well as native influences on American colonial history.

Karen Ordahl Kupperman. *Indians and English: Facing Off in Early America.* Ithaca, 2000. Fascinating reconstruction of the early encounters between English and indigenous American peoples, drawing on sources from all parties to the encounters.

Miguel León-Portilla. *The Broken Spears: The Aztec Account of the Conquest of Mexico.* Rev. ed. Boston, 1992. Offers translations of indigenous accounts of the Spanish conquest of the Aztec empire.

Kathleen Ann Meyers. *Neither Saints nor Sinners: Writing the Lives of Women in Spanish America.* New York, 2003. Examines female self-representation through the life writings of six seventeenth-century women in Latin America.

Gary B. Nash. *Red, White, and Black: The Peoples of Early America.* 3rd ed. Englewood Cliffs, N.J., 1992. Outstanding survey of early American history focusing on the interactions between peoples of European, African, and American ancestry.

James Pritchard. *The French in the Americas, 1670–1730.* Cambridge, 2004. Valuable study of French settlers and imperial policies in the Americas.

Matthew Restall, Lisa Sousa, and Kevin Terraciano, eds. *Mesoamerican Voices: Native Language Writings from Colonial Mexico, Yucatan, and Guatemala.* Cambridge, 2005. Composed between the sixteenth and eighteenth centuries, this collection of texts offers access to an important historical source.

Susan Migden Socolow. *The Women of Colonial Latin America.* Cambridge, 2000. An introductory survey of the female experience in the colonial societies of Spain and Brazil.

David J. Weber. *Bárbaros: Spaniards and Their Savages in the Age of Enlightenment.* New Haven, 2005. Pathbreaking and nuanced study of how Spanish administrators tried to forge a more enlightened policy toward native peoples.

———. *The Spanish Frontier in North America.* New Haven, 1992. A comprehensive study of Spanish efforts to explore and colonize lands north of Mexico.

Richard White. *The Middle Ground: Indians, Empires, and Republics in the Great Lakes Region, 1650–1815.* Cambridge, 1991. Insightful study of relations between French, English, and indigenous peoples in the Great Lakes region.

Africa and the Atlantic World

chapter25

Below decks on an illegal slave ship seized by a British antislavery patrol in 1846.

EYEWITNESS:
A Slave's Long, Strange Trip Back to Africa

Between 1760 and 1792, a west African man known to history as Thomas Peters crossed the Atlantic Ocean four times. In 1760, slave raiders captured Peters, whose original African name is unknown, marched him to the coast, and sold him to French slave merchants. He traveled in a slave ship to the French colony of Louisiana, where he probably worked on a sugar plantation. But Peters was not a docile servant. He attempted to escape at least three times, and his master punished him by beating him, branding him with a hot iron, and forcing him to wear shackles around his legs. During the 1760s his French master sold Peters to an English planter, and about 1770 a Scottish landowner in North Carolina bought him.

During the 1770s, as English colonists in North America prepared to rebel against the British government in the interests of "life, liberty, and the pursuit of happiness," slaves of African ancestry considered their own prospects and looked for ways to obtain personal freedom. Peters was among them. When war broke out, he made his way with his wife and daughter to British lines and joined the Black Pioneers, a company of escaped slaves who fought to maintain British rule in the colonies. When the colonists won the war, Peters escaped to Nova Scotia with his family and many other former slaves.

Blacks were legally free in Nova Scotia, but the white ruling elites forced them to till marginal lands and live in segregated villages. In hopes of improving their lot, some two hundred black families designated Peters as their spokesman and sent him to London to petition the government for better treatment or resettlement in a more favorable land. In 1790 Peters sailed to England, where he promoted the establishment of a colony for former slaves in Sierra Leone. His efforts succeeded, and the next year he returned to Nova Scotia to seek recruits for the colony. In 1792 he led 1,196 blacks aboard a convoy of fifteen ships and began his fourth crossing of the Atlantic Ocean. The colonists arrived safely at Freetown, and Peters served as a leader of the black community there. His time in Freetown was tense and short—he experienced the great pressures of settlement and leadership and then died

549

of malarial fever less than four months after arriving in Sierra Leone. Through his own life and experiences, Thomas Peters personified the links connecting the lands of the Atlantic Ocean basin.

For the most part, the peoples of sub-Saharan Africa continued to follow established patterns of life in early modern times. They built states and organized societies based on kinship groups as their Bantu-speaking predecessors had done for centuries. In west Africa and coastal east Africa, they also traded regularly with Muslim merchants from north Africa and southwest Asia.

Yet the establishment of global trade networks brought deep change to sub-Saharan Africa. Commercial opportunities drew European vessels to the coast of west Africa, and maritime trade soon turned west African attention to the Atlantic. Maritime commerce did not put an end to the trans-Saharan caravan trade that linked west Africa to the Mediterranean, but it helped promote the emergence of prosperous port cities and the establishment of powerful coastal kingdoms that traded through the ocean rather than the desert. In central Africa and south Africa, European merchants brought the first substantial opportunities for long-distance trade, since Muslim merchants had not ventured to those regions in large numbers.

Trade through the Atlantic profoundly affected African society because it included trade in human beings. African peoples had made a place for slavery within their societies for centuries, and they had also supplied slaves to Muslim merchants who transported them to markets in the Mediterranean and the Indian Ocean basin. The Atlantic slave trade, however, was vastly larger than the African and Islamic slave trades, and it had more serious consequences for African society. Between the fifteenth and the nineteenth centuries, it not only siphoned millions of people from their societies but also provoked turmoil in much of sub-Saharan Africa, as some peoples raided others' communities in search of captives for sale to slave traders.

The vast majority of Africans sold into the Atlantic slave trade went to destinations in the Caribbean or the Americas. Most worked on plantations cultivating cash crops for export, although some worked as domestic servants, miners, or laborers. Together they made up the largest forced migration in history before the nineteenth century and gave rise to an African diaspora in the western hemisphere. Under the restrictive conditions of slavery, they did not reconstitute African societies, but they also did not join European or Euro-American society. Instead, they preserved some African traditions and blended them with European and American traditions to create hybrid African-American societies.

AFRICAN POLITICS AND SOCIETY IN EARLY MODERN TIMES

For perhaps three millennia (2000 B.C.E. to 1000 C.E.), Bantu-speaking peoples migrated throughout sub-Saharan Africa. Many organized themselves into villages and clans governed by kinship groups rather than formal states. As their numbers grew, they devised political structures and built a series of chiefdoms and regional kingdoms. Muslim merchants, who ventured to sub-Saharan Africa after the eighth century, brought trade that encouraged the formation of large kingdoms and empires in west Africa and thriving city-states in east Africa.

African peoples continued to form states during the early modern era, but under the influence of maritime trade the patterns of state development changed. Regional kingdoms replaced the imperial states of west Africa as peoples organized their societies to take advantage of Atlantic as well as trans-Saharan commerce. The city-states of east Africa fell under the domination of Portuguese merchant-mariners seeking commercial opportunities in the Indian Ocean basin. The extension of trade networks also led to the formation of regional kingdoms in central Africa and south Africa. As the volume of long-distance trade grew, both Islam and Christianity became more prominent in sub-Saharan African societies.

The States of West Africa and East Africa

Between the eighth and the sixteenth centuries, powerful kingdoms and imperial states ruled the savannas of west Africa. The earliest was the kingdom of Ghana, which originated perhaps as early as the fourth or fifth century and established its dominance in the region in the eighth century. By controlling and taxing the trans-Saharan trade in gold, the kings of Ghana gained the financial resources they needed to field a large army and influence affairs in much of west Africa. In the thirteenth century the Mali empire replaced Ghana as the preeminent power in west Africa, but the Mali rulers continued the Ghana policy of controlling trans-Saharan trade.

The Songhay Empire By the fifteenth century the Mali empire had begun to weaken, and the expansive

Timbuktu, the commercial and cultural center of the Mali and Songhay empires, as sketched by a French traveler in 1828. Though long in decline, the city's mosques, mud-brick dwellings, and crowds of people bespeak a prosperous community.

state of Songhay emerged to take its place as the dominant power of the western grasslands. Based in the trading city of Gao, Songhay rulers built a flourishing city-state perhaps as early as the eighth century. In the early fifteenth century, they rejected Mali authority and mounted raids deep into Mali territory. In 1464 the Songhay ruler Sunni Ali (reigned 1464–1493) embarked on a campaign to conquer his neighbors and consolidated the Songhay empire (1464–1591). He brought the important trading cities of Timbuktu and Jenne under his control and used their wealth to dominate the central Niger valley.

Songhay Administration Sunni Ali built an elaborate administrative and military apparatus to oversee affairs in his realm. He appointed governors to oversee provinces and instituted a hierarchy of command that turned his army into an effective military force. He also created an imperial navy to patrol the Niger River, which was an extremely important commercial highway in the Songhay empire. Songhay military might enabled Sunni Ali's successors to extend their authority north into the Sahara, east toward Lake Chad, and west toward the upper reaches of the Niger River.

The Songhay emperors presided over a prosperous land. The capital city of Gao had about seventy-five thousand residents, many of whom participated in the lucrative trans-Saharan trade that brought salt, textiles, and metal goods south in exchange for gold and slaves. The emperors were all Muslims: they supported mosques, built schools to teach the Quran, and maintained an Islamic university at Timbuktu. Like the rulers of Ghana and Mali, the Songhay emperors valued Islam as a cultural foundation for cooperation with Muslim merchants and Islamic states in north Africa. Nevertheless, the Songhay emperors did not abandon traditional religious practices: Sunni Ali himself often consulted pagan diviners and magicians.

Fall of Songhay The Songhay empire dominated west Africa for most of the sixteenth century, but it was the last of the great imperial states of the grasslands. In 1591 a musket-bearing Moroccan army trekked across the Sahara and opened fire on the previously invincible Songhay military machine. Songhay forces withered under the attack, and subject peoples took the opportunity to revolt against Songhay domination.

As the Songhay empire crumbled, a series of small, regional kingdoms and city-states emerged in west Africa. The kingdom of Kanem-Bornu dominated the region around Lake Chad, and the Hausa people established thriving commercial city-states to the west. In the forests south of the grasslands, Oyo and Asante peoples built powerful

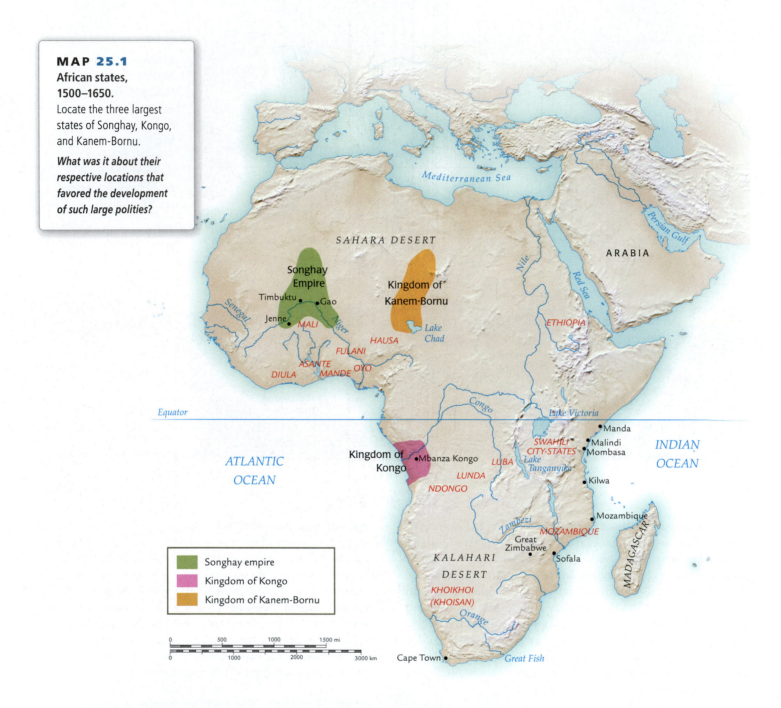

MAP 25.1

African states, 1500–1650.
Locate the three largest states of Songhay, Kongo, and Kanem-Bornu.

What was it about their respective locations that favored the development of such large polities?

Songhay empire

Kingdom of Kongo

Kingdom of Kanem-Bornu

regional kingdoms. On the coasts Diula, Mande, and other trading peoples established a series of states that entered into commercial relations with European merchant-mariners who called at west African ports after the fifteenth century. The increasing prominence of Atlantic trade in west African society worked against the interests of imperial states like Mali and Songhay, which had relied on control of trans-Saharan trade to finance their empires.

Swahili Decline While regional states displaced the Songhay empire in west Africa, the Swahili city-states of

east Africa fell on hard times. When the Portuguese mariner Vasco da Gama made his way up the east African coast en route to India in 1497 and 1498, he skirmished with local forces at Mozambique and Mombasa. On his second voyage to India in 1502, he forced the ruler of Kilwa to pay tribute, and his followers trained their cannons on Swahili ports all along the east African coast. In 1505 a massive Portuguese naval expedition subdued all the Swahili cities from Sofala to Mombasa. Portuguese forces built administrative centers at Mozambique and Malindi and constructed forts throughout the region in hopes of controlling trade in east Africa.

They did not succeed in that effort, but they disrupted trade patterns enough to send the Swahili cities into a decline from which they never fully recovered.

The Kingdoms of Central Africa and South Africa

The Kingdom of Kongo

As trade networks multiplied and linked all regions of sub-Saharan Africa, an increasing volume of commerce encouraged state building in central Africa and south Africa. In central Africa the principal states were the kingdoms of Kongo, Ndongo, Luba, and Lunda in the basin of the Congo River (also known as the Zaire River). Best known of them was the kingdom of Kongo, since abundant written records throw light on its experience in early modern times. The kingdom emerged in the fourteenth century. Its rulers built a centralized state with officials overseeing military, judicial, and financial affairs, and by the late fifteenth century Kongo embraced much of the modern-day Republic of Congo and Angola.

In 1483 a small Portuguese fleet reconnoitered the estuary of the Congo River and initiated commercial relations with the kingdom of Kongo. Within a few years, Portuguese merchants had established a close political and diplomatic relationship with the kings of Kongo. They supplied the kings with advisors, provided a military garrison to support the kings and protect Portuguese interests, and brought tailors, shoemakers, masons, miners, and priests to Kongo.

The kings of Kongo converted to Christianity as a way to establish closer commercial relations with Portuguese merchants and diplomatic relations with the Portuguese monarchy. The kings appreciated the fact that Christianity offered a strong endorsement of their monarchical rule. The new faith was convenient also because the saints of the Roman Catholic church were similar to spirits long recognized in Kongolese religion. King Nzinga Mbemba of Kongo, also known as King Afonso I (reigned 1506–1542), became a devout Roman Catholic and sought to convert all his subjects to Christianity. Portuguese priests in Kongo reported that he attended religious services daily and studied the Bible so zealously that he sometimes neglected to eat. The Kongo capital of Mbanza—known to Europeans as São Salvador—had so many churches during the sixteenth century that contemporaries referred to it as "Kongo of the Bell."

Slave Raiding in Kongo

Relations with Portugal brought wealth and foreign recognition to Kongo but also led eventually to the destruction of the kingdom and the establishment of a Portuguese colony in Angola. In exchange for the textiles, weapons, advisors, and artisans that they brought to Kongo, Portuguese merchants sought high-value merchandise such as copper, ivory, and, most of all, slaves. They sometimes embarked on slaving expeditions themselves, but more often they made alliances with local authorities in interior regions and provided them with

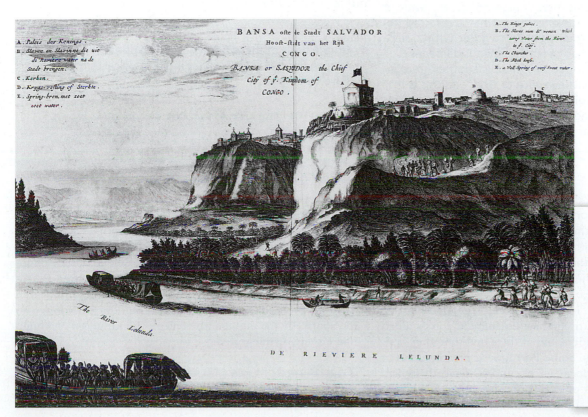

An engraving depicts São Salvador in Angola in the late seventeenth century. A flag flies over the royal palace while the Portuguese citadel (to the right of the palace) guards the city. Churches appear at the center and on the far right side of the engraving.

sources from the past

King Afonso I Protests Slave Trading in the Kingdom of Kongo

King Afonso I of Kongo wrote twenty-four official letters to his fellow monarchs, the kings of Portugal. The letters touch on many themes—relations between Portugal and Kongo, Afonso's devotion to Christianity, and the slave trade. The following excerpts come from two letters of 1526, when Portuguese slave trading was causing serious disruption in Kongo, prompting Afonso to request help in controlling the activities of Portuguese merchants.

And we cannot reckon how great the damage [caused by Portuguese merchants] is, since the mentioned merchants are taking every day our natives, sons of the land and the sons of our noblemen and vassals and our relatives, because the thieves and men of bad conscience grab them wishing to have the things and wares of this Kingdom which they are ambitious of; they grab them and get them to be sold; and so great, Sir, is the corruption and licentiousness that our country is being completely depopulated, and Your Highness should not agree with this nor accept it as in your service. And to avoid it we need from [your] Kingdoms no more than some priests and a few people to teach in schools, and no other goods except wine and flour for the holy sacrament. That is why we beg of Your Highness to help and assist us in this matter, commanding your factors that they should not send here either merchants or wares, because it is *our will that in these Kingdoms there should not be any trade of slaves nor outlet for them.* Concerning what is referred [to] above, again we beg of Your Highness to agree with it, since otherwise we cannot remedy such an obvious damage. . . .

Moreover, Sir, in our Kingdoms there is another great inconvenience which is of little service to God, and this is that many of our people, keenly desirous as they are of the wares and things of your Kingdoms, which are brought here by your people, and in order to satisfy their voracious appetite,

seize many of our people, freed and exempt men, and very often it happens that they kidnap even noblemen and the sons of noblemen, and our relatives, and take them to be sold to the white men who are in our Kingdoms. . . .

And as soon as they are taken by the white men they are immediately ironed and branded with fire, and when they are carried to be embarked, if they are caught by our guards' men the whites allege that they have bought them but they cannot say from whom, so that it is our duty to do justice and to restore to the freemen their freedom, but it cannot be done if your subjects feel offended, as they claim to be.

And to avoid such a great evil we passed a law so that any white man living in our Kingdoms and wanting to purchase goods [i.e., slaves] in any way should first inform three of our noblemen and officials of our court whom we rely upon in this matter, . . . who should investigate if the mentioned goods are captives or free men, and if cleared by them there will be no further doubt nor embargo for them to be taken and embarked. But if the white men do not comply with it they will lose the aforementioned goods. And if we do them this favor and concession it is for the part Your Highness has in it, since we know that it is in your service too that these goods are taken from our Kingdom, otherwise we should not consent to this.

For Further Reflection

■ On the basis of these letters, does it appear that King Afonso opposed all slave trading or only certain kinds of slave trading?

Source: Basil Davidson. *The African Past.* Boston: Little, Brown, 1964, pp. 191–93.

---

weapons in exchange for slaves. Some of their local allies were enemies of the kings of Kongo, while others were royal subordinates. In either case, Portuguese tactics undermined the authority of the kings, who appealed repeatedly but unsuccessfully for the Portuguese to cease or at least to limit their trade in slaves.

In spite of periodic invasions, Kongo remained strong until the mid-seventeenth century. Portuguese forces aided Kongo in expelling invaders, but at the same time they continued to trade in slaves. Some Portuguese merchants even settled in Kongo, took local wives, and henceforth looked more after the interests of their adoptive home than their native land. Over time, though, relations between Kongo

and Portugal deteriorated, particularly after Portuguese agents began to pursue opportunities south of Kongo. By 1665 Portuguese colonists to the south even went to war with Kongo. Portuguese forces quickly defeated the Kongolese army and decapitated the king. Soon thereafter, Portuguese merchants began to withdraw from Kongo in search of more profitable business in the kingdom of Ndongo to the south. By the eighteenth century the kingdom of Kongo had largely disintegrated.

The Kingdom of Ndongo Meanwhile, Portuguese explorers were developing a brisk slave trade to the south in the kingdom of Ndongo, which the Portuguese referred

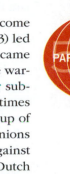

effort to establish a colony that would support large-scale trading in slaves.

Queen Nzinga The conquest of Angola did not come easily. For forty years Queen Nzinga (reigned 1623–1663) led spirited resistance against Portuguese forces. Nzinga came from a long line of warrior kings. She dressed as a male warrior when leading troops in battle and insisted that her subjects refer to her as king rather than queen. She sometimes went so far in playing male roles as to travel with a group of "concubines"—young men dressed as women companions of the "king." She mobilized central African peoples against her Portuguese adversaries, and she also allied with Dutch mariners, who traded frequently on the African coast during the mid-seventeenth century. Her aim was to drive the Portuguese from her land, then expel the Dutch, and finally create a vast central African empire embracing the entire lower Congo basin.

The Portuguese Colony of Angola Although she was a cunning strategist and an effective military leader, Nzinga was unable to oust Portuguese forces from Ndongo. She stymied Portuguese efforts to extend their influence, but with their powerful arms and considerable wealth, Portuguese forces were able to exploit the political divisions that perennially plagued central Africa. When Nzinga died, Portuguese forces faced less capable resistance, and they both extended and tightened their control over Angola, the first European colony in sub-Saharan Africa.

Regional Kingdoms in South Africa Historical records do not shed as much light on the political structures of south Africa as they do on Kongo and Angola, but it is clear that in the south, as in central Africa, regional kingdoms dominated political affairs. Kingdoms had begun to emerge as early as the eleventh century, largely under the influence of trade. Merchants from the Swahili city-states of coastal east Africa sought gold, ivory, and slaves from the interior regions of south Africa. By controlling local commerce, chieftains increased their wealth, enhanced their power, and extended their authority. By 1300 rulers of one such kingdom had built a massive, stone-fortified city known as Great Zimbabwe, near the city of Nyanda in

This is a martial portrait of the warrior Queen Nzinga, produced by European engravers who dubbed her "Anna Singa or Schmga." Queen Nzinga fought the Portuguese in Angola.

to as Angola from the title of the king, *ngola*. During the sixteenth century, Ndongo had grown from a small chiefdom subject to the kings of Kongo to a powerful regional kingdom, largely on the basis of the wealth it was able to attract by trading directly with Portuguese merchants rather than through Kongolese intermediaries. Portuguese merchants founded a small coastal colony in Ndongo as early as 1575. After 1611 they steadily increased their influence inland by allying with neighboring peoples who delivered increasing numbers of war captives to feed the growing slave trade. Over the next several decades, Portuguese forces campaigned in Ndongo in an

thinking about ENCOUNTERS

Queen Nzinga
The Portuguese attempted to establish a colony in Angola in the seventeenth century to promote an even more robust slave trade. Their efforts did not go uncontested, however. What role did Queen Nzinga play in this conflict? What was the outcome of her efforts?

modern Zimbabwe, and they dominated the gold-bearing plain between the Zambesi and Limpopo rivers until the late fifteenth century.

European Arrival in South Africa
After the fifteenth century a series of smaller kingdoms displaced the rulers of Great Zimbabwe, and Portuguese and Dutch mariners began to play a role in south African affairs. In search of commercial opportunities, Europeans struck alliances with local peoples and intervened in disputes with the aim of supporting their allies and advancing their own interests. They became especially active after Dutch mariners built a trading post at Cape Town in 1652. There they encountered the hunting and gathering Khoikhoi people, whom they referred to pejoratively as Hottentots. With the aid of firearms, they claimed lands for themselves and commandeered Khoikhoi labor with relative ease. By 1700 large numbers of Dutch colonists had begun to arrive in south Africa, and by mid-century they had established settlements throughout the region bounded by the Orange and the Great Fish rivers. Their conquests laid the foundation for a series of Dutch and British colonies, which eventually became the most prosperous European possessions in sub-Saharan Africa.

Islam and Christianity in Early Modern Africa

Indigenous religions remained influential throughout sub-Saharan Africa in early modern times. Although many African peoples recognized a supreme, remote creator god, they devoted most of their attention to powerful spirits who were thought to intervene directly in human affairs. African peoples associated many of these spirits with prominent geographic features such as mountains, waters, or forests. Others they thought of as the "living dead"—spirits of ancestors who roamed the world, not only distributing rewards to descendants who led worthy lives and who honored the memories of departed kin, but also meting out punishments to those who did not.

Islam in Sub-Saharan Africa
Although most Africans continued to observe their inherited religions, both Islam and Christianity attracted increasing interest in sub-Saharan Africa. Islam was most popular in the commercial centers of west Africa and the Swahili city-states of east Africa. In the sixteenth century the trading city of Timbuktu had a prominent Islamic university and 180 schools that taught the Quran. Students flocked to Timbuktu by the thousands from all parts of west Africa.

Most African Muslims blended Islam with indigenous beliefs and customs. The result was a syncretic brand of Islam that not only made a place for African beliefs in spirits and magic but also permitted men and women to associate with each other on much more familiar terms than was common in north Africa, Arabia, and southwest Asia. Although it appealed to Africans, this syncretic Islam struck many de-vout Muslims as impure and offensive. Muslim merchants and travelers from north Africa and Arabia often commented on their shock at seeing women in tropical Africa who went out in public with bare breasts and socialized freely with men outside their own families.

The Fulani and Islam
Some Muslims in sub-Saharan Africa also shared these concerns about the purity of Islam. Most important of them were the Fulani, originally a pastoral people who for centuries kept herds of cattle in the savannas of west Africa. By the late seventeenth century, many Fulani had settled in cities, where they observed a strict form of Islam like that practiced in north Africa and Arabia. Beginning about 1680 and continuing through the nineteenth century, the Fulani led a series of military campaigns to establish Islamic states and impose their own brand of Islam in west Africa.

The Fulani did not by any means stamp out African religions, nor did they eliminate indigenous elements from the syncretic Islam practiced in west Africa. But they founded powerful states in what is now Guinea, Senegal, Mali, and northern Nigeria, and they promoted the spread of Islam

"Although many African peoples recognized a supreme, remote creator god, they devoted most of their attention to powerful spirits who were thought to intervene directly in human affairs."

beyond the cities to the countryside. They even established schools in remote towns and villages to teach the Quran and Islamic doctrine. Their campaigns strengthened Islam in sub-Saharan Africa and laid a foundation for new rounds of Islamic state building and conversion efforts in the nineteenth and twentieth centuries.

Christianity in Sub-Saharan Africa
Like Islam, Christianity made compromises with traditional beliefs and customs when it spread in sub-Saharan Africa. The Portuguese community in Kongo and Angola supported priests and missionaries who introduced Roman Catholic Christianity to central Africa. They found strong interest among rulers such as King Afonso I of Kongo and his descendants, who eagerly adopted European-style Christianity as a foundation for commercial and political alliances with Portugal. Beyond the ruling courts, however, Christian teachings blended with African traditions to form syncretic cults. Some Africans regarded Christian missionaries as magicians and wore crosses and other Christian symbols as amulets to ward off danger from angry spirits.

The kings of Kongo retained their Christian faith even after their relations with European merchants and missionaries became strained in the seventeenth century. Here, King Garcia II—with European-style boots and a cross attached to his left sleeve—receives a Dutch embassy in 1642.

The Antonian Movement A particularly influential syncretic cult was the Antonian movement in Kongo, which flourished in the early eighteenth century, when the Kongolese monarchy faced challenges throughout the realm. The Antonian movement began in 1704 when an aristocratic woman named Dona Beatriz proclaimed that St. Anthony of Padua had possessed her and chosen her to communicate his messages. St. Anthony was a thirteenth-century Franciscan missionary and popular preacher. Born in Lisbon, St. Anthony died near Padua in Italy, where his followers built a large church in his honor. He was extremely popular among Portuguese Christians, who introduced his cult to Kongo. Dona Beatriz gained a reputation for working miracles and curing diseases, and she used her prominence to promote an African form of Christianity. She taught that Jesus Christ had been a black African man, that Kongo was the true holy land of Christianity, and that heaven was for Africans. She urged Kongolese to ignore European missionaries and heed her disciples instead, and she sought to harness the widespread popular interest in her teachings and use it to end the wars plaguing Kongo.

Dona Beatriz's movement was a serious challenge to Christian missionaries in Kongo. In 1706 they persuaded King Pedro IV of Kongo to arrest the charismatic prophetess on suspicion of heresy. Upon examining her, the mis-

sionaries satisfied themselves that Dona Beatriz was a false prophet and that she knowingly taught false doctrine. On their recommendation the royal government sentenced her to death and burned her at the stake. Yet the Antonian movement did not disappear: Dona Beatriz's disciples continued working to strengthen the monarchy and reconstruct Kongolese society. In 1708 an army of almost twenty thousand Antonians challenged King Pedro, whom they considered an unworthy ruler. Their efforts illustrate clearly the tendency of Kongolese Christians to fashion a faith that reflected their own needs and concerns as well as the interests of European missionaries.

Social Change in Early Modern Africa

Despite increased state-building activity and political turmoil, African society followed long-established patterns during the early modern era. Kinship groups, for example, the most important social units that emerged after the Bantu migrations, continued to serve as the basis of social organization and sometimes political organization as well. Within agricultural villages throughout sub-Saharan Africa, clans under the leadership of prominent individuals organized the affairs of their kinship groups and disciplined those who violated community standards. In regions where kingdoms and empires had not emerged, clan leaders consulted with one another and governed large regions. Indeed, even in lands ruled by formal states, clan leaders usually implemented state policy at the village level.

Yet interaction with European peoples brought change to African society in early modern times. Trade brought access to European textiles and metal goods. Africans had produced textiles and high-quality steel for centuries before the arrival of Portuguese mariners, but European products of different materials and styles became popular as complements to native African wares.

American Food Crops in Sub-Saharan Africa

Trade also brought new food crops to sub-Saharan Africa. In the mid-sixteenth century, American crops such as manioc, maize, and peanuts arrived in Africa aboard Portuguese ships. These crops supplemented bananas, yams, rice, and millet, the principal staple foods of sub-Saharan Africa. The most important American crop was manioc because of its high yield and because it thrived in tropical soils not well suited to cultivation of the other crops.

Population Growth By the eighteenth century, bread made from manioc flour had become a staple food in much of west Africa and central Africa, where it helped to underwrite steady population growth. In 1500 C.E. the population of sub-Saharan Africa was about thirty-four million. By 1600 it had increased by almost one-third to forty-four million, and it continued climbing to fifty-two million in 1700 and sixty million in 1800. This strong demographic expansion is all the more remarkable because it took place precisely when millions of Africans underwent an involuntary, forced migration to destinations in the Caribbean and the Americas. Despite that migration, American food crops supported expanding populations in all regions of sub-Saharan Africa during early modern times.

THE ATLANTIC SLAVE TRADE

Of all the processes that linked Africa to the larger Atlantic world in early modern times, the most momentous was the Atlantic slave trade. From the fifteenth to the nineteenth century, European peoples looked to Africa as a source of labor for sprawling plantations that they established in the western hemisphere. In exchange for slaves, African peoples received European manufactured products—most notably firearms, which they sometimes used to strengthen military forces that then sought further recruits for the slave trade. Only in the early nineteenth century did the Atlantic slave trade come to an end. During the course of the century, most states abolished the institution of slavery itself.

Foundations of the Slave Trade

Slavery in Africa The institution of slavery appeared in remote antiquity, and until the nineteenth century many settled agricultural peoples made some place for slaves in their societies. Slavery was common throughout Africa after the Bantu migrations spread agriculture to all parts of the continent. As in other societies, most slaves in Africa came from the ranks of war captives, although criminals and individuals expelled from their clans also frequently fell into slavery. Once enslaved, an individual had no personal or civil rights. Owners could order slaves to perform any kind of work, punish them at will, and sell them as chattel. African slaves usually worked as cultivators in societies far from their homes, although some worked as administrators, soldiers, or even highly placed advisors. The Songhay emperors, for example, often employed slaves as administrators and soldiers, since the rulers distrusted free nobles, whom they considered excessively ambitious and undependable. Agricultural plantations in the Songhay empire often had hundreds of slave laborers, many of them working under the management of slave administrators.

Law and society made African slavery different from bondage in Europe, Asia, and other lands. African law did not recognize private property but, rather, vested ownership of land in communities. Thus wealth and power in Africa came not from the possession of land but from control over the human labor that made the land productive. Slaves were a form of private investment, a type of heritable property, and a means of measuring wealth. Those who controlled large numbers of individuals were able to harvest more crops and accumulate more wealth than others. Africans routinely purchased slaves to enlarge their families and enhance their power. Often, they assimilated slaves into their kinship groups, so that within a generation a slave might obtain both freedom and an honorable position in a new family or clan.

The Islamic Slave Trade After the eighth century, Muslim merchants from north Africa, Arabia, and Persia sought African slaves for sale and distribution to destinations in the Mediterranean basin, southwest Asia, India, and even southeast Asia and China. This organized commerce found ready markets for slaves. When traditional sources proved insufficient to satisfy the demand for slaves, merchants created new supplies by raiding villages, capturing innocent individuals, and forcing them into servitude. State officials sometimes allied with the merchants by providing cavalry forces to mount lightning raids on undefended communities. Merchants then transported the freshly recruited slaves across the Sahara desert by camel caravan for distribution in the Mediterranean basin or boarded them on ships at the Swahili port cities of east Africa for delivery to destinations across the Indian Ocean. During a millennium and more of the Islamic slave trade, which lasted into the twentieth century, as many as ten million Africans may have left their homeland in servitude.

By the time Europeans ventured to sub-Saharan Africa in the fifteenth and sixteenth centuries, traffic in slaves was a well-established feature of African society, and a system for capturing, selling, and distributing slaves had functioned effectively for more than five hundred years. When Europeans began to pursue commercial interests in Africa and the Americas, the slave trade expanded dramatically. After 1450, European peoples tapped existing networks and expanded commerce in African slaves from the Mediterranean and the Indian Ocean to the Atlantic Ocean basin. This Atlantic slave trade brought about an enormous involuntary migration that influenced the development of societies throughout the Atlantic Ocean basin.

Human Cargoes

The Atlantic slave trade began small, but it grew steadily and eventually reached enormous proportions. The earliest European slave traders were Portuguese explorers who reconnoitered the west African coast in the mid-fifteenth century. In 1441 a raiding party seized twelve African men and took them to Portugal as slaves. Portuguese mariners encountered stiff resistance when they attempted to capture slaves, as African warriors fired thousands of poison-tipped arrows at gangs of would-be slave raiders. Soon, however, the mariners learned that they could purchase slaves rather than capturing them, and by 1460 they were delivering five hundred slaves per year to Portugal and Spain. In Europe, African slaves usually worked as miners, porters, or domestic servants, since free peasants and serfs cultivated the land.

The Early Slave Trade Slave traders also delivered their human cargoes to Portuguese island colonies in the Atlantic. There was no supply of labor to work plantations in the Azores, Madeiras, Cape Verde Islands, and São Tomé, all of which were uninhabited when explorers discovered them in the fifteenth century. The Portuguese population was too small to provide large numbers of colonists. Sugar planters on the island of São Tomé in particular called for slaves in increasing quantities. They relied on slave labor, and production soared along with the demand for sugar in Europe. By the 1520s some two thousand slaves per year went to São Tomé. Soon thereafter Portuguese entrepreneurs extended the use of slave labor to South Amer-

ica. During the 1530s Portuguese planters imported slaves directly from Kongo and Angola to Brazil, which eventually became the wealthiest of the sugar-producing lands of the western hemisphere.

Meanwhile, Spanish explorers and conquerors also sought laborers to work lands in the Caribbean and the Americas. As imported diseases ravaged indigenous populations in the western hemisphere, the conquerors found themselves in possession of vast stretches of land but few laborers to work it. The Spanish attempted to harness the labor of those who survived the diseases, but native peoples frequently revolted against their overlords or simply escaped into the hinterlands. Gradually, Spanish settlers began to rely on imported African slaves as laborers. In 1518 the first shipment of slaves went directly from west Africa to the Caribbean, where they worked on recently established sugar plantations. During the 1520s Spanish authorities introduced slaves to Mexico, where they worked as cultivators and miners. By the early seventeenth century, English colonists had introduced slaves also to the North American mainland.

Triangular Trade The demand for labor in the western hemisphere stimulated a profitable commerce known as the triangular trade, since European ships often undertook voyages of three legs. On the first leg they carried horses and European manufactured goods—mostly cloth and metalwares, especially firearms—that they exchanged in sub-Saharan Africa for slaves. The second leg took enslaved Africans to Caribbean and American destinations. Upon arrival merchants sold their human cargoes to plantation owners for two to three times what they had cost on the African coast. Sometimes they exchanged slaves for cash, but in sugar-producing regions they often bartered slaves for sugar or molasses. Then they filled their vessels' hulls with American products before embarking on their voyage back to Europe.

At every stage of the process, the slave trade was a brutal and inhumane business. The original capture of slaves in Africa was almost always a violent affair. As European demand for slaves grew, some African chieftains organized raiding parties to seize individuals from

A bronze plaque from Benin offers an early African view of Europeans: it depicts a Portuguese soldier armed with a musket and accompanied by a dog.

neighboring societies. Others launched wars for the purpose of capturing victims for the slave trade. They often snatched individuals right out of their homes, fields, or villages: millions of lives changed instantly, as slave raiders grabbed their quarries and then immediately spirited them away in captivity. Bewilderment and anger was the lot not only of the captives but also of their family members, who would never again see their kin.

The Middle Passage Following capture, enslaved individuals underwent a forced march to the coast, where they lived in holding pens until a ship arrived to transport them to the western hemisphere. Then they embarked on the dreadful "middle passage," the trans-Atlantic journey aboard filthy and crowded slave ships. Enslaved passengers traveled below decks in hideously cramped quarters. Most ships provided slaves with enough room to sit upright, al-

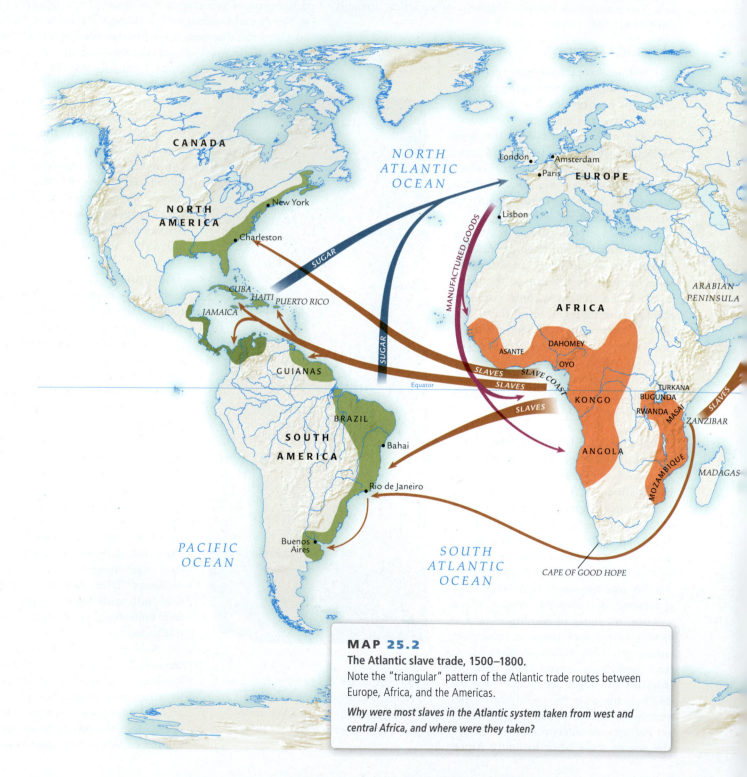

MAP 25.2

The Atlantic slave trade, 1500–1800.

Note the "triangular" pattern of the Atlantic trade routes between Europe, Africa, and the Americas.

Why were most slaves in the Atlantic system taken from west and central Africa, and where were they taken?

though not to stand, but some forced them to lie in chains on shelves with barely half a meter (twenty inches) of space between them. Conditions were so bad that many slaves attempted to starve themselves to death or mounted revolts. Ship crews attempted to preserve the lives of slaves, intending to sell them for a profit at the end of the voyage, but often treated the unwilling passengers with cruelty and contempt. Crew members used tools to pry open the mouths of those who refused to eat and pitched sick individuals into the ocean rather than have them infect others or waste limited supplies of food.

Barring difficulties, the journey to Caribbean and American destinations took four to six weeks, during which heat, cold, and disease levied a heavy toll on the human cargo. During the early days of the slave trade on particularly cramped ships, mortality sometimes exceeded 50 percent. As the volume of the trade grew, slavers built larger ships, carried more water, and provided better nourishment and facilities for their cargoes, and mortality eventually declined to about 5 percent per voyage. Over the course of the Atlantic slave trade, however, approximately 25 percent of individuals enslaved in Africa did not survive the middle passage.

The Impact of the Slave Trade in Africa

Volume of the Slave Trade Before 1600 the Atlantic slave trade operated on a modest scale. Export figures varied considerably from one year to the next, but on average about two thousand slaves left Africa annually during the late fifteenth and sixteenth centuries. During the seventeenth century, slave exports rose dramatically to twenty thousand per year, as European peoples settled in the western hemisphere and called for African labor to cultivate their lands. The high point of the slave trade came in the eighteenth century, when the number of slaves exported to the Americas averaged fifty-five thousand per year. During the 1780s slave arrivals averaged eighty-eight thousand per year, and in some individual years they exceeded one hundred thousand. From beginning to end, the Atlantic slave trade brought about the involuntary migration of about twelve million Africans to the western hemisphere. An additional four million or more died resisting seizure or during captivity before arriving at their intended destination.

The impact of the slave trade varied over time and from one African society to another. The kingdoms of Rwanda and Bugunda on the great lakes and the herding societies of the Masai and Turkana of east Africa largely escaped the slave trade, partly because they resisted it and partly because their lands were distant from the major slave ports on the west African coast. Other societies flourished during early modern times and benefited economically from the slave trade. Those Africans who raided, took captives, and sold slaves to Europeans profited handsomely from the trade, as did the port cities and the states that coordinated trade with European merchants. Asante, Dahomey, and Oyo peoples, for example, took advantage of the slave trade to obtain firearms from European merchants and build powerful states in west Africa. In the nineteenth century, after the abolition of slavery, some African merchants complained bitterly about losing their livelihood and tried to undermine the efforts of the British navy to patrol Atlantic waters and put an end to slave trading.

Social Effects of the Slave Trade On the whole, however, sub-Saharan Africa suffered serious losses from

INDIA

DIAN
EAN

→ Slaves
→ Sugar
→ Manufactured goods
■ Source areas of African slaves
■ Slave settlement areas

sources from the past

Olaudah Equiano on the Middle Passage

Olaudah Equiano (1745–1797) was a native of Benin in west Africa. When he was ten years old, slave raiders seized him and his sister at home while their parents were tending the fields. He spent the next twenty-one years as a slave. Then Equiano purchased his freedom and worked against the slave trade for the rest of his life. In his autobiography of 1789, Equiano described the horrors of the middle passage.

The first object which saluted my eyes when I arrived on the coast was the sea, and a slave ship which was then riding at anchor and waiting for its cargo. These filled me with astonishment, which was soon converted into terror when I was carried on board. I was immediately handled and tossed up to see if I were sound by some of the crew, and I was now persuaded that I had gotten into a world of bad spirits and that they were going to kill me. . . .

I was not long suffered to indulge my grief; I was soon put down under the decks, and there I received such a salutation in my nostrils as I had never experienced in my life: so that with the loathsomeness of the stench and crying together, I became so sick and low that I was not able to eat, nor had I the least desire to taste anything. I now wished for the last friend, death, to relieve me; but soon, to my grief, two of the white men offered me eatables, and on my refusing to eat, one of them held me fast by the hands and laid me across I think the windlass and tied my feet while the other flogged me severely. I had never experienced anything of this kind before, and although not being used to the water I naturally feared that element the first time I saw it, yet nevertheless if I could have gotten over the nettings I would have jumped over the side, but I could not; and besides, the crew used to watch very closely over those of us who were not chained down to the decks, lest we should leap into the water: and I have seen some of these poor African prisoners most severely cut for attempting to do so, and hourly whipped for not eating. This indeed was often the case with myself. . . .

One day when we had a smooth sea and moderate wind, two of my wearied countrymen who were chained together (I was near them at the time), preferring death to such a life of misery, somehow made through the nettings and jumped into the sea: immediately another quite dejected fellow, who on account of his illness was suffered to be out of irons, also followed their example; and I believe many more would very soon have done the same if they had not been prevented by the ship's crew, who were instantly alarmed. Those of us that were the most active were in a moment put down under the deck, and there was such a noise and confusion amongst the people of the ship as I never heard before, to stop her and get the boat to go after the slaves. However, two of the wretches were drowned, but they got the other and afterwards flogged him unmercifully for thus attempting to prefer death to slavery. In this manner we continued to undergo more hardships than I can now relate, hardships which are inseparable from this accursed trade.

For Further Reflection

■ On the basis of Equiano's account, what measures did the crews of slave ships take to ensure maximum profits from their business of transporting human cargoes?

Source: Olaudah Equiano. *The Interesting Narrative of the Life of Olaudah Equiano, or Gustavus Vassa, the African, Written by Himself.* 2 vols. London, 1789. (Translation slightly modified.)

the slave trade. The Atlantic slave trade alone deprived African societies of about sixteen million individuals, in addition to several million others consumed by the continuing Islamic slave trade during the early modern era. Although total African population rose during the early modern era, partly because American food crops enriched diets, several individual societies experienced severe losses because of the slave trade. West African societies between Senegal and Angola were especially vulnerable to slave raiding because of their proximity to the most active slave ports.

Gender and Slavery While diverting labor from subSaharan Africa to other lands, the slave trade also distorted sex ratios both in the Americas and in Africa. Approximately two-thirds of all slaves were young men between fourteen and thirty-five years of age. This reflected European preferences, because men in their physical prime had the best potential to repay their buyers' investments by providing heavy labor over an extended period of time. It also coincided with the desire of African slavers to retain female slaves for use in households. The resulting gender imbalance effectively militated against slaves reproducing in most places of colonial America. This, in turn, made it imperative for plantation owners and slavers to look constantly to Africa as a source for new slaves. This need to replenish the male slave populations was especially acute on Carib-

Armed escorts march a group of freshly captured Africans to the coast for sale on slave markets. Chained together are African men, women, and children. Why would some African peoples enslave other Africans?

bean sugar plantations, where death rates were especially high. The preference for male slaves also had implications for sub-Saharan societies. By the late eighteenth century, for example, women made up more than two-thirds of the adult population of Angola, encouraging Angolans to embrace polygyny, the practice of having more than one wife at a time. Women by necessity took on duties that earlier had been the responsibility of men.

Political Effects of the Slave Trade Apart from its demographic and social effects, the slave trade brought turmoil to African societies. During early modern times, African peoples fought many wars for reasons that had little or nothing to do with the slave trade, but it encouraged them to participate also in conflicts that might never have occurred in the absence of the trade.

Violence escalated especially after the late seventeenth century, when African peoples increasingly exchanged slaves for European firearms. When the kingdom of Dahomey obtained effective firearms, for example, its armies were able to capture slaves from unarmed neighboring societies and exchange them for more weapons. During the eighteenth century, Dahomey expanded rapidly and absorbed neighboring societies by increasing its arsenal of

firearms and maintaining a constant flow of slaves to the coast. Indeed, the Dahomey army, which included a regiment of women soldiers, became largely a slave-raiding force. By no means did all African states take such advantage of the slave trade, but Dahomey's experience illustrates the potential of the slave trade to alter the patterns of African politics and society.

THE AFRICAN DIASPORA

Some slaves worked as urban laborers or domestic servants, and in Mexico and Peru many worked also as miners. The vast majority, however, provided agricultural labor on plantations in the Caribbean or the Americas. There they cultivated cash crops that made their way into commercial arteries linking lands throughout the Atlantic Ocean basin. Although deprived of their freedom, slaves often resisted their bondage, and they built hybrid cultural traditions compounded of African, European, and American elements. Most European and American states ended the slave trade and abolished slavery during the nineteenth century. By that time the African diaspora—the dispersal of African peoples and their descendants—had left a permanent mark throughout the western hemisphere.

Plantation Societies

Most African slaves went to plantations in the tropical and subtropical regions of the western hemisphere. When European peoples arrived in the Caribbean and the Americas, they found vast stretches of fertile land and soon began to envision huge profits from plantations that would satisfy the growing European demand for sugar and other agricultural commodities. Spanish colonists established the first of these plantations in 1516 on the island of Hispaniola (which embraces modern Haiti and the Dominican Republic) and soon extended them to Mexico as well. Beginning in the 1530s Portuguese entrepreneurs organized plantations in Brazil, and by the early seventeenth century English, Dutch, and French plantations had also appeared in the Caribbean and the Americas.

Cash Crops Many of these plantations produced sugar, which was one of the most lucrative cash crops of early modern times. But plantations produced other crops as well. During the seventeenth century, tobacco rivaled sugar as a profitable product. Rice also became a major planta-

tion product, as did indigo. By the eighteenth century many plantations concentrated on the cultivation of cotton, and coffee had begun to emerge as a plantation specialty.

Regardless of the crops they produced, Caribbean and American plantations had certain elements in common. All of them specialized in the production of some agricultural crop in high demand. Plantations often maintained gardens that produced food for the local community, but their purpose was to profit from the production and export of commercial crops. In efforts to operate efficiently and profitably, plantations relied almost exclusively on slave labor. Plantation communities often included a hundred or more slaves, whose uncompensated labor services helped keep their agricultural products competitive. Plantations also featured a sharp, racial division of labor. Small numbers of European or Euro-American supervisors governed plantation affairs, and large numbers of African or African-American slaves performed most of the community's physical labor.

Regional Differences In spite of their structural similarities, plantation societies differed considerably from one

In an engraving of 1667, a European supervisor (lower right) directs slaves on a sugar plantation in Barbados as they haul cane, crush it to extract its juice, boil it to produce molasses, and distill the product into rum.

Slaves were vulnerable to cruel treatment that often provoked them to run away from their plantations or even mount revolts. A French visitor to Brazil in the early nineteenth century depicted a Portuguese overseer administering a brutal whipping to a bound slave on a plantation near Rio de Janeiro.

region to another. In the Caribbean and South America, slave populations usually were unable to sustain their numbers by natural means. Many slaves fell victim to tropical diseases such as malaria and yellow fever. On the plantations, they faced brutal working conditions and low standards of sanitation and nutrition. Moreover, slaves had low rates of reproduction because plantation owners mostly imported male slaves and allowed only a few to establish families. Thus, in the Caribbean and South America, plantation owners imported continuing streams of slaves from Africa to maintain their workforces. Of all the slaves delivered from Africa to the western hemisphere, about half went to the Caribbean, and about one-third went to Brazil. Smaller numbers went to other destinations in South America and Central America.

Only about 5 percent of enslaved Africans went to North American destinations. Diseases there were less threatening than in the Caribbean and Brazil, and in some ways the conditions of slaves' lives were less harsh than in the more southerly regions. North American planters imported larger numbers of female slaves and encouraged their slaves to form families and bear children. Their support for slave families was especially strong in the eighteenth century, when the prices of fresh slaves from Africa rose dramatically.

Resistance to Slavery No matter where they lived, slaves did not meekly accept their servile status, but like Thomas Peters resisted it in numerous ways. Some forms of

resistance were mild but costly to slave owners: slaves often worked slowly for their masters but diligently in their own gardens, for example. They occasionally sabotaged plantation equipment or work routines. A more serious form of resistance involved running away from the plantation community. Runaways known as *maroons* gathered in mountainous, forested, or swampy regions and built their own self-governing communities. Maroons often raided nearby plantations for arms, tools, provisions, and even slaves to increase their own numbers or to provide labor for their communities. Many maroons had gained military experience in Africa, and they organized escaped slaves into effective military forces. Maroon communities flourished throughout slave-holding regions of the western hemisphere, and some of them survived for centuries. In present-day Suriname, for example, the Saramaka people maintain an elaborate oral tradition that traces their descent from eighteenth-century maroons.

Slave Revolts The most dramatic form of resistance to slavery was the slave revolt. Slaves far outnumbered others in most plantation societies, and they had the potential to organize and overwhelm their masters. Slave revolts brought stark fear to plantation owners and supervisors, and they often resulted in widespread death and destruction. Yet slave revolts almost never brought slavery itself to an end, because the European and Euro-American ruling elites had access to arms, horses, and military forces that extinguished most rebellions. Only in the French sugar colony of Saint-Domingue did a slave revolt abolish slavery as an institution (1793). Indeed, the slaves of Saint-Domingue declared independence from France, renamed the land Haiti, and established a self-governing republic (1804). The Haitian revolution terrified slave owners and inspired slaves throughout the western hemisphere, but no other slave rebellion matched its accomplishments.

Slavery and Economic Development The physical labor of African and African-American slaves made crucial contributions to the building of new societies in the Americas and also to the making of the early modern world as a whole. Slave labor cultivated many of the crops and extracted many of the minerals that made their way around the world in the global trade networks of the early modern era. Slaves themselves did not enjoy the fruits of their labors, which flowed disproportionately to European peoples and their Euro-American descendants. Except for the labor of enslaved African peoples and their African-American descendants, however, it would have been impossible for prosperous new societies to emerge in the Americas during the early modern era.

The Making of African-American Cultural Traditions

Enslaved Africans did not enjoy the luxury of maintaining their inherited cultural traditions in the western hemisphere. They often preserved African traditions, including languages and religions, but had to adapt to societies compounded of various European and American as well as African elements. When packed in slave ships for the middle passage, they found themselves in the company of Africans from societies other than their own. When sold to masters in the Caribbean and the Americas, they joined societies shaped by European and American traditions. In adapting to new circumstances, slaves constructed distinctive African-American cultural traditions.

African and Creole Languages European languages were the dominant tongues in the slave societies of the western hemisphere, but African languages also influenced communication. Occasionally, African slaves from a particular region were numerous enough to speak among themselves in their native tongues. More often, they spoke a creole tongue that drew on several African and European languages. In the low country of South Carolina and Georgia, for example, slaves made up about three-quarters of the population in the eighteenth century and regularly communicated in the creole languages Gullah and Geechee, respectively.

African-American Religions Like their languages, slaves' religions also combined elements from different societies. Some slaves shipped out of Africa were Christians, and many others converted to Christianity after their arrival in the western hemisphere. Most Africans and African-Americans did not practice European Christianity, however, but rather a syncretic faith that made considerable room for African interests and traditions. Because they developed mostly in plantation societies under conditions of slavery, these syncretic religions usually did not create an institutional structure or establish a hierarchy of priests and other church officials. Yet in several cases—most notably Vodou in Haiti, Santeria in Cuba, and Candomblé in Brazil—they became exceedingly popular among slaves.

All the syncretic, African-American religions drew inspiration from Christianity: they met in parish churches, sought personal salvation, and made use of European Christian paraphernalia such as holy water, candles, and statues. Yet they also preserved African traditions. They associated African deities with Christian saints and relied heavily on African rituals such as drumming, dancing, and sacrificing animals. Indeed, the core of these syncretic faiths was often participation in rituals like those observed in Africa. They also preserved beliefs in spirits and supernatural powers: magic, sorcery, witchcraft, and spirit possession all played prominent roles in African-American religions.

African-American Music As in their languages and religions, slaves relied on their African traditions in creating musical forms attuned to the plantation landscape. For many of these involuntary laborers, the playing of African music brought a sense of home and community to mind. It represented precisely what the slaves had lost—a sense of cultural grounding and belonging. African slaves in the Americas adapted African musical traditions, including both their rhythmic and their oratorical elements, to their new environments as a means of buffering the shock of transition, as a way to survive and to resist the horrid conditions of their new lives. In the process, they managed to create musical forms that made their influence felt not just in the slave quarters but also in the multicultural societies of the Caribbean and the Americas.

Slaves fashioned a new sense of identity and strength by bending west African instruments and musical traditions to European languages, Christian religion, and the work routines of American plantations. Slave musicians played drums and stringed instruments such as banjos that closely resembled traditional African instruments. They adapted west African call-and-response patterns of singing to the rhythms of field work on plantations. The call-and-response format also found its way into the music of spirituals that blended Christian, European, and African influences.

Many slave owners dismissed drumming and African-influenced music as heathenism, and some sought to ban music out of fear that it harbored subversive potential. Slave owners in South Carolina recalled, for example, that slaves had used drums to signal one another to rise up during the Stono rebellion of 1739. Despite efforts to suppress African influences, the music of slaves and later of their free de-

thinking about TRADITIONS

Creole Culture

The horrors of the institution of slavery made the preservation of African culture extremely difficult for those enslaved. African traditions nonetheless survived in blended or creole forms of culture in the Americas. What forms of culture best expressed this fusion? How did language and music in particular embody creole customs?

scendants survived and testified to the continuing relevance of music as a means of shaping community identity and resistance to oppression. From work songs and spirituals to the blues, jazz, and soul, African-American music evolved to mirror the difficult and often chaotic circumstances of black life in the Americas.

African-American Cultural Traditions African traditions also made their effects felt throughout much of the western hemisphere. Slaves introduced African foods to Caribbean and American societies and helped give rise to distinctive hybrid cuisines. They combined African okra, for example, with European-style sautéed vegetables and American shellfish to produce magnificent gumbos, which found their way to Euro-American as well as African-American tables. (*Okra* and *gumbo* are both African words.) Slaves introduced rice cultivation to tropical and subtropical regions, including South Carolina, Georgia, and Louisiana, and added variety to American diets. They also built houses, fashioned clay pots, and wove grass baskets in west African styles. In many ways, the African diaspora influenced the ways all peoples lived in plantation societies.

The End of the Slave Trade and the Abolition of Slavery

Almost as old as the Atlantic slave trade itself were voices calling for its abolition. The American and French revolutions stimulated the abolitionist cause. The American call for "life, liberty, and the pursuit of happiness" and the French appeal for "liberty, equality, and fraternity" suggested that

there was a universal human right to freedom and equality.

Olaudah Equiano Africans also took up the struggle to abolish commerce in human beings. Frequent slave revolts in the eighteenth and nineteenth centuries made the institution of slavery an expensive and dangerous business. Some freed slaves contributed to the abolitionist cause by writing books that exposed the brutality of institutional slavery. Most notable of them was the west African Olaudah Equiano (1745–1797), who in 1789 published an autobiography detailing his experiences as a slave and a free man. Captured at age ten in his native Benin (in modern Nigeria), Equiano worked as a slave in the West Indies, Virginia, and Pennsylvania. He accompanied one of his masters on several campaigns of the Seven Years' War before purchasing his freedom in 1766. Equiano's book became a best-seller, and the author traveled throughout the British isles giving speeches and denouncing slavery as an evil institution. He lobbied government officials and members of Parliament, and his efforts strengthened the antislavery movement in England.

The Economic Costs of Slavery Quite apart from moral and political arguments, economic forces contributed to the end of slavery and the slave trade. Plantations, slavery, and the slave trade continued to flourish as long as they were profitable, notwithstanding the efforts of abolitionists. Yet it gradually became clear that slave labor did not come cheap. The possibility of rebellion forced slave societies to maintain expensive military forces. Even in peaceful times slaves often worked unenthusiastically, but owners had to care for them throughout their lives no matter how hard they worked. Furthermore, in the late eighteenth century a rapid expansion of Caribbean sugar production led to declining prices. About the same time, African slave traders and European merchants sharply increased the prices they charged for fresh slaves.

As the profitability of slavery declined, Europeans began to shift their investments from sugarcane and slaves to newly emerging manufacturing industries. Investors soon found that wage labor in factories was cheaper

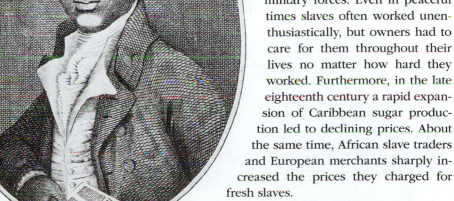

Olaudah Equiano as depicted in the first edition of his autobiography (1789).

than slave labor on plantations. As an additional benefit, free workers spent much of their income on manufactured goods. Meanwhile, European investors realized that leaving Africans in Africa where they could secure raw materials and buy manufactured goods in exchange was good business. Thus European entrepreneurs began to look upon Africa as something other than a source of slave labor.

End of the Slave Trade

In 1803 Denmark abolished the trade in slaves, and other lands followed the Danish example: Great Britain in 1807, the United States in 1808, France in 1814, the Netherlands in 1817, and Spain in 1845. The end of the legal commerce in slaves did not abolish the institution of slavery itself, however, and as long as plantation slavery continued, a clandestine trade shipped slaves across the Atlantic. British naval squadrons sought to prevent this trade by patrolling the west coast of Africa and conducting search and seizure operations, so gradually the illegal slave trade ground to a halt. The last documented ship that carried slaves across the Atlantic arrived in Cuba in 1867.

The Abolition of Slavery

The abolition of the institution of slavery itself was a long and drawn-out process: emancipation of all slaves came in 1833 in British colonies, 1848 in French colonies, 1865 in the United States, 1886 in Cuba, and 1888 in Brazil. Saudi Arabia and Angola abolished slavery in the 1960s. Officially, slavery no longer exists, but millions of people live in various forms of servitude even today. According to the Anti-Slavery Society for the Protection of Human Rights, debt bondage, contract labor, sham adoptions, servile marriages, and other forms of servitude still oppress more than two hundred million people, mostly in Africa, south Asia, and Latin America. Meanwhile, the legacy of the Atlantic slave trade remains visible throughout much of the western hemisphere, where the African diaspora has given rise to distinctive African-American communities.

in**perspective**

During the early modern era, the peoples of sub-Saharan Africa organized societies on the basis of kinship groups as they had since the early days of the Bantu migrations. They also built states and traded with Islamic societies as they had since the eighth century C.E. Yet African peoples also experienced dramatic changes as they participated in the formation of an integrated Atlantic Ocean basin. The principal agents of change were European merchant-mariners who sought commercial opportunities in sub-Saharan Africa. They brought European manufactured goods and introduced American food crops that fueled population growth throughout Africa. But they also encouraged a vast expansion of existing slave-trading networks as they sought laborers for plantations in the western hemisphere. The Atlantic slave trade violently removed sixteen million or more individuals from their home societies, and it led to political turmoil and social disruption throughout much of sub-Saharan Africa. Enslaved Africans and their descendants were mostly unable to build states or organize societies in the western hemisphere. But they formed an African diaspora that maintained some African traditions and profoundly influenced the development of societies in all slave-holding regions of the Caribbean and the Americas. They also collaborated with others to bring about an end to the slave trade and the abolition of slavery itself. ●

CHRONOLOGY	
1441	Beginning of the Portuguese slave trade
1464–1493	Reign of Sunni Ali
1464–1591	Songhay empire
1506–1542	Reign of King Afonso I of Kongo
1623–1663	Reign of Queen Nzinga of Ndongo
1706	Execution of Dona Beatriz
1745–1797	Life of Olaudah Equiano
1793–1804	Haitian revolution
1807	End of the British slave trade
1865	Abolition of slavery in the United States

For Further Reading

Paul Bohannan and Philip D. Curtin. *Africa and Africans.* 3rd ed. Prospect Heights, Ill., 1988. General discussion of African society, religion, and history by an anthropologist and a historian.

Judith A. Carney. *Black Rice: The African Origin of Rice Cultivation in the Americas.* Cambridge, Mass., 2001. Fascinating study demonstrating how African slaves introduced a sophisticated agricultural technology to the low country of Carolina and Georgia.

Michael L. Conniff and Thomas J. Davis. *Africans in the Americas: A History of the Black Diaspora.* New York, 1994. A comprehensive survey of African-European relations, the slave trade, and the African diaspora.

Philip D. Curtin. *The Rise and Fall of the Plantation Complex: Essays in Atlantic History.* 2nd ed. Cambridge, 1998. Examines plantation societies and slavery as institutions linking lands throughout the Atlantic Ocean basin.

————, ed. *Africa Remembered: Narratives by West Africans from the Era of the Slave Trade.* Madison, 1967. Translations of works in which ten enslaved Africans recounted their memories of early modern Africa.

David Brion Davis. *Slavery and Human Progress.* New York, 1984. A rich and thoughtful book that places African slavery in a larger historical context.

Christopher Ehret. *The Civilizations of Africa: A History to 1800.* Charlottesville, Va., 2002. An important contribution that views Africa in the context of world history.

David Eltis. *The Rise of African Slavery in the Americas.* Cambridge, 1999. Emphasizes both the economic and the cultural foundations of Atlantic slavery.

Olaudah Equiano. *Equiano's Travels.* Ed. by Paul Edwards. Oxford, 1967. An abridged and conveniently available edition of Equiano's autobiography.

Leland Ferguson. *Uncommon Ground: Archaeology and Early African America, 1650–1800.* Washington, D.C., 1992. Enriches the understanding of slave society in the southeastern United States on the basis of archaeological discoveries.

Philip Gould. *Barbaric Traffic: Commerce and Antislavery in the Eighteenth-Century Atlantic World.* Cambridge, 2003. Compelling study of Anglo-American antislavery literature that suggests the discourse was less a debate over the morality of slavery than a concern with the commercial aspects of the slave trade.

Joseph E. Harris, ed. *Global Dimensions of the African Diaspora.* 2nd ed. Washington, D.C., 1993. A collection of scholarly essays on Africans in the Americas and the larger world.

Anne Hilton. *The Kingdom of Kongo.* Oxford, 1985. A valuable synthesis.

Patrick Manning. *Slavery and African Life: Occidental, Oriental, and African Slave Trades.* Cambridge, 1990. Concentrates on the impact of the slave trade on Africa.

Sidney W. Mintz. *Sweetness and Power: The Place of Sugar in Modern History.* New York, 1985. Important study of sugar, slavery, politics, and society by a prominent anthropologist.

———— and Richard Price. *The Birth of African-American Culture: An Anthropological Perspective.* Boston, 1992. A provocative study analyzing the forging of African-American cultural traditions under the influence of slavery.

Richard Price. *First-Time: The Historical Vision of an Afro-American People.* Baltimore, 1983. Fascinating reconstruction of the experiences and historical self-understanding of the Saramaka maroons of modern Suriname.

Elias N. Saad. *Social History of Timbuktu: The Role of Muslim Scholars and Notables, 1400–1900.* Cambridge, 1983. Emphasizes the role of Muslim scholars in one of west Africa's most important commercial and cultural centers.

Mechal Sobel. *The World They Made Together: Black and White Values in Eighteenth Century Virginia.* Princeton, 1987. Argues persuasively that African-American slaves deeply influenced the development of early American society.

James H. Sweet. *Recreating Africa: Culture, Kinship, and Religion in the African-Portuguese World, 1441–1770.* Chapel Hill, 2006. Engaging study of African slave culture in Portuguese Brazil and the process of creolization.

Robert Farris Thompson. *Flash of the Spirit: African and African-American Art and Philosophy.* New York, 1983. Fascinating study that documents and analyzes the maintenance and adaptation of African cultural traditions in the Americas.

John Thornton. *Africa and Africans in the Making of the Atlantic World, 1400–1800.* 2nd ed. New York, 1997. A rich analysis of African peoples and their roles in the Atlantic Ocean basin.

————. *The Kongolese Saint Anthony: Dona Beatriz Kimpa Vita and the Antonian Movement, 1684–1706.* Cambridge, 1998. Excellent scholarly study of Dona Beatriz and the Antonian movement in the kingdom of Kongo.

Dale W. Tomich. *Through the Prism of Slavery: Labor, Capital, and World Economy.* Lanham, Md., 2004. Brief overview of slavery's role in the development of global capitalism.

Jan Vansina. *Kingdoms of the Savanna.* Madison, 1966. The best history of central Africa in early modern times.

————. *Paths in the Rainforest: Toward a History of Political Tradition in Equatorial Africa.* Madison, 1990. A thoughtful analysis that considers both native traditions and external influences on African history.

Tradition and Change in East Asia

chapter26

European-style buildings on the waterfront in eighteenth-century Guangzhou, where foreign merchants conducted their business.

PART 5

EYEWITNESS:
Matteo Ricci and Chiming Clocks in China

In January 1601 a mechanical clock chimed the hours for the first time in the city of Beijing. In the early 1580s, devices that Chinese called "self-ringing bells" had arrived at the port of Macau, where Portuguese merchants awed local authorities with their chiming clocks. Reports of them soon spread throughout southern China and beyond to Beijing. The Roman Catholic missionary Matteo Ricci conceived the idea of capturing the emperor's attention with mechanical clocks and then persuading him and his subjects to convert to Christianity. From his post at Macau, Ricci let imperial authorities know that he could supply the emperor with a chiming clock. When the emperor Wanli granted him permission to travel to Beijing and establish a mission, Ricci took with him both a large mechanical clock intended for public display and a smaller, self-ringing bell for the emperor's personal use.

Chiming mechanical clocks enchanted Wanli and his court and soon became the rage in elite society throughout China. Wealthy Chinese merchants did not hesitate to pay handsome sums for the devices, and Europeans often found that their business in China went better if they presented gifts of self-ringing bells to the government officials they dealt with. By the eighteenth century the imperial court maintained a workshop to manufacture and repair mechanical clocks and watches. Most Chinese could not afford to purchase mechanical clocks, but commoners also had opportunities to admire self-ringing bells. Outside their residence in Beijing, Matteo Ricci and his missionary colleagues installed a large mechanical clock that regularly attracted crowds of curious neighbors when it struck the hours.

Chiming clocks did not have the effect that Ricci desired. The emperor showed no interest in Christianity, and the missionaries attracted only small numbers of Chinese converts. Yet, by opening the doors of the imperial court to the missionaries, the self-ringing bells symbolized the increasing engagement between Asian and European peoples.

By linking all the world's regions and peoples, the European voyages of exploration inaugurated a new era in world history. Yet transoceanic connections influenced different societies in very different ways. In contrast to sub-Saharan Africa, where the Atlantic slave trade bred instability and provoked turmoil, east Asian lands benefited greatly from long-distance trade, since it brought silver that stimulated their economies. East Asian societies benefited also from American plant crops that made their way across the seas as part of the Columbian exchange.

Unlike the Americas, where Europeans profoundly influenced historical development from the time of their arrival, east Asian societies largely controlled their own affairs until the nineteenth century. Europeans were active on the coastlines, but they had little influence on internal affairs in the region. Because of its political and cultural preeminence, China remained the dominant power in east Asia. Established during the Qin (221–206 B.C.E.) and Han (206 B.C.E.–220 C.E.) dynasties, long-standing political, social, and cultural traditions endowed Chinese society with a sense of stability and permanence. China was also a remarkably prosperous land. Indeed, with its huge population, enormous productive capacity, and strong demand for silver, China was a leading economic powerhouse driving world trade in early modern times. By the late eighteenth century, however, China was experiencing social and economic change that eventually caused problems both for state authorities and for Chinese society as a whole.

During the seventeenth and eighteenth centuries, Japan also underwent major transformations. The Tokugawa shoguns unified the Japanese islands for the first time and laid a foundation for long-term economic growth. While tightly restricting contacts and relations with the larger world, Tokugawa Japan generated a distinctive set of social and cultural traditions. Those developments helped fashion a Japan that would play a decisive role in global affairs by the twentieth century.

THE QUEST FOR POLITICAL STABILITY

During the thirteenth and fourteenth centuries, China experienced the trauma of rule by the Yuan dynasty (1279–1368) of nomadic Mongol warriors. Mongol overlords ignored Chinese political and cultural traditions, and they displaced Chinese bureaucrats in favor of Turkish, Persian, and other foreign administrators. When the Yuan dynasty came to an end, the Ming emperors who succeeded it sought to erase all signs of Mongol influence and restore traditional ways to China. Looking to the Tang and Song dynasties for inspiration, they built a powerful imperial state, revived the civil service staffed by Confucian scholars, and promoted Confucian thought. Rulers of the succeeding Qing dynasty were themselves Manchus of nomadic origin, but they too worked zealously to promote Chinese ways. Ming and Qing emperors alike were deeply conservative: their principal concern was to maintain stability in a large agrarian society, so they adopted policies that favored Chinese political and cultural traditions. The state that they fashioned governed China for more than half a millennium.

The Ming Dynasty

Ming Government When the Yuan dynasty collapsed, the Ming dynasty (1368–1644) restored native rule to China. Hongwu (reigned 1368–1398), founder of the Ming ("brilliant") dynasty, drove the Mongols out of China and built a tightly centralized state. As emperor, Hongwu made extensive use of mandarins, imperial officials who traveled throughout the land and oversaw implementation of government policies. He also placed great trust in eunuchs on the thinking that they could not generate families and hence would not build power bases that would challenge imperial

authority. The emperor Yongle (reigned 1403–1424) launched a series of naval expeditions that sailed throughout the Indian Ocean basin and showed Chinese colors as far away as Malindi in east Africa. Yongle's successors discontinued the expensive maritime expeditions but maintained the tightly centralized state that Hongwu had established.

The Ming emperors were determined to prevent new invasions. In 1421 Yongle moved the capital from Nanjing in the south to Beijing so as to keep closer watch on the Mongols and other nomadic peoples in the north. The early Ming emperors commanded powerful armies that controlled the Mongols militarily, but by the mid-fifteenth century they had lost their effectiveness. Mongol forces massacred several Chinese armies in the 1440s, and in 1449 they captured the Ming emperor himself.

The Great Wall The later Ming emperors sought to protect their realm by building new fortifications, including the Great Wall of China, along the northern border. The Great Wall had precedents dating back to the fourth century B.C.E., and the first emperor of the Qin dynasty had ordered construction of a long defensive wall during the third century B.C.E. Those early walls had all fallen into ruin, however, and the Great Wall was a Ming-dynasty project. Workers by the hundreds of thousands labored throughout the late fifteenth and sixteenth centuries to build a formidable stone and brick barrier that ran some 2,500 kilometers (1,550 miles). The Great Wall was 10 to 15 meters (33 to 49 feet) high, and it featured watch towers, signal towers, and accommodations for troops deployed on the border.

The Ming emperors also set out to eradicate Mongol and other foreign influences and to create a stable society in the image of the Chinese past. With Ming encouragement,

MAP 26.1

Ming China, 1368–1644.

Locate the old Ming capital at Nanjing and the new Ming capital at Beijing.

Why would the Ming emperors have wanted to move so far north?

for example, individuals abandoned the Mongol names and dress that many had adopted during the Yuan dynasty. Respect for Chinese traditions facilitated the restoration of institutions that the Mongols had ignored or suppressed. The government sponsored study of Chinese cultural traditions, especially Confucianism, and provided financial support for imperial academies and regional colleges. Most important, the Ming state restored the system of civil service examinations that Mongol rulers had neglected.

Ming Decline The vigor of early Ming rule did not survive beyond the mid-sixteenth century, when a series of problems weakened the dynasty. From the 1520s to the 1560s, pirates and smugglers operated almost at will along the east coast of China. (Although Ming officials referred to the pirates as Japanese, in fact most of them were Chinese.) Both the Ming navy and coastal defenses were ineffective, and conflicts with pirates often led to the disruption of coastal communities and sometimes even interior regions. In 1555, for example, a band of sixty-seven pirates went on a three-month rampage during which they looted a dozen cities in three provinces and killed more than four thousand people.

Suppression of pirates took more than forty years, partly because of an increasingly inept imperial government. The later Ming emperors lived extravagantly in the Forbidden City, a vast imperial enclave in Beijing, and received news about the outside world from eunuch servants and administrators. The emperors sometimes ignored government affairs for decades on end while satisfying their various appetites. Throughout his long reign, for example, the emperor Wanli (1572–1620) refused to meet with government officials. Instead, while indulging his taste for wine, he conducted business through eunuch intermediaries. Powerful eunuchs won the favor of the later Ming emperors by procuring concubines for them and providing for their amusement. The eunuchs then used their power and position to enrich themselves and lead lives of luxury. As their influence increased, corruption and inefficiency spread throughout the government and weakened the Ming state.

Ming Collapse When a series of famines struck China during the early seventeenth century, the government was unable to organize effective relief efforts. Peasants in famine-struck regions ate grass roots and tree bark. During the 1630s peasants organized revolts throughout China, and they

The emperor Yongle designed the Forbidden City as a vast, walled imperial retreat in central Beijing. Here a sculptured lion guards the Forbidden City's Gate of Supreme Harmony.

gathered momentum as one city after another withdrew its loyalty from the Ming dynasty. To complicate matters further, Manchu forces invaded from the north in search of opportunities for expansion in China. In 1644, rebel forces captured the Ming capital at Beijing. Manchu invaders allied with an army loyal to the Ming, crushed the rebels, and recovered Beijing. The Manchus portrayed themselves as avengers who saved the capital from dangerous rebels, but they neglected to restore Ming rule. Instead, they moved their own capital to Beijing and simply displaced the Ming dynasty.

The Qing Dynasty

The Manchus When the Ming dynasty fell, Manchus poured into China from their homeland of Manchuria north of the Great Wall. The victors proclaimed a new dynasty, the Qing ("pure"), which ruled China until the early twentieth century (1644–1911).

The Manchus mostly were pastoral nomads, although many had turned to agriculture and settled in the rich farmlands of southern Manchuria. Their remote ancestors had traded with China since the Qin dynasty, and they had frequently clashed with their neighbors over land and resources in northern China and southern Manchuria. During the late sixteenth and early seventeenth centuries, an ambitious chieftain named Nurhaci (reigned 1616–1626) unified Manchu tribes into a centralized state, promulgated a code of laws, and organized a powerful military force. During the 1620s and 1630s, the Manchu army expelled Ming garrisons in Manchuria, captured Korea and Mongolia, and launched small-scale invasions into China. After their seizure of Beijing in 1644, the Manchus moved to extend their authority throughout China. For almost forty years they waged campaigns against Ming loyalists and other rebels in southern China until by the early 1680s the Manchus had consolidated the Qing dynasty's hold throughout the land.

The establishment of the Qing dynasty was due partly to Manchu military prowess and partly to Chinese support for the Manchus. During the 1630s and 1640s, many Chinese generals deserted the Ming dynasty because of its corruption and inefficiency. Confucian scholar-bureaucrats also worked against the Ming, since they despised the eunuchs who dominated the imperial court. The Manchu ruling elites were schooled in Chinese language and Confucian thought, and they often enjoyed more respect from the scholar-bureaucrats than did the emperor and high administrators of the Ming dynasty itself.

The Manchus were careful to preserve their own ethnic and cultural identity. They not only outlawed intermarriage

MAP 26.2

The Qing empire, 1644–1911.

Compare this map with Map 26.1.

Why would the Qing emperors have wanted to incorporate such extensive territories in Mongolia and Tibet into their empire?

between Manchus and Chinese but also forbade Chinese from traveling to Manchuria and from learning the Manchurian language. Qing authorities also forced Chinese men to shave the front of their heads and grow a Manchu-style queue as a sign of submission to the dynasty.

Kangxi and His Reign Until the nineteenth century, strong imperial leadership muted tensions between Manchu rulers and Chinese subjects. The long reigns of two particularly effective emperors, Kangxi (1661–1722) and Qianlong (1736–1795), helped the Manchus consolidate their hold on China. Kangxi was a Confucian scholar as well as an enlightened ruler. He was a voracious reader and occasionally composed poems. He studied the Confucian classics and sought to apply their teachings through his policies. Thus, for example, he organized flood-control and irrigation projects in observance of the Confucian precept that rulers should look after the welfare of their subjects and promote agricul-

ture. He also generously patronized Confucian schools and academies.

Kangxi was also a conqueror, and he oversaw the construction of a vast Qing empire. He conquered the island of Taiwan, where Ming loyalists had retreated after their expulsion from southern China, and absorbed it into his empire. Like his predecessors of the Han and Tang dynasties, Kangxi sought to forestall problems with nomadic peoples by projecting Chinese influence into central Asia. His conquests in Mongolia and central Asia extended almost to the Caspian Sea, and he imposed a Chinese protectorate over Tibet. Kangxi's grandson Qianlong continued this expansion of Chinese influence. Qianlong sought to consolidate Kangxi's conquests in central Asia by maintaining military garrisons in eastern Turkestan (the territory now known as Xinjiang province in western China) and encouraging merchants to settle there in hopes that they would stabilize the region. Qianlong also made Vietnam, Burma, and Nepal vassal states of the Qing dynasty.

Qianlong and His Reign Qianlong's reign marked the height of the Qing dynasty. Like Kangxi, Qianlong was a sophisticated and learned man. He reportedly composed more than one hundred thousand poems, and he was a discriminating connoisseur of painting and calligraphy. During his long, stable, and prosperous reign, the imperial treasury bulged so much that on four occasions Qianlong cancelled tax collections. Toward the end of his reign, Qianlong paid less attention to imperial affairs and delegated many responsibilities to his favorite eunuchs. His successors continued that practice, devoting themselves to hunting and the harem, and by the nineteenth century the Qing dynasty faced serious difficulties. Throughout the reign of Qianlong, however, China remained a wealthy and well-organized land.

The Son of Heaven and the Scholar-Bureaucrats

Although Qing rulers usually appointed Manchus to the highest political posts, they relied on the same governmental apparatus that the Ming emperors had established. Both the Ming and the Qing dynasties presided over a tightly centralized state, which they administered through a bureaucracy staffed by Confucian scholars. For more than five hundred years, the autocratic state created by the Ming emperor Hongwu governed China's fortunes.

The Son of Heaven   If the emperor of China during the Ming and Qing dynasties was not quite a god, he certainly was more than a mere mortal. Chinese tradition held that he was the "Son of Heaven," the human being designated by heavenly powers to maintain order on the earth. He led a privileged life within the walls of the Forbidden City. Hundreds of concubines resided in his harem, and thousands of eunuchs looked after his desires. His daily activities were carefully choreographed performances in the form of inspections, audiences, banquets, and other official duties. Everything about his person and the institution he represented conveyed a sense of awesome authority. The imperial wardrobe and personal effects bore designs forbidden to all others, for instance, and the written characters of the emperor's name were taboo throughout the realm. Individuals who had the rare privilege of a personal audience with the emperor had to perform the kowtow—three kneelings and nine head knockings. Those who gave even minor offense faced severe punishment. Even the highest official could have his bare buttocks flogged with bamboo canes, a punishment that sometimes brought victims to the point of death.

Though painted in the nineteenth century, this portrait depicts Kangxi in his imperial regalia as he looked at about age fifty. Kangxi reigned for sixty-one years, making him the longest-ruling emperor in Chinese history.

The Scholar-Bureaucrats   Day-to-day governance of the empire fell to scholar-bureaucrats appointed by the emperor. With few exceptions these officials came from the class of well-educated and highly literate men known as the scholar-gentry. These men had earned academic degrees by passing rigorous civil service examinations, and they dominated China's political and social life.

Preparations for the examinations began at an early age. Sometimes they took place in local schools, which like the civil service examinations were open only to males. Wealthy families often engaged the services of tutors, who made formal education available also to girls. By the time students were eleven or twelve years old, they had memorized several thousand characters that were necessary to deal with the Confucian curriculum, including the *Analects* of Confucius and other standard works. They followed those studies with instruction in calligraphy, poetry, and essay composition. Diligent students also acquainted themselves with a large corpus of commentaries, histories, and literary works in preparing for civil service examinations.

Civil Service Examinations   The examinations consisted of a battery of tests administered at the district, provincial, and metropolitan levels. Stiff official quotas restricted the number of successful candidates in each examination—only three hundred students could pass metropolitan examinations—and students frequently took the examinations several times before earning a degree.

Writing the examinations was a grueling ordeal. At the appointed hour, candidates presented themselves at the examination compound. Each candidate brought a water pitcher, a chamber pot, bedding, food, an inkstone, ink, and brushes. After guards had verified their identities and searched them for hidden printed materials, the new arrivals proceeded along narrow lanes to a honeycomb of small, cell-like rooms barely large enough to accommodate one man and his possessions. Aside from a bench, a makeshift bed, and boards that served as a desk, the rooms were empty. For the next three days and two nights, the cramped rooms were home to the candidates, who spent all their time writing "eight-legged essays"—literary compositions with eight distinct sections—on questions posed by the examiners. There were

Qiu Ying, a prominent Chinese artist of the sixteenth century, captured this image of candidates who had taken the civil service exams as they waited at the wall where officials would post the scores.

no interruptions, nor was there any communication between candidates. If someone died during the examination period, officials wrapped his body in a straw mat and tossed it over the high walls that ringed the compound.

The Examination System and Chinese Society

The possibility of bureaucratic service—with prospects for rich social and financial rewards—ensured that competition for degrees was ferocious at all levels. As a result, cheating candidates and corrupt examiners occasionally compromised the system. Yet a degree did not ensure government service. During the Qing dynasty the empire's one million degree holders competed for twenty thousand official civil service positions. Those who passed only the district exams had few opportunities for bureaucratic employment and usually spent their careers "plowing with the writing brush"

by teaching in local schools or serving as family tutors. Those who passed the metropolitan examinations, however, could look forward to powerful positions in the imperial bureaucracy.

The examination system was a pivotal institution. By opening the door to honor, power, and rewards, the examinations encouraged serious pursuit of a formal education. Furthermore, since the system did not erect social barriers before its recruits, it provided an avenue for upward social mobility. Years of education and travel to examination sites were expensive, so candidates from wealthy families enjoyed advantages over others, but the exams themselves were open to all males regardless of age or social class. Finally, in addition to selecting officials for government service, the education and examination system molded the personal values of those who managed day-to-day affairs in imperial China.

By concentrating on Confucian classics and neo-Confucian commentaries, the examinations guaranteed that Confucianism would be at the heart of Chinese education and that Confucians would govern the state.

ECONOMIC AND SOCIAL CHANGES

By modeling their governmental structure on the centralized imperial states of earlier Chinese dynasties, the Ming and Qing emperors succeeded in their goal of restoring and maintaining traditional ways in China. They also sought to preserve the traditional hierarchical and patriarchal social order. Yet, while the emperors promoted conservative political and social policies, China experienced economic and social changes, partly as a result of influences from abroad. Agricultural production increased dramatically—especially after the introduction of new food crops from the Americas—and fueled rapid population growth. Meanwhile, global trade brought China enormous wealth, which stimulated the domestic economy by encouraging increased trade, manufacturing, and urban growth. These developments deeply influenced Chinese society and partly undermined the stability that the Ming and Qing emperors sought to preserve.

The Patriarchal Family

Filial Piety Moralists portrayed the Chinese people as one large family, and they extended family values to the larger society. Filial piety, for example, implied not only duties of children toward their fathers but also loyalty of subjects toward the emperor. Like the imperial government, the Chinese family was hierarchical, patriarchal, and authoritarian. The father was head of the household, and he passed leadership of the family to his eldest son. The veneration of ancestors, which the state promoted as a matter of Confucian propriety, strengthened the authority of the patriarchs by honoring the male line of descent in formal family rituals. Filial piety was the cornerstone of family values. Children had the duty to look after their parents' happiness and well-being, and a crucial obligation was to support parents in their old age. Young children heard stories of sons who went so far as to cut off parts of their bodies to ensure that their parents had enough to eat!

The social assumptions of the Chinese family extended into patrilineal descent groups such as the clan. Sometimes numbering into the thousands, clan members came from all social classes, though members of the gentry usually dominated a given clan. Clans assumed responsibilities that exceeded the capacities of the nuclear family, such as the maintenance of local order, organization of local economies, and provision for welfare. Clan-supported education gave poor but promising relatives the opportunity to succeed in the civil service examinations. The principal motives behind this charity were corporate self-interest as well as altruism. A government position brought prestige and prosperity to the entire clan, so educational support was a prudent investment. Finally, clans served as a means for the transmission of Confucian values from the gentry leaders to all social classes within the clan.

Gender Relations Within the family, Confucian principles subjected women to the authority of men. The subordination of females began at an early age. Chinese parents preferred boys over girls. Whereas a boy might have the opportunity to take the official examinations, become a government official, and thereby bring honor and financial reward to the entire clan, parents regarded a girl as a social and financial liability. After years of expensive upbringing, most girls would marry and become members of other households. Under those circumstances it was not surprising that life was precarious for newborn girls, who were the primary victims of infanticide.

During the Ming and Qing dynasties, patriarchal authority over females probably became tighter than ever before in China. Since ancient times, relatives had discouraged widows from remarriage, but social pressures increased during the Ming dynasty. Friends and relatives not only encouraged widows to honor the memory of their departed husbands but also heaped posthumous honors on those who committed suicide and followed their spouses to the grave.

Foot Binding Moreover, foot binding, a custom that probably originated in the Song dynasty, became exceptionally popular during the late Ming and Qing dynasties. Tightly constrained and even deformed by strips of linen, bound feet could not grow naturally and so would not support the weight of an adult woman. Bound feet were small and dainty, and they sometimes inspired erotic arousal among men. The practice of foot binding became most widespread among the wealthy classes, since it demonstrated an ability to support women who could not perform physical labor, but commoners sometimes bound the feet of especially pretty girls in hopes of arranging favorable marriages that would enhance the family's social standing.

Marriage itself was a contractual affair whose principal purpose was to continue the male line of descent. A bride

---

thinking about TRADITIONS

Chinese Women
Women had for long centuries lived under the strictures of a Confucian society. How did Confucian ideals in the Ming and Qing dynasties affect attitudes about women? What did the practice of foot binding suggest about gender relations in late imperial China?

To encourage widows to remain unmarried, the Ming and Qing governments constructed arches in honor of those who remained chaste. These arches erected during the Qing dynasty still stand in Anhui province in the Yangzi River valley.

became a member of the husband's family, and there was no ambiguity about her position in the household. On her wedding day, as soon as she arrived at her husband's home, the bride performed ritual acts demonstrating subservience to her husband and her new family. Women could not divorce their husbands, but men could put aside their wives in cases where there was no offspring or where the wife was guilty of adultery, theft, disobedience to her husband's family, or even being too talkative.

Thus custom and law combined to strengthen patriarchal authority in Chinese families during the Ming and Qing dynasties. Yet, while family life continued to develop along traditional lines, the larger Chinese society underwent considerable change between the sixteenth and the eighteenth centuries.

Population Growth and Economic Development

China was a predominantly agricultural society, a fact that meshed agreeably with the Confucian view that land was the source of everything praiseworthy. The emperor himself acknowledged the central importance of agriculture by plowing the first furrow of the season. Yet only a small fraction of China's land is suitable for planting: even today only about 11 percent is in cultivation. To feed the country's large population, China's farmers relied on intensive, garden-style agriculture that was highly productive. On its strong agrarian foundation, China supported a large population and built the most highly commercialized economy of the preindustrial world.

American Food Crops By intensively cultivating every available parcel of land, Chinese peasants increased their yields of traditional food crops—especially rice, wheat, and millet—until the seventeenth century. Beginning about the mid-seventeenth century, as peasants approached the upper limits of agricultural productivity, Spanish merchants coming by way of the Philippines introduced American food crops to China. American maize, sweet potatoes, and peanuts permitted Chinese farmers to take advantage of soils that previously had gone uncultivated. The introduction of new crops increased the food supply and supported further population growth.

Population Growth In spite of recurring epidemic diseases such as plague, which claimed the lives of millions, China's population rose rapidly from 100 million in 1500 to 160 million in 1600. Partly because of rebellion and war, it fell to 140 million in the mid-seventeenth century, but returned to 160 million by 1700 and then surged to 225 million by 1750, thus registering a more than 40 percent increase in half a century. This rapid demographic growth set the stage for economic and social problems, since agricultural production could not keep pace with population over a long term. Acute problems did not occur until the nineteenth century, but per capita income in China began to decline as early as the reign of Qianlong.

While an increasing population placed pressure on Chinese resources, the growing commercial market offered opportunities for entrepreneurs. Because of demographic

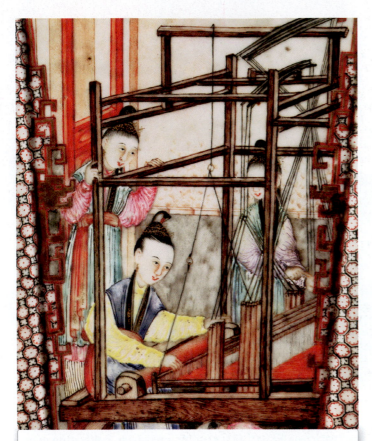

A Ming-era vase painting depicts a woman weaving silk as an attendant pours tea. Silk and tea were among the exports China produced for global trade.

During the early fifteenth century, the Ming emperor Yongle sought to establish a Chinese presence in the Indian Ocean basin, and he sponsored a series of seven massive maritime expeditions (1405–1433) led by the eunuch admiral Zheng He. The Chinese fleets included as many as 317 vessels and 28,000 men. Zheng He called at ports from Java to Malindi, suppressed pirates in southeast Asian waters, intervened in local conflicts in Sumatra and Ceylon, intimidated local authorities with shows of force in southern Arabia and Mogadishu, and made China's presence felt throughout the Indian Ocean basin.

After the reign of Yongle, however, the Ming government withdrew its support for expensive maritime expeditions and even tried to prevent Chinese subjects from dealing with foreign peoples. In its effort to pacify southern China during the later seventeenth century, the Qing government tried to end maritime activity altogether. An imperial edict of 1656 forbade "even a plank from drifting to the sea," and in 1661 the emperor Kangxi ordered evacuation of the southern coastal regions. Those policies had only a limited effect—small Chinese vessels continued to trade actively in Japan and southeast Asian ports—and when Qing forces pacified southern China in the 1680s, government authorities rescinded the strictest measures. Thereafter, however, Qing authorities closely supervised the activities of foreign merchants in China. They permitted Portuguese merchants to operate only at the port of Macau, and British agents had to deal exclusively with the official merchant guild in Guangzhou.

While limiting the activities of foreign merchants, government policies also discouraged the organization of large-scale commercial ventures by Chinese merchants. In the absence of government approval, it was impossible, for example, to maintain shipyards that could construct large sailing ships like the mammoth, nine-masted treasure ships that Zheng He had led throughout the Indian Ocean. Similarly, it was impossible to organize large trading firms like the English East India Company or the Dutch VOC.

Trade and Migration to Southeast Asia

Nevertheless, thousands of Chinese merchants worked either individually or in partnerships, plying the waters of the China seas to link China with global trade networks. Chinese merchants were especially prominent in Manila, where they exchanged silk and porcelain for American silver that came across the Pacific Ocean with the Manila galleons. They were also frequent visitors at the Dutch colonial capital of Batavia, where they supplied the VOC with silk and porcelain in exchange for silver and Indonesian spices. Entrepreneurial Chinese merchants ventured also to lands throughout southeast Asia—the Philippines, Borneo, Sumatra, Malaya, Thailand, and elsewhere—in search of exotic tropical products for Chinese consumers. Indeed, the early modern era was an age when merchants established a prominent Chinese presence throughout southeast Asia.

expansion, entrepreneurs had access to a large labor force that was both occupationally and geographically mobile, so they were able to recruit workers readily at low cost. After the mid-sixteenth century, the Chinese economy benefited also from the influx of Japanese and American silver, which stimulated trade and financed further commercial expansion.

Foreign Trade

Global trade brought prosperity to China, especially during the early Qing dynasty. Chinese workers produced vast quantities of silk, porcelain, lacquerware, and tea for consumers in the Indian Ocean basin, central Asia, and Europe. The silk industry was especially well organized: weavers worked in workshops for regular wages producing fine satins and brocades for export. Chinese imports were relatively few: they included spices from Maluku, exotic products such as birds and animal skins from tropical regions, and small quantities of woolen textiles from Europe. Compensation for exports came most importantly in the form of silver bullion, which supported the silver-based Chinese economy and fueled manufacturing.

Economic growth and commercial expansion took place mostly in an atmosphere of tight government regulation.

sources from the past

Qianlong on Chinese Trade with England

Qing administrators tightly restricted foreign trade. Foreign merchants had to deal with government-approved agents outside the city walls of Guangzhou and had to depart as soon as they had completed their business. In 1793 a British diplomat representing King George III of England bestowed gifts on the emperor Qianlong and petitioned for the right to trade at ports other than Guangzhou. In a letter to King George, Qianlong outlined his views on Chinese trade with England. His letter also bespeaks clearly the importance of government policy for commerce and economic affairs in China.

You, O king, from afar have yearned after the blessings of our civilization, and in your eagerness to come into touch with our influence have sent an embassy across the sea bearing a memorandum. I have already taken note of your respectful spirit of submission, have treated your mission with extreme favor and loaded it with gifts, besides issuing a mandate to you, O king, and honoring you with the bestowal of valuable presents. . . .

Yesterday your ambassador petitioned my ministers to memorialize me regarding your trade with China, but his proposal is not consistent with our dynastic usage and cannot be entertained. Hitherto, all European nations, including your own country's barbarian merchants, have carried on their trade with our Celestial Empire at Guangzhou. Such has been the procedure for many years, although our Celestial Empire possesses all things in prolific abundance and lacks no product within its own borders. There was therefore no need to import the manufactures of outside barbarians in exchange for our own produce. But as the tea, silk, and porcelain which the Celestial Empire produces are absolute necessities to European nations and to yourselves, we have permitted, as a signal mark of favor, that trading agents should be established at Guangzhou, so that your wants might be supplied and your country thus participate in our beneficence. But your ambassador has now put forward new requests which completely fail to recognize our throne's principle to "treat strangers from afar with indulgence," and to exercise a pacifying control over barbarian tribes the world over. . . . Your England is not the only nation trading at Guangzhou. If other nations, following your bad example, wrongfully importune my ear with further impossible requests, how will it be possible for me to treat them with easy indulgence? Nevertheless, I do not forget the lonely remoteness of your island, cut off from the world by intervening wastes of sea, nor do I overlook your excusable ignorance of the usages of our Celestial Empire. I have consequently commanded my ministers to enlighten your ambassador on the subject, and have ordered the departure of the mission. . . .

If, after the receipt of this explicit decree, you lightly give ear to the representations of your subordinates and allow your barbarian merchants to proceed to Zhejiang and Tianjin, with the object of landing and trading there, the ordinances of my Celestial Empire are strict in the extreme, and the local officials, both civil and military, are bound reverently to obey the law of the land. Should your vessels touch the shore, your merchants will assuredly never be permitted to land or to reside there, but will be subject to instant expulsion. In that event your barbarian merchants will have had a long journey for nothing. Do not say that you were not warned in due time! Tremblingly obey and show no negligence! A special mandate!

For Further Reflection

■ What considerations might have prompted the Chinese government to take such a restrictive approach to foreign trade?

Source: J. O. P. Bland. *Annals and Memoirs of the Court of Peking.* Boston: Houghton Mifflin, 1914, pp. 325–31. (Translation slightly modified.)

Government and Technology China's economic expansion took place largely in the absence of technological innovation. During the Tang and Song dynasties, Chinese engineers had produced a veritable flood of inventions, and China was the world's leader in technology. Yet by early Ming times, technological innovation had slowed. Imperial armed forces adopted European cannons and advanced firearms for their own uses—thus borrowing forms of gunpowder technology that had originated in China and that Europeans had refined and improved—but little innovation in agricultural and industrial technologies occurred during the Ming and Qing dynasties.

Part of the explanation for the slowdown has to do with the role of the government. During the Tang and Song dynasties, the imperial government had encouraged technological innovation as a foundation of military and economic strength. In contrast, the Ming and Qing regimes favored political and social stability over technological innovation, which they feared would lead to unsettling change. Alongside government policy, the abundance and ready availability of skilled workers also discouraged technological innovation. When employers wanted to increase production, they found that hiring additional workers was less costly than making large investments in new technologies. In the short term this tactic maintained relative prosperity in China while keeping most of the population gainfully employed. Over the longer term, however, it ensured that China lost technological ground to European peoples, who embarked on a round of stunning technological innovation beginning about the mid-eighteenth century.

Gentry, Commoners, Soldiers, and Mean People

Privileged Classes Except for the emperor and his family, scholar-bureaucrats and gentry occupied the most exalted positions in Chinese society. Because of their official positions, the scholar-bureaucrats ranked slightly above gentry. Nevertheless, scholar-bureaucrats had much in common with the gentry: they came largely from gentry ranks, and after leaving government service they usually rejoined gentry society. The scholar-bureaucrats and gentry functioned as intermediaries between the imperial government and local society. By organizing water control projects and public security measures, they played a crucial role in the management of local society.

Scholar-bureaucrats and gentry were easy to identify. They wore distinctive clothing—black gowns with blue borders adorned with various rank insignia—and commoners addressed them with honorific terms. They received favorable legal treatment that reflected their privileged status. As a rule, commoners could not call members of privileged classes to appear as witnesses in legal proceedings. They also enjoyed immunity from corporal punishment and exemption from labor service and taxes.

Most of the gentry owned land, which was their major source of income. As long as they did not have to perform physical labor, some gentry also supplemented their income by operating pawn and rice shops. Many of them were also silent business partners of merchants and entrepreneurs. Their principal source of income, however, came from the government service to which only they had access by virtue of their

This late-eighteenth-century drawing depicts Chinese men treading the pole of a device that raises irrigation water. The men all wear the braided queue that Manchus required of Chinese men.

academic degrees. In contrast to landed elites elsewhere, who often lived on rural estates, China's gentry resided largely in cities and towns, where they tended to political, social, and financial affairs.

Working Classes Confucian tradition ranked three broad classes of commoners below the gentry: peasants, artisans or workers, and merchants. By far the biggest class consisted of peasants, a designation that covered everyone from day laborers to tenant farmers to petty landlords. Confucian principles regarded peasants as the most honorable of the three classes, since they performed honest labor and provided the food that supported the entire population.

The category of artisans and workers encompassed a wide spectrum of occupations. Despite their lower status, crafts workers, tailors, barbers, physicians, and workers in manufacturing plants generally enjoyed higher income than peasants did. Artisans and workers were usually employees of the state or of gentry and merchant families, but they also pursued their occupations as self-employed persons.

Merchants Merchants, from street peddlers to individuals of enormous wealth and influence, ranked at the bottom level of the Confucian social hierarchy. Because moralists looked upon them as unscrupulous social parasites, merchants enjoyed little legal protection, and government policy was always critically important to their pursuits. Yet Chinese merchants often garnered official support for their enterprises, either through bribery of government bureaucrats or through profit-sharing arrangements with gentry families. Indeed, the participation of gentry families in commercial ventures such as warehousing, money lending, and pawnbroking blurred the distinction between gentry and merchants. Merchants blurred the distinction further by providing their sons with an education that prepared them for government examinations, which in turn could result in promotion to gentry status and appointment to civil service positions.

The prominence of artisans and merchants pointed up the social and economic development of China since the time of Confucius. Although China was still a basically agri-

The elegant clothing of this Chinese merchant suggests the wealth and power of merchants in late imperial China.

Lower Classes Beyond the Confucian social hierarchy were members of the military forces and the so-called mean people. Confucian moralists regarded armed forces as a wretched but necessary evil and attempted to avoid military dominance of society by placing civilian bureaucrats in the highest command positions, even at the expense of military effectiveness. The mean people included slaves, indentured servants, entertainers, prostitutes, and other marginal groups such as the "beggars of Jiangsu" and the "boat people of Guangdong."

THE CONFUCIAN TRADITION AND NEW CULTURAL INFLUENCES

The Ming and Qing emperors looked to Chinese traditions for guidance in framing their cultural as well as their political and social policies. They provided generous support for Confucianism, particularly in the form of neo-Confucianism articulated by the twelfth-century scholar Zhu Xi, and they ensured that formal education in China revolved around Confucian thought and values. Yet the Confucian tradition was not the only cultural alternative in Ming and Qing China. Demographic and urban growth encouraged the emergence of a vibrant popular culture in Chinese cities, and European missionaries reintroduced Roman Catholic Christianity to China and acquainted Chinese intellectuals with European science and technology as well.

Neo-Confucianism and Pulp Fiction

Imperial sponsorship of Chinese cultural traditions meant primarily support for the Confucian tradition, especially as systematized by the Song dynasty scholar Zhu Xi, the most prominent architect of neo-Confucianism. Zhu Xi combined the moral, ethical, and political values of Confucius with the logical rigor and speculative power of Buddhist philosophy. He emphasized the values of self-discipline, filial piety, and obedience to established rulers, all of which appealed to Ming and Qing emperors seeking to maintain stability in their vast realm. Cultural policies of the Ming and Qing dynasties made the neo-Confucian tradition the reigning imperial ideology from the fourteenth to the early twentieth century.

Confucian Education To promote Confucian values, the Ming and Qing emperors supported educational programs at several levels. They funded the Hanlin Academy, a research institute for Confucian scholars in Beijing, and maintained provincial schools throughout China where promising students could study for the civil service examinations. The exams themselves encouraged the cultivation of Confucian values, since they focused largely on Confucian texts and neo-Confucian commentaries.

Ming and Qing courts also provided generous funding for other projects emphasizing Chinese cultural traditions. The Ming emperor Yongle sponsored the compilation

cultural land, manufacturing and commerce had become much more economically important than in ancient times. As a result, those who could recognize and exploit opportunities had the potential to lead comfortable lives and even to climb into the ranks of the privileged gentry class. Yet Chinese merchants and artisans did not forge cooperative relationships with government authorities like the political-commercial alliances formed in the English and Dutch states in early modern times. Late Ming and Qing authorities permitted Chinese merchants to engage in small-scale commerce, and they allowed foreigners to trade through the official merchant guild in Guangzhou. Their principal concern, however, was to preserve the stability of a large agrarian society, not to promote rapid economic development through trade. Thus, unlike some of their European counterparts, Chinese authorities did not adopt policies designed to strengthen both merchants and the state by authorizing merchants to pursue their efforts aggressively in the larger world.

of the *Yongle Encyclopedia*, a vast collection of Chinese philosophical, literary, and historical texts that filled almost twenty-three thousand scrolls. During the Qing dynasty both Kangxi and Qianlong organized similar projects. Kangxi's *Collection of Books* was smaller than the *Yongle Encyclopedia*, but it was more influential because the emperor had it printed and distributed, whereas Yongle's compilation was available only in three manuscript copies. Qianlong's *Complete Library of the Four Treasuries* was too large to publish—it ran to 93,556 pamphlet-size volumes—but the emperor deposited manuscript copies in seven libraries throughout China.

Popular Culture While the imperial courts promoted Confucianism, a lively popular culture took shape in the cities of China. Most urban residents did not have an advanced education and knew little about Confucius, Zhu Xi, or other intellectual luminaries. Many of them were literate merchants, however, and they preferred entertainment and diversion more intellectually engaging than that found in local teahouses and wine shops. Popular novels met their needs.

Popular Novels Confucian scholars looked down on popular novels as crude fiction that had little to do with the realities of the world. Printing made it possible to produce books cheaply and in mass quantities, however, and urban residents eagerly consumed the fast-paced novels that flooded Chinese cities during the Ming and Qing eras. Many of the novels had little literary merit, but their tales of conflict, horror, wonder, excitement, and sometimes unconcealed pornography appealed to readers.

Yet many popular novels also offered thoughtful reflections on the world and human affairs. The historical novel *The Romance of the Three Kingdoms,* for example, explored the political intrigue that followed the collapse of the Han dynasty. *The Dream of the Red Chamber* told the story of cousins deeply in love who could not marry because of their families' wishes. Through the prism of a sentimental love story, the novel shed fascinating light on the dynamics of wealthy scholar-gentry families. In a different vein, *Journey to the West* dealt with the seventh-century journey to India of the famous Buddhist monk Xuanzang. In the popular novel, Xuanzang's traveling companion was a monkey with magical powers who among other things could jump 10,000 kilometers (6,215 miles) in

Italian Jesuit Matteo Ricci (left) with Xu Quangqi, his most famous Chinese disciple. Both men wear the distinctive gowns of educated, refined scholar-gentry. A distinguished scholar who held an appointment at the Hanlin Academy, Xu helped Ricci translate Euclid's geometrical works into Chinese.

a single bound. While promoting Buddhist values, *Journey to the West* also made the trickster monkey a wildly popular and celebrated character in Chinese literature. As recently as 1987, Chinese-American novelist Maxine Hong Kingston adapted this character to modern times in her novel *Tripmaster Monkey.*

The Return of Christianity to China

Nestorian Christians had established churches and monasteries in China as early as the seventh century C.E., and Roman Catholic communities were prominent in Chinese commercial centers during the Yuan dynasty. After the outbreak of epidemic plague and the collapse of the Yuan dynasty in the fourteenth century, however, Christianity disappeared from China. When Roman Catholic missionaries returned in the sixteenth century, they had to start from scratch in their efforts to win converts and establish a Christian community.

Matteo Ricci The most prominent of the missionaries were the Jesuits, who worked to strengthen Roman Catholic Christianity in Europe and also to spread their faith abroad. Founder of the mission to China was the Italian Jesuit Matteo Ricci (1552–1610), who had the ambitious goal of converting China to Christianity, beginning with the Ming emperor Wanli. Ricci was a brilliant and learned man as well as a polished diplomat, and he became a popular figure at the Ming court. Upon arrival at Macau in 1582, Ricci immersed himself in the study of the Chinese language and the Confucian classics. He had a talent for languages, and his phenomenal memory enabled him to master the thousands of characters used in literary Chinese writing. By the time he first traveled to Beijing and visited the imperial court in 1601, Ricci was able to write learned Chinese and converse fluently with Confucian scholars.

Ricci's mastery of Chinese language and literature opened doors for the Jesuits, who then dazzled their hosts with European science, technology, and mechanical gadgetry. Ricci and his colleagues had an advanced education in mathematics and astronomy, and they were able to correct Chinese calendars that consistently miscalculated solar eclipses. The Jesuits also prepared maps of the world—with China placed diplomatically at the center—on the basis of geographic knowledge that Europeans had gained during their voyages through the world's seas. The Jesuits even supervised the casting of high-quality bronze cannons for Ming and early Qing armies.

Confucianism and Christianity The Jesuits piqued Chinese curiosity also with mechanical devices. Finely ground glass prisms became popular because of their refraction of sunlight into its component parts. Harpsichords also drew attention, and Jesuits with musical talents often composed songs for their hosts. Most popular of all, however, were the devices that Chinese called "self-ringing bells"—spring-driven mechanical clocks that kept tolerably accurate time, chimed the hours, and sometimes even struck the quarter hours as well.

The Jesuits sought to capture Chinese interest with European science and technology, but their ultimate goal was always to win converts. They portrayed Christianity as a faith very similar to Chinese cultural traditions. Ricci, for example, wrote a treatise entitled *The True Meaning of the Lord of Heaven* in which he argued that the doctrines of Confucius and Jesus were very similar, if not identical. Over the years, according to Ricci, neo-Confucian scholars had altered Confucius's own teachings, so adoption of Christianity by Chinese would represent a return to a more pure and original Confucianism. The Jesuits also held religious services in the Chinese language and allowed converts to continue the time-honored practice of venerating their ancestors.

In spite of their tolerance, flexibility, and genuine respect for their hosts, the Jesuits attracted few converts in China. By the mid-eighteenth century, Chinese Christians numbered about 200,000—a tiny proportion of the Chinese population of 225 million. Chinese hesitated to adopt Christianity partly because of its exclusivity: for centuries, Chinese had honored Confucianism, Daoism, and Buddhism at the same time. Like Islam, though, Christianity claimed to be the only true religion, so conversion implied that Confucianism, Daoism, and Buddhism were inferior or even fallacious creeds—a proposition most Chinese were unwilling to accept.

End of the Jesuit Mission Ultimately, the Roman Catholic mission in China came to an end because of squabbles between the Jesuits and members of the Franciscan and Dominican orders, who also sought converts in China. Jealous of the Jesuits' presence at the imperial court, the Franciscans and Dominicans complained to the pope about their rivals' tolerance of ancestor veneration and willingness to conduct Chinese-language services. The pope sided with the critics and in the early eighteenth century issued several proclamations ordering missionaries in China to suppress ancestor veneration and conduct services according to European standards. In response to that demand, the emperor Kangxi ordered an end to the preaching of Christianity in China. Although he did not strictly enforce the ban, the mission weakened, and by the mid-eighteenth century it had effectively come to an end.

The Roman Catholic mission to China did not attract large numbers of Chinese converts, but it nonetheless had important cultural effects. Besides making European science and technology known in China, the Jesuits made China known in Europe. In letters, reports, and other writings distributed widely throughout Europe, the Jesuits described China as an orderly and rational society. The Confucian civil service system attracted the attention of European rulers, who began to design their own civil service bureaucracies in the eighteenth century. The rational morality of Confucianism also appealed to the Enlightenment philosophes, who sought alternatives to Christianity as the foundation for ethics and morality. For the first time since Marco Polo, the Jesuits made firsthand observations of China available to Europeans and stimulated strong European interest in east Asian societies.

THE UNIFICATION OF JAPAN

During the late sixteenth and early seventeenth centuries, the political unification of Japan ended an extended period of civil disorder. Like the Ming and Qing emperors in China, the **Tokugawa** shoguns sought to lay a foundation for long-term political and social stability, and they provided generous support for neo-Confucian studies in an effort to promote traditional values. Indeed, the shoguns went even further than their Chinese counterparts by promoting conservative values and tightly restricting foreign influence in Japan. As in China, however, demographic expansion and economic growth fostered social and cultural change in Japan, and merchants introduced Chinese and European influences into Japan.

The Tokugawa Shogunate

From the twelfth through the sixteenth century, a *shogun* ("military governor") ruled Japan through retainers who received political rights and large estates in exchange for military services. Theoretically, the shogun ruled as a temporary stand-in for the Japanese emperor, the ultimate source of political authority. In fact, however, the emperor was nothing more than a figurehead, and the shogun sought to monopolize power. After the fourteenth century the conflicting ambitions of shoguns and retainers led to constant turmoil, and by the sixteenth century Japan was in a state of civil war. Japanese historians often refer to the sixteenth century as the era of *sengoku*—"the country at war."

Tokugawa Ieyasu Toward the end of the sixteenth century, powerful states emerged in several regions of Japan, and a series of military leaders brought about the unification of the land. In 1600 the last of these chieftains, Tokugawa Ieyasu (reigned 1600–1616), established a military government known as the Tokugawa *bakufu* ("tent government,"

Tokugawa (TOH-koo-GAH-wah)

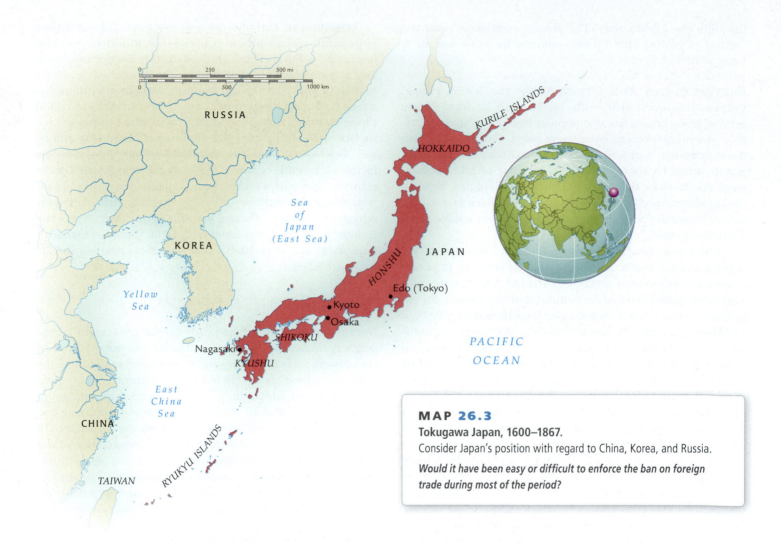

MAP 26.3
Tokugawa Japan, 1600–1867.
Consider Japan's position with regard to China, Korea, and Russia.

Would it have been easy or difficult to enforce the ban on foreign trade during most of the period?

since it theoretically was only a temporary replacement for the emperor's rule). Ieyasu and his descendants ruled the *bakufu* as shoguns from 1600 until the end of the Tokugawa dynasty in 1867.

The principal aim of the Tokugawa shoguns was to stabilize their realm and prevent the return of civil war. Consequently, the shoguns needed to control the **daimyo** ("great names"), powerful territorial lords who ruled most of Japan from their vast, hereditary landholdings. The 260 or so daimyo functioned as near-absolute rulers within their domains. Each maintained a government staffed by military subordinates, supported an independent judiciary, established schools, and circulated paper money. Moreover, after the mid-sixteenth century, many daimyo established relationships with European mariners, from whom they learned how to manufacture and use gunpowder weapons. During the last decades of the *sengoku* era, cannons and personal firearms had played prominent roles in Japanese conflicts.

daimyo (DEYEM-yoh)

Control of the Daimyo From the castle town of Edo (modern Tokyo), the shogun governed his personal domain and sought to extend his control to the daimyo. The shoguns instituted the policy of "alternate attendance," which required daimyo to maintain their families at Edo and spend every other year at the Tokugawa court. This policy enabled the shoguns to keep an eye on the daimyo, and as a side effect it encouraged daimyo to spend their money on lavish residences and comfortable lives in Edo rather than investing it in military forces that could challenge the *bakufu*. The shoguns also subjected marriage alliances between daimyo families to *bakufu* approval, discouraged the daimyo from visiting one another, and required daimyo to obtain permits for construction work on their castles. Even meetings between the daimyo and the emperor required the shogun's permission.

In an effort to prevent European influences from destabilizing the land, the Tokugawa shoguns closely controlled relations between Japan and the outside world. They knew that Spanish forces had conquered the Philippine Islands in the sixteenth century, and they feared that Europeans might jeopardize the security of the *bakufu* itself. Even if Europeans did not conquer Japan, they could cause serious problems by making alliances with daimyo and supplying them with weapons.

Control of Foreign Relations Thus during the 1630s the shoguns issued a series of edicts sharply restricting Japanese relations with other lands that remained in effect for more than two centuries. The policy forbade Japanese from going abroad on pain of death and prohibited the construction of large ships. It expelled Europeans from Japan, prohibited foreign merchants from trading in Japanese ports, and even forbade the import of foreign books. The policy allowed carefully controlled trade with Asian lands, and it also permitted small numbers of Chinese and Dutch merchants to trade under tight restrictions at the southern port city of Nagasaki.

During the seventeenth century, Japanese authorities strictly enforced that policy. In 1640 a Portuguese merchant ship arrived at Nagasaki in hopes of engaging in trade in spite of the ban. Officials beheaded sixty-one of the party and spared thirteen others so that they could relate the experience to their compatriots. Yet authorities gradually loosened the restrictions, and the policy never led to the complete isolation of Japan from the outside world. Throughout the Tokugawa period, Japan carried on a flourishing trade with China, Korea, Taiwan, and the Ryukyu Islands, and Dutch merchants regularly brought news of European and larger world affairs.

Economic and Social Change

By ending civil conflict and maintaining political stability, the Tokugawa shoguns set the stage for economic growth in Japan. Ironically, peace and a booming economy encouraged social change that undermined the order that the *bakufu* sought to preserve.

Economic growth had its roots in increased agricultural production. New crop strains, new methods of water control and irrigation, and the use of fertilizer brought increased yields of rice. Production of cotton, silk, indigo, and sake also increased dramatically. In many parts of Japan, villages moved away from subsistence farming in favor of production for the market. Between 1600 and 1700, agricultural production doubled.

Population Growth Increased agricultural production brought about rapid demographic growth: during the seventeenth century the Japanese population rose by almost one-third, from twenty-two million to twenty-nine million. Thereafter, however, Japan underwent a demographic transition, as many families practiced population control to maintain or raise their standard of living. Between 1700 and 1850 the Japanese population grew moderately, from twenty-nine

million to thirty-two million. Contraception, late marriage, and abortion all played roles in limiting population growth, but the principal control measure was infanticide, euphemistically referred to as "thinning out the rice shoots." Japanese families resorted to those measures primarily because Japan was land poor. During the seventeenth century, populations in some areas strained resources, causing financial difficulties for local governments and distress for rural communities.

The Tokugawa era was an age of social as well as demographic change in Japan. Because of Chinese cultural influence, the Japanese social hierarchy followed Confucian precepts in ranking the ruling elites—including the shogun, daimyo, and samurai warriors—as the most prominent and privileged class of society. Beneath them were peasants and artisans. Merchants ranked at the bottom, as they did in China.

Social Change The extended period of peace ushered in by Tokugawa rule undermined the social position of the ruling elites. Since the twelfth century the administration of local affairs had fallen mostly to daimyo and samurai

Dutch sailing ships and smaller Japanese vessels mingle in Nagasaki harbor. Dutch merchants conducted their business on the artificial island of Deshima, at left.

warriors. Once Japan was stable, however, the interest of Tokugawa authorities was to reduce the numbers of armed professional warriors, so they pushed daimyo and samurai to become bureaucrats and government functionaries. They even encouraged daimyo and samurai to turn their talents to scholarship, a pursuit that their martial ancestors would have utterly despised. As they lost their accustomed place in society, many of the ruling elite also fell into financial difficulty. Their principal income came in the form of rice collected from peasant cultivators of their lands. They readily converted rice into money through brokers, but the price of rice did not keep pace with other costs. Moreover, daimyo and samurai lived in expensive and sometimes ostentatious style—particularly daimyo who sought to impress others with their wealth while residing at Edo in alternate years. Many of them became indebted to rice brokers and gradually declined into genteel poverty.

Meanwhile, as in China, merchants in Japan became increasingly wealthy and prominent. Japanese cities flourished throughout the Tokugawa era—the population of Edo approached one million by 1700—and merchants prospered handsomely in the vibrant urban environment. Rice dealers, pawnbrokers, and sake merchants soon controlled more wealth than the ruling elites did. Those who became especially wealthy sometimes purchased elite ranks or contracted marriages with elite families in efforts to improve their social standing. Others did not go to such lengths but won respect anyway, in spite of occupations that ranked low in the ideal Confucian social order.

Neo-Confucianism and Floating Worlds

Japan had gone to school in China, and the influence of China continued throughout the Tokugawa era. Formal education began with study of Chinese language and literature. As late as the nineteenth century, many Japanese scholars wrote their philosophical, legal, and religious works in Chinese. The common people embraced Buddhism, which had come to Japan from China, and Confucianism was the most influential philosophical system.

Neo-Confucianism in Japan
Like the Ming and Qing emperors in China, the Tokugawa shoguns promoted the neo-Confucianism of Zhu Xi. With its emphasis on filial piety and loyalty to superiors, neo-Confucianism provided a respectable ideological underpinning for the *bakufu*. The shoguns patronized scholars who advocated neo-Confucian views, which figured prominently in the educational curriculum. All those who had a formal education—including the sons of merchants as well as offspring of government officials—received constant exposure to neo-Confucian values. By the early eighteenth century, neo-Confucianism had become the official ideology of the Tokugawa *bakufu*.

Native Learning
Yet even with Tokugawa sponsorship, neo-Confucianism did not dominate intellectual life in Japan. Although most scholars recognized Japan's debt to Chinese intellectual traditions, some sought to establish a sense of Japanese identity that did not depend on cultural kinship with China. Particularly during the eighteenth century,

The courtesan district of Kyoto hummed with activity in the mid-seventeenth century. In this woodblock print, courtesans await clients behind the wooden grill while urban residents fill the streets.

A colored woodcut by Okumura Masanobu depicts the audience at a seventeenth-century kabuki theater. Enthusiastic actors often ran down wooden ramps and played their roles among the audience.

scholars of "native learning" scorned neo-Confucianism and even Buddhism as alien cultural imports and emphasized instead the importance of folk traditions and the indigenous Shinto religion for Japanese identity. Many scholars of native learning viewed Japanese people as superior to all others and xenophobically regarded foreign influence as perverse. They urged the study of Japanese classics and glorified the supposed purity of Japanese society before its adulteration by Chinese and other foreign influences.

While scholars of neo-Confucianism and native learning debated issues of philosophy and Japanese identity, the emergence of a prosperous merchant class encouraged the development of a vibrant popular culture. During the seventeenth and eighteenth centuries, an exuberant middle-class culture flourished in cities such as Kyoto, the imperial capital; Edo, Japan's largest city and home to bureaucrats and daimyo; and Osaka, the commercial hub of the islands. In those and other cities, Japan's finest creative talents catered to middle-class appetites.

Floating Worlds   The centers of Tokugawa urban culture were the *ukiyo* ("floating worlds"), entertainment and pleasure quarters where teahouses, theaters, brothels, and public baths offered escape from social responsibilities and the rigid rules of conduct that governed public behavior in Tokugawa society. In contrast to the solemn, serious proceedings of the imperial court and the *bakufu,* the popular culture of urban residents was secular, satirical, and even scatological. The main expressions of this lively culture were prose fiction and new forms of theater.

Ihara Saikaku (1642–1693), one of Japan's most prolific poets, helped create a new genre of prose literature, the "books of the floating world." Much of his fiction revolved around the theme of love. In *The Life of a Man Who Lived for Love,* for example, Ihara chronicled the experiences of a townsman who devoted his life, beginning at the tender age of eight, to a quest for sexual pleasure. Ihara's treatment of love stressed the erotic rather than the aesthetic, and the brief, episodic stories that made up his work appealed to literate urban residents who were not inclined to pore over dense neo-Confucian treatises.

Beginning in the early seventeenth century, two new forms of drama became popular in Japanese cities. One was *kabuki* theater, which usually featured several acts consisting of lively and sometimes bawdy skits where stylized acting combined with lyric singing, dancing, and spectacular staging. A crucial component of kabuki was the actor's ability to improvise and embellish the dialogue, for the text of plays served only as guides for the dramatic performance. The other new dramatic form was *bunraku,* the puppet theater. In bunraku, chanters accompanied by music told a story acted out by puppets. Manipulated by a team of three, each puppet could

thinking about ENCOUNTERS

Crucifixions in Japan

The Jesuits came to Japan in 1549 and enjoyed some success in their early efforts to convert the Japanese to Christianity. Their continued success over time had major repercussions for Japanese converts. How and why did the Tokugawa *bakufu* respond to this Christian influence? What measures did the Japanese government take to stem the conversions?

execute the subtlest and most intricate movements, such as brushing a tear from the eye with the sleeve of a kimono. Both kabuki and bunraku attracted enthusiastic audiences in search of entertainment and diversion.

Christianity and Dutch Learning

Christian Missions Alongside neo-Confucianism, native learning, and middle-class popular culture, Christian missionaries and European merchants contributed their own distinctive threads to the cultural fabric of Tokugawa Japan. The Jesuit Francis Xavier traveled to Japan in 1549 and opened a mission to seek converts to Christianity. In the early decades of their mission, Jesuits experienced remarkable success in Japan. Several powerful daimyo adopted Christianity and ordered their subjects to do likewise. The principal interest of the daimyo was to establish trade and military alliances with Europeans, but many Japanese converts became enthusiastic Christians and worked to convert their compatriots to the new faith. By the 1580s about 150,000 Japanese had converted to Christianity, and by 1615 Japanese Christians numbered about 300,000.

Although Christians were only a tiny minority of the Japanese population, the popularity of Christianity generated a backlash among government officials and moralists seeking to preserve Japanese religious and cultural traditions. The Tokugawa shoguns restricted European access to Japan largely because of concerns that Christianity might serve as a cultural bridge for alliances between daimyo and European adventurers, which in turn could lead to destabilization of Japanese society and even threats to the bakufu. Meanwhile, Buddhist and Confucian scholars resented the Christian conviction that their faith was the only true doctrine. Some Japanese converts to Christianity themselves eventually rejected their adopted faith out of frustration because European missionaries refused to allow them to become priests or play leadership roles in the mission.

Anti-Christian Campaign Between 1587 and 1639, shoguns promulgated several decrees ordering a halt to Christian missions and commanding Japanese Christians to renounce their faith. In 1612 the shoguns began rigorous enforcement

A seventeenth-century European painting provides an emotional representation of Franciscans being crucified in Nagasaki.

sources from the past

Fabian Fucan Rejects Christianity

Fabian Fucan was a Japanese Buddhist who converted to Christianity and entered the Jesuit order as a novice in 1586. In the early seventeenth century, however, his relations with the Jesuits soured, and he eventually left the order. In 1620 he composed a treatise entitled Deus Destroyed *that leveled a spirited attack at Christianity and its God ("Deus" in Latin). His work reveals deep concerns about European imperial expansion as well as Christian doctrine.*

I joined this creed at an early age; diligently, I studied its teachings and pursued its practices. Due to my stupidity, however, I was long unable to realize that this was a perverse and cursed faith. Thus fruitlessly I spent twenty years and more! Then one day I clearly perceived that the words of the adherents of Deus were very clever and appeared very near reason—but in their teaching there was little truth. So I left their company. Some fifteen years have passed since: every morning I have lamented my desertion of the Great Holy True Law [of Buddhism]; every evening I have grieved over my adherence to the crooked path of the barbarians. All that effort to no effect! But I had a friend who remonstrated with me, saying: "'If you have made a mistake, do not be afraid of admitting the fact and amending your ways' [a Confucian precept]. Here, this is the Confucians' golden rule of life—act on it! Before, you learned all about the cursed faith of Deus; take pen in hand now, commit your knowledge to writing, and counter their teachings. Not only will you thereby gain the merit of destroying wickedness and demonstrating truth; you will also supply a guide toward new knowledge."

All right. Though I am not a clever man, I shall by all means try to act on this advice. I shall gather the important points about the teachings of the Deus sect and shall skip what is not essential; my aim is to write concisely. Thus shall I mount my attack; and I shall call my volume DEUS DESTROYED. . . .

Japan is the Land of the Gods. The generations of our rulers have received the Imperial Dignity from [the gods] Amaterasu Omikami, through U-gaya-fuki-awsezu no Mikoto and his August Child Jimmu Tenno, who became the progenitor of our Hundred Kings. The Three Divine Regalia [symbols of rule received from the gods] became the protectors of the Empire, so that among all the customs of our land there is not one which depends not on the Way of the Gods. . . .

And this, the adherents of Deus plan to subvert! They bide their time with the intent to make all of Japan into their own sectarians, to destroy the Law of Buddha and the Way of the Gods. Because the Law of Buddha and the Way of the Gods are planted here, the Royal Sway also flourishes; and since the Royal Sway is established here the glory of the Buddhas and the gods does grow. And therefore the adherents of Deus have no recourse but to subvert the Royal Sway, overthrow the Buddhas and the gods, eliminate the customs of Japan, and then to import the customs of their own countries; thus only will advance the plot they have concocted to usurp the country themselves.

They have dispatched troops and usurped such countries as Luzon [the Philippines] and Nova Hispania [Mexico], lands of barbarians with nature close to animal. But our land by far surpasses others in fierce bravery; and therefore the ambition to diffuse their faith in every quarter and thus to usurp the country, even if it take a thousand years, has penetrated down to the very marrow of their bones. Ah!—but what a gloomy prospect awaits them! For the sake of their faith they value their lives less than trash, than garbage. *Martyr,* they call this. When a wise sovereign rules the Empire good is promoted and evil is chastised. Rewards promote good and punishments chastise evil. There is no greater punishment than to take away life; but the adherents of Deus, without even fearing that their lives be cut, will not change their religion. How horrible, how awful it is!

For Further Reflection

■ Discuss the various religious, cultural, historical, political, and social aspects of Fabian Fucan's attack on Christianity.

Source: George Elison. *Deus Destroyed: The Image of Christianity in Early Modern Japan.* Cambridge, Mass.: Harvard University Press, 1973, pp. 259–60, 283–84.

of those decrees. They tortured and executed European missionaries who refused to leave the islands as well as Japanese Christians who refused to abandon their faith. They often executed victims by crucifixion or burning at the stake, which Tokugawa authorities regarded as especially appropriate punishments for Christians. The campaign was so effective that even some European missionaries abandoned Christianity. Most notable of them was the Portuguese Jesuit Christóvão Ferreira, head of the Jesuit mission in Japan, who gave up Christianity under torture, adopted Buddhism, and interrogated many Europeans who fell into Japanese hands in the mid-seventeenth century. By the late seventeenth century, the anti-Christian campaign had claimed tens of thousands of lives, and Christianity survived as a secret, underground religion observed only in rural regions of southern Japan.

Dutch Learning Tokugawa policies ensured that Christianity would not soon reappear in Japan, but they did not entirely prevent contacts between Europeans and Japanese. After 1639, Dutch merchants trading at Nagasaki became Japan's principal source of information about Europe and the world beyond east Asia. A small number of Japanese scholars learned Dutch in order to communicate with the foreigners. Their studies, which they called "Dutch learning," brought considerable knowledge of the outside world to Japan. After 1720, Tokugawa authorities lifted the ban on foreign books, and Dutch learning began to play a significant role in Japanese intellectual life.

European art influenced Japanese scholars interested in anatomy and botany because of its accurate representations of objects. Scholars translated Dutch medical and scientific treatises into Japanese and learned to draw according to the principles of linear perspective, which enabled them to prepare textbooks that were more accurate than the Chinese works they had previously used. European astronomy was also popular in Japan, since it enabled scholars to improve calendars and issue accurate predictions of eclipses and other celestial events. By the mid-eighteenth century, the Tokugawa shoguns themselves had become enthusiastic proponents of Dutch learning, and schools of European medicine and Dutch studies flourished in several Japanese cities.

in perspective

Both China and Japan controlled their own affairs throughout the early modern era and avoided the turmoil that afflicted societies in the Americas and much of sub-Saharan Africa. After driving the Mongols to the steppe lands of central Asia, rulers of the Ming dynasty built a powerful centralized state in China. They worked diligently to eradicate all vestiges of Mongol rule and restore traditional ways by reviving Chinese political institutions and providing state sponsorship for neo-Confucianism. In the interest of stability, authorities also restricted foreign merchants' access to China and limited the activities of Christian missionaries. The succeeding Qing dynasty pursued similar policies. The Ming and Qing dynasties both brought political stability, but China experienced considerable social and economic change in early modern times. American food crops helped increase agricultural production, which fueled rapid population growth, and global trade stimulated the Chinese economy, which improved the position of merchants and artisans in society. The experience of the Tokugawa era in Japan was much like that of the Ming and Qing eras in China. The Tokugawa *bakufu* brought political order to the Japanese islands and closely controlled foreign relations, but a vibrant economy promoted social change that enhanced the status of merchants and artisans. ●

CHRONOLOGY	
1368–1644	Ming dynasty (China)
1368–1398	Reign of Hongwu
1403–1424	Reign of Yongle
1552–1610	Life of Matteo Ricci
1572–1620	Reign of Emperor Wanli
1600–1867	Tokugawa shogunate (Japan)
1616–1626	Reign of Nurhaci
1642–1693	Life of Ihara Saikaku
1644–1911	Qing dynasty (China)
1661–1722	Reign of Kangxi
1736–1795	Reign of Qianlong
1793	British trade mission to China

For Further Reading

Timothy Brook. *The Chinese State in Ming Society.* London and New York, 2004. An important collection of essays on commercialism and social networks, and the role they played in the development of a stable society.

———. *The Confusions of Pleasure: Commerce and Culture in Ming China.* Berkeley, 1998. Fascinating social and cultural analysis of Ming China focusing on the role of commerce as an agent of social change.

George Elison. *Deus Destroyed: The Image of Christianity in Early Modern Japan.* Cambridge, Mass., 1973. Scholarly study of the Jesuit mission in Japan and its end during the early Tokugawa era.

Mark C. Elliott. *The Manchu Way: The Eight Banners and Ethnic Identity in Late Imperial China.* Stanford, 2001. Important scholarly study focusing on relations between Manchus and Chinese during the Qing dynasty.

Benjamin A. Elman. *A Cultural History of Civil Examinations in Late Imperial China.* Berkeley, 2000. A meticulous study of one of the most important institutions in Chinese history.

Jacques Gernet. *China and the Christian Impact.* Trans. by J. Lloyd. Cambridge, 1985. A careful study of the Jesuit mission in China, concentrating on the cultural differences between Chinese and Europeans.

Harry D. Harootunian. *Things Seen and Unseen: Discourse and Ideology in Tokugawa Nativism.* Chicago, 1988. A challenging scholarly analysis of the efforts by Tokugawa thinkers to construct a distinctive Japanese identity.

Donald Keene. *The Japanese Discovery of Europe, 1720–1830.* Rev. ed. Stanford, 1969. A highly readable account of Japanese encounters with Europe by way of Dutch merchants.

Susan Mann and Yu-Ying Cheng, eds. *Under Confucian Eyes: Writings on Gender in Chinese History.* Berkeley, 2001. A rich anthology of primary texts documenting the lives of women in imperial China.

Ichisada Miyazaki. *China's Examination Hell: The Civil Service Examinations in Imperial China.* Trans. by Conrad Schirokauer. New Haven, 1981. Explores all aspects of the labyrinthine civil service examination system.

Susan Naquin and Evelyn S. Rawski. *Chinese Society in the Eighteenth Century.* New Haven, 1987. A lucid and well-organized discussion of Chinese social history.

Kenneth Pomeranz. *The Great Divergence: China, Europe, and the Making of the Modern World Economy.* Princeton, 2000. Pathbreaking scholarly study that illuminates the economic history of the early modern world through comparison of economic development in Asian and European lands.

Evelyn S. Rawski. *The Last Emperors: A Social History of Qing Imperial Institutions.* Berkeley, 1998. A nuanced study of the Manchu rulers and the politics of assimilation.

Jonathan D. Spence. *The Death of Woman Wang.* New York, 1978. Engaging reconstruction of life in rural China during the early Qing dynasty.

———. *Emperor of China: Self-Portrait of K'ang-Hsi.* New York, 1974. Outstanding introduction to the reign of Kangxi based partly on numerous documents, some written by the emperor himself.

Ronald P. Toby. *State and Diplomacy in Early Modern Japan: Asia in the Development of the Tokugawa Bakufu.* Princeton, 1984. An important study dealing with Japanese trade and relations with other lands under Tokugawa rule.

H. Paul Varley. *Japanese Culture.* 4th ed. Honolulu, 2000. Places the cultural history of the Tokugawa era in its larger historical context.

Arthur Waldron. *The Great Wall of China: From History to Myth.* Cambridge, 1990. Fascinating work that places the Great Wall of Ming China in the context of earlier efforts to build defensive walls.

The Islamic Empires

chapter27

This equestrian portrait of Shah Jahan (reigned 1628–1658) is emblematic of the Mughal art promoted by Shah Jahan. Builder of the Taj Mahal, Shah Jahan here is shown in a rich and heroic light, symbolized by the ring of light, his clothing and weaponry, and the horse's exquisite appointments.

EYEWITNESS:

Shah Jahan's Monument to Love and Allah

In 1635 Shah Jahan, the emperor of Mughal India, took his seat on the Peacock Throne. Seven years in the making, the Peacock Throne is probably the most spectacular seat on which any human being has rested. Shah Jahan ordered the throne encrusted with ten million rupees' worth of diamonds, rubies, emeralds, and pearls. Atop the throne itself stood a magnificent, golden-bodied peacock with a huge ruby and a fifty-carat, pear-shaped pearl on its breast and a brilliant elevated tail fashioned of blue sapphires and other colored gems.

Yet, for all its splendor, the Peacock Throne ranks a distant second among Shah Jahan's artistic projects: pride of place goes to the incomparable Taj Mahal. Built over a period of eighteen years as a tomb for Shah Jahan's beloved wife, Mumtaz Mahal, who died during childbirth in 1631, the Taj Mahal is a graceful and elegant monument both to the departed empress and to Shah Jahan's Islamic faith.

The emperor and his architects conceived the Taj Mahal as a vast allegory in stone symbolizing the day when Allah would cause the dead to rise and undergo judgment before his heavenly throne. Its gardens represented the gardens of paradise, and the four water channels running through them symbolized the four rivers of the heavenly kingdom. The domed marble tomb of Mumtaz Mahal represented the throne of Allah, and the four minarets surrounding the structure served as legs supporting the divine throne. Craftsmen carved verses from the Quran throughout the Taj Mahal. The main gateway to the structure features the entire text of the chapter promising that on the day of judgment, Allah will punish the wicked and gather the faithful into his celestial paradise.

The Peacock Throne and the Taj Mahal testify to the wealth of the Mughal empire, and the tomb of Mumtaz Mahal bespeaks also the fundamentally Islamic character of the ruling dynasty. But the Mughal empire, which ruled most of the Indian subcontinent for more than three hundred years, was not the only well-organized Islamic empire of early modern times. The Ottoman empire was a dynastic Muslim state centered in what is today Turkey. At the height of its power, it controlled a vast area from southeastern Europe to western Asia and North Africa. It was also the longest-lived of the Muslim empires, not disbanding until the early twentieth century. On the eastern borders of the Ottoman empire lay the ancient lands of Persia, where yet another Muslim empire emerged during the early sixteenth century. Ruled by the Safavid dynasty, this state never expanded far beyond its heartland of present-day Iran, but its Shiite rulers challenged the Sunni Ottomans for dominance in southwest Asia. The Safavid realm prospered from its place in trade networks linking China, India, Russia, southwest Asia, and the Mediterranean basin.

All three Islamic empires of early modern times had Turkish ruling dynasties. The Ottomans, Safavids, and Mughals came from nomadic, Turkish-speaking peoples of central Asia who conquered the settled agricultural lands of Anatolia, Persia, and India, respectively. All three dynasties retained political and cultural traditions that their ancestors had adopted while leading nomadic lives on the steppes, but they also adapted readily to the city-based agricultural societies that they conquered. The Ottoman dynasty made especially effective use of the gunpowder weapons that transformed early modern warfare, and the Safavids and the Mughals also incorporated gunpowder weapons into their arsenals. All three dynasties officially embraced Islam and drew cultural guidance from Islamic values.

During the sixteenth and early seventeenth centuries, the three Islamic empires presided over expansive and prosperous societies. About the mid-seventeenth century, however, they all began to weaken. Their waning fortunes reflected the fact that they had ceased to expand territorially and gain access to new sources of wealth. Instead, each empire waged long, costly wars that drained resources without bringing compensating benefits. The empires also faced domestic difficulties. Each of them was an ethnically and religiously diverse realm, and each experienced tensions when conservative Muslim leaders lobbied for strict observance of Islam while members of other communities sought greater freedom for themselves. Furthermore, the Islamic empires made little investment in economic and technological development. By the mid-eighteenth century, the Safavid empire had collapsed, and the Ottoman and Mughal realms were rapidly falling under European influence.

FORMATION OF THE ISLAMIC EMPIRES

By the sixteenth century, Turkish warriors had transformed the major Islamic areas of the world into vast regional empires. Three empires divided up the greater part of the Islamic world: the Ottoman empire, which was distinguished by its multiethnic character; the Safavid empire of Persia, which served as the center of Shiite Islam; and the Mughal empire, which had been imposed over a predominantly Hindu Indian subcontinent. The creation of these durable and powerful political entities brought to an end a century and a half of Muslim political disunity.

The Islamic empires began as small warrior principalities in frontier areas. They expanded at varying rates and with varying degrees of success at the expense of neighboring states. As they grew, they devised elaborate administrative and military institutions. Under the guidance of talented and energetic rulers, each empire organized an effective governmental apparatus and presided over a prosperous society.

The Ottoman Empire

Osman The Ottoman empire was an unusually successful frontier state. The term *Ottoman* derived from Osman Bey, founder of the dynasty that continued in unbroken succession from 1289 until the dissolution of the empire in 1923.

Osman was *bey* (chief) of a band of seminomadic Turks who migrated to northwestern Anatolia in the thirteenth century. Osman and his followers sought above all to become *ghazi,* Muslim religious warriors. In his encomium of the Ottomans, the poet Ahmadi described their ethos: "The Ghazi is the instrument of the religion of Allah, a servant of God who purifies the earth from the filth of polytheism; the Ghazi is the sword of God, he is the protector and the refuge of the believers. If he becomes a martyr in the ways of God, do not believe that he has died—he lives in beatitude with Allah, he has eternal life."

Ottoman Expansion The Ottomans' location on the borders of the Byzantine empire afforded them ample opportunity to wage holy war. Their first great success came in 1326 with the capture of the Anatolian city of Bursa, which became the capital of the Ottoman principality. Around 1352 they established a foothold in Europe when they seized the fortress of Gallipoli while aiding a claimant to the Byzantine throne. Numerous *ghazi,* many of them recent converts, soon flocked to join the Ottomans. The city of Edirne (Adrianople) became a second Ottoman capital and served as a base for further expansion into the Balkans. As warriors settled in frontier districts and pushed their boundaries forward, they took spoils and gathered revenues that enriched both the *ghazi* and the central government.

MAP 27.1

The Islamic empires, 1500–1800.
Locate the Ottoman capital of Istanbul, the Safavid capital of Isfahan, and the Mughal capital of Delhi.

What strategic or commercial purposes did each of these capitals fulfill, and how would their locations have aided or hindered imperial administration?

Bursa developed into a major commercial and intellectual center with inns, shops, schools, libraries, and mosques.

A formidable military machine drove Ottoman expansion. Ottoman military leaders initially organized *ghazi* recruits into two forces: a light cavalry and a volunteer infantry. As the Ottoman state became more firmly established, it added a professional cavalry force equipped with heavy armor and financed by land grants. After expanding into the Balkans, the Ottomans created a supremely important force composed of slave troops. Through an institution known as the *devshirme,* the Ottomans required the Christian population of the Balkans to contribute young boys to become slaves of the sultan. The boys received special training, learned Turkish, and converted to Islam. According to individual ability, they entered either the Ottoman civilian administration or the military. Those who became soldiers were known as Janissaries, from the Turkish *yeni cheri* ("new troops"). The Janissaries quickly gained a reputation for esprit de corps, loyalty to the sultan, and readiness to employ new military technology. Besides building powerful military forces, the Ottomans outfitted their forces with gunpowder weapons and used them effectively in battles and sieges.

Mehmed the Conqueror The capture of Constantinople in 1453 by Mehmed II (reigned 1451–1481)—known as Mehmed the Conqueror—opened a new chapter in Otto-

man expansion. With its superb location and illustrious heritage, Constantinople became the new Ottoman capital, subsequently known as Istanbul, and Mehmed worked energetically to stimulate its role as a commercial center. With the capture of the great city behind him, Mehmed presented himself not just as a warrior-sultan but also as a true emperor, ruler of the "two lands" (Europe and Asia) and the "two seas" (the Black Sea and the Mediterranean). He laid the foundations for a tightly centralized, absolute monarchy, and his army faced no serious rival. He completed the conquest of Serbia, moved into southern Greece and Albania, eliminated the last Byzantine outpost at Trebizond, captured Genoese ports in the Crimea, initiated a naval war with Venice in the Mediterranean, and reportedly hoped to cross the Strait of Otranto, march on Rome, and capture the pope himself. Toward the end of his life, he launched an invasion of Italy and briefly occupied Otranto, but his successors abandoned Mehmed's plans for expansion in western Europe.

Süleyman the Magnificent The Ottomans continued their expansion in the early sixteenth century when

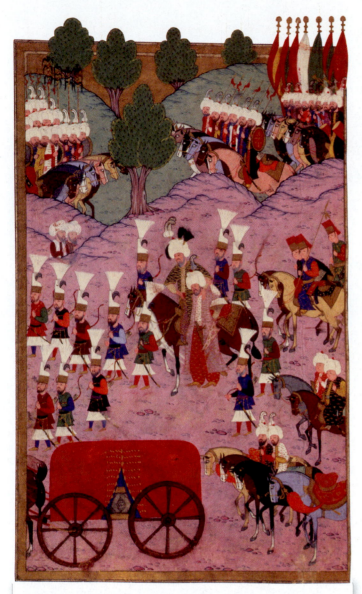

Sultan Süleyman (center, on horse) leads Ottoman forces as they march on Europe. How does this illustration promote the power and prominence of Süleyman and his Ottoman forces?

Danube, and in 1529 subjected the Habsburgs' prized city of Vienna to a brief but nonetheless terrifying siege.

Under Süleyman the Ottomans also became a major naval power. In addition to their own Aegean and Black Sea fleets, the Ottomans inherited the navy of the Mamluk rulers of Egypt. A Turkish corsair, Khayr al-Din Barbarossa Pasha, who had challenged Spanish forces in Tunisia and Algeria, placed his pirate fleet under the Ottoman flag and became Süleyman's leading admiral. Thus Süleyman was able to challenge Christian vessels throughout the Mediterranean as well as Portuguese fleets in the Red Sea and the Indian Ocean. The Ottomans seized the island of Rhodes from the Knights of St. John, besieged Malta, secured Yemen and Aden, and even dispatched a squadron to attack the Portuguese fleet at Diu in India.

The Safavid Empire

In 1499 a twelve-year-old boy named Ismail left the swamps of Gilan near the Caspian Sea, where he had hidden from the enemies of his family for five years, to seek his revenge. Two years later he entered Tabriz at the head of an army and laid claim to the ancient Persian imperial title of shah. The young Shah Ismail (reigned 1501–1524) also proclaimed that the official religion of his realm would be Twelver Shiism, and he proceeded to impose it, by force when necessary, on the formerly Sunni population. Over the next decade he seized control of the Iranian plateau and launched expeditions into the Caucasus, Anatolia, Mesopotamia, and central Asia.

The Safavids   For propaganda purposes, Shah Ismail and his successors carefully controlled accounts of their rise to power—and expediently changed the story when circumstances warranted. They traced their ancestry back to Safi al-Din (1252–1334), leader of a Sufi religious order in northwestern Persia. Sufism, a mystical belief and practice, formed an important Islamic tradition. The goal of a Sufi mystic, such as Safi al-Din, was to recover the lost intimacy between God and the human soul, and to find the truth of divine knowledge and love through a direct personal experience of God. The famous tomb and shrine of Safi al-Din at Ardabil became the home of Shah Ismail's family (named "Safavids" after the holy man himself), the headquarters of his religious movement, and the center of a determined, deliberate conspiracy to win political power for his descendants. The Safavids changed their religious preferences several times in the hope of gaining popular support before settling on a form of Shiism that appealed to the nomadic Turkish tribes moving into the area in the post-Mongol era.

Twelver Shiism   Twelver Shiism held that there had been twelve infallible imams (or religious leaders) after Muhammad, beginning with the prophet's cousin and son-in-law Ali. The twelfth, "hidden," imam had gone into hiding around 874 to escape persecution, but the Twelver Shiites believed he was still alive and would one day return to take

sultan Selim the Grim (reigned 1512–1520) occupied Syria and Egypt. Ottoman imperialism climaxed in the reign of **Süleyman** the Magnificent (reigned 1520–1566). Süleyman vigorously promoted Ottoman expansion both in southwest Asia and in Europe. In 1534 he conquered Baghdad and added the Tigris and Euphrates valleys to the Ottoman domain. In Europe he kept the rival Habsburg empire on the defensive throughout his reign. He captured Belgrade in 1521, defeated and killed the king of Hungary at the battle of Mohács in 1526, consolidated Ottoman power north of the

Süleyman (SOO-lee-mahn)

sources from the past

Ghislain de Busbecq's Concerns about the Ottoman Empire

Ogier Ghislain de Busbecq was a diplomat who traveled to Istanbul in 1555 as a representative of Habsburg King Ferdinand of Hungary and Bohemia to negotiate a border dispute between Ferdinand and Sultan Süleyman the Magnificent. In a series of four letters to a friend, Ghislain commented on Ottoman state, society, customs, and military forces. His observations left him deeply concerned about the prospects of Christian Europe in the event of conflict with the Ottoman realm.

The Sultan, when he sets out on a campaign, takes as many as 40,000 camels with him, and almost as many baggage-mules, most of whom, if his destination is Persia, are loaded with cereals of every kind, especially rice. Mules and camels are also employed to carry tents and arms and warlike machines and implements of every kind. . . . They are careful, however, to avoid touching the supplies which they carry with them as long as they are marching against their foes, but reserve them, as far as possible, for their return journey, when the moment for retirement comes and they are forced to retrace their steps through regions which the enemy has laid waste, or which the immense multitude of men and baggage animals has, as it were, scraped bare, like a swarm of locusts. It is only then that the Sultan's store of provisions is opened, and just enough food to sustain life is weighed out each day to the Janissaries and the other troops in attendance upon him. The other soldiers are badly off, if they have not provided food for their own use; most of them, having often experienced such difficulties during their campaigns—and this is particularly true of the cavalry—take a horse on a leading-rein loaded with many of the necessities of life. These include a small piece of canvas to use as a tent, which may protect them from the sun or a shower of rain, also some clothing and bedding and a private store of provisions, consisting of a leather sack or two of the finest flour, a small jar of butter, and some spices and salt; on these they support life when they are reduced to the extremes of hunger. They take a few spoonfuls of flour and place them in water, adding a little butter, and then flavour the mixture with salt and spices. This, when it is put on the fire, boils and swells up so as to fill a large bowl. They eat of it once or twice a day, according to the quantity, without any bread, unless they have with them some toasted bread or biscuit. They thus contrive to live on short rations for a month or even longer, if necessary. . . .

All this will show you with what patience, sobriety, and economy the Turks struggle against the difficulties which beset them, and wait for better times. How different are our soldiers, who on campaign despise ordinary food and expect dainty dishes (such as thrushes and beccaficoes) and elaborate meals. If these are not supplied, they mutiny and cause their own ruin; and even if they are supplied, they ruin themselves just the same. . . . I tremble when I think of what the future must bring when I compare the Turkish system with our own; one army must prevail and the other be destroyed, for certainly both cannot remain unscathed. On their side are the resources of a mighty empire, strength unimpaired, experience and practice in fighting, a veteran soldiery, habituation to victory, endurance of toil, unity, order, discipline, frugality, and watchfulness. On our side is public poverty, private luxury, impaired strength, spirit, lack of endurance and training; the soldiers are insubordinate, the officers avaricious; there is contempt for discipline; licence, recklessness, drunkenness, and debauchery are rife; and worst of all, the enemy is accustomed to victory, and we to defeat. Can we doubt what the result will be?

For Further Reflection

■ Why might Ghislain de Busbecq have assumed that conflict between Turkish and Habsburg forces was inevitable?

Source: Ghislain de Busbecq. *The Turkish Letters of Ogier Ghislain de Busbecq.* Trans. by E. S. Foster. Oxford: Clarendon Press, 1927, pp. 209–14.

power and spread his true religion. Ismail's father had instructed his Turkish followers to wear a distinctive red hat with twelve pleats in memory of the twelve Shiite imams, and they subsequently became known as the *qizilbash* ("red heads"). Safavid propaganda also suggested that Ismail was himself the hidden imam, or even an incarnation of Allah. Although most Muslims, including most Shiites, would have regarded those pretensions as utterly blasphemous, the *qizilbash* enthusiastically accepted them, since they resembled traditional Turkish conceptions of leadership that associated military leaders with divinity. The *qizilbash* believed that Ismail would make them invincible in battle, and they became fanatically loyal to the Safavid cause.

Battle of Chaldiran   Shah Ismail's curious blend of Shiism and Turkish militancy gave his regime a distinctive identity, particularly since he made conversion to Shiite Islam mandatory for the largely Sunni population, but it also created some powerful enemies. Foremost among them were the staunchly Sunni Ottomans who detested the Shiite Safavids and feared the spread of Safavid propaganda among the nomadic Turks in their territory. As soon as Selim the Grim became sultan, he launched a persecution of Shiites in the Ottoman empire and prepared for a full-scale invasion of Safavid territory.

At the critical battle on the plain of Chaldiran (1514), the Ottomans deployed heavy artillery and thousands of Janissaries equipped with firearms behind a barrier of carts. Although the Safavids knew about gunpowder technology and had access to firearms, they declined to use devices that they saw as unreliable and unmanly. Trusting in the protective charisma of Shah Ismail, the *qizilbash* cavalry fearlessly attacked the Ottoman line and suffered devastating casualties. Ismail had to slip away, and the Ottomans temporarily occupied his capital at Tabriz. The Ottomans badly damaged the Safavid state but lacked the resources to destroy it, and the two empires remained locked in intermittent conflict for the next two centuries.

Later Safavid rulers recovered from the disaster at Chaldiran. They relied more heavily than Ismail had on the Persian bureaucracy and its administrative talents. Ismail's successors abandoned the extreme Safavid ideology that associated the emperor with Allah in favor of more conventional Twelver Shiism, from which they still derived legitimacy as descendants and representatives of the imams. They also assigned land grants to the *qizilbash* officers to retain their loyalty and give them a stake in the survival of the regime.

Shah Abbas the Great   Shah Abbas the Great (reigned 1588–1629) fully revitalized the Safavid empire. He moved the capital to the more central location of Isfahan, encouraged trade with other lands, and reformed the administrative and military institutions of the empire. He incorporated

Shah Ismail and the *qizilbash*. This miniature painting from a Safavid manuscript depicts the shah and his *qizilbash* warriors wearing the distinctive red pleated cap that was their emblem of identity.

"slaves of the royal household" into the army, increased the use of gunpowder weapons, and sought European assistance against the Ottomans and the Portuguese in the Persian Gulf. With newly strengthened military forces, Shah Abbas led the Safavids to numerous victories. He attacked and defeated the nomadic Uzbeks in central Asia, expelled the Portuguese from Hormuz, and harassed the Ottomans mercilessly in a series of wars from 1603 to the end of his reign. His campaigns brought most of northwestern Iran, the Caucasus, and Mesopotamia under Safavid rule.

The Mughal Empire

Babur   In 1523 Zahir al-Din Muhammad, known as Babur ("the Tiger"), a Chaghatai Turk who claimed descent from both Chinggis Khan and Tamerlane, suddenly appeared in northern India. Unlike the Ottomans, who sought to be renowned *ghazis,* or the Safavids, who acted as champions of Shiism, Babur made little pretense to be anything more than an adventurer and soldier of fortune in the manner of his illustrious ancestors. His father had been the prince of Farghana, and Babur's great ambition was to transform his inheritance into a glorious central Asian empire. Yet envious relatives and Uzbek enemies frustrated his ambitions.

Never able to extend his authority much beyond Kabul and Qandahar and reduced at times to hardship and a handful of followers, Babur turned his attention to India. With the aid of gunpowder weapons, including both artillery and firearms, Babur mounted invasions in 1523 and 1525, and he took Delhi in 1526. Ironically, Babur cared little for the land he had conquered. Many in his entourage wanted to take their spoils of war and leave the hot and humid Indian climate, which ruined their finely crafted compound bows, but Babur elected to stay. He probably hoped to use the enormous wealth of India to build a vast central Asian empire like that of Tamerlane—an elusive dream that his successors would nonetheless continue to cherish. By the time of his death in 1530, Babur had built a loosely knit empire that

This colorful scene at a spring in Kabul highlights Babur (1483–1530), founder of the Mughal dynasty, who stands in a central position near the life-giving water.

This manuscript illustration from about 1590 depicts Akbar (at top, shaded by attendants) inspecting construction of a new imperial capital at Fatehpur Sikri.

stretched from Kabul through the Punjab to the borders of Bengal. He founded a dynasty called the *Mughal* (a Persian term for "Mongol"), which expanded to embrace almost all the Indian subcontinent.

Akbar The real architect of the Mughal empire was Babur's grandson Akbar (reigned 1556–1605), a brilliant and charismatic ruler. Akbar gathered the reins of power in his own hands in 1561 following an argument with Adham Khan, a powerful figure at the imperial court and commander of the Mughal army. Akbar threw Adham Khan out a window, then dragged him back from the palace courtyard, and tossed him out again to make sure he was dead. Thereafter Akbar

took personal control of the Mughal government and did not tolerate challenges to his rule. He created a centralized administrative structure with ministries regulating the various provinces of the empire. His military campaigns consolidated Mughal power in Gujarat and Bengal. He also began to absorb the recently defeated Hindu kingdom of Vijayanagar, thus laying the foundation for later Mughal expansion in southern India.

Although he was a no-nonsense ruler, Akbar was also a thoughtful, reflective man deeply interested in religion and philosophy. He pursued a policy of religious toleration that he hoped would reduce tensions between Hindu and

sources from the past

A Conqueror and His Conquests: Babur on India

Babur was a talented writer as well as a successful warrior. His memoirs make fascinating reading and provide a unique perspective on early Mughal India. His writings include his reflections on the territories he conquered in India, which he compared unfavorably to his central Asian homeland, and on his decision to stay in India and found an empire.

Most of the inhabitants of India are infidels, called Hindus, believing mainly in the transmigration of souls; all artisans, wage-earners, and officials are Hindus. In our countries the desert dwellers get tribal names; here people settled in the cultivated villages also get tribal names. Again, every artisan follows the trade handed down to him from his forefathers.

India is a country of few charms. The people lack good looks and good manners. They have no social life or exchange of visits. They have no genius or intelligence, no polite learning, no generosity or magnanimity, no harmony or proportion in their arts and crafts, no lead-wire or carpenter's square. They lack good horses and good dogs; grapes, melons, and any good fruit; ice and cold water; good food or good bread in the markets. They have no baths and no advanced educational institutions. . . . There are no running streams in their gardens or residences, no waters at all except the large rivers and the swamps in the ravines and hollows. Their residences have no pleasant and salubrious breezes, and in their construction [there is] no form or symmetry. . . .

Among the charms that India does possess is that it is a large country, with large quantities of gold and silver. Its air in the rainy season is very fine. Sometimes it rains ten or fifteen or even twenty times a day, and in such torrents that rivers flow where no water was previously. While it rains, and throughout the rainy season, the air is remarkably fine, not to be surpassed for mildness and pleasantness. Its only fault is its great humidity, which spoils bows. . . .

It was the hot season when we came to Agra. All the inhabitants had run away in terror. We could find neither grain for ourselves nor corn for our horses. The villages, out of hostility and hatred for us, had taken to thieving and highway-robbery, and it was impossible to travel on the roads. We had not yet the opportunity to distribute the treasure and to assign men in strength to each district. Moreover, the year was a very hot one, pestilential simooms [sandstorms] were striking people down in heaps, and masses were beginning to die off.

For all these reasons, most of the best warriors were unwilling to stay in India; in fact, they determined to leave. . . .

When I discovered this unsteadiness among my people, I summoned all the leaders and took counsel. I said, "Without means and resources there is no empire and conquest, and without lands and followers there is no sovereignty and rule. By the effort of long years, through much tribulation and the crossing of distant lands, by flinging ourselves into battle and danger, we have through God's favor overcome so many enemies and conquered such vast lands. And now, what force compels us, what necessity has arisen, that we should, without cause, abandon a country taken at such risk of life? And if we returned to Kabul, we would again be left in poverty and weakness. Henceforth, let no well-wisher of mine speak of such things! But let not those turn back from going who cannot bear the hardship and have determined to leave." With such words I reasoned with them and made them, willy-nilly, quit their fears.

For Further Reflection

■ What does Babur's reaction to India suggest about his views of his own central Asian homeland?

Source: Babur. *The Babur-nama in English (Memoirs of Babur).* Trans. by Annette Susannah Beveridge. London: Luzac, 1922. (Translation slightly modified.)

Muslim communities in India. Although illiterate (probably due to dyslexia), he was extremely intelligent and had books read to him daily. Instead of imposing Islam on his subjects, he encouraged the elaboration of a syncretic religion called the "divine faith" that focused attention on the emperor as a ruler common to all the religious, ethnic, and social groups of India.

Aurangzeb The Mughal empire reached its greatest extent under Aurangzeb (reigned 1659–1707). During his long reign, Aurangzeb waged a relentless campaign to push Mu-

ghal authority deep into southern India. By the early eighteenth century, Mughals ruled the entire subcontinent except for a small region at the southern tip.

Although he greatly expanded Mughal boundaries, Aurangzeb presided over a troubled empire. He faced rebellions throughout his reign, and religious tensions generated conflicts between Hindus and Muslims. Aurangzeb was a devout Muslim, and he broke with Akbar's policy of religious toleration. He demolished several famous Hindu temples and replaced them with mosques. He also imposed a tax on Hindus in an effort to encourage conversion to Islam.

His promotion of Islam appealed strongly to the Mughals themselves and other Indian Muslims as well, but it provoked deep hostility among Hindus and enabled local leaders to organize movements to resist or even rebel against Mughal authority.

IMPERIAL ISLAMIC SOCIETY

Despite their ethnically and religiously diverse populations, there were striking similarities in the development of Ottoman, Safavid, and Mughal societies. All relied on bureaucracies that drew inspiration from the steppe traditions of Turkish and Mongol peoples as well as from the heritage of Islam. They adopted similar economic policies and sought ways to maintain harmony in societies that embraced many different religious and ethnic groups. Rulers of all the empires also sought to enhance the legitimacy of their regimes by providing for public welfare and associating themselves with literary and artistic talent.

The Dynastic State

The Ottoman, Safavid, and Mughal empires were all military creations, regarded by their rulers as their personal possessions by right of conquest. The rulers exercised personal command of the armies, appointed and dismissed officials at will, and adopted whatever policies they wished. In theory, the emperors owned all land and granted use of it to peasant families on a hereditary basis in return for the payment of fixed taxes. The emperors and their families derived revenues from crown lands, and revenues from other lands supported military and administrative officials.

The Emperors and Islam In the Ottoman, Safavid, and Mughal empires, the prestige and authority of the dynasty derived from the personal piety and the military prowess of the ruler and his ancestors. The Safavids were prominent leaders of a Sufi religious order, and the Ottomans and Mughals associated closely with famous Sufis. Devotion to Islam encouraged rulers to extend their faith to new lands. The *ghazi* ideal of spreading Islam by fighting infidels or heretics resonated with the traditions of Turkish and Mongolian peoples: on the steppes fighting was routine, and successful warriors became charismatic leaders.

Steppe Traditions The autocratic authority wielded by the rulers of the Islamic empires also reflected steppe traditions. The early emperors largely did as they pleased, irrespective of religious and social norms. The Ottoman sultans, for example, unilaterally issued numerous legal edicts. The greatest of these were the many *kanun* ("laws") issued by Süleyman—Europeans called him Süleyman the Magnificent, but the Ottomans referred to him as Süleyman Kanuni, "the Lawgiver." Safavid and Mughal rulers went even further than the Ottomans in asserting their spiritual authority. Shah Ismail did not hesitate to force his Shiite religion on his sub-jects. Akbar issued a decree in 1579 claiming broad authority in religious matters, and he promoted his own eclectic religion, which glorified the emperor as much as Islam.

Steppe practices also brought succession problems. In the steppe empires the ruler's relatives often managed components of the states, and succession to the throne became a hot contest between competing members of the family. The Mughal empire in particular became tied up in family controversies: conflicts among Mughal princes and rebellions of sons against fathers were recurrent features throughout the history of the empire. The Safavids also engaged in murderous struggles for the throne. Shah Abbas himself lived in fear that another member of the family would challenge him. He kept his sons confined to the palace and killed or blinded relatives he suspected, almost wiping out his family in the process.

The early Ottomans assigned provinces for the sultan's sons to administer but kept the empire as a whole tightly unified. After the fifteenth century, however, the sultans moved to protect their position by eliminating family rivals. Mehmed the Conqueror decreed that a ruler could legally kill off his brothers after taking the throne. His successors observed that tradition in Turko-Mongol style—by strangling victims with a silk bow string so as not to shed royal blood—until 1595, when the new sultan executed nineteen brothers, many of them infants, as well as fifteen expectant mothers. After that episode, sultans confined their sons in special quarters of the imperial harem and forbade them to go outside except to take the throne.

Women and Politics Even though Muslim theorists universally agreed that women should have no role in public affairs and decried the involvement of women in politics as a sure sign of decadence, women played important roles in managing the Islamic empires. Many Ottoman, Safavid, and Mughal emperors followed the example of Chinggis Khan, who revered his mother and his first wife. In the Islamic empires the ruler's mother and his chief wife or favorite concubine enjoyed special privileges and authority. Ottoman courtiers often complained loudly about the "rule of women," thus offering eloquent testimony to the power that women could wield. Süleyman the Magnificent, for example, became infatuated with Hürrem Sultana (also known as Roxelana), a concubine of Ukrainian origin. Süleyman elevated her to the status of a legal wife, consulted her on state policies, and deferred to her judgment even to the point of executing his eldest son for treason when Hürrem wanted him eliminated to secure the succession of her own child. After Hürrem's death, Süleyman constructed a mausoleum for her next to his own in the courtyard of the great mosque in Istanbul.

Women also played prominent political roles in the Safavid and Mughal empires. In Safavid Persia, Mahd-e Olya, the wife of one shah, was the de facto ruler. Her efforts to limit the power of the *qizilbash* so enraged them that they murdered her. The aunt of another shah scolded the ruler for neglecting his duties and used her own money to raise an army to put down a revolt. The Mughal emperor Jahangir was content to let his wife Nur Jahan run the government, and even the conscientious Muslim Aurangzeb listened to his daughter's political advice. Shah Jahan's devotion to his wife, Mumtaz Mahal, has become world-famous because of the Taj Mahal.

Agriculture and Trade

Food Crops
Productive agricultural economies were the foundations of all the Islamic empires. Each empire extracted surplus agricultural production and used it to finance armies and bureaucracies. Mostly the Islamic empires relied on crops of wheat and rice that had flourished for centuries in the lands they ruled. The Columbian exchange brought American crops to all the Islamic empires but without the same dramatic effects as in Europe, east Asia, and Africa. European merchants introduced maize, potatoes, tomatoes, and other crops to the Islamic empires, and the new arrivals soon found a place in regional cuisines. Potatoes appeared in the curries of southern India, and tomatoes enlivened dishes in the Ottoman empire as well as other Mediterranean lands. Maize did not appeal to human palates in the Islamic empires, but it became popular as feed for animal stocks, especially in the Ottoman empire.

The Columbian exchange strongly encouraged consumption of coffee and tobacco, especially in the Ottoman and Safavid empires. Although native to Ethiopia and cultivated in southern Arabia, coffee did not become popular in Islamic lands until the sixteenth century. Like sugar, it traveled to Europe and from there to the Americas, where plantations specialized in the production of tropical crops for the world market. By the eighteenth century, American producers and European merchants supplied Muslim markets with both coffee and sugar.

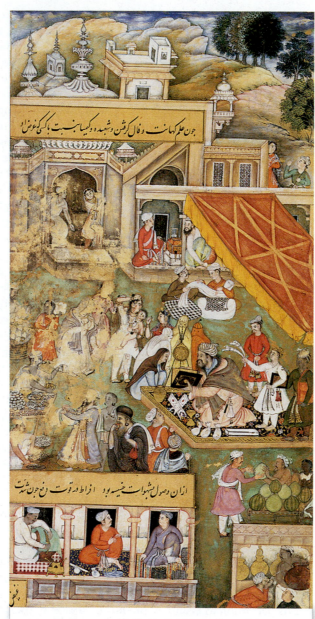

A bustling bazaar in Mughal India. At the center of this painting, a soothsayer attracts a crowd as he consults a manual while telling fortunes. Sacks of coins at his side suggest that he has done good business. Elsewhere in the market consumers buy watermelons, cloth, and peanuts.

Tobacco
According to the Ottoman historian Ibrahim Pechevi, English merchants introduced tobacco around 1600, claiming it was useful for medicinal purposes. Within a few decades it had spread throughout the Ottoman empire. The increasing popularity of coffee drinking and pipe smoking encouraged entrepreneurs to establish coffeehouses where customers could indulge their appetites for caffeine and nicotine at the same time. The popularity of coffeehouses provoked protest from moralists who worried that these popular attractions were dens of iniquity that distracted habitués from their religious duties and attracted crowds of idlers and riffraff. Pechevi complained about the hideous odor of tobacco, the messy ashes, and the danger that smoking could cause fires, and religious leaders claimed that coffee was an illegal beverage and that it was worse to frequent a coffeehouse than a tavern. Sultan Murad IV went so far as to outlaw coffee and tobacco and to execute those who continued to partake. That effort, however, was a losing battle. Both pastimes eventually won widespread acceptance, and the coffeehouse became a prominent social institution in the Islamic empires.

Population Growth
American food crops had less demographic effect in the Islamic empires than in other parts of the world. The population of India surged during early modern times, growing from 105 million in 1500 to 135 million in 1600, 165 million in 1700, and 190 million in 1800. But population growth in India resulted more from intensive agriculture along traditional lines than from the influence of new crops. The Safavid population grew less rapidly, from 5 million in 1500 to 6 million in 1600, and to 8 million in 1800. Ottoman numbers grew from 9 million in 1500 to 28 million in 1600, as the empire enlarged its boundaries to include populous regions in the Balkans, Egypt, and south-

In this anonymous painting produced about 1670, Dutch and English ships lie at anchor in the harbor of the busy port of Surat in northwestern India. Surat was the major port on the west coast of India, and it served as one of the chief commercial cities of the Mughal empire.

west Asia. After 1600, however, the Ottoman population declined to about 24 million, where it remained until the late 1800s. The decline reflected loss of territory more than a shrinking population, but even in the heartland of Anatolia, Ottoman numbers did not expand nearly as dramatically as those of other lands in early modern times. From 6 million in 1500, the population of Anatolia rose to 7.5 million in 1600, 8 million in 1700, and 9 million in 1800.

Trade The Islamic empires ruled lands that had figured prominently in long-distance trade for centuries and participated actively in global trade networks in early modern times. In the Ottoman empire, for example, the early capital at Bursa was also the terminus of a caravan route that brought raw silk from Persia to supply the Italian market. The Ottomans also granted special trading concessions to merchants from England and France to cement alliances against common enemies in Spain and central Europe. Aleppo became an emporium for foreign merchants engaged primarily in the spice trade and served as local headquarters for the operations of the English Levant Company.

Shah Abbas promoted Isfahan as a commercial center, extending trading privileges to foreign merchants and even allowing Christian monastic orders to set up missions there to help create a favorable environment for trade. European merchants sought Safavid raw silk, carpets, ceramics, and high-quality craft items. The English East India Company, the French East India Company, and the Dutch VOC all traded actively with the Safavids. To curry favor with them, the English company sent military advisors to introduce gunpowder weapons to Safavid armed forces and provided a navy to help them retake Hormuz in the Persian Gulf from the Portuguese.

The Mughals did not pay as much attention to foreign trade as the Ottomans and the Safavids did, partly because of the enormous size and productivity of the domestic Indian economy and partly because the Mughal rulers concentrated on their land empire and had little interest in maritime affairs. Nevertheless, the Mughal treasury derived significant income from foreign trade. The Mughals allowed the creation of trading stations and merchant colonies by Portuguese, English, French, and Dutch merchants. Meanwhile, Indian merchants formed trading companies of their own, ventured overland as far as Russia, and sailed the waters of the Indian Ocean to port cities from Persia to Indonesia.

Religious Affairs in the Islamic Empires

Religious Diversity All the Islamic empires had populations that were religiously and ethnically diverse, and imperial rulers had the daunting challenge of maintaining harmony between different religious communities. The Ottoman empire included large numbers of Christians and Jews in the Balkans, Armenia, Lebanon, and Egypt. The Safavid empire embraced sizable Zoroastrian and Jewish communities as well as many Christian subjects in the Caucasus. The Mughal empire was especially diverse. Most Mughal subjects were Hindus, but large numbers of Muslims lived alongside smaller communities of Jains, Zoroastrians, Christians, and devotees of syncretic faiths such as Sikhism.

Christian Mission in India

Portuguese Goa became the center of a Christian mission in India. Priests at Goa sought to attract converts to Christianity and established schools that provided religious instruction for Indian children. In 1580 several Portuguese Jesuits traveled to the Mughal court at Akbar's invitation. They had visions of converting the emperor to Christianity and then spreading their faith throughout India, but their hopes went unfulfilled. Akbar received the Jesuits cordially and welcomed their participation in religious and philosophical discussions at his court, but he declined to commit to an exclusive faith that he thought would alienate many of his subjects.

Akbar's Divine Faith

Indeed, Akbar was cool even to his Islamic faith. In his efforts to find a religious synthesis that would serve as a cultural foundation for unity in his diverse empire, he supported the efforts of the early Sikhs, who combined elements of Hinduism and Islam in a new syncretic faith. He also attempted to elaborate his own "divine faith" that emphasized loyalty to the emperor while borrowing eclectically from different religious traditions. Akbar never explained his ideas systematically, but it is clear that they drew most heavily on Islam. The divine faith was strictly monotheistic, and it reflected the influence of Shiite and Sufi teachings. But it also glorified the emperor: Akbar even referred to himself as the "lord of wisdom," who would guide his subjects to understanding of the world's creator god. The divine faith was tolerant of Hinduism, and it even drew inspiration from Zoroastrianism in its effort to bridge the gaps between Mughal India's many cultural and religious communities.

In a seventeenth-century painting, the emperor Akbar presides over discussions between representatives of various religious groups. Two Jesuits dressed in black robes kneel at the left.

Status of Religious Minorities

The Islamic empires relied on a long-established model to deal with subjects who were not Muslims. They did not require conquered peoples to convert to Islam but extended to them the status of *dhimmi* ("protected people"). In return for their loyalty and payment of a special tax known as *jizya, dhimmi* communities retained their personal freedom, kept their property, practiced their religion, and handled their legal affairs. In the Ottoman empire, for example, autonomous religious communities known as *millet* retained their civil laws, traditions, and languages. *Millet* communities usually also assumed social and administrative functions in matters concerning birth, marriage, death, health, and education.

The situation in the Mughal empire was different, since its large number of religious communities made a *millet* system impractical. Mughal rulers reserved the most powerful military and administrative positions for Muslims, but in the day-to-day management of affairs, Muslims and Hindus cooperated closely. Some Mughal emperors sought to forge links between religious communities. Akbar in particular worked to integrate Muslim and Hindu elites. In an effort to foster communication and understanding among the different religious communities of his realm, he abolished the *jizya,* tolerated all faiths, and sponsored discussions and debates between Muslims, Hindus, Jains, Zoroastrians, and Christians.

thinking about TRADITIONS

Religious Diversity

An overarching feature of all three Islamic empires was the ethnic and religious diversity of the subject populations. What measures did the rulers of the Ottoman, Safavid, and Mughal states take to maintain harmony among the different ethnic and religious communities?

Promotion of Islam Policies of religious tolerance were not popular with many Muslims, who worried that they would lose their religious identity and that toleration might lead to their absorption into Hindu society as another caste. They therefore insisted that Mughal rulers create and maintain an Islamic state based on Islamic law. When Aurangzeb reached the Mughal throne in 1659, this policy gained strength. Aurangzeb reinstated the *jizya* and promoted Islam as the official faith of Mughal India. His policy satisfied zealous Muslims but at the cost of deep bitterness among his Hindu subjects. Tension between Hindu and Muslim communities in India persisted throughout the Mughal dynasty and beyond.

Cultural Patronage of the Islamic Emperors

As the empires matured, the Islamic rulers sought to enhance their prestige through public works projects and patronage of scholars. They competed to attract outstanding religious scholars, poets, artists, and architects to their courts. They lavished resources on mosques, palaces, government buildings, bridges, fountains, schools, hospitals, and soup kitchens for the poor.

Istanbul Capital cities and royal palaces were the most visible expressions of imperial majesty. The Ottomans beautified both Bursa and Edirne, but they took particular pride in Istanbul. Dilapidated and deserted after the conquest, it quickly revived and became a bustling, prosperous city of more than a million people. At its heart was the great Topkapi palace, which housed government offices, such as the mint, and meeting places for imperial councils. At its core was the sultan's residence with its harem, gardens, pleasure pavilions, and a repository for the most sacred possessions of the empire, including the mantle of the prophet Muhammad. Sultan Süleyman the Magnificent was fortunate to be able to draw on the talents of the architectural genius Sinan Pasha (1489–1588) to create the most celebrated of all the monuments of Istanbul. Sinan built a vast religious complex called the Süleymaniye, which blended Islamic and Byzantine architectural elements. It combined tall, slender mina-

rets with large domed buildings supported by half domes in the style of the Byzantine church Hagia Sofia (which the Ottomans converted into the mosque of Aya Sofya).

Isfahan Shah Abbas made his capital, Isfahan, into the queen of Persian cities and one of the most precious jewels of urban architectural development anywhere in the world: its inhabitants still boast that "Isfahan is half the world." Abbas concentrated markets, the palace, and the royal mosque around a vast polo field and public square. Broad, shaded avenues and magnificent bridges linked the central city to its suburbs. Safavid architects made use of monumental entryways, vast arcades, spacious courtyards, and intricate, colorful decoration. Unlike the sprawling Ottoman and Mughal palaces, the Safavid palaces in Isfahan were relatively small and emphasized natural settings with gardens and pools. They were also much more open than Topkapi, with its series of

The massive Süleymaniye mosque built for Sultan Süleyman the Magnificent by the Ottoman architect Sinan Pasha in 1556.

Fatehpur Sikri, built by Akbar in the 1570s, commemorated the emperor's military conquests and housed the tomb of his religious guide. It included a palace, an audience hall where Akbar attended religious and philosophical debates, and a great mosque.

inner courts and gates. Ali Qapu, the palace on the square in Isfahan, had a striking balcony, and most of the palaces had large, open verandas. The point was not only to enable the shah to observe outside activities but also to emphasize his visibility and accessibility, qualities long esteemed in the Persian tradition of kingship.

To some extent, in accordance with steppe traditions, the early Mughals regarded the capital as wherever the ruler happened to camp. Yet they too came to sponsor urban development. Their work skillfully blended central Asian traditions with elements of Hindu architecture, and they built on a scale that left no doubt about their wealth and resources. They constructed scores of mosques, fortresses, and palaces and sometimes created entire cities.

Fatehpur Sikri

Fatehpur Sikri The best example was Fatehpur Sikri, a city planned and constructed by Akbar that served as his capital from 1569 to 1585. It commemorated his conquest of the prosperous commercial province of Gujarat in a campaign that enabled Akbar to head off both Portuguese attacks and Ottoman intervention there. With its mint, records office, treasury, and audience hall, the new city demonstrated Akbar's strength and imperial ambitions. Fatehpur Sikri was also a private residence and retreat for the ruler, reproducing in stone a royal encampment with exquisite pleasure palaces where Akbar indulged his passions for music and conversation with scholars and poets. At yet another level, it was a dramatic display of Mughal piety and devotion, centered on the cathedral mosque and the mausoleum of Akbar's Sufi guru, Shaykh Salim Chisti. Despite their intensely Islamic character, many of the buildings consciously incorporated Indian elements such as verandas supported by columns and

decorations of stone elephants. Even the tomb of Shaykh Chisti bore some resemblance to a Hindu shrine. Unfortunately, Akbar selected a poor site for the city and soon abandoned it because of its bad water supply.

The Taj Mahal The most famous of the Mughal monuments—and one of the most prominent of all Islamic edifices—was the Taj Mahal. Shah Jahan had twenty thousand workers toil for eighteen years to erect the exquisite white marble mosque and tomb. He originally planned to build a similar mausoleum out of black marble for himself, but his son Aurangzeb deposed him before he could carry out the project. Shah Jahan spent his last years confined to a small cell with a tiny window, and only with the aid of a mirror was he able to catch the sight of his beloved wife's final resting place.

THE EMPIRES IN TRANSITION

The Islamic empires underwent dramatic change between the sixteenth and the eighteenth centuries. The Safavid empire disappeared entirely. In 1722 a band of Afghan tribesmen marched all the way to Isfahan, blockaded the city until its starving inhabitants resorted to cannibalism, forced the shah to abdicate, and executed thousands of Safavid officials as well as many members of the royal family. After the death of Aurangzeb in 1707, Mughal India experienced provincial rebellions and foreign invasions. By mid-century the subcontinent was falling under British imperial rule. By 1700 the Ottomans, too, were on the defensive: the sultans lost control over remote provinces such as Lebanon and Egypt, and throughout the eighteenth and nineteenth cen-

The Taj Mahal was a sumptuous mosque and tomb built between 1632 and 1649 by Shah Jahan in memory of his wife, Mumtaz Mahal.

turies European and Russian states placed political, military, and economic pressure on the shrinking Ottoman realm.

The Deterioration of Imperial Leadership

Strong and effective central authority was essential to the Islamic empires, and Muslim political theorists never tired of emphasizing the importance of rulers who were diligent, virtuous, and just. Weak, negligent, and corrupt rulers would allow institutions to become dysfunctional and social

order to break down. The Ottomans were fortunate in having a series of talented sultans for three centuries, and the Safavids and Mughals produced their share of effective rulers as well.

Dynastic Decline Eventually, however, all three dynasties had rulers who were incompetent or more interested in spending vast sums of money on personal pleasures than in tending to affairs of state. Moreover, all three dynasties faced difficulties because of suspicion and fighting among competing members of their ruling houses. The Ottomans sought to limit problems by confining princes in the palace, but that measure had several negative consequences. The princes had no opportunity to gain experience in government, but they were exposed to plots and intrigues of the various factions maneuvering to bring a favorable candidate to the throne. Notorious examples of problem rulers included Süleyman's successor Selim the Sot (reigned 1566–1574) and Ibrahim the Crazy (reigned 1640–1648), who taxed and spent to such excess that government officials deposed and murdered him. Several energetic rulers and talented ministers attempted to keep the government on track. Nonetheless, after the late seventeenth century, weak rule increasingly provoked mutinies in the army, provincial revolts, political corruption, economic oppression, and insecurity throughout the Ottoman realm.

Religious Tensions Political troubles often arose from religious tensions. Conservative Muslim clerics strongly objected to policies and practices that they considered affronts to Islam. Muslim leaders had considerable influence in the Islamic empires because of their monopoly of education and their deep involvement in the everyday lives and legal affairs of ordinary subjects. The clerics mistrusted the emperors' interests in unconventional forms of Islam such as Sufism, complained bitterly when women or subjects who were not Muslims played influential political roles, and protested any exercise of royal authority that contradicted Islamic law.

In the Ottoman empire, disaffected religious students often joined the Janissaries in revolt. A particularly serious threat came from the Wahhabi movement in Arabia, which denounced the Ottomans as dangerous religious innovators who were unfit to rule. Conservative Muslims fiercely protested the construction of an astronomical observatory in Istanbul and forced the sultan to demolish it in 1580. In 1742 they also forced the closure of the Ottoman printing press, which they regarded as an impious technology.

The Safavids, who began their reign by crushing Sunni religious authorities, fell under the domination of the very Shiites they had supported. Shiite leaders pressured the shahs to persecute Sunnis, non-Muslims, and even the Sufis who had helped establish the dynasty. Religious tensions also afflicted Mughal India. Already in the seventeenth century, the conservative Shaykh Ahmad Sirhindi (1564–1624) fearlessly rebuked Akbar for his policy of religious tolerance and his interest in other faiths. In the mid-eighteenth century, as he struggled to claim the Mughal throne, Aurangzeb drew on Sirhindi's ideas when he required non-Muslims to pay the poll tax and ordered the destruction of Hindu temples. Those measures inflamed tensions between the various Sunni, Shiite, and Sufi branches of Islam and also fueled animosity among Hindus and other Mughal subjects who were not Muslims.

Economic and Military Decline

In the sixteenth century, all the Islamic empires had strong domestic economies and played prominent roles in global trade networks. By the eighteenth century, however, domestic economies were under great stress, and foreign trade had declined dramatically or had fallen under the control of European powers. The Islamic empires were well on their way to becoming marginal lands that depended on goods produced elsewhere.

Economic Difficulties The high cost of maintaining an expensive military and administrative apparatus helped

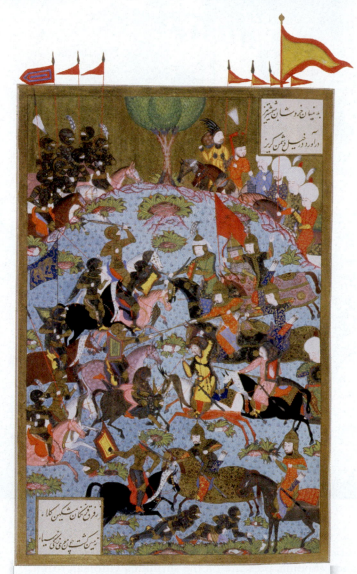

All the Islamic empires fought numerous wars, many of which exhausted resources without adding to the productive capacities of the empires. This illustration depicts Ottoman forces (right) clashing with heavily armored Austrian cavalry near Budapest in 1540.

to bring about economic decline in the Islamic empires. As long as the empires were expanding, they were able to finance their armies and bureaucracies with fresh resources extracted from newly conquered lands. When expansion slowed, ceased, or reversed, however, they faced the problem of supporting their institutions with limited resources. The long, costly, and unproductive wars fought by the Ottomans with the Habsburgs in central Europe, by the Safavids and the Ottomans in Mesopotamia, and by Aurangzeb in southern India, exhausted the treasuries of the Islamic empires without making fresh resources available to them. As early as 1589 the Ottomans tried to pay the Janissaries in debased coinage and immediately provoked a mutiny. The next 150 years witnessed at least six additional military revolts.

As expansion slowed and the empires lost control over remote provinces, officials reacted to the loss of revenue by raising taxes, selling public offices, accepting bribes, or resorting to simple extortion. All those measures were counterproductive. Although they might provide immediate cash, they did long-term economic damage. To make matters worse, the governments viewed foreign trade as just another opportunity to bring in revenue. The Ottomans expanded the privileges enjoyed by foreign merchants, and the Mughals encouraged the establishment of Dutch and English trading outposts and welcomed the expansion of their business in India. Imperial authorities were content to have foreign traders come to them. None made serious efforts to establish commercial stations abroad, although Indian merchants organized their own private trading companies.

Military Decline As they lost initiative to western European peoples in economic and commercial affairs, the Islamic empires also experienced military decline because they did not seek actively to improve their military technologies. As early as the fifteenth century, the Ottomans had relied heavily on European technology in gunnery; indeed, the cannon that Mehmed the Conqueror used in 1453 to breach the defensive wall of Constantinople was the product of a Hungarian gun-founder. During the sixteenth and early seventeenth centuries, the Islamic empires

were able to purchase European weapons in large numbers and attract European expertise that kept their armies supplied with powerful gunpowder weapons. In 1605, for example, the cargo of an English ship bound for Anatolia included seven hundred barrels of gunpowder, one thousand musket barrels, five hundred fully assembled muskets, and two thousand sword blades, alongside wool textiles and bullion.

By about the mid-seventeenth century, European military technology was advancing so rapidly that the Islamic empires could not keep pace. None of the empires had a large armaments industry, so they had to rely on foreign suppliers. They still were able to purchase European weapons and expertise, but their arsenals became increasingly dated, since they depended on technologies that European peoples had already replaced. By the late eighteenth century, the Ottoman navy, which had long influenced maritime affairs in the Mediterranean, Red Sea, Persian Gulf, and Arabian Sea, was closing its shipbuilding operations and ordering new military vessels from foreign shipyards.

Cultural Conservatism

While experiencing economic and military decline, the Islamic empires also neglected cultural developments in the larger world. Europeans who visited the Islamic empires attempted to learn as much as possible about the language, religion, social customs, and history of the host countries. They published accounts of their travels that became extremely popular in their homelands, and they advocated serious study of Islamic lands. In the early seventeenth century, for example, the English scholar William Bedwell described Arabic as the only important language of trade, diplomacy, and religion from Morocco to the China seas.

Piri Reis To some extent, information also flowed in the other direction. During the sixteenth century, just as European mariners were scouting Atlantic waters, Ottoman mariners reconnoitered the Indian Ocean basin from east Africa to Indonesia—a project that reflected military concerns about European and other naval forces in the region. Ottoman geographers also manifested great interest in European

Ottoman cartographer Piri Reis drew on European charts when preparing this map of the Atlantic Ocean basin in 1513. Caribbean and South American coastlines are visible at left, while Iberian and west African coastlines appear in the upper right corner.

thinking about ENCOUNTERS

Islamic Mapmaking

Muslims evinced a generalized wariness about knowledge deriving from European contacts. One notable exception to this was Piri Reis, an Ottoman cartographer. Why did he draw on European sources for his maps? Why were maps seen as so strategically useful in an age of cross-cultural contacts?

knowledge of geography, some of which had considerable military value. The Ottoman admiral and cartographer Piri Reis produced several large-scale maps and a major navigational text, the *Book of Seafaring,* which drew on reports and maps from European mariners and explorers. Piri Reis even managed to consult a copy of a chart drawn by Christopher Columbus during his first voyage to the western hemisphere. Some of Piri Reis's maps included the Atlantic coast of North America and the lands visited by Columbus, which the cartographer probably learned about from Spanish sailors captured in naval conflicts with Ottoman forces.

Cultural Confidence Yet few Muslims traveled willingly to the infidel lands of "the Franks." Muslim rulers and their Muslim subjects were confident of their superiority and believed that they had nothing to learn from Europeans. As a result, most Muslims remained largely oblivious to European cultural and technological developments. Not until 1703 was there an attempt to introduce European scientific instruments such as the telescope into astronomical observatories. Then conservative Muslim clerics soon forced the removal of the foreign implements, which they considered impious and unnecessary.

The Printing Press The early experience of the printing press in the Islamic empires illustrates especially well the resistance of conservative religious leaders to cultural imports from western Europe. Jewish refugees from Spain introduced the first printing presses to Anatolia in the late fifteenth century. Ottoman authorities allowed them to operate presses in Istanbul and other major cities as long as they did not print books in the Turkish or Arabic language. Armenian and Greek printers soon established presses in the Ottoman realm and published books in their own languages. Not until 1729 did government authorities lift the ban on the printing of books in the Turkish and Arabic languages. During the next thirteen years, a Turkish press published seventeen books dealing mostly with history, geography, and language before conservative Muslims forced its closure in 1742. Only in 1784 did a new Turkish press open, and printing spread throughout the Ottoman empire soon thereafter.

Printing also caught on slowly in Mughal India. Jesuit missionaries in Goa published books, including translations of the Bible into Indian and Arabic languages, as early as the 1550s. Yet Mughal rulers displayed little interest in the press, and printing did not become prominent in Indian society until the establishment of British colonial rule in Bengal in the eighteenth century.

To some extent, aesthetic considerations stood in the way of the printing press: particularly in the Ottoman and Safavid empires, as in many other Muslim lands, scholars and general readers alike simply preferred elegant handwritten books to cheaply produced printed works, especially when the book in question was the Quran. Yet resistance to printing also reflected the concerns of conservative religious leaders that readily available printed books would introduce all manner of new and dangerous ideas to the public—indeed, that an active publishing industry might spread inconvenient questions about the organization of Muslim societies or even about the Islamic faith itself.

Thus, like imperial China and Tokugawa Japan, the Islamic empires resisted the introduction of cultural influences from western European societies. Rulers of the Islamic empires readily accepted gunpowder weapons as enhancements to their military and political power, but they and their subjects drew little inspiration from European religion, science, or ideas. Moreover, under the influence of conservative religious leaders, Islamic authorities actively discouraged the circulation of ideas that might pose unsettling challenges to the social and cultural order of the Islamic empires. Like the Ming, Qing, and Tokugawa rulers, the Ottoman, Safavid, and Mughal emperors preferred political and social stability to the risks that foreign cultural innovations might bring.

in**perspective**

Like China and Japan, the Islamic empires largely retained control of their own affairs throughout the early modern era. Ruling elites of the Ottoman, Safavid, and Mughal empires came from nomadic Turkish stock, and they all drew on steppe traditions in organizing their governments. But the rulers also adapted steppe traditions to the needs of settled agricultural societies and devised institutions that maintained order over a long term. During the sixteenth and seventeenth centuries, all the Islamic empires enjoyed productive economies that enabled merchants to participate actively in the global trade networks of early modern times. By the early eighteenth century, however, these same empires were experiencing economic difficulties that led to political and military decline. Like the Ming, Qing, and Tokugawa rulers in east Asia, the Islamic emperors mostly sought to limit foreign and especially European influences in their realms. The Islamic emperors ruled lands that were religiously and ethnically diverse, and most of them worried that the expansion of foreign religious and cultural traditions would threaten political and social stability. They allowed their subjects to practice faiths other than Islam, and the Mughal emperor Akbar even promoted a syncretic religion in hopes that it would defuse tensions between Hindus and Muslims. For the most part, however, rulers of the Islamic empires followed the advice of conservative Muslim clerics, who promoted Islamic values and fought the introduction of foreign cultural imports, such as the printing press and European science, that might undermine their authority. By the late eighteenth century, the Safavid empire had collapsed, and economic difficulties and cultural insularity had severely weakened the Ottoman and Mughal empires. ●

CHRONOLOGY	
1289–1923	Ottoman dynasty
1451–1481	Reign of Mehmed the Conqueror
1453	Ottoman conquest of Constantinople
1501–1524	Reign of Shah Ismail
1501–1722	Safavid dynasty
1514	Battle of Chaldiran
1520–1566	Reign of Süleyman the Magnificent
1526–1858	Mughal dynasty
1556–1605	Reign of Akbar
1588–1629	Reign of Shah Abbas the Great
1659–1707	Reign of Aurangzeb

For Further Reading

Esin Atil. *The Age of Sultan Süleyman the Magnificent.* Washington, D.C., 1987. Richly illustrated volume that emphasizes Süleyman's role as a patron of the arts.

Franz Babinger. *Mehmed the Conqueror and His Time.* Trans. by R. Manheim. Princeton, 1978. A magisterial biography of the sultan who conquered Constantinople.

Jonathan P. Berkey. *The Formation of Islam: Religion and Society in the Near East, 600–1800.* New York, 2002. Broad survey of the history of Islam and Islamic civilization.

Stephen Frederic Dale. *Indian Merchants and Eurasian Trade, 1600–1750.* Cambridge, 1994. Examines the workings of an Indian trading community that conducted business in Persia, central Asia, and Russia.

Suraiya Faroghi. *Towns and Townsmen of Ottoman Anatolia.* Cambridge, 1989. A valuable contribution to an understanding of the Ottoman domestic economy.

Carter Vaughn Findley. *The Turks in World History.* New York, 2005. A highly readable account that connects the two-thousand-year history of the Turkic peoples with larger global processes.

Dina Le Gall. *A Culture of Sufism: Naqshbandis in the Ottoman World, 1450–1700.* Albany, N.Y., 2005. Study of the cultural practices and religious beliefs of an important Sufi brotherhood.

Halil Inalçik. *The Ottoman Empire: The Classical Age, 1300–1600.* New York, 1973. A reliable survey by the foremost historian of the early Ottoman empire.

———— and Donald Quataert, eds. *An Economic and Social History of the Ottoman Empire, 1300–1914.* Cambridge, 1994. An exhaustive survey of Ottoman economic history.

Çemal Kafadar. *Between Two Worlds: The Construction of the Ottoman State.* Berkeley, 1995. Studies the origins and early development of the Ottoman empire.

Kemal H. Karpat. *The Politicization of Islam: Reconstructing Identity, State, Faith, and Community in the Late Ottoman State.* New York, 2001. Scholarly study of the Ottoman state's role in constructing Muslim identity.

Bernard Lewis. *The Muslim Discovery of Europe.* New York, 1982. An important study that charts Muslim interest in European affairs.

Bruce Masters. *The Origins of Western Economic Dominance in the Middle East: Mercantilism and the Islamic Economy in Aleppo, 1600–1750.* New York, 1988. A stimulating case study of an important trading city caught between a central government in chaos and European mercantile pressure.

David Morgan. *Medieval Persia, 1040–1797.* London, 1988. A brief and insightful survey that examines Persian history through the Safavid dynasty.

Leslie Pierce. *The Imperial Harem: Women and Sovereignty in the Ottoman Empire.* Oxford, 1993. Challenges many stereotypes about the role of women in the imperial Ottoman elite.

Gabriel Piterberg. *An Ottoman Tragedy: History and Historiography at Play.* Berkeley, 2003. Analysis of the Ottoman empire in the seventeenth century that also examines the evolution of Ottoman historiography.

John F. Richards. *The Mughal Empire.* Cambridge, 1993. A concise and reliable overview of Mughal history, concentrating on political affairs.

Roger Savory. *Iran under the Safavids.* Cambridge, 1980. A rich and authoritative survey of Safavid history, especially interesting for its views on Safavid origins, culture, and commercial relations.

Madeline Zilfi. *The Politics of Piety: The Ottoman Ulema in the Postclassical Age, 1600–1800.* Minneapolis, 1988. Examines the influence and changing role of the Ottoman religious leadership.

State of the World

Changing Views of the World, Changing Worldviews

Whether signaled by a young Mexican woman serving as an interpreter for Spanish conquerors or by the sounds of chiming clocks in China, novel cross-cultural experiences—on both an intimately human and a coldly technological level—symbolized the intense global transformations taking place in the early modern world. One of the most stunning alterations after 1500 involved the very way humans could now envision a world so perilously and profitably interconnected. Mariners and voyagers from as far afield as east Asia, the Ottoman empire, and western Europe charted the vast expanses of the world's oceans and opened up new human vistas on a world where two previously isolated hemispheres coexisted in an ever-tightening web of global interaction. Detailed maps of the Americas, Oceania, the Indian Ocean basin, and western Africa added to the world's cartographic knowledge and stood as two-dimensional emblems of this changed view of the world—and of the changed worldviews impelled by that new world understanding.

Few societies could withstand the impulses of change emanating from this new, globally intertwined world. Western Europeans in the vanguard of global voyaging in the early modern era consolidated their global influence by establishing empires and settler colonies in the Americas and by setting off a complex process of voluntary and forced human migrations that changed both the world and the worldviews of those involved. Indigenous Americans and Pacific Islanders suffered mass die-offs from epidemics and the consequent dimming of their strength, while the African slaves who replaced them as laborers likewise had their worldviews rudely adjusted during their forced migrations through the Atlantic Ocean basin. And, as the far-flung travels of Thomas Peters suggested, Africans experienced exposure to a complex mixture of worldviews shaped by indigenous African, American, and European ideologies. In this early modern era of interconnectedness, worldviews took on an increasingly cross-cultural cast.

The imperative to change in this era had both external global and internal cultural elements. This was nowhere more evident than in western European societies, where intercontinental outreach was matched by an internal questioning of traditions, whether religious, intellectual, or political. In the age of revolution after 1750, the external and internal pulses of change in Europe would collide and provide it with even more explosive global power. The prosperous societies in the early modern era, such as China, Japan, and the Islamic empires, succeeded in shielding their traditions and their worldviews from the intensifying impulses of change through much of this period. The chimes of those clocks in China, however, served as harbingers of a more deafening weapons technology that threatened imperial intrusion and the further altering of worldviews.

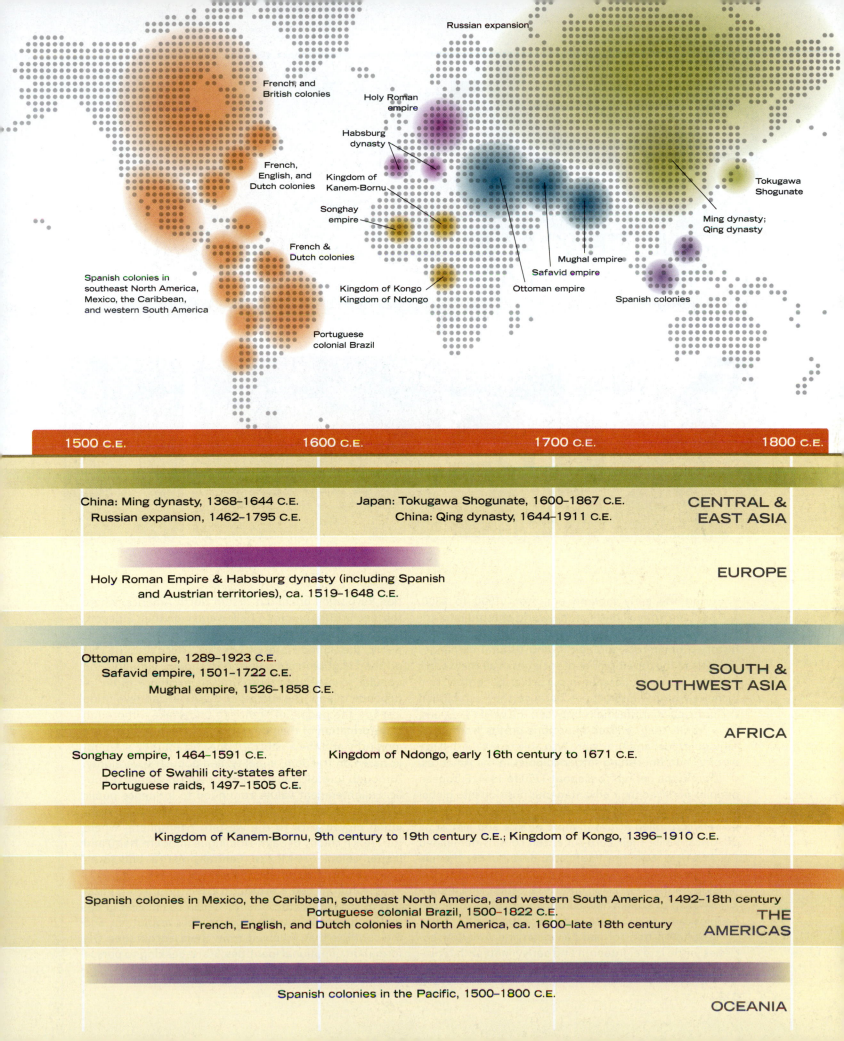

1500 C.E.   **1600 C.E.**   **1700 C.E.**   **1800 C.E.**

CENTRAL & EAST ASIA

China: Ming dynasty, 1368–1644 C.E.   Japan: Tokugawa Shogunate, 1600–1867 C.E.
Russian expansion, 1462–1795 C.E.   China: Qing dynasty, 1644–1911 C.E.

EUROPE

Holy Roman Empire & Habsburg dynasty (including Spanish
and Austrian territories), ca. 1519–1648 C.E.

SOUTH & SOUTHWEST ASIA

Ottoman empire, 1289–1923 C.E.
Safavid empire, 1501–1722 C.E.
Mughal empire, 1526–1858 C.E.

AFRICA

Songhay empire, 1464–1591 C.E.   Kingdom of Ndongo, early 16th century to 1671 C.E.
Decline of Swahili city-states after
Portuguese raids, 1497–1505 C.E.

Kingdom of Kanem-Bornu, 9th century to 19th century C.E.; Kingdom of Kongo, 1396–1910 C.E.

THE AMERICAS

Spanish colonies in Mexico, the Caribbean, southeast North America, and western South America, 1492–18th century
Portuguese colonial Brazil, 1500–1822 C.E.
French, English, and Dutch colonies in North America, ca. 1600–late 18th century

OCEANIA

Spanish colonies in the Pacific, 1500–1800 C.E.

part 6

AN AGE OF REVOLUTION, INDUSTRY, AND EMPIRE, 1750 TO 1914

During the early modern era, from 1500 to 1800, peoples from all parts of the world entered into sustained interactions with one another for the first time in history. Commercial, biological, and cultural exchanges influenced the development of societies in all the world's regions. European peoples in particular benefited from increased global interactions because they established the principal maritime links between the world's regions. As a result, they realized enormous profits from interregional trade, and they were also able to establish large empires and flourishing settler colonies in the Americas.

During the period from about 1750 to 1914, European peoples parlayed their advantageous position into global hegemony: by the late nineteenth century, European powers controlled affairs in most of Asia and almost all of Africa, while their Euro-American cousins dominated the Americas. Even tiny Pacific islands fell under the rule of European and Euro-American peoples. Three historical developments—revolution, industrialization, and imperialism—help to explain how European and Euro-American peoples came to dominate so much of the world.

Revolution transformed European and American societies in the late eighteenth and early nineteenth centu-ries. Revolution broke out first in North America, where thirteen British colonies rebelled and won their independence. These colonies joined together to form a new republic, the United States of America, which drew heavily on the Enlightenment values of freedom, equality, and popular sovereignty in justifying its existence as an independent land. The success of the American revolution inspired the people of France to undertake a thorough transformation of their own society: after abolishing the monarchy and the aristocracy, they established a republic based on freedom, equality, and popular sovereignty. Although turmoil soon brought down the French republic, Enlightenment values continued to influence public affairs in France after the revolution. From France, revolution moved back to the western hemisphere, where the French colony of Saint-Domingue (modern Haiti) and Iberian colonies in Mexico, Central America, and South America won their independence.

Revolutions had a profound effect on the organization of societies in the Atlantic Ocean basin. First in Europe and later in the Americas as well, revolutions and the conflicts that followed from them encouraged the formation of national identities. States seeking to pursue the interests of national communities were able to mobilize popular support on a scale never before achieved and often enjoyed success in conflicts with neighboring peoples who had not been able to organize effective national states. The idea of organizing states around national communities eventually influenced political development throughout the world.

While organizing themselves into national states,

western European and North American peoples also embarked on processes of industrialization. By harnessing inanimate sources of energy and organizing production in factories, industrialists were able to produce high-quality goods at low cost. Because industrialization encouraged continuous innovation, industrial societies were also able to improve constantly on their economic performance. Industrialization caused a great deal of discomfort and dislocation as workers adjusted from the rhythms of agricultural society to the demands of factories, machines, and managers seeking efficiencies in production. Over time, however, industrial societies became economically much stronger than agricultural societies, and industrial production brought about general improvement in material standards of living. After originating in Britain in the late eighteenth century, industrialization spread rapidly to western Europe and North America and, by the late nineteenth century, to Russia and Japan as well. Even the lands that did not undergo processes of industrialization until the twentieth century immediately felt the effects of industrialization as demand rose for agricultural products and natural resources needed by industrial societies.

Alongside increased material standards of living, industrialization also brought political, military, and economic strength. Particularly in western Europe and the United States, where it occurred alongside the formation of national communities, industrialization helped underwrite processes of imperialism and colonialism. Industrial lands developed powerful transportation, communication, and military technologies that agricultural societies could not match. Railroads, steamships, telegraphs, and lethal weapons enabled western European peoples to impose their rule in most of Asia and Africa in the nineteenth century, just as Euro-American settlers relied on industrial technologies to drive the indigenous peoples of North America and South America onto marginal lands. Toward the end of the nineteenth century, the United States and Japan each used their industrial technologies to increase their presence in the larger world and thus joined western European lands as global imperial and colonial powers.

Revolution, industrialization, and imperialism had effects that were felt around the world. Western European and North American lands vastly strengthened their position in the world by exercising political or economic influence over other societies. In some lands, particularly the Ottoman empire, Russia, China, and Japan, reformers worked to restructure their societies and increase their influence in global affairs by building national states that harnessed the energies of their populations. In doing so they studied the experience of western European societies and sought to adapt the principles of European political and social organization to their societies. In the absence of a revolution that toppled ruling elites, however, critics found it difficult to bring about meaningful reform, since privileged classes resisted change that threatened their position in their societies. Colonized peoples had even less opportunity to bring about political and social reform, but they frequently resisted imperial powers by mounting rebellions and organizing anticolonial movements. Revolution, industry, and empire fueled conflict throughout the world in the nineteenth century, and in combination they forced the world's peoples to deal with each other more systematically than ever before in history.

Revolutions and National States in the Atlantic World

chapter28

Liberty, personified as a woman, leads the French people in a famous painting by Eugène Delacroix.

EYEWITNESS:
Olympe de Gouges Declares the Rights of Women

Marie Gouze was a French butcher's daughter who educated herself by reading books, moved to Paris, and married a junior army officer. Under the name Olympe de Gouges, she won some fame as a journalist, actress, and playwright. Gouges was as flamboyant as she was talented, and news of her well-publicized love affairs scandalized Parisian society.

Gouges was also a revolutionary and a strong advocate of women's rights. She responded enthusiastically when the French revolution broke out in July 1789, and she applauded in August when revolutionary leaders proclaimed freedom and equality for all citizens in the *Declaration of the Rights of Man and the Citizen.* It soon became clear, however, that in the view of revolutionary leaders, freedom and equality pertained only to male citizens. They welcomed women's contributions to the revolution but withheld the right to vote and left women under the patriarchal authority of their fathers and husbands.

Gouges campaigned fervently to raise the standing of women in French society. She called for more education and demanded that women share equal rights in family property. She challenged patriarchal authority and appealed to Queen Marie Antoinette to use her influence to advance women's rights. In 1791 Gouges published a *Declaration of the Rights of Woman and the Female Citizen,* which claimed the same rights for women that revolutionary leaders had granted to men in August 1789. She asserted that freedom and equality were inalienable rights of women as well as men, and she insisted on the rights of women to vote, speak their minds freely, participate in the making of law, and hold public office.

Gouges's declaration attracted a great deal of attention but little support. Revolutionary leaders dismissed her appeal as a publicity stunt and refused to put women's rights on their political agenda. In 1793 they executed her because of her affection for Marie Antoinette and her persistent crusade for women's rights. Yet Gouges's campaign illustrated the power of the Enlightenment ideals of freedom and equality. Revolutionary leaders stilled her voice, but once they had proclaimed freedom and equality as universal human rights, they were unable to suppress demands to extend them to new constituencies.

Violence rocked lands throughout much of the Atlantic Ocean basin in the late eighteenth and early nineteenth centuries as a series of revolutions and wars of independence brought dramatic political and social change. Royal subjects attempted to restructure their societies—if necessary by violent means—by abolishing traditional social and political institutions and replacing them with novel ones. The notion of a divinely ordained division between ruler and ruled ceased to exist, as the politically activated masses not only sought to participate in government but also actually viewed it as their inherent right to do so. Each revolution broke out in its own context and had its own specific causes. Yet all derived, directly or indirectly, their inspiration and rationalization from the Enlightenment.

Revolution broke out first in the British colonies of North America, where colonists asserted their independence and founded a new republic. A few years later, revolutionaries abolished the French monarchy and thoroughly reorganized French society. Revolutionary ideas soon spread to other lands. They inspired popular movements throughout Europe and prompted Latin American peoples to seek independence from Spanish and Portuguese colonial rule. In Saint-Domingue, revolution led to the abolition of slavery as well as independence from French rule. By the 1830s, peoples had reorganized political and social structures throughout western Europe and the Americas.

Apart from affecting individual lands, the revolutions of the late eighteenth and early nineteenth centuries had two results of deep global significance. First, they helped to spread a cluster of Enlightenment ideas concerning freedom, equality, and popular sovereignty. Revolutionary leaders argued that political authority arose from the people and worked to establish states in the interests of the people rather than the rulers. Usually, they instituted republican forms of government, in which constituents selected delegates to represent their interests. In fact, early revolutionaries extended political rights to a privileged group of white men, but they justified their actions in general terms that invited new constituencies to seek enfranchisement. Ideas about freedom, equality, and popular sovereignty spread globally after the American and French revolutions as social reformers and revolutionaries struggled throughout the nineteenth and twentieth centuries to make freedom and equality a reality for oppressed groups and subject peoples throughout the world. By the mid-twentieth century, nearly every state in the world formally recognized the freedom and equality of all its citizens—even if they did not always honor their official positions—and claimed authority to rule on the basis of popular sovereignty.

While promoting Enlightenment values, revolutions also encouraged the consolidation of national states as the principal form of political organization. As peoples defended their states from enemies and sometimes mounted attacks on foreign lands, they developed a powerful sense of identity with their compatriots, and nationalist convictions inspired them to work toward the foundation of states that would advance the interests of the national community. During the nineteenth century, strong national identities and movements to build national states profoundly influenced the political experiences of European states. Strong nationalist sentiments created problems for multicultural states such as the Austrian empire, which embraced several distinct linguistic and ethnic communities, but also fueled movements to unify lands such as Italy and Germany, which previously had no national state. During the late nineteenth and twentieth centuries, efforts to harness nationalist sentiments and form states based on national identity became one of the most powerful and dynamic movements in world history.

POPULAR SOVEREIGNTY AND POLITICAL UPHEAVAL

Drawing on Enlightenment ideals, revolutionaries of the eighteenth and nineteenth centuries sought to fashion an equitable society by instituting governments that were responsive to the needs and interests of the peoples they governed. In justifying their policies, revolutionaries attacked monarchical and aristocratic regimes and argued for popular sovereignty—the notion that legitimate political authority resides not in kings but, rather, in the people who make up a society. In North America, colonists declared independence from British rule and instituted a new government founded on the principle of popular sovereignty. Soon thereafter, French revolutionaries abolished the monarchy and revamped the social order. Enlightenment ideals had

given focus to a combination of social and political factors that motivated French revolutionaries, including their resentment of royal, noble, and clerical privileges as well as their own aspirations for freedom of religion, liberty, and republicanism. Yet revolutionaries in France were unable to devise a stable alternative to the monarchy, and French society experienced turmoil for more than twenty years. In the early nineteenth century, Napoleon Bonaparte imposed military rule on France and helped spread revolutionary ideas to much of western Europe.

Enlightened and Revolutionary Ideas

Throughout history, kings or emperors ruled almost all settled agricultural societies. Small societies occasionally instituted democratic governments, in which all citizens participated in political affairs, or republican governments, in which delegates represented the interests of various constituencies. Some societies, especially those with weak central leadership, also relied on aristocratic governments, in which privileged elites supervised public affairs. But hierarchical rule flowing from a king or an emperor was by far the most common form of government in settled agricultural societies.

In justifying their rule, kings and emperors throughout the world often identified themselves with deities or claimed divine sanction for their authority. Some rulers were priests, and most others cooperated closely with religious authorities. On the basis of their association with divine powers, kings and emperors claimed sovereignty—political supremacy and the authority to rule. In imperial China, for example, dynastic houses claimed to rule in accordance with the "mandate of heaven," and in early modern Europe centralizing monarchs often asserted a "divine right of kings" to rule as absolute monarchs.

Popular Sovereignty During the seventeenth and eighteenth centuries, philosophes and other advocates of Enlightenment ideas (discussed in chapter 23) began to question long-standing notions of sovereignty. The philosophes rarely challenged monarchical rule, but sought instead to make kings responsible to the people they governed. They commonly regarded government as the result of a contract between rulers and ruled. The English philosopher John Locke (1632–1704) formulated one of the most influential theories of contractual government. In his *Second Treatise of Civil Government,* published in 1690, Locke held that government arose in the remote past when people decided to work together, form civil society, and appoint rulers to protect and promote their common interests. Individuals granted political rights to their rulers but retained personal rights to life, liberty, and property. Any ruler who violated those rights was subject to deposition. Furthermore, according to Locke, because individuals voluntarily formed society and established government, rulers derived their authority from the consent of those whom they governed. If subjects withdrew their consent, they had the right to replace their rulers. In effect, Locke's political thought relocated sovereignty, removing it from rulers as divine agents and vesting it in the people of a society.

Individual Freedom Enlightenment thinkers addressed issues of freedom and equality as well as sovereignty. Philosophes such as Voltaire (1694–1778) resented the persecution of religious minorities and the censorship of royal officials, who had the power to prevent printers from publishing works that did not meet the approval of political and religious authorities. Philosophes called for religious toleration and freedom to express their views openly. When censors prohibited the publication of their writings in France, they often worked with French-speaking printers in Switzerland or the Netherlands who published their books and smuggled them across the border into France.

Political and Legal Equality Many Enlightenment thinkers also called for equality. They condemned the legal and social privileges enjoyed by aristocrats, who in the philosophes' view made no more contribution to the larger society than a peasant, an artisan, or a crafts worker. They recommended the creation of a society in which all individuals would be equal before the law. The most prominent advocate of political equality was the French-Swiss thinker Jean-Jacques Rousseau (1712–1778), who identified with simple working people and deeply resented the privileges enjoyed by elite classes. In his influential book *The Social Contract* (1762), Rousseau argued that members of a society were collectively the sovereign. In an ideal society all individuals would participate directly in the formulation of policy and the creation of laws. In the absence of royalty, aristocrats, or other privileged elites, the general will of the people would carry the day.

Enlightenment thought on freedom, equality, and popular sovereignty reflected the interests of educated and talented men who sought to increase their influence and enhance their status in society. Most Enlightenment thinkers were of common birth but comfortable means. Although seeking to limit the prerogatives of ruling and aristocratic classes, they did not envision a society in which they would share political rights with women, children, peasants, laborers, slaves, or people of color.

Global Influence of Enlightenment Values Nevertheless, Enlightenment thought constituted a serious challenge to long-established notions of political and social order. Revolutionary leaders in Europe and the Americas readily adopted Enlightenment ideas when justifying their efforts to overhaul the political and social structures they inherited. Over time, Enlightenment political thought influenced the organization of states and societies throughout the world. Enlightenment ideals did not spread naturally or inevitably. Rather, they spread when social reformers and revolutionaries claimed rights previously denied to them by ruling authorities and elite classes. Arguments for freedom, equality, and popular sovereignty originally served the interests of relatively privileged European and Euro-American men, but many other groups made effective use of them in seeking the extension of political rights.

The American Revolution

In the mid-eighteenth century there was no sign that North America might become a center of revolution. Residents of the thirteen British colonies there regarded themselves as British subjects: they recognized British law, read English-language books, and often braved the stormy waters of the North Atlantic Ocean to visit friends and family in England. Trade brought prosperity to the colonies, and British military forces protected colonists' interests. From 1754 to 1763, for example, British forces waged an extremely expensive conflict in North America known as the French and Indian War. This conflict merged with a larger contest for imperial supremacy, the Seven Years' War (1756–1763), in which British and French forces battled each other in Europe and India as well as North America. Victory in the Seven Years' War ensured that Britain would dominate global trade and that British possessions, including the North American colonies, would prosper.

Tightened British Control of the Colonies

After the mid-1760s, however, North American colonists became increasingly disenchanted with British imperial rule, in some measure because colonists had become accustomed to a degree of autonomy. The geographic distance separating England and the colonies as well as the inevitable inefficiency of the imperial bureaucracy had weakened royal power. Nearly every colony had an elective legislative assembly that had gained control over legislation affecting taxation and defense and that ultimately controlled the salaries paid to royal officials. The colonists resisted once the British attempted to reinvigorate imperial control. Faced with staggering financial difficulties arising from the Seven Years' War, the British Parliament passed legislation to levy new taxes and bring order to a far-flung trading empire. Parliament expected that the North American colonies would bear a fair share of the empire's tax burden and respect imperial trade policies. But parliamentary legislation proved extremely unpopular in North America. Colonists especially resented the imposition of taxes on molasses by the Sugar Act (1764), on publications and legal documents by the Stamp Act (1765), on a wide variety of imported items by the Townshend Act (1767), and on tea by the Tea Act (1773). They objected to strict enforcement of navigation laws—some of them a century old, but widely disregarded—that required cargoes to travel in British ships and clear British customs. Colonists also took offense at the Quartering Act (1765), which required them to provide housing and accommodations for British troops.

In responding to British policies, the colonists argued that Parliament could do nothing in the colonies that it could

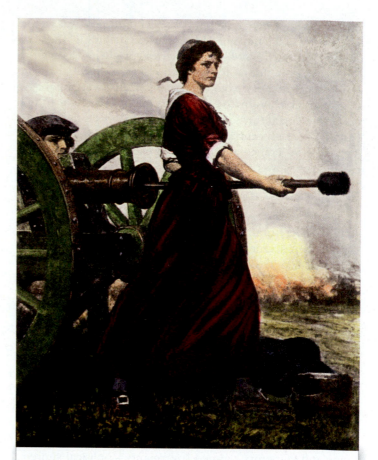

In this painting by C. Y. Turner, Molly Pitcher, an imaginary heroine of the American revolution, is shown at the 1778 battle of Monmouth loading a cannon. Many historians regard Molly Pitcher as folklore, as a composite image inspired by the actions of a number of real women. The name itself may have originated as a nickname given to women who carried water to men on the battlefield.

not do in Britain because the Americans were protected by all the common-law rights of the British. The colonists in effect embraced legal traditions that were first demonstrated during the English Civil War (1641–1651), establishing the constitutional precedent that an English monarch cannot govern without Parliament's consent. This concept was legally enshrined in the Bill of Rights (1689), which established among other rights that the consent of Parliament is required for the implementation of any new taxes. Thus, the colonists responded to new parliamentary levies with the slogan "no taxation without representation." They boycotted British products, physically attacked British officials, and mounted protests such as the Boston Tea Party (1773), in which colonists dumped a cargo of tea into Boston harbor rather than pay duties under the Tea Act. They also organized the Continental Congress (1774), which coordinated the colonies' resistance to British policies. By 1775 tensions were so high that British troops and a colonial militia skirmished at the village of Lexington, near Boston. The war of American independence had begun.

The Declaration of Independence

On 4 July 1776 the Continental Congress adopted a document entitled "The unanimous Declaration of the thirteen united States of America." This Declaration of Independence drew deep inspiration from Enlightenment political thought in justifying the colonies' quest for independence. The document asserted "that all men are created equal, that they are endowed by their Creator with certain unalienable Rights, that among these are Life, Liberty, and the pursuit of Happiness." It echoed John Locke's contractual theory of government in arguing that individuals established governments to secure those rights and in holding that governments derive their power and authority from "the consent of the governed." When any government infringes upon individuals' rights, the document continued, "it is the Right of the People to alter or abolish it, and to institute new Government." The Declaration of Independence presented a long list of specific abuses charged to the British crown and concluded by proclaiming the colonies "Free and Independent States" with "full Power to levy War, conclude Peace, contract Alliances, establish Commerce, and to do all other Acts and Things which Independent States may of right do."

Divided Loyalties

It was one thing to declare independence, but a different matter altogether to make independence a reality. At the beginning of the war for independence, Britain enjoyed many advantages over the rebels: a strong government with clear lines of authority, the most powerful navy in the world, a competent army, a sizable population of loyalists in the colonies, and an overall colonial population with mixed sentiments about revolution. In their political views and attitudes, the colonial population was far from homogeneous. Political loyalties varied between and within regions and communities and frequently shifted during the course of the revolution. Although "patriots," those who supported the revolution, were in the majority, not every colonist favored a violent confrontation with the British empire. An estimated 20 percent of the white population of the colonies were "loyalists" or "Tories" who remained loyal to the

Washington Crossing the Delaware is an 1851 oil-on-canvas painting by German American artist Emanuel Leutze. It commemorates Washington's crossing of the Delaware on 25 December 1776, during the American revolutionary war. A copy of this painting hangs in the West Wing reception area of the White House.

British monarchy. A minority of people tried to stay neutral in the conflict, most notably the Religious Society of Friends of Pennsylvania, a religious movement better known as the Quakers. Native Americans were divided in their loyalties. Tribes that depended on colonial trade usually threw their weight behind the patriots, but most native Americans east of the Mississippi distrusted the colonists, and thus supported the British cause. African-Americans understood the political rhetoric of the times as promising freedom and equality, but their hopes were not realized. British promises of freedom for service were at best halfhearted. The British faced a dilemma: how to exploit the colonists' fear of slave revolts while also reassuring loyal slave owners and wealthy planters that their slave property would remain secure. Rather than advocating slave revolts, the British more commonly lampooned American advocates of independence for their hypocritical calls for freedom while many of their leaders were slave holders.

Nonetheless, Britain also faced some real difficulties in suppressing the revolution. Waging a war in a distant land full of opponents, Britain had to ship supplies and reinforcements across a stormy ocean. Meanwhile, the rebels benefited from the military and economic support of European states that were eager to chip away at British hegemony in the Atlantic Ocean basin: France, Spain, the Netherlands, and several German principalities contributed to the American quest for independence. Moreover, George Washington (1732–1799) provided strong and imaginative military leadership for the colonial army while local militias employed guerrilla tactics effectively against British forces.

By 1780 all combatants were weary of the conflict. In the final military confrontation of the war, American and French forces under the command of George Washington surrounded the British forces of Charles Cornwallis at Yorktown, Virginia. After a twenty-day siege, the British forces surrendered in October 1781, and major military hostilities ceased from that point forward. In September 1783 diplomats concluded the Peace of Paris, by which the British government formally recognized American independence.

Building an Independent State
The leaders of the fledgling republic organized a state that reflected Enlightenment principles. In 1787 a constitutional convention drafted the blueprint for a new system of government—the Constitution of the United States—which emphasized the rights of

MAP 28.1

The American revolution.
Note both the location of the major towns and cities in the colonies and the location of the major battles that occurred during the revolution.

Why were both situated so close to the eastern coast?

individuals. American leaders based the federal government on popular sovereignty, and they agreed to follow this written constitution that guaranteed individual liberties such as freedom of speech, of the press, and of religion. They did not grant political and legal equality to all inhabitants of the newly independent land. They accorded full rights only to men of property, withholding them from landless men, women, slaves, and indigenous peoples. Over time, however, disenfranchised groups claimed and struggled for political and legal rights. Their campaigns involved considerable personal sacrifice and sometimes led to violence, since those in possession of rights did not always share them readily with others. With the extension of civil rights, American society broadened the implications of the Enlightenment values of freedom and equality as well as popular sovereignty.

The French Revolution

French revolutionaries also drew inspiration from Enlightenment political thought, but the French revolution was a more radical affair than its American counterpart. American revolutionary leaders sought independence from British imperial rule, but they were content to retain British law and much of their British social and cultural heritage. In contrast, French revolutionary leaders repudiated existing society, often referred to as the *ancien régime* ("old order"), and sought to replace it with new political, social, and cultural structures. But, unlike their American counterparts, French revolutionaries lacked experience with self-government.

The Estates General Serious fiscal problems put France on the road to revolution. In the 1780s approximately half of the French royal government's revenue went to pay off war debts—some of them arising from French support for colonists in the war of American independence—and an additional quarter went to French armed forces. King Louis XVI (reigned 1774–1793) was unable to raise more revenue from the overburdened peasantry, so he sought to increase taxes on the French nobility, which had long been exempt from many levies. Aristocrats protested that effort and forced Louis to summon the Estates General, an assembly that represented the entire French population through groups known as estates. In the ancien régime there were three estates, or political classes. The first estate consisted of about one hundred thousand Roman Catholic clergy, and the second included some four hundred thousand nobles. The third estate embraced the rest of the population—about twenty-four million serfs, free peasants, and urban residents ranging from laborers, artisans, and shopkeepers to physicians, bankers, and attorneys. Though founded in 1303, the Estates General had not met since 1614. The third estate had as many delegates as the other two estates combined, but that numerical superiority offered no advantage when the assembly voted on issues, because voting took place by estate—one vote for each—not by individuals.

In May 1789 King Louis called the Estates General into session at the royal palace of Versailles in hopes that it would authorize new taxes. Louis never controlled the assembly. Representatives of the third estate arrived at Versailles demanding political and social reform. Although some members of the lower clergy and a few prominent nobles supported reform, the first and second estates stymied efforts to push measures through the Estates General.

The National Assembly On 17 June 1789, after several weeks of fruitless debate, representatives of the third estate took the dramatic step of seceding from the Estates General

A contemporary print depicts the storming of the Bastille in 1789. The deeds of common people working in crowds became a favorite theme of artists after the outbreak of the French revolution.

sources from the past

Declaration of the Rights of Man and the Citizen

While developing their program of reform, members of the National Assembly consulted closely with Thomas Jefferson, the principal author of the American Declaration of Independence, who was the U.S. ambassador to France in 1789. Thus it is not surprising that the Declaration of the Rights of Man and the Citizen *reflects the influence of American revolutionary ideas.*

First Article. Men are born and remain free and equal in rights. Social distinctions may be based only on common utility.

Article 2. The goal of every political association is the preservation of the natural and inalienable rights of man. These rights are liberty, property, security, and resistance to oppression.

Article 3. The principle of all sovereignty resides essentially in the nation. No body and no individual can exercise authority that does not flow directly from the nation.

Article 4. Liberty consists in the freedom to do anything that does not harm another. The exercise of natural rights of each man thus has no limits except those that assure other members of society their enjoyment of the same rights. These limits may be determined only by law.

Article 6. Law is the expression of the general will. All citizens have the right to participate either personally or through their representatives in the making of law. The law must be the same for all, whether it protects or punishes. Being equal in the eyes of the law, all citizens are equally eligible for all public honors, offices, and occupations, according to their abilities, without any distinction other than that of their virtues and talents.

Article 7. No person shall be accused, arrested, or imprisoned except in the cases and according to the forms prescribed by law. Any one soliciting, transmitting, executing, or causing to be executed, any arbitrary order, shall be pun-ished. But any citizen summoned or arrested in virtue of the law shall submit without delay, as resistance constitutes an offense.

Article 9. As all persons are held innocent until they shall have been declared guilty, if arrest shall be deemed indispensable, all harshness not essential to the securing of the prisoner's person shall be severely repressed by law.

Article 11. The free communication of thoughts and opinions is one of the most precious rights of man: every citizen may thus speak, write, and publish freely, but will be responsible for abuse of this freedom in cases decided by the law.

Article 13. For the maintenance of public military force and for the expenses of administration, common taxation is necessary: it must be equally divided among all citizens according to their means.

Article 15. Society has the right to require from every public official an accounting of his administration.

Article 16. Any society in which guarantees of rights are not assured and separation of powers is not defined has no constitution at all.

Article 17. Property is an inviolable and sacred right. No one may be deprived of property except when public necessity, legally determined, clearly requires it, and on condition of just and prearranged compensation.

For Further Reflection

■ In what ways do the principles established in the Declaration reflect the political transformations taking place throughout the age of Atlantic revolutions?

Source: *Déclaration des droits de l'homme et du citoyen.* Translated by Jerry H. Bentley.

---

and proclaiming themselves to be the National Assembly. Three days later, meeting in an indoor tennis court, members of the new Assembly swore not to disband until they had provided France with a new constitution. On 14 July 1789 a Parisian crowd, fearing that the king sought to undo events of the previous weeks, stormed the Bastille, a royal jail and arsenal, in search of weapons. The military garrison protecting the Bastille surrendered to the crowd but only after killing many of the attackers. To vent their rage, members of the crowd hacked the defenders to death. One assailant used his pocketknife to sever the garrison commander's head, which the victorious crowd mounted on a pike and paraded around the streets of Paris. News of the event soon spread, sparking insurrections in cities throughout France.

Emboldened by popular support, the National Assembly undertook a broad program of political and social reform. The *Declaration of the Rights of Man and the Citizen,* which the National Assembly promulgated in August 1789, articulated the guiding principles of the program. Reflecting the influence of American revolutionary ideas, the *Declaration of the Rights of Man and the Citizen* proclaimed the equality of all men, declared that sovereignty resided in the people, and asserted individual rights to liberty, property, and security.

Liberty, Equality, and Fraternity Between 1789 and 1791 the National Assembly reconfigured French society. Taking "liberty, equality, and fraternity" as its goals, the As-

sembly abolished the old social order along with the many fees and labor services that peasants owed to their landlords. It dramatically altered the role of the church in French society by seizing church lands, abolishing the first estate, defining clergy as civilians, and requiring clergy to take an oath of loyalty to the state. It also promulgated a constitution that made the king the chief executive official but deprived him of legislative authority. France became a constitutional monarchy in which men of property—about half the adult male population—had the right to vote in elections to choose legislators. Thus far, the French revolution represented an effort to put Enlightenment political thought into practice.

The Convention The revolution soon took a radical turn. Efforts by the French nobility to mobilize foreign powers in support of the king and the restoration of the ancien régime gave the Assembly the pretext to declare war against Austria and Prussia in April 1792. Adding to the military burden of France, revolutionary leaders declared war in the following year on Spain, Britain, and the Netherlands. Fearing military defeat and counterrevolution, revolutionary leaders created the Convention, a new legislative body elected by universal manhood suffrage, which abolished the monarchy and proclaimed France a republic. The Convention rallied the French population by instituting the *levée en masse* ("mass levy"), or universal conscription that drafted people and resources for use in the war against invading forces. The Convention also rooted out enemies at home. It made frequent use of the guillotine, a recently invented machine that brought about supposedly humane executions by quickly severing a victim's head. In 1793 King Louis XVI and his wife, Queen Marie Antoinette, themselves went to the guillotine when the Convention found them guilty of treason.

Revolutionary chaos reached its peak in 1793 and 1794 when Maximilien Robespierre (1758–1794) and the radical Jacobin party dominated the Convention. A lawyer by training, Robespierre had emerged during the revolution as a ruthless but popular radical known as "the Incorruptible," and he dominated the Committee of Public Safety, the executive authority of the Republic. The Jacobins believed passionately that France needed complete restructuring, and they unleashed a campaign of terror to promote their revolutionary agenda. They sought to eliminate the influence of Christianity in French society by closing churches and forcing priests to take wives. They promoted a new "cult of reason" as a secular alternative to Christianity. They reorganized the calendar, keeping months of thirty days but replacing seven-day weeks with ten-day units that recognized no day of religious observance. The Jacobins also proclaimed the inauguration of a new historical era with the Year I, which began with the declaration of the First Republic on 22 September 1792. They encouraged citizens to display their revolutionary zeal by wearing working-class clothes. They granted increased rights to women by permitting them to inherit property and divorce their husbands, although they did not allow women to vote or participate in political affairs. The Jacobins also made frequent use of the guillotine: between the summer of 1793 and the summer of 1794, they executed about forty thousand people and imprisoned three hundred thousand suspected enemies of the revolution. Even the feminist Olympe de Gouges (1748–1793) was a victim of the Jacobins, who did not appreciate her efforts to extend the rights of freedom and equality to women.

The Directory Many victims of this reign of terror were fellow radicals who fell out of favor with Robespierre and the Jacobins. The instability of revolutionary leadership eventually undermined confidence in the regime itself. In July 1794 the Convention arrested Robespierre and his allies, convicted them of tyranny, and sent them to the guillotine. A group of conservative men of property then seized power and ruled France under a new institution known as the Directory (1795–1799). Though more pragmatic than previous revolutionary leaders, members of the Directory were unable to resolve the economic and military problems that plagued revolutionary France. In seeking a middle way between the ancien régime and radical revolution, they lurched from one policy to another, and the Directory faced constant challenges to its authority. It came to an end in November 1799 when a young general named Napoleon Bonaparte staged a coup d'état and seized power.

The Reign of Napoleon

Born to a minor noble family of Corsica, a Mediterranean island annexed by France in 1768, Napoleon Bonaparte (1769–1821) studied at French military schools and became an officer in the army of King Louis XVI. A brilliant military leader, he became a general at age twenty-four. He was a fervent supporter of the revolution and defended the Directory against a popular uprising in 1795. In a campaign of 1796–1797, he drove the Austrian army from northern Italy and established French rule there. In 1798 he mounted an invasion of Egypt to gain access to the Red Sea and threaten British control of the sea route to India, but the campaign ended in a complete British victory. Politically ambitious, Napoleon returned to France in 1799, overthrew the Directory, and set up a new government, the Consulate. Although ostensibly he shared power with two other consuls, it was Napoleon who was henceforth the real master of France. Having established a dictatorship, he crowned himself emperor in 1802.

Napoleonic France Napoleon brought political stability to a land torn by revolution and war. He made peace with the Roman Catholic church and in 1801 concluded an agreement with the pope. The pact, known as the Concordat, provided that the French state would retain church lands seized during the revolution, but the state agreed to pay clerics' salaries, recognize Roman Catholic Christianity as the preferred faith of France, and extend freedom of religion to Protestant Christians and Jews. This

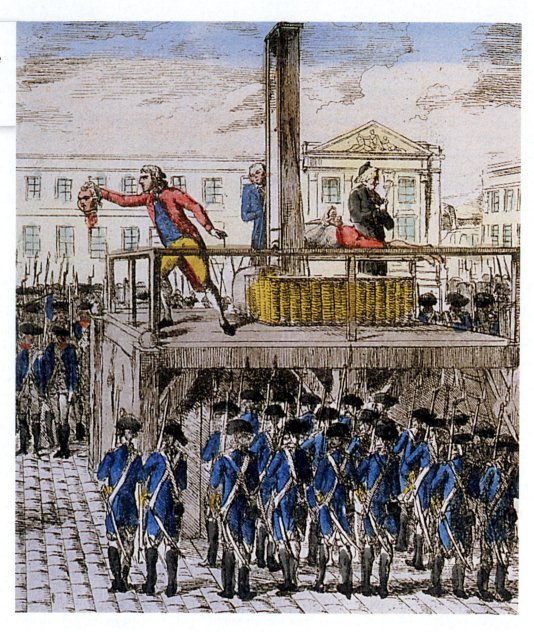

The guillotine was an efficient killing machine. In this contemporary print the executioner displays the just-severed head of King Louis XVI to the crowd assembled to witness his execution.

measure won Napoleon a great deal of support from people who supported the political and social goals of the revolution but balked at radicals' efforts to replace Christianity with a cult of reason.

In 1804 Napoleon promulgated the Civil Code, a revised body of civil law, which also helped stabilize French society. The Civil Code affirmed the political and legal equality of all adult men and established a merit-based society in which individuals qualified for education and employment because of talent rather than birth or social standing. The code protected private property, and Napoleon allowed aristocratic opponents of the revolution to return to France and reclaim some of their lost property. The Civil Code confirmed many of the moderate revolutionary policies of the National Assembly but retracted measures passed by the more radical Convention. The code restored patriarchal authority in the

family, for example, by making women and children subservient to male heads of households. French civil law became the model for the civil codes of Québec Province, Canada, the Netherlands, Italy, Spain, some Latin American republics, and the state of Louisiana.

Although he approved the Enlightenment ideal of equality, Napoleon was no champion of intellectual freedom or representative government. He limited free speech and routinely censored newspapers and other publications. He established a secret police force that relied heavily on spies and detained suspected political opponents by the thousands. He made systematic use of propaganda to manipulate public opinion. He ignored elective bodies and surrounded himself with loyal military officers who ensured that representative assemblies did not restrict his authority. When he crowned himself emperor, he founded a dy-

Jacques-Louis David's *Napoleon on Horseback at the St. Bernard Pass* (1800) presents a famously heroic image of Napoleon's attack on Italy in 1800. David's art clearly served the interests of Napoleon's political regime. The powerful and dynamic image was intended to convey Napoleon's greatness and his place in the history of conquering heroes.

nasty that set his family above and apart from the people in whose name they ruled.

Napoleon's Empire While working to stabilize France, Napoleon also sought to extend his authority throughout Europe. Napoleon's armies conquered the Iberian and Italian peninsulas, occupied the Netherlands, and inflicted humiliating defeats on Austrian and Prussian forces. Napoleon sent his brothers and other relatives to rule the conquered and occupied lands, and he forced Austria, Prussia, and Russia to ally with him and respect French hegemony in Europe. Napoleon's empire began to unravel in 1812, when he decided to invade Russia. Convinced that the tsar was conspiring with his British enemies, Napoleon led a Grand Army of six hundred thousand soldiers to Moscow. He captured the city, but the tsar withdrew and refused to surrender. Russians set Moscow ablaze, leaving Napoleon's massive army without adequate shelter or supplies.

The Fall of Napoleon Napoleon's disastrous Russian campaign emboldened his enemies. A coalition of British,

Austrian, Prussian, and Russian armies converged on France and forced Napoleon to abdicate his throne in April 1814. The victors restored the French monarchy and exiled Napoleon to the tiny Mediterranean island of Elba, near Corsica. But Napoleon's adventure had not yet come to an end. In March 1815 he escaped from Elba, returned to France, and reconstituted his army. For a hundred days he ruled France again before a British army defeated him at Waterloo in Belgium. Unwilling to take further chances with the wily general, European powers banished Napoleon to the remote and isolated island of St. Helena in the South Atlantic Ocean, where he died of natural causes in 1821.

THE INFLUENCE OF REVOLUTION

The Enlightenment ideals promoted by the American and French revolutions—freedom, equality, and popular sovereignty—appealed to peoples throughout Europe and the Americas. In the Caribbean and Latin America, they inspired revolutionary movements: slaves in the French colony of Saint-Domingue rose against their overlords and established the independent republic of Haiti, and revolutionary leaders mounted independence movements in Mexico, Central America, and South America. The ideals of the American and French revolutions also encouraged social reformers to organize broader programs of liberation. Whereas the American and French revolutions guaranteed political and legal rights to white men, social reformers sought to extend those rights to women and slaves of African ancestry. During the nineteenth century all European and American states abolished slavery, but former slaves and their descendants remained an underprivileged and often oppressed class in most of the Atlantic world. The quest for women's rights also proceeded slowly during the nineteenth century.

The Haitian Revolution

The only successful slave revolt in history took place on the Caribbean island of Hispaniola in the aftermath of the French revolution. By the eighteenth century, Hispaniola was a major center of sugar production with hundreds of prosperous plantations. The Spanish colony of Santo Domingo occupied the eastern part of the island (modern Dominican Republic), and the French colony of Saint-Domingue occupied the western part (modern Haiti). Saint-Domingue was one of the richest of all European colonies in the Caribbean: sugar, coffee, and cotton produced there accounted for almost one-third of France's foreign trade.

Saint-Domingue Society On the eve of the Haitian revolution, the population of Saint-Domingue comprised three major groups. There were about forty thousand white colonials, subdivided into several classes: European-born Frenchmen who monopolized colonial administrative posts; a class of plantation owners, chiefly minor aristocrats who hoped to return to France as soon as possible; and lower-class

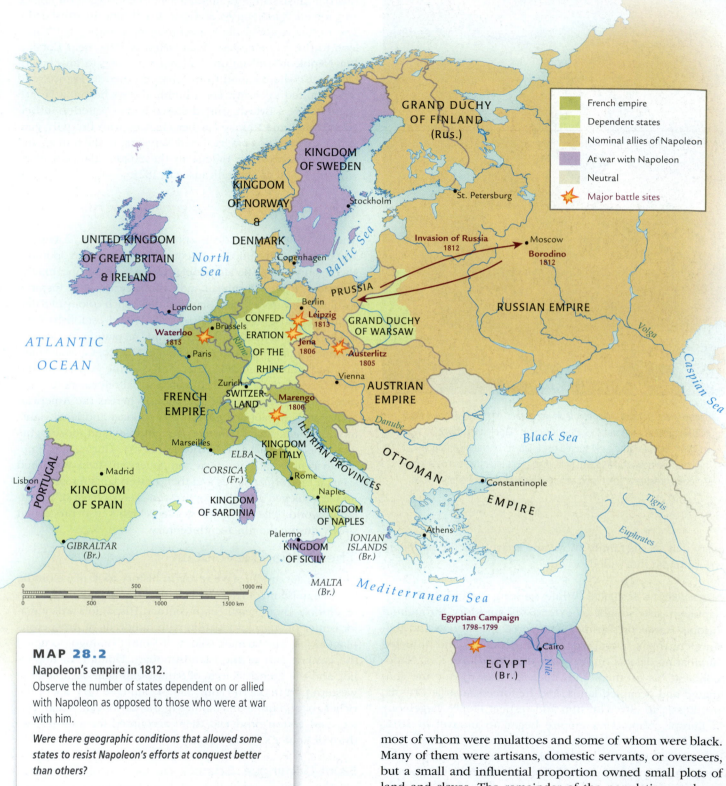

MAP 28.2

Napoleon's empire in 1812.

Observe the number of states dependent on or allied with Napoleon as opposed to those who were at war with him.

Were there geographic conditions that allowed some states to resist Napoleon's efforts at conquest better than others?

whites, which included artisans, shopkeepers, slave dealers, and day laborers. A second group comprised about twenty-eight thousand *gens de couleur* (French for "people of color"), most of whom were mulattoes and some of whom were black. Many of them were artisans, domestic servants, or overseers, but a small and influential proportion owned small plots of land and slaves. The remainder of the population made up the third group, consisting of some five hundred thousand slaves, some of whom were mulattoes but most of whom were African-born.

Most of the colony's slaves toiled in fields under brutal conditions. Planters worked their slaves so hard and pro-

Former slave and effective military leader, Toussaint Louverture led the Haitian revolution.

vided them with so little care that mortality was very high. Not surprisingly, white planters and black slaves frequently had violent conflicts. Aware that they were outnumbered by slaves by a factor of more than ten, plantation owners lived in constant fear of slave rebellion. Many slaves ran away into the mountains. By the late eighteenth century, Saint-Domingue had many large communities of maroons, who maintained their own societies and sometimes attacked plantations in search of food, weapons, tools, and additional recruits. As planters lost laborers, they imported new slaves from Africa and other Caribbean islands. This pattern continued throughout the eighteenth century, until prices of new slaves from Africa rose dramatically.

The American and French revolutions prepared the way for a violent political and social revolution in Saint-Domingue. Because French policy supported North American colonists against British rule, colonial governors in Saint-Domingue sent about five hundred *gens de couleur* to fight in the American war of independence. They returned to Saint-Domingue with the intention of reforming society there. When the French revolution broke out in 1789, white settlers in Saint-

Domingue sought the right to govern themselves, but they opposed proposals to grant political and legal equality to the *gens de couleur.* By May 1791 civil war had broken out between white settlers and *gens de couleur.*

Slave Revolt
The conflict expanded dramatically when a charismatic Vodou priest named Boukman organized a slave revolt. In August 1791 some twelve thousand slaves began killing white settlers, burning their homes, and destroying their plantations. Within a few weeks the rebels attracted almost one hundred thousand slaves into their ranks. Saint-Domingue quickly descended into chaos as white, *gens de couleur,* and slave factions battled one another. Many slaves were battle-tested veterans of wars in Africa, and they drew on their military experience to organize large armies. Slave leaders also found recruits and reinforcements in Saint-Domingue's maroon communities. Foreign armies soon complicated the situation: French troops arrived in 1792 to restore order, and British and Spanish forces intervened in 1793 in hopes of benefiting from France's difficulties.

Toussaint Louverture
Boukman died while fighting shortly after launching the revolt, but slave forces eventually overcame white settlers, *gens de couleur,* and foreign armies. Their successes were due largely to the leadership of François-Dominique Toussaint (1744–1803), who after 1791 called himself Louverture—from the French *l'ouverture,* meaning "the opening," or the one who created an opening in enemy ranks. The son of slaves, Toussaint learned to read and write from a Roman Catholic priest. Because of his education and intelligence, he rose to the position of livestock overseer on the plantation and subsequently planted coffee on leased land with rented slaves. A free man since 1776, Toussaint was also an astute judge of human character. When the slave revolt broke out in 1791, Toussaint helped his masters escape to a safe place, then left the plantation and joined the rebels.

Toussaint was a skilled organizer, and by 1793 he had built a strong, disciplined army. He shrewdly played French, British, and Spanish forces against one another while also jockeying for power with other black and mulatto generals. By 1797 he led an army of twenty thousand that controlled most of Saint-Domingue. In 1801 he promulgated a constitution that granted equality and citizenship to all residents of Saint-Domingue. He stopped short of declaring independence from France, however, because he did not want to provoke Napoleon into attacking the island.

The Republic of Haiti
Nevertheless, in 1802 Napoleon dispatched forty thousand troops to restore French authority in Saint-Domingue. Toussaint attempted to negotiate a peaceful settlement, but the French commander arrested him and sent him to France, where he died in jail of mistreatment in 1803. By the time he died, however, yellow fever had ravaged the French army in Saint-Domingue, and the black generals who succeeded Toussaint had defeated the

The slave rebellion in Saint-Domingue struck fear in the hearts of European and Euro-American peoples. This French print depicts outnumbered white settlers under attack on a plantation.

remaining troops and drove them out of the colony. Late in 1803 they declared independence, and on 1 January 1804 they proclaimed the establishment of Haiti, meaning "land of mountains," which became the second independent republic in the western hemisphere.

Wars of Independence in Latin America

Latin American Society
Revolutionary ideals traveled beyond Saint-Domingue to the Spanish and Portuguese colonies in the Americas. Though governed by *peninsulares* (colonial officials from Spain or Portugal), the Iberian colonies all had a large, wealthy, and powerful class of Euro-American *criollos,* or creoles. In 1800 the *peninsulares* numbered about 30,000, and the creole population was 3.5 million. The Iberian colonies also had a large population—about 10 million in all—of less privileged classes. Black slaves formed a majority in Brazil, but elsewhere indigenous peoples and individuals of mixed ancestry such as mestizos and mulattoes were most numerous.

Creoles benefited greatly during the eighteenth century as they established plantations and ranches in the colonies and participated in rapidly expanding trade with Spain and Portugal. Yet the creoles also had grievances. Like British colonists in North America, the creoles resented administrative control and economic regulations imposed by the Iberian powers. They drew inspiration from Enlightenment political thought and occasionally took part in tax revolts and popular uprisings. The creoles desired neither social reform like that promoted by Robespierre nor the establishment of an egalitarian society like Haiti. Basically, they sought to displace the *peninsulares* but retain their privileged position in society: political independence on the model of the United States in North America struck them as an attractive alternative to colonial status. Between 1810 and 1825, creoles led

BRITISH NORTH AMERICA (Br.)

OREGON
TERRITORY

San Francisco

Mississippi

UNITED STATES

ATLANTIC OCEAN

Independent
Latin American
states in 1830

San Antonio

Rio Grande

MEXICO
1821

*Gulf of
Mexico*

PACIFIC OCEAN

Havana

BAHAMA ISLANDS (Br.)

CUBA (Sp.)

HAITI (1804)

Mexico City   Veracruz

BRITISH
HONDURAS (Br.)

PUERTO RICO (Sp.)

JAMAICA (Br.)

Guatemala City

Caribbean Sea

Caracas

TRINIDAD (Br.)

UNITED PROVINCES OF
CENTRAL AMERICA
1823–1839

Panama City

VENEZUELA
1830

BRITISH GUIANA (Br.)

DUTCH GUIANA (Neth.)

GRAN COLOMBIA
1819–1830   Bogotá

Orinoco

FRENCH GUIANA (Fr.)

Quito   COLOMBIA

*GALAPAGOS
ISLANDS*

ECUADOR
1803

Amazon

EMPIRE OF BRAZIL
1822

Lima

PERU
1821

Paraguay

Bahia

La Paz

BOLIVIA
1825

PARAGUAY
1811

Rio de Janeiro

CHILE
1817

Paraná

URUGUAY
1828

Santiago

Buenos Aires

ARGENTINA
1816

Montevideo

PATAGONIA
(Disputed between
Argentina and Chile)

*ISLAS MALVINAS/
FALKLAND ISLANDS (Argentina)*

0   500   1000   1500 mi
0   1000   2000   3000 km

Original area of slave revolt, 1791

Border of Saint-Domingue/
Santo Domingo 1790

Border of Haiti/Santo Domingo
1820

BAHAMAS

Napoleonic forces
attack, 1802

Caribbean Sea

CUBA
(Spain)   Port-de-Paix

HISPANIOLA

Le Cap   Fort Dauphin

British invade,
1794

SAINT-
DOMINGUE

Haitian revolutionary
forces invade (1801–1802)

Jérémie

Port-au-Prince

SANTO DOMINGO
(Spain)

*PUERTO
RICO*

0   100   200 mi
0   200   400 km

MAP 28.3

Latin America in 1830.

Note the dates each state won its independence.

Since most states became independent in very close succession, what conditions prevented Latin American states from joining together in a federation like that in the United States?

movements that brought independence to all Spanish colonies in the Americas—except Cuba and Puerto Rico—and established creole-dominated republics.

Mexican Independence

The struggle for independence began in the wake of Napoleon's invasion of Spain and Portugal (1807), which weakened royal authority in the Iberian colonies. By 1810, revolts against Spanish rule had broken out in Argentina, Venezuela, and Mexico. The most serious was a peasant rebellion in Mexico led by a parish priest, Miguel Hidalgo y Costilla (1753–1811), who rallied indigenous peoples and mestizos against colonial rule. Many contemporaries viewed Hidalgo's movement for independence from Spanish rule as social and economic warfare by the masses against the elites of Mexican society, particularly since he rallied people to his cause by invoking the name of the popular and venerated Virgin of Guadalupe and by calling for the death of Spaniards. Conservative creoles soon captured Hidalgo and executed him, but his rebellion continued to flare for three years after his death. Hidalgo became the symbol of Mexican independence, and the day on which he proclaimed his revolt—16 September 1810—is Mexico's principal national holiday.

Colonial rule came to an end in 1821, when the creole general Augustín de Iturbide (1783–1824) declared independence from Spain. In the following year, he declared himself emperor of Mexico. Neither Iturbide nor his empire survived for long. Though an able general, Iturbide was an incompetent administrator, and in 1823 creole elites deposed him and established a republic. Two years later the southern regions of the Mexican empire declared their own independence. They formed a Central American Federation until 1838, when they split into the independent states of Guatemala, El Salvador, Honduras, Nicaragua, and Costa Rica.

Simón Bolívar

In South America, creole elites such as Simón Bolívar (1783–1830) led the movement for independence. Born in Caracas (in modern Venezuela), Bolívar was a fervent republican steeped in Enlightenment ideas about popular sovereignty. Inspired by the example of George Washington, he took up arms against Spanish rule in 1811. In the early days of his struggle, Bolívar experienced many reversals and twice went into exile. In 1819, however, he as-

Simón Bolívar, creole leader of the independence movement in Latin America, was a favorite subject of painters in the nineteenth century. This portrait depicts him as a determined and farsighted leader.

sembled an army that surprised and crushed the Spanish army in Colombia. Later, he campaigned in Venezuela, Ecuador, and Peru, coordinating his efforts with other creole leaders, such as José de San Martín (1778–1850) in Argentina and Bernardo O'Higgins (1778–1842) in Chile. By 1825 creole forces had overcome Spanish armies and deposed Spanish rulers throughout South America.

Bolívar's goal was to weld the former Spanish colonies of South America into a great confederation like the United States in North America. During the 1820s independent Venezuela, Colombia, and Ecuador formed a republic called Gran Colombia, and Bolívar attempted to bring Peru and Bolivia (named for Bolívar himself) into the confederation. By 1830, however, strong political and regional differences had undermined Gran Colombia. As the confederation disintegrated, a bitterly disappointed Bolívar pronounced South America "ungovernable" and lamented that "those who have served the revolution have plowed the sea." Shortly after the breakup of Gran Colombia, Bolívar died of tuberculosis while en route to self-imposed exile in Europe.

Brazilian Independence

Independence came to Portuguese Brazil at the same time as to Spanish colonies, but by a different process. When Napoleon invaded Portugal in 1807, the royal court fled Lisbon and established a government in exile in Rio de Janeiro. In 1821 the king returned to Portugal, leaving his son Pedro in Brazil as regent. The next year Brazilian creoles called for independence from Portugal, and Pedro agreed to their demands. When the Portuguese *Cortes* (parliament) tried to curtail his power, Pedro declared Brazil's independence and accepted appointment as Emperor Pedro I (reigned 1822–1834).

Creole Dominance

Although Brazil achieved independence as a monarchy rather than a republic, creole elites dominated Brazilian society just as they did in former Spanish colonies. Indeed, independence brought little social change in Latin America. The *peninsulares* returned to Europe, but Latin American society remained as rigidly stratified as it had been in 1800. The newly independent states granted military authority to local charismatic strongmen, known as **caudillos,** allied with creole elites. The new states also permitted the continuation of slavery, confirmed the wealth and authority of the Roman Catholic church, and re-

caudillos (KAW-dee-ohs)

pressed the lower orders. The principal beneficiaries of independence in Latin America were the creole elites.

The Emergence of Ideologies: Conservatism and Liberalism

While inspiring revolutions and independence movements in other lands, the American and French revolutions also prompted political and social theorists to crystallize the modern ideologies of conservatism and liberalism. An *ideology* is a coherent vision of human nature, human society, and the larger world that proposes some particular form of political and social organization as ideal. Some ideologies seek to justify the current state of affairs, whereas others sharply criticize the status quo in arguing for movement toward an improved society. In all cases, ideologists seek to design a political and social order appropriate for their communities.

Conservatism The modern ideology of conservatism arose as political and social theorists responded to the challenges of the American and especially the French revolutions. Conservatives viewed society as an organism that changed slowly over the generations. The English political philosopher Edmund Burke (1729–1797) held, for example, that society was a compact between a people's ancestors, the present generation, and their descendants as yet unborn. While admitting the need for gradual change that came about by general consensus, Burke condemned radical or revolutionary change, which in his view could only lead to anarchy. Thus Burke approved of the American revolution, which he took as an example of natural change in keeping with the historical development of North American society, but he denounced the French revolution as a chaotic and irresponsible assault on society.

Liberalism In contrast to conservatives, liberals took change as normal and welcomed it as the agent of progress. They viewed conservatism as an effort to justify the status quo, maintain the privileges enjoyed by favored classes, and avoid dealing with injustice and inequality in society. For liberals the task of political and social theory was not to stifle change but, rather, to manage it in the best interests of society. Liberals championed the Enlightenment values of freedom and equality, which they believed would lead to higher standards of morality and increased prosperity for the whole society. They usually favored republican forms of government in which citizens elected representatives to legislative bodies, and they called for written constitutions that guaranteed freedom and equality for all citizens and that precisely defined the political structure and institutions of their societies.

The liberalism that emerged from the Atlantic revolutions was concerned about civil rights, less so about political and social rights. Most liberals, for example, held the view that voting was more of a privilege than a right, and

therefore was legitimately subject to certain qualifications. Limitations on the franchise long characterized suffrage in postrevolutionary societies, with citizens being disenfranchised on the basis of class, age, gender, and race, among other factors. But as the nineteenth century passed, liberalism changed its character. As the masses of people became more assertive, liberalism could not concern itself mainly with interests of the more privileged strata of society. Consequently, there was a shift from early classical liberalism to a more democratic variety. Equality before the law was supplemented by equality before the ballot box. Liberalism's traditional emphasis on minimizing the role and power of government was reversed, and by the end of the nineteenth century, liberals started to look to government to minimize or correct the problems that accompanied industrialization.

The most prominent exponent of early liberalism was John Stuart Mill (1806–1873), an English philosopher, economist, and social reformer. Mill tirelessly promoted the freedom of individuals to pursue economic and intellectual interests. He tried to ensure that powerful minorities, such as wealthy businessmen, would not curb the freedoms of the poorly organized majority, but he also argued that it was improper for the majority to impose its will on minorities with different interests and values. He advocated universal suffrage as the most effective way to advance individual freedom, and he called for taxation of business profits and high personal incomes to forestall the organization of wealthy classes into groups that threatened individual liberties. Mill went further than most liberals in seeking to extend the rights of freedom and equality to women and working people as well as men of property.

Voting Rights and Restrictions As Mill recognized, the age of revolutions in the Atlantic world illustrated the centrality of suffrage in establishing a people's and a nation's sense of democratic legitimacy and political sovereignty. Defined as either the right or the privilege to vote, in order to elect public officials or to adopt laws, suffrage derived its revolutionary significance from Enlightenment notions about self-government and about governments deriving authority from the consent of the governed. Voting rights and restrictions evolved into powerful political concerns during and after the age of revolutions.

Testing the Limits of Revolutionary Ideals: Slavery

The Enlightenment ideals of freedom and equality were watchwords of revolution in the Atlantic Ocean basin. Yet different revolutionaries understood the implications of freedom and equality in very different ways. In North America revolution led to political independence, a broad array of individual freedoms, and the legal equality of adult white men. In France it destroyed the hierarchical order of the ancien régime and temporarily extended political and legal rights to all citizens, although Napoleon and later rulers effectively curbed some of those rights. In Haiti revolution brought independence from French rule and the end of slavery. In South America it led to independence from Iberian rule and societies dominated by creole elites. In the wake of the Atlantic revolutions, social activists in Europe and the Americas considered the possibility that the ideals of freedom and equality might have further implications as yet unexplored. They turned their attention especially to the issues of slavery and women's rights.

thinking about TRADITIONS

Revolution and Slavery

North Atlantic political economies were organized at least in part around the institution of slavery. How did political revolutions in the Atlantic Ocean basin affect or alter the institution of slavery and the lives of slaves? What were the long-term consequences of revolutionary ideologies for peoples of color?

Movements to End the Slave Trade The campaign to end the slave trade and abolish slavery began in the eighteenth century. Freed slaves such as Olaudah Equiano (1745–1797) were among the earliest critics of slavery. Beginning in the 1780s European Christian moralists also voiced opposition to slavery.

Only after the American, French, and Haitian revolutions, however, did the antislavery movement gain momentum. The leading spokesman of the movement was William Wilberforce (1759–1833), a prominent English philanthropist elected in 1780 to a seat in Parliament. There he tirelessly attacked slavery on moral and religious grounds. After the Haitian revolution he attracted supporters who feared that continued reliance on slave labor would result in more and larger slave revolts, and in 1807 Parliament passed Wilberforce's bill to end the slave trade. Under British pressure, other states also banned commerce in slaves: the United States in 1808, France in 1814, the Netherlands in 1817, and Spain in 1845. The British navy, which dominated the North Atlantic Ocean, patrolled the west coast of Africa to ensure compliance with the law. But the slave trade died slowly, as illegal trade in African slaves continued on a small scale: the last documented ship to carry slaves across the Atlantic Ocean arrived in Cuba in 1867.

Movements to Abolish Slavery The abolition of slavery itself was a much bigger challenge than ending the slave trade because owners had property rights in their slaves. Planters and merchant elites strongly resisted efforts to alter the system that provided them with abundant supplies of inexpensive labor. Nevertheless, the end of the slave trade doomed the institution of slavery in the Americas. In Haiti the end of slavery came with the revolution. In much of South America, slavery ended with independence from Spanish rule, as Simón Bolívar freed slaves who joined his forces and provided constitutional guarantees of free status for all residents of Gran Colombia. In Mexico slavery was abolished in 1829, though not solely for humanitarian reasons. It served as a mechanism to stop the influx of residents from the southern United States coming in with their slaves to grow cotton.

Meanwhile, as they worked to ban traffic in human labor, Wilberforce and other moralists also launched a campaign to free slaves and abolish the institution of slavery itself. In 1833, one month after Wilberforce's death, Parliament provided twenty million pounds sterling as compensation to slave owners and abolished slavery throughout the British empire. Other states followed the British example: France abolished slavery in 1848, the United States in 1865, Cuba in 1886, and Brazil in 1888.

Freedom without Equality Abolition brought legal freedom for African and African-American slaves, but it did not bring political equality. In most lands other than Haiti, African-American peoples had little influence in society. Property requirements, literacy tests, poll taxes, and campaigns of intimidation effectively prevented them from voting. Nor did emancipation bring social and economic improvements for former slaves and their descendants. White creole elites owned most of the property in the Americas, and they kept blacks in subordination by forcing them to accept low-paying work. A few African-Americans owned small plots of land, but they could not challenge the economic and political power of creole elites.

Testing the Limits of Revolutionary Ideals: Women's Rights

Women participated alongside men in the movement to abolish slavery, and their experience inspired feminist social reformers to seek equality with men. They pointed out that women suffered many of the same legal disabilities as slaves: they had little access to education, they could not enter professional occupations that required advanced education, and they were legally deprived of the right to vote. They drew on Enlightenment thought in making a case for women's rights, but in spite of support from prominent liberals such as John Stuart Mill, they had little success before the twentieth century.

Enlightenment Ideals and Women Enlightenment thought called for the restructuring of government and society, but the philosophes mostly held conservative views on women and their roles in family and society. Rousseau, for example, advised that girls' education should prepare them to become devoted wives and mothers. Yet social reformers found Enlightenment thought extremely useful in argu-

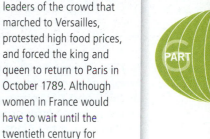

Parisian women were the leaders of the crowd that marched to Versailles, protested high food prices, and forced the king and queen to return to Paris in October 1789. Although women in France would have to wait until the twentieth century for political rights fully equal to those of men, women laid a foundation for future gains by drawing on the ideas of the Enlightenment to argue for equality.

ing for women's rights. Drawing on the political thought of John Locke, for example, the English writer Mary Astell (1666–1731) suggested that absolute sovereignty was no more appropriate in a family than in a state. Astell also reflected Enlightenment influence in asking why, if all men were born free, all women were born slaves.

During the eighteenth century, advocates of women's rights were particularly active in Britain, France, and North America. Among the most prominent was the British writer Mary Wollstonecraft (1759–1797). Although she had little schooling, Wollstonecraft avidly read books at home and gained an informal self-education. In 1792 she published an influential essay entitled *A Vindication of the Rights of Woman*. Like Astell, Wollstonecraft argued that women possessed all the rights that Locke had granted to men. She insisted on the right of women to education: it would make them better mothers and wives, she said, and would enable them to contribute to society by preparing them for professional occupations and participation in political life.

Women and Revolution Women played crucial roles in the revolutions of the late eighteenth and early nineteenth centuries. Some women supported the efforts of men by sewing uniforms, rolling bandages, or managing farms, shops, and businesses. Others actively participated in revolutionary activities. In October 1789, for example, about six thousand Parisian women marched to Versailles to protest the high price of bread. Some of them forced their way into the royal apartments and demanded that the king and queen return with them to Paris—along with the palace's supply of flour. In the early 1790s, pistol-wielding

members of the Republican Revolutionary Women patrolled the streets of Paris. The fate of Olympe de Gouges made it clear, however, that revolutionary women had little prospect of holding official positions or playing a formal role in public affairs.

Under the National Assembly and the Convention, the French revolution brought increased rights for women. The republican government provided free public education for girls as well as boys, granted wives a share of family property, and legalized divorce. Yet the revolution did not bring women the right to vote or to play major roles in public affairs. Under the Directory and Napoleon's rule, women lost even the rights that they had won in the early days of the revolution. In other lands, women never gained as much as they did in revolutionary France. In the United States and the independent states of Latin America, revolution brought legal equality and political rights only for adult white men, who retained patriarchal authority over their wives and families.

Women's Rights Movements Nevertheless, throughout the nineteenth century social reformers pressed for women's rights as well as the abolition of slavery. The American feminist Elizabeth Cady Stanton (1815–1902) was an especially prominent figure in this movement. In 1840 Stanton went to London to attend an antislavery conference but found that the organizers barred women from participation. Infuriated, Stanton returned to the United States and began to build a movement for women's rights. She organized a conference of feminists who met at Seneca Falls, New York, in 1848. The conference passed twelve resolutions demanding that lawmakers grant women rights equivalent to those

sources from the past

Declaration of the Rights of Woman and the Female Citizen

In 1791 Olympe de Gouges, a butcher's daughter and playwright of some note, wrote and published the Declaration of the Rights of Woman and the Female Citizen. *She directly challenged the inferiority presumed of women by the 1789* Declaration of the Rights of Man and the Citizen, *which limited citizenship to males. By publicly asserting the equality of women, Gouges breached barriers that most revolutionary leaders wanted to perpetuate. Charged with treason during the rule of the National Convention, Gouges went to the guillotine on 3 November 1793.*

Article 1. Woman is born free and lives equal to man in her rights. Social distinctions can be based only on the common utility.

Article 2. The purpose of any political association is the conservation of the natural and impresciptible rights of woman and man; these rights are liberty, property, security, and especially resistance to oppression.

Article 3. The principle of all sovereignty rests essentially with the nation, which is nothing but the union of woman and man; no body and no individual can exercise any authority which does not come expressly from it (the nation).

Article 4. Liberty and justice consist of restoring all that belongs to others; thus, the only limits on the exercise of the natural rights of woman are perpetual male tyranny; these limits are to be reformed by the laws of nature and reason.

Article 6. The law must be the expression of the general will; all female and male citizens must contribute either personally or through their representatives to its formation; it must be the same for all: male and female citizens, being equal in the eyes of the law, must be equally admitted to all honors, positions, and public employment according to their capacity and without other distinctions besides those of their virtues and talents.

Article 7. No woman is an exception; she is accused, arrested, and detained in cases determined by law. Women, like men, obey this rigorous law.

Article 11. The free communication of thoughts and opinions is one of the most precious rights of woman, since that liberty assures recognition of children by their fathers. Any female citizen thus may say freely, I am the mother of a child which belongs to you, without being forced by a barbarous prejudice to hide the truth; (an exception may be made) to respond to the abuse of this liberty in cases determined by law.

Article 13. For the support of the public force and the expenses of administration, the contributions of woman and man are equal; she shares all the duties and all the painful tasks; therefore, we must have the same share in the distribution of positions, employment, offices, honors, and jobs.

Article 14. Female and male citizens have the right to verify, either by themselves or through their representatives, the necessity of the public contribution. This can only apply to women if they are granted an equal share, not only of wealth, but also of public administration, and in the determination of the proportion, the base, the collection, and the duration of the tax.

Article 17. Property belongs to both sexes whether united or separate; for each it is an inviolable and sacred right; no one can be deprived of it, since it is the true patrimony of nature, unless the legally determined public need obviously dictates it, and then only with a just and prior indemnity.

For Further Reflection

■ How does Olympe de Gouges's feminist restatement of the *Declaration of the Rights of Man and the Citizen* intensify its radical precepts?

Source: Darline Gay Levy, Harriet Branson Applewhite, and Mary Durham Johnson. *Women in Revolutionary Paris, 1789–1795.* Urbana: University of Illinois Press, 1979, pp. 90–92.

enjoyed by men. The resolutions called specifically for women's rights to vote, attend public schools, enter professional occupations, and participate in public affairs.

The women's rights movement experienced limited success in the nineteenth century. More women received formal education than before the American and French revolutions, and women in Europe and North America participated in academic, literary, and civic organizations. Rarely did they enter the professions, however, and nowhere did they enjoy the right to vote. Yet, by seeking to extend the promises of Enlightenment political thought to blacks and women as well as white men, social reformers of the nineteenth century laid a foundation that would lead to large-scale social change in the twentieth century.

THE CONSOLIDATION OF NATIONAL STATES IN EUROPE

The Enlightenment ideals of freedom, equality, and popular sovereignty inspired political revolutions in much of the Atlantic Ocean basin, and the revolutions in turn helped spread Enlightenment values. The wars of the French revolution and the Napoleonic era also inspired the development of a particular type of community identity that had little to do with Enlightenment values—nationalism. Revolutionary wars involved millions of French citizens in the defense of their country against foreign armies and the extension of French influence to neighboring states. Wartime experiences encouraged peoples throughout Europe to think of themselves as members of distinctive national communities. Throughout the nineteenth century, European nationalist leaders worked to fashion states based on national identities and mobilized citizens to work in the interests of their own national communities, sometimes by fostering jealousy and suspicion of other national groups. By the late nineteenth century, national identities were so strong that peoples throughout Europe responded enthusiastically to ideologies of nationalism, which promised glory and prosperity to those who worked in the interests of their national communities.

Nations and Nationalism

One of the most influential concepts of modern political thought is the idea of the nation. The word *nation* refers to a type of community that became especially prominent in the nineteenth century. At various times and places in history, individuals have associated themselves primarily with families, clans, cities, regions, and religious faiths. During the nineteenth century, European peoples came to identify strongly with communities they called nations. Members of a nation considered themselves a distinctive people born into a unique community that spoke a common language, observed common customs, inherited common cultural traditions, held common values, and shared common historical experiences. Often, they also honored common religious beliefs, although they sometimes overlooked differences of faith and construed the nation as a political, social, and cultural, rather than religious, unit.

Intense feelings of national identity fueled ideologies of nationalism. Advocates of nationalism insisted that the nation must be the focus of political loyalty. Zealous nationalist leaders maintained that members of their national communities had a common destiny that they could best advance by organizing independent national states and resolutely pursuing their national interests. Ideally, in their view, the boundaries of the national state embraced the territory occupied by the

national community, and its government promoted the interests of the national group, sometimes through conflict with other peoples.

Cultural Nationalism Early nationalist thought often sought to deepen appreciation for the historical experiences of the national community and foster pride in its cultural accomplishments. During the late eighteenth century, for example, Johann Gottfried von Herder (1744–1803) sang the praises of the German *Volk* ("people") and their powerful and expressive language. In reaction to Enlightenment thinkers and their quest for a scientific, universally valid understanding of the world, early cultural nationalists such as Herder focused their attention on individual communities and relished their uniqueness. They emphasized historical scholarship, which they believed would illuminate the distinctive characteristics of their societies. They also valued the study of literature, which they considered the best guide to the *Volksgeist,* the popular soul or spirit or essence of their community. For that reason the German brothers Jakob and Wilhelm Grimm collected popular poetry, stories, songs, and tales as expressions of the German *Volk.*

Political Nationalism During the nineteenth century, nationalist thought became much more strident than the cultural nationalism of Herder or the brothers Grimm. Advocates of nationalism demanded loyalty and solidarity from members of the national group. In lands where they were minorities or where they lived under foreign rule, they sought to establish independent states to protect and advance the interests of the national community.

In Italy, for example, the nationalist activist Giuseppe Mazzini (1805–1872) formed a group called Young Italy that promoted independence from Austrian and Spanish rule and the establishment of an Italian national state. Mazzini likened the nation to a family and the nation's territory to the family home. Austrian and Spanish authorities forced Mazzini to lead much of his life in exile, but he used the opportunity to encourage the organization of nationalist movements in new lands. By the mid-nineteenth century, Young Italy had inspired the development of nationalist movements in Ireland, Switzerland, and Hungary.

While it encouraged political leaders to work toward the establishment of national states for their communities, nationalism also had strong potential to stir up conflict between different

A portrait of the Italian nationalist leader Giuseppe Mazzini as a disappointed but determined idealist. By the mid-nineteenth century, Mazzini's views had inspired nationalist movements not only in Italy but in other European lands as well.

groups of people. The more nationalists identified with their own national communities, the more they distinguished themselves both from peoples in other lands and from minority groups within their societies.

Nationalism and Anti-Semitism

Nationalism and Anti-Semitism This divisive potential of nationalism helps to explain the emergence of Zionism, a political movement that holds that the Jewish people constitute a nation and have the right to their own national homeland. Unlike Mazzini's Italian compatriots, Jews did not inhabit a well-defined territory but, rather, lived in states throughout Europe and beyond. As national communities tightened their bonds, nationalist leaders often became distrustful of minority populations. Suspicion of Jews fueled anti-Semitism in many parts of Europe. Whereas anti-Semitism was barely visible in countries such as Italy and the Netherlands, it operated openly in those such as Austria-Hungary and Germany. In eastern

thinking about ENCOUNTERS

Nationalism on the March

The Napoleonic wars that followed the French revolution brought both French troops and revolutionary ideals to the regions of Europe involved in those wars. What ideals were exported from France? How did clashes between the French and other peoples of Europe, such as the Italians and the Germans, reshape the nationalist sentiments of those peoples?

Europe, anti-Semitism often turned violent. In Russia and in the Russian-controlled areas of Poland, the persecution of Jews climaxed in a series of pogroms. Beginning in 1881 and lasting into the early twentieth century, these massacres claimed the lives and property of thousands of Jews.

During the late nineteenth and twentieth centuries, millions of Jews migrated to other European lands or to North America to escape persecution and violence. Anti-Semitism was not as severe in France as in central and eastern Europe, but it reached a fever pitch there after a military court convicted Alfred Dreyfus, a Jewish army officer, of spying for Germany in 1894. Although he was innocent of the charges and eventually had the verdict reversed on appeal, Dreyfus was the focus of bitter debates about the trustworthiness of Jews in French society. The trial also became a key event in the evolution of Zionism.

Zionism Among the reporters at the Dreyfus trial was a Jewish journalist from Vienna, Theodor Herzl (1860–1904). As Herzl witnessed mobs shouting "Death to the Jews" in the land of enlightenment and liberty, he concluded that anti-Semitism was a persistent feature of human society that assimilation could not solve. In 1896 Herzl published the pamphlet *Judenstaat,* which argued that the only defense against anti-Semitism lay in the mass migration of Jews from all over the world to a land that they could call their own. In the following year, Herzl organized the first Zionist Congress in Basel, Switzerland, which founded the World Zionist Organization. The delegates at Basel formulated the basic platform of the Zionist movement, declaring that "Zionism seeks to establish a home for the Jewish people in Palestine," the location of the ancient Kingdom of Israel. During the next half century, Jewish migrants trickled into Palestine, and in 1948 they won recognition for the Jewish state of Israel. Although it arose in response to exclusive nationalism in Europe, Zionism in turn provoked a resentful nationalism among Palestinian Arabs displaced by Jewish settlers. Conflicts between Jews and Palestinians continue to the present day.

A determined Theodor Herzl founded the Zionist movement, which sought to confront anti-Semitism in Europe by establishing a home for the Jews in Palestine.

The Emergence of National Communities

The French revolution and the wars that followed it heightened feelings of national identity throughout Europe. In

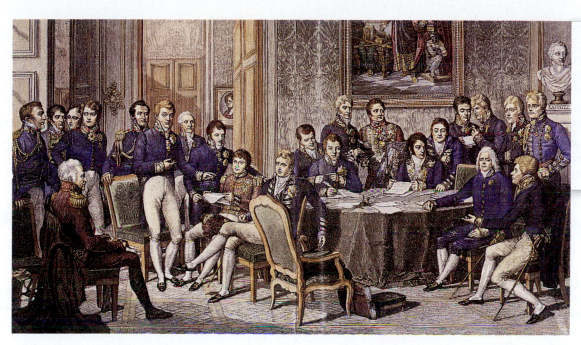

The charming and polished courtier Prince Klemens von Metternich (standing at left center) dominated the Congress of Vienna. Here, delegates to the Congress are gathered at the Habsburg palace in Vienna.

France the establishment of a republic based on liberty, equality, and fraternity inspired patriotism and encouraged citizens to rally to the defense of the revolution when foreign armies threatened it. Revolutionary leaders took the tricolored flag as a symbol of the French nation, and they adopted a rousing marching tune, the "Marseillaise," as an anthem that inspired pride in and identity with the national community. In Spain, the Netherlands, Austria, Prussia, and Russia, national consciousness surged in reaction to the arrival of revolutionary and Napoleonic armies. Opposition to Napoleon and his imperial designs also inspired national feeling in Britain.

The Congress of Vienna After the fall of Napoleon, conservative political leaders feared that heightened national consciousness and ideas of popular sovereignty would encourage further experimentation with revolution and undermine European stability. Meeting as the Congress of Vienna (1814–1815), representatives of the "great powers" that defeated Napoleon—Britain, Austria, Prussia, and Russia—attempted to restore the prerevolutionary order. Under the guidance of the influential foreign minister of Austria, Prince Klemens von Metternich (1773–1859), the Congress dismantled Napoleon's empire, returned sovereignty to Europe's royal families, restored them to the thrones they had lost during the Napoleonic era, and created a diplomatic order based on a balance of power that prevented any one state from dominating the others. A central goal of Metternich himself was to suppress national consciousness, which he viewed as a serious threat to the multicultural Austrian empire that included Germans, Italians, Magyars, Czechs, Slovaks, Poles, Serbs, and Croats among its subjects.

The efforts of Metternich and the Congress of Vienna to restore the ancien régime had limited success. The European balance of power established at Vienna survived for almost a century, until the outbreak of a general continental and global war in 1914. Metternich and the conservative rulers installed by the Congress of Vienna took measures to forestall further revolution: they censored publications to prevent communication of seditious ideas and relied on spies to identify nationalist and republican activists. By 1815, however, it was impossible to suppress national consciousness and ideas of popular sovereignty.

Nationalist Rebellions From the 1820s through the 1840s, a wave of rebellions inspired by nationalist sentiments swept through Europe. The first uprising occurred in 1821 in the Balkan peninsula, where the Greek people sought independence from the Ottoman Turks, who had ruled the region since the fifteenth century. Many western Europeans sympathized with the Greek cause. The English poet Lord Byron even joined the rebel army and in 1824 died (of a fever) while serving in Greece. With the aid of Britain, France, and Russia, the rebels overcame the Ottoman forces in the Balkans by 1827 and won formal recognition of Greek independence in 1830.

In 1830 rebellion showed its face throughout Europe. In France, Spain, Portugal, and some of the German principalities, revolutionaries inspired by liberalism called for constitutional government based on popular sovereignty. In Belgium, Italy, and Poland, they demanded independence and the formation of national states as well as popular sovereignty. Revolution in Paris drove Charles X from the throne, while uprisings in Belgium resulted in independence from the

MAP 28.4

The unification of Italy and Germany.
The unification of Italy and Germany (see map on page 645) as national states in the nineteenth century fundamentally altered the balance of power in Europe.

Why did unification result from diplomacy and war conducted by conservative statesmen rather than popular nationalist action?

Netherlands. By the mid-1830s authorities had put down the uprisings elsewhere, but in 1848 a new round of rebellions shook European states. The uprisings of 1848 brought down the French monarchy and seriously threatened the Austrian empire, where subject peoples clamored for constitutions and independence. Prince Metternich resigned his office as Austrian foreign minister and unceremoniously fled Vienna as rebels took control of the city. Uprisings also rocked cities in Italy, Prussia, and German states in the Rhineland.

By the summer of 1849, the veteran armies of conservative rulers had put down the last of the rebellions. Advocates of national independence and popular sovereignty remained active, however, and the potential of their ideals to mobilize popular support soon became dramatically apparent.

The Unifications of Italy and Germany

The most striking demonstration of the power that national sentiments could unleash involved the unification of Italy and of Germany. Since the fall of the Roman empire, Italy and Germany had been disunited lands. A variety of regional kingdoms, city-states, and ecclesiastical states ruled the Italian peninsula for more than a thousand years, and princes divided Germany into more than three hundred semiautonomous jurisdictions. The Holy Roman Empire claimed authority over Germany and much of Italy, but the emperors were rarely strong enough to enforce their claims.

As they dismantled Napoleon's empire and sought to restore the ancien régime, delegates at the Congress of Vienna placed much of northern Italy under Austrian rule. Southern Italy was already under close Spanish supervision because of

dynastic ties between the Kingdom of the Two Sicilies and the Spanish Bourbon monarchy. As national sentiment surged throughout nineteenth-century Europe, Italian political leaders worked to win independence from foreign rule and establish an Italian national state. Mazzini's Young Italy movement attracted discontented idealists throughout the peninsula. In 1820, 1830, and 1848, they mounted major uprisings that threatened but did not dislodge foreign rule in Italy.

Cavour and Garibaldi The unification of Italy came about when practical political leaders such as Count Camillo di Cavour (1810–1861), prime minister to King Vittore Emmanuele II of Piedmont and Sardinia, combined forces with nationalist advocates of independence. Cavour was a cunning diplomat, and the kingdom of Piedmont and Sardinia was the most powerful of the Italian states. In alliance with France, Cavour expelled Austrian authorities from most of northern Italy in 1859. Then he turned his attention to south-

ern Italy, where Giuseppe Garibaldi (1807–1882), a dashing soldier of fortune and a passionate nationalist, led the unification movement. With an army of about one thousand men outfitted in distinctive red shirts, Garibaldi swept through Sicily and southern Italy, outmaneuvering government forces and attracting enthusiastic recruits. In 1860 Garibaldi met King Vittore Emmanuele near Naples. Not ambitious to rule, Garibaldi delivered southern Italy into Vittore Emmanuele's hands, and the kingdom of Piedmont and Sardinia became the kingdom of Italy. During the next decade the new monarchy absorbed several additional territories, including Venice, Rome, and their surrounding regions.

In Germany as in Italy, unification came about when political leaders harnessed nationalist aspirations. The Congress of Vienna created a German Confederation composed of thirty-nine states dominated by Austria. Metternich and other conservative German rulers stifled nationalist movements, and the suppression of the rebellions of 1848 left German nationalists frustrated at their inability to found a national state.

Otto von Bismarck In 1862 King Wilhelm I of Prussia appointed a wealthy landowner, Otto von Bismarck (1815–1898), as his prime minister. Bismarck was a master of *Realpolitik* ("the politics of reality"). He succinctly expressed his realistic approach in his first speech as prime minister: "The great questions of the day will not be settled by speeches or majority votes—that was the great mistake of 1848 and 1849—but by blood and iron."

It was indeed blood and iron that brought about the unification of Germany. As prime minister, Bismarck reformed and expanded the Prussian army. Between 1864 and 1870 he intentionally provoked three wars—with Denmark, Austria, and France—and whipped up German sentiment against the enemies. In all three conflicts Prussian forces quickly shattered their opponents, swelling German pride. In 1871 the Prussian king proclaimed himself emperor of the Second Reich—meaning the Second German Empire, following the Holy Roman Empire—which embraced almost all German-speaking peoples outside Austria and Switzerland in a powerful and dynamic national state.

Wearing a white jacket, Otto von Bismarck (center) witnesses the crowning of King Wilhelm I of Prussia as German emperor. The coronation followed the victory of Prussia over France in 1871, and it took place in the royal palace at Versailles.

The unification of Italy and Germany made it clear that when coupled with strong political, diplomatic, and military leadership, nationalism had enormous potential to mobilize people who felt a sense of national kinship. Italy, Germany, and other national states went to great lengths to foster a sense of national community. They adopted national flags to serve as symbols of unity, national anthems to inspire patriotism, and national holidays to focus public attention on individuals and events of special importance for the national community. They established bureaucracies that took censuses of national populations and tracked vital national statistics involving birth, marriage, and death. They built schools that instilled patriotic values in students, and they recruited young men into armies that defended national interests and sometimes went on the offensive to enhance national prestige. By the end of the nineteenth century, the national state had proven to be a powerful model of political organization in Europe. By the mid-twentieth century, it had become well-nigh universal as political leaders adopted the national state as the principal form of political organization throughout the world.

in**perspective**

The Enlightenment ideals of freedom, equality, and popular sovereignty inspired revolutionary movements throughout much of the Atlantic Ocean basin in the late eighteenth and early nineteenth centuries. In North America colonists threw off British rule and founded an independent federal republic. In France revolutionaries abolished the monarchy, established a republic, and refashioned the social order. In

Saint-Domingue rebellious slaves threw off French rule, established an independent Haitian republic, and granted freedom and equality to all citizens. In Latin America creole elites led movements to expel Spanish and Portuguese colonial authorities and to found independent republics. During the nineteenth century, adult white men were the main beneficiaries of movements based on Enlightenment ideals, but social reformers launched campaigns to extend freedom and equality to Africans, African-Americans, and women.

Meanwhile, as they fought each other in wars sparked by the French revolution, European peoples developed strong feelings of national identity and worked to establish states that advanced the interests of national communities. Nationalist thought was often divisive: it pitted national groups against one another and fueled tensions especially in large multicultural states. But nationalism also had strong potential to contribute to state-building movements, and nationalist appeals played prominent roles in the unification of Italy and Germany. During the nineteenth and twentieth centuries, peoples throughout the world drew inspiration from Enlightenment ideals and national identities when seeking to build or restructure their societies. ●

CHRONOLOGY

1632–1704	Life of John Locke
1694–1778	Life of Voltaire
1712–1778	Life of Jean-Jacques Rousseau
1744–1803	Life of Toussaint Louverture
1748–1793	Life of Olympe de Gouges
1753–1811	Life of Miguel Hidalgo y Costilla
1769–1821	Life of Napoleon Bonaparte
1773–1859	Life of Klemens von Metternich
1774–1793	Reign of King Louis XVI
1775–1781	American revolution
1783–1830	Life of Simón Bolívar
1789–1799	French revolution
1791–1803	Haitian revolution
1799–1814	Reign of Napoleon
1805–1872	Life of Giuseppe Mazzini
1807–1882	Life of Giuseppe Garibaldi
1810–1825	Wars of independence in Latin America
1810–1861	Life of Camillo di Cavour
1814–1815	Congress of Vienna
1815–1898	Life of Otto von Bismarck
1821–1827	War of Greek independence
1859–1870	Unification of Italy
1864–1871	Unification of Germany

For Further Reading

Benedict Anderson. *Imagined Communities: Reflections on the Origin and Spread of Nationalism.* Rev. ed. London, 1991. A pioneering work that analyzes the means and the processes by which peoples came to view themselves as members of national communities.

Bernard Bailyn. *The Ideological Origins of the American Revolution.* 2nd ed. Cambridge, Mass., 1992. A fundamental study of pamphlets and other publications that criticized British colonial policy in North America.

David A. Bell. *The Cult of the Nation in France: Inventing Nationalism, 1680–1800.* Cambridge, Mass., 2001. Looks at how patriotism and national sentiment were grafted onto religious forms of community in the context of the eighteenth century and the French revolution.

———. *The First Total War: Napoleon's Europe and the Birth of Warfare as We Know It.* Boston, 2007. A fine work that argues that nearly every "modern" aspect of war was born in the Revolutionary and Napoleonic wars.

Reinhard Bendix. *Kings or People: Power and the Mandate to Rule.* Berkeley, 1978. A challenging but important comparative study of popular sovereignty and its displacement of monarchical authority.

Linda Colley. *Britons: Forging the Nation, 1707–1837.* New Haven, 1992. A detailed analysis of the emergence of British national identity.

Laureant Dubois. *Avengers of the New World: The Story of the Haitian Revolution.* Cambridge, Mass., 2005. Comprehensive study of how the French slave colony of Saint-Domingue became a unique example of a successful black revolution that challenged the boundaries of freedom, citizenship, and empire.

Susan Dunn. *Sister Revolutions: French Lightning, American Light.* New York, 1999. An accessible and stimulating work that traces the different legacies of the American and French revolutions of the eighteenth century.

Geoffrey Ellis. *Napoleon.* New York, 1997. An excellent biography of a pivotal figure in modern European history.

Eric Hobsbawm. *Nations and Nationalism Since 1780: Programme, Myth, and Reality.* 2nd ed. Cambridge, 1992. A brief interpretation of nationalism in Europe and the larger world.

——— and Terence Ranger, eds. *The Invention of Tradition.* Cambridge, 1983. A fascinating collection of essays examining the rituals and other traditions that modern states have relied on to enhance their authority.

Lynn Hunt. *Politics, Culture, and Class in the French Revolution.* Berkeley and Los Angeles, 1984. Continues to be a touchstone for the history of the French revolution's political culture and of the meanings of the revolution's symbols to the course of events.

Colin Jones. *The Great Nation: France from Louis XV to Napoleon.* London and New York, 2003. An excellent economic and political history of a society opposed to absolutism.

Lester D. Langley. *The Americas in the Age of Revolution, 1750–1850.* New Haven, 1997. A comparative study of revolutions and wars of independence in the western hemisphere.

Mary Beth Norton. *Liberty's Daughters: The Revolutionary Experience of American Women, 1750–1800.* Boston, 1980. Focuses on the role of women in the American revolution and the early republic.

Robert Palmer. *The Age of the Democratic Revolution: A Political History of Europe and America, 1760–1800.* 2 vols. Princeton, 1959–64. A classic study of the American and French revolutions and their influence in Europe and the Americas.

Simon Schama. *Citizens: A Chronicle of the French Revolution.* New York, 1989. Detailed narrative of the French revolution focusing on the experiences and decisions made by individual actors.

Eric Van Young. *The Other Rebellion: Popular Violence, Ideology, and the Mexican Struggle for Independence, 1810–1821.* Stanford, 2001. An exhaustive account of Mexico's movement toward independence from Spain that stresses the importance of domestic struggles that pitted classes and ethnic groups against one another.

Gordon S. Wood. *The Radicalism of the American Revolution.* New York, 1991. A comprehensive synthesis emphasizing the role of republican and democratic ideas in the overthrow of monarchical institutions.

The Making of Industrial Society

chapter 29

Young woman at work in a mechanized mill in the 1830s.

EYEWITNESS:

Betty Harris, a Woman Chained in the Coal Pits

In 1827, shortly after marrying at the age of twenty-three, Betty Harris took a job as a drawer in a coal pit near Manchester, England. A drawer's job involved crawling down narrow mine shafts and hauling loads of coal from the bottom of the pit, where miners chipped it from the earth, to the surface. From there the coal went to fuel the steam engines that powered the factories and the mills of early industrial society. Drawers performed unskilled labor for low wages, but their work was essential for the emergence of industrial production.

While working, Harris wore a heavy belt around her waist. Hitched to the belt was a chain that passed between her legs and attached to the coal cart that she pulled through the mine shafts, often while creeping along on hands and knees. The belt strained against her body, and the mine shafts were steep and slippery. Yet every work day, even when she was pregnant, Harris strapped on her belt and chain at 6:00 A.M., removing her bindings only at the end of the shift twelve hours later.

Work conditions for Betty Harris were less than ideal. She labored in the coal pit with six other women and six boys and girls. All members of the crew experienced hardships and exploitation. Harris reported that drawing coal was "very hard work for a woman," and she did not exaggerate. She and her companions often had to crawl through water that collected in the mine shafts during rainstorms, and the men who mined coal in the pits showed scant respect for the lowly, ill-paid drawers. The belts and chains worn by drawers often chafed their skin raw, and miners contributed to their physical discomfort by beating them for slow or clumsy work. The miners, many of whom shed their clothes and worked naked in the hot, oppressive coal pits, also took sexual liberties with the women and girl drawers: Harris personally knew several illegitimate children conceived during forced sexual encounters in the coal pits.

Betty Harris faced her own sexual problems once she arrived home. Exhausted from twelve hours of work, with only a one-hour break for a midday meal consisting of bread and butter, she often tried to discourage her husband's advances. Her husband had little patience, however, and Harris remarked that "my feller has beaten me many a time for not being ready." Harris's work schedule made comfortable family life impossible. A cousin had to care for her two children during the day, and Harris tended to them and her husband at night. The grinding demands of the coal pit took a toll: at age thirty-seven, after fourteen years in the mines, Harris admitted that "I am not so strong as I was, and cannot stand my work so well as I used to."

Not all industrial workers suffered the indignities that coal drawers endured, but Betty Harris's experience nonetheless illustrates some of the deep changes that industrialization wrought in patterns of work and family life. Beginning in the late eighteenth century, workers and their families had to adjust to the sometimes harsh demands of the machine age. First in Britain, then in western Europe, North America, Russia, and Japan, machines and factories transformed agricultural societies into industrial societies. At the heart of this transformation were technological changes based on newly developed, inanimate sources of power that led to the extensive use of machinery in manufacturing. Machine production raised worker productivity, encouraged economic specialization, and promoted the growth of large-scale enterprise. Industrial machinery transformed economic production by turning out high-quality products quickly, cheaply, and efficiently. The process of industrialization encouraged rapid technological innovation and over the long term raised material standards of living in much of the world.

But the impact of industrialization went beyond economics, generating widespread and often unsettling social change as well. Early industrialists created a new work environment, the factory, which concentrated large numbers of workers under one roof to operate complicated machinery. The concentration of workers made it possible to rely on inanimate motive power such as waterwheels or steam engines. Factories also enabled managers to impose work discipline and closely supervise the quality of production at their plants. By moving work outside the home, however, factories drew fathers, mothers, and children in different directions, altered traditional patterns of domestic life, and strained family relations in the industrial era.

Industrialization encouraged rapid urbanization and migration. New cities mushroomed to house workers who left the countryside for jobs in factories. Millions of migrants traveled even farther, crossing the seas in search of opportunities in new lands. Often, however, early industrial workers found themselves living in squalor and laboring under dangerous conditions.

Social critics and reformers worked to alleviate the problems of early industrial society. Most scathing and influential of the critics were the German theorists Karl Marx and Friedrich Engels, who called for the destruction of capitalism and the establishment of a more just and equitable socialist society. Despite their appeals, capitalism and industrialization flourished and spread rapidly from Britain to continental Europe, North America, and Asia. Although industrialization spread unevenly around the globe, it profoundly influenced social and economic conditions throughout the world, since industrial societies created a new international division of labor that made most African, Asian, and American lands dependent on the export of raw materials.

PATTERNS OF INDUSTRIALIZATION

Industrialization refers to a process that transformed agrarian and handicraft-centered economies into economies distinguished by industry and machine manufacture. The principal features of this process were technological and organizational changes that transformed manufacturing and led to increased productivity. Critical to industrialization were technological developments that made it possible to produce goods by machines rather than by hand and that harnessed inanimate sources of energy such as coal and petroleum. Organizational changes accompanied technological developments. By the end of the nineteenth century, the factory had become the predominant site of industrial production in Europe, the United States, and Japan. Factory production strongly encouraged the emergence of new divisions of labor as interchangeable parts and belt-driven assembly lines made the mass production of goods a hallmark of industrialized societies. The need to invest in increasingly expensive equipment encouraged the formation of large businesses: by the mid-nineteenth century, many giant corporations had joined together to control trade through trusts and cartels.

Foundations of Industrialization

By the mid-eighteenth century, several areas of the world—Great Britain in western Europe, the Yangzi Delta in China,

Japan—exhibited growing and dynamic economies that shared many common features. High agricultural productivity in those regions resulted in significant population growth. High population densities in turn encouraged occupational specialization and permitted many individuals to work at tasks other than cultivation. Navigable rivers and networks of canals facilitated trade and transport, and cities and towns were home to sophisticated banking and financial institutions. At the same time, these commercially sophisticated economies ran up against difficult ecological obstacles—especially soil depletion and deforestation—that threatened continued population growth and consumption levels. First Great Britain and subsequently the other regions of western Europe transcended those ecological constraints by exploiting coal deposits fortuitously found at home and natural resources found abroad.

Coal and Colonies Coal played a crucial role in the industrialization of Great Britain. Until the eighteenth century, wood had served as the primary source of fuel for iron production, home heating, and cooking. Prodigious uses of wood, however, had also hastened deforestation, causing serious wood shortages. Geographic luck had placed some of western Europe's largest coal deposits in Great Britain, within easy reach of water transport, centers of commerce, and pools of skilled labor. The fortunate conjunction of coal deposits and the skills necessary to extract this fuel encouraged the substitution of coal for wood, thus creating a promising framework for industrialization. In the absence of easily accessible coal deposits, it was unlikely that the economy could have supported an expanding iron production and the application of steam engines to mining and industry—both crucial to the industrial process in Great Britain. In that respect, Britain's experience proved unique and differed from that of China, where the breakthrough to industrialization occurred at a later time. In China, geography conspired against an important early shift from wood to coal, because the main coal-producing regions of northwest China were too distant from the Yangzi Delta, economically China's most promising region.

Ecological Relief The unique economic relationship between Europe and the Americas gave Great Britain additional ecological relief. The conquered and colonized lands of the Americas lifted European land constraints by supplying European societies with a growing volume of primary products. During the eighteenth century the slave-based plantations of northeastern Brazil, the Caribbean islands, and later the southern United States supplied Europe with huge amounts of sugar and cotton; the former increased available food calories while the latter kept emerging textile industries going. Neither of these products could have been grown in Europe. The plantation economies of the Caribbean islands in particular also created significant markets for manufactured imports from Europe, the poverty of slaves notwithstanding.

Almost one-half of the proceeds from sugar exports paid for the importation of manufactured goods from Europe, including cheap cotton cloth for slaves to wear. The significance of valuable American resources grew after 1830, when large amounts of grain, timber, and beef traveled across the Atlantic to European destinations. All these products grew on colonial acreage, which expanded Europe's land base. Later in the century, American lands also served as outlets for Europe's surplus population.

Access to coal deposits and the exploitation of overseas resources provided a context—one not yet available to societies such as China's—that increased the odds for an industrial breakthrough. This industrial expansion, in fact, started with Britain's textiles. Beginning about the mid-eighteenth century, consumer demand encouraged a transformation of the British cotton industry.

During the seventeenth century, English consumers had become fond of calicoes—inexpensive, brightly printed textiles imported from India. Cotton cloth came into demand because it was lighter, easier to wash, and quicker to dry than wool, which was the principal fabric of European clothes before the nineteenth century. Threatened by the popularity of cotton products, British wool producers persuaded Parliament to pass a series of laws to protect the domestic wool industry. The Calico Acts of 1720 and 1721 prohibited imports of printed cotton cloth and restricted the sale of calicoes at home. Parliament even passed a law requiring corpses to be buried in woolen shrouds, but legislation did not dampen consumers' enthusiasm for cotton. Consumer demand for cotton products drove the development of a British cotton textile industry.

Mechanization of the Cotton Industry Demand for cotton was so strong that producers had to speed up spinning and weaving to supply growing domestic and foreign markets. To increase production, they turned to inventions that rapidly mechanized the cotton textile industry. In the early 1730s, artisans began to develop labor-saving devices for spinning and weaving cotton, thereby moving away from hand-based techniques derived from the wool and linen industries. The first important technological breakthrough came in 1733 when Manchester mechanic John Kay invented the flying shuttle. This device speeded up the weaving process and stimulated demand for thread. Within a few years, competitions among inventors resulted in the creation of several mechanical spinning devices. The most important was Samuel Crompton's "mule," built in 1779. Adapted for steam power by 1790, the mule became the device of choice for spinning cotton. A worker using a steam-driven mule could produce a hundred times more thread than a worker using a manual spinning wheel.

The new spinning machines created an imbalance in manufacturing because weavers could not keep up with the production of thread, so innovators turned their attention next to weaving. In 1785 Edmund Cartwright, a clergyman

An 1835 engraving depicts female workers at a textile factory. The shift to machine-based manufacturing commonly started with the mechanization of the textile industries, not only in Great Britain, but also in other industrializing lands, such as the United States and Japan.

without training or experience in either mechanics or textiles, patented a water-driven power loom that inaugurated an era of mechanical weaving. Within two decades steam moved the power loom, and by the 1820s it had largely supplanted hand weavers in the cotton industry. Collectively, these technological developments permitted the production of textile goods in great volume and variety and at low cost. By 1830 half a million people worked in the cotton business, Britain's leading industry, which accounted for 40 percent of exports.

Steam Power

The most crucial technological breakthrough of the early industrial era was the development of a general-purpose steam engine in 1765 by James Watt, an instrument maker at the University of Glasgow in Scotland. Steam engines burned coal to boil water and create steam, which drove mechanical devices that performed work. Even before Watt's time, primitive steam engines had powered pumps that drew water out of coal mines, but those devices consumed too much fuel to be useful for other purposes. Watt's version relied on steam to force a piston to turn a wheel, whose rotary motion converted a simple pump into an engine that had multiple uses. Watt's contemporaries used the term *horsepower* to measure the energy generated by his steam engine, which did the work of numerous animals. By 1800 more than a thousand of Watt's steam engines were in use in the British isles. They were especially prominent in the textile industry, where their application resulted in greater productivity for manufacturers and cheaper prices for consumers.

Iron and Steel

Innovation did not stop with cotton production and steam engines. The iron and steel industries also benefited from technological refinement, and the availability of inexpensive, high-quality iron and steel reinforced the move toward mechanization. After 1709, British smelters began to use coke (a purified form of coal) rather than more expensive charcoal as a fuel to produce iron. Deforestation in England had made wood—the principal source of charcoal—scarce. Besides being cheaper than charcoal, coke made it possible for producers to build bigger blast furnaces and turn out larger lots of iron. As a result, British iron production skyrocketed during the eighteenth century, and prices to consumers fell. Inexpensive iron fittings and parts made industrial machinery stronger, and iron soon became common in bridges, buildings, and ships.

The nineteenth century was an age of steel rather than iron. Steel is much harder, stronger, and more resilient than iron, but until the nineteenth century it was very expensive to produce. Between 1740 and 1850 a series of improvements simplified the process. In 1856 Henry Bessemer built a refined blast furnace known as the Bessemer converter that made it possible to produce steel cheaply and in large quantities. Steel production rose sharply, and steel quickly began to replace iron in tools, machines, and structures that required high strength.

Transportation

Steam engineering and metallurgical innovations both contributed to improvements in transportation technology. James Watt's steam engine did not adapt well to transportation uses because it consumed too much coal.

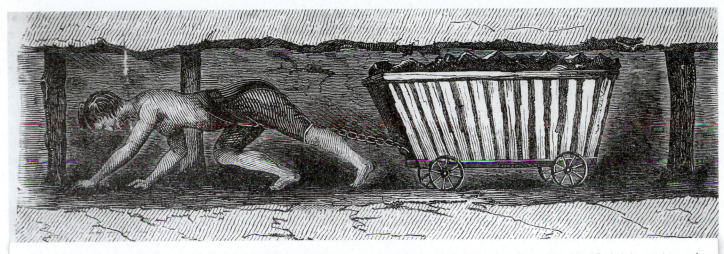

A woman working as a drawer in a British coal mine drags her coal cart with the aid of a belt and chain. Manually produced coal fueled the machines of early industrial society. What specific risks might have been associated with this kind of job?

After his patent expired, however, inventors devised high-pressure engines that required less fuel. In 1815 George Stephenson, a self-educated Englishman, built the first steam-powered locomotive. In 1829 his Rocket won a contest by reaching a speed of 45 kilometers (28 miles) per hour. Although they were more efficient than Watt's invention, Stephenson's engines still burned too much coal for use at sea. Sailing ships remained the most effective means of transport over the seas until the middle of the nineteenth century, when refined engines of high efficiency began to drive steamships.

Because they had the capacity to carry huge cargoes, railroads and steamships dramatically lowered transportation costs. They also contributed to the creation of dense transportation networks that linked remote interior regions and distant shores more closely than ever before. Between 1830 and 1870, British entrepreneurs laid about 20,000 kilometers (13,000 miles) of railroads, which linked industrial centers, coalfields, iron deposits, and port cities throughout the land—and also carried some 322 million passengers as well as cargoes of raw materials and manufactured goods. Steamships proved their own versatility by advancing up rivers to

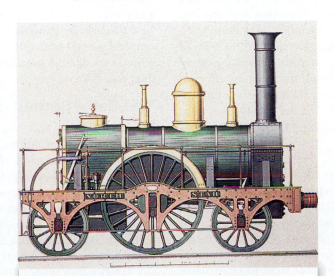

George Stephenson's North Star engine of 1837. Although Stephenson did not invent the locomotive, his refinements of locomotive technology, his application of civil engineering to the development of efficient railroad lines, and his vision of the future impact of railway systems on commerce earned him the nickname "Father of the Railways."

points that sailboats could not reach because of inconvenient twists, turns, or winds. Railroads and steamships benefited from the innovations that drove the industrialization process and in turn encouraged continuing industrialization by providing rapid and inexpensive transport.

The Factory System

In the emerging capitalist society of early modern Europe (discussed in chapter 23), most manufacturing took place under the putting-out system. To avoid guild restrictions on prices and wages, entrepreneurs in early modern Europe paid individuals to work on materials in their households. That protoindustrial system of production centered on the household and usually involved fewer than ten people. During the seventeenth and early eighteenth centuries, new and larger units of production supplemented the putting-out system. Rising demand for certain products such as textiles and the growing use of water and wind power led to the formation of protoindustrial factories, where workers performed specialized tasks under one roof. Nevertheless, the largest preindustrial workforces consisted of unskilled laborers in mines and slaves on plantations.

The Factory The factory system replaced both the putting-out system and protoindustrial factories and became the characteristic method of production in industrial economies. It began to emerge in the late eighteenth century, when technological advances transformed the British textile industry, and by the mid-nineteenth century most cotton production took place in factories. Many of the newly developed machines were too large and expensive for home use, and it became necessary to move work to locations where entrepreneurs and engineers built complicated machinery for large-scale production. This centralization of production brought together more workers doing specialized tasks than ever before. Most industrial workers hailed from the countryside. A combination of factors provided a plentiful supply of cheap labor for the burgeoning factories, including rural overpopulation, declining job opportunities, and the financial difficulties of small farmers who had to sell their land to large landowners.

The factory system with its new machines demanded a rational organization of job functions that differed from earlier forms of industrial organization. The factory became associated with a new division of labor, one that called for a production process in which each worker performed a single task, rather than one in which a single worker completed the entire job, as was typical of handicraft traditions. In the first chapter of the *Wealth of Nations* (1776), Adam Smith used a pin factory to describe the new system of manufacture. "One man draws out the wire, another straights it, a third cuts it, a fourth points it, a fifth grinds it at the top for receiving the head; . . . and the important business of making a pin is, in this manner, divided into about eighteen distinct operations." Factories also enabled managers to impose strict work discipline and closely supervise employees. Thus Josiah Wedgwood (1730–1795), an Englishman with a wooden leg and who owned a pottery plant, held his employees to high standards in an effort to produce the highest quality pottery. When he spotted inferior work, he frequently dumped it on the factory floor and crushed it with his peg leg saying, "This will not do for Josiah Wedgwood!"

Working Conditions With its new divisions of labor, the factory system allowed managers to improve worker productivity and realize spectacular increases in the output of manufactured goods. But the new environment also had unsettling effects on the nature of work. The factory system led to the emergence of an owner class whose capital financed equipment and machinery that were too expensive for workers to acquire. Industrial workers themselves became mere wage earners who had only their labor services to offer and who depended on their employers for their livelihood. In addition, any broad-range skills that workers may have previously acquired as artisans often became obsolete in a work environment that rewarded narrowly defined skills. The repetitive and boring nature of many industrial jobs, moreover, left many workers alienated or estranged from their work and the products of their labor.

Equally disturbing was the new work discipline and the pace of work. Those accustomed to rural labor soon learned that the seasons, the rising and setting of the sun, and fluctuations in the weather no longer dictated work routines. Instead, clocks, machines, and shop rules established new rhythms of work. Industrial workers commonly labored six days a week for twelve to fourteen hours daily. The factory whistle sounded the beginning and the end of the working day, and throughout the day workers had to keep pace with the monotonous movements of machines. At the same time, they faced strict and immediate supervision, which made little allowance for a quick nap or socializing with friends. Floor managers pressured men, women, and children to speed up production and punished them when they did not meet expectations. Because neither the machines nor the methods of work took safety into account, early industrial workers constantly faced the possibility of maiming or fatal accidents.

Industrial Protest In some instances, machine-centered factories sparked violent protest. Between 1811 and 1816, organized bands of English handicraft workers known as Luddites went on a rampage and destroyed textile machines that they blamed for their low wages and unemployment. They called their leader King Lud, after a legendary boy named Ludlam who broke a knitting frame to spite his father. The movement broke out in the hosiery and lace industries around Nottingham and then spread to the wool and cotton mills of Lancashire. The Luddites usually wore masks and operated at night. Because they avoided violence against people, they enjoyed considerable popular support. Nevertheless, by hanging fourteen Luddites in 1813, the government served notice that it was unwilling to tolerate violence even against machines, and the movement gradually died out.

The Early Spread of Industrialization

Industrialization and the technological, organizational, and social transformations that accompanied it might have originated in many parts of the world where abundant craft skills, agricultural production, and investment capital could support the industrialization process. For half a century, however, industrialization took place only in Great Britain. Aware of their head start, British entrepreneurs and government officials forbade the export of machinery, manufacturing techniques, and skilled workers.

Yet Britain's monopoly on industrialization did not last forever, because enterprising entrepreneurs recognized profitable opportunities in foreign lands and circumvented government regulations to sell machinery and technical know-how abroad. Moreover, European and North American businesspeople did their best to become acquainted with British industrial techniques and lure British experts to their lands. European and North American entrepreneurs

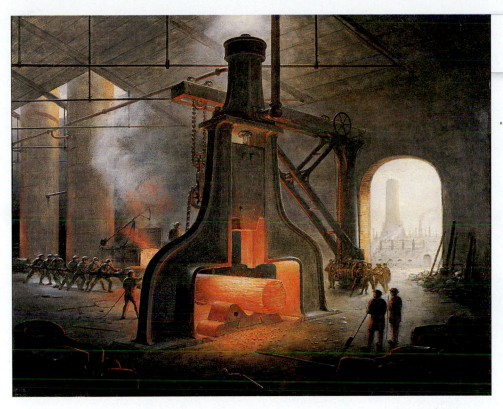

Workers tend to a massive steam hammer under dangerous conditions.

German industrialization proceeded more slowly than did Belgian and French, partly because of political instability resulting from competition between the many German states. After the 1840s, however, German coal and iron production soared, and by the 1850s an extensive railroad network was under construction. After unification in 1871, Bismarck's government sponsored rapid industrialization in Germany. In the interests of strengthening military capacity, Bismarck encouraged the development of heavy industry, and the formation of huge businesses became a hallmark of German industrialization. The giant Krupp firm, for example, dominated mining, metallurgy, armaments production, and shipbuilding.

did not hesitate to bribe or even kidnap British engineers, and they also smuggled advanced machinery out of the British isles. Sometimes they got poor value for their investments: they found that it was difficult to attract the best British experts to foreign lands and had to make do with drunkards or second-rate specialists who demanded high pay but made little contribution to industrialization.

Industrialization in Western Europe Nevertheless, by the mid-nineteenth century, industrialization had spread to France, Germany, Belgium, and the United States. The French revolution and the Napoleonic wars helped set the stage for industrialization in western Europe by abolishing internal trade barriers and dismantling guilds that discouraged technological innovation and restricted the movement of laborers. The earliest continental center of industrial production was Belgium, where coal, iron, textile, glass, and armaments production flourished in the early nineteenth century. About the same time, France also moved toward industrialization. By 1830, French firms employed about fifteen thousand skilled British workers who helped establish mechanized textile and metallurgical industries in France. By the mid-nineteenth century, French engineers and inventors were devising refinements and innovations that led to greater efficiencies especially in metallurgical industries. Later in the century a boom in railroad construction stimulated economic development while also leading to decreased transportation costs.

Industrialization in North America Industrialization transformed North America as well as western Europe in the nineteenth century. In 1800 the United States possessed abundant land and natural resources but few laborers and little money to invest in business enterprises. Both labor and investment capital came largely from Europe: migrants crossed the Atlantic in large numbers throughout the nineteenth century, and European bankers and businesspeople eagerly sought opportunities to invest in businesses that made use of American natural resources. American industrialization began in the 1820s when entrepreneurs lured British crafts workers to New England and built a cotton textile industry. By mid-century well over a thousand mills were producing fabrics from raw cotton grown in the southern states, and New England had emerged as a site for the industrial production also of shoes, tools, and handguns. In the 1870s heavy iron and steel industries emerged in areas such as western Pennsylvania and central Alabama where there were abundant supplies of iron ore and coal. By 1900 the United States had become an economic powerhouse, and industrialization had begun to spill over into southern Canada.

The vast size of the United States was advantageous to industrialists because it made abundant natural resources available to them, but it also hindered travel and communication between the regions. To facilitate transportation

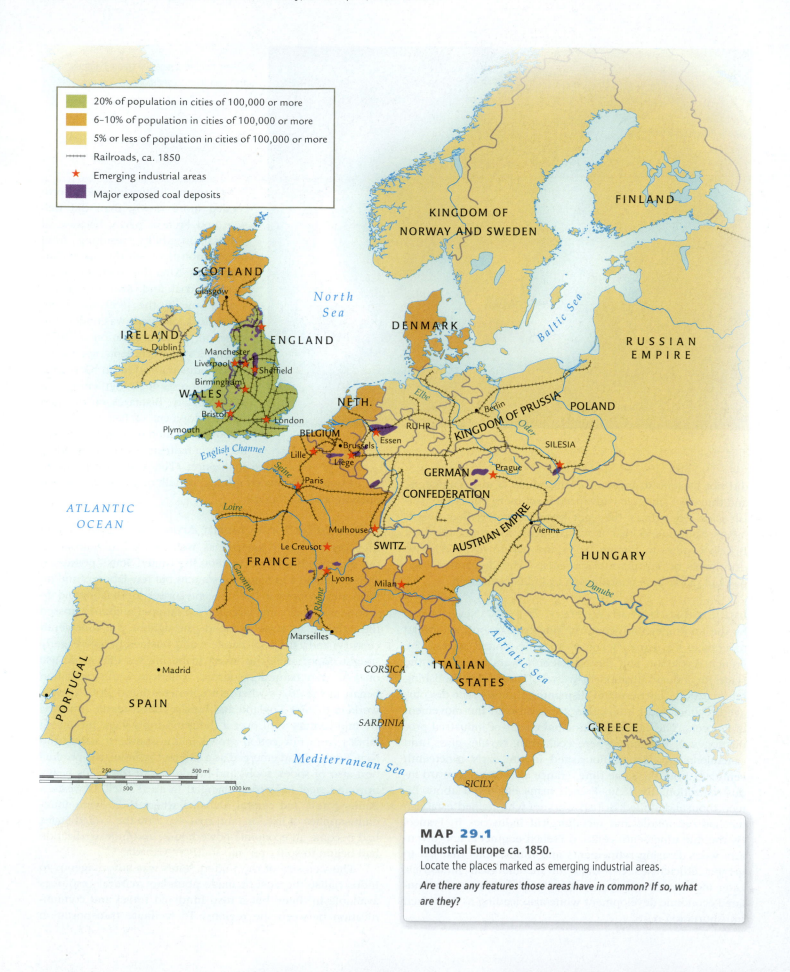

MAP 29.1

Industrial Europe ca. 1850.
Locate the places marked as emerging industrial areas.

Are there any features those areas have in common? If so, what are they?

and distribution, state governments built canals, and private investors established steamship lines and railroad networks. By 1860 rails linked the industrial northeast with the agricultural south and the midwestern cities of St. Louis and Chicago, where brokers funneled wheat and beef from the plains to the more densely populated eastern states. As in other lands, railroad construction in the United States spurred industrialization by providing cheap transportation and stimulating coal, iron, and steel industries.

Industrial Capitalism

Mass Production
Cotton textiles were the major factory-made products during the early phase of industrialization, but new machinery and techniques soon made it possible to extend the factory system to other industries. Furthermore, with refined manufacturing processes, factories could mass-produce standardized articles. An important contribution to the evolving factory system came from the American inventor Eli Whitney (1765–1825). Though best remembered as the inventor of the cotton gin (1793), Whitney also developed the technique of using machine tools to produce large quantities of interchangeable parts in the making of firearms. In conventional methods a skilled worker made a complete musket, forming and fitting each unique part; Whitney designed machine tools with which unskilled workers made only a particular part that fit every musket of the same model. Before long, entrepreneurs applied Whitney's method to the manufacture of everything from clocks and sewing machines to uniforms and shoes. By the middle of the nineteenth century, mass production of standardized articles was becoming the hallmark of industrial societies.

In 1913 Henry Ford improved manufacturing techniques further when he introduced the assembly line to automobile production. Instead of organizing production around a series of stations where teams of workers assembled each individual car using standardized parts, Ford designed a conveyor system that carried components past workers at the proper height and speed. Each worker performed a specialized task at a fixed point on the assembly line, which churned out a complete chassis every 93 minutes—a task that previously had taken 728 minutes. The subdivision of labor and the coordination of operations resulted in enormous productivity gains, enabling Ford Motor Company to produce half the world's automobiles in the early twentieth century. With gains in productivity, car prices plummeted, allowing millions of people to purchase automobiles. The age of the motor car had arrived.

Big Business
As the factory evolved, so too did the organization of business. Industrial machinery and factories were expensive investments, and they encouraged businesses to organize on a large scale. Thus industrialization spurred the continuing development of capitalist business organization. Entrepreneurs in early modern Europe formed private businesses in the hopes of profiting from market-oriented production and trade. Some businesses, such as the English East India Company and other commercial concerns, organized joint-stock companies in the interests of spreading risk, achieving efficiency, and maximizing profits. With industrialization, manufacturers followed the lead of merchants by organizing on a large scale.

The Corporation
During the 1850s and 1860s, government authorities in Britain and France laid the legal foundations for the modern corporation, which quickly became the most common form of business organization in industrial societies. By the late nineteenth century, corporations controlled most businesses requiring large investments in land, labor, or machinery, including railroads, shipping lines, and industrial concerns that produced iron, steel, and armaments. Meanwhile, an array of investment banks, brokerage firms, and other financial businesses arose to serve the needs of industrial capitalists organized in corporations.

Monopolies, Trusts, and Cartels
To protect their investments, some big businesses of the late nineteenth century sought not only to outperform their competitors in the capitalist marketplace but also to eliminate competition. Business firms formed associations to restrict markets or establish monopolies in their industries. Large-scale business organizations formed trusts and cartels. The difference between the two was largely a technical one, and both shared a common goal: to control the supply of a product and hence its price in the marketplace. Some monopolists sought to control industries through vertical organization, by which they would dominate all facets of a single industry. The industrial empire of the American petroleum producer John D. Rockefeller, for example, which he ruled through Standard Oil Company and Trust, controlled almost all oil drilling, processing, refining, marketing, and distribution in the United States. Control over all aspects of the petroleum industry enabled Standard Oil to operate efficiently, cut costs, and undersell its competitors. Vertical organization of this kind offered large corporations great advantages over smaller companies.

Other monopolists tried to eliminate competition by means of horizontal organization, which involved the consolidation or cooperation of independent companies in the same business. Thus cartels sought to ensure the prosperity of their members by absorbing competitors, fixing prices, regulating production, or dividing up markets. The German firm IG Farben, the world's largest chemical concern until the middle of the twentieth century, grew out of a complex merger of chemical and pharmaceutical manufacturers that controlled as much as 90 percent of production in chemical industries. By the end of the nineteenth century, some governments outlawed these combinations and broke them up. Yet, when governments proved unwilling to confront large businesses, or when the public remained ignorant or indifferent, monopolistic practices continued well into the twentieth century.

This is a 1911 photograph of Standard Oil's refinery in Richmond, California. Established in 1870 as an Ohio corporation, Standard Oil was the largest oil refiner in the world and operated as a major company trust. It was one of the world's first and largest multinational corporations until it was broken up by the United States Supreme Court in 1911. John D. Rockefeller, the company's founder, became the richest man in history.

INDUSTRIAL SOCIETY

Industrialization brought material benefits in its train: inexpensive manufactured products, rising standards of living, and population growth. Yet industrialization also unleashed dramatic and often unsettling social change. Massive internal and external migrations took place as millions of people moved from the countryside to work in new industrial cities, and European migrants crossed the Atlantic by the tens of millions to seek opportunities in the less densely populated lands of the western hemisphere. Industrialization encouraged the emergence of new social classes—especially the middle class and the working class—and forced men, women, and children to adjust to distinctly new patterns of family and work life. Reformers sought to alleviate the social and economic problems that accompanied industrialization. The most influential critics were the socialists, who did not object to industrialization per se but worked toward the building of a more equitable and just society.

Industrial Demographics

Industrialization brought efficiencies in production that flooded markets with affordable manufactured goods. In 1851 the bounty of industry went on display in London at the Crystal Palace, a magnificent structure made of iron and glass that enclosed trees, gardens, fountains, and manufactured products from around the world. Viewers flocked to the exhibition to see industrial products such as British textiles, iron goods, and machine tools. Colt revolvers and sewing machines from the United States also attracted attention as representatives of the "American system of manufacture," which used interchangeable parts in producing large quantities of standardized goods at low prices. Observers marveled at the Crystal Palace exhibits and congratulated themselves on the achievements of industrial society.

In many ways, industrialization raised material standards of living. Industrial production led to dramatic reductions in the cost of clothing, for example, so individuals were able to add variety to their wardrobes. By the early nineteenth century, all but the desperately poor could afford several changes of clothes, and light, washable underwear came into widespread use with the availability of inexpensive manufactured cotton. Industrial factories turned out tools that facilitated agricultural work, while steam-powered locomotives delivered produce quickly and cheaply to distant markets, so industrialization contributed as well to a decline in the price of food. Consumers in early industrial Europe also filled their homes with more furniture, cabinets, porcelain, and decorative objects than any but the most wealthy of their ancestors.

Exhibitors from around the world displayed fine handicrafts and manufactured goods at the Crystal Palace exhibition of 1851 in London. Industrial products from Britain and the United States particularly attracted the attention of visitors to the enchanting and futuristic exhibition hall.

Population Growth The populations of European and Euro-American peoples rose sharply during the eighteenth and nineteenth centuries, and they reflected the rising prosperity and standards of living that came with industrialization. Between 1700 and 1800 the population of Europe increased from 105 million to 180 million, and during the nineteenth century it more than doubled to 390 million. Demographic growth in the western hemisphere—fueled by migration from Europe—was even more remarkable. Between 1700 and 1800 the population of North America and South America rose from 13 million to 24 million and then surged to 145 million by 1900. Demographic growth was most spectacular in the temperate regions of the west-

ern hemisphere. In Argentina, for example, population expanded from 300,000 in 1800 to 4.75 million in 1900—a 1,583 percent increase. In temperate North America—what is now the United States—population rose from 6 million to 76 million (1,266 percent) during the 1800s.

The rapid population growth in Europe and the Americas reflected changing patterns of fertility and mortality. In most preindustrial societies fertility was high, but famines and epidemics resulted in high mortality, especially child mortality, which prevented explosive population growth.

Medical advances over time supplied the means to control disease and reduce mortality. A case in point was smallpox, an ancient, highly contagious, and often fatal viral disease that had killed more people than any other malady in world history. The experiments of the English physician Edward Jenner dealt an effective blow against smallpox. Knowing that milkmaids often contracted cowpox, in 1797 Jenner inoculated an eight-year-old boy with cowpox and followed it six weeks later with the smallpox virus. The boy became ill but soon recovered fully, leading Jenner to deduce that cowpox conferred immunity against smallpox. Later called vaccination (from *vacca,* the Latin word for "cow"), Jenner's procedure not only created a powerful weapon in the war against smallpox but also laid the foundation for scientific immunology. Over time, physicians developed vaccines that prevented sickness and death from polio, tetanus, typhoid, whooping cough, and many other diseases that once plagued humankind.

High birthrates were common also in early industrializing societies, but death rates fell markedly because better diets and improved disease control reduced child mortality. Because more infants survived to adulthood, the population of early industrializing societies grew rapidly. By the late nineteenth century, better diets and improved sanitation led to declining levels of adult as well as child mortality, so populations of industrial societies expanded even faster. Britain and Germany, the most active sites of early industrialization, experienced especially fast population growth. Between 1800 and 1900 the British population increased

from 10.5 million to 37.5 million while German numbers rose from 18 million to 43 million.

The Demographic Transition Beginning in the nineteenth century, industrializing lands experienced a social change known as the demographic transition, which refers to shifting patterns of fertility and mortality. As industrialization transformed societies, fertility began a marked decline. In the short run, mortality fell even faster than fertility, so the populations of industrial societies continued to increase. Over time, however, declining birthrates led to lower population growth and relative demographic stability. The principal reason for declining fertility in industrial lands was voluntary birth control through contraception.

Birth Control For thousands of years, people tried to find deliberate ways of preventing or reducing the probability of pregnancy resulting from sexual intercourse. Some of the methods, such as coitus interruptus, proved not to be particularly reliable, and others, such as sexual abstinence,

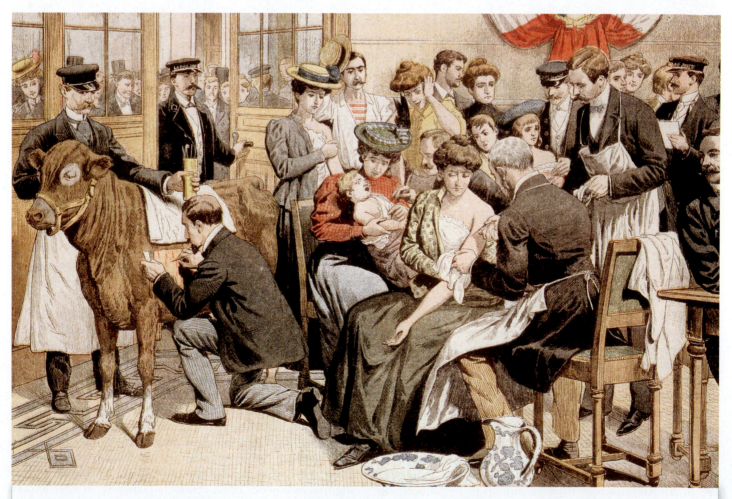

A French newspaper sponsored free smallpox vaccinations in 1905; the serum of a cow infected with cowpox is being injected into waiting Parisians.

turned out to be unrealistic. More ingenious methods of birth control such as vaginal depositories, cervical caps, or drinkable concoctions designed to prevent pregnancies or induce miscarriages usually carried serious health risks for women. Because none of those methods proved effective, people throughout the world had resorted to abortion or infanticide.

The first efficient means of contraception without negative side effects was the male condom. Initially made of animal intestines, it came into use in the seventeenth century. In reference to its place of origin, the Italian adventurer and womanizer Casanova called the condom an "English riding coat." The effectiveness and popularity of the condom soared in the mid-nineteenth century with the arrival of the latex condom, which served both as a contraceptive device and as a barrier against syphilis, a much-feared venereal disease. Since then, a plethora of contraceptive devices has become available.

Married couples might have chosen to have fewer offspring because raising them cost more in industrial than in agricultural societies or because declining child mortality meant that any children born were more likely to survive to adulthood. In any case, the demographic transition accompanied industrialization in western Europe, the United States, Japan, and other industrializing lands as well.

Urbanization and Migration

Industrialization and population growth strongly encouraged migration and urbanization. Within industrial societies, migrants flocked from the countryside to urban centers in search of work. Industrial Britain led the world in urbanization. In 1800 about one-fifth of the British population lived in towns and cities of 10,000 or more inhabitants. During the following century a largely rural society became predominantly urban, with three-quarters of the population working and living in cities. That pattern repeated itself in continental Europe, the United States, Japan, and the rest of the industrialized world. By 1900 at least 50 percent of the population in industrialized lands lived in towns with populations of 2,000 or more. The increasing size of cities reflected this internal migration. In 1800 there were barely twenty cities in Europe with populations as high as 100,000, and there were none in the western hemisphere. By 1900 there were more than 150 large cities in Europe and North America combined. With a population of 6.5 million, London was the largest city in the world, followed by New York with 4.2 million, Paris with 3.3 million, and Berlin with 2.7 million.

The Urban Environment With urbanization came intensified environmental pollution. Although cities had always been putrid and unsanitary places, the rapid increase in urban populations during the industrial age dramatically increased the magnitude and severity of water and air pollution. The widespread burning of fossil fuels, such as wood and coal, fouled the air with vast quantities of chemicals and particulate matter. This pollution led to typical occupa-

tional diseases among some trades. Chimney sweeps, for instance, contracted cancer of the scrotum from hydrocarbon deposits found in chimney soot. Effluents from factories and mills and an increasing amount of untreated sewage dirtied virtually every major river. No part of a city was immune to the constant stench coming from air and water pollution. Worse, tainted water supplies and unsanitary living conditions led to periodic epidemics of cholera and typhus, and dysentery and tuberculosis were also common maladies. Until the latter part of the nineteenth century, urban environments remained dangerous places in which death rates commonly exceeded birthrates, and only the constant stream of new arrivals from the country kept cities growing.

Income determined the degree of comfort and security offered by city life. The wealthy typically tried to insulate themselves the best they could from urban discomforts by retreating to their elegant homes in the newly growing suburbs. The working poor, in contrast, crowded into the centers of cities to live in shoddy housing constructed especially for them. The rapid influx of people to expanding industrial cities such as Liverpool and Manchester encouraged the quick but slipshod construction of dwellings close to the mills and factories. Industrial workers and their families occupied overcrowded tenements lacking in comfort and amenities. The cramped spaces in apartments obliged many to share the same bed, increasing the likelihood of incestuous relationships and the ease of disease transmission. The few open spaces outside the buildings were usually home to herds of pigs living in their own dung or were depositories for pools of stagnant water and human waste. Whenever possible, the inhabitants of such neighborhoods flocked to parks and public gardens.

By the later nineteenth century, though, government authorities were tending to the problems of the early industrial cities. They improved municipal water supplies, expanded sewage systems, and introduced building codes that outlawed the construction of rickety tenements to accommodate poorly paid workers. Those measures made city life safer and brought improved sanitation that helped to eliminate epidemic disease. City authorities also built parks and recreational facilities to make cities more livable.

Transcontinental Migration While workers moved from the countryside to urban centers, rapid population growth in Europe encouraged massive migration to the Americas, especially to the United States. During the nineteenth and early twentieth centuries, about fifty million Europeans migrated to the western hemisphere, and this flow of humanity accounts for much of the stunning demographic growth of the Americas. Many of the migrants intended to stay for only a few years and fully expected to return to their homelands with a modest fortune made in the Americas. Indeed, some did return to Europe: about one-third of Italian migrants to the Americas made the trip back across the Atlantic. The vast majority, however, remained in the western

sources from the past

Thomas Malthus on Population

The Reverend Thomas R. Malthus (1766–1834), English economist and pioneer of modern population study, generated controversy with his pessimistic predictions regarding the future of humanity. In his famous Essay on the Principle of Population *(1798, rev. ed. 1803), he insisted that poverty and distress are the inevitable consequences of unchecked population growth. Malthus argued that demand for food will invariably exceed the means of subsistence.*

The principal object of the present essay is to examine the effects of one great cause intimately united with the very nature of man; which, though it has been constantly and powerfully operating since the commencement of society, has been little noticed by the writers who have treated this subject. . . . The cause to which I allude is the constant tendency in all animated life to increase beyond the nourishment prepared for it.

This is incontrovertibly true. Through the animal and vegetable kingdoms Nature has scattered the seeds of life abroad with the most profuse and liberal hand; but has been comparatively sparing in the room and the nourishment necessary to rear them. The germs of existence contained in this earth, if they could freely develop themselves, would fill millions of worlds in the course of a few thousand years. Necessity, that imperious, all pervading law of nature, restrains them within the prescribed bounds. The race of plants and the race of animals shrink under this great restrictive law; and man cannot by any efforts of reason escape from it.

It may safely be pronounced, therefore, that population, when unchecked, goes on doubling itself every twenty-five years, or increases in a geometrical ratio. . . . It may fairly be pronounced, therefore, that considering the present average state of the earth, the means of subsistence, under circumstances the most favorable to human industry, could not possibly be made to increase faster than in an arithmetical ratio.

The ultimate check to population appears then to be want of food, arising necessarily from the different ratios according to which population and food increase. But this ultimate check is never the immediate check, except in the cases of actual famine.

The immediate check may be stated to consist in all those customs and diseases, which seem to be generated by a scarcity of the means of subsistence; and all those causes, independent of this scarcity, whether of a moral or physical nature, which tend prematurely to weaken and destroy the human frame.

These checks to population which are constantly operating with more or less force in every society, and keep down the number to the level of the means of subsistence, may be classed under two general heads—the preventative and positive checks.

The preventative check, as far as it is voluntary, is peculiar to man, and arises from that distinctive superiority in his reasoning faculties which enables him to calculate distant consequences. . . . These considerations are calculated to prevent, and certainly do prevent, a great number of persons in all civilised nations from pursuing the dictate of nature in an early attachment to one woman. . . . [T]he restraint from marriage which is not followed by irregular gratifications may properly be termed moral restraint.

The positive checks to population are extremely various, and include every cause, whether arising from vice or misery, which in any degree contributes to shorten the natural duration of human life. Under this head, therefore, may be enumerated all unwholesome occupations, severe labor and exposure to the seasons, extreme poverty, bad nursing of children, great towns, excesses of all kinds, the whole train of common diseases, and epidemics, wars, plague, and famine.

For Further Reflection

■ Were Malthus's fears about a lack of food realized during the age of industrialization, or did aspects of the new industrial society in fact help to prevent those fears from being realized?

Source: Thomas R. Malthus. *An Essay on Population.* London: J. M. Dent, 1914, pp. 6–15.

---

hemisphere. They and their descendants transformed the Americas into Euro-American lands.

Most of the migrants came from the British isles in the early nineteenth century, from Germany, Ireland, and Scandinavia in the middle decades, and from eastern and southern Europe in the late nineteenth century. Migration reflected difficult political, social, and economic circumstances in Europe: British migrants often sought to escape

dangerous factories and the squalor of early industrial cities, most Irish migrants departed during the potato famines of the 1840s, and millions of Jews left the Russian empire in the 1890s because of the tsar's anti-Semitic policies. Many of those migrants entered the workforce of the United States, where they settled in new industrial centers such as New York, Pittsburgh, and Cleveland. Indeed, labor from abroad made it possible for the United States to undergo rapid in-

Gustave Dore, a French book illustrator, sketched an image of Wentworth Street, Whitechapel, in London. By the middle of the nineteenth century, population shifts from rural areas to London made Whitechapel synonymous with poverty and overcrowding. Small dark avenues such as Wentworth Street contained the greatest suffering, filth, and danger.

dustrialization in the late nineteenth century.

Industry and Society

As millions of people moved from the countryside to industrial centers, society underwent a dramatic transformation. Before industrialization, the vast majority of the world's peoples worked in rural areas as cultivators or herders. Rulers, aristocrats, priests, and a few others enjoyed privileged status, and small numbers of people worked in cities as artisans, crafts workers, bureaucrats, or professionals. Many societies also made use of slave labor, occasionally on a large scale.

Industrialization radically altered traditional social structures. It encouraged the disappearance of slavery in lands undergoing industrialization, partly because the economics of industrial society did not favor slave labor. Slaves were generally poor, so they did not consume the products of industrial manufacturers in large quantities. Industrialists preferred free wage laborers who spent their money on products that kept their factories busy.

New Social Classes Industrialization also helped bring new social classes into being. Captains of industry and enterprising businesspeople became fabulously wealthy and powerful enough to overshadow the military aristocracy and other traditionally privileged classes. Less powerful than this new elite was the middle class, consisting of small business owners, factory managers, engineers, accountants, skilled employees of large corporations, and professionals such as teachers, physicians, and attorneys. Industrial production generated great wealth, and a large portion of it flowed to the middle class, which was a principal beneficiary of industrialization. Meanwhile, masses of laborers who toiled in factories and mines constituted a new working class. Less skilled than the artisans and crafts workers of earlier times, the new workers tended to machines or provided heavy labor for low wages. Concentrated in mining and industrial centers, the working class began to influence political affairs by the mid-nineteenth century.

Industrial Families The most basic unit of social organization—the family—also underwent fundamental change during the industrial age. In preindustrial societies the family was the basic productive unit. Whether engaged in agriculture, domestic manufacturing, or commerce, family members worked together and contributed to the welfare of the larger group. Industrialization challenged the family economy and reshaped family life by moving economic production outside the home and introducing a sharp distinction between work and family life. During the early years of industrialization, family economies persisted as fathers, mothers, and children pooled their wages and sometimes even worked together in factories. Over time, however, it became less common for family members to work in groups. Workers left their homes each day to labor an average of fourteen hours in factories, and family members led increasingly separate lives.

Work and Play Men gained increased stature and responsibility in the industrial age as work dominated public life. When production moved outside the home, some men became owners or managers of factories, although the majority served as wageworkers. Industrial work seemed to be far more important than the domestic chores traditionally carried out by women, or even the agricultural and light industrial work performed by women and children. Men's wages also constituted the bulk of their families' income. Upper-class and middle-class men especially enjoyed increased prestige at home, since they usually were the sole providers who made their families' comfortable existence possible.

Internalizing the work ethic of the industrial age, professional men dedicated themselves to self-improvement even in their leisure hours. They avidly read books and attended lectures on business or cultural themes. They also strove to instill their values in the industrial workforce and to impose work discipline on the laborers under their supervision. Threats of fines, beatings, and dismissal coerced workers into accepting factory rules against absenteeism, tardiness, and swearing. Through their support for churches and Sunday schools, factory owners sought to persuade workers to adopt middle-class norms of respectability and morality.

For their part, industrial workers often resisted the work discipline and moral pressures they encountered at the factory. They frequently observed "Holy Monday" and stayed home to lengthen their weekly break from work on Sundays. In their leisure time they flocked to sporting events: European soccer and American baseball both became popular sports during the industrial era. They also gambled, socialized at bars and pubs, and staged fights between dogs or roosters. The middle and upper classes tried to suppress these activities and established urban police forces to control workers' public behavior. But efforts at regulation had limited success, and workers persistently pursued their own interests.

Women at Home and Work Like men, women had worked long hours in preindustrial times. Agriculture and domestic manufacturing could easily accommodate women's dual role as mothers and workers, since the workplace

A small group of Englishmen find entertainment in a cockfight, a blood sport between two roosters. Cockfighting was a pastime already practiced in the Indus Valley by 2000 B.C.E. Banned outright in England and Wales and in the British Overseas Territories with the Cruelty to Animals Act in 1835, it nonetheless remains a popular form of entertainment worldwide.

thinking about TRADITIONS

Family and Factory

Most families had for long centuries lived according to the rhythms of nature and agrarianism. The age of industrialization introduced a machine-driven world and radically altered family life. What transformations occurred once factories organized life and work? Did changes equally affect men, women, and children?

was either at home or nearby. Industrialization dramatically changed the terms of work for women. When industry moved production from the home to the factory, married women were unable to work unless they left their homes and children in someone else's care. By the late nineteenth century, industrial society neither expected nor wanted women to engage in labor but, instead, encouraged women to devote themselves to traditional pursuits such as the raising of children, the management of the home, and the preservation of traditional family values.

Working-Class Women Working-class women, however, typically were expected to work at least until marriage, and often even after marriage, usually to compensate for their husbands' insufficient wages. Since women commonly earned less money than men, working-class women rarely could support themselves, let alone their families. Although most women in the cities went into domestic service in middle-class households, an important minority labored in industry. Particularly during the early stages of industrialization, early manufacturers employed women in greater numbers than men. This was especially true for the flourishing low-wage textile industry, where labor-saving devices made their first appearance. Both inventors and manufacturers mistakenly believed that women (and also children) were best suited to operate the new machines because their small hands and fingers gave them superior dexterity. By the middle of the nineteenth century, women made up the majority of the British industrial workforce. Ironically, the labor-saving devices that initially increased female employment were also responsible for their elimination from the workforce. In the long term, most labor-saving devices replaced jobs women had done. The first spinning jenny, for example, replaced ten workers for every worker it employed. A similar pattern held for the power looms that replaced weavers.

Most working-class women found employment in domestic service. Industrialization increased the demand for domestic servants as the middle class grew in both numbers and wealth. One of every three European women became a domestic servant at some point in her life. Rural women sometimes had to move long distances to take positions in middle-class homes in cities, where they experienced ad-

venture and independence from family control. Their employers replaced their parents as guardians, but high demand for servants ensured that women could switch jobs readily in search of more attractive positions. Young women servants often sent some of their earnings home, but many also saved wages for personal goals: amassing a dowry, for example, or building funds to start careers as clerks or secretaries.

Middle-Class Women Middle-class women generally did not work outside the home. For them, industrialization brought stringent confinement to the domestic sphere and pressure to conform to new models of behavior revolving around their roles as mothers and wives. In a book entitled *Woman in Her Social and Domestic Character* (1833), Mrs. John Sandford—who referred to herself by her husband's name rather than her own—described the ideal British woman. "Domestic life is the chief source of her influence," Sandford proclaimed, adding that "there is, indeed, something unfeminine in independence." (By *independence* Sandford meant taking a job or "acting the Amazon.") The model woman "knows that she is the weaker vessel" and takes pride in her ability to make the home a happy place for her husband and children.

Child Labor Industrialization profoundly influenced the childhood experience. Like their elders, children in pre-industrial societies had always worked in and around the family home. Industrial work, which took children away from home and parents for long hours with few breaks, made child labor seem especially pitiable and exploitative. Early reports from British textile mills described sensational abuses by overseers who forced children to work from dawn until dark and beat them to keep them awake. Yet many families needed their children's wages to survive, so they continued to send their offspring to the factories and mines. By the 1840s the British Parliament began to pass laws regulating child labor and ultimately restricted or removed children from the industrial workforce. In the long term, industrial society was responsible for removing children from the labor process altogether, even in the home. Whereas agricultural settings continued to demand that children make a contribution to the family income, urban industrial societies redefined the role of children. Motivated in part by moral concerns and in part by the recognition that modern society demanded a highly skilled and educated labor force, governments established the legal requirement that education, and not work for monetary gain, was the principal task of childhood. In England, for instance, education for children age five to ten became mandatory by 1881.

The Socialist Challenge

Among the most vocal and influential critics of early industrial society were the socialists, who worked to alleviate the

This 1909 photograph shows a young girl being instructed by a male supervisor on how to use a spinning machine. Women, not men, made up the bulk of the early labor force in the textile industry, principally because women were presumed easier to discipline than men and because women's smaller hands allegedly made them better suited for working with machines.

social and economic problems generated by capitalism and industrialization. Socialists deplored economic inequalities, as represented by the vast difference in wealth between a captain of industry and a factory laborer, and they condemned the system that permitted the exploitation of laborers, especially women and children. Early socialists sought to expand the Enlightenment understanding of equality: they understood equality to have an economic as well as a political, legal, and social dimension, and they looked to the future establishment of a just and equitable society. Although most socialists shared this general vision, they held very different views on the best way to establish and maintain an ideal socialist society.

Utopian Socialists The term *socialism* first appeared around 1830, when it referred to the thought of social critics such as Charles Fourier (1772–1837) and Robert Owen (1771–1858). Often called utopian socialists, Fourier, Owen, and their followers worked to establish ideal communities that would point the way to an equitable society. Fourier spent most of his life as a salesman, but he loathed the competition of the market system and called for social transformations that would better serve the needs of humankind. He painstakingly planned model communities held together by love rather than coercion in which everyone performed work in accordance with personal temperament and inclination. Owen, a successful businessman, transformed a

squalid Scottish cotton mill town called New Lanark into a model industrial community. At New Lanark, Owen raised wages, reduced the workday from seventeen to ten hours, built spacious housing, and opened a store that sold goods at fair prices. Despite the costs of those reforms, the mills of New Lanark generated profits. Out of the two thousand residents of the community, five hundred were young children from the poorhouses of Glasgow and Edinburgh, and Owen devoted special attention to their education. He kept young children out of the factories and sent them to a school that he opened in 1816. Owen's indictment of competitive capitalism, his stress on cooperative control of industry, and his advocacy of improved educational standards for children left a lasting imprint on the socialist tradition.

The ideas of the utopian socialists resonated widely in the nineteenth century, and their disciples established experimental communities from the United States to Romania. Despite the enthusiasm of the founders, most of the communities soon encountered economic difficulties and political problems that forced them to fold. By the mid-nineteenth century, most socialists looked not to utopian communities but to large-scale organization of working people as the best means to bring about a just and equitable society.

Marx and Engels Most prominent of the nineteenth-century socialists were the German theorists Karl Marx (1818–1883) and Friedrich Engels (1820–1895). They scorned the

Once held almost exclusively by men, clerical jobs increasingly went to women as industrial society matured. Men assumed positions as managers who supervised their female employees.

utopian socialists as unrealistic dabblers whose ideal communities had no hope of resolving the problems of the early industrial era. Marx and Engels believed that social problems of the nineteenth century were inevitable results of a capitalist economy. They held that capitalism divided people into two main classes, each with its own economic interests and social status: the capitalists, who owned industrial machinery and factories (which Marx and Engels called the means of production), and the proletariat, consisting of wageworkers who had only their labor to sell. Intense competition between capitalists trying to realize a profit resulted in ruthless exploitation of the working class. To make matters worse, according to Marx and Engels, the state and its coercive institutions, such as police forces and courts of law, were agencies of the capitalist ruling class. Their function was to maintain capitalists in power and enable them to continue their exploitation of the proletariat. Even music, art, literature, and religion served the purposes of capitalists, according to Marx and Engels, since they amused the working classes and diverted attention from their misery. Marx once referred to religion as "the opiate of the masses" because it encouraged workers to focus on a hypothetical realm of existence beyond this world rather than trying to improve their lot in society.

The *Communist Manifesto* Marx developed those views fully in a long, theoretical work called *Capital*. Together with Engels, Marx also wrote a short, spirited tract entitled *Manifesto of the Communist Party* (1848). In the *Manifesto* Marx and Engels aligned themselves with the communists, who worked toward the abolition of private property and the institution of a radically egalitarian society. The *Manifesto* asserted that all human history has been the history of struggle between social classes. It argued that the future lay with the working class because the laws of history dictated that capitalism would inexorably grind to a halt. Crises of overproduction, underconsumption, and diminishing profits would shake the foundations of the capitalist order. Meanwhile, members of the constantly growing and thoroughly exploited proletariat would come to view the forcible overthrow of the existing system as the only alternative available to them. Marx and Engels believed that a socialist revolution would result in a "dictatorship of the proletariat," which would abolish private property and destroy the capitalist order. After the revolution was secure, the state would wither away. Coercive institutions would also disappear, since there would no longer be an exploiting class. Thus socialism would lead to a fair, just, and egalitarian society infinitely more humane than the capitalist order.

The doctrines of Marx and Engels came to dominate European and international socialism, and socialist parties grew rapidly throughout the nineteenth century. Political parties, trade unions, newspapers, and educational associations all worked to advance the socialist cause. Yet socialists disagreed strongly on the best means to reform society. Revolutionary socialists such as Marx, Engels, and other communists urged workers to seize control of the state, confiscate the means of production, and distribute wealth equitably throughout society. Doubting that a revolution could

sources from the past

Marx and Engels on Bourgeoisie and Proletarians

Karl Marx and Friedrich Engels were the most scathing critics of early industrial society. Indeed, their critique extended to industrial capitalism in general. In their view, contemporary society pitted capitalists (whom they called the bourgeoisie in their Manifesto of the Communist Party*) against proletarians. Marx and Engels argued that in the short term capitalists would exploit the proletarians, but that over the longer term proletarians would become aware of their misery, rise up, and destroy capitalist society.*

The history of all hitherto existing society is the history of class struggles.

Freeman and slave, patrician and plebeian, lord and serf, guild-master and journeyman, in a word, oppressor and oppressed, stood in constant opposition to one another, carried on an uninterrupted, now hidden, now open fight, a fight that each time ended, either in a revolutionary reconstitution of society at large, or in the common ruin of the contending classes. . . .

The modern bourgeois society that has sprouted from the ruins of feudal society has not done away with class antagonisms. It has but established new classes, new conditions of oppression, new forms of struggle in place of the old ones.

Our epoch, the epoch of the bourgeoisie, possesses, however, this distinctive feature: it has simplified the class antagonisms. Society as a whole is more and more splitting up into two great hostile camps, into two great classes directly facing each other: Bourgeoisie and Proletariat. . . .

The bourgeoisie has stripped of its halo every occupation hitherto honoured and looked up to with reverent awe. It has converted the physician, the lawyer, the priest, the poet, the man of science, into its paid wage-labourers. . . .

The need for a constantly expanding market for its products chases the bourgeoisie over the whole surface of the globe. It must nestle everywhere, settle everywhere, establish connexions everywhere. . . .

The weapons with which the bourgeoisie felled feudalism to the ground are now turned against the bourgeoisie itself.

But not only has the bourgeoisie forged the weapons that bring death to itself; it has also called into existence the men who are to wield those weapons—the modern working class—the proletarians.

In proportion as the bourgeoisie, i.e., capital, is developed, in the same proportion is the proletariat, the modern working class, developed—a class of labourers, who live only so long as they find work, and who find work only so long as their labour increases capital. These labourers, who must sell themselves piecemeal, are a commodity, like every other article of commerce, and are consequently exposed to all the vicissitudes of competition, to all the fluctuations of the market. . . .

The advance of industry, whose involuntary promoter is the bourgeoisie, replaces the isolation of the labourers, due to competition, by their revolutionary combination, due to association. The development of Modern Industry, therefore, cuts from under its feet the very foundation on which the bourgeoisie produces and appropriates products. What the bourgeoisie, therefore, produces, above all, is its own grave-diggers. Its fall and the victory of the proletariat are equally inevitable.

For Further Reflection

■ How did Marx and Engels's historical embrace of the concept of class struggle shape their understanding of the great forces clashing during this industrial age?

Source: Karl Marx and Friedrich Engels. *Manifesto of the Communist Party.* Trans. by Samuel Moore. London: W. Reeves, 1888.

---

succeed, evolutionary socialists placed their hopes in representative governments and called for the election of legislators who supported socialist reforms.

Social Reform Although socialists did not win control of any government until the Russian revolution of 1917, their critiques—along with those of conservatives and liberals—persuaded government authorities to attack the abuses of early industrialization and provide security for the working classes. Parliament prohibited underground employment for women, like the drawer Betty Harris, as well as for boys and girls under age ten and stipulated that children under age nine not work more than nine hours a day. The 1830s and 1840s saw the inception of laws that regulated women's working hours, while leaving men without protection and constraints. The intention behind this legislation was to protect women's family roles, but it also reduced women's economic opportunities on the grounds of their special frailty. Coming under pressure from the voting public and labor unions, governments increasingly accepted that the state was responsible for the social and economic welfare of its citizens. Beginning in the late nineteenth century, European countries, led by Germany, adopted social reform programs, including retirement pensions, minimum wage laws,

Contemporary photograph of Karl Marx, German political philosopher and founder of modern socialism. His most important theoretical work, *Das Kapital* (*Capital*, in the English translation), is an extensive treatise on political economy that offers a highly critical analysis of capitalism.

sidered trade unions illegal associations whose purpose was to restrain trade. Tensions ran high when union members went on strike, especially when employers sought to keep their businesses going by hiring replacement workers. In those cases, violence frequently broke out, prompting government authorities to send in police or military forces to maintain order. Over the longer run, though, trade unions gradually improved the lives of working people and reduced the likelihood that a disgruntled proletariat would mount a revolution to overthrow industrial capitalist society. Indeed, trade unions became an integral part of industrial society because they did not seek to destroy capitalism but, rather, to make employers more responsive to their employees' needs and interests.

Global Effects of Industrialization

Early industrialization was a British, western European, and North American affair. By the late nineteenth century, Russia and Japan were beginning to industrialize (see chapter 31). Quite apart from its spread beyond western Europe, industrialization had deep global implications because industrial powers used their tools, technologies, business organization, financial influence, and transportation networks to obtain raw materials from preindustrial societies around the world. Many lands that possessed natural resources became increasingly oriented to exporting raw materials but maintained little control over them because representatives of industrial countries dominated the commercial and financial institutions associated with the trade. Some societies saw their home markets flooded with inexpensive manufactured products from industrial lands, which devastated traditional industries and damaged local economies.

The International Division of Labor Industrialization brought great economic and military strength to societies that reconfigured themselves and relied on mechanized production. Their power encouraged other societies to work toward industrialization. Before the mid-twentieth century, however, those efforts had limited results outside Europe, North America, and Japan. In India, for example, entrepreneurs established a thriving industry in the production of jute—a natural, hemplike fiber used for making carpets, upholstery, and burlap bags—as well as a small domestic steel

sickness, accident, and unemployment insurance, and the regulation of hours and conditions of work. These reforms of liberal capitalist society were a prelude to the modern welfare state.

Trade Unions Trade unions also sought to advance the quest for a just and equitable society. As governments regulated businesses and enhanced social security, trade unions struggled to eliminate abuses of early industrial society and improve workers' lives by seeking higher wages and better working conditions for their members. Through most of the nineteenth century, both employers and governments con-

thinking about ENCOUNTERS

Class Struggle

The reconfiguration of an industrial economy resulted in the formation of antagonistic social and economic classes. What confrontations took place between industrial-capitalists and the working class? What institutions and ideologies arose to represent these opposing interests?

Robert Koehler's painting *The Strike* depicts a situation verging toward violence as workers mill about in a confrontation with factory owners and one angry laborer crouches to pick up a stone.

industry. But fledgling Indian industries lacked government support, and private investment capital was insufficient to bankroll industrialization on a large scale.

Nevertheless, industrialization had deep global ramifications. The industrialization process influenced the economic and social development of many societies because it promoted a new international division of labor. Industrial societies needed minerals, agricultural products, and other raw materials from sometimes distant regions of the world. Representatives of industrial societies searched the globe for raw materials to supply their factories.

Demand for Raw Materials

Large-scale global trade in agricultural products was nothing new. From the sixteenth through the eighteenth century, European countries had imported sugar, spices, tobacco, tea, coffee, cotton, and other products grown mostly on plantations. In the nineteenth century, demand for these products increased sharply because of population growth. But industrial society fueled the demand for additional products as British, European, and U.S. industrialists sought the natural resources and agricultural products of Africa, the Americas, Asia, Australia, and eastern Europe. The mechanization of the textile industry, for example, produced a demand for large quantities of raw cotton, which came mostly from India, Egypt, and the southern rim of the United States. Similarly, new industrial technologies increased demand for products such as rubber, the principal ingredient of belts and tires that were essential to industrial machinery, which came from Brazil, Malaya, and the Congo River basin.

Economic Development

In some lands, specialization in the production and export of primary goods paved the way for economic development and eventual industrialization. This pattern was especially noticeable in lands settled by European colonists, including Canada, Argentina, Uruguay, South Africa, Australia, and New Zealand, each of which experienced economic growth through the export of primary products and the infusion of foreign capital and labor. The same societies had an additional advantage in that they were high-wage economies. High incomes fostered economic development in two ways: they created flourishing markets, and

An Eastern Steamboat, a watercolor by Pavel Petrovich Svinin, depicted Robert Fulton's steamboat the *Paragon*. Steamboats transported passengers and cargo and helped spread industrialization around the world.

they encouraged entrepreneurs to counteract high wages and labor scarcity by inventing labor-saving technologies.

Economic Interdependence Other lands were less fortunate. The peoples of Latin America, sub-Saharan Africa, south Asia, and southeast Asia also exported primary products but attracted little foreign investment and developed little mechanical industry. Export-oriented agriculture dominated these lands, where the major cash crops were sugar, cotton, and rubber. Foreign owners controlled the plantations that produced these crops, and most of the profits went abroad, depriving domestic economies of funds that might otherwise have contributed to the building of markets and industries. The low wages of plantation workers made the situation worse by dampening demand for manufactured goods. The result was a concentration of wealth in the hands of small groups that contributed little to economic development through consumption or investment. To compound the problem, the dominant financial interests adopted free-trade policies allowing unrestricted entry of foreign manufactures, which supported continuing industrialization in foreign lands but sharply limited opportunities for indigenous industrialization.

The new geographic division of labor, in which some of the world's peoples provided raw materials while others processed and consumed them, increased the volume of world trade and led to increased transportation on both sea and land. Bigger ships, larger docks, and deeper canals facilitated trade and transport. The benefits of this new system flowed primarily to Europe, North America, and Japan. Other lands realized few benefits from the process of industrialization, but the process nevertheless increasingly linked the fortunes of all the world's peoples.

in**perspective**

The process of industrialization involved the harnessing of inanimate sources of energy, the replacement of handicraft production with machine-based manufacturing, and the generation of new forms of business and labor organization. Along with industrialization came demographic growth, large-scale migration, and rapid urbanization, which increased the demand for manufactured goods by the masses of working people. Societies that underwent industrialization enjoyed sharp increases in economic productivity: they produced large quantities of high-quality goods at low prices, and their increased productivity translated into higher material standards of living. Yet industrialization brought costs, in the form of unsettling social problems, as well as benefits. Family life changed dramatically in the industrial age as men, women, and children increasingly left their homes to work in factories and mines, often under appalling conditions. Socialist critics sought to bring about a more just and equitable society, and government authorities curtailed the worst abuses of the early industrial era. Governments and labor unions both worked to raise living standards and provide security for working people. Meanwhile, industrialization increasingly touched the lives of peoples around the world. Western European, North American, and Japanese societies followed Britain's lead into industrialization, while many African, Asian, and Latin American lands became dependent on the export of raw materials to industrial societies. ●

CHRONOLOGY	
1730–1795	Life of Josiah Wedgwood
1733	John Kay develops the flying shuttle
1765	James Watt patents an improved steam engine
1765–1825	Life of Eli Whitney
1779	Samuel Crompton develops the spinning mule
1785	Edmund Cartwright develops the power loom
1797	Eli Whitney introduces interchangeable parts to the manufacturing process
1829	George Stephenson's locomotive, the Rocket, attains a speed of 45 kilometers (28 miles) per hour
1832	Reform Bill expands electorate to House of Commons
1833	Factory Act restricts employment of women and children in textile factories
1842	Mines Act restricts employment of women and children in mines
1848	Karl Marx and Friedrich Engels publish *Manifesto of the Communist Party*
1851	Crystal Palace exhibition in London
1856	Bessemer converter developed
1913	Henry Ford introduces the assembly line to the manufacture of automobiles

For Further Reading

Sean Patrick Adams. *Old Dominion, Industrial Commonwealth: Coal, Politics, and Economy in Antebellum America.* Baltimore, 2004. Shrewd and innovative analysis of the development of the coal industry in Virginia and Pennsylvania.

T. S. Ashton. *The Industrial Revolution, 1760–1830.* New York, 1968. A brief and readable survey of early industrialization in the British isles.

Jeffrey Auerbach. *The Great Exhibition of 1851: A Nation on Display.* New Haven, 1999. Analyzes the significance of the first world's fair and industrial exhibit held at London's Crystal Palace.

François Crouzet. *A History of the European Economy, 1000–2000.* Charlottesville, Va., 2000. A clear overview of European economic development that emphasizes European integration rather than the experiences of individual countries.

Daniel R. Headrick. *The Tentacles of Progress: Technology Transfer in the Age of Imperialism, 1850–1940.* New York, 1988. Concentrates on the political and cultural obstacles that hindered transfer of European technologies to colonial lands.

A. G. Kenwood and A. L. Lougheed. *Technological Diffusion and Industrialisation before 1914.* London, 1982. A balanced interpretation drawing on different theoretical perspectives raised by industrialization worldwide.

David S. Landes. *The Unbound Prometheus: Technological Change and Industrial Development in Western Europe from 1750 to the Present.* Cambridge, 1969. A comprehensive study of industrialization concentrating on the role of technological innovation.

————. *The Wealth and Poverty of Nations: Why Some Are So Rich and Some So Poor.* New York, 1998. A wide-ranging analysis arguing that social and cultural attitudes serve as the foundation of economic development.

Penelope Lane, Neil Raven, and K. D. M. Snell, eds. *Women, Work and Wages in England, 1600–1850.* Rochester, N.Y., 2004. Study of women's contributions to British industrialization and how it was rewarded.

Karl Marx and Friedrich Engels. *The Communist Manifesto.* Trans. by Samuel Moore. Harmondsworth, 1967. English translation of the most important tract of nineteenth-century socialism, with an excellent introduction by historian A. J. P. Taylor.

David R. Meyer. *The Roots of American Industrialization.* Baltimore, 2003. Interdisciplinary study that ties America's industrialization to increasing agricultural productivity of the antebellum period.

Joel Mokyr. *The Lever of Riches: Technological Creativity and Economic Progress.* New York, 1990. Examines European technological development in a comparative context.

Lawrence A. Peskin. *Manufacturing Revolution: The Intellectual Origins of Early American Industry.* Baltimore, 2003. The intellectual foundations of industrialization and economic growth take center stage.

Kenneth Pomeranz. *The Great Divergence: China, Europe, and the Making of the Modern World Economy.* Princeton, 2000. Argues that the fortuitous location of coal deposits and access to the resources of the Americas created a uniquely advantageous framework for English industrialization.

Mikulas Teich and Roy Porter, eds. *The Industrial Revolution in National Context: Europe and the USA.* Cambridge, 1996. A collection of essays by leading scholars who reappraise industrialization and explore the new approaches that have emerged.

E. P. Thompson. *The Making of the English Working Class.* New York, 1966. A classic work that analyzes the formation of working-class consciousness in England from the 1790s to the 1830s.

Louise A. Tilly. *Industrialization and Gender Inequality.* Washington, D.C., 1993. A brief historiographical survey of debates on gender and industrialization in England, France, Germany, the United States, Japan, and China.

The Americas in the Age of Independence

chapter30

Chinese migrants toil at various tasks, from sifting soil and panning to carrying water, in their search for wealth in the California gold mines.

EYEWITNESS:

Fatt Hing Chin Searches for Gold from China to California

A village fish peddler, Fatt Hing Chin often roamed the coast of southern China in search of fish to sell at market. One day at the wharves, he heard a tale of mysterious but enticing mountains of gold beckoning young Chinese to cross the ocean. At nineteen years of age, Chin felt restless, and he longed for the glittering mountains. He learned that he could purchase passage on a foreign ship, but he also needed to be cautious. He did not want to alarm his parents, nor did he want to draw the attention of the authorities, who were reportedly arresting individuals seeking to leave China. Eventually, he reconciled his parents to his plans, and in 1849 he boarded a Spanish ship to sail to California and join the gold rush.

Chin felt some uncertainty once at sea. Surprised at the large number of young Chinese men crammed in with him in the ship's hold, he shared their dismay as they remained confined for weeks to the vomit-laden cargo areas of the ship. Ninety-five days and nights passed before the hills of San Francisco came into view. Upon arrival the travelers met Chinese veterans of life in the United States who explained the need to stick together if they were to survive and prosper.

Chin hired out as a gold miner and headed for the mountains of gold. After digging and sifting for two years, he had accumulated his own little pile of gold. He wrote to his brothers and cousins, urging them to join him, and thus helped fuel the large-scale overseas migration of workers. Having made his fortune, though, Chin decided to return to China. Wealthy, he traveled more comfortably this time around, with a bunk and other amenities—and temptations. He participated in the gambling that took place at sea and lost half his gold by the time the ship docked in Guangzhou. What remained still amounted to a small fortune. California gold provided him with the means to take a wife, build a house, and buy some land.

Although settled and prosperous, Chin remained restless and longed for the excitement of California. Leaving his pregnant wife, he sailed for California again after only a year in China. He returned to mining with his brother, but the gold was more difficult to find. Inspired by the luck of another migrant, Tong Ling, who managed to get one dollar for

677

each meal he sold, Chin's cousins in San Francisco decided to open a restaurant. As one of them said, "If the foreign devils will eat his food, they will eat ours." Chin found the city much more comfortable than the mountains. "Let the others go after the gold in the hills," he said. "I'll wait for the gold to come to the city."

Fatt Hing Chin was one of the earliest Chinese migrants to settle in the Americas. His career path—from a miner in search of quick riches to an urban resident committed to a new homeland and hoping to profit from the service industry—was quite typical of Chinese migrants to the United States. Some went from mining to railroad construction or agricultural labor, but all contributed to the transformation of the Americas. Along with millions of others from Europe and Asia, Chinese migrants increased the ethnic diversity of American populations and stimulated political, social, and economic development in the western hemisphere.

During the late eighteenth and early nineteenth centuries, almost all the lands of the western hemisphere won their independence from European colonial powers. American peoples then struggled throughout the nineteenth century to build states and societies that realized their potential in an age of independence. The United States built the most powerful state in the western hemisphere and embarked on a westward push that brought most of the temperate regions of North America under U.S. control. Canada built a federal state under British Canadian leadership. The varied lands of Latin America built smaller states that often fell under the sway of local military leaders. One issue that most American peoples wrestled with, regardless of their region, was the legacy of the Enlightenment. The effort to build societies based on freedom, equality, and constitutional government was a monumental challenge only partially realized in lands characterized by enormous social, economic, and cultural diversity. Both the institution of slavery and its ultimate abolition complicated the process of building societies in the Americas, particularly in regard to defining and diversifying a new type of workforce for free and increasingly industrial economies. Asian and European migrants joined freed slaves and native-born workers in labor systems—from plantations and factories to debt peonage—that often betrayed American promises of welcome and freedom.

The age of independence for the United States, Canada, and Latin America was a contentious era characterized by continuous mass migration and explosive economic growth, occasionally followed by deep economic stagnation, and punctuated with civil war, ethnic violence, class conflict, and battles for racial and sexual equality. Independence did not solve all the political and social problems of the western hemisphere but, rather, created a new context in which American peoples struggled to build effective states, enjoy economic prosperity, and attain cultural cohesion. Those goals were elusive throughout the nineteenth century and in many ways remain so even in the present day. Nevertheless, the histories of these first lands to win independence from colonial powers inspired other peoples who later sought freedom from imperial rule, but they also served as portents of the difficulties faced by newly free states.

THE BUILDING OF AMERICAN STATES

After winning independence from Britain, the United States fashioned a government and began to expand rapidly to the west. By mid-century the new republic had absorbed almost all the temperate lands of North America. Yet the United States was an unstable society composed of varied regions with diverse economic and social structures. Differences over slavery and the rights of individual states as opposed to the federal government sparked a devastating civil war in the 1860s. That conflict resulted in the abolition of slavery and the strengthening of the federal state. The experience of Canada was very different from that of the United States. Canada gained independence from Britain without fighting a war, and even though Canada also was a land of great diversity, it avoided falling into a civil war. Although intermittently nervous about the possibility that the United States might begin to expand to the north, Canada established a relatively weak federal government, which presided over provinces that had considerable power over local affairs. Latin American lands were even more diverse than their counterparts to the north, and there was never any real possibility that they could join together in a confederation. Throughout the nineteenth century Latin America was a politically fragmented region, and many individual states faced serious problems and divisions within their own societies.

The United States: Westward Expansion and Civil War

After gaining independence the United States faced the need to construct a framework of government. During the 1780s leaders from the rebellious colonies drafted a constitution that entrusted responsibility for general issues to a federal government, reserved authority for local issues for individual states, and provided for the admission of new states and territories to the confederation. Although the Declaration of Independence had declared that "all men are created equal," most individual states limited the vote to men of property. But the Enlightenment ideal of equality encouraged political leaders to extend the franchise: by the late 1820s most property qualifications had disappeared, and by mid-century almost all adult white men were eligible to participate in the political affairs of the republic.

Westward Expansion and Manifest Destiny

While working to settle constitutional issues, residents of the United States also began to expand rapidly to the west. After the American revolution, Britain ceded to the new republic all lands between the Appalachian Mountains and the Mississippi River, and the United States doubled in size. In 1803 Napoleon Bonaparte needed funds immediately to protect revolutionary France from its enemies, and he allowed the United States to purchase France's Louisiana Territory, which extended from the Mississippi River to the Rocky Mountains. Overnight the United States doubled in size again. Between 1804 and 1806 a geographic expedition led by Meriwether Lewis and William Clark mapped the territory and surveyed its resources. Settlers soon began to flock west in search of cheap land to cultivate. By the 1840s westward expansion was well under way, and many U.S. citizens spoke of a "manifest destiny." According to this idea, the United States was destined, even divinely ordained, to expand across the North American continent from the Atlantic seaboard to the Pacific and beyond. Manifest destiny was often invoked to justify U.S. annexations.

Conflict with Indigenous Peoples

Westward expansion brought settlers and government forces into conflict with the indigenous peoples of North America, who resisted efforts to push them from their ancestral lands and hunting grounds. Native peoples forged alliances among themselves and also sought the backing of British colonial officials in Canada, but U.S. officials and military forces supported Euro-American settlers and gradually forced the continent open to white expansion. With the Indian Removal Act of 1830, the United States government determined to move all native Americans west of the Mississippi River into "Indian Territory" (Oklahoma). Among the tribes affected by this forced removal from the east were the Seminoles, some of whom managed to avoid capture and the long march to Oklahoma by resisting and retreating to Florida's swampy lowlands. The Cherokees also suffered a harrowing 800-mile migration from the eastern woodlands to Oklahoma

thinking about TRADITIONS

Vanishing Ways of Life

For millennia indigenous peoples throughout the Americas had established their own cultural and economic patterns of life. What happened to those traditions once the consolidating nation-states in North America and Latin America committed to an expansion of their territories? How did indigenous peoples resist such conquest?

Sitting Bull (ca. 1831–1890) was a Hunkpapa Lakota Sioux holy man, who also led his people as a war chief during years of resistance to United States government policies. The Battle of the Little Bighorn, also known by the indigenous Americans as the Battle of Greasy Grass Creek, was the most famous action of the Great Sioux War of 1876–1877. It was an overwhelming victory for the Lakota and Northern Cheyenne, overseen by Sitting Bull.

| United States 1783 | Ceded by Great Britain 1818 | Annexation of Texas 1845 | Ceded by Mexico 1848 |
| Louisiana Purchase 1803 | Treaty with Spain 1819 | Agreement with Great Britain 1846 | Gadsden Purchase 1853 |

MAP 30.1

Westward expansion of the United States during the nineteenth century.

Note the large land claims ceded by Britain, France, and Mexico.

Why were there no portions of North America purchased from or ceded by native Americans?

on the Trail of Tears (1838–1839), so known because thousands died from disease, starvation, and the difficulties of relocation.

After 1840 the site of conflict between Euro-American and indigenous peoples shifted to the plains region west of the Mississippi River. Settlers and ranchers in the trans-Mississippi west encountered peoples such as the Sioux, Comanche, Pawnee, and Apache, who possessed firearms and outstanding equestrian skills. The native peoples of the plains offered effective resistance to encroachment by white settlers and at times celebrated powerful victories over U.S. forces. In 1876, for example, thousands of Lakota Sioux and their allies annihilated an army under the command of Colonel George Armstrong Custer in the battle of Little Big Horn (in southern Montana). Despite occasional successes in battle, native Americans on the plains ultimately lost the war against the forces of U.S. expansionism. The techno-

logically sophisticated weaponry employed against native peoples included cannons and deadly, rapid-fire Gatling guns. Those weapons aided U.S. forces in breaking native resistance and opened the western plains to U.S. conquest.

One last forbidding and symbolic conflict took place in 1890 at Wounded Knee Creek in South Dakota. Frightened and threatened by the Sioux adoption of the Ghost Dance, an expression of religious beliefs that included a vision of an afterlife in which all white peoples disappeared, whites wanted these religious ceremonies suppressed. U.S. cavalry forces chased the Sioux who were fleeing to safety in the South Dakota Badlands. At Wounded Knee Creek, a Sioux man accidentally shot off a gun, and the cavalry overreacted badly, slaughtering more than two hundred men, women, and children with machine guns. Emblematic of harsh U.S. treatment of native peoples, Wounded Knee represented the place where "a people's dream died," as a later native leader put it.

The Mexican-American War Westward expansion also generated tension between the United States and Mexico, whose territories included Texas, California, and New Mexico (the territory that is now the American southwest). Texas declared independence from Mexico in 1836, largely because the many U.S. migrants who had settled there

This photograph of an 1890s Plains Indian camp in South Dakota offers an idealized, pastoral, and peaceful image of the disappearing indigenous societies in the United States.

wanted to run their own affairs. In 1845 the United States accepted Texas as a new state—against vigorous Mexican protest—and moved to consolidate its hold on the territory. Those moves led to conflicts that rapidly escalated into the Mexican-American War (1846–1848), or, as it is known in Mexico, *la intervención norteamericano* (the North American Intervention) or *la guerra del 47* (the War of 1847). U.S. forces instigated the war and then inflicted a punishing defeat on the Mexican army. By the Treaty of Guadalupe Hidalgo (1848), the United States took possession of approximately one-half of Mexico's territory, paying a mere fifteen million dollars in exchange for Texas north of the Rio Grande, California, and New Mexico. Thousands of U.S. and Mexican soldiers died in the conflict, and thousands of

Mexican families found themselves stranded in the territories annexed by the United States. Some returned to Mexico, but most stayed put and attained U.S. citizenship. This conflict nonetheless fueled Mexican nationalism, as well as disdain for the United States.

While satisfying desires for the United States to realize its manifest destiny, westward expansion also created problems within the republic by aggravating tensions between regions. The most serious and divisive issue had to do with slavery, which had vexed American politics since independence. The Enlightenment ideal of equality clearly suggested that the appropriate policy was to abolish slavery, but the leaders of the American revolution and framers of the Constitution recognized the sanctity of private property, including slaves. U.S. independence initially promoted a surge of antislavery sentiment, as states from Delaware north abolished slavery within their jurisdictions. Abolition did not bring full equality for free blacks in northern states, but it hardened divisions between slave and free states. Westward expansion aggravated tensions further by raising the question of whether settlers could extend slavery to newly acquired territories.

Sectional Conflict Opponents of slavery had dreamed that the institution would die a natural death with the decline of tobacco cultivation. Their hopes faded, however, with the invigoration of the slave system by the rise of cotton as a cash crop in the early nineteenth century, followed by westward expansion. The U.S. slave population rose sharply, from five hundred thousand in 1770 to almost two million in 1820. As the numbers of slaves grew, antislavery forces fought to limit the spread of slavery to new territories. Beginning with the Missouri Compromise of 1820, a series of political compacts attempted to maintain a balance between slave and free states as the republic admitted new states carved out of western territories. Those compromises ultimately proved too brittle to endure, as proslavery and antislavery forces became more strident. Abraham Lincoln (1809–1865) predicted in 1858 that "a house divided against itself cannot stand," and he made the connection to slavery explicit: "I believe this government cannot endure permanently half *slave* and half *free*. . . . It will become *all* one thing, or *all* the other."

The election of Abraham Lincoln to the presidency in 1860 was the spark that ignited war between the states (1861–1865). Lincoln was an explicitly sectional candidate, was convinced that slavery was immoral, and was committed to free soil—territories without slavery. Although slavery stood at the center of the conflict, President Lincoln had insisted from the beginning of the war that his primary aim was the restoration of the Union, not the abolition of slavery. He was therefore reluctant to adopt an abolitionist policy. There were reasons for his hesitancy. Not only had Lincoln been elected on a platform of noninterference with slavery within the states, but he also doubted the constitutionality of any federal action. He was also concerned about the difficulties

of assimilating four million freed slaves into the nation's social and political fabric. Most important, Lincoln feared that an abolitionist program would have the effect of inducing border states to join the Confederacy and upsetting the loyalty of Delaware, Maryland, Kentucky, and Missouri—the four slave states that remained in the Union. The Civil War also revolved around issues central to the United States as a society: the nature of the Union, states' rights as opposed to the federal government's authority, and the imperatives of a budding industrial-capitalist system against those of an export-oriented plantation economy.

The U.S. Civil War Eleven southern states withdrew from the Union in 1860 and 1861, affirming their right to dissolve the Union and their support for states' rights. Slavery and the cultivation of cotton as a cash crop had isolated the southern states from economic developments in the rest of the United States. By the mid-nineteenth century, the southern states were the world's major source of cotton, and the bulk of the crop went to the British isles. Manufactured goods consumed in the southern states came mostly from Britain, and almost all food came from the region's farms. Southerners considered themselves self-sufficient and believed that they did not need the rest of the United States. Northerners saw the situation differently. They viewed secession as illegal insurrection and an act of betrayal. They fought not only against slavery but also against the concept of a state subject to blackmail by its constituent parts. They also fought for a way of life—their emerging industrial society—and an expansive western agricultural system based on free labor.

The first two years of the war ended in stalemate. The war changed character, however, when Abraham Lincoln signed the Emancipation Proclamation, making the abolition of slavery an explicit goal of the war. As the war progressed, Lincoln increasingly viewed the destruction of slavery as the only way to preserve the Union. Five days after the Union victory at Antietam, President Lincoln issued a preliminary Emancipation

LINCOLN'S ADDRESS AT GETTYSBURG.

This early-twentieth-century postcard offered an idealized depiction of Abraham Lincoln delivering his Gettysburg Address, which commemorated the Union soldiers who fell in that crucial battle.

The grotesquely twisted bodies of dead northern soldiers lay near a fence outside Antietam, Maryland, in 1862. The Civil War was the most costly in U.S. history in terms of lives lost.

Proclamation. The final version, issued 1 January 1863, freed the slaves in those states that had rebelled. Ironically, in the states that remained loyal to the Union, slavery was protected by the U.S. Constitution. A looming problem was that the slaves freed by emancipation would have risked re-enslavement after the war unless their liberty was quickly reaffirmed. The solution to this problem, one that Lincoln urged, was the Thirteenth Amendment to the Constitution, ratified in 1865, which completely abolished slavery throughout the United States.

Ultimately, the northern states prevailed in the Civil War, after the bloody battle at Gettysburg in July 1863 had turned the military tide against southern forces. The northern states brought considerable resources to the war effort—some 90 percent of the country's industrial capacity and approximately two-thirds of its railroad lines—but still they fought four bitter years against a formidable enemy. The victory of the northern states ended slavery in the United States. Moreover, it ensured that the United States would remain politically united, and it enhanced the authority of the federal government in the republic. Thus, as European lands were building powerful states on the foundations of revolutionary ideals, liberalism, and nationalism, the United States also forged a strong central government to supervise westward expansion and deal with the political and social issues that divided the nation. That strength came at a horrible cost for both sides, however, especially in terms of the enormous human casualties. About 1,556,000 soldiers served in the Union armies and suffered a total of over 634,000 casualties, 360,000 of whom died. Approximately 800,000 men served in the Confederate forces, which sustained approximately 483,000 casualties, including 258,000 dead.

The Canadian Dominion: Independence without War

Autonomy and Division Canada did not fight a war for independence, and in spite of deep regional divisions, it did not experience bloody internal conflict. Instead, Canadian independence came gradually as Canadians and the British government agreed on general principles of autonomy. The distinctiveness of the two dominant ethnic groups, the British Canadians and the French Canadians, ensured that the process of building an independent society would not be smooth, but intermittent fears of U.S. expansion and concerns about the possibility of an invasion from the south helped submerge ethnic differences. By the late nineteenth century, Canada was a land in control of its own destiny, despite continuing ties to Britain and the looming presence of the United States to the south.

Originally colonized by trappers and settlers from both Britain and France, the colony of New France passed into the British empire after the British victory in the Seven Years' War (1756–1763). Until the late eighteenth century, however, French Canadians outnumbered British Canadians, so imperial officials made large concessions to their subjects of French descent to forestall unnecessary strife. Officials recognized the Roman Catholic church and permitted continued observance of French civil law in Quebec and other areas of French Canadian settlement, which they governed through appointed councils staffed by local elites. British Canadians, in contrast, were Protestants who lived mostly in Ontario, followed British law, and governed themselves through elected representatives. After 1781 large numbers of British loyalists fled the newly formed United States to

MAP 30.2

The Dominion of Canada in the nineteenth century.
Note the provinces that make up the modern state of Canada and the dates in which they were incorporated into the Dominion.

At what date were eastern and western Canada geographically united?

the south and sought refuge in Canada, thus greatly enlarging the size of the English-speaking community there.

The War of 1812
Ethnic divisions and political differences could easily have splintered Canada, but the War of 1812 stimulated a sense of unity against an external threat. The United States declared war on Britain in retaliation for encroachments on U.S. rights during the Napoleonic wars, and the British colony of Canada formed one of the front

lines of the conflict. U.S. military leaders assumed that they could easily invade and conquer Canada to pressure their foes. Despite the greater resources of the United States, however, Canadian forces repelled U.S. incursions. Their victories promoted a sense of Canadian pride, and anti-U.S. sentiments became a means for covering over differences among French Canadians and British Canadians.

After the War of 1812, Canada experienced an era of rapid growth. Expanded business opportunities drew English-speaking migrants, who swelled the population. That influx threatened the identity of Quebec, and discontent in Canada reached a critical point in the 1830s. The British imperial governors of Canada did not want a repeat of the American revolution, so between 1840 and 1867 they defused tensions by expanding home rule in Canada and

permitting the provinces to govern their own internal affairs. Inspiring this imperial move toward Canadian autonomy was the Durham Report, issued in 1839 by John George Lambton (1782–1840), the first earl of Durham and the recent governor-general and lord high commissioner of Canada. He advocated a good deal of self-government for a united Canada, and his report became a model for British imperial policy and colonial self-rule in other states, including Australia and New Zealand.

Dominion Westward expansion of the United States and the U.S. Civil War pushed Canada toward political autonomy. Fear of U.S. expansion helped stifle internal conflicts among Canadians and prompted Britain to grant independence to Canada. The British North America Act of 1867 joined Quebec, Ontario, Nova Scotia, and New Brunswick and recognized them as the Dominion of Canada. Other provinces joined the Dominion later. Each province had its own seat of government, provincial legislature, and lieutenant governor representing the British crown. The act created a federal government headed by a governor-general who acted as the British representative. An elected House of Commons and appointed Senate rounded out the framework of governance. Provincial legislatures reserved certain political matters for themselves, whereas others fell within the purview of the federal government. Without waging war, the Dominion of Canada had won control over all Canadian internal affairs, and Britain retained jurisdiction over foreign affairs until 1931.

John A. Macdonald (1815–1891) became the first prime minister of Canada, and he moved to incorporate all of British North America into the Dominion. He negotiated the purchase of the huge Northwest Territories from the Hudson's Bay Company in 1869, and he persuaded Manitoba, British Columbia, and Prince Edward Island to join the Dominion. Macdonald believed, however, that Canada's Dominion would remain symbolic—a mere "geographic expression," as he put it—until the government took concrete action to make Canadian unity and independence a reality. To strengthen the union, he oversaw construction of a transcontinental railroad, completed in 1885. The railroad facilitated transportation and communications throughout Canada and eventually helped bring new provinces into the Dominion: Alberta and Saskatchewan in 1905 and Newfoundland in 1949. Internal conflicts never disappeared, but the Dominion provided a foundation for Canadian independence and unity. Although maintaining ties to Britain and struggling to forge an identity distinct from that of its powerful neighbor to the south, Canada developed as a culturally diverse yet politically unified society.

Latin America: Fragmentation and Political Experimentation

Political unity was short-lived in Latin America. Simón Bolívar (1783–1830), hailed as South America's liberator, worked for the establishment of a large confederation that would provide Latin America with the political, military, and economic strength to resist encroachment by foreign powers. The wars of independence that he led encouraged a sense of solidarity in Latin America. But Bolívar once admitted that "I fear peace more than war," and after the defeat of the common colonial enemy, solidarity was impossible to sustain. Bolívar's Gran Colombia broke into its three constituent parts—Venezuela, Colombia, and Ecuador—and the rest of Latin America fragmented into numerous independent states.

Creole Elites and Political Instability Following the example of the United States, creole elites usually established republics with written constitutions for the newly independent states of Latin America. Yet constitutions were much more difficult to frame in Latin America than in the United States. Before gaining independence, Latin American leaders had less experience with self-government because Spanish and Portuguese colonial regimes were far more autocratic than was the British imperial government in North America. Creole elites responded enthusiastically to Enlightenment values and republican ideals, but they had little experience putting their principles into practice. As a result, several Latin American lands lurched from one constitution to another as leaders struggled to create a machinery of government that would lead to political and social stability.

Creole elites also dominated the newly independent states and effectively prevented mass participation in public affairs. Less than 5 percent of the male population was active in Latin American politics in the nineteenth century, and millions of indigenous peoples lived entirely outside the political system. Without institutionalized means of expressing discontent or opposition, those disillusioned with the system had little choice beyond rebellion. Aggravating political instability were differences among elites. Whether they were urban merchants or rural landowners, Latin American elites divided into different camps as liberals or conservatives, centralists or federalists, secularists or Roman Catholics.

Conflicts with Indigenous Peoples One thing elites agreed on was the policy of claiming American land for agriculture and ranching. That meant pushing aside indigenous peoples and establishing Euro-American hegemony in Latin America. Conflict was most intense in Argentina and Chile, where cultivators and ranchers longed to take over the South American plains. During the mid-nineteenth century, as the United States was crushing native resistance to western expansion in North America, Argentine and Chilean forces brought modern weapons to bear in their campaign to conquer the indigenous peoples of South America. By the 1870s, they had pacified the most productive lands and forced indigenous peoples either to assimilate to Euro-American society or to retreat to marginal lands that were unattractive to cultivators and ranchers.

Caudillos Although creole elites agreed on the policy of conquering native peoples, division and discord in the

UNITED STATES

UTAH

CALIFORNIA

Colorado

NEW
MEXICO

San Diego

TEXAS

Rio Grande

BAJA
CALIFORNIA

Gulf of
Mexico

MEXICO
1821

Mexico City

ATLANTIC
OCEAN

Caribbean Sea

BR. HONDURAS
HONDURAS 1838
MOSQUITO COAST
(Br.; Nicaragua, 1860)

GUATEMALA 1838
EL SALVADOR 1838
NICARAGUA 1838
COSTA RICA 1838

PANAMA
(1903)

Caracas

NEW
GRANADA
1831

VENEZUELA
1830

BRITISH GUIANA
DUTCH GUIANA
FRENCH GUIANA

Orinoco

GALAPAGOS IS.
(Ecuador)

Bogotá

COLOMBIA
1886

Quito

ECUADOR
1803

Amazon

PACIFIC

OCEAN

ANDES MOUNTAINS

Lima

PERU
1821

BRAZIL
kingdom, 1815,
empire, 1822,
republic, 1889

São Francisco

La Paz

BOLIVIA
1825

BRAZILIAN HIGHLANDS

Rio de Janeiro

São Paulo

United Provinces of Central America,
1823–38

Republic of Colombia, 1819–30

Mexico, 1867

CHILE
1818

Paraná

PARAGUAY
1811

Uruguay

ARGENTINA
1810

URUGUAY
1828

0   500   1000   1500 mi

0   1000   2000   3000 km

Santiago

Buenos Aires

Rio de la Plata

Colorado

PATAGONIA

FALKLAND IS.
Sp., 1770–1820,
Arg., 1820–33,
Br., 1833

SOUTH GEORGIA
ISLAND (Br.)

Tierra
del Fuego

Cape Horn

SOUTH ORKNEY
ISLAND (Br.)

MAP 30.3

**Latin America in the nineteenth century. Date is year of
independence.**

Note the many states that emerged from the independence movements early in the century.

*Why was it difficult for large, federated republics, such as the Republic
of Colombia, founded by Simón Bolívar, to survive?*

newly independent states helped caudillos, or regional military leaders, come to power in much of Latin America. The wars of independence had lasted well over a decade, and they provided Latin America with military rather than civilian heroes. After independence, military leaders took to the political stage, appealing to populist sentiments and exploiting the discontent of the masses. One of the most notable caudillos was Juan Manuel de Rosas, who from 1829 to 1852 ruled an Argentina badly divided between the cattle-herding and gaucho society of the pampas (the interior grasslands) and the urban elite of Buenos Aires. Rosas himself emerged from the world of cattle ranching, and he used his skills to subdue other caudillos and establish control in Buenos Aires. Rosas called for regional autonomy in an attempt to reconcile competing interests, but he worked to centralize the government he usurped. He quelled rebellions, but he did so in bloody fashion. Critics often likened Rosas to historically infamous figures, calling him "the Machiavelli of the pampas" and "the Argentine Nero," and they accused him of launching a reign of terror to stifle opposition. One writer exiled by the caudillo compiled a chart that counted the number of Rosas's victims and the violent ways they met their ends; of the 22,404 total victims killed, most met their end in armed clashes but others died by poisoning, hanging, and assassination.

Rosas did what caudillos did best: he restored order. In doing so, however, he made terror a tool of the government, and he ruled as a despot through his own personal army.

Rosas also, however, embodied the winning personality traits most exemplified by caudillos. He attained great popularity through his identification with the people and with gauchos, and he demonstrated his physical strength and machismo. Although caudillo rule often limited freedom and undermined republican ideals, it sometimes also gave rise to an opposition that aimed to overthrow the caudillos and work for liberal reforms that would promote democratic forms of government.

Mexico: War and Reform Independent Mexico experienced a succession of governments, from monarchy to republic to caudillo rule, but it also generated a liberal reform movement. The Mexican-American War caused political turmoil in Mexico and helped the caudillo General Antonio López de Santa Anna (1797–1876) perpetuate his intermittent rule. After the defeat and disillusion of the war, however, a liberal reform movement attempted to reshape Mexican society. Led by President Benito Juárez (1806–1872), a Mexican of indigenous ancestry, La Reforma of the 1850s aimed to limit the power of the military and the Roman Catholic church in Mexican society. Juárez and his followers called for liberal reform, designed in part to create a rural middle class. The Constitution of 1857 set forth the ideals of La Reforma. It curtailed the prerogatives of priests and military elites, and it guaranteed universal male suffrage and other civil liberties, such as freedom of speech. Land reform efforts centered on dismantling corporate properties, which

Edouard Manet's painting depicts the execution by firing squad of Emperor Maximilian, whose death in 1867 ended attempted French rule in Mexico.

had the effect of parceling out communal Indian lands and villages as private property, much of which ended up in the hands of large landowners, not indigenous peoples.

Mexico: Revolution

La Reforma challenged some of the fundamental conservatism of Mexican elites, who led spirited opposition to political, social, and economic reform. Liberals and conservatives in Mexico stayed bitterly divided, and conservatives forced the Juárez government out of Mexico City until 1861, when Juárez struggled to establish order in his country. To lessen Mexico's financial woes, Juárez chose to suspend loan payments to foreign powers, and that led to French, British, and Spanish intervention as Europeans sought to recover and protect their investments in Mexico. France's Napoleon III proved especially persistent and intrusive. His attempts to end Mexican disorder by re-creating a monarchy met unexpected resistance in Puebla, where Mexican forces beat back the French invaders on 5 May 1862, a date thereafter celebrated as Cinco de Mayo. Napoleon III then sent tens of thousands of troops and proclaimed a Mexican empire, although he had to withdraw those forces in 1867. A Mexican firing squad killed the man he had appointed emperor, the Austrian archduke Maximilian (1832–1867). Juárez managed to restore a semblance of liberal government, but Mexico remained beset by political divisions.

By the early twentieth century, Mexico was a divided land moving toward civil war. The Mexican revolution (1910–1920), a bitter and bloody conflict, broke out when middle-class Mexicans joined with peasants and workers to overthrow the powerful dictator Porfirio Díaz (1830–1915). The revolt in Mexico, which was the first major, violent effort in Latin America to attempt to topple the grossly unequal system of landed estates—whereby fully 95 percent of all peasants remained landless—turned increasingly radical as those denied land and representation armed themselves and engaged in guerrilla warfare against government forces. The lower classes took up weapons and followed the revolutionary leaders Emiliano Zapata (1879–1919) and Francisco (Pancho) Villa (1878–1923), charismatic agrarian rebels who organized massive armies fighting for *tierra y libertad* (land and liberty), which were Zapata's stated revolutionary goals. Zapata, the son of a mestizo peasant, and

Zapata, hailing from the southern state of Morelos, was the very picture of a revolutionary leader, heavily armed and sporting his dashing, trademark moustache.

Villa, the son of a field worker, embodied the ideals and aspirations of the indigenous Mexican masses and enjoyed tremendous popular support. They discredited timid governmental efforts at reform and challenged governmental political control; Zapata confiscated hacienda lands and began distributing the lands to the peasants, while Villa attacked and killed U.S. citizens in retaliation for U.S. support of Mexican government officials—and succeeded in eluding capture by either U.S. or Mexican forces.

Despite the power and popularity enjoyed by Zapata and Villa, they were unable to capture Mexico's major cities, and they did not command the resources and wealth to which government forces had access. The Mexican revolution came to an end soon after government forces ambushed and killed Zapata in 1919. Villa was killed a few years later, assassinated in 1923 while driving in the town of Hidalgo de Parral, his car and body riddled with bullets. Government forces regained control over Mexico, a land battered and devastated by long years of war and by the death of as many as two million Mexicans. Although radicals such as Zapata and Villa were ultimately defeated, the Mexican Constitution of 1917 had already addressed some of the concerns of the revolutionaries by providing for land redistribution, universal suffrage, state-supported education, minimum wages and maximum hours for workers, and restrictions on foreign ownership of Mexican property and mineral resources. Although these constitutional provisions were not soon implemented, they provided important guarantees for the future.

In the form of division, rebellion, caudillo rule, and civil war, instability and conflict plagued Latin America throughout the nineteenth century. Many Latin American peoples lacked education, profitable employment, and political representation. Simón Bolívar himself once said that "independence is the only blessing we have gained at the expense of all the rest."

AMERICAN ECONOMIC DEVELOPMENT

During the nineteenth and early twentieth centuries, two principal influences—mass migration and British investment—shaped economic development throughout the Americas. But American states reacted in different ways to migration and foreign investment. The United States and

sources from the past

Ponciano Arriaga Calls for Land Reform

During the era of La Reforma in Mexico, the leftist liberal Ponciano Arriaga voiced demands for land reform on behalf of the Mexican masses, reflecting the broader problem of land control throughout Latin American societies. At the Constitutional Convention of 1856–1857, Arriaga spoke about the troubles resulting from an aristocratic monopoly on land and argued passionately for reform.

One of the most deeply rooted evils of our country—an evil that merits the close attention of legislators when they frame our fundamental law—is the monstrous division of landed property.

While a few individuals possess immense areas of uncultivated land that could support millions of people, the great majority of Mexicans languish in a terrible poverty and are denied property, homes, and work.

Such a people cannot be free, democratic, much less happy, no matter how many constitutions and laws proclaim abstract rights and beautiful but impracticable theories—impracticable by reason of an absurd economic system.

There are Mexican landowners who occupy (if one can give that name to a purely imaginary act) an extent of land greater than the area of some of our sovereign states, greater even than that of one or several European states.

In this vast area, much of which lies idle, deserted, abandoned, awaiting the arms and labor of men, live four or five million Mexicans who know no other industry than agriculture, yet are without land or the means to work it, and who cannot emigrate in the hope of bettering their fortunes. They must either vegetate in idleness, turn to banditry, or accept the yoke of a landed monopolist who subjects them to intolerable conditions of life. . . .

How can a hungry, naked, miserable people practice popular government? How can we proclaim the equal rights of men and leave the majority of the nation in conditions worse than those of helots or pariahs? How can we condemn slavery in words, while the lot of most of our fellow citizens is more grievous than that of the black slaves of Cuba or the United States? When will we begin to concern ourselves with the fate of the proletarians, the men we call Indians, the laborers and peons of the countryside, who drag the heavy chains of serfdom established not by Spanish laws—which were so often flouted and infringed—but by the arbitrary mandarins of the colonial regime? Would it not be more logical and honest to deny our four million poor Mexicans all share in political life and public offices, all electoral rights, and declare them to be things, not persons, establishing a system of government in which an aristocracy of wealth, or at most of talent, would form the basis of our institutions?

For one of two things is inevitable: either our political system will continue to be dominated for a long time to come by a *de facto* aristocracy—no matter what our fundamental laws may say—and the lords of the land, the privileged caste that monopolizes the soil and profits by the sweat of its serfs, will wield all power and influence in our civil and political life; or we will achieve a reform, shatter the trammels and bonds of feudal servitude, bring down all monopolies and despotisms, end all abuses, and allow the fruitful element of democratic equality, the powerful element of democratic sovereignty—to which alone authority rightfully belongs—to penetrate the heart and veins of our political institutions. The nation wills it, the people demand it; the struggle has begun, and sooner or later that just authority will recover its sway. The great word "reform" has been pronounced, and it is vain to erect dykes to contain those torrents of truth and light.

For Further Reflection

■ In studies of life not just in Mexico but throughout the Americas, how can patterns of land ownership illuminate societies' economic and political power structures?

Source: "A Mexican Radical: Ponciano Arriaga." In Benjamin Keen, ed., *Latin American Civilization History and Society, 1492 to the Present,* 6th ed., revised and updated. New York: Westview Press, 1996, pp. 273–74.

Canada absorbed waves of migrants, exploited British capital, built industrial societies, and established economic independence. The fragmented states of Latin America were unable to follow suit, however, as they struggled with the legacies of colonialism, slavery, and economic dependence on single export crops. Migrants to Latin America mostly worked not in factories but on plantations. The importation of migrant laborers for agricultural work in South America and the Caribbean indicated some of the major alterations in labor systems taking place throughout the Americas in the wake of slavery's abolition. Freedom for slaves did not necessarily bring about freer forms of labor, because many migrants arrived under contract or as indentured laborers. Although some freed slaves became small landowning farmers, more found themselves still subject to landowning elite control in the form of debt peonage or sharecropping. Life and labor in the Americas, whether for

Italian migrants construct a railway in New York. Italians were just one of many European groups coming to the Americas in the nineteenth century.

freedmen and freedwomen, migrants, or industrial workers, often proved arduous and at times heartbreaking, even as those American workers contributed to the economic development of the region.

Migration to the Americas

Underpinning the economic development of the Americas was large-scale migration of European and Asian peoples to the United States, Canada, and Latin America. Internal migration within the Americas also contributed to a new economic landscape, particularly as Latin Americans journeyed to the United States in search of work and financial well-being. Gold discoveries drew prospectors hoping to make a quick fortune: the California gold rush of 1849 drew the largest crowd, but Canadian gold also lured migrants by the tens of thousands. Outnumbering gold prospectors were millions of European and Asian migrants who made their way to the factories, railroad construction sites, and plantations of the Americas. Following them were others who offered the support services that made life for migrant workers more comfortable and at the same time transformed the ethnic and cultural landscape of the Americas. Fatt Hing Chin's restaurant in San Francisco's Chinatown fed Chinese migrants, but it also helped introduce Chinese cuisine to American society. Migrants from other parts of the world found similar comforts as their foods, religious beliefs, and cultural traditions migrated with them to the Americas.

Industrial Migrants After the mid-nineteenth century, European migrants flocked to North America, where they filled the factories of the growing industrial economy of the United States. Their lack of skills made them attractive to industrialists seeking workers to operate machinery or perform heavy labor at low wages. By keeping labor costs down, migrants helped increase the profitability and fuel the expansion of U.S. industry.

In the 1850s European migrants to the United States numbered 2.3 million—almost as many as had crossed the Atlantic during the half century from 1800 to 1850—and the volume of migration surged until the early twentieth century. Increasing rents and indebtedness drove cultivators from Ireland, Scotland, Germany, and Scandinavia to seek opportunities in North America. Some of them moved to the Ohio and Mississippi River valleys in search of cheap and abundant land, but many stayed in the eastern cities and contributed to the early industrialization of the United

thinking about ENCOUNTERS

Mass Migration
The nineteenth century witnessed a mass migration of Asians and Europeans to the Americas. How did those migrants contribute to a redefinition of work and culture in the Americas? How in turn did their experience in the Americas—North, Central, and South—change migrants and their cultural practices?

States. By the late nineteenth century, most European migrants were coming from southern and eastern Europe. Poles, Russian Jews, Slavs, Italians, Greeks, and Portuguese were most prominent among the later migrants, and they settled largely in the industrial cities of the eastern states. They dominated the textile industries of the northeast, and without their labor, the remarkable industrial expansion that the United States experienced in the late nineteenth century would have been inconceivable.

Asian migrants further swelled the U.S. labor force and contributed to the construction of an American transportation infrastructure. Chinese migration grew rapidly after the 1840s, when British gunboats opened China to foreign influences. Officials of the Qing government permitted foreigners to seek indentured laborers in China and approved their migration to distant lands. Between 1852 and 1875 some two hundred thousand Chinese migrated to California. Some, like Fatt Hing Chin, negotiated their own passage and sought to make their fortune in the gold rush, but most traveled on indentured labor contracts that required them to cultivate crops or work on the Central Pacific Railroad. An additional five thousand Chinese entered Canada to search for gold in British Columbia or work on the Canadian Pacific Railroad.

Plantation Migrants

Whereas migrants to the United States contributed to the development of an industrial society, those who went to Latin American lands mostly worked on agricultural plantations. Some Europeans figured among these migrants. About four million Italians sought opportunities in Argentina in the 1880s and 1890s, for example, and the Brazilian government paid Italian migrants to cross the Atlantic and work for coffee growers, who experienced a severe labor shortage after the abolition of slavery there (1888). Many Italian workers settled permanently in Latin America, especially Argentina, but some, popularly known as *golondrinas* ("swallows") because of their regular migrations, traveled back and forth annually between Europe and South America to take advantage of different growing seasons in the northern and southern hemispheres.

Other migrants who worked on plantations in the western hemisphere came from Asian lands. More than fifteen thousand indentured laborers from China worked in the sugarcane fields of Cuba during the nineteenth century, and Indian migrants traveled to Jamaica, Trinidad, Tobago, and Guyana. Laborers from both China and Japan migrated to Peru, where they worked on cotton plantations in coastal regions, mined guano deposits for fertilizer, and built railroad lines. After the middle of the nineteenth century, expanding U.S. influence in the Pacific islands also led to Chinese, Japanese, Filipino, and Korean migrations to Hawai`i, where planters sought indentured laborers to tend sugarcane. About twenty-five thousand Chinese went to Hawai`i during the 1850s and 1860s, and later 180,000 Japanese also made their way to island plantations.

Economic Expansion in the United States

British Capital

British investment capital in the United States proved crucial to the early stages of industrial development by helping businesspeople establish a textile industry. In the late nineteenth century, it also spurred a vast expansion of U.S. industry by funding entrepreneurs, who opened coal and iron ore mines, built iron and steel factories, and constructed railroad lines. The flow of investment monies was a consequence of Britain's own industrialization, which generated enormous wealth and created a need for investors to find profitable outlets for their funds. Stable, white-governed states and colonies were especially fertile grounds for British investment, which often provided the impetus for industrial expansion and economic independence in those regions. In the case of the United States, it helped create a rival industrial power that would eventually outperform Britain's economy.

After the 1860s, U.S. businesses made effective use of foreign investment capital as the reunited land recovered from the Civil War. The war determined that the United States would depend on wage labor rather than slavery, and entrepreneurs set about tapping American resources and building a continental economy.

Railroads

Perhaps the most important economic development of the later nineteenth century was the construction of railroad lines that linked all U.S. regions and helped create an integrated national economy. Because of its enormous size and environmental diversity, the United States offered an abundance of natural resources for industrial exploitation. But vast distances made it difficult to maintain close economic ties between regions until a boom in railroad construction created a dense transportation, communication, and distribution network. Before the Civil War the United States had about 50,000 kilometers (31,000 miles) of railroad lines, most of them short routes east of the Mississippi River. By 1900 there were more than 320,000 kilometers (200,000 miles) of track, and the U.S. rail network stretched from coast to coast. Most prominent of the new lines was a transcontinental route, completed in 1869, running from Omaha, where connections provided access to eastern states, to San Francisco.

Railroads decisively influenced U.S. economic development. They provided cheap transportation for agricultural commodities, manufactured goods, and individual travelers as well. Railroads hauled grain, beef, and hogs from the plains states, cotton and tobacco from the south, lumber from the northwest, iron and steel from the mills of Pittsburgh, and finished products from the eastern industrial cities. Quite apart from the transportation services they provided, railroads spurred the development of other industries: they required huge amounts of coal, wood, glass, and rubber, and by the 1880s some 75 percent of U.S. steel went to the railroad industry. Railroads also required the development of new managerial skills to operate large, complicated businesses. In 1850 few if any U.S. businesses had more than a thousand employees. By the early 1880s, however, the Pennsylvania Railroad alone employed almost fifty thousand people, and the size of the business called for organization and coordination on an unprecedented scale. Railroads were the testing grounds where managers developed the techniques they needed to run big businesses.

Space and Time   Railroads led to drastic changes in the ways people organized and controlled space and time. Railroads altered the landscape in often extreme fashion, and the transformations consequent to the building of railroads—in land control and development, the transportation of migrants and settlers to the west, and the exploitation of natural resources—only furthered the environmental impact of the railroad. The westward expansion driven by the railroad led to broadscale land clearing and the extension of farming and mining lands, and brought about both

human suffering for indigenous peoples and environmental damage through soil erosion and pollution. Irrigation and the politics of water also sparked trouble, especially as settlers and farmers entered the drier plains and even desert regions. The dark smoke emanating from railroad engines undoubtedly represented progress to industrial promoters, but it also symbolized an ever-widening intrusion into the natural environment.

Railroads even shaped the sense of time in the United States. Until rapid and regular rail transportation became available, communities set their clocks by the sun. As a result, New York time was eleven minutes and forty-five seconds behind Boston time. When the clock showed 12 noon in Chicago, it was 11:50 A.M. in St. Louis and 12:18 P.M. in Detroit. Those differences in local sun times created scheduling nightmares for railroad managers, who by the 1880s had to keep track of more than fifty time standards. Observance of local time also created hazards because a small miscalculation in scheduling could bring two massive trains

AMERICAN EXPRESS TRAIN.

In this lithograph of Frances F. Palmer's well-known painting *American Express Train* (ca. 1864), the railroad demonstrates its domination of the natural landscape and its role as the harbinger of change and industry.

hurtling unexpectedly toward each other on the same track. To simplify matters, in 1883 railroad companies divided the North American continent into four zones in which all railroad clocks read precisely the same time. The general public quickly adopted "railroad time" in place of local sun time, and in 1918 the U.S. government legally established the four time zones as the nation's official framework of time.

Economic Growth Led by railroads, the U.S. economy expanded at a blistering pace between 1870 and 1900. Inventors designed new products and brought them to market: electric lights, telephones, typewriters, phonographs, film photography, motion picture cameras, and electric motors all made their appearance during this era. Strong consumer demand for those and other products fueled rapid industrial expansion and suggested to observers that the United States had found the road to continuous progress and prosperity.

Yet the march of U.S. industrialization did not go entirely unopposed: large-scale labor unions emerged alongside big business in the period from 1870 to 1900, and confrontations between business owners seeking profits and workers seeking higher wages or job security sometimes grew ugly. A nationwide, coordinated strike of rail workers in 1877 shut down two-thirds of the nation's railroads. Violence stemming from the strike took the lives of one hundred people and resulted in ten million dollars' worth of property damage. Nevertheless, big business prevailed in its disputes with workers during the nineteenth century, often with support from federal or state governments, and by the early twentieth century the United States had emerged as one of the world's major industrial powers.

Canadian Prosperity

British investment deeply influenced the development of the Canadian as well as the U.S. economy in the nineteenth and early twentieth centuries. Canadian leaders, like U.S. leaders, took advantage of British capital to industrialize without allowing their economy to fall under British control. During the early nineteenth century, Britain paid relatively high prices for Canadian agricultural products and minerals, partly to keep the colony stable and discourage the formation of separatist movements. As a result, white Canadians enjoyed a high standard of living even before industrialization.

The National Policy After the establishment of the Dominion, politicians started a program of economic development known as the National Policy. The idea was to attract migrants, protect nascent industries through tariffs, and build national transportation systems. The centerpiece of the transportation network was the transcontinental Canadian Pacific Railroad, built largely with British investment capital and completed in 1885. The Canadian Pacific Railroad opened the western prairie lands to commerce, stimulated the development of other industries, and promoted the emergence of a Canadian national economy. The National

Policy created some violent altercations with indigenous peoples who resisted encroachment on their lands and with trappers who resented disruption of their way of life, but it also promoted economic growth and independence. In Canada as in the United States, the ability to control and direct economic affairs was crucial to limiting the state's dependence on British capital.

As a result of the National Policy, Canada experienced booming agricultural, mineral, and industrial production in the late nineteenth and early twentieth centuries. Canadian population surged as a result of both migration and natural increase. Migrants flocked to Canada's shores from Asia and especially from Europe: between 1903 and 1914 some 2.7 million eastern European migrants settled in Canada. Fueled in part by this population growth, Canadian economic expansion took place on the foundation of rapidly increasing wheat production and the extraction of rich mineral resources, including gold, silver, copper, nickel, and asbestos. Industrialists also tapped Canadian rivers to produce the hydroelectric power necessary for manufacturing.

U.S. Investment Canada remained wary of its powerful neighbor to the south but did not keep U.S. economic influence entirely at bay. British investment dwarfed U.S. investment throughout the nineteenth century: in 1914 British investment in Canada totaled $2.5 billion, compared with $700 million from the United States. Nevertheless, the U.S. presence in the Canadian economy grew. By 1918, Americans owned 30 percent of all Canadian industry, and thereafter the U.S. and Canadian economies became increasingly interdependent. Canada began to undergo rapid industrialization after the early twentieth century, as the province of Ontario benefited from the spillover of U.S. industry in the northeastern states.

Latin American Investments

Latin American states did not undergo industrialization or enjoy economic development like that of the United States and Canada. Colonial legacies help explain the different economic development in Latin American lands. Even when Spain and Portugal controlled the trade and investment policies of their American colonies, their home economies were unable to supply sufficient quantities of the manufactured goods that colonial markets demanded. As a result, they opened the colonies to European trade, which snuffed out local industries that could not compete with British, French, and German producers of inexpensive manufactured goods. Moreover, both in colonial times and after independence, Latin American elites—urban merchants and large landholders—retained control over local economies. Elites profited handsomely from European trade and investment and thus had little incentive to seek different economic policies or work toward economic diversification. Thus foreign investment and trade had more damaging effects in Latin America than in the United States or Canada.

British Investment The relatively small size of Latin American markets limited foreign influence, which generally took the form of investment or what could be termed informal imperialism. British merchants had little desire to transform Latin American states into dependent trading partners for the simple reason that they offered no substantial market for British goods. Nevertheless, British investors took advantage of opportunities that brought them profits and considerable control over Latin American economic affairs. In Argentina, for example, British investors encouraged the development of cattle and sheep ranching. After the 1860s and the invention of refrigerated cargo ships, meat became Argentina's largest export. British investors controlled the industry and reaped the profits, however, as Argentina became Britain's principal supplier of meat. Between 1880 and 1914, European migrants labored in the new export industries and contributed to the explosive growth of urban areas such as Buenos Aires: by 1914 the city's population exceeded 3.5 million. Although migrant laborers rarely shared in the profits controlled by elites, the domination of urban labor by European migrants represented yet another form of foreign influence in Latin American economic affairs.

Attempted Industrialization In a few lands, ruling elites made attempts to encourage industrialization, but with only limited success. The most notable of those efforts came when the dictatorial general Porfirio Díaz ruled Mexico (1876–1911). Díaz represented the interests of large landowners, wealthy merchants, and foreign investors. Under his rule, railroad tracks and telegraph lines connected all parts of Mexico, and the production of mineral resources surged. A small steel industry produced railroad track and construction materials, and entrepreneurs also established glass, chemical, and textile industries. The capital, Mexico City, underwent a transformation during the Díaz years: it acquired paved streets, streetcar lines, and electric streetlights. But the profits from Mexican enterprises did not support continuing industrial development. Instead, they went into the pockets of the Mexican oligarchy and foreign investors who supported Díaz, while a growing and discontented urban working class seethed with resentment at low wages, long hours, and foreign managers. Even as agriculture, railroad construction, and mining were booming, the standard of living for average Mexicans had begun to decline by the early twentieth century. Frustration with that state of affairs helps explain the sudden outbreak of violent revolution in 1910.

Despite a large proportion of foreign and especially British control, Latin American economies expanded rapidly in the late nineteenth century. Exports drove that growth: copper and silver from Mexico, bananas and coffee from Central America, rubber and coffee from Brazil, beef and wheat from Argentina, copper from Chile, and tobacco and sugar from Cuba. Other areas in the world also developed many of those same products for export, however, and competition for markets often led to lower prices for those commodities. As in the United States and Canada, foreign investment in Latin America provided capital for development, but unlike the situation in the northern lands, control over industries and exports remained in foreign hands. Latin American economies were thus subject to decisions made in the interests of foreign investors, and unstable governments could do little in the face of strong foreign intervention. Controlled by the very elites who profited from foreign intervention at the expense of their citizens, Latin

British and U.S. investors underwrote economic and industrial development in Latin America during the late nineteenth century, but most of the profits flowed outside the region. This copper mine in northwestern Mexico was built with U.S. investments.

American governments helped account for the region's slower economic development, despite growth in industrial and export economies.

AMERICAN CULTURAL AND SOCIAL DIVERSITY

In his "Song of Myself" (1855), a poetic celebration of himself as well as the vast diversity of his nation, U.S. poet Walt Whitman asked:

> Do I contradict myself?
> Very well then I contradict myself,
> (I am large, I contain multitudes.)

Much of the allure of the Americas derived from their vast spaces and diverse populations. The Americas were indeed large, and they contained multitudes. While diversity distinguished the Americas, it also provided abundant fuel for conflicts between ethnic groups, social classes, and those segregated into rigid castes based on race and gender. The social and cultural diversity of American societies challenged their ability to achieve cultural cohesion as well as political unity and democratically inclusive states. The lingering legacies of European conquest, slavery, migration, and patriarchy highlighted contradictions between the Enlightenment ideals of freedom and equality and the reali-

ties of life for native and African-American peoples as well as recent migrants and women. American societies experienced ample strife in the age of independence. In efforts to maintain their own position and preserve social stability, the dominant political forces in the Americas often repressed demands for recognition by dispossessed groups.

Societies in the United States

By the late nineteenth century, the United States had become a boisterous multicultural society—the most culturally diverse land of the western hemisphere—whose population included indigenous peoples, Euro-American settlers, African-American laborers, and growing numbers of migrants from Europe and Asia. Walt Whitman described the United States as "not merely a nation but a teeming nation of nations." Yet political and economic power rested almost exclusively with white male elites of European ancestry. The United States experienced tension and occasional conflict as members of various constituencies worked for dignity, prosperity, and a voice in society. During the nineteenth century, cultural and social tension swirled especially around indigenous peoples, African-American slaves and their descendants, women, and migrants.

Native Peoples As they expanded to the west, Euro-American settlers and ranchers pushed indigenous peoples

The Apache youths at the Carlisle Indian School offer stark faces to the camera, suggesting their discontent with reform efforts directed at assimilation through education.

onto reservations. Although promising to respect those lands, the U.S. government permitted settlers and railroads to encroach on the reservations and force native peoples into increasingly cramped and marginal territories. Begrudging native Americans even these meager lands, the United States embarked in the latter half of the nineteenth century on a policy designed to reduce native autonomy even further through laws and reforms aimed at assimilating tribes to the white way of life. The U.S. government and private citizens acted to undermine or destroy outright the bases of native cultural traditions. Native tribes on the plains, for example, had developed material cultures largely centered on the hunting of bison, or buffalo, and the skillful exploitation of those animal resources. Beginning in 1850 but accelerating after the Civil War, white migrants, railroad employees, hunters, and "wild west" men such as Buffalo Bill Cody shot and killed hundreds of thousands of bison, effectively exterminating the buffalo and the economy of the Plains Indians. Herds numbering at least 15 million had been reduced to a mere thousand by 1875.

Other U.S. actions also attempted to sever native Americans' ties to their communal traditions and cultural practices. The Dawes Severalty Act of 1887 shifted land policies away from collective tribal reservations and toward individual tracts of land meant to promote the family farms once common in white U.S. society and now becoming increasingly less competitive. Even more traumatically, government officials removed native children from their families and tribes and enrolled them in white-controlled boarding schools. These schools, such as the Carlisle Indian School and the Toledo Indian School, illustrated the extent to which white society sought to eliminate tribal influences and inculcate Christian, U.S. values. Tribal languages as well as native dress and hair fashions were banned, further distancing the children from their cultures. Native Americans, however, resisted these forms of assimilation, often fleeing from boarding schools or refusing to agree to new governmental land policies. Native land control diminished as a result, but over the following decades tribes rebuilt and reaffirmed native identities.

Freed Slaves The Civil War ended slavery, but it did not bring about instant equality for freed slaves and their African-American descendants. In an effort to establish a place for

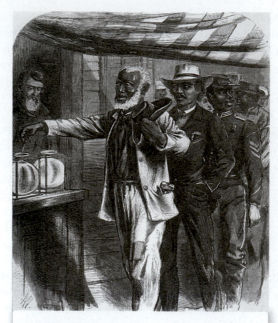

A lithograph from *Harper's Weekly* after the Civil War. A black artisan, a middle-class African-American, and a black Union soldier are in the process of voting, perhaps for the first time in their lives.

freed slaves in American society, northern forces sent armies of occupation to the southern states and forced them to undergo a program of social and political Reconstruction (1867–1877). They extended civil rights to freed slaves and provided black men with voting rights. Black and white citizens in southern states elected biracial governments for the first time in U.S. history, and freed slaves participated actively in the political affairs of the republic.

After Reconstruction, however, the armies of occupation went back north, and a violent backlash soon dismantled the program's reforms. Freed slaves had not received land grants or any other means of economic support, so many had to work as sharecroppers for former slave owners. Under those circumstances it was relatively easy for white southerners to take away the political and civil liberties that former slaves had gained under Reconstruction. By the turn of the century, U.S. blacks faced violence and intimidation when they tried to vote. Southern states fashioned a rigidly segregated society that deprived the African-American population of educational, economic, and political opportunities. Although freedom was better than slavery, it was far different from the hopeful visions of the slaves who had won their emancipation.

Women Even before the Civil War, a small but growing women's movement had emerged in the United States. At the Seneca Falls Convention in 1848, feminists issued a "declaration of sentiments" modeled on the Declaration of Independence—"We hold these truths to be self-evident: that all men and women are created equal"—and they demanded equal political and economic rights for U.S. women:

> Now, in view of this entire disenfranchisement of one-half the people of this country, their social and religious degradation—in view of the unjust laws above mentioned, and because women do feel themselves aggrieved, oppressed, and fraudulently deprived of their most sacred rights, we insist that they have immediate admission to all the rights and privileges which belong to them as citizens of the United States.

Women fought for equal rights throughout the nineteenth century, and new opportunities for education and employment offered alternatives to marriage and domesticity. Women's colleges, reform activism, and professional in-

This photograph from the late nineteenth century captures the busy street life in San Francisco's Chinatown. Migrants flocked to urban centers and created ethnic enclaves such as Chinatown for comfort and protection, transforming the urban landscapes of the Americas in the process.

dustrial jobs allowed some women to pursue careers over marriage. Yet meaningful economic and political opportunities for women awaited the twentieth century.

Migrants Between 1840 and 1914 some twenty-five million European migrants landed on American shores, and in the late nineteenth century most of them hailed from southern and eastern European countries. Migrants introduced new foods, music, dances, holidays, sports, and languages to U.S. society and contributed to the cultural diversity of the western hemisphere. Yet white, native-born citizens of the United States began to feel swamped by the arrival of so many migrants. Distaste for foreigners often resulted in hostility to the migrants who flooded into the expanding industrial cities. Migrants and their families tended to concentrate in certain districts, such as Little Italy and Chinatown—partly out of choice, since they preferred neighbors with

familiar cultural traditions, but partly also because native-born citizens discouraged the migrants from moving into other neighborhoods. Concerns about growing numbers of migrants with different cultural and social traditions eventually led to the exclusion of new arrivals from Asian lands: the U.S. government ordered a complete halt to migration from China in 1882 and from Japan in 1907.

Canadian Cultural Contrasts

Ethnic Diversity British and French settlers each viewed themselves as Canada's founding people. This cleavage, which profoundly influenced Canadian political development, masked much greater cultural and ethnic diversity in Canada. French and British settlers displaced the indigenous peoples, who remain a significant minority of Canada's population today. Slavery likewise left a mark on Canada. Slavery was legal in the British empire until 1833, and many early settlers brought their slaves to Canada. After the 1830s, escaped slaves from the United States also reached Canada by way of the Underground Railroad. Blacks in Canada were free but not equal, segregated and isolated from the political and cultural mainstream. Chinese migrants also came to Canada; lured by gold rushes such as the Fraser River rush of 1858 and by opportunities to work on the Canadian Pacific Railway in the 1880s, Chinese migrants lived mostly in segregated Chinatowns in the cities of British Columbia, and like blacks they had little voice in public affairs. In the late nineteenth and early twentieth centuries, waves of migrants brought even greater ethnic diversity to Canada. Between 1896 and 1914 three million migrants from Britain, the United States, and eastern Europe arrived in Canada.

Despite the heterogeneity of Canada's population, communities descended from British and French settlers dominated Canadian society, and conflict between the two communities was the most prominent source of ethnic tension throughout the nineteenth and twentieth centuries. After 1867, as British Canadians led the effort to settle the Northwest Territories and incorporate them into the Dominion, frictions between the two groups intensified. Westward expansion brought British Canadian settlers and cultivators into conflict with French Canadian fur traders and lumberjacks. The fur traders in particular often lived on the margins between European and indigenous societies. They frequently married or consorted with native women, giving rise to the métis, individuals of mixed European and indigenous ancestry.

The Métis and Louis Riel A major outbreak of civil strife took place in the 1870s and 1880s. Native peoples and métis had moved west throughout the nineteenth century to preserve their land and trading rights, but the drive of British Canadians to the west threatened them. Louis Riel (1844–1885) emerged as the leader of the métis and indigenous peoples of western Canada. A métis himself, Riel abandoned his studies for the priesthood in Montreal and

sources from the past

The Meaning of Freedom for an Ex-Slave

Even before the conclusion of the Civil War brought slavery to an end in the United States, Jourdan Anderson had taken the opportunity to run away and claim his freedom. After the war his former master, Colonel P. H. Anderson, wrote a letter asking him to return to work on his Tennessee plantation. In responding from his new home in Dayton, Ohio, Anderson respectfully refers to the colonel as "my old master" and addresses him as "sir." Yet Anderson's letter makes it clear that his family's freedom and welfare were his principal concerns.

I want to know particularly what the good chance is you propose to give me. I am doing tolerably well here; I get $25 a month, with victuals and clothing; have a comfortable home for Mandy (the folks here call her Mrs. Anderson), and the children, Milly, Jane and Grundy, go to school and are learning well; the teacher says Grundy has a head for a preacher. They go to Sunday-School, and Mandy and me attend church regularly. We are kindly treated; sometimes we overhear others saying, "Them colored people were slaves" down in Tennessee. The children feel hurt when they hear such remarks, but I tell them it was no disgrace in Tennessee to belong to Col. Anderson. Many darkies would have been proud, as I used to was, to call you master. Now, if you will write and say what wages you will give me, I will be better able to decide whether it would be to my advantage to move back again.

As to my freedom, which you say I can have, there is nothing to be gained on that score, as I got my free-papers in 1864 from the Provost-Marshal-General of the Department at Nashville. Mandy says she would be afraid to go back without some proof that you are sincerely disposed to treat us justly and kindly—and we have concluded to test your sincerity by asking you to send us our wages for the time we served you. This will make us forget and forgive old scores, and rely on your justice and friendship in the future. I served you faithfully for thirty-two years and Mandy twenty years. At $25 a month for me, and $2 a week for Mandy, our earnings would amount to $11,680. Add to this the interest for the time our wages has been kept back and deduct what you paid for our clothing and three doctor's visits to me, and pulling a tooth for Mandy, and the balance will show what we are in justice entitled to. Please send the money by Adams Express, in care of V. Winters, esq, Dayton, Ohio. If you fail to pay us for faithful labors in the past we can have little faith in your promises in the future. We trust the good Maker has opened your eyes to the wrongs which you and your fathers have done to me and my fathers, in making us toil for you for generations without recompense. Here I draw my wages every Saturday night, but in Tennessee there was never any pay day for the negroes any more than for the horses and cows. Surely there will be a day of reckoning for those who defraud the laborer of his hire.

In answering this letter please state if there would be any safety for my Milly and Jane, who are now grown up and both good-looking girls. You know how it was with poor Matilda and Catherine. I would rather stay here and starve and die if it comes to that than have my girls brought to shame by the violence and wickedness of their young masters. You will also please state if there has been any schools opened for the colored children in your neighborhood, the great desire of my life now is to give my children an education, and have them form virtuous habits.

For Further Reflection

■ In what clever ways does Jourdan Anderson test the seriousness of his former owner's offer of employment, and what does his approach say about the meaning of black freedom?

Source: Leon F. Litwack. *Been in the Storm So Long: The Aftermath of Slavery.* New York: Knopf, 1979, pp. 334–35.

returned to his home in the Red River Settlement (in the southern part of modern Manitoba). Sensitive to his community's concern that the Canadian government threatened local land rights, Riel assumed the presidency of a provisional government in 1870. He led his troops in capturing Fort Garry (modern Winnipeg) and negotiated the incorporation of the province of Manitoba into the Canadian Dominion. Canadian government officials and troops soon outlawed his government and forced Riel into years of exile, during which he wandered through the United States and Quebec, even suffering confinement in asylums.

Work on the Canadian Pacific Railroad in the 1880s renewed the threat of white settlement to indigenous and métis society. The métis asked Riel to lead resistance to the railroad and British Canadian settlement. In 1885 he organized a military force of métis and native peoples in the Saskatchewan river country and led an insurrection known as the Northwest Rebellion. Canadian forces quickly subdued the makeshift army, and government authorities executed Riel for treason.

Although the Northwest Rebellion never had a chance of success, the execution of Riel nonetheless reverberated throughout Canadian history. French Canadians took it as an indication of the state's readiness to subdue individuals who were culturally distinct and politically opposed to the drive for a nation dominated by British Canadian elites. In the very year when completion of the transcontinental railroad signified for some the beginnings of Canadian national unity, Riel's execution foreshadowed a long term of cultural conflict between Canadians of British, French, and indigenous ancestry.

Ethnicity, Identity, and Gender in Latin America

The heritage of Spanish and Portuguese colonialism and the legacy of slavery inclined Latin American societies toward the establishment of hierarchical distinctions based on ethnicity and color. At the top of society stood the creoles, individuals of European ancestry born in the Americas, while indigenous peoples, freed slaves, and their black descendants occupied the lowest rungs of the social ladder. In between were various groups of mixed ancestry, such as mestizos, mulattoes, zambos, and castizos. Although most Latin American states ended the legal recognition of these groups, the distinctions themselves persisted after independence and limited the opportunities available to peoples of indigenous, African, or mixed ancestry.

Migration and Cultural Diversity Large-scale migration brought added cultural diversity to Latin America in the nineteenth century. Indentured laborers who went from Asian lands to Peru, Brazil, Cuba, and other Caribbean destinations carried with them many of their native cultural practices. When their numbers were relatively small, as in the case of Chinese migrants to Cuba, they mostly intermarried and assimilated into the working classes without leaving much foreign influence on the societies they joined. When they were relatively more numerous, however, as in the case of Indian migrants to Trinidad and Tobago, they formed distinctive communities in which they spoke their native languages, prepared foods from their homelands, and observed their inherited cultural and social traditions. Migration of European workers to Argentina brought a lively diversity to the

Engraving of Louis Riel, the rebellious Canadian métis. Riel fought through political and military means on behalf of the métis and indigenous peoples of western Canada.

capital of Buenos Aires, which was perhaps the most cosmopolitan city of nineteenth-century Latin America. With its broad avenues, smart boutiques, and handsome buildings graced with wrought iron, Buenos Aires enjoyed a reputation as "the Paris of the Americas."

Latin American intellectuals seeking cultural identity usually saw themselves either as heirs of Europe or as products of the American environment. One spokesperson who identified with Europe was the Argentine president Domingo Faustino Sarmiento (1811–1888). Sarmiento despised the rule of caudillos that had emerged after independence and worked for the development of the best society based on European values. In his widely read book *Facundo: Civilization and Barbarism* (1845), Sarmiento argued that it was necessary for Buenos Aires to bring discipline to the disorderly Argentine countryside. Deeply influenced by the Enlightenment, he characterized books, ideas, law, education, and art as products of cities, and he argued that only when cities dominated the countryside would social stability and genuine liberty be possible.

Gauchos Sarmiento admired the bravery and independence of Argentina's *gauchos* ("cowboys"), but he considered it imperative that urban residents rather than ranchers make society's crucial decisions. Although the mystique of the gaucho did not extend throughout all of Latin America, observers did see gauchos as one symbol of Latin American identity. Most gauchos were mestizos or castizos, but there were also white and black gauchos. For all intents and purposes, anyone who adopted gaucho ways became a gaucho, and gaucho society acquired an ethnic egalitarianism rarely found elsewhere in Latin America. Gauchos were most prominent in the Argentine pampas, but their cultural practices linked them to the cowboys, or vaqueros, found throughout the Americas. As pastoralists herding cattle and horses on the pampas, gauchos stood apart from both the indigenous peoples and the growing urban and agricultural elites who gradually displaced them with large landholdings and cattle ranches that spread to the pampas.

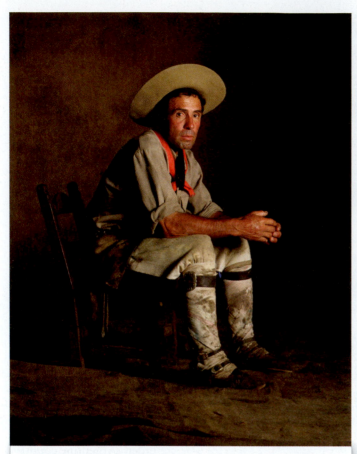

Pedro Damian Alegre as an Argentinian gaucho, dressed traditionally and striking a solitary pose symbolic of gaucho individualism.

The gauchos led independent and self-sufficient lives that appealed broadly in hierarchical Latin American society. Gauchos lived off their own skills and needed only their horses to survive. They dressed distinctively, with sashed trousers, ponchos, and boots. Countless songs and poems lauded their courage, skills, and lovemaking bravado. Yet independence and caudillo rule disrupted gaucho life as the cowboys increasingly entered armies, either voluntarily or under compulsion, and as settled agriculture and ranches surrounded by barbed wire enclosed the pampas. The gauchos did not leave the pampas without resistance. The poet José Hernandez offered a romanticized vision of the gaucho life and protested its decline in his epic poem *The Gaucho Martín Fierro* (1873). Hernandez conveyed the pride of gauchos, particularly those who resisted assimilation into Euro-American society, by having Martín Fierro proclaim his independence and assert his intention to stay that way:

> I owe nothin' to nobody;
> I don't ask for shelter, or give it;
> and from now on, nobody
> better try to lead me around by a rope.

Nevertheless, by the late nineteenth century, gauchos were more echoes of the Latin American past than makers of a viable society.

Male Domination Even more than in the United States and Canada, male domination was a central characteristic of Latin American society in the nineteenth century. Women could not vote or hold office, nor could they work or manage estates without permission from their male guardians. In rural areas, women were liable to rough treatment and assault by gauchos and other men steeped in the values of *machismo*—a social ethic that honored male strength, courage, aggressiveness, assertiveness, and cunning. A few women voiced their discontent with male domination and machismo. In her poem "To Be Born a Man" (1887), for example, the Bolivian poet Adela Zamudio lamented bitterly that talented women could not vote, but ignorant men could, just by learning how to sign their names. Although Latin American lands had not yet generated a strong women's movement, they did begin to expand educational opportunities for girls and young women after the mid-nineteenth century. In large cities most girls received some formal schooling, and women usually filled teaching positions in the public schools that proliferated throughout Latin America in the late nineteenth century.

Female Activism Women did carve spaces for themselves outside or alongside the male world of machismo, and this was especially true in the home and in the marketplace, where Latin American women exerted great influence and control. In the early twentieth century, women served in conjunction with men in the Mexican revolution, most famously as Zapatistas, or followers of Emiliano Zapata. Many women supporting Zapata labored within the domestic realm to provide food for the soldiers, and others breached the domestic barrier to become soldiers and officers themselves. Although those women who became *soldaderas* (female soldiers or supporters of soldiers) demonstrated the most extreme forms of activism during the Mexican revolution, Mexican women on the whole made major contributions to the success of the revolution and shared in the radical spirit of change that characterized much of early-twentieth-century Latin America.

in perspective

After gaining independence from European colonial powers, the states of the western hemisphere worked to build stable and prosperous societies. The independent American states faced difficult challenges—including vast territories, diverse populations, social tensions, and cultural differences—as they sought to construct viable societies on the Enlightenment principles of freedom, equality, and constitutional government. The United States and Canada built large federal societies in North America, whereas a series of smaller states governed affairs in Latin America. The United States in particular was an expansive society, absorbing Texas, California, and the northern territories of Mexico while extending its authority from the Atlantic to the Pacific Ocean. Throughout the hemisphere, descendants of European settlers subdued indigenous American peoples and built societies dominated by Euro-American peoples. They established agricultural economies, exploited natural resources, and in some lands launched processes of industrialization. They accepted streams of European and Asian migrants, who contributed not only to American cultural diversity but also to the transformations in labor practices necessitated by the abolition of slavery and the rise of industry. All American lands experienced tensions arising from social, economic, cultural, and ethnic differences, which led occasionally to violent civil conflict and often to smoldering resentments and grievances. The making of independent American societies was not a smooth process, but it reflected the increasing interdependence of all the world's peoples. ●

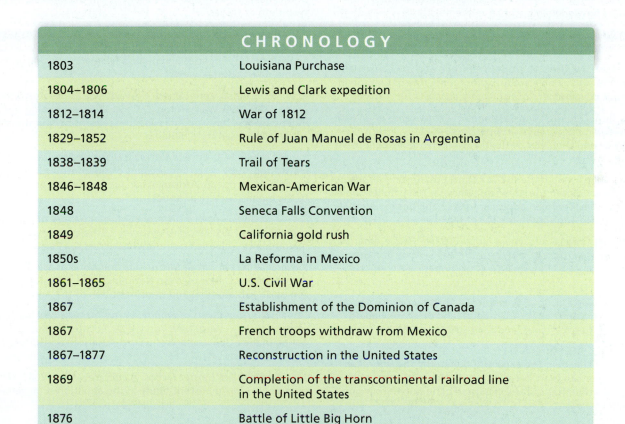

CHRONOLOGY	
1803	Louisiana Purchase
1804–1806	Lewis and Clark expedition
1812–1814	War of 1812
1829–1852	Rule of Juan Manuel de Rosas in Argentina
1838–1839	Trail of Tears
1846–1848	Mexican-American War
1848	Seneca Falls Convention
1849	California gold rush
1850s	La Reforma in Mexico
1861–1865	U.S. Civil War
1867	Establishment of the Dominion of Canada
1867	French troops withdraw from Mexico
1867–1877	Reconstruction in the United States
1869	Completion of the transcontinental railroad line in the United States
1876	Battle of Little Big Horn
1876–1911	Rule of Porfirio Díaz in Mexico
1885	Completion of the Canadian Pacific Railroad
1885	Northwest Rebellion
1890	Massacre at Wounded Knee
1910–1920	Mexican revolution

For Further Reading

Richard Buel Jr. *America on the Brink: How the Political Struggle over the War of 1812 Almost Destroyed the Young Republic.* New York, 2004. Scholarly examination of the conflicts between Federalists and Jeffersonians that culminated in the War of 1812.

Colin G. Calloway. *First Peoples: A Documentary Survey of American Indian History.* Boston, 1999. A fine text on native American history, written by a knowledgeable scholar in the field.

Roderic Ai Camp. *Politics in Mexico: The Democratic Transformation.* 4th ed. New York, 2004. The best introduction to Mexican politics.

William Cronon. *Nature's Metropolis: Chicago and the Great West.* New York, 1991. A valuable study exploring the role of Chicago in the economic development of the American west.

Ellen C. DuBois. *Feminism and Suffrage: The Emergence of an Independent Women's Movement in America, 1848–1869.* Ithaca, 1984. Traces the rise and character of the U.S. women's movement in the nineteenth century.

David Barry Gaspar and Darlene Clark Hine, eds. *Beyond Bondage: Free Women of Color in the Americas.* Chicago, 2004. Collection of essays on free black women and their unique abilities to negotiate social and legal institutions in the era of slavery.

Tom Holm. *The Great Confusion in Indian Affairs: Native Americans and Whites in the Progressive Era.* Austin, 2005. Study of native American resistance to the American government's attempts at subjugation.

Joseph Kinsey Howard. *Strange Empire: A Narrative of the Northwest.* Westport, Conn., 1974. An in-depth and often moving account of Louis Riel, the métis, and their struggles with the Canadian government.

Patricia Nelson Limerick. *The Legacy of Conquest: The Unbroken Past of the American West.* New York, 1987. A provocative work exploring the influences of race, class, and gender in the conquest of the American west.

James M. McPherson. *Battle Cry of Freedom: The Civil War Era.* New York, 1988. A balanced account of the Civil War by a renowned scholar.

J. R. Miller. *Skyscrapers Hide the Heavens: A History of Indian-White Relations in Canada.* Toronto, 1989. An important study of Canadian policies toward indigenous peoples.

Walter Nugent. *Crossings: The Great Transatlantic Migrations, 1870–1914.* Bloomington, 1992. Provides an overview and analysis of the mass migrations to North America in the nineteenth and twentieth centuries.

Marc Reisner. *Cadillac Desert: The American West and Its Disappearing Water.* Revised and updated ed. New York, 1993. An incisive analysis of water policies and politics from an engaging and environmentalist point of view.

Robert L. Scheina. *Latin American Wars.* Vol. 1: *The Age of the Caudillos, 1791–1899.* Washington, D.C., 2003. By examining the wars of independence, this work uncovers the reasons behind the failures of Latin American state building.

Ronald Takaki. *A Different Mirror: A History of Multicultural America.* Boston, 1993. A spirited account of the contributions made by peoples of European, African, Asian, and native American ancestry to the modern American society.

————. *Strangers from a Different Shore: A History of Asian Americans.* Boston, 1989. Fascinating survey of the experiences of Asian migrants who came to North America across the Pacific Ocean.

Richard White. *"It's Your Misfortune and None of My Own": A History of the American West.* Norman, Okla., 1991. Surveys the conquest, exploitation, and transformation of the American west.

Donald Worster. *Rivers of Empire: Water, Aridity, and the Growth of the American West.* New York, 1985. Focuses on the role of irrigation in the establishment of a Euro-American agricultural society in the arid west.

Jean Fagan Yellin. *Harriet Jacobs: A Life.* New York, 2003. Scholarly biography of an important figure in the abolitionist movement.

chapter 31

太皇禧慈國

European portrait of China's Empress Dowager Cixi from 1903. Beginning her political career as a concubine in the harem of the Xianfeng emperor, she developed into a powerful and charismatic figure who became the de facto ruler of the Manchu Qing dynasty in China for over forty years, from 1861 until her death in 1908.

EYEWITNESS:

"Heavenly King" Hong Xiuquan, Empress Dowager Cixi, and Qing Reform

Hong Xiuquan, the third son of a poor family, grew up in a farming village in southern China about 50 kilometers (31 miles) from Guangzhou. Although he was arrogant and irritable, he showed intellectual promise. His neighbors made him village teacher so that he could study and prepare for the civil service examinations, the principal avenue to government employment, since a position in the Qing bureaucracy would bring honor and wealth to both his family and his village. Between 1828 and 1837, Hong took the exams three times but failed to obtain even the lowest degree. This outcome was not surprising, since thousands of candidates competed for a degree, which only a few obtained. Yet the disappointment was too much for Hong. He suffered an emotional collapse, lapsed into a delirium that lasted about forty days, and experienced visions.

Upon recovering from his breakdown, Hong resumed his position as village teacher. After failing the civil service examinations a fourth time in 1843, he began studying the works of a Chinese missionary who explained the basic elements of Christianity. As he pondered the religious tracts, Hong came to believe that during his illness he had visited heaven and learned from God that he was the younger brother of Jesus Christ. He believed further that God had revealed to him that his destiny was to reform China and pave the way for the heavenly kingdom. Inspired by these convictions, Hong baptized himself and worked to build a community of disciples.

Hong's personal religious vision soon evolved into a political program: Hong believed that God had charged him with the establishment of a new order, one that necessitated the destruction of the Qing dynasty, which had ruled China since 1644. In 1847 he joined the Society of God Worshipers, a religious group recently founded by disgruntled peasants and miners. Hong soon emerged as the group's guiding force, and in the summer of 1850 he led about ten thousand followers in rebellion against the Qing dynasty. On his thirty-seventh birthday, 11 January 1851, he assumed the title of "Heavenly King" and proclaimed his own dynasty, the **Taiping** tianguo ("Heavenly Kingdom of Great Peace"). Hong's followers, known as the Taipings, quickly grew from a ragtag band to a disciplined and zealous army of over one million men and women who pushed the Qing dynasty to the brink of extinction.

One of the more radical beliefs of the Taipings was the equality of men and women before God and on earth, and that belief was ironically illustrated in the political rise of a woman destined to be part of the Taipings' downfall: the Dowager Empress Cixi. Rising to behind-the-throne power in the early 1860s, Cixi helped to institute changes—putting Chinese, not Manchus, in charge of armies, for example—that worked to quell the Taiping rebels. Both the Hong-led Taiping rebellion and the imperial power of Cixi suggested the internal turmoil of a China reaching a crossroads in its history.

China was not the only land that faced serious difficulties in the nineteenth century: the Ottoman empire, the Russian empire, and Tokugawa Japan experienced problems similar to those of China during the late Qing dynasty. One problem common to the four societies was military weakness that left them vulnerable to foreign threats. The Ottoman, Russian, Qing, and Tokugawa armies all fought wars or engaged in military confrontations with the industrial lands of western Europe and the United States, and all discovered suddenly and unexpectedly that they were militarily much weaker than the industrial powers. European lands occasionally seized territories outright and either absorbed them into their own possessions or ruled them as colonies. More often, however, European and U.S. forces used their power to squeeze concessions out of militarily weak societies. They won rights for European and U.S. businesses to seek opportunities on favorable terms and enabled industrial capitalists to realize huge profits from trade and investment in militarily weak societies.

Another problem common to the four societies was internal weakness that was due to population pressure, declining agricultural productivity, famine, falling government revenue, and corruption at all levels of government. Ottoman, Russian, Chinese, and Japanese societies all experienced serious domestic turmoil, especially during the second half of the nineteenth century, as peasants mounted rebellions, dissidents struggled for reform, and political factions fought among themselves or conspired to organize coups. Military weakness often left leaders of the four societies unable to respond effectively to domestic strife, which sometimes provided western European powers and the United States with an excuse to intervene to protect their business interests.

Thus, by the late nineteenth century, the Ottoman empire, the Russian empire, Qing China, and Tokugawa Japan were societies at crossroads. Even if they undertook a program of thoroughgoing political, social, and economic reform, they might continue to experience domestic difficulties and grow progressively weaker in relation to industrial lands. Reformers in all four societies promoted plans to introduce written constitutions, limit the authority of rulers, make governments responsive to the needs and desires of the people, guarantee equality before the law, restructure educational systems, and begin processes of industrialization. Many reformers had traveled in Europe and the United States, where they experienced constitutional government and industrial society firsthand, and they sought to remodel their own societies along the lines of the industrial lands.

Vigorous reform movements emerged in all four lands, but they had very different results. In the Ottoman empire, the Russian empire, and Qing China, ruling elites and wealthy classes viewed reform warily and opposed any changes that might threaten their status. Reform in those three lands was halting, tentative, and sometimes abortive, and by the early twentieth century, the Ottoman, Romanov, and Qing dynasties were on the verge of collapse. In Japan, however, the Tokugawa dynasty fell and so was unable to resist change. Reform there was much more thorough than in the other lands, and by the early twentieth century, Japan was an emerging industrial power poised to expand its influence in the larger world.

Taiping (TEYE-pihng)

THE OTTOMAN EMPIRE IN DECLINE

During the eighteenth century the Ottoman empire experienced military reverses and challenges to its rule. By the early nineteenth century, the Ottoman state could no longer ward off European economic penetration or prevent territorial dismemberment. As Ottoman officials launched reforms to regenerate imperial vigor, Egypt and other north African provinces declared their independence, and European states seized territories in the northern and western parts of the Ottoman empire. At the same time, pressure from ethnic, religious, and nationalist groups threatened to fragment the polyglot empire. The once-powerful realm slipped into decline, its sovereignty maintained largely by the same European powers that exploited its economy.

The Nature of Decline

Military Decline

By the late seventeenth century, the Ottoman empire had reached the limits of its expansion. Ottoman armies suffered humiliating defeats on the battlefield, especially at the hands of Austrian and Russian foes. Ottoman forces lagged behind European armies in strategy, tactics, weaponry, and training. Equally serious was a breakdown in the discipline of the elite Janissary corps, which had served as the backbone of the imperial armed forces since the fifteenth century. The Janissaries repeatedly masterminded palace coups during the seventeenth and eighteenth centuries and by the nineteenth century had become a powerful political force within the Ottoman state. The Janissaries neglected their military training and turned a blind eye to advances in weapons technology. As its military capacity declined, the Ottoman realm became vulnerable to its more powerful neighbors.

Loss of military power translated into declining effectiveness of the central government, which was losing power in the provinces to its own officials. By the early nineteenth century, semi-independent governors and local notables had formed private armies of mercenaries and slaves to support the sultan in Istanbul in return for recognition of autonomy. Increasingly these independent rulers also turned fiscal and administrative institutions to their own interests, collecting taxes for themselves and sending only nominal payments to the imperial treasury, thus depriving the central state of revenue.

Territorial Losses

The Ottoman government managed to maintain its authority in Anatolia (present-day Turkey), the heart of the empire, as well as in Iraq, but it suffered serious territorial losses elsewhere. Russian forces took over poorly defended territories in the Caucasus and in central Asia, and the Austrian empire nibbled away at the western frontiers. Nationalist uprisings forced Ottoman rulers to recognize the independence of Balkan provinces, notably Greece (1830) and Serbia (1867).

Most significant, however, was the loss of Egypt. In 1798 the ambitious French general Napoleon invaded Egypt

By the latter part of the nineteenth century, European imperialism directly affected the fortunes of the Ottoman empire. This undated political cartoon shows England as a lion and Russia as a bear threatening Turkey (shown as a turkey). The illustration is labeled "Be my ally, or I'll give you the worst thrashing you ever had in your life."

in hopes of using it as a springboard for an attack on the British empire in India. His campaign was a miserable failure: Napoleon had to abandon his army and sneak back to France, where he proceeded to overthrow the Directory. But the invasion sparked turmoil in Egypt, as local elites battled to seize power after Napoleon's departure. The ultimate victor was the energetic general Muhammad Ali, who built a powerful army modeled on European forces and ruled Egypt from 1805 to 1848. He drafted peasants to serve as infantry, and he hired French and Italian officers to train his troops. He also launched a program of industrialization, concentrating on cotton textiles and armaments. Although he remained nominally subordinate to the Ottoman sultan, by 1820 he had established himself as the effective ruler of Egypt, which was the most powerful land in the Muslim world. He even invaded Syria and Anatolia, threatening to capture Istanbul and topple the Ottoman state. Indeed, the Ottoman dynasty survived only because British forces intervened out of fear that Ottoman collapse would result in a sudden and dangerous expansion of Russian influence. Nevertheless, Muhammad Ali made Egypt an essentially autonomous region within the Ottoman empire.

Economic ills aggravated the military and political problems of the Ottoman state. The volume of trade passing through the Ottoman empire declined throughout the

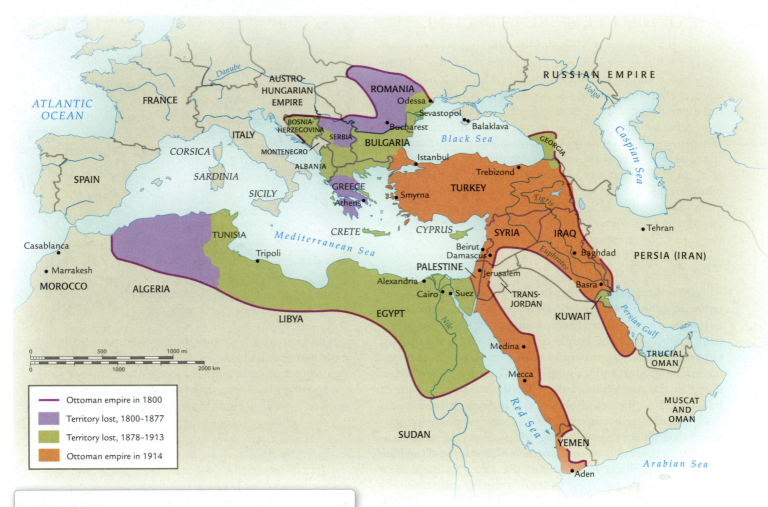

MAP 31.1

Territorial losses of the Ottoman empire, 1800–1923.

Compare the borders of the Ottoman empire in 1800 with what was left of the empire in 1914.

What might have been the strategic value of the remaining Ottoman territories?

later seventeenth and eighteenth centuries, as European merchants increasingly circumvented Ottoman intermediaries and traded directly with their counterparts in India and China. By the eighteenth century the focus of European trade had shifted to the Atlantic Ocean basin, where the Ottomans had no presence at all.

Economic Difficulties

Meanwhile, as European producers became more efficient in the eighteenth and nineteenth centuries, their textiles and manufactured goods began to flow into the Ottoman empire. Because those items were inexpensive and high-quality products, they placed considerable pressure on Ottoman artisans and crafts workers, who frequently led urban riots to protest foreign im-

ports. Ottoman exports consisted largely of raw materials such as grain, cotton, hemp, indigo, and opium, but they did not offset the value of imported European manufactures. Gradually, the Ottoman empire moved toward fiscal insolvency and financial dependency. After the middle of the nineteenth century, economic development in the Ottoman empire depended heavily on foreign loans, as European capital financed the construction of railroads, utilities, and mining enterprises. Interest payments grew to the point that they consumed more than half of the empire's revenues. In 1882 the Ottoman state was unable to pay interest on its loans and had no choice but to accept foreign administration of its debts.

The Capitulations

Nothing symbolized foreign influence more than the capitulations, agreements that exempted European visitors from Ottoman law and provided European powers with extraterritoriality—the right to exercise jurisdiction over their own citizens according to their own laws. The practice dated back to the sixteenth century, when Ottoman sultans signed capitulation treaties to avoid the burden of administering justice for communities of foreign merchants. By the nineteenth century, however, Ottoman officials regarded the capitulations as humiliating intrusions on their sovereignty. Capitulations also served as instruments of economic penetration by European businesspeople who established tax-exempt banks and commercial enterprises in the Ottoman empire, and they permitted foreign governments to levy duties on goods sold in Ottoman ports.

By the early twentieth century, the Ottoman state lacked the resources to maintain its costly bureaucracy. Expenditures exceeded revenues, and the state experienced growing difficulty paying the salaries of its employees in the palace household, the military, and the religious hierarchy. Declining incomes led to reduced morale, recruitment difficulties, and a rise in corruption. Increased taxation designed to offset revenue losses only led to increased exploitation of the peasantry and a decline in agricultural production. The Ottoman empire was ailing, and it needed a major restructuring to survive.

Reform and Reorganization

In response to recurring and deepening crises, Ottoman leaders launched a series of reforms designed to strengthen and preserve the state. Reform efforts began as early as the seventeenth century, when sultans sought to limit taxation, increase agricultural production, and end official corruption. Reform continued in the eighteenth century, as Sultan Selim III (reigned 1789–1807) embarked on a program to remodel his army along the lines of European forces. But the establishment of a new crack fighting force, trained by European instructors and equipped with modern weapons, threatened the elite Janissary corps, which reacted violently by rising in revolt, killing the new troops, and locking up the sultan. When Selim's successor tried to revive the new military force, rampaging Janissaries killed all male members of the dynasty save one, Selim's cousin Mahmud II, who became sultan (reigned 1808–1839).

The Reforms of Mahmud II

The encroachment of European powers and the separatist ambitions of local rulers persuaded Mahmud to launch his own reform program. Politically savvy,

Sultan Abdül Hamid II ruled the Ottoman empire from 1876 to 1909, when the Young Turks deposed him and sent him into exile.

Mahmud ensured that his reforms were perceived not as dangerous infidel innovations but, rather, as a restoration of the traditional Ottoman military. Nevertheless, his proposal for a new European-style army in 1826 brought him into conflict with the Janissaries. When the Janissaries mutinied in protest, Mahmud had them massacred by troops loyal to the sultan. That incident cleared the way for a series of reforms that unfolded during the last thirteen years of Mahmud's reign.

Mahmud's program remodeled Ottoman institutions along western European lines. Highest priority went to the creation of a more effective army. European drill masters dressed Ottoman soldiers in European-style uniforms and instructed them in European weapons and tactics. Before long, Ottoman recruits were studying at military and engineering schools that taught European curricula. Mahmud's reforms went beyond military affairs. His government created a system of secondary education for boys to facilitate the transition from mosque schools, which provided most primary education, to newly established scientific, technical, and military academies. Mahmud also tried to transfer power from traditional elites to the sultan and his cabinet by taxing rural landlords, abolishing the system of military land grants, and undermining the ulama, the Islamic leadership. To make his authority more effective, the sultan established European-style ministries, constructed new roads, built telegraph lines, and inaugurated a postal service. By the time of Mahmud's death in 1839, the Ottoman empire had shrunk in size, but it was also more manageable and powerful than it had been since the early seventeenth century.

Legal and Educational Reform Continuing defeats on the battlefield and the rise of separatist movements among subject peoples prompted the ruling classes to undertake more radical restructuring of the Ottoman state. The tempo of reform increased rapidly during the Tanzimat ("reorganization") era (1839–1876). Once again, the army was a principal target of reform efforts, but legal and educational reforms also had wide-ranging implications for Ottoman society. In designing their program, Tanzimat reformers drew considerable inspiration from Enlightenment thought and the constitutional foundations of western European states.

Tanzimat reformers attacked Ottoman law with the aim of making it acceptable to Europeans so they could have the capitulations lifted and recover Ottoman sovereignty. Using the French legal system as a guide, reformers promulgated a commercial code (1850), a penal code (1858), a maritime code (1863), and a new civil code (1870–1876). Tanzimat reformers also issued decrees designed to safeguard the rights of subjects. Key among them were measures that guaranteed public trials, rights of privacy, and equality before the law for all Ottoman subjects, whether Muslim or not. Matters pertaining to marriage and divorce still fell under religious law. But because state courts administered the new laws, legal reform undermined the ulama and enhanced the authority of the Ottoman state. Educational reforms also undermined the ulama, who controlled religious education for Muslims. A comprehensive plan for educational reform, introduced in 1846, provided for a complete system of primary and secondary schools leading to university-level instruction, all under the supervision of the state ministry of education. A still more ambitious plan, inaugurated in 1869, provided for free and compulsory primary education.

Opposition to the Tanzimat Although reform and reorganization strengthened Ottoman society, the Tanzimat provoked spirited opposition from several distinct quarters. Harsh criticism came from religious conservatives, who argued that reformers posed a threat to the empire's Islamic foundation. Many devout Muslims viewed the extension of legal equality to Jews and Christians as an act contrary to the basic principles of Islamic law. Even some minority leaders opposed legal equality, fearing that it would diminish their own position as intermediaries between their communities and the Ottoman state. Criticism arose also from a group known collectively as the Young Ottomans. Although they did not share a common political or religious program—their views ranged from secular revolution to uncompromising Islam—Young Ottomans agitated for individual freedom, local autonomy, and political decentralization. Many Young Ottomans desired the establishment of a constitutional government along the lines of the British system. A fourth and perhaps the most dangerous critique of Tanzimat emerged from within the Ottoman bureaucracy itself. In part because of their exclusion from power, high-level bureaucrats were determined to impose checks on the sultan's power by forcing him to accept a constitution and, if necessary, even to depose the ruler.

The Young Turk Era

Reform and Repression In 1876 a group of radical dissidents from the Ottoman bureaucracy seized power in a coup, formed a cabinet that included partisans of reform, and installed Abdül Hamid II as sultan (reigned 1876–1909). Convinced of the need to check the sultan's power, reformers persuaded Abdül Hamid to accept a constitution that limited his authority and established a representative government. Within a year, however, the sultan suspended the constitution, dissolved parliament, exiled many liberals, and executed others. For thirty years he ruled autocratically in an effort to rescue the empire from dismemberment by European powers. He continued to develop the army and administration according to Tanzimat

Young Turks celebrate the success of their coup, which forced the sultan to establish a constitutional government in 1908.

sources from the past

Proclamation of the Young Turks

Beginning in the 1890s the Ottoman Society for Union and Progress, better known as the Young Turk Party, started agitating for the resignation of the Ottoman sultan Abdül Hamid and the restoration of the constitution of 1876. After years of underground activity, the Young Turks forced the sultan to reestablish a parliamentary government and reinstate the constitution in 1908. Shortly thereafter the Young Turks outlined their plans for a new Turkish state.

1. The basis for the Constitution will be respect for the predominance of the national will. One of the consequences of this principle will be to require without delay the responsibility of the minister before the Chamber, and, consequently, to consider the minister as having resigned, when he does not have a majority of the votes of the Chamber.

2. Provided that the number of senators does not exceed one third the number of deputies, the Senate will be named (which is not provided for in article 62 of the Constitution) as follows: one third by the Sultan and two thirds by the nation, and the term of senators will be of limited duration.

3. It will be demanded that all Ottoman subjects having completed their twentieth year, regardless of whether they possess property or fortune, shall have the right to vote. Those who have lost their civil rights will naturally be deprived of this right.

4. It will be demanded that the right freely to constitute political groups be inserted in a precise fashion in the constitutional charter, in order that article 1 of the Constitution of 1293 (1876) be respected. . . .

7. The Turkish tongue will remain the official state language. Official correspondence and discussion will take place in Turk. . . .

9. Every citizen will enjoy complete liberty and equality, regardless of nationality or religion, and be submitted to the same obligations. All Ottomans, being equal before the law as regards rights and duties relative to the State, are eligible for government posts, according to their individual capacity and their education. Non-Muslims will be equally liable to the military law.

10. The free exercise of the religious privileges which have been accorded to different nationalities will remain intact. . . .

14. Provided that the property rights of landholders are not infringed upon (for such rights must be respected and must remain intact, according to the law), it will be proposed that peasants be permitted to acquire land, and they will be accorded means to borrow money at a moderate rate. . . .

16. Education will be free. Every Ottoman citizen, within the limits of the prescriptions of the Constitution, may operate a private school in accordance with the special laws.

17. All schools will operate under the surveillance of the state. In order to obtain for Ottoman citizens an education of a homogeneous and uniform character, the official schools will be open, their instruction will be free, and all nationalities will be admitted. Instruction in Turk will be obligatory in public schools. In official schools, public instruction will be free.

Secondary and higher education will be given in the public and official schools indicated above; it will use the Turkish tongue as a basis. . . . Schools of commerce, agriculture and industry will be opened with the goal of developing the resources of the country.

For Further Reflection

■ How do the plans of the Young Turks privilege their own age cohort within the Ottoman empire, particularly in regard to voting rights and education?

Source: Rondo Cameron, ed. *Civilization since Waterloo: A Book of Source Readings.* Itasca, Ill.: F. E. Peacock, 1971, pp. 245–46.

principles, and he oversaw the formation of a police force, educational reforms, economic development, and the construction of railroads.

Abdül Hamid's despotic rule generated many liberal opposition groups. Though intended to strengthen the state, reform and reorganization actually undermined the position of the sultan. As Ottoman bureaucrats and army officers received an education in European curricula, they not only learned modern science and technology but also became acquainted with European political, social, and cultural traditions. Many of them fell out of favor with Abdül Hamid and spent years in exile, where they experienced European society firsthand. Educated subjects came to believe that the biggest problem of the Ottoman empire was the political structure that vested unchecked power in the sultan. For these dissidents, Ottoman society was in dire need of political reform and especially of a written constitution that defined and limited the sultan's power.

The Young Turks The most active dissident organization was the Ottoman Society for Union and Progress, better known as the Young Turk Party, although many of its members were neither young nor Turkish. Founded in 1889 by exiled Ottoman subjects living in Paris, the Young Turk Party vigorously promoted reform, and its members made effective use of recently established newspapers to spread their message. Young Turks called for universal suffrage, equality before the law, freedom of religion, free public education, secularization of the state, and the emancipation of women. In 1908 the Young Turks inspired an army coup that forced Abdül Hamid to restore parliament and the constitution of 1876. In 1909 they dethroned him and established Mehmed V Rashid (reigned 1909–1918) as a puppet sultan. Throughout the Young Turk era (1908–1918), Ottoman sultans reigned but no longer ruled.

While pursuing reform within Ottoman society, the Young Turks sought to maintain Turkish hegemony in the larger empire. They worked to make Turkish the official language of the empire, even though many subjects spoke Arabic or a Slavic language as their native tongue. Thus Young Turk policies aggravated tensions between Turkish rulers and subject peoples outside the Anatolian heartland of the Ottoman empire. Syria and Iraq were especially active regions of Arab resistance to Ottoman rule. In spite of their efforts to shore up the ailing empire, reformers could not turn the tide of decline: Ottoman armies continued to lose wars, and subject peoples continued to seek autonomy or independence. By the early twentieth century, the Ottoman empire survived principally because European diplomats could not agree on how to dispose of the empire without upsetting the European balance of power.

Legend:
- Russian empire, 1801–1855
- Acquisitions through 1855
- Acquisitions through 1914
- Boundary of Russian empire, 1914

MAP 31.2

The Russian empire, 1801–1914.

Note the sheer size of Russian territory in this period, and that the state included part of Europe, central Asia, and east Asia.

How would straddling so much space and so many cultures have affected the process of industrialization and nationalism in Russia?

THE RUSSIAN EMPIRE UNDER PRESSURE

Like the Ottoman empire, the Russian empire experienced battlefield reverses that laid bare the economic and technological disparity between Russia and western European powers. Determined to preserve Russia's status as a great land power, the tsarist government embarked on a program of reform. The keystone of those efforts was the emancipation of the serfs. Social reform paved the way for government-sponsored industrialization, which began to transform Russian society during the last decades of the nineteenth century. Political liberalization did not accompany social and economic reform, because the tsars refused to yield their autocratic powers. The oppressive political environment sparked opposition movements that turned increasingly radical in the late nineteenth century. In the early twentieth century, domestic discontent reached crisis proportions and exploded in revolution.

Military Defeat and Social Reform

The nineteenth-century tsars ruled a multiethnic, multilingual, multicultural empire that stretched from Poland to the Pacific Ocean. Only about half the population spoke the Russian language or observed the Russian Orthodox faith. The Romanov tsars ruled their diverse and sprawling realm through an autocratic regime in which all initiative came from

the central administration. The tsars enjoyed the support of the Russian Orthodox church and a powerful class of nobles who owned most of the land and were exempt from taxes and military duty. Peasants made up the vast majority of the population, and most of them were serfs bound to the lands that they cultivated. Serfdom was almost as cruel and exploitative as slavery, but most landowners, including the state, considered it a guarantee of social stability.

The Crimean War A respected and feared military power, Russia maintained its tradition of conquest and expansion. During the nineteenth century the Russian empire expanded in three directions: east into Manchuria, south into the Caucasus and central Asia, and southwest toward the Mediterranean. This last thrust led to interference in the Balkan provinces of the Ottoman empire. After defeating Turkish forces in a war from 1828 to 1829, Russia tried to establish a protectorate over the weakening Ottoman empire. This expansive effort threatened to upset the balance of power in Europe, which led to military conflict between Russia and a coalition including Britain, France, the kingdom of Sardinia, and the Ottoman empire. The Crimean War (1853–1856) clearly revealed the weakness of the Russian empire, which could hold its own against Ottoman and Qing forces, but not against the industrial powers of western Europe. In September 1854, allied forces mounted a campaign against Sevastopol in the Crimean peninsula, headquarters of Russia's Black Sea Fleet. Unable to mobilize, equip, and transport troops to defeat European forces that operated under a mediocre command, Russian armies suffered devastating and humiliating defeats on their own territory. Russia's economy could not support the tsars' expansionist ambitions, and the Crimean War clearly demonstrated the weakness of an agrarian economy based on unfree labor. Military defeat compelled the tsarist autocracy to reevaluate the Russian social order and undertake an extensive restructuring program.

Emancipation of the Serfs The key to social reform in Russia was emancipation of the serfs. Opposition to serfdom had grown steadily since the eighteenth century, not only among radicals, but also among high officials. Although some Russians objected to serfdom on moral grounds, many believed that it had become an obstacle to economic development and a viable state. Besides being economically inefficient, serfdom was a source of rural instability and peasant revolt: hundreds of insurrections broke out during the first four decades of the nineteenth century. As Tsar Alexander II (reigned 1855–1881) succinctly suggested to the nobility of Moscow, "It is better to abolish serfdom from above than to wait until the serfs begin to liberate themselves from below." Accordingly, in 1861 the tsar abolished the institution of serfdom, though it remained in practice for decades to come.

The government sought to balance the interests of lords and serfs, but on balance the terms of emancipation were unfavorable to most peasants. The government compensated

landowners for the loss of their land and the serfs who had worked it. Serfs won their freedom, had their labor obligations gradually canceled, and gained opportunities to become landowners. But the peasants won few political rights, and they had to pay a redemption tax for most of the lands they received. Many disappointed peasants believed that their rulers forced them to pay for land that was theirs by right. A few peasants prospered and improved their position as the result of emancipation, but most found themselves in debt for the rest of their lives—a source of alienation and radicalization. Emancipation resulted in little if any increase in agricultural production.

Political and Legal Reform   Other important reforms came in the wake of the serfs' emancipation. To deal with local issues of health, education, and welfare, the government created elected district assemblies, or *zemstvos,* in 1864. Although all classes, including peasants, elected representatives to these assemblies, the *zemstvos* remained subordinate to the tsarist autocracy, which retained exclusive authority over national issues, and the landowning nobility, which possessed a disproportionately large share of both votes and seats. Legal reform was more fruitful than experi-

mentation with representative government. The revision of the judiciary system in 1864 created a system of law courts based on western European models, replete with independent judges and a system of appellate courts. Legal reforms also instituted trial by jury for criminal offenses and elected justices of the peace who dealt with minor offenses. These reforms encouraged the emergence of attorneys and other legal experts, whose professional standards contributed to a decline in judicial corruption.

Industrialization

Social and political reform coincided with industrialization in nineteenth-century Russia. Tsar Alexander II emancipated the serfs partly with the intention of creating a mobile labor force for emerging industries, and the tsarist government encouraged industrialization as a way of strengthening the Russian empire. Thus, although Russian industrialization took place within a framework of capitalism, it differed from western European industrialization in that the motivation for development was political and military and the driving force was government policy rather than entrepreneurial initiative. Industrialization proceeded slowly at first, but it surged during the last two decades of the nineteenth century.

The Witte System   The prime mover behind Russian industrialization was Count Sergei Witte, minister of finance from 1892 to 1903. His first budget, submitted to the government in 1893, outlined his aims as "removing the unfavorable conditions which hamper the economic development of the country" and "kindling a healthy spirit of enterprise." Availing himself of the full power of the state, Witte implemented policies designed to stimulate economic development. The centerpiece of his industrial policy was an ambitious program of railway construction, which linked the far-flung regions of the Russian empire and also stimulated the development of other industries. Most important of the new lines was the trans-Siberian railway, which opened Siberia to large-scale settlement, exploitation, and industrialization. To raise domestic capital for industry, Witte remodeled the state bank and encouraged the establishment of savings banks. Witte supported infant industries with high protective tariffs while also securing large foreign loans from western Europe to finance industrialization. His plan worked. French and Belgian capital played a key role in developing the steel and coal industries, and British funds supported the booming petroleum industry in the Caucasus.

Tsar Alexander II of Russia. After signing the Treaty of Paris in 1856, ending the Crimean War, Alexander abolished serfdom in the Russian empire.

Industrial Discontent   For a decade the Witte system played a crucial role in the industrialization of Russia, but peasant rebellions and strikes by industrial workers indicated that large segments of the population were unwilling to tolerate the low standard of living that Witte's policy entailed. Recently freed serfs often did not appreciate factory work, which forced them to follow new routines and adapt to the rhythms of industrial machinery. Industrial growth

Russian merchants in nineteenth-century Novgorod wear both western European and traditional Russian dress while taking tea. What does this mixed fashion suggest about the Russian society and its economic evolution?

began to generate an urban working class, which endured conditions similar to those experienced by workers in other societies during the early stages of industrialization. Employers kept wages of overworked and poorly housed workers at the barest minimum. The industrial sections of St. Petersburg and Moscow became notorious for the miserable working and living conditions of factory laborers. In 1897 the government limited the maximum working day to 11.5 hours, but that measure did little to alleviate the plight of workers. The government prohibited the formation of trade unions and outlawed strikes, which continued to occur in spite of the restrictions. Economic exploitation and the lack of political freedom made workers increasingly receptive to revolutionary propaganda, and underground movements soon developed among them.

Not everyone was dissatisfied with the results of intensified industrialization. Besides foreign investors, a growing Russian business class benefited from government policy that protected domestic industries and its profits. Russian entrepreneurs reaped rich rewards for their roles in economic development, and they had little complaint with the political system. In contrast to western European capitalists, who had both material and ideological reasons to challenge the power of absolute monarchs and the nobility, Russian businesspeople generally did not challenge the tsarist autocracy.

Repression and Revolution

Protest During the last three decades of the nineteenth century, antigovernment protest and revolutionary activity increased. Hopes aroused by government reforms gave impetus to reform movements, and social tensions arising from industrialization fueled protest by groups whose aims became increasingly radical. Peasants seethed with discontent because they had little or no land and, increasingly, mobile dissidents spread rebellious ideas between industrial cities. At the center of opposition were university students and a class of intellectuals collectively known as the intelligentsia. Their goals and methods varied, but they generally sought substantial political reform and thorough social change. Most dissidents drew inspiration from western European socialism, but they despised the individualism, materialism, and unbridled capitalism of western Europe and thus worked toward a socialist system more in keeping with Russian cultural traditions. Many revolutionaries were anarchists, who on principle opposed all forms of government and believed that individual freedom cannot be realized until all government is abolished. Some anarchists relied on terror tactics and assassination to achieve their goals. Insofar as they had a positive political program, the anarchists wanted to vest all authority in local governing councils elected by universal suffrage.

Repression Some activists saw the main potential for revolutionary action in the countryside, and between 1873 and 1876 hundreds of anarchists and other radicals traveled to rural areas to enlighten and rouse the peasantry. The peasants did not understand their impassioned speeches, but the police did and soon arrested the idealists. Tsarist authorities sentenced some to prison and banished others to the remote provinces of Siberia. Frightened by manifestations of radicalism, tsarist authorities resorted to repression: they censored publications and sent secret police to infiltrate and break up dissident organizations. Repression, however, only radicalized

Japanese infantry charging during the Russo-Japanese war.

revolutionaries further and encouraged them to engage in conspiratorial activities.

In the Baltic provinces, Poland, the Ukraine, Georgia, and central Asia, dissidents opposed the tsarist autocracy on ethnic as well as political and social grounds. In those lands, subject peoples speaking their own languages often used schools and political groups as foundations for separatist movements as they sought autonomy or independence from the Russian empire. Tsarist officials responded with a heavy-handed program of Russification to repress the use of languages other than Russian and to restrict educational opportunities to those loyal to the tsarist state. Throughout the Russian empire, Jews also were targets of suspicion, and tsarist authorities tolerated frequent pogroms (anti-Jewish riots) by subjects jealous of their Jewish neighbors' success in business affairs. To escape this violence, Jews migrated by the hundreds of thousands to western Europe and the United States in the late nineteenth century.

Terrorism In 1876 a recently formed group called the Land and Freedom Party began to promote the assassination of prominent officials as a means to pressure the government into political reform. In 1879 a terrorist faction of the party, the People's Will, resolved to assassinate Alexander II, who had emancipated the serfs and had launched a program of political and social reform. After several unsuccessful attempts, an assassin exploded a bomb under Alexander's carriage in 1881. The first blast did little damage, but as Alexander inspected his carriage, a second and more powerful explosion killed the reforming tsar. The attack brought the era of reform to an end and prompted the tsarist autocracy to adopt an uncompromising policy of repression.

In 1894 Nicholas II (reigned 1894–1917) ascended the throne. A well-intentioned but weak ruler, Nicholas championed oppression and police control. To deflect attention from domestic issues and neutralize revolutionary movements, the tsar's government embarked on expansionist ventures in east Asia. Russian designs on Korea and Manchuria clashed with similar Japanese intentions, leading to a rivalry that ended in war. The Russo-Japanese war began

with a Japanese surprise attack on the Russian naval squadron at Port Arthur in February 1904 and ended in May 1905 with the destruction of the Russian navy.

The Revolution of 1905 Russian military defeats brought to a head simmering political and social discontent and triggered widespread disturbances. In January 1905 a group of workers marched on the tsar's Winter Palace in St. Petersburg to petition Nicholas for a popularly elected assembly and other political concessions. Government troops met the petitioners with rifle fire, killing 130. The news of this Bloody Sunday massacre caused an angry uproar throughout the empire that culminated in labor unrest, peasant insurrections, student demonstrations, and mutinies in both the army and the navy. Organizing themselves at the village level, peasants discussed seizing the property of their landlords. Urban workers created new councils known as soviets to organize strikes and negotiate with employers and government authorities. Elected delegates from factories and workshops served as members of these soviets.

Revolutionary turmoil paralyzed Russian cities and forced the government to make concessions. Sergei Witte, whom Nicholas had appointed to conduct peace negotiations with Japan, urged the tsar to create an elected legislative assembly. The tsar reluctantly consented and permitted the establishment of the Duma, Russia's first parliamentary institution. Although the Duma lacked the power to create or bring down governments, from the Romanov perspective this act was a major concession. Still, the creation of the Duma did not end unrest. Between 1905 and 1907 disorder continued, and violence flared especially in the Baltic provinces, Poland, the Ukraine, Georgia, and central Asia, where ethnic tensions added to revolutionary sentiments. Through bloody reprisals the government eventually restored order, but the hour was late for the Romanov dynasty.

THE CHINESE EMPIRE UNDER SIEGE

The Chinese empire and the Qing dynasty experienced even more difficulties than did the Ottoman and Russian empires during the nineteenth century. European powers inflicted military defeats on Qing forces and compelled China's leaders to accept a series of humiliating treaties. The provisions of these treaties undermined Chinese sovereignty, carved China into spheres of influence that set the stage for economic exploitation, and handicapped the Qing dynasty's ability to deal with domestic disorder. As the government tried to cope with foreign challenges, it also faced dangerous internal upheavals, the most important of which was the Taiping rebellion. Caught between aggressive foreigners and insurgent rebels, China's ruling elites developed reform programs to maintain social order, strengthen the state, and preserve the Qing dynasty. The reforms had limited effect, however, and by the early twentieth century, China was in a seriously weakened condition.

The Opium War and the Unequal Treaties

In 1759 the Qianlong emperor restricted the European commercial presence in China to the waterfront at Guangzhou, where European merchants could establish warehouses. There, Chinese authorities controlled not only European merchants but also the terms of trade. Foreign merchants could deal only with specially licensed Chinese firms known as *cohongs,* which bought and sold goods at set prices and operated under strict regulations established by the government. Besides the expense and inconvenience of the *cohong* system, European merchants had to cope with a market that had little demand for European products. As a result, European merchants paid for Chinese silk, porcelain, lacquerware, and tea largely with silver bullion.

The Opium Trade Seeking increased profits in the late eighteenth century, officials of the British East India Company sought alternatives to bullion to exchange for Chinese goods. They gradually turned to trade in a product that was as profitable as it was criminal—opium. Using Turkish and Persian expertise, the East India Company grew opium in India and shipped it to China, where company officials exchanged it for Chinese silver coin. The silver then flowed back to British-controlled Calcutta and London, where company merchants used it to buy Chinese products in Guangzhou. The opium trade expanded rapidly: annual imports of opium in the early nineteenth century amounted to about 4,500 chests, each weighing 60 kilograms (133 pounds), but by 1839 some 40,000 chests of opium entered China annually to satisfy the habits of drug addicts. With the help of this new commodity, the East India Company easily paid for luxury Chinese products.

Trade in opium was illegal, but it continued unabated for decades because Chinese authorities made little effort to enforce the law. Indeed, corrupt officials often benefited personally by allowing the illegal trade to go on. By the late 1830s, however, government officials had become aware that China had a trade problem and a drug problem as well. The opium trade not only drained large quantities of silver bullion from China but also created serious social problems in southern China. When government authorities took steps in 1838 to halt the illicit trade, British merchants started losing money. In 1839 the Chinese government stepped up its campaign by charging the incorruptible Lin Zexu with the task of destroying the opium trade. Commissioner Lin acted quickly, confiscating and destroying some 20,000 chests of opium. His uncompromising policy ignited a war that ended in a humiliating defeat for China.

The Opium War Outraged by the Chinese action against opium, British commercial agents pressed their government into a military retaliation designed to reopen the opium trade. The ensuing conflict, known as the Opium War (1839–1842), made plain the military power differential between Europe and China. In the initial stages of the conflict, British

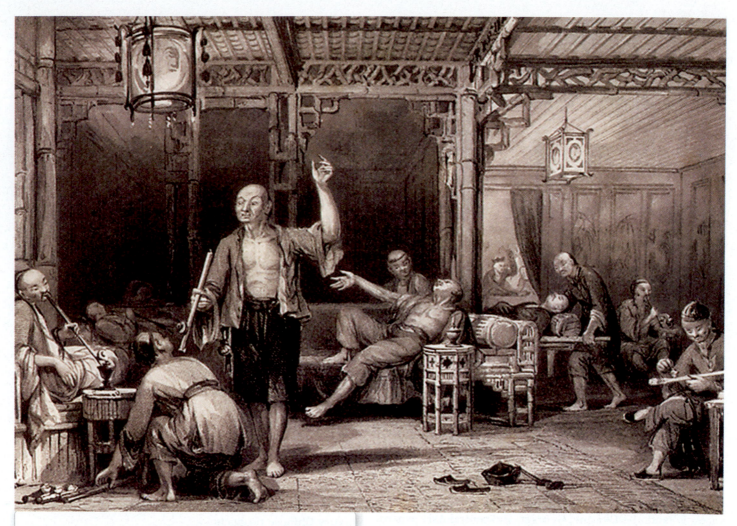

Chinese opium smokers. Chinese efforts to stop opium imports led to a humiliating defeat in the Opium War.

naval vessels easily demonstrated their superiority on the seas. Meanwhile, equipped only with swords, knives, spears, and occasionally muskets, the defenders of Chinese coastal towns were no match for the controlled firepower of well-drilled British infantry armed with rifles. But neither the destruction of Chinese war fleets nor the capture of coastal forts and towns persuaded the Chinese to sue for peace.

British forces broke the military stalemate when they decided to strike at China's jugular vein—the Grand Canal, which linked the Yangzi and Yellow River valleys—with the aid of steam-powered gunboats. Armed, shallow-draft steamers could travel speedily up and down rivers, projecting the military advantage that European ships enjoyed on the high seas deep into interior regions. In May 1842 a British armada of seventy ships—led by the gunboat *Nemesis*—advanced up the Yangzi River. The British fleet encountered little resistance, and by the time it reached the intersection of the river and the Grand Canal, the Chinese government had sued for peace. China experienced similar military setbacks throughout the second half of the nineteenth century in conflicts with Britain and France (1856–1858), France (1884–1885), and Japan (1894–1895).

Unequal Treaties In the wake of those confrontations came a series of pacts collectively known in China as unequal treaties, which curtailed China's sovereignty. Beginning with the Treaty of Nanjing, which Britain forced China to accept at the conclusion of the Opium War in 1842, these agreements guided Chinese relations with foreign states until 1943. The Treaty of Nanjing (1842) ceded Hong Kong Island in perpetuity to Britain, opened five Chinese ports—including Guangzhou and Shanghai—to commerce and residence, compelled the Qing government to extend most-favored-nation status to Britain, and granted extraterritoriality to British subjects, which meant they were not subject to Chinese laws. The Treaty of Nanjing governed relations only between Britain and China, but France, Germany, Den-

sources from the past

Letter of Lin Zexu to Queen Victoria

In 1838 Qing emperor Daoguang sent Lin Zexu to Guang-zhou to put an end to imports of opium into China. A leading Confucian scholar, Lin worked to persuade Chinese and foreigners alike that opium was a harmful and evil drug. In 1839 he composed a letter to Great Britain's Queen Victoria seeking her support in halting the flow of opium. Although never delivered, the letter illustrates Lin's efforts to stem the flow of opium by reason and negotiation before he resorted to sterner measures.

You have traded in China for almost 200 years, and as a result, your country has become wealthy and prosperous.

As this trade has lasted for a long time, there are bound to be unscrupulous as well as honest traders. Among the unscrupulous are those who bring opium to China to harm the Chinese; they succeed so well that this poison has spread far and wide in all the provinces. You, I hope, will certainly agree that people who pursue material gains to the great detriment of the welfare of others can be neither tolerated by Heaven nor endured by men. . . .

I have heard that the areas under your direct jurisdiction such as London, Scotland, and Ireland do not produce opium; it is produced instead in your Indian possessions such as Bengal, Madras, Bombay, Patna, and Malwa. In these possessions the English people not only plant opium poppies that stretch from one mountain to another but also open factories to manufacture this terrible drug. As months accumulate and years pass by, the poison they have produced increases in its wicked intensity, and its repugnant odor reaches as high as the sky. Heaven is furious with anger, and all the gods are moaning with pain! It is hereby suggested that you destroy and plow under all of these opium plants and grow food crops instead, while issuing an order to punish severely anyone who dares to plant opium poppies again. If you adopt this policy of love so as to produce good and exterminate evil, Heaven will protect you, and gods will bring you good fortune. Moreover, you will enjoy a long life and be rewarded with a multitude of children and grandchildren! . . .

The present law calls for the imposition of the death sentence on any Chinese who has peddled or smoked opium. Since a Chinese could not peddle or smoke opium if foreigners had not brought it to China, it is clear that the true culprits of a Chinese's death as a result of an opium conviction are the opium traders from foreign countries. Being the cause of other people's death, why should they themselves be spared from capital punishment? A murderer of one person is subject to the death sentence; just imagine how many people opium has killed! This is the rationale behind the new law which says that any foreigner who brings opium to China will be sentenced to death by hanging or beheading. Our purpose is to eliminate this poison once and for all and to the benefit of all mankind. . . .

Our Celestial Empire towers over all other countries in virtue and possesses a power great and awesome enough to carry out its wishes. But we will not prosecute a person without warning him in advance; that is why we have made our law explicit and clear. If the merchants of your honorable country wish to enjoy trade with us on a permanent basis, they must fearfully observe our law by cutting off, once and for all, the supply of opium. Under no circumstance should they test our intention to enforce the law by deliberately violating it.

For Further Reflection

■ How does Lin Zexu convey his distaste for opium in the descriptive terms he attaches to the drug, and how do the punishments inflicted on opium peddlers suggest Lin Zexu's perception of opium's threat to China?

Source: Dan J. Li. *China in Transition*. New York: Van Nostrand, 1969, pp. 64–67.

mark, the Netherlands, Spain, Belgium, Austria-Hungary, the United States, and Japan later concluded similar unequal treaties with China. Collectively these treaties broadened the concessions given to foreign powers; they legalized the opium trade, permitted the establishment of Christian missions throughout China, and opened additional treaty ports. To ease sales of foreign goods, various treaties also prevented the Qing government from levying tariffs on imports to protect domestic industries. By 1900 ninety Chinese ports were under the effective control of foreign powers, foreign merchants controlled much of the Chinese economy, Christian missionaries sought converts throughout China, and foreign gunboats patrolled Chinese waters. Several treaties also released Korea, Vietnam, and Burma (now known as Myanmar) from Chinese authority and thereby dismantled the Chinese system of tributary states.

The Taiping Rebellion

The debilitation of the Chinese empire at the end of the nineteenth century was as much a result of internal turmoil

MAP 31.3

East Asia in the nineteenth century.
Notice the division of China, which technically remained a sovereign nation, into spheres of influence by various European nations and Japan.

What impact would such spheres of influence have had on the Chinese government in Beijing?

as it was a consequence of foreign intrusion. Large-scale rebellions in the later nineteenth century reflected the increasing poverty and discontent of the Chinese peasantry. Between 1800 and 1900 China's population rose by almost 50 percent, from 330 million to 475 million. The amount of land under cultivation increased only slowly during the same period, so population growth strained Chinese resources. The concentration of land in the hands of wealthy elites aggravated peasant discontent, as did widespread corruption of government officials and increasing drug addiction. After 1850, rebellions erupted throughout China: the Nian rebellion (1851–1868) in the northeast, the Muslim rebellion (1855–1873) in the southwest, and the Tungan rebellion (1862–1878) in the northwest. Most dangerous of all was the Taiping rebellion (1850–1864), which raged throughout most of China and brought the Qing dynasty to the brink of collapse.

The Taiping Program The village schoolteacher Hong Xiuquan provided both inspiration and leadership for the Taiping rebellion. His call for the destruction of the Qing dynasty and his program for the radical transformation of Chinese society appealed to millions of men and women. The Qing dynasty had ruled China since 1644, and Qing elites had adapted to Chinese ways, but many native Chinese subjects despised the Manchu ruling class as foreigners. The Taiping reform program contained many radical features that appealed to discontented subjects, including the abolition of private property, the creation of communal wealth to be shared according to needs, the prohibition of footbinding and concubinage, free public edcation, simplification of the written language, and literacy for the masses. Some Taiping leaders also called for the establishment of democratic political institutions and the building of an industrial society. Although they divided their army into separate divisions of men and women soldiers, the Taipings decreed the equality of men and women. Taiping regulations prohibited sexual intercourse among their followers, including married couples, but Hong and other high leaders maintained large harems.

After sweeping through southeastern China, Hong and his followers in the Society of God Worshipers took Nanjing in 1853 and made it the capital of their Taiping ("Great Peace") kingdom. From Nanjing they campaigned throughout China, and as the rebels passed through the countryside whole towns and villages joined them—often voluntarily, but sometimes under coercion. By 1855 a million Taipings were poised to attack Beijing. Qing forces repelled them, but five years later, firmly entrenched in the Yangzi River valley, the Taipings threatened Shanghai.

Taiping Defeat The radical nature of the Taiping program ensured that the Chinese gentry would side with the Qing government to support a regime dedicated to the preservation of the established order. After imperial forces consisting of Manchu soldiers failed to defeat the Taipings, the Qing government created regional armies staffed by Chinese instead of Manchu soldiers and commanded by members of the scholar-gentry class, a shift encouraged by the empress dowager Cixi (1835–1908), a former imperial concubine who established herself as effective ruler of China during the last fifty years of the Qing dynasty. With the aid of European advisors and weapons, these regional armies gradually overcame the Taipings. By 1862 Hong Xiuquan had largely withdrawn from public affairs, as he sought solace

The final assault on the Taipings at Nanjing by Qing forces in 1864, an operation that caught common people and their livestock in the crossfire.

in religious reflection and diversion in his harem. After a lingering illness, he committed suicide in June 1864. In the following months Nanjing fell, and government forces slaughtered some one hundred thousand Taipings. By the end of the year, the rebellion was over. But the Taiping rebellion had taken a costly toll. It claimed twenty million to thirty million lives, and it caused such drastic declines in agricultural production that populations in war-torn regions frequently resorted to eating grass, leather, hemp, and even human flesh.

Reform Frustrated

The Taiping rebellion altered the course of Chinese history. Contending with aggressive foreign powers and lands ravaged by domestic rebellion, Qing rulers recognized that changes were necessary for the empire to survive. From 1860 to 1895, Qing authorities tried to fashion an efficient and benevolent Confucian government to solve social and economic problems while also adopting foreign technology to strengthen state power.

The Self-Strengthening Movement Most imaginative of the reform programs was the Self-Strengthening Movement (1860–1895), which flourished especially in the 1860s and 1870s. Empowered with imperial grants of authority that permitted them to raise troops, levy taxes, and run bureaucracies, several local leaders promoted military and economic reform. Adopting the slogan "Chinese learning at the base, Western learning for use," leaders of the Self-Strengthening Movement sought to blend Chinese cultural traditions with European industrial technology. While holding to Confucian values and seeking to reestablish a stable agrarian society, movement leaders built modern shipyards, constructed railroads, established weapons industries, opened steel foundries with blast furnaces, and founded academies to develop scientific expertise.

Although it laid a foundation for industrialization, the Self-Strengthening Movement brought only superficial change to the Chinese economy and society. It did not introduce enough industry to bring real military and economic strength

Empress Dowager Cixi diverted government funds intended for the construction of modern warships to the construction of a huge marble vessel to decorate a lake in the gardens of the Summer Palace near Beijing.

to China. It also encountered obstacles in the imperial government: the empress dowager Cixi diverted funds intended for the navy to build a magnificent marble boat to grace a lake in the imperial gardens. Furthermore, the movement foundered on a contradiction: industrialization would bring fundamental social change to an agrarian land, and education in European curricula would undermine the commitment to Confucian values.

Spheres of Influence

In any case, the Self-Strengthening Movement also did not prevent continuing foreign intrusion into Chinese affairs. During the latter part of the nineteenth century, foreign powers began to dismantle the Chinese system of tributary states. In 1885 France incorporated Vietnam into its colonial empire, and in 1886 Great Britain detached Burma from Chinese control. In 1895 Japan forced China to recognize the independence of Korea and cede the island of Taiwan and the Liaodong Peninsula in southern Manchuria. By 1898 foreign powers had carved China

ÉVÉNEMENTS DE CHINE
Quatorze têtes de Boxers aux murs de Tchio-Tchao

A French journal discussing events in China included an illustration of the Chinese rebels' severed heads being displayed on a wall in 1900.

into spheres of economic influence. Powerless to resist foreign demands, the Qing government granted exclusive rights for railway and mineral development to Germany in Shandong Province, to France in the southern border provinces, to Great Britain in the Yangzi River valley, to Japan in the southeastern coastal provinces, and to Russia in Manchuria. Only distrust among the foreign powers prevented the total dismemberment of the Middle Kingdom.

The Hundred Days Reforms

Those setbacks sparked the ambitious but abortive Hundred Days reforms of 1898. The leading figures of the reform movement were the scholars Kang Youwei (1858–1927) and Liang Qichao (1873–1929), who published a series of treatises reinterpreting Confucian thought in a way that justified radical changes in the imperial system. Kang and Liang did not seek to preserve an agrarian society and its cultural traditions so much as to remake China and turn it into a powerful modern industrial society. Impressed by their ideas, the young and open-minded Emperor Guangxu launched a sweeping program to transform China into a constitutional monarchy, guarantee civil liberties, root out corruption, remodel the educational system, encourage foreign influence in China, modernize military forces, and stimulate economic development. The broad range of reform edicts produced a violent reaction from members of the imperial household, their allies in the gentry, and the young emperor's aunt, the ruthless and powerful empress dowager Cixi. After a period of 103 days, Cixi nullified the reform decrees, imprisoned the emperor in the Forbidden City, and executed six leading reformers. Kang and Liang, the spiritual guides of the reform movement, escaped to Japan.

The Boxer Rebellion

Believing that foreign powers were pushing for her retirement, Cixi threw her support behind an antiforeign uprising known as the Boxer rebellion, a violent movement spearheaded by militia units calling themselves the Society of Righteous and Harmonious Fists. The foreign press referred to the rebels as Boxers. In 1899 the Boxers organized to rid China of "foreign devils" and their influences. With the empress dowager's encouragement, the Boxers went on a rampage in northern China, killing foreigners and Chinese Christians as well as Chinese who had ties to foreigners. Confident that foreign weapons could not harm them, some 140,000 Boxers besieged foreign embassies in Beijing in the summer of 1900. A heavily armed force of British, French, Russian, U.S., German, and Japanese troops quickly crushed the Boxer movement in bloody retaliation for the assault. The Chinese government had to pay a punitive indemnity and allow foreign powers to station troops in Beijing at their embassies and along the route to the sea.

Because Cixi had instigated the Boxers' attacks on foreigners, many Chinese regarded the Qing dynasty as bankrupt. Revolutionary uprisings gained widespread public support throughout the country, even among conservative Chinese gentry. Cixi died in November 1908, one day after the sudden, unexpected, and mysterious death of the emperor. In her last act of state, the empress dowager appointed the two-year-old boy Puyi to the imperial throne. But Puyi never had a chance to rule: revolution broke out in the autumn of 1911, and by early 1912 the last emperor of the Qing dynasty had abdicated his throne.

THE TRANSFORMATION OF JAPAN

In 1853 a fleet of U.S. warships steamed into Tokyo Bay and demanded permission to establish trade and diplomatic relations with Japan. Representatives of European lands soon joined U.S. agents in Japan. Heavily armed foreign powers intimidated the Tokugawa shogun and his government, the bakufu, into signing unequal treaties providing political and economic privileges similar to those obtained earlier from the Qing dynasty in China. Opposition forces in Japan used the humiliating intrusion of foreigners as an excuse to overthrow the discredited shogun and the Tokugawa bakufu. After restoring the emperor to power in 1868, Japan's new rulers worked for the transformation of Japanese society to achieve political and economic equality with foreign powers. The changes initiated during the Meiji period turned Japan into the political, military, and economic powerhouse of east Asia.

From Tokugawa to Meiji

Crisis and Reform
By the early nineteenth century, Japanese society was in turmoil. Declining agricultural productivity, periodic crop failures and famines, and harsh taxation contributed to economic hardship and sometimes even led to starvation among the rural population. A few cultivators prospered during this period, but many had to sell their land and become tenant farmers. Economic conditions in towns and cities, where many peasants migrated in search of a better life, were hardly better than those in the countryside. As the price of rice and other commodities rose, the urban poor experienced destitution and hunger. Even samurai and daimyo faced hardship because they fell into debt to a growing merchant class. Under those conditions, Japan experienced increasing peasant protest and rebellion during the late eighteenth and early nineteenth centuries.

The Tokugawa bakufu responded with conservative reforms. Between 1841 and 1843 the shogun's chief advisor, Mizuno Tadakuni, initiated measures to stem growing social and economic decline and to shore up the Tokugawa government. Mizuno canceled debts that samurai and daimyo owed to merchants, abolished several merchant guilds, and compelled peasants residing in cities to return to the land and cultivate rice. Most of his reforms were ineffective, and they provoked strong opposition that ultimately drove him from office.

A Japanese view of an audience of the first U.S. consul, Townsend Harris, with the Tokugawa shogun and his officials in 1859.

Foreign Pressure Another problem facing the Tokugawa bakufu was the insistence on the establishment of diplomatic and commercial relations by foreign lands. Beginning in 1844, British, French, and U.S. ships visited Japan seeking to establish relations. The United States in particular sought ports where its Pacific merchant and whaling fleets could stop for fuel and provisions. Tokugawa officials refused all those requests and stuck to the policy of excluding all European and American visitors to Japan except for a small number of Dutch merchants, who carried on a carefully controlled trade in Nagasaki. In the later 1840s the bakufu began to make military preparations to resist potential attacks.

The arrival of a U.S. naval squadron in Tokyo Bay in 1853 abruptly changed the situation. The American commander, Commodore Matthew C. Perry, trained his guns on the bakufu capital of Edo (modern Tokyo) and demanded that the shogun open Japan to diplomatic and commercial relations and sign a treaty of friendship. The shogun had no good alternative and so quickly acquiesced to Perry's demands. Representatives of Britain, the Netherlands, and Russia soon won similar rights. Like Qing diplomats a few years earlier, Tokugawa officials agreed to a series of unequal treaties that opened Japanese ports to foreign commerce, deprived the government of control over tariffs, and granted foreigners extraterritorial rights.

The End of Tokugawa Rule The sudden intrusion of foreign powers precipitated a domestic crisis in Japan that resulted in the collapse of the Tokugawa bakufu and the restoration of imperial rule. When the shogun complied with the demands of U.S. and European representatives, he aroused the opposition of conservative daimyo and the emperor, who resented the humiliating terms of the unequal treaties and questioned the shogun's right to rule Japan as "subduer of barbarians." Opposition to Tokugawa authority spread rapidly, and the southern domains of Choshu and Satsuma became centers of discontented samurai. By 1858 the imperial court in Kyoto—long excluded from playing an active role in politics—had become the focal point for opposition. Dissidents there rallied around the slogan "Revere the emperor, expel the barbarians."

The Meiji Restoration Tokugawa officials did not yield power quietly. Instead, they vigorously responded to their opponents by forcibly retiring dissident daimyo and executing or imprisoning samurai critics. In a brief civil war, however, bakufu armies suffered repeated defeats by dissident militia units trained by foreign experts and armed with imported weapons. With the Tokugawa cause doomed, the shogun resigned his office. On 3 January 1868 the boy emperor Mutsuhito—subsequently known by his regnal name, Meiji ("Enlightened Rule")—took the reins of power. Emperor Meiji (1852–1912) reigned during a most eventful period in Japan's history.

Japanese artist Miyagawa Shuntei offered a late-nineteenth-century pointed contrast in fashion in his depiction of two women at the seaside. One wears European swimwear, and the other has donned a kimono.

Meiji Reforms

The Meiji restoration returned authority to the Japanese emperor and brought an end to the series of military governments that had dominated Japan since 1185. It also marked the birth of a new Japan. Determined to gain parity with foreign powers, a conservative coalition of daimyo, imperial princes, court nobles, and samurai formed a new government dedicated to the twin goals of prosperity and strength: "rich country, strong army." The Meiji government looked to the industrial lands of Europe and the United States to obtain the knowledge and expertise to strengthen Japan and win revisions of the unequal treaties. The Meiji government sent many students and officials abroad to study everything from technology to constitutions, and it also hired foreign experts to facilitate economic development and the creation of indigenous expertise.

thinking about ENCOUNTERS

Opening Doors

In 1853 Commodore Matthew Perry sailed into Edo Bay and inaugurated a new era in Japan's history. Why did the arrival of American forces prompt change in Japan? In what ways did the Japanese respond?

Foreign Influences Among the most prominent of the Meiji-era travelers were Fukuzawa Yukichi (1835–1901) and Ito Hirobumi (1841–1909). Fukuzawa began to study English soon after Perry's arrival in Japan, and in 1860 he was a member of the first Japanese mission to the United States. Later, he traveled in Europe, and he reported his observations of foreign lands in a series of popular publications. He lauded the constitutional government and modern educational systems that he found in the United States and western Europe, and he argued strongly for equality before the law in Japan. Ito ventured abroad on four occasions. His most important journey came in 1882 and 1883, when he traveled to Europe to study foreign constitutions and administrative systems, as Meiji leaders prepared to fashion a new government. He was especially impressed with recently united Germany, and he drew inspiration from the German constitution in drafting a governing document for Japan.

Abolition of the Social Order The first goal of the Meiji leaders was to centralize political power, a ticklish task that required destruction of the old social order. After persuading daimyo to yield their lands to the throne in exchange for patents of nobility, reformers replaced the old domains with prefectures and metropolitan districts controlled by the central government. Reformers then appointed new prefectural governors to prevent the revival of old domain loyalties. As a result, most daimyo found themselves effectively removed from power. The government also abolished the samurai class and the stipends that supported it. Gone as well were the rights of daimyo and samurai to carry swords and wear their hair in the distinctive topknot that signified their military status. When Meiji leaders raised a conscript army, they deprived the samurai of the military monopoly they had held for centuries. Many samurai felt betrayed by these actions, and Meiji officials sought to ease their discontent by awarding them government bonds. As the bonds diminished in value because of inflation, former warriors had to seek employment or else suffer impoverishment. Frustrated by these new circumstances, some samurai rose in rebellion, but the recently created national army crushed all opposition. By 1878 the national government no longer feared military challenges to its rule.

Revamping the Tax System Japan's new leaders next put the regime on secure financial footing by revamping the tax system. Peasants traditionally paid taxes in grain, but because the value of grain fluctuated with the price of rice, so did government revenue. In 1873 the Meiji government converted the grain tax into a fixed-money tax, which provided the government with predictable revenues and left peasants to deal with market fluctuations in grain prices. The state also began to assess taxes on the potential productivity of arable land, no matter how much a cultivator actually produced. This measure virtually guaranteed that only those who maximized production could afford to hold on to their land. Others had to sell their land to more efficient producers.

Constitutional Government The reconstruction of Japanese society continued in the 1880s under mounting domestic pressure for a constitution and representative government. Those demands coincided with the rulers' belief that constitutions gave foreign powers their strength and unity. Accordingly, in 1889 the emperor promulgated the Meiji constitution as "a voluntary gift" to his people. Drafted under the guidance of Ito Hirobumi, this document established a constitutional monarchy with a legislature, known as the Diet, composed of a house of nobles and an elected lower house. The constitution limited the authority of the Diet and reserved considerable power to the executive branch of government. The "sacred and inviolable" emperor commanded the armed forces, named the prime minister, and appointed the cabinet. Both the prime minister and the cabinet were responsible to the emperor rather than the lower house, as in European parliamentary systems. The emperor also had the right to dissolve the parliament, and whenever the Diet was not in session he had the prerogative of issuing ordinances. Effective power thus lay with the emperor, whom the parliament could advise but never control. The Meiji constitution recognized individual rights, but it provided that laws could limit those rights in the interests of the state, and it established property restrictions on the franchise, ensuring that delegates elected to the lower house represented the most prosperous social classes. In the elections of 1890 less than 5 percent of the adult male population was eligible to cast ballots. Despite its conservative features, the Meiji constitution provided greater opportunity for debate and dissent than ever before in Japanese society.

Remodeling the Economy Economic initiatives matched efforts at political reconstruction. Convinced that a powerful economy was the foundation of national strength, the Meiji government created a modern transportation, communications, and educational infrastructure. The establishment of telegraph, railroad, and steamship lines tied local

and regional markets into a national economic network. The government also removed barriers to commerce and trade by abolishing guild restrictions and internal tariffs. Aiming to improve literacy rates—40 percent for males and 15 percent for females in the nineteenth century—the government introduced a system of universal primary and secondary education. Universities provided advanced instruction for the best students, especially in scientific and technical fields. This infrastructure supported rapid industrialization and economic growth. Although most economic enterprises were privately owned, the government controlled military industries and established pilot programs to stimulate industrial development. During the 1880s the government sold most of its enterprises to private investors who had close ties to government officials. The result was a concentration of enormous economic

This Japanese illustration of Emperor Mutsohito demonstrates the visual and martial transformations in Meiji Japan.

power in the hands of a small group of people, collectively known as *zaibatsu,* or financial cliques. By the early twentieth century, Japan had joined the ranks of the major industrial powers.

Costs of Economic Development

Economic development came at a price, as the Japanese people bore the social and political costs of rapid industrialization. Japanese peasants, for example, supplied much of the domestic capital that supported the Meiji program of industrialization. The land tax of 1873, which cost peasants 40 to 50 percent of their crop yields, produced almost 90 percent of government revenue during the early years of Meiji development. Foreign exchange to purchase industrial equipment came chiefly from the export of textiles produced in a labor-intensive industry staffed by poorly paid workers.

The difficult lot of peasants came to the fore in 1883 and 1884 with a series of peasant uprisings aimed at moneylenders and government offices holding records of loans. The Meiji government deployed military police and army units to put down these uprisings, and authorities imprisoned or executed many leaders of the rebellions. Thereafter, the government did virtually nothing to alleviate the suffering of the rural population. Hundreds of thousands of families lived in destitution, haunted by malnutrition, starvation, and infanticide. Those who escaped rural society to take up work in the burgeoning industries learned that the state did not tolerate labor organizations that promoted the welfare of workers: Meiji law treated the formation of unions and the organization of strikes as criminal activities, and the government crushed a growing labor movement in 1901.

Nevertheless, in a single generation Meiji leaders transformed Japan into a powerful industrial society poised to play a major role in world affairs. Achieving political and economic equality with western European lands and the United States was the prime goal of Meiji leaders, who sought an end to humiliating treaty provisions. Serving as symbols of Japan's remarkable development were the ending of extraterritoriality in 1899, the conclusion of an alliance with Britain as an equal power in 1902, and convincing displays of military prowess in victories over the Chinese empire (1894–1895) and the Russian empire (1904–1905).

in**perspective**

During the nineteenth century, Ottoman, Russian, Chinese, and Japanese societies faced severe challenges on both foreign and domestic fronts. Confrontations with western European and U.S. forces showed that the agrarian societies were militarily much weaker than industrializing lands. Ottoman, Russian, Chinese, and Japanese societies suffered also from domestic weaknesses brought on by growing populations, the slowing of agricultural productivity, official corruption, and declining imperial revenues. All those societies embarked on ambitious reform programs that drew inspiration from western European and U.S. models to solve the crises caused by domestic discontent and foreign intrusions on their sovereignty. But reform programs had very different results in different lands. In the Ottoman, Russian, and Chinese empires, conservative ruling elites were able to limit the scope of reform: although they generally supported industrialization and military reform, they stifled political and social reforms that might threaten their positions in society. In Japan, however, dissent led to the collapse of the Tokugawa bakufu, and reformers had the opportunity to undertake a much more thorough program of reform than did their counterparts in Ottoman, Russian, and Chinese societies. By the early twentieth century, on the basis of reforms implemented by Meiji leaders, Japan was becoming a political, military, and economic powerhouse. ●

CHRONOLOGY

1805–1848	Reign of Muhammad Ali in Egypt
1808–1839	Reign of Sultan Mahmud II
1814–1864	Life of Taiping leader Hong Xiuquan
1839–1842	Opium War
1839–1876	Tanzimat era
1850–1864	Taiping rebellion
1853	Arrival of Commodore Perry in Japan
1853–1856	Crimean War
1855–1881	Reign of Tsar Alexander II
1860–1895	Self-Strengthening Movement
1861	Emancipation of the Russian serfs
1868	Meiji restoration
1876	Promulgation of the Ottoman constitution
1889	Promulgation of the Meiji constitution
1894–1917	Reign of Tsar Nicholas II
1898	Hundred Days reforms
1900	Boxer rebellion
1904–1905	Russo-Japanese war
1905	Revolution of 1905 in Russia
1908–1918	Young Turk era

For Further Reading

Michael R. Auslin. *Negotiating with Imperialism: The Unequal Treaties and the Culture of Japanese Diplomacy.* Cambridge, Mass., 2004. Diplomatic history that examines Japan's interaction with Western imperialism and the country's emergence as a world power.

David Anthony Bello. *Opium and the Limits of Empire: Drug Prohibition in the Chinese Interior, 1729–1850.* Cambridge, Mass., 2005. Explores Qing China's efforts at controlling and prohibiting the domestic opium trade.

William L. Blackwell. *The Industrialization of Russia: An Historical Perspective.* New York, 1982. A useful overview.

Carter V. Findley. *Bureaucratic Reform in the Ottoman Empire: The Sublime Porte, 1789–1922.* Princeton, 1980. An important scholarly work on bureaucratic reform and the development of the Ottoman civil service.

Yukichi Fukuzawa. *The Autobiography of Yukichi Fukuzawa.* Trans. by E. Kiyooka. New York, 1966. Fascinating autobiography of the former samurai who introduced Japan to the larger world on the basis of his travels in Europe and the United States.

Marius B. Jansen and Gilbert Rozman, eds. *Japan in Transition: From Tokugawa to Meiji.* Princeton, 1986. Important collection of essays exploring economic and social change during the era of the Meiji restoration.

Rebecca E. Karl. *Staging the World: Chinese Nationalism at the Turn of the Twentieth Century.* Durham, 2002. Intellectual history arguing that Chinese nationalism resulted from global interactions.

Peter Kolchin. *Unfree Labor: American Slavery and Russian Serfdom.* Cambridge, Mass., 1987. A remarkable and stimulating comparative study of American slavery and Russian serfdom.

Tetsuo Najita and J. Victor Koschmann, eds. *Conflict in Modern Japanese History: The Neglected Tradition.* Princeton, 1982. Explores the role of conflict rather than consensus in Japanese society.

Sevket Pamuk. *The Ottoman Empire and European Capitalism, 1820–1913: Trade, Investment, and Production.* Cambridge, 1987. Closely examines complex economic entanglements.

James M. Polachek. *The Inner Opium War.* Cambridge, Mass., 1992. A scholarly treatment of the Opium War and its effects in China.

Hans Rogger. *Russia in the Age of Modernisation and Revolution, 1881–1917.* New York, 1983. An important study of Russian social and economic development.

Jonathan D. Spence. *God's Chinese Son: The Taiping Heavenly Kingdom of Hong Xiuquan.* New York, 1996. A readable work on the Taiping rebellion.

John W. Steinberg, ed. *The Russo-Japanese War in Global Perspective: World War Zero.* Boston, 2005. Collection of essays that examines the Russo-Japanese War as a harbinger of World War I.

Conrad D. Totman. *The Collapse of the Tokugawa Bakufu, 1862–1868.* Honolulu, 1980. A detailed political history of the bakufu's decline and fall.

Arthur Waley. *The Opium War through Chinese Eyes.* Stanford, 1968. Fascinating perspective on the Opium War drawing on eyewitness accounts by Chinese participants and observers.

Francis William Wcislo. *Reforming Rural Russia: State, Local Society, and National Politics, 1855–1914.* Princeton, 1990. Beginning with emancipation of the serfs, this work traces agrarian and political problems in Russian society.

R. B. Wong. *China Transformed: Historical Change and the Limits of European Experience.* Ithaca, N.Y., 2002. A sophisticated work that explores similarities and differences between Chinese and European development over the long term.

Richard Wortman. *Scenarios of Power: Myth and Ceremony in the Russian Monarchy.* Princeton, 1995. An innovative study exploring the means by which Romanov rulers held on to their autocratic prerogatives despite fundamental changes in Russian society.

Peter Zarrow. *China in War and Revolution, 1895–1949.* New York, 2005. Study of the impact of Qing China's loss of Korea on the formation of modern China.

The Building of Global Empires

chapter32

The battle of Omdurman on the Nile River, 2 September 1898.

EYEWITNESS:
Cecil John Rhodes Discovers
Imperial Diamonds Are Forever

Few Europeans had traveled to south Africa by the mid-nineteenth century, but the discovery of diamonds and rich gold deposits brought both European settlers and dramatic change to the region. European prospectors flocked to south Africa to seek their fortune.

Among the arrivals was Cecil John Rhodes, an eighteen-year-old student at Oxford University, who in 1871 went to south Africa in search of a climate that would relieve his tuberculosis. Rhodes was persistent, systematic, and ambitious. He carefully supervised African laborers who worked his claims in the diamond fields, and he bought the rights to others' claims when they looked promising. By 1889, at age thirty-five, he had almost completely monopolized diamond mining in south Africa, and he controlled 90 percent of the world's diamond production. With ample financial backing, Rhodes built up a healthy stake in the gold-mining business, although he did not seek to monopolize gold the way he did diamonds. He also entered politics, serving as prime minister (1890–1896) of the British Cape Colony.

Yet Rhodes's ambitions went far beyond business and local politics. In his vision the Cape Colony would serve as a base of operations for the extension of British control to all of Africa, from Cape to Cairo. Rhodes led the movement to enlarge the colony by absorbing territories to the north settled by Dutch farmers. Under Rhodes's guidance, the colony annexed Bechuanaland (modern Botswana) in 1885, and in 1895 it added Rhodesia (modern Zambia and Zimbabwe) to its holdings. But Rhodes's plan did not stop with Africa: he urged the expansion of the British empire until it embraced all the world, and he even hoped to bring the United States of America back into the British fold. Rhodes considered British society the most noble, moral, and honorable in the world, and he regarded imperial expansion as a duty to humankind: "We are the finest race in the world," he said in 1877, "and the more of the world we inhabit, the better it is for the human race." In his sense of superiority to other peoples as well as his restless energy, his compulsion to expand, and his craving to extract mineral wealth from distant parts of the world, Rhodes represented well the views of European imperialists who carved the world into colonies during the nineteenth century.

Throughout history strong societies have often sought to dominate their weaker neighbors by subjecting them to imperial rule. They have built empires for various reasons: to gain control over natural resources, to subdue potential enemies, to seize wealth, to acquire territory for expansion, and to win glory. From the days of ancient Mesopotamia and Egypt to the present, imperialism has been a prominent theme of world history.

During the second half of the nineteenth century, as the Ottoman and Qing empires weakened, a handful of western European states wrote a new chapter in the history of imperialism. Strong nationalist sentiments enabled them to mobilize their populations for purposes of overseas expansion. Industrialization equipped them with the most effective tools and the most lethal weapons available anywhere in the world. Three centuries of experience with maritime trade in Asia, Africa, the Americas, and Oceania provided them with unparalleled knowledge of the world and its peoples. With those advantages, western European peoples conquered foreign armies, overpowered local rulers, and imposed their hegemony throughout the world. Toward the end of the century, the United States and Japan joined European states as new imperial powers.

The establishment of global empires had far-reaching effects. In many ways, imperialism tightened links between the world's societies. Imperial powers encouraged trade between dominant states and their overseas colonies, for example, and they organized mass migrations of laborers to work in agricultural and industrial ventures. Yet imperialism also fostered divisions between the world's peoples. Powerful tools, deadly weapons, and global hegemony tempted European peoples to consider themselves superior to their subjects throughout the world: modern racism is one of the legacies of imperialism. Another effect of imperialism was the development of nationalism in subject lands. Just as the incursion of Napoleonic armies stimulated the development of nationalism in Europe, so the imposition of foreign rule provoked nationalist responses in colonized lands. Although formal empires almost entirely dissolved in the twentieth century, the influence of global imperialism continues to shape the contemporary world.

FOUNDATIONS OF EMPIRE

Even under the best of circumstances, campaigns to conquer foreign lands have always been dangerous and expensive ventures. They have arisen from a sense that foreign conquest is essential, and they have entailed the mobilization of political, military, and economic resources. In nineteenth-century Europe, proponents of empire advanced a variety of political, economic, and cultural arguments to justify the conquest and control of foreign lands. The imperialist ventures that they promoted enjoyed dramatic success partly because of the increasingly sophisticated technologies developed by European industry.

Motives of Imperialism

Modern Imperialism
The building of empires is an old story in world history. By the nineteenth century, however, European observers recognized that empires of their day were different from those of earlier times. Accordingly, about mid-century they began to speak of *imperialism,* and by the 1880s the recently coined term had made its way into popular speech and writing throughout western Europe. In contemporary usage, imperialism refers to the domination of European powers—and later the United States and Japan as well—over subject lands in the larger world. Sometimes that domination came in the old-fashioned way, by force of arms, but often it arose from trade, investment, and business activities that enabled imperial powers to profit from subject societies and influence their affairs without going to the trouble of exercising direct political control.

Modern Colonialism
Like the building of empires, the establishment of colonies in foreign lands is a practice dating from ancient times. In modern parlance, however, colonialism refers not just to the sending of colonists to settle new lands but also to the political, social, economic, and cultural structures that enabled imperial powers to dominate subject lands. In some lands, such as North America, Chile, Argentina, Australia, New Zealand, and south Africa, European powers established settler colonies populated largely by migrants from the home societies. Yet contemporary scholars also speak of European colonies in India, southeast Asia, and sub-Saharan Africa, even though European migrants did not settle there in large numbers. European agents, officials, and businesspeople effectively turned those lands into colonies and profoundly influenced their historical development by controlling their domestic and foreign policies, integrating local economies into the net-

work of global capitalism, introducing European business techniques, transforming educational systems according to European standards, and promoting European cultural preferences.

During the second half of the nineteenth century, many Europeans came to believe that imperial expansion and colonial domination were crucial for the survival of their states and societies—and sometimes for the health of their personal fortunes as well. European merchants and entrepreneurs sometimes became fabulously wealthy from business ventures in Asia or Africa, and they argued for their home states to pursue imperialist policies partly to secure and enhance their own enterprises. After making his fortune mining diamonds and gold, for example, Cecil Rhodes (1853–1902) worked tirelessly on behalf of British imperial expansion.

Economic Motives of Imperialism It is not difficult to understand why entrepreneurs such as Rhodes would promote overseas expansion, but their interests alone could not have driven the vast imperialist ventures of the late nineteenth century. In fact, a wide range of motives encouraged European peoples to launch campaigns of conquest and control. Some advocates argued that imperialism was in the economic interests of European societies as well as individuals. They pointed out that overseas colonies could serve as reliable sources of raw materials not available in Europe that came into demand because of industrialization: rubber, tin, and copper were vital products, for example, and by the late nineteenth century petroleum had also become a crucial resource for industrialized lands. Rubber trees were indigenous to the Amazon River basin, but imperialists established colonial rubber plantations in the Congo River

basin and Malaya. Abundant supplies of tin were available from colonies in southeast Asia and copper in central Africa. The United States and Russia supplied most of the world's petroleum in the nineteenth century, but the oil fields of southwest Asia attracted the attention of European industrialists and imperialists alike.

Proponents of imperialism also held that colonies would consume manufactured products and provide a haven for migrants in an age of rapidly increasing European population. In fact, manufactured goods did not flow to most colonies in large quantities, and European migrants went overwhelmingly to independent states in the Americas rather than to overseas colonies. Nevertheless, arguments arising from national economic interest generated considerable support for imperialism.

Political Motives of Imperialism As European states extended their influence overseas, a geopolitical argument for imperialism gained prominence. Even if colonies were not economically beneficial, imperialists held, it was crucial for political and military reasons to maintain them. Some overseas colonies occupied strategic sites on the world's sea lanes, and others offered harbors or supply stations for commercial and naval ships. Advocates of imperialism sought to gain those advantages for their own states and—equally important—to deny them to rivals.

Imperialism had its uses also for domestic politics. In an age when socialists and communists directly confronted industrialists, European politicians and national leaders sought to defuse social tension and inspire patriotism by focusing public attention on foreign imperialist ventures. Cecil Rhodes himself once observed that imperialism was an attractive alternative to civil war, and the German chancellor Otto von

Cecil Rhodes resting in the goldfields of south Africa, about 1897. His dominating economic, cultural, and political influence on southern African territories for personal and British gain was a model of European imperialist values.

thinking about TRADITIONS

New Imperialism?
The building of empires stretched back historically as far as the beginning of written history. How did the so-called new imperialism of the nineteenth and twentieth centuries differ from earlier imperial traditions?

Bismarck worked to persuade both industrialists and workers that overseas expansion would benefit them all. By the end of the nineteenth century, European leaders frequently organized colonial exhibitions where subject peoples displayed their dress, music, and customs for tourists and the general public in imperial lands, all in an effort to win popular support for imperialist policies.

Cultural Justifications of Imperialism

Even spiritual motives fostered imperialism. Like the Jesuits in the early modern era, missionaries flocked to African and Asian lands in search of converts to Christianity. Missionaries often opposed imperialist ventures and defended the interests of their converts against European entrepreneurs and colonial officials. Nevertheless, their spiritual campaigns provided a powerful religious justification for imperialism. Furthermore, missionaries often facilitated communications between imperialists and subject peoples, and they sometimes provided European officials with information they needed to maintain control of overseas colonies. Missionary settlements also served as convenient meeting places for Europeans overseas and as distribution centers for European manufactured goods.

While missionaries sought to introduce Christianity to subject peoples, other Europeans worked to bring them "civilization" in the form of political order and social stability. French imperialists routinely invoked the *mission civilisatrice* ("civilizing mission") as justification for their expansion into Africa and Asia, and the English writer and poet Rudyard Kipling (1864–1936) defined the "white man's burden" as the duty of European and Euro-American peoples to bring order and enlightenment to distant lands.

Tools of Empire

Even the strongest motives would not have enabled imperialists to impose their rule throughout the world without the powerful technological advantages that industrialization conferred on them. Ever since the introduction of gunpowder in the thirteenth century, European states had competed vigorously to develop increasingly powerful military technologies. Industrialization enhanced those efforts by making it possible to produce huge quantities of advanced weapons and tools. During the nineteenth century, industrialists devised effective technologies of transportation, commu-

nication, and war that enabled European imperialists to have their way in the larger world.

Transportation Technologies

The most important innovations in transportation involved steamships and railroads. Small steamboats plied the waters of the United States and western Europe from the early nineteenth century. During the 1830s British naval engineers adapted steam power to military uses and built large, ironclad ships equipped with powerful guns. These steamships traveled much faster than any sailing vessel, and as an additional advantage they could ignore the winds and travel in any direction. Because they could travel much farther upriver than sailboats, which depended on convenient winds, steamships enabled imperialists to project power deep into the interior regions of foreign lands. Thus in 1842 the British gunboat *Nemesis* led an expedition up the Yangzi River that brought the Opium War to a conclusion. Steam-powered gunboats later introduced European power to inland sites throughout Africa and Asia.

The construction of new canals enhanced the effectiveness of steamships. Both the Suez Canal (constructed 1859–1869) and the Panama Canal (constructed 1904–1914) facilitated the building and maintenance of empires by enabling naval vessels to travel rapidly between the world's seas and oceans. They also lowered the costs of trade between imperial powers and subject lands.

Once imperialists had gained control of overseas lands, railroads helped them to maintain their hegemony and organize local economies to their own advantage. Rail transportation enabled colonial officials and armies to travel quickly through the colonies. It also facilitated trade in raw materials and the distribution of European manufactured goods in the colonies.

Military Technologies

European industrialists also churned out enormous quantities of increasingly powerful weapons. The most advanced firearms of the early nineteenth century were smoothbore, muzzle-loading muskets. When large numbers of infantry fired their muskets at once, the resulting volley could cause havoc among opponents. Yet it took a skilled musketeer about one minute to reload a weapon, and because of its smoothbore, the musket was not a very accurate firearm. By mid-century European armies were using breech-loading firearms with rifled bores that were far more accurate and reliable than muskets. By the 1870s Europeans were experimenting with rifled machine guns, and in the 1880s they adopted the Maxim gun, a light and powerful weapon that fired eleven bullets per second.

Those firearms provided European armies with an arsenal vastly stronger than any other in the world. Accurate rifles and machine guns devastated opposing overseas forces, enabling European armies to impose colonial rule almost at will. In 1898, for example, a British army with twenty ma-

sources from the past

Rudyard Kipling on the White Man's Burden

Rudyard Kipling lived in northern India for the first six years of his life. He grew up speaking Hindi, and he mixed easily with Indian subjects of the British empire. After attending a boarding school in England, he returned to India in 1882 and became a journalist and writer. Many of his works express his deep enchantment with India, but he also believed strongly in imperial rule. Indeed, he wrote his famous poem titled "The White Man's Burden" to encourage the United States to impose colonial rule in the Philippines. While recognizing the unpopularity of foreign rule, Kipling considered it a duty to bring order to colonial lands and to serve subject peoples.

Take up the White Man's burden—
   Send forth the best ye breed—
Go bind your sons to exile
   To serve your captives' need;
To wait in heavy harness,
   On fluttered folk and wild—
Your new-caught, sullen peoples,
   Half-devil and half-child.

Take up the White Man's burden—
   In patience to abide,
To veil the threat of terror
   And check the show of pride;
By open speech and simple,
   An hundred times made plain,
To seek another's profit,
   And work for another's gain.

Take up the White Man's burden—
   The savage wars of peace—
Fill full the mouth of Famine
   And bid the sickness cease;
And when your goal is nearest
   The end for others sought,
Watch Sloth and heathen Folly
   Bring all your hope to nought.

Take up the White Man's burden—
   No tawdry rule of kings,
But toil of serf and sweeper—
   The tale of common things.

The ports ye shall not enter,
   The roads ye shall not tread,
Go make them with your living,
   And mark them with your dead.

Take up the White Man's burden—
   And reap his old reward:
The blame of those ye better,
   The hate of those ye guard—
The cry of hosts ye humor
   (Ah, slowly!) toward the light;—
"Why brought ye us from bondage,
   "Our loved Egyptian night?"

Take up the White Man's burden—
   Ye dare not stoop to less—
Nor call too loud on Freedom
   To cloak your weariness;
By all ye cry or whisper,
   By all ye leave or do,
The silent, sullen peoples
   Shall weigh your Gods and you.

Take up the White Man's burden—
   Have done with childish days—
The lightly proffered laurel,
   The easy, ungrudged praise.
Comes now, to search your manhood
   Through all the thankless years,
Cold, edged with dear-bought wisdom,
   The judgment of your peers!

For Further Reflection

■ Compare and contrast the sorts of adjectives Kipling uses to describe native peoples as opposed to Europeans; how does his very language usage convey his sense of white superiority?

Source: Rudyard Kipling. "The White Man's Burden." *McClure's Magazine* 12, no. 4 (1899): 290–91.

chine guns and six gunboats encountered a Sudanese force at Omdurman, near Khartoum on the Nile River. During five hours of fighting, the British force lost a few hundred men while machine guns and explosive charges fired from gunboats killed thousands of Sudanese. The battle of Omdurman opened the door for British colonial rule in Sudan.

Communications Technologies Communications also benefited from industrialization. Oceangoing steamships reduced the time required to deliver messages from imperial capitals to colonial lands. In the 1830s it took as long as two years for a British correspondent to receive a reply to a letter sent to India by sailing ship. By the 1850s, however, after the introduction of steamships, correspondence could make the round-trip between London and Bombay in four months. After the opening of the Suez Canal in 1869, steamships traveled from Britain to India in less than two weeks.

The invention of the telegraph made it possible to exchange messages even faster. Telegraph wires carried communications over land from the 1830s, but only in the 1850s did engineers devise reliable submarine cables for the transmission of messages through the oceans. By 1870, submarine cables carried messages between Britain and India in about five hours. By 1902, cables linked all parts of the British empire throughout the world, and other European states maintained cables to support communications with their own colonies. Their monopoly on telegraphic communications provided imperial powers with distinct advantages over their subject lands. Imperial officials could rapidly mobilize forces to deal with troubles, and merchants could respond quickly to developments of economic and commercial significance. Rapid communication was an integral structural element of empire.

Thousands of spectators gathered on the banks of the Suez Canal in 1869 to watch a parade of ships that opened the canal by proceeding from the Mediterranean to the Red Sea. The Suez and Panama canals became the most strategic waterways in the world because they significantly shortened maritime routes both between Europe and the lands bordering the Indian and Pacific oceans and between one coast of North America and ports on the other side of South America.

EUROPEAN IMPERIALISM

Aided by powerful technologies, European states launched an unprecedented round of empire building in the second half of the nineteenth century. Imperial expansion began with the British conquest of India. Competition between imperial powers led to European intrusion into central Asia and the establishment of colonies in southeast Asia. Fearful that rivals might gain control over some region that remained free of imperial control, European states embarked on a campaign of frenzied expansion in the 1880s that brought almost all of Africa and Pacific Ocean territories into their empires.

The British Empire in India

The British empire in south Asia and southeast Asia grew out of the mercantile activities of the English East India Company, which enjoyed a monopoly on English trade with India. The East India Company obtained permission from the Mughal emperors of India to build fortified posts on the coastlines. There, company agents traded for goods and stored commodities in warehouses until company ships arrived to transport them to Europe. In the seventeenth century, company merchants traded mostly for Indian pepper and cotton, Chinese silk and porcelain, and fine spices from southeast Asia. During the eighteenth century, tea and coffee became the most prominent trade items, and European consumers acquired a taste for both beverages that they have never lost.

Company Rule After the death of the emperor Aurangzeb in 1707, the Mughal state entered a period of decline, and many local authorities asserted their independence of Mughal rule. The East India Company took advantage of Mughal weakness to strengthen and expand its trading posts. In the 1750s company officials embarked on the outright conquest of India. Through diplomacy or military campaigns, the company conquered autonomous Indian kingdoms and reduced Mughal rule to only a small area around Delhi. Part of the British policy of expansion was the "doctrine of lapse," greatly resented by Indians. If an Indian ruler failed to produce a biological male heir to the throne, his territories lapsed to the company upon his death. By the mid-nineteenth century, the English East India Company had annexed huge areas of India and had established control over present-day Pakistan, Bangladesh, Burma, and Sri Lanka. Company rule was enforced by a small British army and a large number of Indian troops known as sepoys.

Indian Rebellion

Not all of the Indian population was willing to cooperate with foreign rule, however, and the English East India Company faced a deadly uprising in 1857 that threatened the British empire in India. Sepoy discontent came to a head when rumors circulated among the troops that cartridges for newly issued rifles were lubricated with a mixture of pig and cow fat. To load their rifles, sepoys had to bite off the ends of the lubricated cartridges, thus making oral contact with a substance that was offensive and insulting to both Muslims and Hindus. In several isolated cases, soldiers refused to use these cartridges, but they were promptly convicted of mutiny.

In response to the harsh treatment meted out by the British, several sepoy regiments joined what became a large-scale mutiny, rapidly igniting a general anti-British revolution in central and north India. Sepoys were now joined by Indian princes and their followers, whose territories had been annexed by the British, and people whose ways of life and sources of income had been disrupted by British trade, missionary activities, and misguided social reforms. What had begun as a rebellion by Indian troops in the employ of the English East India Company turned into a full-fledged war of independence against British rule. In the course of the conflict, both sides committed widespread atrocities against combatants and noncombatants alike. After several months of inconclusive battles, British forces finally gained the upper hand by late 1857, and peace was officially declared on 8 July 1858.

British Imperial Rule

The widespread but unsuccessful rebellion against British rule in India had far-reaching consequences. The British government officially abolished the Mughal empire and exiled the emperor Muhammad Bahadur Shah to Burma. To stabilize affairs and forestall future problems, the British crown abolished the East India Company in favor of the direct rule of India by the British government. In 1858 Queen Victoria (reigned 1837–1901) assigned responsibility for Indian policy to the newly established office of secretary of state for India. A viceroy represented British royal

A contemporary British print depicts what the British perceived as atrocities at Cawnpore. At left, independence-seeking sepoys kill British troops and men from the garrison, while women and children fall in the foreground.

authority in India and administered the colony through an elite Indian civil service staffed almost exclusively by the English. Indians served in low-level bureaucratic positions, but British officials formulated all domestic and foreign policy in India.

Under both the East India Company and direct colonial administration, British rule transformed India. As they extended their authority to all parts of India and Ceylon (modern Sri Lanka), British officials cleared forests, restructured landholdings, and encouraged the cultivation of crops, such as tea, coffee, and opium, that were especially valuable trade items. They built extensive railroad and telegraph networks that tightened links between India and the larger global economy. They also constructed new canals, harbors, and irrigation systems to support commerce and agriculture. British colonial authorities made little effort to promote Christianity, but they established English-style schools for the children of Indian elites, whom they sought as supporters of their rule.

Imperialism in Central Asia and Southeast Asia

As the East India Company and British colonial agents tightened their grip on India, competition among European states kindled further empire-building efforts. Beginning in the early nineteenth century, French and Russian strategists sought ways to break British power and establish their own colonial presence in India. The French bid stalled after the fall of Napoleon, but Russian interest in India fueled a prolonged contest for power in central Asia.

Russian forces had probed central Asia as early as the sixteenth century, but only in the nineteenth century did they undertake a systematic effort to extend Russian authority south of the Caucasus. The weakening of the Ottoman and Qing empires turned central Asia into a political vacuum and invited Russian expansion into the region. By the 1860s cossacks had overcome Tashkent, Bokhara, and Samarkand, the great caravan cities of the silk roads, and approached the ill-defined northern frontier of British India. For the next half century, military officers and imperialist adventurers engaged in a risky pursuit of influence and intelligence that British agents referred to as the "Great Game."

The Great Game Russian and British explorers ventured into parts of central Asia never before visited by Euro-

MAP 32.1

Imperialism in Asia, ca. 1914. Date is year of conquest.
Note the claims made by various industrial powers.

Which territories remained unclaimed, and why? Which power claimed the most imperial territory in Asia?

peans. They mapped terrain, scouted mountain passes, and sought alliances with local rulers from Afghanistan to the Aral Sea—all in an effort to prepare for the anticipated war for India. In fact, the outbreak of global war in 1914 and the collapse of the tsarist state in 1917 ensured that the contest for India never took place. Nevertheless, imperial expansion brought much of central Asia into the Russian empire and subjected the region to a Russian hegemony that persisted until the disintegration of the Soviet Union in 1991.

Competition among European powers led also to further imperialism in southeast Asia. The Philippines had come under Spanish colonial rule in the sixteenth century, and many southeast Asian islands fell under Dutch rule in the seventeenth century. As imperial rivalries escalated in the nineteenth century, Dutch officials tightened their control and extended their authority throughout the Dutch East Indies, the archipelago that makes up the modern state of Indonesia. Along with cash crops of sugar, tea, coffee, and

tobacco, exports of rubber and tin made the Dutch East Indies a valuable and productive colony.

British Colonies in Southeast Asia In the interests of increasing trade between India, southeast Asia, and China, British imperialists moved in the nineteenth century to establish a presence in southeast Asia. As early as the 1820s, colonial officials in India came into conflict with the kings of Burma (modern Myanmar) while seeking to extend their influence to the Irrawaddy River delta. By the 1880s they had established colonial authority in Burma, which became a source of teak, ivory, rubies, and jade. In 1824 Thomas Stamford Raffles founded the port of Singapore, which soon became the busiest center of trade in the Strait of Melaka. Administered by the colonial regime in India, Singapore served as the base for the British conquest of Malaya (modern Malaysia) in the 1870s and 1880s. Besides offering outstanding ports that enabled the British navy to

Warships provide covering fire as British troops prepare to storm the Burmese port of Rangoon in 1824. By the 1880s the British had established colonial authority in Burma and were using it as a source of such valuable commodities as teak, ivory, rubies, and jade.

control sea lanes linking the Indian Ocean with the South China Sea, Malaya provided abundant supplies of tin and rubber.

French Indochina

Although foiled in their efforts to establish themselves in India, French imperialists built the large southeast Asian colony of French Indochina, consisting of the modern states of Vietnam, Cambodia, and Laos, between 1859 and 1893. Like their British counterparts in India, French colonial officials introduced European-style schools and sought to establish close connections with native elites. Unlike their rivals, French officials also encouraged conversion to Christianity, and as a result the Roman Catholic church became prominent throughout French Indochina, especially in Vietnam. By century's end, all of southeast Asia had come under European imperial rule except for the kingdom of Siam (modern Thailand), which preserved its independence largely because colonial officials regarded it as a convenient buffer state between British-dominated Burma and French Indochina.

The Scramble for Africa

The most striking outburst of imperialism took place in Africa. As late as 1875, European peoples maintained a limited presence in Africa. They held several small coastal colonies and fortified trading posts, but their only sizable possessions were the Portuguese colonies of Angola and Mozambique, the French settler colony in northern Algeria, and a cluster of settler colonies populated by British and Dutch migrants in south Africa. After the end of the slave trade, a lively commerce developed around the exchange of African gold, ivory, and palm oil for European textiles, guns, and manufactured goods. This trade brought considerable prosperity and economic opportunity, especially to west African lands.

Between 1875 and 1900, however, the relationship between Africa and Europe dramatically changed. Within a quarter century, European imperial powers partitioned and colonized almost the entire African continent. Prospects of exploiting African resources and nationalist rivalries between European powers help to explain this frenzied quest for empire, often referred to as the "scramble for Africa."

European Explorers in Africa

European imperialists built on the information compiled by a series of adventurers and explorers who charted interior regions of Africa that Europeans had never before visited. Some went to Africa as missionaries. Best known of them was Dr. David Livingstone, a Scottish minister, who traveled through much of central and southern Africa in the mid-nineteenth century in search of suitable locations for mission posts. Other travelers were adventurers such as the American journalist Henry Morton Stanley, who undertook a well-publicized expedition to find Livingstone and report on his activities. Meanwhile, two English explorers, Richard Burton and John Speke, ventured into east Africa seeking the source of the Nile River. The geographic information compiled by these travelers held great interest for merchants eager to exploit business opportunities in Africa.

Especially exciting was reliable information about the great African rivers—the Nile, Niger, Congo, and Zambesi—and the access they provided to inland regions. In the 1870s King Leopold II of Belgium (reigned 1865–1909) employed Henry Morton Stanley to help develop commercial ventures and establish a colony called the Congo Free State (modern-day Democratic Republic of the Congo) in the basin of the Congo River. To forestall competition from Belgium's much larger and more powerful European neighbors, Leopold announced that the Congo region would be a free-trade zone accessible to merchants and businesspeople from all European lands. In fact, however, he carved out a personal colony and filled it with lucrative rubber plantations run by forced labor. Working conditions in the Congo Free State were so brutal, taxes so high, and abuses so many that humanitarians protested Leopold's colonial regime. Predatory rule had culminated in the death of four to eight million Africans. In 1908 the Belgian government took control of the colony, known thereafter as Belgian Congo.

As Leopold colonized central Africa, Britain established an imperial presence in Egypt. As Muhammad Ali and other Egyptian rulers sought to build up their army, strengthen the economy, and distance themselves from Ottoman authority, they borrowed heavily from European lenders. In the 1870s crushing debt forced Egyptian officials to impose high taxes, which provoked popular unrest

Henry Morton Stanley spent a great deal of time in the field, but here he appears, along with his gun bearer Kalulu, in front of a painted backdrop in a photographer's studio.

and a military rebellion. In 1882 a British army occupied Egypt to protect British financial interests and ensure the safety of the Suez Canal, which was crucial to British communications with India.

South Africa

Long before the nineteenth-century scramble, a European presence had grown at the southern tip of the African continent, where the Dutch East India Company had established Cape Town (1652) as a supply station for ships en route to Asia. Soon after, former company employees plus newly arrived settlers from Europe moved into lands beyond company control to take up farming and ranching. Many of these settlers, known first as Boers (the Dutch word for "farmer") and then as Afrikaners (the Dutch word for "African"), believed that God had predestined them to claim the people and resources of the Cape. The area under white settler control ex-

This 1912 photograph shows a stark portrait of the Belgian king's inhumane treatment of Africans in the Congo.

panded during the eighteenth century as a steady stream of European migrants—chiefly Dutch, Germans, and French Huguenots fleeing religious persecution—continued to swell the colony's population. As European settlers spread beyond the reaches of the original colony, they began encroaching on lands occupied by Khoikhoi and Xhosa peoples. Competition for land soon led to hostility, and by the early eighteenth century, warfare, enslavement, and smallpox epidemics had led to the virtual extinction of the Khoikhoi. After a century of intermittent warfare, the Xhosa too had been decimated, losing lives, land, and resources to European settlers.

The British takeover of the Cape during the Napoleonic Wars (1799–1815) encouraged further Afrikaner expansion into the interior of south Africa. The establishment of British rule in 1806 deeply disrupted Afrikaner society, for in its wake came the imposition of English law and language. The institution of slavery—a key defining feature of rural Afrikaner society—developed into the most contentious issue between British administrators and Afrikaner settlers. When the British abolished slavery in 1833, they not only eliminated the primary source of labor for white farmers but also dealt a crippling blow to Afrikaner financial viability and lifestyles. Chafing under British rule, Afrikaners started to leave their farms in Cape Colony and gradually migrated east in what they called the Great Trek. That colonial expansion sometimes led to violent conflict with indigenous

peoples, but the superior firepower of Afrikaner *voortrekkers* (Afrikaans for "pioneers") overcame first Ndebele and then Zulu resistance. The colonizers interpreted their successful expansion as evidence that God approved of their dominance in south Africa. By the mid-nineteenth century, *voortrekkers* had created several independent republics: the Republic of Natal, annexed by the British in 1843; the Orange Free State in 1854; and the South African Republic (Transvaal territories) in 1860.

Britain's lenient attitude toward Afrikaner statehood took a drastic turn with the discovery of large mineral deposits in Afrikaner-populated territories—diamonds in 1867 and gold in 1886. The influx of thousands of British miners and prospectors led to tensions between British authorities and Afrikaners, culminating in the South African War (1899–1902; sometimes called the Boer War). Although the brutal conflict pitted whites against whites, it also took a large toll on black Africans, who served both sides as soldiers and laborers. The internment of 100,000 black Africans in British concentration camps, for example, left more than 10,000 dead. The Afrikaners conceded defeat in 1902, and by 1910 the British government had reconstituted the four former colonies as provinces in the Union of South Africa, a largely autonomous British dominion. British attempts at improving relations between English speakers and Afrikaners centered on shoring up the privileges of white colonial society and the domination of black Africans.

The Berlin Conference

Tensions between those European powers who were seeking African colonies led to the Berlin West Africa Conference (1884–1885), during which the delegates of twelve European states as well as the United States and the Ottoman empire—not a single African was present—devised the ground rules for the colonization of Africa. Half the nations represented, including the United States, had no colonial ambitions on the continent, but they had been invited to give the proceedings a veneer of unbiased international approval. The Berlin Conference produced agreement for future claims on African lands: each colonial power had to notify the others of its claims, and each claim had to be followed up by "effective occupation" of the claimed territory. Occupation was commonly accomplished either by getting a signed agreement from a local African ruler or by military conquest. Conference participants also spelled out noble-minded objectives for colonized lands: an end to the slave trade, the extension of civilization and Christianity, and commerce and trade. Although the conference did not parcel out African lands among the participant nations, it nevertheless served public notice that European powers were poised to carve the continent into colonies.

During the next twenty-five years, European imperialists sent armies to consolidate their claims and impose colonial rule. Armed with the latest weapons technology, including the newly developed machine gun and artillery with explosive shells, they rarely failed to defeat African forces. All too often, battles were one-sided. In 1898, at Omdurman, a city in central Sudan near the junction of the White and Blue Nile rivers, British forces killed close to 20,000 Sudanese in a matter of hours while suffering only minor losses themselves. The only indigenous African state to resist colonization successfully was Ethiopia. In 1895, Italian forces invaded Ethiopia, anticipating an easy victory. But any designs to establish a colony were abandoned when the well-equipped Ethiopian army annihilated the Italians at the battle of Adwa in 1896. Besides Ethiopia, the only African state to remain independent was Liberia, a small

MAP 32.2

Imperialism in Africa, ca. 1914.

By 1914, only Ethiopia and Liberia remained free of European control.

How was it possible for Europeans to gain such domination?

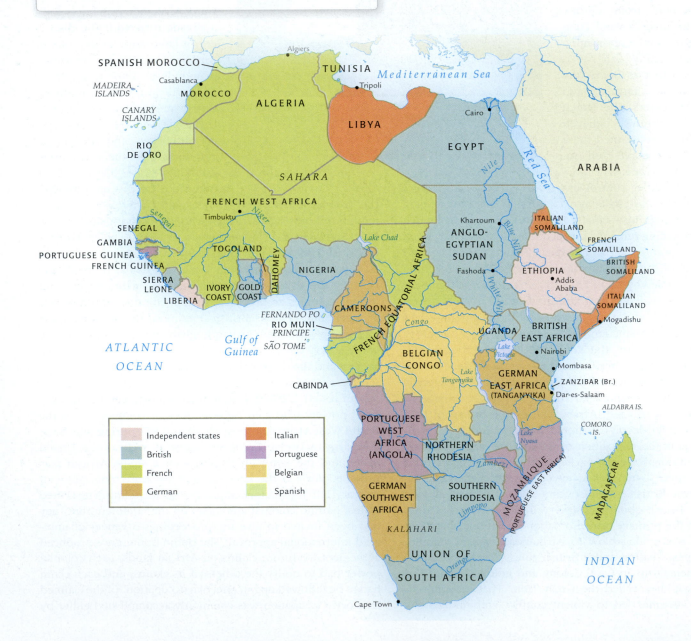

republic in west Africa populated by freed slaves that was effectively a dependency of the United States.

Systems of Colonial Rule

In the wake of rapid conquest came problems of colonial occupation. Imperial powers commonly assumed that, following an initial modest investment, colonial administration would become financially self-sufficient. For decades, Europeans struggled to identify the ideal system of rule, only to learn that colonial rule in Africa could be maintained only through exceedingly high expenditures.

The earliest approach to colonial rule involved "concessionary companies." European governments typically granted private companies large concessions of territory and empowered them to undertake economic activities such as mining, plantation agriculture, or railroad construction. Concessionary companies also had permission to implement systems of taxation and labor recruitment. Although that approach allowed European governments to colonize and exploit immense territories with only a modest investment in capital and personnel, company rule also brought liabilities. The brutal use of forced labor, which provoked a public outcry in Europe, and profits smaller than anticipated persuaded most European governments by the early twentieth century to curtail the powers of private companies and to establish their own rule, which took the form of either direct rule, typical of French colonies, or indirect rule, characteristic of British colonies.

Under direct rule, colonies featured administrative districts headed by European personnel who assumed responsibility for tax collection, labor and military recruitment, and the maintenance of law and order. Administrative boundaries intentionally cut across existing African political and ethnic boundaries to divide and weaken potentially powerful indigenous groups. Direct rule aimed at removing strong kings and other leaders and replacing them with more malleable persons. Underlying the principle of direct rule was the desire to keep African populations in check and to permit European administrators to engage in a "civilizing mission." However, that approach to colonial rule presented its own difficulties. Key among them was the constant shortage of European personnel. For example, in French West Africa some thirty-six hundred Europeans tried to rule over an African population of more than nine million. The combination of long distances and slow transport limited effective communication between regional authorities and officials in remote areas. An inability to speak local languages and a limited understanding of local customs among European officials further undermined their effective administration.

The British colonial administrator Frederick D. Lugard (1858–1945) was the driving force behind the doctrine of indirect rule, which the British employed in many of their African colonies. In his book *The Dual Mandate in British Tropical Africa* (1922), he stressed the moral and financial advantages of exercising control over subject populations through indigenous institutions. He was particularly keen on using existing "tribal" authorities and "customary laws" as the foundation for colonial rule. Forms of indirect rule worked in regions where Africans had already established strong and highly organized states, but elsewhere erroneous assumptions concerning the "tribal" nature of African societies weakened the effectiveness of indirect rule. Bewildered by the complexities of African societies, colonial officials frequently imposed their own ideas of what constituted "tribal boundaries" or "tribal authorities." The invention of rigid tribal categories and the establishment of artificial tribal boundaries became one of the greatest obstacles to nation building and regional stability in much of Africa during the second half of the twentieth century.

European Imperialism in the Pacific

While scrambling for Africa, European imperial powers did not overlook opportunities to establish their presence in the Pacific Ocean basin. Imperialism in the Pacific took two main forms. In Australia and New Zealand, European powers established settler colonies and dominant political institutions. In most of the Pacific islands, however, they sought commercial opportunities and reliable bases for their operations but did not wish to go to the trouble or expense of outright colonization. Only in the late nineteenth century did they begin to impose direct colonial rule on the islands.

Settler Colonies in the Pacific

European mariners reconnoitered Australia and made occasional landfalls from the early sixteenth century, but only after the Pacific voyages of Captain James Cook did Europeans travel to the southern continent in large numbers. In 1770 Cook anchored his fleet for a week at Botany Bay, near modern Sydney, and reported that the region would be suitable for settlement. In 1788 a British fleet with about one thousand settlers, most of them convicted criminals, arrived at Sydney harbor and established the colony of New South Wales. The migrants supported themselves mostly by herding sheep. Lured by opportunity, voluntary migrants outnumbered convicts by

---

thinking about ENCOUNTERS

Forays into the Pacific

Oceania had remained largely outside the purview of European and American imperialists until the nineteenth century. What resulted once European and American traders, missionaries, and settlers arrived on the shores of islands as far afield as Australia and Hawai`i? How did the indigenous peoples respond to these intruders?

sources from the past

The Royal Niger Company Mass-Produces Imperial Control in Africa

The 1880s proved a crucial time for sub-Saharan African societies and European imperial adventurers. European nations at the Berlin Conference set forth the rules by which they would partition and rule African states, and then those nations—such as Great Britain—commissioned companies like the Royal Niger Company to assert imperial prerogatives. To fend off French competitors in the Niger River delta, the British-controlled Royal Niger Company had local rulers sign its "standard treaty," a mass-produced, fill-in-the-blank document that essentially ceded trade and political control to the company, and thus to Britain, in what became the British colony of Nigeria.

We, the undersigned Chiefs of _____, with the view to the bettering of the condition of our country and our people, do this day cede to the Royal Niger Company, for ever, the whole of our territory from _____.

We also give to the said Royal Niger Company full power to settle all native disputes arising from any cause whatever, and we pledge ourselves not to enter into any war with other tribes without the sanction of the said Royal Niger Company.

We understand that the said Royal Niger Company have full power to mine, farm, and build in any portion of our country.

We bind ourselves not to have any intercourse with any strangers or foreigners except through the said Royal Niger Company.

In consideration of the foregoing, the said Royal Niger Company (Chartered and Limited) bind themselves not to interfere with any of the native laws or customs of the country, consistently with the maintenance of order and good government.

The said Royal Niger Company agree to pay native owners of land a reasonable amount for any portion they may require.

The said Royal Niger Company bind themselves to protect the said Chiefs from the attacks of any neighboring aggressive tribes.

The said Royal Niger Company also agree to pay the said Chiefs _____ measures native value.

We, the undersigned witnesses, do hereby solemnly declare that the _____ Chiefs whose names are placed opposite their respective crosses have in our presence affixed their crosses of their own free will and consent, and that the said _____ has in our presence affixed his signature.

Done in triplicate at _____, this _____ day of _____, 188__.

Declaration by interpreter I, _____, of _____, do hereby solemnly declare that I am well acquainted with the language of the country, and that on the _____ day of _____, 188__, I truly and faithfully explained the above Agreement to all the Chiefs present, and that they understood its meaning.

For Further Reflection

■ What did this "standard treaty" promise to Nigerian leaders, and what was expected in return? Given language barriers and imperial greed, do you believe Nigerians received true and faithful explanations of the treaty's meaning?

Source: Alfred J. Andrea and James H. Overfield, eds. *The Human Record: Sources of Global History,* 3rd ed., vol. 2. Boston: Wadsworth, 1998, pp. 299–300.

---

the 1830s, and the discovery of gold in 1851 brought a surge in migration to Australia. European settlers established communities also in New Zealand. Europeans first visited New Zealand while hunting whales and seals, but the islands' fertile soils and abundant stands of timber soon attracted their attention and drew large numbers of migrants.

European migration rocked the societies of Australia and New Zealand. Diseases such as smallpox and measles devastated indigenous peoples at the same time that European migrants flooded into their lands. The aboriginal population of Australia fell from about 650,000 in 1800 to 90,000 in 1900, whereas the European population rose from

a few thousand to 3.75 million during the same period. Similarly, the population of indigenous Maori in New Zealand fell from about 200,000 in 1800 to 45,000 a century later, while European numbers climbed to 750,000.

Increasing migration also fueled conflict between European settlers and native populations. Large settler societies pushed indigenous peoples from their lands, often following violent confrontations. Because the nomadic foraging peoples of Australia did not occupy lands permanently, British settlers considered the continent *terra nullius*—"land belonging to no one"—that they could seize and put to their own uses. They undertook brutal military campaigns to evict aboriginal

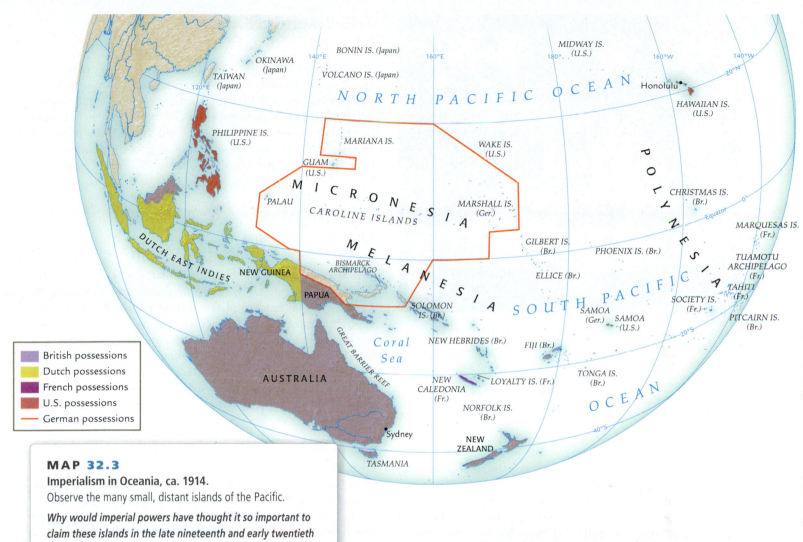

MAP 32.3

Imperialism in Oceania, ca. 1914.

Observe the many small, distant islands of the Pacific.

Why would imperial powers have thought it so important to claim these islands in the late nineteenth and early twentieth centuries?

peoples from lands suitable for agriculture or herding. Despite native resistance, by 1900 the British had succeeded in displacing most indigenous Australians from their traditional lands and dispersing them throughout the continent.

A similarly disruptive process transpired in New Zealand. Representatives of the British government encouraged Maori leaders in 1840 to sign the Treaty of Waitangi, presumably designed to place New Zealand under British protection. Interpreted differently by the British and the Maori, the treaty actually signaled the coming of official British colonial control in New Zealand (1841) and thereafter inspired effective and long-lasting Maori opposition to British attempts to usurp their land and sovereignty. Conflicts over land confiscations and disputed land sales, for example, helped to spark the New Zealand Wars, a series of military confrontations between autonomous Maori groups and British troops and settlers that extended from the mid- to the late nineteenth century. Various Maori also cooperated in the Maori King Movement (or *Kingitanga*), beginning in 1856, as a means of forwarding Maori unity and sovereignty. While political and military battles continued, the British managed by the end of the century to force many Maori into poor rural communities separated from European settlements.

Imperialists in Paradise Even though imported diseases ravaged indigenous populations, the Pacific islands mostly escaped the fate of Australia and New Zealand, where settlers overwhelmed and overpowered native populations. During the nineteenth century the principal European visitors to Pacific islands were whalers, merchants, and missionaries. Whalers frequented ports where they could relax, refit their ships, and drink rum. Merchants sought fragrant sandalwood and succulent sea slugs, both of which fetched high prices in China. Missionaries established both Roman Catholic and Protestant churches throughout the Pacific Ocean basin. Naval vessels sometimes made a show of force or intervened in disputes between islanders and Europeans—or between competing groups of Europeans. Through most of the nineteenth century, however, imperialist powers had no desire to establish direct colonial rule over Pacific islands.

An anonymous contemporary painting depicts the signing of the Treaty of Waitangi on 6 February 1840. British military and colonial officials look on as about fifty Maori chiefs put their names to the document.

THE EMERGENCE OF NEW IMPERIAL POWERS

Nineteenth-century imperialism was mostly a European affair. Toward the end of the century, however, two new imperial powers appeared on the world stage: the United States and Japan. Both lands experienced rapid industrialization in the late nineteenth century, and both built powerful armed forces. As European imperial powers planted their flags throughout the world, leaders of the United States and Japan decided that they too needed to establish a global imperial presence.

U.S. Imperialism in Latin America and the Pacific

The very existence of the United States was due to European imperialism. After the new republic had won its independence, U.S. leaders pursued their manifest destiny and brought almost all the temperate regions of North America under their authority. Like British migrants in Australia and New Zealand, Euro-American cultivators pushed indigenous peoples onto marginal lands and reservations. This domination of the North American continent represents a part of the larger story of European and Euro-American imperialism.

The Monroe Doctrine   The fledgling United States also tried to wield power outside North America. In 1823 President James Monroe (in office 1817–1825) issued a proclamation that warned European states against imperialist designs in the western hemisphere. In essence Monroe claimed the Americas as a U.S. protectorate, and his proclamation, known as the Monroe Doctrine, served as a justification for later U.S. intervention in hemispheric affairs. Until the late nineteenth century, the United States mostly exercised informal influence in the Americas and sought to guarantee free trade in the region. That policy benefited U.S. entrepreneurs and their European counterparts who worked to bring the natural resources and agricultural products of the Americas to the world market.

As the United States consolidated its continental holdings, U.S. leaders became interested in acquiring territories beyond the temperate regions of North America. In 1867 the United States purchased Alaska from Russia and in 1875 it claimed a protectorate over the islands of Hawai`i, where U.S. entrepreneurs had established highly productive sugarcane plantations. The Hawaiian kingdom survived until 1893, when a group of planters and businesspeople overthrew the last monarch, Queen Lili`uokalani (reigned 1891–1893), and invited the United States to annex the islands. U.S. president Grover Cleveland (in office 1885–1889 and 1893–1897) opposed annexation, but his successor, William McKinley (in office 1897–1901), was more open to American expansion and agreed to acquire the islands as U.S. possessions in 1898.

That situation changed in the late nineteenth century. Just as nationalist rivalries drove the scramble for Africa, so they encouraged imperialist powers to stake their claims in the Pacific. In an era of global imperialism, European states sought reliable coaling stations for their steamships and ports for their navies. France established a protectorate in Tahiti, the Society Islands, and the Marquesas as early as 1841 and imposed direct colonial rule in 1880. France also annexed New Caledonia in 1853. Britain made Fiji a crown colony in 1874, and Germany annexed several of the Marshall Islands in 1876 and 1878. At the Berlin Conference, European diplomats agreed on a partition of Oceania as well as Africa, and Britain, France, Germany, and the United States proceeded to claim almost all of the Pacific islands. By 1900 only the kingdom of Tonga remained independent, and even Tonga accepted British protection against the possibility of encroachments by other imperial powers.

Quite apart from their value as ports and coaling stations, the Pacific islands offered economic benefits to imperial powers. Hawai`i and Fiji were the sites of productive sugarcane plantations. Samoa, French Polynesia, and many Melanesian and Micronesian islands were sources of copra—dried coconut, which produced high-quality vegetable oil for the manufacture of soap, candles, and lubricants. New Caledonia had rich veins of nickel, and many small Pacific islands had abundant deposits of guano—bird droppings that made excellent fertilizer.

The Spanish-Cuban-American War The United States emerged as a major imperial and colonial power after the brief Spanish-Cuban-American War (1898–1899). War broke out as anticolonial tensions mounted in Cuba and Puerto Rico—the last remnants of Spain's American empire—where U.S. business interests had made large investments. In 1898 the U.S. battleship *Maine* exploded and sank in Havana harbor. U.S. leaders claimed sabotage and declared war on Spain. The United States easily defeated Spain and took control and possession of Cuba and Puerto Rico. After the U.S. navy destroyed the Spanish fleet at Manila in a single day, the United States also took possession of Guam and the Philippines, Spain's last colonies in the Pacific, to prevent them from falling under German or Japanese control.

The United States quickly established colonial governments in most of its new possessions. Instability and disorder prompted the new imperial power to intervene also in the affairs of Caribbean and Central American lands, even those that were not U.S. possessions, to prevent rebellion and protect American business interests. U.S. military forces occupied Cuba, the Dominican Republic, Nicaragua, Honduras, and Haiti in the early twentieth century.

The consolidation of U.S. authority in the Philippines was an especially difficult affair. The Spanish-Cuban-American War coincided with a Filipino revolt against Spanish rule, and U.S. forces promised to support independence of the Philippines in exchange for an alliance against Spain. After the victory over Spain, however, President William McKinley decided to bring the Philippines under American control. The United States paid Spain twenty million dollars for rights to the colony, which was important to American businesspeople and military leaders because of its strategic position in the South China Sea. Led by Emilio Aguinaldo—known to his followers as the George Washington of his country—Filipino rebels turned their arms against the new intruders. The result was a bitter insurrection that raged until 1902 and flared sporadically until 1906. The conflict claimed the lives of 4,200 American soldiers, 15,000 rebel troops, and some 200,000 Filipino civilians.

Queen Lili`uokalani, last monarch of Hawai`i, before her deposition in 1893. Wearing a European dress, the queen sits on a throne covered with a traditional royal cape made of bird feathers.

The Panama Canal To facilitate communication and transportation between the Atlantic and the Pacific oceans, the United States sought to build a canal across some narrow stretch of land in Central America. Engineers identified the isthmus of Panama in northern Colombia as the best site for a canal, but Colombia was unwilling to cede land for the project. Under President Theodore Roosevelt (in office 1901–1909), an enthusiastic champion of imperial expansion, the United States supported a rebellion against Colombia in 1903 and helped rebels establish the breakaway state of Panama. In exchange for this support, the United States won the right to build a canal across Panama and to control the adjacent territory, known as the Panama Canal Zone. Given this expansion of U.S. interests in Latin America, Roosevelt added a corollary to the Monroe Doctrine in 1904. The "Roosevelt Corollary" exerted the U.S. right to intervene in the domestic affairs of nations within the hemisphere if they demonstrated an inability to maintain the security deemed necessary to protect U.S. investments. The Roosevelt Corollary, along with the Panama Canal when it opened in 1914, strengthened U.S. military and economic claims.

Imperial Japan

Strengthened by rapid industrialization during the Meiji era, Japan joined the ranks of imperial powers in the late nineteenth century. Japanese leaders deeply resented the unequal treaties that the United States and European powers forced them to accept in the 1860s. They resolved to eliminate the diplomatic handicaps imposed by the treaties and to raise Japan's profile in the world. While founding representative political institutions to demonstrate their trustworthiness to American and European diplomats, Japanese leaders also made a bid to stand alongside the world's great powers by launching a campaign of imperial expansion.

Early Japanese Expansion The Japanese drive to empire began in the east Asian islands. During the 1870s Japanese leaders consolidated their hold on Hokkaido and the Kurile Islands to the north, and they encouraged Japanese migrants to populate the islands to forestall Russian expansion there. By 1879 they had also established their hegemony over Okinawa and the Ryukyu Islands to the south.

In 1876 Japan purchased modern warships from Britain, and the newly strengthened Japanese navy immediately began to flex its muscles in Korea. After a confrontation between the Korean navy and a Japanese surveying vessel, Meiji officials dispatched a gunboat expedition and forced Korean leaders to submit to the same kind of unequal treaty that the United States and European states had imposed on Japan. As European and U.S. imperialists divided up the world in the 1880s and 1890s, Meiji political and military leaders made plans to project Japanese power abroad. They developed contingency plans for a conflict with China, staged maneuvers in anticipation of a continental war, and built a navy with the capacity to fight on the high seas.

The Sino-Japanese War

Conflict erupted in 1894 over the status of Korea. Taking advantage of the unequal treaty of 1876, Japanese businesses had substantial interests in Korea. When an antiforeign rebellion broke out in Korea in 1893, Meiji leaders feared that the land might fall into anarchy and become an inviting target of European and U.S. imperialism. Qing rulers sent an army to restore order and reassert Chinese authority in Korea, but Meiji leaders were unwilling to recognize Chinese control over a land so important to Japanese business interests. Thus in August 1894 they declared war on China. The Japanese navy quickly gained control of the Yellow Sea and demolished the Chinese fleet in a battle lasting a mere five hours. The Japanese army then pushed Qing forces out of the Korean peninsula. Within a few months the conflict was over. When the combatants made peace in April 1895, Qing authorities recognized the independence of Korea, thus making it essentially a dependency of Japan. They also ceded Taiwan, the Pescadores Islands, and the Liaodong peninsula, which strengthened Japanese control over east Asian waters. Alongside territorial acquisitions, Japan gained unequal treaty rights in China like those enjoyed by European and American powers.

The unexpected Japanese victory startled European imperial powers, especially Russia. Tensions between Japan and Russia soon mounted, as both imperial powers had territorial ambitions in the Liaodong peninsula, Korea, and Manchuria. During the late 1890s Japanese military leaders vastly strengthened both their navy and their army with an eye toward a future conflict with Russia.

The Russo-Japanese War

War broke out in 1904, and Japanese forces overran Russian installations before reinforcements could arrive from Europe. The enhanced Japanese navy destroyed the Russian Baltic fleet, which had sailed halfway around the world to support the war effort. By 1905 the war was over, and Japan won international recognition of its colonial authority over Korea and the Liaodong peninsula. Furthermore, Russia ceded the southern half

The Japanese painter Kobayashi Kiyochika celebrates a Japanese naval victory over the Chinese fleet. China's defeat in the Sino-Japanese war showed how the Qing dynasty had been weakened militarily, especially by the Opium War, and demonstrated how successful modernization had been for Japan since the Meiji restoration.

of Sakhalin island to Japan, along with a railroad and economic interests in southern Manchuria. Victory in the Russo-Japanese War transformed Japan into a major imperial power.

LEGACIES OF IMPERIALISM

Imperialism and colonialism profoundly influenced the development of world history. In some ways, they tightened links between the world's peoples: trade and migration increased dramatically as imperial powers exploited the resources of subject lands and recruited labor forces to work in colonies throughout the world. Yet imperialism and colonialism also brought peoples into conflict and heightened senses of difference between peoples. European, Euro-American, and Japanese imperialists all came to think of themselves as superior to the peoples they overcame. Meanwhile, foreign intrusion stimulated the development of national identities in colonized lands, and over time these national identities served as a foundation for anticolonial independence movements.

Empire and Economy

One of the principal motives of imperialism was the desire to gain access to natural resources and agricultural products. As imperial powers consolidated their hold on foreign lands, colonial administrators reorganized subject societies so they would become efficient suppliers of timber, rubber, petroleum, gold, silver, diamonds, cotton, tea, coffee, cacao, and other products as well. As a result, global trade in those commodities surged during the nineteenth and early twentieth centuries. The advantages of that trade went mostly to the colonial powers, whose policies encouraged their subject lands to provide raw materials for processing in the industrialized societies of Europe, North America, and Japan.

Economic and Social Changes Sometimes colonial rule transformed the production of crops and commodities that had long been prominent in subject societies. In India,

for example, the cultivation of cotton began probably before 5000 B.C.E. For most of history, cultivators spun thread and wove their own cotton textiles or else supplied local artisans with raw materials. In the nineteenth century, however, colonial administrators reoriented the cultivation of cotton to serve the needs of the emerging British textile industry. They encouraged cultivators to produce cotton for export rather than for local consumption, and they built railroads deep into the subcontinent to transport raw cotton to the coast quickly, before rain and dust could spoil the product. They shipped raw cotton to England, where mechanized factories rapidly turned out large volumes of high-quality textiles. They also allowed the import of inexpensive British textiles, which undermined Indian cotton cloth production. The value of raw cotton exported from India went from 10 million rupees in 1849 to 60 million rupees in 1860 and 410 million rupees in 1913, whereas the value of finished cotton products imported into India rose from 50,000 rupees in 1814 to 5.2 million rupees in 1829 and 30 million rupees in 1890. Thus colonial policies transformed India from the world's principal center of cotton manufacture to a supplier of raw cotton and a consumer of textiles produced in the British isles.

In some cases, colonial rule led to the introduction of new crops that transformed both the landscape and the social order of subject lands. In the early nineteenth century, for example, British colonial officials introduced tea bushes from China to Ceylon and India. The effect on Ceylon was profound. British planters felled trees in much of the island, converted rain forests into tea plantations, and recruited Ceylonese women by the thousands to carry out the labor-intensive work of harvesting mature tea leaves. Consumption of tea in India and Ceylon was almost negligible, so increased supplies met the growing demand for tea in Europe, where the beverage became accessible to individuals of all social classes. The value of south Asian tea exports rose from about 309,000 pounds sterling in 1866 to 4.4 million pounds sterling in 1888 and 6.1 million pounds sterling in 1900. Malaya and Sumatra underwent a similar social

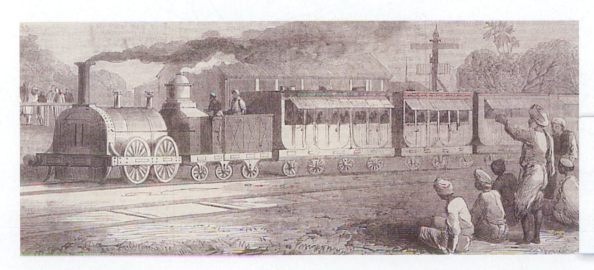

An engraving depicts the East India Railway about 1863. Though originally built to transport goods, railroads quickly became a popular means of passenger travel in India.

transformation after British colonial agents planted rubber trees there in the 1870s and established plantations to meet the growing global demand for rubber products.

Labor Migrations

Efforts to exploit the natural resources and agricultural products of subject lands led imperial and colonial powers to encourage mass migrations of workers during the nine-

teenth and early twentieth centuries. Two patterns of labor migration were especially prominent during the imperial and colonial era. European migrants went mostly to temperate lands, where they worked as free cultivators or industrial laborers. In contrast, migrants from Asia, Africa, and the Pacific islands moved largely to tropical and subtropical lands, where they worked as indentured laborers on plantations or manual laborers for mining enterprises or large-scale construction projects. Between them, these two streams of labor migration profoundly influenced the development of societies, especially in the Americas and the Pacific basin.

European Migration Between 1800 and 1914 some fifty million European migrants left their homes and sought opportunities overseas. Most of those migrants left the relatively poor agricultural societies of southern and eastern Europe, especially Italy, Russia, and Poland, although siz-

MAP 32.4

Imperialism and migration during the nineteenth and early twentieth centuries.

An unprecedented intercontinental migration of people characterized the age of imperialism.

What factors encouraged and facilitated migration on this extraordinary scale?

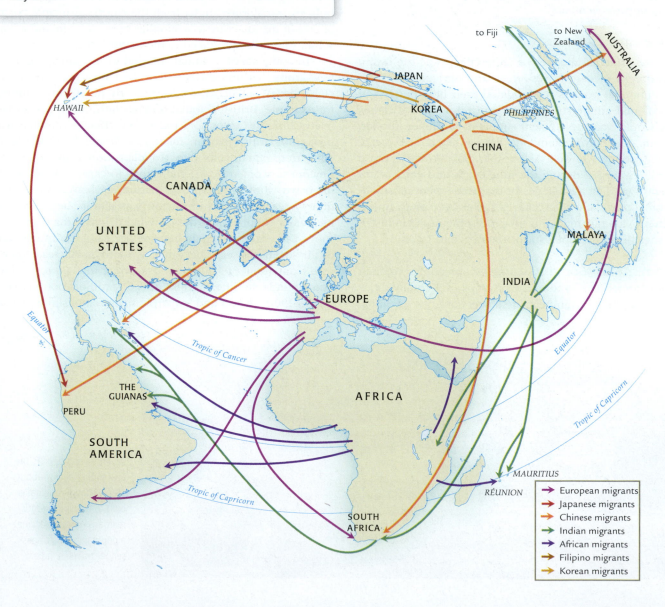

able numbers came also from Britain, Ireland, Germany, and Scandinavia. A majority of the migrants—about thirty-two million—went to the United States. Many of the early arrivals went west in search of cheap land to cultivate. Later migrants settled heavily in the northeast, where they provided the labor that drove U.S. industrialization after the 1860s. Settler colonies in Canada, Argentina, Australia, New Zealand, and south Africa also drew large numbers of European migrants, who mostly became free cultivators or herders but sometimes found employment as skilled laborers in mines or fledgling industries. Most European migrants traveled as free agents, but some went as indentured laborers. All of them were able to find opportunities in temperate regions of the world because of European and Euro-American imperialism in the Americas, south Africa, and Oceania.

Indentured Labor Migration In contrast to their European counterparts, migrants from Asia, Africa, and the Pacific islands generally traveled as indentured laborers. As the institution of slavery went into decline, planters sought large numbers of laborers to replace slaves who left the plantations. The planters relied primarily on indentured laborers recruited from relatively poor and densely populated lands. Between 1820 and 1914 about 2.5 million indentured laborers left their homes to work in distant parts of the world. Labor recruiters generally offered workers free passage to their destinations and provided them with food, shelter, clothing, and modest compensation for their services in exchange for a commitment to work for five to seven years. Sometimes recruiters also offered free return passage to workers who completed a second term of service.

The majority of the indentured laborers came from India, but sizable numbers also came from China, Japan, Java, Africa, and the Pacific islands. Indentured laborers went mostly to tropical and subtropical lands in the Americas, the Caribbean, Africa, and Oceania. The indentured labor trade began in the 1820s when French and British colonial officials sent Indian migrants to work on sugar plantations in the Indian Ocean islands of Réunion and Mauritius. The arrangement worked well, and large numbers of Indian laborers later went to work on rubber plantations in Malaya and sugar plantations in south Africa, the Pacific island of Fiji, the Guianas, and the Caribbean islands of Trinidad, Tobago, and Jamaica. After the Opium War, recruiters began to seek workers in China. Large numbers of Chinese laborers went to sugar plantations in Cuba and Hawai`i, guano mines in Peru, tin mines in Malaya, gold mines in south Africa and Australia, and railroad construction sites in the United States, Canada, and Peru. After the Meiji restoration in Japan, a large contingent of Japanese laborers migrated to Hawai`i to work on sugar plantations, and a smaller group went to work in guano mines in Peru. Indentured laborers from Africa went mostly to sugar plantations in Réunion, the Guianas, and Caribbean islands. Those from Pacific islands went mostly to plantations in other Pacific islands and Australia.

Empire and Migration All those large-scale migrations of the nineteenth century reflected the global influence of imperial powers. European migrations were possible only because European and Euro-American peoples had established settler societies in temperate regions around the world. Movements of indentured laborers were possible because colonial officials were able to recruit workers and dispatch them to distant lands where their compatriots had already established plantations or opened mines. In combination the nineteenth-century migrations profoundly influenced societies around the world by depositing large communities of people with distinctive ethnic identities in lands far from their original homes.

Empire and Society

Colonial Conflict The policies adopted by imperial powers and colonial officials forced peoples of different societies to deal with one another on a regular and systematic basis. Their interactions often led to violent conflicts between colonizers and subject peoples. The sepoy rebellion was the most prominent effort to resist British colonial authority in India, but it was only one among thousands of insurrections organized by discontented Indian subjects between the mid-nineteenth and the mid-twentieth centuries. Colonized lands in southeast Asia and Africa also became hotbeds of resistance, as subject peoples revolted against foreign rule, tyrannical behavior of colonial officials, the introduction of European schools and curricula, high taxation, and requirements that subject peoples cultivate certain crops or provide compulsory labor for colonists' enterprises.

Many rebellions drew strength from traditional religious beliefs, and priests or prophets often led resistance to colonial rule. In Tanganyika, for example, a local prophet organized the large-scale Maji Maji rebellion (1905–1906) to expel German colonial authorities from east Africa. Rebels sprinkled themselves with *maji-maji* ("magic water"), which they believed would protect them from German weapons. The magic water was ineffective, and as many as seventy-five thousand insurgents died in the conflict. Nevertheless, rebellion was a constant threat to colonial rule. Even when subject peoples dared not revolt, since they could not match European weaponry, they resisted colonial rule by boycotting European goods, organizing political parties and pressure groups, publishing anticolonial newspapers and magazines, and pursuing anticolonial policies through churches and religious groups.

Colonial policies also led to conflicts among peoples brought together artificially into multicultural societies. When indentured laborers from different societies congregated on plantations, for example, tensions quickly developed between workers and their supervisors and among different groups of workers themselves. In Hawai`i, one of the most diverse multicultural societies created by the labor migrations of the nineteenth century, workers on sugar plantations came primarily from China, Japan, and Portugal, but there were also sizable contingents from the Philippines, Korea, and other Pacific islands. Workers and their families normally lived in villages dominated by their own ethnic groups, but there were plentiful opportunities for individuals and groups to mix with one another at work, at play, or in the larger society. Although the various ethnic communities readily adopted their neighbors' foods and sometimes took spouses from other groups, linguistic, religious, and cultural differences provided a foundation for strong ethnic identities throughout the plantation era and beyond.

Scientific Racism

Social and cultural differences were the foundation of an academic pursuit known as scientific racism, which became prominent especially after the 1840s. Theorists such as the French nobleman Count Joseph Arthur de Gobineau (1816–1882) took race as the most important index of human potential. In fact, there is no such thing as a biologically pure race, but nineteenth-century theorists assumed that the human species consisted of several distinct racial groups. In his dense, four-volume *Essay on the Inequality of the Human Races* (1853–1855), Gobineau divided humanity into four main racial groups, each of which had its own peculiar traits. Gobineau characterized Africans as unintelligent and lazy; Asians as smart but docile; the native peoples of the Americas as dull and arrogant; and Europeans as intelligent, noble, and morally superior to others. Throughout the later nineteenth and early twentieth centuries, racist thinkers sought to identify racial groups on the basis of skin color, bone structure, nose shape, cranial capacity, and other physical characteristics. Agreeing uniformly that Europeans were superior to other peoples, race theorists clearly reflected the dominance of European imperial powers in the larger world.

After the 1860s, scientific racists drew heavily from the writings of Charles Darwin (1809–1882), an English biologist whose book *The Origin of Species* (1859) argued that all living species had evolved over thousands of years in a ferocious contest for survival. Species that adapted well to their

Apollo Belvidere

Greek

Negro

Creole Negro

Young chimpanzee

Young chimpanzee

Scientific racists often argued that Europeans had reached a higher stage of evolution than other peoples. An illustration from a popular book by Josiah Clark Nott and G. R. Glidden, *Indigenous Races of the Earth,* deliberately distorted facial and skull features to suggest a close relationship between African peoples and chimpanzees.

environment survived, reproduced, and flourished, according to Darwin, whereas others declined and went into extinction. The slogan "survival of the fittest" soon became a byword for Darwin's theory of evolution. Theorists known as social Darwinists seized on those ideas, which Darwin had applied exclusively to biological matters, and adapted them to explain the development of human societies. The English philosopher Herbert Spencer (1820–1903) relied on theories of evolution to explain differences between the strong and the weak: successful individuals and races had competed better in the natural world and consequently evolved to higher states than did other, less fit peoples. On the basis of that reasoning, Spencer and others justified the domination of European imperialists over subject peoples as the inevitable result of natural scientific principles.

Popular Racism

On a more popular level, there was no need for elaborate scientific theories to justify racist prejudices. Representatives of imperial and colonial powers routinely adopted racist views on the basis of personal experience, which seemed to teach their superiority to subject peoples. In 1896, for example, the British military officer Colonel Francis Younghusband reflected on differences between peoples that he noticed during his travels throughout China, central Asia, and India. He granted that Asian peoples were physically and intellectually equal to Europeans, but he held that

no European can mix with non-Christian races without feeling his moral superiority over them. He feels, from the first contact with them, that whatever may be their relative positions from an intellectual point of view, he is stronger morally than they are. And facts show that this feeling is a true one. It is not because we are any cleverer than the natives of India, because we have more brains or bigger heads than they have, that we rule India; but because we are stronger morally than they

are. Our superiority over them is not due to mere sharpness of intellect, but to that higher moral nature to which we have attained in the development of the human race.

Racist views were by no means a monopoly of European imperialists: U.S. and Japanese empire builders also developed a sense of superiority over the peoples they conquered and ruled. U.S. forces in the Philippines disparaged the rebels they fought there as "gooks," and they did not hesitate to torture enemies in a conflict justified by President McKinley as an effort to "civilize and Christianize" the Filipinos. In the 1890s Japanese newspapers portrayed Chinese and Korean peoples as dirty, backward, stupid, and cowardly. Some scholars concocted speculative theories that the Japanese people were more akin to the "Aryans," who supposedly had conquered much of the Eurasian landmass in ancient times, than to the "Mongolians" who populated China and Korea. After their victory in the Russo-Japanese War, political and military leaders came to believe that Japan had an obligation to oversee the affairs of their backward neighbors and help civilize their little Asian brothers.

Nationalism and Anticolonial Movements

While imperialists convinced themselves of their racial superiority, colonial rule provoked subject peoples to develop a sense of their own identities. Just as Napoleon's invasions aroused national feelings and led to the emergence of nationalist movements in Europe, so imperial expansion and colonial domination prompted the formation of national identities and the organization of anticolonial movements in subject lands. The potential of imperialism and colonialism to push subject peoples toward nationalism was most evident in India.

Ram Mohan Roy

During the nineteenth century, educated Indian elites helped forge a sense of Indian identity. Among the most influential of them was Ram Mohan Roy (1772–1833), a prominent Bengali intellectual sometimes called the "father of modern India." Roy argued for the construction of a society based on both modern European science and the Indian tradition of devotional Hinduism. He supported some British colonial policies, such as the campaign to end the practice of sati, and he worked with Christian social reformers to improve the status of women by providing them with education and property rights. Yet Roy saw himself as a Hindu reformer who drew inspiration from the Vedas and Upanishads and who sought to bring Hindu spirituality to bear on the problems and conditions of his own time. During the last two decades of his life, Roy tirelessly published newspapers and founded societies to mobilize educated Hindus and advance the cause of social reform in colonial India.

Reform societies flourished in nineteenth-century India. Most of them appealed to upper-caste Hindus, but some were Muslim organizations, and a few represented the interests of peasants, landlords, or lower castes. After mid-century, reformers increasingly called for self-government or at least greater Indian participation in government. Their leaders often had received an advanced education at British universities, and they drew inspiration from European Enlightenment values such as equality, freedom, and popular sovereignty. But they invoked those values to criticize the British colonial regime in India and to call for political and social reform.

The Indian National Congress

The most important of the reform groups was the Indian National Congress,

Much of western India experienced severe famine in 1896–1897, and epidemics of bubonic plague broke out among weakened populations. British relief efforts were often heavy-handed and insensitive, and they did little to alleviate the problems.

founded in 1885, with British approval, as a forum for educated Indians to communicate their views on public affairs to colonial officials. Representatives from all parts of the subcontinent aired grievances about Indian poverty, the transfer of wealth from India to Britain, trade and tariff policies that harmed Indian businesses, the inability of colonial officials to provide effective relief for regions stricken by drought or famine, and British racism toward Indians. By the end of the nineteenth century, the congress openly sought Indian self-rule within a larger imperial framework. In 1916 the congress joined forces with the All-India Muslim League, the most prominent organization working to advance the political and social interests of Muslims, who made up about 25 percent of the Indian population.

Faced with increasing demands for Indian participation in government, in 1909 colonial authorities granted a limited franchise that allowed wealthy Indians to elect representatives to local legislative councils. By that time, however, the drive for political reform had become a mass movement. Indian nationalists called for immediate independence, mounted demonstrations to build support for their cause, and organized boycotts of British goods. A few zealous nationalists turned to violence and sought to undermine British rule by bombing government buildings and assassinating colonial officials. Going into the twentieth century, Indian nationalism was a powerful movement that would bring independence from colonial rule in 1947.

Although local experiences varied considerably, Indian nationalism and independence movements served as models for anticolonial campaigns in other lands. In almost all cases, the leaders of those movements were European-educated elites who absorbed Enlightenment values and then turned those values into an attack on European colonial rule in foreign lands.

in**perspective**

The construction of global empires in the nineteenth century noticeably increased the tempo of world integration. Armed with powerful transportation, communication, and military technologies, European peoples imposed their rule on much of Asia and almost all of Africa. They wielded enormous influence throughout the world, even where they did not establish imperial control, because of their wealth and economic power. Toward the end of the nineteenth century, the United States and Japan joined European states as global imperialists. All the imperial powers profoundly influenced the development of the societies they ruled. They shaped the economies and societies of their colonies by pushing them to supply natural resources and agricultural commodities in exchange for manufactured products. They created multicultural societies around the world by facilitating the movement of workers to lands where there was high demand for labor on plantations or in mines. They unintentionally encouraged the emergence of independence movements by provoking subject peoples to develop a sense of national identity. From the early twentieth century forward, much of global history has revolved around issues stemming from the world order of imperialism and colonialism. ●

CHRONOLOGY

1772–1833	Life of Ram Mohan Roy
1809–1882	Life of Charles Darwin
1816–1882	Life of Count Joseph Arthur de Gobineau
1824	Founding of Singapore by Thomas Stamford Raffles
1840	Treaty of Waitangi
1853–1902	Life of Cecil Rhodes
1857	Sepoy rebellion
1859–1869	Construction of the Suez Canal
1860–1864	Land wars in New Zealand
1865–1909	Reign of King Leopold II of Belgium
1884–1885	Berlin West Africa Conference
1885	Founding of the Indian National Congress
1894–1895	Sino-Japanese War
1897–1901	Term of office of U.S. president William McKinley
1898–1899	Spanish-Cuban-American War
1899–1902	South African War (Boer War)
1901–1909	Term of office of U.S. president Theodore Roosevelt
1904–1905	Russo-Japanese War
1904–1914	Construction of the Panama Canal
1905–1906	Maji Maji rebellion
1906	Founding of All-India Muslim League

For Further Reading

Michael Adas. *Machines as the Measure of Men: Science, Technology, and Ideologies of Western Dominance.* Ithaca, 1988. Argues that European imperialists judged other peoples on the basis of their technological expertise.

————. *Prophets of Rebellion: Millenarian Protest Movements against the European Colonial Order.* Cambridge, 1987. Fascinating study focusing on five rebellions against European colonial rule led by religious leaders.

Benedict Anderson. *Imagined Communities: Reflections on the Origin and Spread of Nationalism.* Rev. ed. London, 1991. Examines the emergence of nationalism in Europe and its spread to other parts of the world during the era of imperialism.

A. Adu Boahen. *African Perspectives on Colonialism.* Baltimore, 1987. A valuable synthetic work that examines African responses to imperial intrusions and colonial regimes.

Sugata Bose. *A Hundred Horizons: The Indian Ocean in the Age of Global Empires.* Cambridge, Mass., 2006. A bold interregional history that argues that the peoples of the Indian Ocean littoral shared a common historical destiny.

H. V. Bowen. *The Business of Empire: The East India Company and Imperial Britain, 1756–1833.* Cambridge, 2006. Detailed history of the company's rise to power in India.

Jane Burbank and Frederick Cooper. *Empires in World History: Power and the Politics of Difference.* Princeton, 2010. A major study that considers modern empires in historical context.

John M. Carroll. *Edge of Empires: Chinese Elites and British Colonials in Hong Kong.* Cambridge, Mass., 2005. Study of the commercial and social interaction between Chinese and British in the formation of Hong Kong.

Ken S. Coates. *A Global History of Indigenous Peoples: Struggle and Survival.* Houndmills, 2004. Stressing the active role of indigenous peoples, this work examines the dynamics of colonial encounters.

Bernard S. Cohn. *Colonialism and Its Forms of Knowledge: The British in India.* Princeton, 1996. Insightful essays on the cultural and intellectual manifestations of imperialism.

Philip D. Curtin. *The World and the West: The European Challenge and the Overseas Response in the Age of Empire.* Cambridge and New York, 2000. A work that focuses on cultural change as it examines how various peoples have responded to the establishment of European empires.

Ranajit Guha and Gayatri Chakravorty Spivak, eds. *Selected Subaltern Studies.* New York, 1988. A collection of essays dealing with the experiences of women, minorities, peasants, workers, rebels, and subordinate groups in colonial India.

Daniel R. Headrick. *The Tentacles of Progress: Technology Transfer in the Age of Imperialism, 1850–1940.* New York, 1988. Argues that imperial powers reserved the benefits of technological innovation for themselves by limiting the expertise that they shared with subject peoples.

————. *The Tools of Empire: Technology and European Imperialism in the Nineteenth Century.* New York, 1981. Surveys the role of transportation, communication, military, and medical technologies in the making of global empires.

Adam Hochschild. *King Leopold's Ghost: A Story of Greed, Terror, and Heroism in Colonial Africa.* Boston, 1998. A ghastly story of nearly forgotten greed and crime.

Peter H. Hoffenberg. *An Empire on Display: English, Indian, and Australian Exhibitions from the Crystal Palace to the Great War.* Berkeley, 2001. An imaginative work that shows how exhibitions shaped culture and society within and across borders of the British empire.

Zine Magubane. *Bringing the Empire Home: Race, Class, and Gender in Britain and Colonial South Africa.* Chicago, 2004. Study of the ways that colonial England used racial stereotypes to justify its own social hierarchies as well as the colonial project.

David Northrup. *Indentured Labor in the Age of Imperialism, 1834–1922.* Cambridge, 1995. Careful study of indentured labor migrations and working conditions.

Thomas Pakenham. *The Scramble for Africa, 1876–1912.* New York, 1991. Detailed popular history of empire building in sub-Saharan Africa.

H. L. Wesseling. *The European Colonial Empires: 1815–1919.* New York, 2004. Puts the process of colonization into a comparative and long-term perspective.

Kathleen Wilson, ed. *A New Imperial History: Culture, Identity, and Modernity in Britain and the Empire, 1660–1840.* New York, 2004. Study of the cultural impact of colonialism on Britain.

Louise Young. *Japan's Total Empire: Manchuria and the Culture of Wartime Imperialism.* Berkeley, 1988. An important work that analyzes the transforming power imperialism had on both the colonized and the colonizer.

State of the World
The World Turned Upside Down

At the 1781 British surrender to colonial American troops in Yorktown, the British band reputedly played the march "The World Turned Upside Down." Whether that is a true story or not, the tune's title offered an appropriate commentary on how the state of the world was indeed experiencing dramatic changes, not just by political revolutions, but also by industrialization and the new imperialism. When the much-underrated colonial and guerrilla forces defeated the brash, imperial army of Great Britain, the most powerful nation in the world, that world did indeed seem upside down. A subject population of the British empire had bested its rulers and overthrown monarchy in favor of a republican form of government.

As "the people" became the source for national sovereignty in much of the Atlantic basin, revolution brought about the beheading of a king and a queen in France and the elevation of slaves to the status of national leaders in Haiti. Throughout Europe, the Caribbean, and Latin America, old governments fell under the pressure of revolutionary ideals and a new sort of nationalism. Similarly, the economic transformations linked to industrialization contributed to a world seemingly upended, whereby machines, factories, and inanimate sources of power and energy ruled over human life and nature. Industrialization likewise promoted mass migrations of Europeans and Asians to the Americas, literally repositioning human populations across hemispheres. Migrants, indigenous peoples, freed slaves, and women agitated for their democratic rights and equality in these new industrial and expansionist national states, but most of the world did not immediately undergo revolution inspired by Enlightenment of ideals of liberty, equality, and popular sovereignty.

Some of the oldest, most prestigious, and most powerful territories in the world, from the Ottoman empire and Africa to Russia, China, and Japan, found themselves challenged by the upstart new imperialists in Europe and the United States, their sovereignty and freedom impinged upon by the powerful combination of nationalism, industry, and militarism. Resistance to this world turned upside down persisted, however. On the foundation of thoroughgoing reform, Japan managed to attain parity with European empires. Colonial subjects from India to Africa engaged in large-scale rebellion and small acts of resistance. What North American colonists began in the late eighteenth century, colonial peoples in Africa and Asia finished in the twentieth century. After Europe imploded from within during two cataclysmic world wars, colonized peoples would turn the world upside down once again.

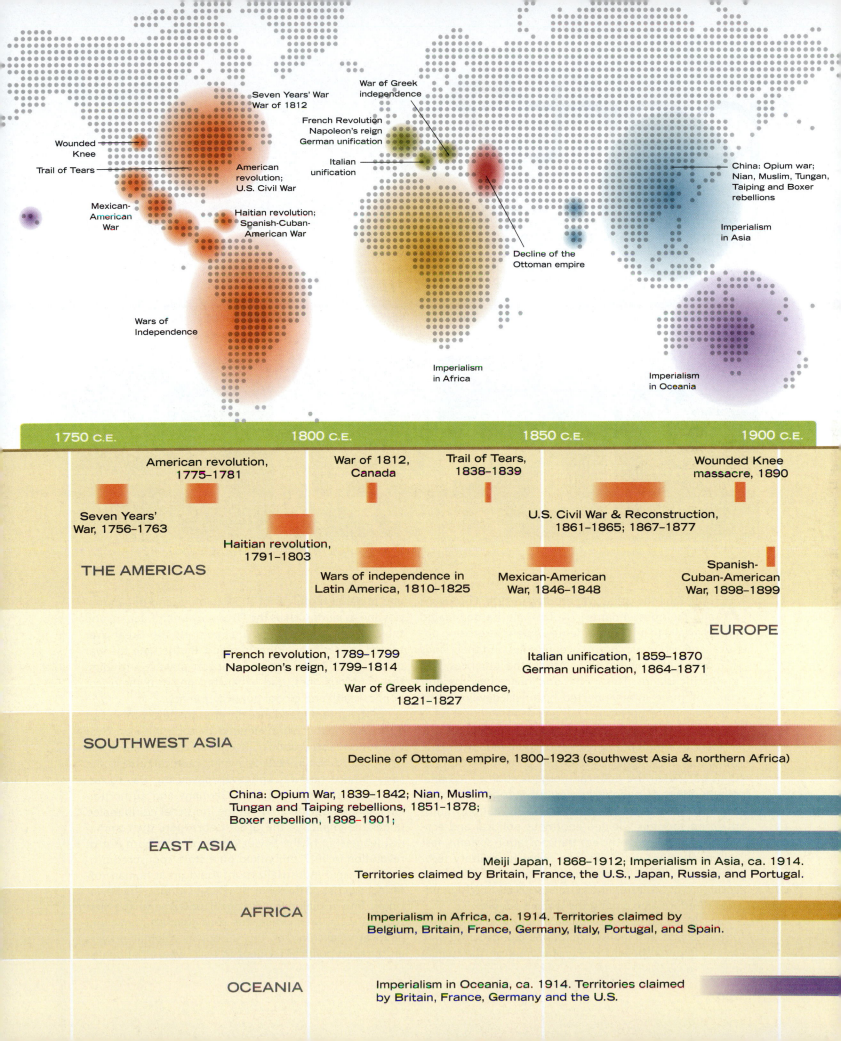

Wounded Knee

Trail of Tears

Seven Years' War
War of 1812

War of Greek independence

French Revolution
Napoleon's reign
German unification

Italian unification

American revolution;
U.S. Civil War

China: Opium war;
Nian, Muslim, Tungan,
Taiping and Boxer
rebellions

Mexican-American War

Haitian revolution;
Spanish-Cuban-American War

Imperialism in Asia

Decline of the Ottoman empire

Wars of Independence

Imperialism in Africa

Imperialism in Oceania

1750 C.E.	1800 C.E.	1850 C.E.	1900 C.E.

American revolution, 1775–1781

War of 1812, Canada

Trail of Tears, 1838–1839

Wounded Knee massacre, 1890

Seven Years' War, 1756–1763

U.S. Civil War & Reconstruction, 1861–1865; 1867–1877

Haitian revolution, 1791–1803

THE AMERICAS

Wars of independence in Latin America, 1810–1825

Mexican-American War, 1846–1848

Spanish-Cuban-American War, 1898–1899

EUROPE

French revolution, 1789–1799
Napoleon's reign, 1799–1814

Italian unification, 1859–1870
German unification, 1864–1871

War of Greek independence, 1821–1827

SOUTHWEST ASIA

Decline of Ottoman empire, 1800–1923 (southwest Asia & northern Africa)

China: Opium War, 1839–1842; Nian, Muslim, Tungan and Taiping rebellions, 1851–1878; Boxer rebellion, 1898–1901;

EAST ASIA

Meiji Japan, 1868–1912; Imperialism in Asia, ca. 1914. Territories claimed by Britain, France, the U.S., Japan, Russia, and Portugal.

AFRICA

Imperialism in Africa, ca. 1914. Territories claimed by Belgium, Britain, France, Germany, Italy, Portugal, and Spain.

OCEANIA

Imperialism in Oceania, ca. 1914. Territories claimed by Britain, France, Germany and the U.S.

part 7

CONTEMPORARY GLOBAL REALIGNMENTS, 1914 TO THE PRESENT

At the time the Great War erupted in 1914, Europeans and their descendants in North America dominated global affairs to an unprecedented extent, exercising political and economic control over peoples and their lands in most of Asia, nearly all of Africa, the Americas, and the Pacific islands. This global dominance was the outcome of three interconnected historical developments that took place between 1750 and 1914. Political revolutions in the Atlantic Ocean basin had encouraged the formation of national states, which could mobilize large-scale popular support. Extensive economic transformations paralleled the political reorganization of national communities, as peoples in western Europe and North America initiated processes of industrialization. Industrializing societies wielded enormous political and economic power. Their efficient transportation systems, fast communications networks, and powerful military technology supported imperial and colonial expansion. The ensuing cross-cultural encounters resulted in a high degree of interaction among the world's peoples.

In 1914 a Europe torn by national rivalries, colonial disputes, and nationalist aspirations plunged into war. As the imperial powers of Europe drew on the human and material resources of their colonies and dependencies and as lands such as the Ottoman empire, Japan, and the United States became belligerents, the Great War turned increasingly global in scope. By the time the war ended in 1918, the major European powers, including the victorious ones, had exhausted much of their economic wealth and global political primacy.

Global interdependence ensured that after the Great War most of the world needed to cope with postwar frustrations and economic instability, culminating in the Great Depression in 1929. Spawning political turmoil and social misery, postwar upheavals paved the way to fascist dictatorships in Italy and Germany and authoritarian regimes elsewhere. While the industrial world reeled under the impact of the Great Depression, the communist leadership of the Soviet Union, a state born out of revolution in 1917, embarked on a state-sponsored program of rapid industrialization. Amid great human suffering, a series of five-year plans transformed the Soviet Union into a major international power and the first socialist state. Meanwhile, the continued economic and political weakening of the European colonial powers encouraged political ferment in Asia, where nationalist movements tried to forge new identities free from imperial domination.

Sparked as a result of the Great War and the Great Depression, World War II began in China in 1931 when Japanese forces established a colonial empire on Chinese territory. The conflict spread to Europe in the late 1930s when the Nazi regime embarked on a policy of territorial expansion. By 1941 all the world's major powers

had been sucked into a maelstrom of violence and suffering that engulfed most European societies, almost all of Asia and the Pacific, and parts of Africa. World War II proved to be more destructive than any previous war and counted among its victims more civilians than soldiers. With the United States and the Soviet Union playing the lead roles, the Allied forces brought the conflict to a victorious end in 1945.

World War II completed the economic and political weakening of European societies and led to a second major realignment in the contemporary era. Two events—the immediate outbreak of the cold war and the dismantling of colonial empires—created and realigned the world of the late twentieth and twenty-first centuries. Because European powers no longer had the wherewithal to rule the world and their empires, two new superpowers filled a global void. The cold war, therefore, significantly contributed to global political transformations after World War II. It was a strategic struggle that

developed between the United States and its allies on the one hand and the Soviet Union and its allied countries on the other. The conflict between the forces of capitalism and communism produced a new set of global relationships, shaping the foreign policies, economic systems, and political institutions of nations throughout the world. The cold war ended suddenly in the late 1980s as the Soviet-dominated regimes of central and eastern Europe dissolved under the impact of mostly peaceful revolutions.

Although the cold war complicated the task of building nations from the wreckage of empires, in the three decades after World War II an irresistible wave of independence movements swept away colonies and empires and led to the establishment of new nations in Africa and Asia. This end of empire was one of the most important outcomes of World War II and was perhaps the most spectacular phase of contemporary global realignments, but the initial euphoria that accompanied freedom from imperial control was tempered by neocolonial and post-colonial problems such as rapid population growth, lack of economic development, and regional and ethnic conflicts among the former colonial lands.

Other transforming forces were also at work, among them globalization, a process that widened the extent and forms of cross-cultural interaction among the world's peoples. Technological advances dissolved old political, social, and economic barriers and promoted globalization. Improvements in information, communication, and transportation technologies, for instance, eased the movement of peoples, diseases, and cultural preferences across political and geographic borders. In this highly interdependent world, the task of dealing with problems of a global magnitude—such as human rights, epidemic diseases, gender equity, and environmental pollution—increasingly required international cooperation. Greater global integration encouraged similar economic and political preferences and fostered common cultural values, but forces promoting distinct cultural traditions and political identities also arose to challenge the universalizing effects of globalization.

The Great War: The World in Upheaval

chapter 33

This 1914 painting depicts the assassination of Archduke Francis Ferdinand and his wife, the Duchess Sophie. The gun in the killer's hand triggered what became the bloodiest war in history to date.

EYEWITNESS:
A Bloodied Archduke and a Bloody War

Archduke Francis Ferdinand (1863–1914) was aware that his first official visit to Sarajevo was fraught with danger. That ancient city was the capital of Bosnia-Herzegovina, twin provinces that had been under Ottoman rule since the fifteenth century and then occupied in 1878 and finally annexed by Austria-Hungary in 1908. These provinces became the hotbed of pan-Serbian nationalism. Ferdinand was on record as favoring greater autonomy for the provinces, but his words carried little weight with most Serbian nationalists, who hated the dynasty and the empire represented by the heir to the throne of Austria-Hungary.

It was a warm and radiant Sunday morning when Ferdinand's motorcade made its way through the narrow streets of Sarajevo. Waiting for him along the designated route were seven assassins armed with bombs and revolvers. The first would-be assassin did nothing, but the next man in line had more resolve and threw a bomb into the open car. Glancing off Ferdinand's arm, the bomb exploded near another vehicle and injured dozens of spectators. Trying to kill himself, the bomb thrower swallowed cyanide and jumped into a nearby river. The old poison only made him vomit, and the water was too shallow for drowning.

Undeterred, Ferdinand went on to a reception at city hall; after the reception he instructed his driver to take him to the hospital where those wounded in the earlier attack were being treated. While Ferdinand was on his way to the hospital, a young Bosnian Serb named Gavrilo Princip (1894–1918) lunged at the archduke's car and fired a revolver. The first bullet blew a gaping hole in the side of Ferdinand's neck. A second bullet intended for the governor of Bosnia went wild and entered the stomach of the expectant Duchess Sophie, the wife of the archduke. Turning to his wife, the archduke pleaded: "Sophie dear! Don't die! Stay alive for our children!" By the time medical aid arrived, however, the archduke and the duchess were dead.

In the meantime, Princip swallowed poison, which also only made him sick. When he tried to turn the gun on himself, a crowd intervened. After rescuing Princip from the mob, the police inflicted their own torture on the assassin: they kicked him, beat him, and scraped the skin from his neck with the edges of their swords. Three months later a court found Princip guilty of treason and murder, but because he committed his crime before his twentieth birthday, he could not be executed. Sentenced to twenty years in prison, Princip died in April 1918 from tuberculosis.

The assassination on 28 June 1914 brought to a head the tensions between the Austro-Hungarian empire and the neighboring kingdom of Serbia. As other European powers took sides, the stakes far outgrew Austro-Serbian conflicts. Nationalist aspirations, international rivalries, and an inflexible alliance system transformed that conflict into a general European war and ultimately into a global struggle involving thirty-two nations. Twenty-eight of those nations, collectively known as the Allies and the Associated Powers, fought the coalition known as the Central Powers, which consisted of Germany, Austria-Hungary, the Ottoman empire, and Bulgaria. The shell-shocked generation that survived the carnage called this clash of arms the Great War. Sadly, though, a subsequent generation of survivors renamed the conflict World War I, because it was only the first of two wars that engulfed the world in the first half of the twentieth century.

The Great War lasted from August 1914 to November 1918 and ushered in history's most violent century. In geographic extent the conflict surpassed all previous wars, compelling men, women, and children on five continents to participate directly or indirectly in a struggle that many did not understand. The Great War also had the distinction of being the first total war in human history, as governments mobilized every available human and material resource for the conduct of war. This scope contrasted with those of past wars, which, though frequently waged with ruthlessness and savage efficiency, were less destructive because they rarely engaged the passions of entire nations. Moreover, total war depended on industrial nations' capacity to fight with virtually unlimited means and to conduct combat on a vast scale. The industrial nature of the conflict meant that it was the bloodiest in the annals of organized violence. It took the lives of millions of combatants and civilians, physically maimed untold multitudes, and emotionally scarred an entire generation. The military casualties passed a threshold beyond previous experience: approximately fifteen million soldiers died, and an additional twenty million combatants suffered injuries.

The war of 1914–1918 did more than destroy individual lives. It seriously damaged national economies. The most visible signs of that damage were huge public debts and soaring rates of inflation. The international economy witnessed a shift in power away from western Europe. By the end of the conflict, the United States loomed as an economic world power that, despite its self-imposed isolation during the 1920s and 1930s, played a key role in global affairs in the coming decades. Politically, the war led to the redrawing of European boundaries and caused the demise of four dynasties and their empires—the Ottoman empire, the Russian empire, the Austro-Hungarian empire, and the German empire. The Great War also gave birth to nine new nations: Yugoslavia, Austria, Hungary, Czechoslovakia, Poland, Lithuania, Latvia, Estonia, and Finland. The war helped unleash the Bolshevik Revolution of 1917, which set the stage for an ideological conflict between capitalism and communism that endured to the end of the twentieth century. Finally, the Great War was responsible for an international realignment of power. It undermined the preeminence and prestige of European society, signaling an end to Europe's global primacy.

THE DRIFT TOWARD WAR

The catalyst for war was the assassination of Archduke Francis Ferdinand, heir to the throne of the Austro-Hungarian empire, by a Serbian nationalist. Yet without deeper underlying developments, the assassin's bullets would have had limited effect. The underlying causes for the war of 1914–1918 were many, including intense nationalism, frustrated national ambitions and ethnic resentments, the pursuit of exclusive economic interests, abrasive colonial rivalries, and a general struggle over the balance of power in Europe and in the world at large. Between 1871 and 1914, European governments adopted foreign policies that increased steadily the danger of war. So as to not find themselves alone in a hostile world, national leaders sought alignments with other powers. The establishment and maintenance in

Europe of two hostile alliances—the Allies and the Central Powers—helped spread the war from the Balkans.

Nationalist Aspirations

The French revolution and subsequent Napoleonic conquests spread nationalism throughout most of Europe (see chapter 28). Inherent in nationalism was the idea that peoples with the same ethnic origins, language, and political ideals had the right to form sovereign states; this concept is termed *self-determination*. The dynastic and reactionary powers that dominated European affairs during the early nineteenth century either ignored or opposed the principle of self-determination, thereby denying national autonomy to Germans, Italians, and Belgians, among others. Before long, however, a combination of powerful nationalistic movements, revolutions, and wars allowed Belgians to gain independence from the Netherlands in 1830, promoted the unification of Italy in 1861, and secured the unification of Germany in 1871. Yet at the end of the nineteenth century, the issue of nationalism remained unresolved in other areas of Europe, most notably in eastern Europe and the Balkans. There the nationalist aspirations of subject minorities threatened to tear apart the multinational empires of the Ottoman, Habsburg, and Russian dynasties and with them the regional balance of power. In those instances, opposition to foreign rule played a large role in the construction of national identities and demands for self-determination.

The Ottoman empire had controlled the Balkan peninsula since the fifteenth century, but after 1829 the Turkish empire shriveled. European powers, especially Austria and Russia, were partly responsible for the shrinking of Ottoman territories in Europe, but the slicing away of Turkish territory resulted mostly from nationalist revolts by the sultan's subjects. Greece was the first to gain independence (in 1830), but within a few decades Serbia, Romania, and Bulgaria followed suit.

As the Ottoman territories succumbed to the forces of nationalism, Austria-Hungary confronted the nationalist aspirations of Slavic peoples—Poles, Czechs, Slovaks, Serbs, Croats, and Slovenes. Most menacing and militant were the Serbs, who pressed for unification with the independent kingdom of Serbia. Russia added fuel to this volatile situation by promoting Pan-Slavism, a nineteenth-century movement that stressed the ethnic and cultural kinship of the various Slav peoples of eastern and east central Europe and that sought to unite those peoples politically. Pan-Slavism, as advocated by Russian leaders, supported Slav nationalism in lands occupied by Austria-Hungary. The purpose behind that policy was to promote secession by Slav areas, thereby weakening Austrian rule and perhaps preparing territories for future Russian annexation. Russia's support of Serbia, which supported Slav nationalism, and Germany's backing of Austria-Hungary, which tried desperately to counter the threat of national independence, helped set the stage for international conflict.

National Rivalries

Aggressive nationalism was also manifest in economic competition and colonial conflicts, fueling dangerous rivalries among the major European powers. The industrialized nations of Europe competed for foreign markets and engaged in tariff wars, but the most unsettling economic rivalry involved Great Britain and Germany. By the twentieth century, Germany's rapid industrialization threatened British economic predominance. In 1870 Britain, the first industrial nation, produced almost 32 percent of the world's total industrial output, compared with Germany's share of 13 percent, but by 1914 Britain's share had dropped to 14 percent, roughly equivalent to that of Germany. British reluctance to accept the relative decline of British industry vis-à-vis German industry strained relations between the two economic powers.

The Naval Race An expensive naval race further exacerbated tensions between the two nations. Germans and Britons convinced themselves that naval power was imperative to secure trade routes and protect merchant shipping. Moreover, military leaders and politicians saw powerful navies as a means of controlling the seas in times of war, a control they viewed as decisive in determining the outcome of any war. Thus, when Germany's political and military leaders announced their program to build a fleet with many large battleships, they seemed to undermine British naval supremacy. The British government moved to meet the German threat through the construction of super battleships known as *dreadnoughts*. Rather than discouraging the Germans from their naval buildup, the British determination to retain naval superiority stimulated the Germans to build their own flotilla of dreadnoughts. This expensive naval race contributed further to international tensions and hostilities between nations.

Colonial Disputes Economic rivalries fomented colonial competition. During the late nineteenth and early twentieth centuries, European nations searched aggressively for new colonies or dependencies to bolster economic performance. In their haste to conquer and colonize, the imperial powers stumbled over each other, repeatedly clashing in one corner of the globe or another: Britain and Russia faced off in Persia (modern-day Iran) and Afghanistan; Britain and France in Siam (modern-day Thailand) and the Nile valley; Britain and Germany in east and southwest Africa; Germany and France in Morocco and west Africa.

Virtually all the major powers engaged in the scramble for empire, but the competition between Britain and Germany and that between France and Germany were the most intense and dangerous. Germany, a unified nation only since 1871, embarked on the colonial race belatedly but aggressively, insisting that it too must have its "place in the sun." German imperial efforts were frustrated, however, by the simple fact that British and French imperialists had already carved up most of the world. German-French antagonisms and German-British rivalries went far toward shaping the international alliances that contributed to the spread of war after 1914.

Between 1905 and 1914, a series of international crises and two local wars raised tensions and almost precipitated a general European war. The first crisis resulted from a French-German confrontation over Morocco in 1905. Trying to isolate the French diplomatically, the German government announced its support of Moroccan independence, which French encroachment endangered. The French responded to German intervention by threatening war. An international conference in Algeciras, Spain, in the following year prevented a clash of arms, but similar crises threatened the peace in subsequent years. Contributing to

the growing tensions in European affairs were the Balkan wars. Between 1912 and 1913, the states of the Balkan peninsula—including Bulgaria, Greece, Montenegro, Serbia, and Romania—fought two consecutive wars for possession of European territories held by the Ottoman empire. The Balkan wars strained European diplomatic relations and helped shape the tense circumstances that led to the outbreak of the Great War.

Public Opinion Public pressure also contributed to national rivalries. Characteristic of many European societies was a high degree of political participation and chauvinism on the part of citizens who identified strongly with the state. These citizens wanted their nation to outshine others, particularly in the international arena. New means of communication nourished the public's desire to see their country "come in first," whether in the competition for colonies or in the race to the South Pole. The content of cheap, mass-produced newspapers, pamphlets, and books fueled feelings

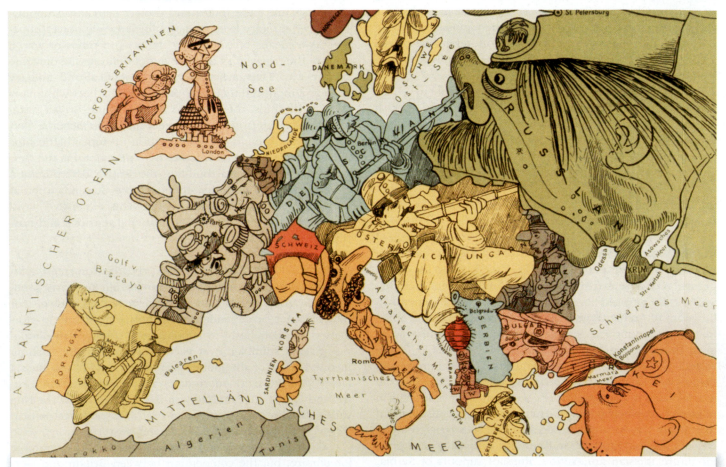

Dissident cartoonist Walter Trier's satirical map of Europe in 1914. Trier's work stands in stark contrast to the press of the time, which fueled the chauvinist desires of competing national publics. What message was Trier trying to convey with this map?

of national arrogance and aggressive patriotism. However, public pressure calling for national greatness placed policy-makers and diplomats in an awkward situation. Compelled to achieve headline-grabbing foreign policy successes, these leaders ran the risk of paying for short-lived triumphs with long-lasting hostility from other countries.

Understandings and Alliances

In addition to a basic desire for security, escalating national rivalries and nationalist aspirations of subject minorities spawned a system of entangling alliances. While national in-terests guided the search for allies, each nation viewed its ful-fillment of treaty obligations as crucial to self-preservation. Moreover, the complexity of those obligations could not hide the common characteristic underlying all the alliances: they outlined the circumstances under which countries would go to war to support one another. Intended to preserve the peace, rival alliance systems created a framework whereby even a small international crisis could set off a chain reaction leading to global war. Thus by 1914 Europe's major powers had transformed themselves into two hostile camps—the Triple Alliance and the Triple Entente.

The Central Powers
The Triple Alliance, also known as the Central Powers, grew out of the close relation-ship that developed between the leaders of Germany and Austria-Hungary during the last three decades of the nine-teenth century. In 1879 the governments of the two empires formed the Dual Alliance, a defensive pact that ensured re-ciprocal protection from a Russian attack and neutrality in case of an attack from any other power. Fear of a hostile France motivated Germans to enter into this pact, whereas Austrians viewed it as giving them a free hand in pursuing their Balkan politics without fear of Russian intervention. Italy, fearful of France, joined the Dual Alliance in 1882, thereby transforming it into the Triple Alliance. From the outset, however, the Italian policy of aggrandizement at the expense of the Ottoman empire and Italy's rivalry with Austria-Hungary in the Balkans threatened to wreck the alliance. Thus the Italian declaration of war on the Otto-man empire in 1911 and the subsequent drive to annex the Tripoli region of northern Africa strained the Triple Alliance because the German government tried to cultivate friendly relations with the Turks.

The Allies
The Central Powers sought to protect the po-litical status quo in Europe, but the leaders of other nations viewed this new constellation of power with suspicion. This response was especially true of French leaders, who neither forgot nor forgave France's humiliating defeat during the Franco-Prussian War of 1870–1871. The French government was determined to curb the growing might of Germany.

The tsarist regime of Russia was equally disturbed by the new alignment of powers, especially by Germany's sup-port of Austria, and British leaders were traditionally sus-picious of any nation that seemed to threaten the balance of power on the Continent. The result was that the most unlikely bedfellows formed the Triple Entente, a combina-tion of nations commonly referred to as the Allies. The Tri-ple Entente originated in a series of agreements between Britain and France (1904) and between Britain and Russia (1907) that aimed to resolve colonial disputes. Between 1907 and 1914 cooperation between the leaders of Britain, France, and Russia led to the signing of a military pact in the summer of 1914. Reciprocal treaty obligations, which the governments felt compelled to honor lest they face the risk of being alone in a hostile world, made it difficult for diplomats to contain what otherwise might have been rela-tively small international crises.

War Plans
The preservation of peace was also difficult because the military staffs of each nation had devised inflex-ible military plans and timetables to be carried out in the event of war. For example, French military strategy revolved around Plan XVII, which amounted to a veritable celebration of offensive maneuvers. The French master plan could be summed up in one word, *attack,* to be undertaken always and everywhere. This strategy viewed the enemy's intentions as inconsequential and gave no thought to the huge number of casualties that would invariably result. German war plans in particular played a crucial role in the events leading to the Great War. Germany's fear of encirclement encouraged its military planners to devise a strategy that would avoid a war on two fronts. It was based on a strategy developed in 1905 by General Count Alfred von Schlieffen (1833–1913). The Schlieffen plan called for a swift knockout of France, fol-lowed by defensive action against Russia. German planners predicated their strategy on the knowledge that the Russians could not mobilize their soldiers and military supplies as quickly as the French, thus giving German forces a few pre-cious weeks during which they could concentrate their full power on France. However brilliantly conceived, the Schlief-fen plan raised serious logistical problems, not the least of which was moving 180,000 soldiers and their supplies into France and Belgium on five hundred trains, with fifty wag-ons each. More important, Germany's military strategy was a serious obstacle to those seeking to preserve the peace. In the event of Russian mobilization, Germany's leaders would feel compelled to stick to their war plans, thereby setting in motion a military conflict of major proportions.

GLOBAL WAR

War came to Europe during harvest time, and most ordinary people heard the news as they worked in the fields. They reacted not with enthusiasm but with shock and fear. Other people, especially intellectuals and young city dwellers, met the news with euphoria. Many of them had long expected

This British recruiting poster reflects the enthusiasm that many British people felt at the beginning of the Great War, when they believed it would be a short and glorious adventure—an expectation that was very quickly dashed.

war and saw it as a liberating release of pressure that would resolve the various political, social, and economic crises that had been building for years. The philosopher Bertrand Russell observed that the average Englishman positively wanted war, and the French writer Alain-Fournier noted that "this war is fine and just and great." In the capitals of Europe, people danced in the streets when their governments announced formal declarations of war. When the first contingents of soldiers left for the front, jubilant crowds threw flowers at the feet of departing men, who expected to return victorious after a short time.

Reality crushed any expectations of a short and triumphant war. On most fronts the conflict quickly bogged down and became a war of attrition in which the firepower of modern weapons slaughtered soldiers by the millions. For the first time in history, belligerent nations engaged in total war. Even in democratic societies, governments assumed dictatorial control to marshal the human and material resources required for continuous war. One result was increased participation of women in the labor force. Total war had repercussions that went beyond the borders of Europe. Imperial ties drew millions of Asians, Africans, and residents of the British dominions into the war to serve as soldiers and laborers. Struggles over far-flung colonies further underlined the global dimension of this war. Last, the war gained a global flavor through the entry of Japan, the United States, and the Ottoman empire, nations whose leaders professed little direct interest in European affairs.

The Guns of August

The shots fired from Gavrilo Princip's revolver on that fateful day of 28 June 1914 were heard around the world, for they triggered the greatest war in human history up to that point. By July, Austrian investigators had linked the assassins to a terrorist group known as the Black Hand. Centered in neighboring Serbia, this organization was dedicated to the unification of all south Slavs, or Yugoslavs, to form a greater Serbia. As far as Serbian nationalists were concerned, the principal obstacle to Slavic unity was the Austro-Hungarian empire, which explains why the heir to the Habsburg throne was a symbolic victim. This viewpoint also explains Austria's unyielding and violent response to the murder.

Declarations of War The assassination set in motion a flurry of diplomatic activity that quickly escalated into war. Austrian leaders in Vienna were determined to teach the unruly Serbs a lesson, and on 23 July the Austrians issued a nearly unacceptable ultimatum to the government of Serbia. The Serbian government accepted all the terms of the ultimatum except one, which infringed on its sovereignty. The ultimatum demanded that Austrian officials take part in any Serbian investigation of persons found on Serbian territory connected to the assassination of Francis Ferdinand. On 28 July, after declaring the Serbian reply to be unsatisfactory, Austria-Hungary declared war on Serbia. The war had begun, and politicians and generals discovered that it could not be easily arrested. The subsequent sequence of events was largely determined by two factors: complex mobilization plans and the grinding logic of the alliance system. Mobilization called for the activation of military forces for imminent battle and the redirection of economic and social activities to support military efforts. Thus military planners were convinced that the timing of mobilization orders and adherence to precise timetables were crucial to the successful conduct of war.

On 29 July the Russian government mobilized its troops to defend its Serbian ally and itself from Austria. The tsar of Russia then ordered mobilization against Germany. Nicholas II (1868–1918) took that decisive step reluctantly and only after his military experts had convinced him that a partial mobilization against the Austrians would upset complex

This photograph from August 1914 documents the famous "guns of August" that sparked the Great War. Dogs carted this machine gun to the front in Belgium.

military plans and timetables. Delayed mobilization might invite defeat, they advised, should the Germans enter the war. That action precipitated a German ultimatum to Russia on 31 July, demanding that the Russian army cease its mobilization immediately. Another ultimatum addressed to France demanded to know what France's intentions were in case Germany and Russia went to war. The Russians replied with a blunt "impossible," and the French never answered. Thus on 1 August the German government declared war on Russia, and France started to mobilize.

After waiting two more days, the Germans declared war on France, on 3 August. On the same day, German troops invaded Belgium in accordance with the Schlieffen plan. Key to this plan was an attack on the weak left flank of the French army by a massive German force through Belgium. The Belgian government, which had refused to permit the passage of German troops, called on the signatories of the treaty of 1839, which guaranteed Belgium's neutrality. On 4 August the British government, one of the signatories, sent an ultimatum to Germany demanding that Belgian neutrality be respected. When Germany's wartime leaders refused, the British immediately declared war. A local conflict had become a general European war.

Mutual Butchery

Everyone expected the war to be brief. In the first weeks of August 1914, twenty million young men donned uniforms, took up rifles, and left for the front. Many of them looked forward to heroic charges, rapid promotions, and a quick homecoming. Some dreamed of glory and honor, and they believed that God was on their side. The inscription on the belt buckle of German recruits read *Gott mit uns* ("God is with us"), a sentiment echoed by Russian troops, who fought for "God and Tsar," and British soldiers, who went into battle "For God, King, and Country." Several years later Americans felt called on to "make the world safe for democracy." Similar attitudes prevailed among the political and military leaders of the belligerent nations. The war strategies devised by the finest military thinkers of the time paid little attention to matters of defense. Instead, they were preoccupied with visions of sweeping assaults, envelopments, and, above all, swift triumphs.

The Western Front The German thrust toward Paris in August 1914 came to a grinding halt along the river Marne, and both sides then undertook flanking maneuvers, a "race to the sea" that took them to the Atlantic coast. For the next three years, the battle lines remained virtually stationary, as both sides dug in and slugged it out in a war of attrition that lasted until the late autumn of 1918. Each belligerent tried to wear down the enemy by inflicting continuous damage and casualties, only to have their own forces suffer heavy losses in return. Trenches on the western front ran from the English Channel to Switzerland. Farther south, Italy left the Triple Alliance in favor of neutrality but entered the war on the side of the Allies in 1915. By the terms of the Treaty

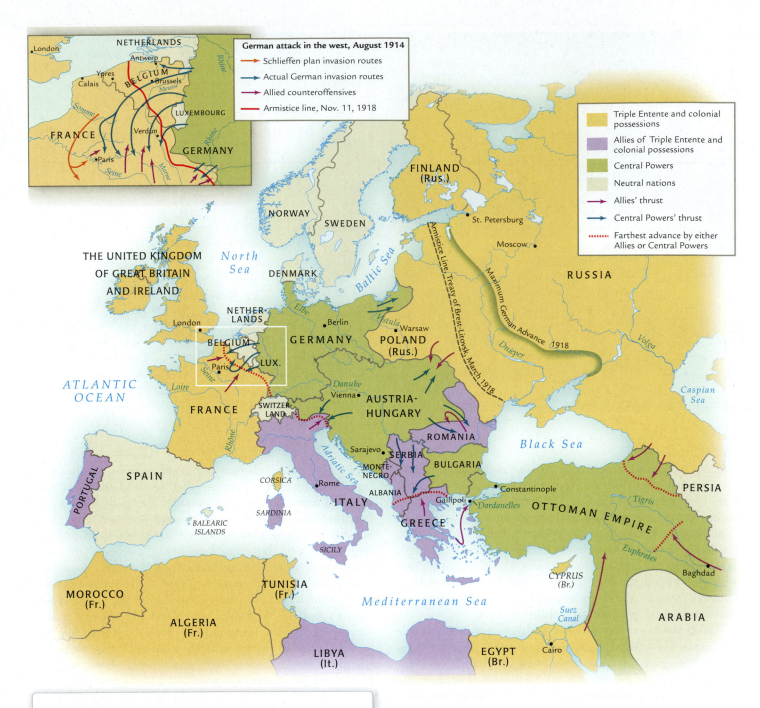

MAP 33.1

The Great War in Europe and southwest Asia, 1914–1918.
Note the locations of both the eastern and the western fronts in Europe during the war.

Why didn't the same kind of trench warfare immobilize opposing armies on the eastern front the way it did on the western front?

of London, the Allies promised, once victory was secured, to cede to Italy Austro-Hungarian-controlled territories, specifically south Tyrol and most of the Dalmatian coast. Allied hopes that the Italians would pierce Austrian defenses quickly faded. After the disastrous defeat at Caporetto in 1917, Italian forces maintained a defensive line only with the help of the French and the British.

Stalemate and New Weapons The stalemate on the western and southern fronts reflected technological developments that favored defensive tactics. Barbed wire, which had confined cattle on America's Great Plains, proved highly effective in frustrating the advance of soldiers across "no-man's-land," the deadly territory between opposing trenches. The rapid and continuous fire of machine guns further contributed to the battlefield stalemate, turning in-

thinking about TRADITIONS

Heroic War?

Before the Great War, Europeans in battle usually adhered to certain military traditions and had expectations that conflicts could be settled quickly. How did the Great War alter time-honored military codes of conduct and dash hopes for a quick end to the war? What role did new technologies play in the process of changing the understanding of war?

fantry charges across no-man's-land into suicide missions. First deployed by Confederate troops during the U.S. Civil War, the machine gun had been a key weapon for overcoming resistance to colonial expansion before Europeans trained the weapon on one another during the Great War. The machine gun represented one of the most important advances in military technology and compelled military leaders on all sides to rethink their battlefield tactics.

The immobility of trench warfare and the desire to reintroduce movement to warfare prompted the development of weapons that supplied the power necessary to break the deadly stalemate. Industrial societies subsequently gave birth to many new and potent weapons. The most unconventional weapon was poisonous gas, first used by German troops in January 1915. Especially hated and much feared by troops in the trenches was mustard gas, a liquid agent that, when exposed to air, turned into a noxious yellow gas, hence its name. The effects of mustard gas did not appear for some twelve hours following exposure, but then it rotted the body from both within and without. After blistering the skin and damaging the eyes, the gas attacked the bronchial tubes, stripping off the mucous membrane. Death could occur in four to five weeks. In the meantime, victims endured excruciating pain and had to be strapped to their beds. Like the machine gun, gas proved a potent weapon, and both sides suffered heavy casualties totaling about 1.2 million soldiers. Such destructiveness convinced military leaders of the effectiveness of chemical agents, yet gas attacks failed to deliver the promised strategic breakthroughs, and the anticipated return to more fluid battle lines never materialized.

Other novel weapons developed during the war included tanks and air-

Air-raid warden in helmet and gas mask, holding a wooden gas attack rattle in his gloved hand. The deployment of poison gas represented a technological development of horrific dimension that was designed to break the stalemate of trench warfare by killing, on a massive scale, soldiers otherwise difficult to reach.

planes. The British first introduced tanks in late 1915, and the Allies deployed them to break down defensive trenches and to restore fighting. Despite its proven short-term effectiveness during the final offenses of the war, the tank did not produce the longed-for strategic advantage. As a rule, German counterattacks quickly regained the ground won by tanks. Also of recent origin was the airplane, still in its infancy in 1914. Constantly refined and improved as the war progressed, the airplane by the end of the war showed dramatic improvements in speed, range, and altitude. However, because airplanes could not carry enough weapons to do serious damage to troops or installations on the ground, their real asset during the Great War was aerial reconnaissance. It was, in effect, an attempt to prevent the enemy from conducting aerial reconnaissance that led to the much publicized and glamorized aerial combat of the Great War featuring "ace fighters" and "dogfights." The plane and the tank figured more prominently as important strategic weapons during the Second World War. Other weapons systems, such as the submarine, had made earlier appearances in warfare but did not play a significant role until the Great War. It was not until the Great War, when the German navy deployed its diesel-powered submarine fleet against Allied commercial shipping, that the submarine proved its military effectiveness. Although the German navy relied more heavily on submarines, the allied navies of Great Britain and the United States deployed their own fleets of diesel-powered submarines.

No-Man's-Land The most courageous infantry charges, even when preceded by pulverizing artillery barrages and clouds of poisonous gas, were no match for determined defenders. Shielded by the dirt of their trenches and by barbed wire and gas masks, they unleashed a torrent of lethal metal with their machine guns and repeating rifles. In every sector of the front, those who fought rarely found the glory they sought. Instead, they encountered death. No-man's-land was strewn with shell craters, cadavers, and body parts. The grim realities of trench warfare—the wet, cold, waist-deep mud, gluttonous lice, and corpse-fed rats—contrasted sharply with the ringing phrases of politicians and generals justifying the unrelenting slaughter. War had ceased to be a noble and sporting affair, if it ever was.

A dogfight between German and British planes during the Great War. Dogfights as a new type of combat resulted from the attempt of each contestant to prevent the enemy from conducting aerial reconnaissance.

The Eastern Front

In eastern Europe and the Balkans, the battle lines were more fluid. After a staunch defense, a combination of Austrian and German forces overran Serbia, Albania, and Romania. Farther north, Russia took the offensive early by invading Prussia in 1914. The Central Powers recovered quickly, however, and by the summer of 1915 combined German-Austrian forces drove the Russian armies out of East Prussia and then out of Poland and established a defensive line extending from the Baltic to the Ukraine. Russian counterattacks in 1916 and 1917 collapsed in a sea of casualties. Those Russian defeats undermined the popularity of the tsar and his government and played a significant role in fostering revolutionary ferment within Russian society.

Bloodletting

Many battles took place, but some were so horrific, so devastating, and so futile that their names are synonymous with human slaughter. The casualty figures attested to this bloodletting. In 1916 the Germans tried to break the deadlock with a huge assault on the fortress of Verdun. The French rallying cry was "They shall not pass,"

and they did not—but at a tremendous cost: while the victorious French counted 315,000 dead, the defeated Germans suffered a loss of 280,000. Survivors recovered fewer than 160,000 identifiable bodies. The rest were unrecognizable or had been blown to bits by high explosives and sucked into the mud. To relieve the pressure on Verdun, British forces counterattacked at the Somme, and by November they had gained a few thousand yards at the cost of 420,000 casualties. The Germans suffered similar losses, although in the end neither side gained any strategic advantage.

New Rules of Engagement

Dying and suffering were not limited solely to combatants: the Great War established rules of engagement that made civilians targets of warfare. Because they were crucial to the war effort, millions of people out of uniform became targets of enemy military operations. On 30 August 1914, Parisians looked up at the sky and saw a new weapon of war, a huge, silent German zeppelin (a hydrogen-filled dirigible) whose underbelly rained bombs, eventually killing one person. That event heralded a new kind of warfare—air war against civilians. A less novel but more effective means of targeting civilian populations was the naval blockade. Military leaders on both sides used blockades to deny food to whole populations, hoping that starving masses would force their governments to capitulate. The British blockade of Germany during the war contributed to the deaths of an estimated half-million Germans.

Total War: The Home Front

Helmuth Karl von Moltke (1800–1891), former chief of the Prussian General Staff, showed an uncanny insight long before 1914 when he predicted that future wars would not end with a single battle, because the defeat of a nation would not be acknowledged until the whole strength of its people was broken. He was right. As the Great War ground on, it became a conflict of attrition in which the organization of material and human resources was of paramount importance. War became total, fought between entire societies, not just between armies; and total victory was the only acceptable outcome that might justify the terrible sacrifices made by all sides. The nature of total war created a military front and a home front. The term *home front* expressed the important reality that the outcome of the war hinged on how effectively each nation mobilized its economy and activated its noncombatant citizens to support the war effort.

The Home Front

As the war continued beyond Christmas 1914 and as war weariness and a decline in economic capability set in, the response of all belligerents was to limit individual freedoms and give control of society increasingly over to military leaders. Because patriotism and courage alone could not guarantee victory, the governments of belligerent nations assumed control of the home front. Initially, ministers and generals shrank from compulsive measures, even conscription of recruits, but they quickly changed their minds. Each belligerent government eventually militarized civilian war production by subordinating private enterprises to governmental control and imposing severe discipline on the labor process.

Economic measures were foremost in the minds of government leaders because the war created unprecedented demands for raw materials and manufactured goods. Those material requirements compelled governments to abandon long-cherished ideals of a laissez-faire capitalist market economy and to institute tight controls over economic life. Planning boards reorganized entire industries, set production quotas and priorities, and determined what would be produced and consumed. Government authorities also established wage and price controls, extended work hours, and in some instances restricted the movement of workers. Because bloody battlefields caused an insatiable appetite for soldiers, nations responded by extending military service. In Germany, for example, men between the ages of sixteen and sixty were eligible to serve at the front. By constantly tapping into the available male population, the war created an increasing demand for workers at home. Unemployment—a persistent feature of all prewar economies—vanished virtually overnight.

Women at War As men marched off to war, women marched off to work. Conscription took men out of the labor force, and wartime leaders exhorted women to fill the gaps in the workforce. A combination of patriotism and high wages drew women into formerly "male" jobs. The lives of women changed as they bobbed their hair and left home or domestic service for the workplace. Some women took over the management of farms and businesses left by their husbands, who went off to fight. Others found jobs as postal workers and police officers. Behind the battle lines, women were most visible as nurses, physicians, and communications clerks.

Perhaps the most crucial work performed by women during the war was the making of shells. Several million women, and sometimes children, put in long, hard hours in munitions factories. This work exposed them to severe dangers. The first came from explosions, because keeping sparks away from highly volatile materials was impossible. Many women died in these incidents, although government censorship dur-

Mutilated body on the western front. So tremendous was the number of the dead—over a half-million French and German soldiers perished in the battle of Verdun alone—that many were never recovered or identified.

ing the war made it difficult to know how many women perished in this fashion. The other, more insidious danger came from working with TNT explosives. Although the authorities claimed that this work was not dangerous, exposure to TNT caused severe poisoning, depending on the length of exposure. Before serious illnesses manifested themselves, TNT poisoning marked its victims by turning their skin yellow and their hair orange. The accepted though ineffectual remedy for TNT poisoning was rest, good food, and plenty of fresh milk.

Middle- and upper-class women often reported that the war was a liberating experience, freeing them from older attitudes that had limited their work and their personal lives. At the least, the employment of upper-class women spawned a degree of deliverance from parental control and gave women a sense of mission. They knew that they were important to the war effort. The impact of the Great War on the lives of working-class women, in contrast, was relatively minor. Working-class women in cities had long been accustomed to earning wages, and for them war work proved less than liberating. Most of the belligerent governments promised equal pay for equal work, but in most instances that promise remained unfulfilled. Although women's industrial wages rose during the war, measurable gaps always remained between the incomes of men and women. In the end, substantial female employment was a transitory phenomenon. With few exceptions, the Great War only briefly suspended traditional patterns of work outside the home. Nevertheless, the extension of voting rights to women shortly after the war, in Britain (1918, for women thirty years and older), Germany (1919), and Austria (1919), was in part due to the role women assumed during the Great War. Later in the century, war and revolution continued to serve as at least temporary liberating forces for women, especially in Russia (1917) and China (1949), where new communist governments discouraged the patriarchal family system and supported sexual equality, including birth control.

Propaganda To maintain the spirit of the home front and to counter threats to national unity, governments resorted to the restriction of civil liberties, censorship of bad news, and vilification of the enemy through propaganda campaigns. While some government officials busily censored war news, people who had the temerity to criticize their nation's war

sources from the past

Dulce et Decorum Est

The Great War produced a wealth of poetry. The poetic response to war covered a range of moods, from early romanticism and patriotism to cynicism, resignation, and the angry depiction of horror. Perhaps the greatest of all war poets was Wilfred Owen (1893–1918), whose poems are among the most poignant of the war. Owen, who enlisted for service on the western front in 1915, was injured in March 1917 and sent home. Declared fit for duty in August 1918, he returned to the front. German machine-gun fire killed him on 7 November, four days before the armistice, when he tried to cross the Sambre Canal.

Bent double, like old beggars under sacks,
Knock-kneed, coughing like hags, we cursed through
    sludge,
Till on the haunting flares we turned our backs
And towards our distant rest began to trudge.
Men marched asleep. Many had lost their boots
But limped on, blood-shod. All went lame; all blind;
Drunk with fatigue; deaf even to the hoots
Of gas-shells dropping softly behind.

Gas! GAS! Quick, boys!—An ecstasy of fumbling,
Fitting the clumsy helmets just in time;
But someone still was yelling out and stumbling
And floundering like a man in fire or lime.—
Dim, through the misty panes and thick green light
As under a green sea, I saw him drowning.

In all my dreams, before my helpless sight,
He plunges at me, guttering, choking, drowning.
If in some smothering dreams you too could pace
Behind the wagon that we flung him in,
And watch the white eyes writhing in his face,
His hanging face, like a devil's sick of sin;
If you could hear, at every jolt, the blood
Come gargling from the froth-corrupted lungs,
Obscene as cancer, bitter as the cud
Of vile, incurable sores on innocent tongues,—
My friend, you would not tell with such high zest
To children ardent for some desperate glory,
The old Lie: Dulce et decorum est
Pro patria mori.*

*Author's note: "Sweet and fitting is it to die for one's country" comes from a line by the Roman poet Horace (65–8 B.C.E.)

For Further Reflection

■ How does Owen poetically describe the effects of a gas attack? Is his literary depiction more or less effective than detached descriptions of war's effects?

Source: Edmund Blunden, ed. *The Poems of Wilfred Owen.* London: Chattus & Windus, 1933, p. 66.

effort were prosecuted as traitors. In France, for example, former prime minister Joseph Caillaux spent two years in prison awaiting trial because he had publicly suggested that the best interest of France would be to reach a compromise peace with Germany.

The propaganda offices of the belligerent nations tried to convince the public that military defeat would mean the destruction of everything worth living for, and to that end they did their utmost to discredit and dehumanize the enemy. Posters, pamphlets, and "scientific" studies depicted the enemy as subhuman savages who engaged in vile atrocities. While German propaganda depicted Russians as semi-Asiatic barbarians, French authorities chronicled the atrocities committed by the German "Hun" in Belgium. In 1917 the *Times* of London published a story claiming that Germans converted human corpses into fertilizer and food. With much less fanfare a later news story admitted that this information resulted from a sloppy translation: the German word for *horse* had been mistakenly translated as "human." German propaganda stooped equally low. One widely distributed poster invoked images of bestial black Allied soldiers raping German women, including pregnant women, to suggest the horrors that would follow if the nation's war effort failed. Most atrocity stories originated in the fertile imagination of propaganda officers, and their falsehood eventually engendered public skepticism and cynicism. Ironically, public disbelief of wartime propaganda led to an inability to believe in the abominations perpetrated during subsequent wars.

Conflict in East Asia and the Pacific

To many Asian and African peoples, the Great War was a murderous European civil war that quickly turned into a global conflict. There were three reasons for the war's expansion. First, European governments carried their animosities into their colonies, embroiling them—especially

Women at work in an English munitions factory. The Great War drew huge numbers of men out of the workforce at a time of great industrial need. Women replaced them, for the first time assuming traditionally "male" jobs.

"The Heroes of Belgium 1914." French propaganda poster expresses outrage at the German invasion of Belgium.

African societies—in their war. Second, because Europe's human reserves were not enough to satisfy the appetite of war, the British and the French augmented their ranks by recruiting men from their colonies. Millions of Africans and Asians were drawn into the war. Behind their trenches the French employed laborers from Algeria, China, and French Indochina, and the British did not hesitate to draft Indian and African troops for combat. The British in particular relied on troops furnished by the dominion lands, including Australia, New Zealand, Canada, Newfoundland, and South Africa. Third, the Great War assumed global significance because the desires and objectives of some principal actors that entered the conflict—Japan, the United States, and the Ottoman empire—had little to do with the murder in Sarajevo or the other issues that drove the Europeans to battle.

Japan's Entry into the War On 15 August 1914 the Japanese government, claiming that it desired "to secure firm and enduring peace in Eastern Asia," sent an ultimatum to Germany demanding the handover of the German-leased

territory of Jiaozhou (northeastern China) to Japanese authorities without compensation. The same note also demanded that the German navy unconditionally withdraw its warships from Japanese and Chinese waters. When the Germans refused to comply, the Japanese entered the war on the side of the Allies on 23 August 1914. Japanese forces took the fortress of Qingdao, a German-held port in China's Shandong Province, in November 1914, and between August and November of that year took possession of the German-held Marshall Islands, the Mariana Islands, Palau, and the Carolines. Forces from New Zealand and Australia joined in the Japanese quest for German-held islands in the Pacific, capturing German-held portions of Samoa in August 1914 and German-occupied possessions in the Bismarck Archipelago and New Guinea.

The Twenty-one Demands After seizing German bases on the Shandong peninsula and on Pacific islands, Japan shrewdly exploited Allied support and European preoccupation to advance its own imperial interests in China.

On 18 January 1915 the Japanese presented the Chinese government with twenty-one secret demands. The terms of that ultimatum, if accepted, would have reduced China to a protectorate of Japan. The most important demands were that the Chinese confirm the Japanese seizure of Shandong from Germany, grant Japanese industrial monopolies in central China, place Japanese overseers in key government positions, give Japan joint control of Chinese police forces, restrict their arms purchases to Japanese manufacturers, and make those purchases only with the approval of the Tokyo government. China submitted to most of the demands but rejected others. Chinese diplomats leaked the note to the British authorities, who spoke up for China, thus preventing total capitulation. The Twenty-one Demands reflected Japan's determination to dominate east Asia and served as the basis for future Japanese pressure on China.

An Indian gun crew in the Somme area, 1916. During the Great War, colonial powers relied on millions of Asian and African men to fight or labor for their respective sides.

Battles in Africa and Southwest Asia

The geographic extent of the conflict also broadened beyond Europe when the Allies targeted German colonies in Africa. When the war of 1914–1918 erupted in Europe, all of sub-Saharan Africa (except Ethiopia and Liberia) consisted of European colonies, with the Germans controlling four: Togoland, the Cameroons, German Southwest Africa, and German East Africa. Unlike the capture of German colonies in the Pacific, which Allied forces accomplished during the first three months of the war with relative ease, the conquest of German colonies in Africa was difficult. Togoland fell to an Anglo-French force after three weeks of fighting, but it took extended campaigns ranging over vast distances to subdue the remaining German footholds in Africa. The Allied force included British, French, and Belgian troops and large contingents of Indian, Arab, and African soldiers. Fighting took place on land and sea; on lakes and rivers; in deserts, jungles, and swamps; and in the air. Germs were frequently more deadly than Germans; tens of thousands of Allied soldiers and workers succumbed to deadly tropical diseases. The German flag did not disappear from Africa until after the armistice took effect on 11 November 1918.

Gallipoli The most extensive military operations outside Europe took place in the southwest Asian territories of the Ottoman empire, which was aligned with the Central Powers at the end of 1914. Seeking a way to break the stalemate on the western front, Winston Churchill (1874–1965), first lord of the Admiralty (British navy), suggested that an Allied strike against the Ottomans—a weak ally of the Central Powers—would hurt the Germans. Early in 1915 the British navy conducted an expedition to seize the approach to the Dardanelles Strait in an attempt to open a warm-water supply line to Russia through the Ottoman-controlled strait. After bombing the forts that defended the strait, Allied ships took damage from floating mines and withdrew without accomplishing their mission. After withdrawing the battleships, the British high command decided to land a combined force of English, Canadian, Australian, and New Zealand soldiers on the beaches of the Gallipoli peninsula. The campaign was a disaster. Turkish defenders, ensconced in the cliffs above, quickly pinned down the Allied troops on the beaches. Trapped between the sea and the hills, Allied soldiers dug in and engaged in their own version of trench warfare. The resulting stalemate produced a total of 250,000 casualties on each side. Despite the losses, Allied leaders took nine months to admit that their campaign had failed.

Gallipoli was a debacle with long-term consequences. Although the British directed the ill-fated campaign, it was mostly Canadians, Australians, and New Zealanders who suffered terrible casualties. That recognition led to a weakening of imperial ties and paved the way for emerging national identities. In Australia the date of the fateful landing, 25 April 1915, became enshrined as Anzac Day (an acronym for Australian and New Zealand Army Corps) and remains the country's most significant day of public homage. On the other side, the battle for the strait helped launch the political career of the commander of the Turk-

thinking about ENCOUNTERS

From Civil War to Total War
Many observers considered the Great War a civil war among Europeans. How did the war draw in peoples outside Europe, and what form did contacts between Europeans, Asians, and Africans take?

ish division that defended Gallipoli. Mustafa Kemal (1881–1938) went on to play a crucial role in the formation of the modern Turkish state.

Armenian Massacres

The war provided the pretext for a campaign of extermination against the Ottoman empire's two million Armenians, the last major non-Muslim ethnic group under Ottoman rule seeking autonomy and eventual independence. Friction between Christian Armenians and Ottoman authorities went back to the nineteenth century, when distinct nationalist feelings stirred many of the peoples who lived under Ottoman rule.

Initially, Armenians had relied on government reforms to prevent discrimination against non-Muslim subjects by corrupt officials and extortionist tax collectors. When abuses persisted, Armenians resorted to confrontation. Armenian demonstrations against Ottoman authorities in 1890 and 1895 led to reprisals by a government that had become increasingly convinced that the Armenians were seeking independence, as other Christian minorities of the Balkans had done in previous decades.

After 1913 the Ottoman state adopted a new policy of Turkish nationalism intended to shore up the crumbling imperial edifice. The new nationalism stressed Turkish culture and traditions, which only aggravated tensions between Turkish rulers and non-Turkish subjects of the empire. In particular, the state viewed Christian minorities as an obstacle to Turkism. During the Great War, the Ottoman government branded Armenians as a traitorous internal enemy, who threatened the security of the state, and then unleashed a murderous campaign against them. Forced mass evacuations, accompanied by starvation, dehydration, and exposure, led to the death of tens of thousands of Armenians. An equally deadly assault on the Armenians came by way of government-organized massacres that claimed victims through mass drowning, incineration, or assaults with blunt instruments.

Those wartime atrocities that took place principally between 1915 and 1917 have become known as Armenian genocide. Best estimates suggest that close to a million Armenians perished. Although it is generally agreed that the Armenian genocide did occur, the Turkish government in particular rejects the label of genocide and claims that Armenian deaths resulted not from a state-sponsored plan of mass extermination but from communal warfare perpetrated by Christians and Muslims, disease, and famine.

The Ottoman Empire

After successfully fending off Allied forces on the beaches of Gallipoli in 1915 and in Mesopotamia in 1916, Ottoman armies retreated slowly on all fronts. After yielding to the Russians in the Caucasus, Turkish troops were unable to defend the empire against invading British armies that drew heavily on recruits from Egypt, India, Australia, and New Zealand. As the armies smashed the Ottoman state—one entering Mesopotamia and the other advancing from the Suez Canal toward Palestine—they received signifi-

Australian recruiting poster. The British were keen to augment their forces by recruiting Australians and others to help defeat the Ottoman empire, which had allied itself with the Central Powers.

cant support from an Arab revolt against the Turks. In 1916, abetted by the British, the nomadic bedouin of Arabia under the leadership of Ibn Ali Hussain, sherif of Mecca and king of the Hejaz (1856–1931), and others rose up against Turkish rule. The motivation for the Arab revolt centered on securing independence from the Ottoman empire and subsequently creating a unified Arab nation spanning lands from Syria to Yemen. The British government did not keep its promise of Arab independence after the war.

THE END OF THE WAR

The war produced strains within all the belligerent nations, but most of them managed, often ruthlessly, to cope with food riots, strikes, and mutinies. In the Russian empire, the war amplified existing stresses to such an extent that the Romanov dynasty was forced to abdicate in favor of a provisional government in the spring of 1917. Eight months later, the provisional government yielded power to **Bolshevik** revolutionaries, who took Russia out of the war early in 1918. This blow to the Allies was more than offset by the entry of the United States into the conflict in 1917, which turned the tide of war in 1918. The resources of the United States finally compelled the exhausted Central Powers to sue for peace in November 1918.

In 1919 the victorious Allies gathered in Paris to hammer out a peace settlement that turned out to be a compromise that pleased few of the parties involved. The most significant consequence of the war was Europe's diminished role in the world. The war of 1914–1918 undermined Europe's power and simultaneously promoted nationalist aspirations among colonized peoples who clamored for self-determination and national independence. For the time being, however, the major imperialist powers kept their grip on their overseas holdings.

Revolution in Russia

The March Revolution The Great War had undermined the Russian state. In the spring of 1917, disintegrating armies, mutinies, and food shortages provoked a series of street demonstrations and strikes in Petrograd (St. Petersburg). The inability of police forces to suppress the uprisings, and the subsequent mutiny of troops garrisoned in the capital, persuaded Tsar Nicholas II (reigned 1894–1917) to abdicate the throne. Thus Russia ceased to be a monarchy, and the Romanov dynasty disappeared after more than three hundred years of uninterrupted rule. The March revolution—the first of two revolutions in 1917—was an unplanned and incomplete affair.

The Struggle for Power After its success in Petrograd, the revolution spread throughout the country, and political power in Russia shifted to two new agencies: the provisional government and the Petrograd soviet of Workers' and Soldiers' Deputies. Soviets, which were revolutionary councils organized by socialists, appeared for the first time during the Russian revolution of 1905 (see chapter 31). In 1917, soviets of Workers' and Soldiers' Deputies surfaced all over Russia, wielding considerable power through their control

of factories and segments of the military. The period between March and November witnessed a political struggle between the provisional government and the powerful Petrograd soviet. At first the new government enjoyed considerable public support as it disbanded the tsarist police; repealed all limitations on freedom of speech, press, and association; and abolished laws that discriminated against ethnic or religious groups; but it failed to satisfy popular demands for an end to war and for land reform. It claimed that, being provisional, it could not make fundamental changes such as confiscating land and distributing it among peasants. Any such change had to be postponed for decision by a future constituent assembly. The government also pledged itself to "unswervingly carry out the agreements made with the Allies" and promised to continue the war to a victorious conclusion. The Petrograd soviet, in contrast, called for an immediate peace. Such radicals were the only ones in Russia determined to end the war and hence gained more support from the people of Russia.

Lenin Into this tense political situation stepped Vladimir Ilyich Lenin (1870–1924), a revolutionary Marxist who had been living in exile in Switzerland. Born into a warm and loving family, Lenin grew up in the confines of a moderately prosperous family living in the provincial Russian town of Simbirsk. In 1887, shortly after his father's death, the police arrested and hanged his older brother for plotting to assassinate the tsar, an event that seared Lenin's youth. Following a brief career as a lawyer, Lenin spent many years abroad, devoting himself to studying Marxist thought and writing political pamphlets. In contrast to Marx, Lenin viewed the in-

Vladimir Lenin makes a speech in Red Square on the first anniversary (1918) of the Bolshevik revolution.

dustrial working class as incapable of developing the proper revolutionary consciousness that would lead to effective political action. To Lenin the industrial proletariat required the leadership of a well-organized and highly disciplined party, a workers' vanguard that would serve as the catalyst for revolution and for the realization of a socialist society.

In a moment of high drama, the German High Command transported Lenin and other revolutionaries in 1917 to Russia in a sealed train, hoping that this committed antiwar activist would stir up trouble and bring about Russia's withdrawal from the war. Lenin headed the Bolsheviks, the radical wing of the Russian Social Democratic Party. In April he began calling for the transfer of legal authority to the soviets and advocated uncompromising opposition to the war. Initially, his party opposed his radicalism, but he soon succeeded in converting his fellow Bolsheviks to his proposals.

The November Revolution

The Bolsheviks, who were a small minority among revolutionary working-class parties, eventually gained control of the Petrograd soviet. Crucial to that development was the provisional government's insistence on continuing the war, its inability to feed the population, and its refusal to undertake land reform. Those policies led to a growing conviction among workers and peasants that their problems could be solved only by the soviets. The Bolsheviks capitalized on that mood with effective slogans such as "All Power to the Soviets" and, most famous, "Peace, Land, and Bread." In September, Lenin persuaded the Central Committee of the Bolshevik Party to organize an armed insurrection and seize power in the name of the All-Russian National Congress of Soviets, which was then convening in Petrograd. During the night of 6 November and the following day, armed workers, soldiers, and sailors stormed the Winter Palace, the home of the provisional government. By the afternoon of 7 November, the virtually bloodless insurrection had run its course, and power passed from the provisional government into the hands of Lenin and the Bolshevik Party. The U.S. journalist John Reed (1887–1920), who witnessed the Bolshevik seizure of power, understood the significance of the events when he referred to them as "ten days that shook the world." Lenin and his followers were poised to destroy the traditional patterns and values of Russian society and challenge the institutions of liberal society everywhere.

Treaty of Brest-Litovsk

The Bolshevik rulers ended Russia's involvement in the Great War by signing the Treaty of Brest-Litovsk with Germany on 3 March 1918. The treaty gave the Germans possession or control of much of Russia's territory (the Baltic states, the Caucasus, Finland, Poland, and the Ukraine) and one-quarter of its population. The terms of the treaty were harsh and humiliating, but taking Russia out of the war gave the new government an opportunity to deal with internal problems. Russia's departure from the war meant that Germany could concentrate all its resources on the western front.

U.S. Intervention and Collapse of the Central Powers

The year 1917 was crucial for another reason: it marked the entry of the United States into the war on the side of the Allies. In 1914 the American public firmly opposed intervention in a European war. Woodrow Wilson (1856–1924) was reelected president in 1916 because he campaigned on a nonintervention platform. That sentiment soon changed. After the outbreak of the war, the United States pursued a neutrality that favored the Allies, and as the war progressed, the United States became increasingly committed economically to an Allied victory.

Economic Considerations

During the first two years of the war, the U.S. economy coped with a severe business recession that saw thousands of businesses fail and unemployment reach 15 percent. Economic recovery became dependent on sales of war materials, especially on British orders for munitions. Because U.S. companies sold huge amounts of supplies to the Allies, insistence on neutrality seemed hypocritical at best. With the war grinding on, the Allies took out large loans with American banks, which persuaded some Americans that an Allied victory made good financial sense. Moreover, by the spring of 1917, the Allies had depleted their means of paying for essential supplies from the United States and probably could not have maintained their war effort had the United States remained neutral. An Allied victory and, hence, the ability to pay off Allied war debts could be accomplished only by direct U.S. participation in the Great War.

Submarine Warfare

The official factor in the United States' decision to enter the war was Germany's resumption of unrestricted submarine warfare in February 1917. At the outset of the war, U.S. government officials asserted the traditional doctrine of neutral rights for American ships because they wanted to continue trading with belligerents, most notably the British and the French. With the German surface fleet bottled up in the Baltic, Germany's wartime leaders grew desperately dependent on their submarine fleet to strangle Britain economically and break the British blockade of the Central Powers. German military experts calculated that submarine attacks against the ships of Great Britain and all the ships headed to Great Britain would bring about the defeat of Great Britain in six months. German subs often sank neutral merchant ships without first giving a warning as required by international law. On 7 May 1915, a German submarine sank the British passenger liner *Lusitania* off the Irish coast with a loss of 1,198 lives, including 128 U.S. citizens. Technically, the ship was a legitimate target, because it carried 4,200 cases of ammunition and traveled through a declared war zone. Nevertheless, segments of the American public were outraged, and during the next two years the country's mood increasingly turned against Germany. Allied

In 1915 artist Willy Stower depicted a ship sinking as a result of a submarine attack. The Germans used submarines to great effect to disrupt the shipping of essential supplies to Great Britain.

propaganda, especially British manipulation of information, also swayed public opinion.

America Declares War

Even though the British naval blockade directed at the Central Powers constantly interfered with American shipping, Woodrow Wilson nonetheless moved his nation to war against Germany. In January 1917, with his country still at peace, Wilson began to enumerate U.S. war aims, and on 2 April he urged the Congress of the United States to adopt a war resolution. In his ringing war message, Wilson equated German "warfare against commerce" with "warfare against mankind," intoning that "the world must be made safe for democracy." Republican senator George W. Norris, arguing for U.S. neutrality, countered by saying "I feel that we are about to put the dollar sign upon the American flag." That protest was to no avail, and on 6 April 1917 the United States declared war against Germany. The U.S. entry proved decisive in breaking the stalemate.

Collapsing Fronts

The corrosive effects of years of bloodletting showed. For the first two years of the conflict, most people supported their governments' war efforts, but the continuing ravages of war took their toll everywhere. In April 1916 Irish nationalists mounted the Great Easter Rebellion, which attempted unsuccessfully to overthrow British rule in Ireland. The Central Powers suffered from food shortages as a result of the British blockade, and increasing numbers of people took to the streets to demonstrate against declining food rations. Food riots were complemented by strikes as prewar social conflicts reemerged. Governments reacted harshly to those challenges, pouncing on strikers, suppressing demonstrators, and jailing dissidents. Equally dangerous was the breakdown of military discipline. At the German naval base in Kiel, sailors revolted in the summer of 1917 and again, much more seriously, in the fall of 1918. In the wake of another failed offensive during the spring of 1917, which resulted in ghastly casualties, French soldiers lost confidence in their leadership. When ordered to attack once again, they refused. The extent of the mutiny was enormous: 50,000 soldiers were involved, resulting in 23,385 courts-martial and 432 death sentences. So tight was

German prisoners taken in France in the autumn of 1918. Millions of soldiers had been captured and imprisoned by war's end, and many more had died or been wounded. Over fifteen million had been killed and twenty million wounded by the time of the armistice on 11 November 1918.

French censorship that the Germans, who could have taken advantage of this situation, did not learn about the mutiny until the war was over.

Against the background of civilian disillusionment and deteriorating economic conditions, Germany took the risk of throwing its remaining might at the western front in the spring of 1918. The gamble failed, and as the offensive petered out, the Allies broke through the front and started pushing the Germans back. By that time Germany had effectively exhausted its human and material means to wage war. Meanwhile, Bulgaria capitulated to the invading Allies on 30 September, the Ottomans concluded an armistice on 30 October, and Austria-Hungary surrendered on 4 November. Finally, the Germans accepted an armistice, which took effect on 11 November 1918. At last the guns went silent.

After the War

The immediate effects of the Great War were all too obvious. Aside from the physical destruction, which was most visible in northern France and Belgium, the war had killed, disabled, orphaned, or rendered homeless millions of people. Conservative estimates suggest that the war killed fifteen million people and wounded twenty million others. In the immediate postwar years, millions more succumbed to the effects of starvation, malnutrition, and epidemic diseases.

The Influenza Pandemic of 1918 The end of the Great War coincided with the arrival of one of the worst pandemics ever recorded in human history. No one knows its origins or why it vanished in mid-1919, but by the time this virulent influenza disappeared, it had left more than twenty million dead. The disease killed more people than did the Great War, and it hit young adults—a group usually not severely affected by influenza—with particular ferocity. Contemporaries called it the Spanish flu because the first major documented outbreak of the disease occurred in Spain in late 1918.

The Great War did not cause the flu pandemic of 1918–1919, but wartime traffic on land and sea probably contributed to the spread of the infection. It killed swiftly wherever it went. From the remotest villages in Arctic climates and crowded cities in India and the United States to the battlefields of Europe, men and women were struck down by high fever. Within a few days they were dead. One estimate puts deaths in India alone at seven million. In Calcutta, the postal service and the legal system ground to a halt. In the United States, the flu killed more Americans than all the wars fought in the twentieth century put together. In cutting a swath across west Africa, it left in its deadly path more than one million victims. The Pacific islands suffered worst of all as the flu wiped out up to 25 percent of their entire population.

The influenza plague never discriminated. It struck the rich as fiercely as the poor. It decimated men and women equally. It did not distinguish between the hungry and the well nourished, and it took the sick as well as the healthy. The presence or absence of doctors and nurses never made any difference. There was no cure for the flu of 1918.

The Paris Settlement Before the costs of the war were assessed fully, world attention shifted to Paris. There, in 1919, the victorious powers convened to arrange a postwar settlement and set terms for the defeated nations. At the outset, people on both sides of the war had high hopes for the settlement, but in the end it left a bitter legacy. Because the twenty-seven nations represented at Paris had different and often conflicting aims, many sessions of the conference deteriorated into pandemonium. Ultimately, Georges Clemenceau (1841–1929), Lloyd George (1863–1945), and Woodrow Wilson—the representative leaders of France, Great Britain, and the United States—dominated the deliberations. The Allies did not permit representatives of the Central Powers to participate. In addition, the Allies threatened to renew the war if the terms they laid down were not accepted. Significantly, the Soviet Union was not invited to the conference.

Throughout this time the British blockade of Germany remained in effect, adding a sense of urgency to the proceedings. That situation later gave rise to the charge of a dictated peace, especially because no foreign troops set foot on German soil.

Wilson's Fourteen Points

One year before the opening of the Paris Peace Conference in January 1918, U.S. president Woodrow Wilson forwarded a proposal for a just and enduring postwar peace settlement. Wilson's postwar vision had subsequently prompted the defeated Central Powers to announce their acceptance of his so-called Fourteen Points as the basis for the armistice. They also expected the Allies to use them as the foundation for later peace treaties. Key among Wilson's Fourteen Points were the following recommendations: open covenants (agreements) of peace, openly arrived at; absolute freedom of navigation on the seas in peace and war; the removal of all economic barriers and the establishment of an equality of trade conditions among all nations; adequate guarantees for a reduction in national armaments; adjustments of colonial disputes to give equal weight to the interests of the controlling government and the colonial population; and a call for "a general association of nations." The idealism expressed in the Fourteen Points gave Wilson a position of moral leadership among the Allies. Those same allies also opposed various points of Wilson's peace formula, because those points compromised the secret wartime agreements by which they had agreed to distribute among themselves territories and possessions of the defeated nations. The defeated powers, in turn, later felt betrayed when they faced the harsh peace treaties that so clearly violated the spirit of the Fourteen Points.

The Peace Treaties

The final form of the treaties represented a series of compromises among the victors. The hardest terms originated with the French, who desired the destruction or the permanent weakening of German power. Thus, in addition to requiring Germany to accept sole responsibility and guilt for causing the war, the victors demanded a reduction in the military potential of the former Central Powers. For example, the Treaty of Versailles (1919) denied the Germans a navy and an air force and limited the size of the German army to 100,000 troops. In addition, the Allies prohibited Germany and Austria from entering into any sort of political union. The French and the British agreed that the defeated Central Powers must pay for the cost of the war and required the payment of reparations either in money or in kind. Although the German government and the public decried the Treaty of Versailles as being excessively harsh, it was no more severe in its terms than the Treaty of Brest-Litovsk that the Germans imposed on Russia in 1918.

The Paris peace conference resulted in several additional treaties. Bulgaria accepted the Treaty of Neuilly (1919), ceding only small portions of territory, because the Allies feared that major territorial changes in the Balkans would destabilize the region. That view did not apply to the dual monarchy of Austria-Hungary, whose imperial unity disintegrated under the impact of the war. The peacemakers recognized the territorial breakup of the former empire in two separate treaties: the Treaty of St. Germain (1919), between the Allies and the Republic of Austria, and the Treaty of Trianon (1920), between the Allies and the kingdom of Hungary. Both Austria and Hungary suffered severe territorial losses, which the Allies claimed were necessary in order to find territorial boundaries that accorded closely with the principle of self-determination. For example, the peace settlement reduced Hungarian territory to one-third of its prewar size and decreased the nation's population from 28 to 8 million people.

Arrangements between the defeated Ottoman empire and the Allies proved to be a more complicated and protracted affair. The Treaty of Sèvres (1920) effectively dissolved the empire, calling for the surrender of Ottoman Balkan and Arab provinces and the occupation of eastern and southern Anatolia by foreign powers. The treaty was acceptable to the government of sultan Mohammed VI, but not to Turkish nationalists who rallied around their wartime hero Mustafa Kemal. As head of the Turkish nationalist movement, Mustafa Kemal set out to defy the Allied terms. He organized a national army that drove out Greek, British, French, and Italian occupation forces and abolished the sultanate and replaced it with the Republic of Turkey, with Ankara as its capital. In a great diplomatic victory for Turkish nationalists, the Allied powers officially recognized the Republic of Turkey in a final peace agreement, the Treaty of Lausanne (1923).

Atatürk

As president of the republic, Mustafa Kemal, now known as Atatürk ("Father of the Turks"), instituted an ambitious program of modernization that emphasized economic development and secularism. Gov-

Political leaders sign the Treaty of Versailles, which, among other provisions, controversially compelled the Germans to accept sole responsibility for causing the war.

ernment support of critical industries and businesses, and other forms of state intervention in the economy designed to ensure rapid economic development, resulted in substantial long-term economic progress. The government's policy of secularism dictated the complete separation between the existing Muslim religious establishment and the state. The policy resulted in the replacement of religious with secular institutions of education and justice, the emancipation of women, including their right to vote, the adoption of European-derived law, Hindu-Arabic numerals, the Roman alphabet, and Western clothing. Theoretically heading a constitutional democracy, Atatürk ruled Turkey as a virtual dictator until his death in 1938.

Turkey's postwar transformations and its success in refashioning the terms of peace proved to be something of an exception. In the final analysis, the peace settlement was strategically weak because too few participants had a stake in maintaining it and too many had an interest in revising it. German expansionist aims in Europe, which probably played a role in the nation's decision to enter the Great War, remained unresolved, as did Italian territorial designs in the Balkans and Japanese influence in China. Those issues virtually ensured that the two decades following the peace settlement became merely a twenty-year truce, characterized by power rivalries and intermittent violence that led to yet another global war.

The League of Nations   In an effort to avoid future destructive conflicts, the diplomats in Paris created the League of Nations. The League was the first permanent international security organization whose principal mission was to maintain world peace. At the urging of U.S. president Woodrow Wilson, the Covenant of the League of Nations was made an integral part of the peace treaties, and every signatory to a peace treaty had to accept this new world organization. Initially, the League seemed to be the sign of a new era: twenty-six of its forty-two original members were countries outside Europe, suggesting that it transcended European interests.

The League had two major flaws that rendered it ineffective. First, though designed to solve international disputes through arbitration, it had no power to enforce its decisions. Second, it relied on *collective security* as a tool for the preservation of global peace. The basic premise underlying collective security arrangements was the concept that aggression against any one state was considered aggression against all the other states, which had pledged to aid one another. Shared deterrence could assume different forms, such as diplomatic pressure, economic sanctions, and, ultimately, force. However, the basic precondition for collective security—participation by all the great powers—never materialized, because at any given time one or more of the major powers did not belong to the League. The United States never joined the organization because the U.S. Senate rejected the idea. Germany, which viewed the League as a club

of Allied victors, and Japan, which saw it as an instrument of imperialism, left the League of Nations in 1933, as did some smaller powers. Italy, chastised by the League for imperial adventures in Ethiopia, withdrew from it in 1937. The Soviet Union, which regarded the League as a tool of global capitalism, joined the organization in 1934, only to face expulsion in 1940. Although its failure to stop aggression in the 1930s led to its demise in 1940, the League established the pattern for a permanent international organization and served as a model for its successor, the United Nations.

Self-Determination   One of the principal themes of the peacemaking process was the concept of self-determination, which was promoted most intensely by Woodrow Wilson. Wilson believed that self-determination was the key to international peace and cooperation. With respect to Europe, that principle sometimes translated into reality. For example, Poland, Czechoslovakia, and Yugoslavia (kingdom of Serbs, Croats, and Slovenes until 1929) already existed as sovereign states by 1918, and by the end of the conference, the principle of self-determination had triumphed in many areas that were previously under the control of the Austro-Hungarian and Russian empires. Yet in other instances peacemakers pushed the principle aside for strategic and security reasons, such as in Austria and Germany, whose peoples were denied the right to form one nation. At other times, diplomats violated the notion of self-determination because they found it impossible to redraw national boundaries in accordance with nationalist aspirations without creating large minorities on one side or the other of a boundary line. Poland was one case in point; one-third of the population did not speak Polish. A more complicated situation existed in Czechoslovakia. The peoples who gave the republic its name—the Czechs and the Slovaks—totaled only 67 percent of the population, with the remaining population consisting of Germans (22 percent), Ruthenes (6 percent), and Hungarians (5 percent). On the surface, the creation of Yugoslavia ("Land of the South Slavs") represented a triumph of self-determination, because it politically united related peoples who for centuries had chafed under foreign rule. Beneath that unity, however, there lingered the separate national identities embraced by Serbs, Croats, and Slovenes.

The Mandate System   However imperfect the results, the peacemakers at Paris tried to apply the principle of self-determination and nationality throughout Europe. Elsewhere, however, they did not do so. The unwillingness to apply the principle of self-determination became most obvious when the victors confronted the issue of what to do with Germany's former colonies and the Arab territories of the Ottoman empire. Because the United States rejected the establishment of old-fashioned colonies, the European powers came up with the enterprising idea of trusteeship. Article 22 of the Covenant of the League of Nations referred to the colonies and territories of the former Central Powers as areas

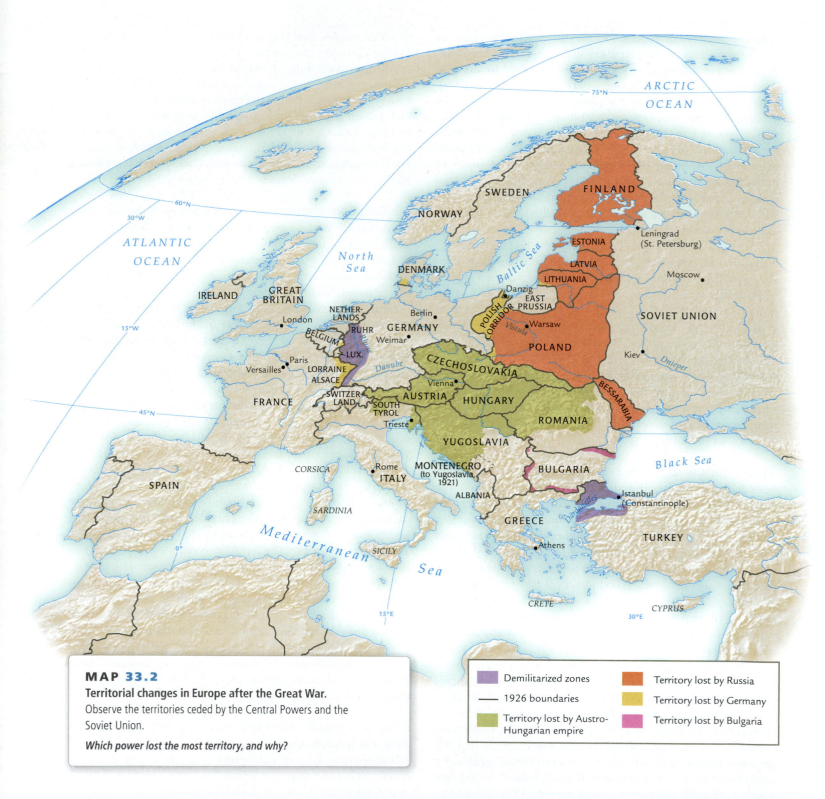

MAP 33.2

Territorial changes in Europe after the Great War.
Observe the territories ceded by the Central Powers and the
Soviet Union.

Which power lost the most territory, and why?

Demilitarized zones
1926 boundaries
Territory lost by Austro-
Hungarian empire
Territory lost by Russia
Territory lost by Germany
Territory lost by Bulgaria

"inhabited by peoples not yet able to stand by themselves under the strenuous conditions of the modern world." As a result, "The tutelage of such peoples should be entrusted to the advanced nations who . . . can best undertake this responsibility." The League divided the mandates into three classes based on the presumed development of their populations in the direction of fitness for self-government. The administration of the mandates fell to the victorious powers of the Great War.

The Germans interpreted the mandate system as a division of colonial booty by the victors, who had conveniently forgotten to apply the tutelage provision to their own colonies. German cynicism was more than matched by Arab outrage. The establishment of mandates in the former ter-

sources from the past

Memorandum of the General Syrian Congress

Article 22 of the League of Nations Covenant established a system of mandates to rule the colonies and territories of the defeated powers, including parts of the former Ottoman empire (comprising present-day Syria, Lebanon, Jordan, and Israel). The mandate system essentially substituted European mandates for Ottoman rule. The news of this arrangement came as a shock to the peoples of the defeated Ottoman empire who had fought alongside the English and the French during the Great War and expected their independence. They quickly denounced the mandate system. The following selection is a memorandum addressed to the King Crane Commission, which was responsible for overseeing the transfer of Ottoman territory.

We the undersigned members of the General Syrian Congress, meeting in Damascus on Wednesday, July 2nd 1919, . . . provided with the credentials and authorizations by the inhabitants of our various districts, Moslems, Christians, and Jews, have agreed upon the following statement of the desires of the people of the country who have elected us. . . .

1. We ask absolutely complete political independence for Syria. . . .

2. We ask that the Government of this Syrian country should be a democratic civil constitutional Monarchy on broad decentralization principles, safeguarding the rights of minorities, and that the King be the Emir Feisal, who carried on a glorious struggle in the cause of liberation and merited our full confidence and entire reliance.

3. Considering that the Arabs inhabiting the Syrian area are not naturally less gifted than other more advanced races

and that they are by no means less developed than the Bulgarians, Serbians, Greeks, and Romanians at the beginning of their independence, we protest against Article 22 of the Covenant of the League of Nations, placing us among the nations in their middle stage of development which stand in need of a mandatory power.

6. We do not acknowledge any right claimed by the French Government in any part whatever of our Syrian country and refuse that she should assist us or have a hand in our country under any circumstances and in any place.

7. We oppose the pretensions of the Zionists to create a Jewish commonwealth in the southern part of Syria, known as Israel, and oppose Zionist migration to any part of our country; for we do not acknowledge their title but consider them a grave peril to our people, from the national, economical, and political points of view. Our Jewish compatriots shall enjoy our common rights and assume the common responsibilities.

For Further Reflection

■ For what specifically was the Syrian Congress asking? Do you think the European powers expected this response to the League of Nations Covenant?

Source: Foreign Relations of the United States: Paris Peace Conference, vol. 12. Washington, D.C.: Government Printing Office, 1919, pp. 780–81. Cited in Philip F. Riley et al., *The Global Experience. Readings in World History,* vol. 2. Englewood Cliffs, N.J.: Prentice Hall, 1992, pp. 193–94.

ritories of the Ottoman empire violated promises (made to Arabs) by French and British leaders during the war. They had promised Arab nationalists independence from the Ottoman empire and had promised Jewish nationalists in Europe a homeland in Palestine. Where the Arabs hoped to form independent states, the French (in Lebanon and Syria) and the British (in Iraq and Palestine) established mandates. The Allies viewed the mandate system as a reasonable compromise between the reality of imperialism and the ideal of self-determination. To the peoples who were directly affected, the mandate system smacked of continued imperial rule draped in a cloak of respectability.

Challenges to European Preeminence

The Great War changed Europe forever, but to most Europeans the larger world and the Continent's role in it remained essentially unchanged. With the imperial powers still ruling over their old colonies and new protectorates, it appeared that European global hegemony was more secure. Yet that picture did not correspond to reality. The Great War did irreparable damage to European power and prestige and set the stage for a process of decolonization that gathered momentum during and after the Second World War. The war of 1914–1918 accelerated the growth of nationalism in the European-controlled parts of the world, fueling desires for independence and self-determination.

Weakened Europe The decline in European power was closely related to diminished economic stature, a result of the commitment to total war. In time, Europe overcame many war-induced economic problems, such as high rates of inflation and huge public debts, but other economic dislocations

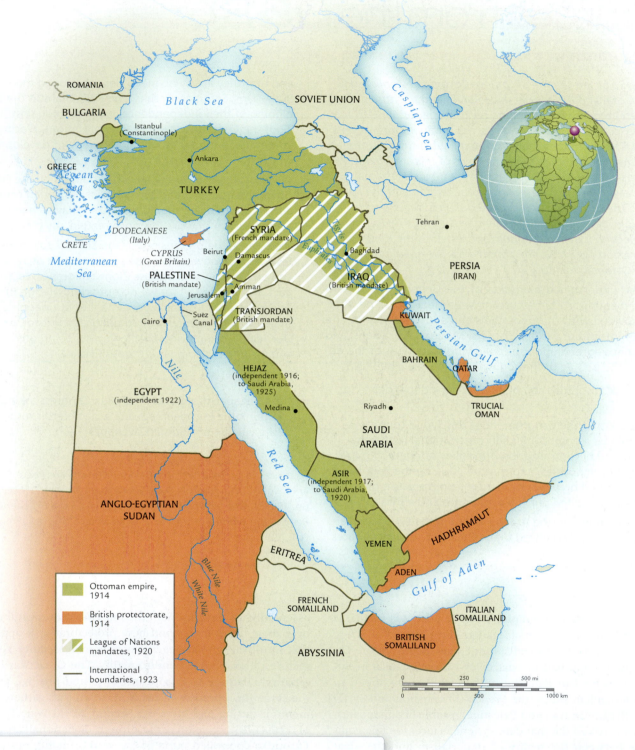

MAP 33.3

Territorial changes in southwest Asia after the Great War.
The Great War completed the process of disintegration of the Ottoman empire and
left much of the region in limbo.

*What was the reaction in the region when European statesmen assigned former Otto-
man territories to French or British control under the League of Nations mandates?*

were permanent and damaging. Most significant was the loss of overseas investments and foreign markets, which had brought huge financial returns. Nothing is more indicative of Europe's reduced economic might than the reversal of the economic relationship between Europe and the United States. Whereas the United States was a debtor nation before 1914, owing billions of dollars to European investors, by 1919 it was a major creditor.

A loss of prestige overseas and a weakening grip on colonies also reflected the undermining of Europe's global hegemony. Colonial subjects in Africa, Asia, and the Pacific often viewed the Great War as a civil war among the European nations, a bloody spectacle in which the haughty bearers of an alleged superior society vilified and slaughtered one another. Because Europe seemed weak, divided, and vulnerable, the white overlords no longer appeared destined to rule over colonized subjects. The colonials who returned home from the war in Europe and southwest Asia reinforced those general impressions with their own first-hand observations. In particular, they were less inclined to be obedient imperial subjects.

Revolutionary Ideas The war also helped spread revolutionary ideas to the colonies. The U.S. war aims spelled out in the Fourteen Points raised the hopes of peoples under imperial rule and promoted nationalist aspirations. The peacemakers repeatedly invoked the concept of self-determination, and Wilson publicly proposed that in all colonial questions "the interests of the native populations be given equal weight with the desires of European governments." Wilson seemed to call for nothing less than national independence and self-rule. Nationalists struggling to organize anti-imperialist resistance also sought inspiration from the Soviet Union, whose leaders denounced all forms of imperialism and pledged their support to independence movements. Taken together, these messages were subversive to imperial control and had a great appeal for colonial peoples. The postwar disappointments and temporary setbacks experienced by nationalist movements did not diminish their desire for self-rule and self-determination.

in**perspective**

The assassination of the Austrian archduke Francis Ferdinand had a galvanizing effect on a Europe torn by national rivalries, colonial disputes, and demands for self-determination. In the summer of 1914, inflexible war plans and a tangled alliance system transformed a local war between Austria-Hungary and Serbia into a European-wide clash of arms. With the entry of the Ottoman empire, Japan, and the United States, the war of 1914–1918 became a global conflict. Although many belligerents organized their societies for total war and drew on the resources of their overseas empires, the war remained at a bloody stalemate until the United States entered the conflict in 1917. The tide turned, and the combatants signed an armistice in November 1918. The Great War, a brutal encounter between societies and peoples, inflicted ghastly human casualties, severely damaged national economies, and discredited established political and cultural traditions. The war also altered the political landscape of many lands as it destroyed four dynasties and their empires and fostered the creation of several new European nations. In Russia the war served as a backdrop for the world's first successful socialist revolution. In the end the Great War sapped the strength of European colonial powers while promoting nationalist aspirations among colonized peoples. ●

CHRONOLOGY

1914	Assassination of Archduke Francis Ferdinand
1915	German submarine sinks the *Lusitania*
1915	Japan makes Twenty-one Demands on China
1915	Gallipoli campaign
1916	Battles at Verdun and the Somme
1917	German resumption of unrestricted submarine warfare
1917	United States declaration of war on Germany
1917	Bolshevik Revolution
1918	Treaty of Brest-Litovsk
1918	Armistice suspends hostilities
1919	Paris Peace Conference
1920	First meeting of the League of Nations
1923	Atatürk proclaims Republic of Turkey

For Further Reading

Jonathan W. Daly. *The Watchful State: Security Police and Opposition in Russia, 1906–1917.* DeKalb, Ill., 2004. Study of the Russian secret police and their policies toward early revolutionary activities.

Belinda Davis. *Home Fires Burning: Food, Politics, and Everyday Life in World War I Berlin.* Chapel Hill, 2000. Effectively covers daily life in wartime and also offers insights into how government policies during the war affected the reconstruction of society following it.

Modris Eckstein. *Rites of Spring: The Great War and the Birth of the Modern Age.* Boston, 1989. An imaginative cultural study that ranges widely.

Niall Ferguson. *The Pity of War: Explaining World War I.* New York, 2000. A stimulating example of revisionist history that shifts the blame for the war away from Germany and onto England.

Paul Fussell. *Great War and Modern Memory.* Oxford, 1975. An original and deeply moving piece of cultural history.

Peter Gatrell. *Russia's First World War: A Social and Economic History.* London, 2005. Traces the impact of World War I on Russian society before the revolution.

Felix Gilbert. *The End of the European Era, 1890 to the Present.* New York, 1979. An information-laden study that argues that the Great War destroyed Europe's centrality in the world.

Paul G. Halpern. *A Naval History of World War I.* Annapolis, 1994. Unlike most other treatments, this work covers all participants in all major theaters.

Margaret Randolph Higonnet et al. *Behind the Lines.* New Haven, 1990. Women's work and the war industry take center stage.

James Joll. *The Origins of the First World War.* 2nd ed. London, 1991. The most lucid and balanced introduction to a complex and controversial subject.

John Keegan. *The First World War.* New York, 1999. A comprehensive and a stunningly vivid account of the Great War.

John Maynard Keynes. *The Economic Consequences of the Peace.* New York, 1920. A classic and devastating critique of the Versailles treaty.

John H. Morrow. *The Great War. An Imperial History.* New York, 2003. A global history of the Great War that places the conflict squarely in the context of imperialism.

Michael S. Neiberg. *Fighting the Great War.* Cambridge, Mass., 2005. A good blend of narrative and analysis, this work highlights the global reach of the conflict.

Richard Pipes. *The Russian Revolution 1899–1919.* 2nd ed. London, 1992. An up-to-date and well-argued interpretation.

Erich Remarque. *All Quiet on the Western Front.* New York, 1958. A fictional account of trench warfare.

Hew Strachan. *The First World War.* Vol. 1: *To Arms.* New York, 2001. The first of three anticipated volumes, this is a masterly work that treats the war in global rather than European terms.

Barbara Tuchman. *The Guns of August.* New York, 1962. Spellbinding narrative of the coming of the war.

Robert Wohl. *The Generation of 1914.* Cambridge, 1979. Elegantly captures the ideas and attitudes of the generations that experienced the Great War.

In his disturbing painting of the *Seven Deadly Sins* (1933), Otto Dix features Hitler, clearly identified by a black moustache, in the guise of envy. Fearing retribution while the Führer remained in power, Dix added the moustache after Hitler's death.

PART

EYEWITNESS:
The Birth of a Monster

Born on a lovely spring day in 1889, in a quaint Austrian village, he was the apple of his mother's eye. He basked in Klara's warmth and indulgence as a youth, enjoying the fine life of a middle-class child. As he grew older, he sensed a tension that long stayed with him, a vague anxiety that stemmed from the competing expectations of his parents. Contented with the dreamy indolence allowed by Klara, he bristled at the demands of his father, Alois. Alois expected him to follow in his footsteps, to study hard and enter the Austrian civil service. He had no desire to become a bureaucrat. In fact, he envisioned a completely different life for himself. He wanted to be an artist. His school grades slipped, and that seemed an appropriate way to express his discontent and sabotage his father's pedestrian plans for his future.

Alois's unexpected death in 1903 freed him from that awful future. He now had the time and the familial sympathy to daydream and indulge his imagination. He left school in 1905, not at all dissatisfied with having achieved only a ninth-grade education, because now he could pursue his heart's desire: an education as an artist. He followed his ambitions to Vienna, only to find bitter disappointment when the Vienna Academy of Fine Arts rejected him as an art student in 1907. His beloved Klara died the following year, and he meandered the city streets of Vienna, living off a pension and the money he inherited from his mother. He immersed himself in Vienna, admiring the architecture of the city and attending the opera when his funds permitted. He especially enjoyed the music of Richard Wagner, whose embrace of heroic German myth matched his own imaginative predilections.

Having finally run through all of his money, he hit bottom and began staying at a homeless shelter. It was interesting, though, to hear the different political points of view spouted by the shelter's other inhabitants. They discussed compelling issues of the day, such as race, and he listened intently to those who hailed the supremacy of the Aryan race and the inferiority of the Jews. He immersed himself in reading, particularly the newspapers and pamphlets that gave him more information about those disturbing political issues. He came to hate Jews and Marxists, whom he thought had formed an evil union with the goal of destroying the world. He also despised liberalism and democracy, and in cheap cafés

This is one of the few known photographs of a young Adolf Hitler, taken in 1923.

he began directing political harangues at anyone who would listen.

Still, he had his art, and he found he could just barely survive on the earnings he made from selling his pretty postcards covered with painted replicas of famous works or his original sketches of Viennese buildings. He believed, too, that his political and social life had become much more exciting, as he was now publicly debating issues and learning to speak up about the concerns of the day—and what anxious, perilous, but interesting times these were. He felt compelled to leave Vienna in 1913, however, if only to avoid the Austrian military draft. He was not willing to serve or die for what he believed was a decaying Austria-Hungary empire.

He found refuge in Munich, Germany, and there volunteered for service in the German army, which had just embarked on its crusade in the greatest war ever fought. He discovered in himself a real talent for military service, and he remained in the army for the duration of the war, 1914–1918. Twice wounded and decorated for bravery, he nonetheless found himself in despair at war's end. He languished in a military hospital, temporarily blinded by the mustard gas that had enveloped him during his last days of fighting. An impotent rage coursed through him when he learned of Germany's defeat. He knew with all his being that the Jews were responsible for this humiliation, and he also knew what he had to do: he had to enter the political arena in his chosen fatherland and save the nation. Adolf Hitler had finally found his mission in life.

Affected by and in turn affecting the anxiety and malaise of the early decades of the twentieth century, Hitler (1889–1945) stood as just one personification of Europe's age of anxiety. Torn between divergent visions of his future and embittered by a sense of dislocation and fear stemming from the drastic changes engulfing the society around him, Hitler dedicated himself to discovering a way out of the anxiety for the nation he had adopted. His solutions ultimately brought about more rather than less anxiety, but the novelty and cruelty of his political and military agendas reflected brilliantly the traumatic consequences of the Great War and the Great Depression.

Just as Adolf Hitler changed as a result of his life experiences in the early twentieth century, so too did European society as a whole. Badly shaken by the effects of years of war, Europeans experienced a shock to their system of values, beliefs, and traditions. Profound scientific and cultural transformations that came to the fore in the postwar decades also contributed to a sense of loss and anxiety. As peoples in Europe and around the world struggled to come to terms with the aftermath of war, an unprecedented economic contraction gripped the international community.

Against the background of the Great Depression, dictators in Russia, Italy, and Germany tried to translate blueprints for utopias into reality. While Joseph Stalin and his fellow communists recast the former tsarist empire into a dictatorship of the proletariat, Benito Mussolini and his fascists along with Adolf Hitler and his Nazi party forged new national communities. These political innovations unsettled many Europeans and much of the world, contributing significantly to the anxiety of the age. Such shifts in political thought matched in their radicalness, however strangely, the vast alterations taking place in the intellectual and cultural realms of European society after the Great War.

PROBING CULTURAL FRONTIERS

The Great War discredited established social and political institutions and long-held beliefs about the superiority of European society. Writers, poets, theologians, and other intellectuals lamented the decline and imminent death of their society. While some wrote obituaries, however, others embarked on bold new cultural paths that established the main tendencies of contemporary thought and taste. Most of these cultural innovators began their work before the war, but it was in the two decades following the war that a revolution in science, psychology, art, and architecture attained its fullest development and potency.

The discoveries of physicists undermined the Newtonian universe, in which a set of inexorable natural laws governed events, with a new and disturbing cosmos. Uncertainty governed this strange universe, which lacked objective reality. Equally discomforting were the insights of psychoanalysis, which suggested that human behavior was fundamentally irrational. Disquieting trends in the arts and architecture paralleled the developments in science and psychology. Especially in painting, an aversion to realism and a pronounced preference for abstraction heralded the arrival of new aesthetic standards.

Postwar Pessimism

"You are all a lost generation," noted Gertrude Stein (1874–1946) to her fellow American writer Ernest Hemingway (1899–1961). Stein had given a label to the group of American intellectuals and literati who congregated in Paris in the postwar years. This "lost generation" expressed in poetry and fiction the malaise and disillusion that characterized U.S. and European thought after the Great War. The vast majority of European intellectuals rallied enthusiastically to the war in 1914, viewing it as a splendid adventure. The brutal realities of industrialized warfare left no room for heroes, however, and most of these young artists and intellectuals quickly became disillusioned. During the 1920s they spat out their revulsion in a host of war novels such as Ernest Hemingway's *A Farewell to Arms* (1929) and Erich Maria Remarque's *All Quiet on the Western Front* (1929), works overflowing with images of meaningless death and suffering.

Postwar writers lamented the decline of Western society. A retired German schoolteacher named Oswald Spengler (1880–1936) made headlines when he published *The Decline of the West* (1918–1922). In this work, which might have been seen as an obituary of civilization, Spengler proposed that all societies pass through a life cycle of growth and decay comparable to the biological cycle of living organisms. His analysis of the history of western Europe led him to conclude that European society had entered the final stage of its existence. All that remained was irreversible decline, marked by imperialism and warfare. Spengler's gloomy predictions provided a kind of comfort to those who sought to rationalize their postwar despair, as did his

conviction that all the nations of the world were equally doomed. In England the shock of war caused the historian Arnold J. Toynbee (1889–1975) to begin his twelve-volume classic, *A Study of History* (1934–1961), that sought to discover how societies develop through time. In this monumental comparative study, Toynbee analyzes the genesis, growth, and disintegration of twenty-six societies.

Religious Uncertainty Theologians joined the chorus of despair. In 1919 Karl Barth (1886–1968), widely recognized as one of the most notable Christian theologians, published a religious bombshell entitled *Epistle to the Romans*. In his work Barth sharply attacked the liberal Christian theology that embraced the idea of progress, that is, the tendency of European thinkers to believe in limitless improvement as the realization of God's purpose. Other Christians joined the fray, reminding a generation of optimists that Christ's kingdom is not of this world. The Augustinian, Lutheran, and Calvinist message of original sin—the depravity of human nature—fell on receptive ears as many Christians refused to accept the idea that contemporary human society was in any way a realization of God's purpose. The Russian orthodox thinker Niokolai Berdiaev (1874–1948) summed up these sentiments: "Man's historical experience has been one of steady failure, and there are no grounds for supposing it will be ever anything else."

Attacks on Progress The Great War destroyed long-cherished beliefs such as belief in the universality of human progress. Many idols of nineteenth-century progress came under attack, especially science and technology. The scientists' dream of leading humanity to a beneficial conquest of nature seemed to have gone awry, because scientists had spent the war making poisonous gas and high explosives. Democracy was another fallen idol. The idea that people should have a voice in selecting the leaders of their government enjoyed widespread support in European societies. By the early twentieth century, the removal of property and educational restrictions on the right to vote resulted in universal male suffrage in most societies. In the years following the Great War, most European governments extended the franchise to women. Those developments led to an unprecedented degree of political participation as millions of people voted in elections and referendums, but many intellectuals abhorred what they viewed as a weak political system that championed the tyranny of the average person. Because they viewed democracy as a product of decay and as lacking in positive values, many people idealized elite rule. In Germany a whole school of conservatives lamented the "rule of inferiors." Common people, too, often viewed democracy as a decaying political system because they associated it with corrupt and ineffective party politics. However, antidemocratic strains were not confined to Germany. The widely read essay "Revolt of the Masses" (1930) by the Spanish philosopher José Ortega y Gasset (1883–1955) warned readers

One of the best-known faces of the twentieth century, Albert Einstein was the symbol of the revolution in physics.

and Mechanical Relationships," which established the "uncertainty principle." According to Heisenberg, it is impossible to specify simultaneously the position and the velocity of a subatomic particle. The more accurately one determines the position of an electron, the less precisely one can determine its velocity, and vice versa. In essence, scientists cannot observe the behavior of electrons objectively, because the act of observation interferes with them. The indeterminacy of the atomic universe demanded that the exact calculations of classical physics be replaced by probability calculations.

It quickly became evident that the uncertainty principle had important implications beyond physics. It also carried broader philosophical ramifications. Heisenberg's theory called into question established notions of truth and violated the fundamental law of cause and effect. Likewise, objectivity as it was understood was no longer a valid concept, because

about the masses who were destined to destroy the highest achievements of Western society.

Revolutions in Physics and Psychology

The postwar decade witnessed a revolution in physics that transformed the character of science. Albert Einstein (1879–1955) struck the first blow with his theory of special relativity (1905), showing that there is no single spatial and chronological framework in the universe. According to the theory, it no longer made sense to speak of space and time as absolutes, because the measurement of those two categories always varies with the motion of the observer. That is, space and time are relative to the person measuring them. To the layperson such notions—usually expressed in incomprehensible mathematical formulas—suggested that science had reached the limits of what could be known with certainty. A commonsense universe had vanished, to be replaced by a radically new one in which reality or truth was merely a set of mental constructs.

The Uncertainty Principle More disquieting even than Einstein's discoveries was the theory formulated by Werner Heisenberg (1901–1976), who in 1927 published a paper, "About the Quantum-Theoretical Reinterpretation of Kinetic

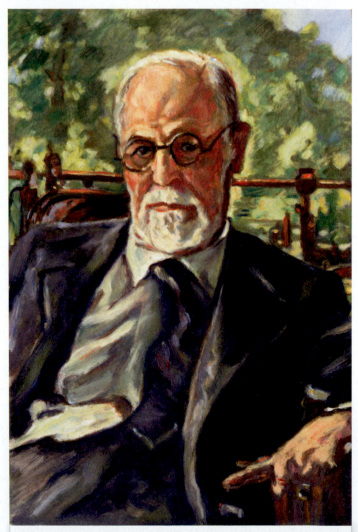

A striking painted portrait of Sigmund Freud. Freud formulated psychoanalysis, a theory and clinical practice to explore the mind and, by extension, its creations, such as literature, religion, art, and history.

Paul Gauguin, *Nafea Fan Ipoipo* ("When are you to be married?"; 1892). Gauguin sought the spiritual meaning for his art in the islands of the South Pacific. This painting of two Tahitian women revealed his debt to impressionism, but also showed his innovations: strong outlines, flat colors, and flattened forms.

the observer was always part of the process under observation. Accordingly, any observer—an anthropologist studying another society, for instance—had to be alert to the fact that his or her very presence became an integral part of the study.

Freud's Psychoanalytic Theory Equally unsettling as the advances in physics were developments in psychology that challenged established concepts of morality and values. In an indeterminate universe governed by relativity, the one remaining fixed point was the human psyche, but the insights of Sigmund Freud (1856–1939) proved disturbing as well. Beginning in 1896, the medical doctor from Vienna embarked on research that focused on psychological rather than physiological explanations of mental disorders. Through his clinical observations of patients, Freud identified a conflict between conscious and unconscious mental processes that lay at the root of neurotic behavior. That conflict, moreover,

suggested to him the existence of a repressive mechanism that keeps painful memories or threatening events away from the conscious mind. Freud believed that dreams held the key to the deepest recesses of the human psyche. Using the free associations of patients to guide him in the interpretation of dreams, he identified sexual drives and fantasies as the most important source of repression. For example, Freud claimed to have discovered a so-called Oedipus complex in which male children develop an erotic attachment to their mother and hostility toward their father.

From dreams Freud analyzed literature, religion, politics, and virtually every other type of human endeavor, seeking always to identify the manifestations of the repressed conscious. He was convinced that his theory, known as *psychoanalysis,* provided the keys to understanding all human behavior. In the end, Freudian doctrines shaped the psychiatric profession and established a powerful presence in literature and the arts. During the 1920s, novelists, poets, and painters acknowledged Freud's influence as they focused on the inner world—the hidden depths of memory and emotion—of their characters. The creators of imaginative literature used Freud's bold emphasis on sexuality as a tool for the interpretation and understanding of human behavior.

Experimentation in Art and Architecture

The roots of contemporary painting go back to nineteenth-century French avant-garde artists who became preoccupied with how a subject should be painted. The common denominator among the various schools was disdain for realism and concern for freedom of expression. The aversion to visual realism was heightened by the spread of photography. When everyone could create naturalistic landscapes or portraits with a camera, it made little sense for artists to do so laboriously with paint and brush. Thus painters began to think of canvas not as a reproduction of reality but as an end in itself. The purpose of a painting was not to mirror reality but to create it.

By the beginning of the twentieth century, the possibilities inherent in this new aesthetic led to the emergence of a bewildering variety of pictorial schools, all of which promised an entirely new art. Regardless of whether they called themselves *les fauves* ("wild beasts"), expressionists, cubists, abstractionists, dadaists, or surrealists, artists generally agreed on a program "to abolish the sovereignty of appearance." Paintings no longer depicted recognizable objects from the everyday world, and beauty was expressed in pure color or shape. Some painters sought to express feelings and emotions through violent distortion of forms and the use of explosive colors; others, influenced by Freudian psychology, tried to tap the subconscious mind to communicate an inner vision or a dream.

Artistic Influences The artistic heritages of Asian, Pacific, and African societies fertilized various strains of contemporary painting. Nineteenth-century Japanese prints, for

Pablo Picasso's *Les Demoiselles d'Avignon* (1907) was the first of what would be called cubist works. This image had a profound influence on subsequent art.

example, influenced French impressionists such as Edgar Degas (1834–1917), whose study of them led him to experiment with visual angles and asymmetrical compositions. The deliberate violation of perspective by Japanese painters and their stress on the flat, two-dimensional surface of the picture, their habit of placing figures off center, and their use of primary colors, encouraged European artists to take similar liberties with realism. In a revolt against rational society, the postimpressionist painter Paul Gauguin (1848–1903) fled to central America and Tahiti. He was inspired by the "primitive" art he found there, claiming that it held a sense of wonder that "civilized" people no longer possessed. In Germany a group of young artists known as the "Bridge" made a point of regularly visiting the local ethnographic museum to be inspired by the boldness and power of indigenous art. The early works of Pablo Picasso (1881–1973), the leading proponent of cubism, displayed the influence of African art forms.

By the third decade of the twentieth century, it was nearly impossible to generalize about the history of contemporary painting. All artists were acknowledged to have a right to their own reality, and generally accepted standards that distinguished between "good" and "bad" art disappeared.

Bauhaus During the first decades of the twentieth century, architecture underwent a revolutionary transformation as designers deliberately set out to create a completely different building style that broke with old forms and traditions. The modernistic trends in architecture coalesced with the opening of the *Bauhaus,* an institution that brought together architects, designers, and painters from several countries. Located first in Weimar and then Dessau, Germany, the Bauhaus

Designed by Walter Gropius in 1925, this building introduced the functional international style of architecture that dominated for the next half century.

was a community of innovators bent on creating a building style and interior designs that were uniquely suited to the urban and industrial landscape of the twentieth century.

The first director of the Bauhaus was Walter Gropius (1883–1969), whose theory of design became the guiding principle first of the Bauhaus and subsequently of contemporary architecture in general. To Gropius, design was functional, based on a marriage between engineering and art. The buildings Gropius designed featured simplicity of shape and extensive use of glass and always embodied the new doctrine that form must follow function. The second director of the Bauhaus, Ludwig Mies von der Rohe (1886–1969), exerted an equally profound influence on modern architecture. He experimented with steel frames around which he stretched non-load-bearing walls of glass. His designs became the basis for the ubiquitous glass-box skyscrapers that first adorned cities such as Chicago and New York and later dominated the skylines of most major cities.

The style initiated by the Bauhaus architects, the international style, gradually prevailed after 1930 because its functionalism was well suited to the construction of large apartment and office complexes. The work of the world-famous Swiss-French architect Le Corbusier (Charles Édouard Jeanneret, 1887–1965) proved the broad appeal of the new architecture. At the request of Jawaharlal Nehru (1889–1964), India's first prime minister, Le Corbusier laid out the new capital city of the Punjab, Chandigarh, and designed for it three concrete government buildings. Governments and businesses eagerly embraced the new style, but the public never quite warmed to the glass box, a cold and impersonal structure that seemed to overwhelm the individual.

GLOBAL DEPRESSION

After the horrors and debilitating upheavals of the Great War, much of the world yearned for a return to normality and prosperity. By the early 1920s the efforts of governments and businesses to rebuild damaged economies seemed to bear fruit. Prosperity, however, was short-lived. In 1929 the world plunged into economic depression that was so long-lasting, so severe, and so global that it has become known as the Great Depression. The old capitalist system of trade and finance collapsed, and until a new system took its place after 1945, a return to worldwide prosperity could not occur.

The Great Depression

By the middle of the 1920s, some semblance of economic normality had returned, and most countries seemed on the way to economic recovery. Industrial productivity had returned to prewar levels as businesses repaired the damages the war had inflicted on industrial plants, equipment, and transportation facilities. But that prosperity was fragile, perhaps false, and many serious problems and dislocations remained in the international economy.

Economic Problems

The economic recovery and well-being of Europe, for example, were tied to a tangled financial system that involved war debts among the Allies, reparations paid by Germany and Austria, and the flow of U.S. funds to Europe. In essence, the governments of Austria and Germany relied on U.S. loans and investment capital to finance reparation payments to France and England. The French and British governments, in turn, depended on those reparation payments to pay off loans taken out in the United States during the Great War. By the summer of 1928, U.S. lenders and investors started to withdraw capital from Europe, placing an intolerable strain on the financial system.

There were other problems as well. Improvements in industrial processes reduced worldwide demand for certain raw materials, causing an increase in supplies and a drop in prices. Technological advances in the production of automobile tires, for instance, permitted the use of reclaimed rubber. The resulting glut of natural rubber had devastating consequences for the economies of the Dutch East Indies, Ceylon, and Malaysia, which relied on the export of rubber. Similarly, the increased use of oil undermined the coal industry, the emergence of synthetics hurt the cotton industry, and the growing adoption of artificial nitrogen virtually ruined the nitrate industry of Chile.

One of the nagging weaknesses of the global economy in the 1920s was the depressed state of agriculture, the result of overproduction and falling prices. During the Great War, when Europe's agricultural output declined significantly, farmers in the United States, Canada, Argentina, and Australia expanded their production. At the end of the war, European farmers resumed their agricultural activity, thereby contributing to worldwide surpluses. Above-average global harvests between 1925 and 1929 aggravated the situation. As production increased, demand declined, and prices collapsed throughout the world. By 1929 the price of a bushel of wheat was at its lowest level in 400 years, and farmers everywhere became impoverished. The reduced income of farm families contributed to high inventories of manufactured goods, which in turn caused businesses to cut back production and to dismiss workers.

The Crash of 1929

The United States enjoyed a boom after the Great War: industrial wages were high, and production and consumption increased. Many people in the United States invested their earnings and savings in speculative ventures, particularly the buying of stock on margin—putting up as little as 3 percent of a stock's price in cash and borrowing the remainder from brokers and banks or by mortgaging their homes. By October 1929, hints of a worldwide economic slowdown and warnings from experts that stock prices were overvalued prompted investors to pull out of the market. On Black Thursday (24 October), a wave of panic selling on the New York Stock Exchange caused stock prices to plummet. Investors who had overextended themselves in a frenzy of speculative stock purchases watched in agony. Thousands of people, from poor widows to industrial tycoons, lost their life savings, and by the end of the day eleven financiers had committed suicide. The crisis deepened when lenders called in loans, thereby forcing more investors to sell their securities at any price.

Economic Contraction Spreads

In the wake of this financial chaos came a drastic decrease in business activity, wages, and employment. Consumer demand no longer sufficed to purchase all the goods that businesses produced, and when businesses realized that they could not sell their inventories, they responded with cutbacks in production and additional layoffs. With so many people unemployed or underemployed, demand plummeted further, causing more business failures and soaring unemployment. In 1930 the slump deepened, and by 1932 industrial production had fallen to half of its 1929 level. National income had dropped by approximately half. Forty-four percent of U.S. banks were out of business, and the deposits of millions of people had disappeared. Because much of the world's prosperity depended on the export of U.S. capital and the strength of U.S. import markets, the contraction of the U.S. economy created a ripple effect that circled the globe.

Most societies experienced economic difficulties throughout the 1930s. Although the severity of the economic contraction varied in intensity, virtually every industrialized society saw its economy shrivel. Nations that relied on exports of manufactured goods to pay for imported fuel and food—Germany and Japan in particular—suffered the most. The depression also spread unevenly to primary producing economies in Latin America, Africa, and Asia. Hardest hit were countries that depended on the export of a few primary products—agricultural goods, such as coffee, sugar, and cotton, and raw materials, such as minerals, ores, and rubber.

Industrial Economies

U.S. investors, shaken by the collapse of stock prices, tried to raise money by calling in loans and liquidating investments, and Wall Street banks refused to extend short-term loans as they became due. Banking houses in Austria and Germany became vulnerable to collapse, because they had been major recipients of U.S. loans. Devastated by the loss of U.S. capital, the German economy experienced a precipitous economic slide that by 1932 resulted in 35 percent unemployment and a 50 percent decrease in industrial production. As the German economy ground to a virtual halt, the rest of Europe—which was closely integrated with the German economy—sputtered and stalled. Although Germany lost the Great War, it remained a leading economic power throughout the postwar years. Because no military engagements took place on German soil, the national economy—its natural resources, infrastructure, and productive capacity—was spared the physical destruction that seri-

ously disrupted the economies of other lands such as France or Russia. Germany did not escape the ravages of the depression. The situation in Europe deteriorated further when businesses, desperate to raise capital by exporting goods to the United States, found that U.S. markets had virtually disappeared behind tariff walls. Foreign trade fell sharply between 1929 and 1932, causing further losses in manufacturing, employment, and per capita income. Because of its great dependence on the U.S. market, the Japanese economy felt the depression's effects almost immediately. Unemployment in export-oriented sectors of the economy skyrocketed as companies cut back on production.

Economic Nationalism The Great Depression destroyed the international financial and commercial network of the capitalist economies. As international cooperation broke down, governments turned to their own resources and practiced economic nationalism. By imposing tariff barriers, import quotas, and import prohibitions, politicians hoped to achieve a high degree of economic self-sufficiency. In an age of global interdependence, such goals remained unobtainable, and economic nationalism invariably backfired. Each new measure designed to restrict imports provoked retaliation by other nations whose interests were affected. After the U.S. Congress passed the Smoot-Hawley Tariff in 1930, which raised duties on most manufactured products to prohibitive levels, the governments of dozens of other nations immediately retaliated by raising tariffs on imports of U.S. products. The result was a sharp drop in international trade. Instead of higher levels of production and income, economic nationalism yielded the opposite. Between 1929 and 1932, world production declined by 38 percent and trade dropped by more than 66 percent.

Despair and Government Action

By 1933 unemployment in industrial societies reached thirty million, more than five times higher than in 1929. Men lost their jobs because of economic contraction, and a combination of economic trends and deliberate government policy caused women to lose theirs also. Unemployment initially affected women less directly than men because employers preferred women workers, who were paid two-thirds to three-quarters the wages of men doing the same work. But before long, governments enacted policies to reduce female employment, especially for married women. The notion that a woman's place was in the home was widespread. In 1931 a British royal commission on unemployment insurance declared that "in the case of married women as a class, industrial employment cannot be regarded as the normal condition." More candid was the French Nobel Prize–winning physician Charles Richet (1850–1935), who insisted that removing women from the workforce would solve the problem of male unemployment and increase the nation's dangerously low birthrate.

Personal Suffering The Great Depression caused enormous personal suffering. The stark, gloomy statistics docu-

In January 1932, ten thousand hunger strikers marched on Washington, D.C., seeking government relief for their misery.

menting the failure of economies do not convey the anguish and despair of those who lost their jobs, savings, and homes, and often their dignity and hope. For millions of people the struggle for food, clothing, and shelter grew desperate. Shantytowns appeared overnight in urban areas, and breadlines stretched for blocks. Marriage, childbearing, and divorce rates declined, while suicide rates rose. The acute physical and social problems of those at the bottom of the economic ladder often magnified social divisions and class hatreds. Workers and farmers especially came to despise the wealthy, who, despite their reduced incomes, were shielded from the worst impact of the economic downturn and continued to enjoy a comfortable lifestyle. Adolescents completing their schooling faced an almost nonexistent job market.

That the Great Depression deflated economies and hope was especially noticeable in the literature of the period. Writers castigated the social and political order, calling repeatedly for a more just society. The U.S. writer John Steinbeck (1902–1968) chillingly captured the official heartlessness and the rising political anger inspired by the depression. In *The Grapes of Wrath* (1939), the Joad family, prototypical "Okies," migrated from Oklahoma to California to escape the dust bowl. In describing their journey Steinbeck commented on the U.S. government's policy of "planned scarcity," in which surplus crops were destroyed

Soup kitchens and breadlines became commonplace in the United States during the earliest, darkest years of the Great Depression. They fed millions of starving and unemployed people.

to raise prices while citizens starved. In one of the novel's most famous passages, Steinbeck portrayed the nation's rising political anguish:

> The people come with nets to fish for potatoes in the river and the guards hold them back; they come in rattling cars to get the dumped oranges, but the kerosene is sprayed. And they stand still and watch potatoes float by, listen to the screaming pigs being killed in a ditch and covered with quicklime, watch the mountains of oranges slop down to a putrefying ooze; and in the eyes of the people there is the failure; and in the eyes of the hungry there is a growing wrath. In the souls of the people the grapes of wrath are filling and growing heavy, growing heavy for the vintage.

Human faces of the Great Depression: children bathing in the Ozark Mountains, Missouri, 1940.

Economic Experimentation

Classical economic thought held that capitalism was a self-correcting system that operated best when left to its own devices. Governments responded to the economic crisis in one of two ways. Initially, most governments did nothing, hoping against all odds that the crisis would resolve itself. When the misery spawned by the depression sparked calls for action, some governments assumed more active roles, pursuing deflationary measures by balancing national budgets and curtailing public spending. In either case, rather than lifting national economies out of the doldrums, the classical prescriptions for economic ills worsened the depression's impact and intensified the plight of millions of people. Far from self-correcting, capitalism seemed to be dying. Many people called for a fundamental revision of economic thought.

sources from the past

Franklin Delano Roosevelt: Nothing to Fear

Franklin Delano Roosevelt (1882–1945) assumed the presidency of the United States on 4 March 1933, during the very depths of the Great Depression. In his inaugural address to the nation, he conveyed both the anxiousness of the times and the seemingly unquenchable optimism that carried him—and his nation—through hard times. A vastly wealthy man serving as president during a time of devastating penury, Roosevelt nonetheless gained the admiration and respect of his people because of his warm eloquence and compassion. Although he hid his condition quite successfully during his time in public, FDR had contracted polio in the 1920s and had lost the use of his legs. This "crippled" president became a metaphor for the United States' economic collapse, but also for its ability to overcome fear itself.

I am certain that my fellow Americans expect that on my induction into the Presidency I will address them with a candor and a decision which the present situation of our Nation impels. This is preeminently the time to speak the truth, the whole truth, frankly and boldly. Nor need we shrink from honestly facing conditions in our country today. This great Nation will endure as it has endured, will revive and will prosper. So, first of all, let me assert my firm belief that the only thing we have to fear is fear itself—nameless, unreasoning, unjustified terror which paralyzes needed efforts to convert retreat into advance. In every dark hour of our national life a leadership of frankness and vigor has met with that understanding and support of the people themselves which is essential to victory. I am convinced that you will again give that support to leadership in these critical days.

In such a spirit on my part and on yours we face our common difficulties. They concern, thank God, only material things. Values have shrunken to fantastic levels; taxes have risen; our ability to pay has fallen; government of all kinds is faced by serious curtailment of income; the means of exchange are frozen in the currents of trade; the withered leaves of industrial enterprise lie on every side; farmers find no markets for their produce; the savings of many years in thousands of families are gone.

More important, a host of unemployed citizens face the grim problem of existence, and an equally great number toil with little return. Only a foolish optimist can deny the dark realities of the moment. . . .

Happiness lies not in the mere possession of money; it lies in the joy of achievement, in the thrill of creative effort. The joy and moral stimulation of work no longer must be forgotten in the mad chase of evanescent profits. These dark days will be worth all they cost us if they teach us that our true destiny is not to be ministered unto but to minister to ourselves and to our fellow men.

For Further Reflection

■ How does Roosevelt believe U.S. citizens can profit from the dark days of the Great Depression, and why is it that all they have to fear is fear itself?

Source: Franklin D. Roosevelt, First Inaugural Address, 4 March 1933, available at The Avalon Project at http://www.yale.edu/lawweb/avalon/president/inaug/froos1.htm.

Keynes John Maynard Keynes (1883–1946), the most influential economist of the twentieth century, offered a novel solution. His seminal work, *The General Theory of Employment, Interest, and Money* (1936), was his answer to the central problem of the depression—that millions of people who were willing to work could not find employment. To Keynes the fundamental cause of the depression was not excessive supply, but inadequate demand. Accordingly, he urged governments to play an active role and stimulate the economy by increasing the money supply, thereby lowering interest rates and encouraging investment. He also advised governments to undertake public works projects to provide jobs and redistribute incomes through tax policy, an intervention which would result in reduced unemployment and increased consumer demand, which would lead to economic revival. Such measures were necessary even if they caused governments to run deficits and maintain unbalanced budgets.

The New Deal Although Keynes's theories did not become influential with policymakers until after World War II, the administration of U.S. president Franklin Delano Roosevelt (1882–1945) applied similar ideas. Roosevelt took aggressive steps to reinflate the economy and ease the worst of the suffering caused by the depression. His proposals for dealing with the national calamity included legislation designed to prevent the collapse of the banking system, to provide jobs and farm subsidies, to give workers the right to organize and bargain collectively, to guarantee minimum wages, and to provide social security in old age. This program of sweeping economic and social reforms was called the "New Deal." Its fundamental premise, that the federal government was justified in intervening to protect the social and economic welfare of the people, represented a major shift in U.S. government policy and started a trend toward social reform legislation that continued long after the depression years. Ultimately, the

thinking about ENCOUNTERS

Poverty, People, and the State
The Great Depression radically transformed the role of government in nations as divergent as the Soviet Union and the United States, and the people had more contact with government representatives and programs than ever before. How did the Great Depression reconfigure the relationships between governments and citizens?

enormous military spending during World War II did more to end the Great Depression in the United States and elsewhere than did the specific programs of the New Deal or similar approaches.

CHALLENGES TO THE LIBERAL ORDER

Amid the gloom and despair of the Great Depression, some voices proclaimed the promise of a better tomorrow. Marxists believed that capitalist society was on its deathbed, and they had faith that a new and better system based on rule by the proletariat was being born out of the ashes of the Russian empire. The new rulers of Russia, Vladimir Ilyich Lenin and then Joseph Stalin, transformed the former tsarist empire into the world's first socialist society, the Union of Soviet Socialist Republics (1922).

Other people, uncomfortable with the abolition of private property and the "dictatorship of the proletariat," found solace in activist political movements that claimed to have an alternative formula for the reconstruction of society. Fascist movements across Europe promoted their alternatives to socialism and offered revolutionary answers to the economic, social, and political problems that seemed to defy solution by traditional liberal democratic means. Among those fascist movements, the Italian and German ones figured most prominently.

Communism in Russia

In 1917 Lenin and his fellow Bolsheviks had taken power in the name of the Russian working class, but socialist victory did not bring peace and stability to the lands of the former Russian empire. After seizing power, Lenin and his supporters had to defend the world's first dictatorship of the proletariat against numerous enemies, including dissident socialists, anti-Bolshevik officers and troops, peasant bands, and foreign military forces.

Civil War Opposition to the Bolshevik Party—by now calling itself the Russian Communist Party—erupted into a civil war that lasted from 1918 to 1920. Operating out of its new capital in Moscow, Lenin's government began a policy

of crushing all opposition. The communists began the Red Terror campaign in which suspected anticommunists known as Whites were arrested, tried, and executed. The secret police killed some 200,000 opponents of the regime. In July 1918 the Bolsheviks executed Tsar Nicholas II, Empress Alexandra, their five children, and their remaining servants because they feared that the Romanov family would fall into the hands of the Whites, thereby strengthening counterrevolutionary forces. White terror was often as brutal as Red terror. The peasantry, although hostile to the communists, largely supported the Bolsheviks, fearing that a victory by the Whites would result in the return of the monarchy. However, foreign military intervention supported White resistance to the communist takeover. Russia's withdrawal from the Great War and anticommunist sentiment inflamed Russia's former allies (notably Britain, France, Japan, and the United States), who sent troops and supplies to aid White forces. Although their numbers were negligible, the foreigners' presence sometimes had the effect of bonding otherwise hostile groups to the Reds. Poorly organized and without widespread support, the Whites were defeated by the Red Army in 1920. Estimates place the number of lives lost in the civil war at ten million, with many more people dying from disease and starvation than from the fighting. The political system that emerged from the civil war bore the imprint of political oppression, which played a significant role in the later development of the Soviet state.

War Communism The new rulers of Russia had no plans to transform the economy, but in the course of the civil war they embarked on a hasty and unplanned course of nationalization, a policy known as *war communism*. After officially annulling private property, the Bolshevik government assumed control or ownership of banks, industry, and other privately held commercial properties. Landed estates and the holdings of monasteries and churches became national property, although the Bolsheviks explicitly exempted the holdings of poor peasants from confiscation. The abolition of private trade was unpopular, and when the party seized crops from peasants to feed people in the cities, the peasants drastically reduced their production. By 1920 industrial production had fallen to about one-tenth of its prewar level and agricultural output to about one-half its prewar level.

In 1921, as the Reds consolidated their military victories, Lenin faced the daunting prospect of rebuilding a society that had been at war since 1914. The workers, in whose name he had taken power, were on strike. Other problems included depopulated cities, destroyed factories, and an army that demobilized soldiers faster than the workforce could absorb them. Lenin and the party tried to take strict control of the country by crushing workers' strikes, peasant rebellions, and a sailors' revolt. Yet Lenin recognized the need to make

peace with those whose skills would rekindle industrial production. Faced with economic paralysis, in the spring of 1921 he decided on a radical reversal of war communism.

The New Economic Policy

Demonstrating his pragmatism and willingness to compromise, Lenin implemented the New Economic Policy (NEP), which temporarily restored the market economy and some private enterprise in Russia. Large industries, banks, and transportation and communications facilities remained under state control, but the government returned small-scale industries (those with fewer than twenty workers) to private ownership. The government also allowed peasants to sell their surpluses at free market prices. Other features of the NEP included a vigorous program of electrification and the establishment of technical schools to train technicians and engineers. Lenin did not live to see the success of the NEP. After suffering three paralytic strokes, he died in 1924. His death was followed by a bitter struggle for power among the Bolshevik leaders.

Joseph Stalin

Many old Bolsheviks continued to argue for a permanent or continuous revolution, asserting that socialism in Russia would fail if socialism did not move from a national to an international stage. Others in the Politburo, the central governing body of the Communist Party, favored establishing socialism in one country alone, thus repudiating the role of the Union of Soviet Socialist Republics as torchbearer of worldwide socialist revolution. Joseph Stalin (1879–1953), who served in the unglamorous bureaucratic position of general secretary, promoted the idea of socialism in one country. A Georgian by birth, an Orthodox seminarian by training, and a Russian nationalist by conviction, Stalin indicated his unified resolve to gain power in his adopted surname, which meant "man of steel." Speaking Russian with a heavy accent, he was an intellectual misfit among the Bolshevik elite. However, by 1928, Stalin lived up to his name and completely triumphed over his rivals in the party, clearing the way for an unchallenged dictatorship of the Soviet Union.

First Five-Year Plan

Stalin decided to replace Lenin's NEP with an ambitious plan for rapid economic development known as the First Five-Year Plan. The basic aims of this and subsequent five-year plans, first implemented in 1929, were to transform the Soviet Union from a predominantly agricultural country to a leading industrial power. The First Five-Year Plan set targets for increased productivity in all spheres of the economy but emphasized heavy industry—especially steel and machinery—at the expense of consumer goods. Through Gosplan, the central state planning agency, Stalin and the party attempted to coordinate resources and the labor force on an unprecedented scale. As the rest of the world teetered on the edge of economic collapse, this blueprint for maximum centralization of the entire national economy offered a bold alternative to market capitalism. Stalin repeatedly stressed the urgency of this monumental endeavor, telling his people, "We are 50 to 100 years behind the advanced countries. Either we do it, or we shall go under."

Collectivization of Agriculture

Integral to the drive for industrialization was the collectivization of agriculture. The Soviet state expropriated privately owned land to create collective or cooperative farm units whose profits were shared by all farmers. The logic of communist ideology demanded the abolition of private property and market choices, but more practical considerations also played a role. Stalin and his regime viewed collectivization as a means of increasing the efficiency of agricultural production and ensuring that industrial workers would be fed. Collectivization was enforced most ruthlessly against *kulaks*—relatively wealthy peasants who had risen to prosperity during the NEP but accounted for only 3 to 5 percent of the peasantry.

In some places, outraged peasants reacted to the government's program by slaughtering their livestock and burning their crops. Millions of farmers left the land and migrated to cities in search of work, thereby further taxing the limited supplies of housing, food, and utilities. Unable to meet production quotas, peasants often starved to death on the land

Joseph Stalin at a Soviet congress in 1936. By 1928 Stalin had prevailed over his opponents to become the dictator of the Soviet Union, a position he held until his death in 1953.

Men and women drive tractors out of one of the Soviet Union's Machine Tractor Stations to work fields where mechanization had been a rare sight.

they once owned. When Stalin called a halt to collectivization in 1931, proclaiming the policymakers "dizzy with success," half the farms in the Soviet Union had been collectivized. Estimates of the number of peasant lives lost have fluctuated wildly, but even the most cautious place it at three million.

The First Five-Year Plan set unrealistically high production targets. Even so, the Soviet leadership proclaimed success after only four years. The Soviet Union industrialized under Stalin even though the emphasis on building heavy industry first and consumer industries later meant that citizens postponed the gratifications of industrialization. Before refrigerators, radios, or automobiles became available, the government constructed steelworks and hydroelectric plants. The scarcity or nonexistence of consumer goods was to some degree balanced by full employment, low-cost utilities, and—when available—cheap housing and food. Set against the collapse of the U.S. stock market and the depression-ridden capitalist world, the ability of a centrally planned economy to create more jobs than workers could fill made it appear an attractive alternative.

The Great Purge Nevertheless, the results of Stalin's First Five-Year Plan generated controversy as the Communist Party prepared for its seventeenth congress in 1934, the self-proclaimed "Congress of Victors." The disaster of collectivization and the ruthlessness with which it was carried out had raised doubts about Stalin's administration. Although themes of unity and reconciliation prevailed, Stalin learned of a plan to bring more pluralism back into leadership. The Congress of Victors became the "Congress of Victims" as Stalin incited a civil war within the party that was climaxed by highly publicized trials of former Bolshevik elites for treason and by a purge of two-thirds of the delegates. Between 1935

and 1938 Stalin removed from posts of authority all persons suspected of opposition, including two-thirds of the members of the 1934 Central Committee and more than one-half of the army's high-ranking officers. The victims faced execution or long-term suffering in labor camps. In 1939 eight million Soviet citizens were in labor camps, and three million were dead as a result of the "cleansing," as Stalin's supporters termed this process.

The outside world watched the events unfolding within the Soviet Union with a mixture of contempt, fear, and admiration. Most observers recognized that the political and social upheavals that transformed the former Russian empire were of worldwide importance. The establishment of the world's first dictatorship of the proletariat challenged the values and institutions of liberal society everywhere and seemed to demonstrate the viability of communism as a social and political system.

The Fascist Alternative

While socialism was transforming the former Russian empire, another political force swept across Europe after the Great War. Fascism, a political movement and ideology that sought to create a new type of society, developed as a reaction against liberal democracy and the spread of socialism and communism. The term *fascism* derives from the *fasces,* an ancient Roman symbol of punitive authority consisting of a bundle of wooden rods strapped together around an axe. In 1919 Benito Mussolini adopted this symbol for the Italian Fascist movement that governed Italy from 1922 to 1943. Movements comparable to Italian fascism subsequently developed and sometimes dominated political life in many European societies, most notably in Germany in the guise of National Socialism (Nazism). Although fascism enjoyed

sources from the past

Goals and Achievements of the First Five-Year Plan

In the aftermath of war, revolution, and civil strife, Vladimir Lenin in 1921 adopted the New Economic Policy (NEP) to prevent the collapse of the Russian economy. In the main, the NEP was successful, but it rankled Marxist purists because it permitted the return of a limited form of capitalism. Lenin's successor, Joseph Stalin, was determined to build "socialism in one country" by replacing the NEP with a planned economy, whereby a centralized bureaucracy guided and regulated production. To that end, Stalin launched a series of Five-Year Plans designed to transform the Soviet Union into a modern, powerful state. In the following report, delivered to the Central Committee of the Communist Party of the Soviet Union in January 1933, Stalin outlined the goals and the achievements of the First Five-Year Plan.

The fundamental task of the five-year plan was to convert the U.S.S.R. from an agrarian and weak country, dependent upon the caprices of the capitalist countries, into an industrial and powerful country, fully self-reliant and independent of the caprices of world capitalism.

The fundamental task of the five-year plan was, in converting the U.S.S.R. into an industrial country, to completely oust the capitalist elements, to widen the front of socialist forms of economy, and to create the economic basis for the abolition of classes in the U.S.S.R., for the building of a socialist society.

The fundamental task of the five-year plan was to transfer small and scattered agriculture on to the lines of large-scale collective farming, so as to ensure the economic basis of socialism in the countryside and thus to eliminate the possibility of the restoration of capitalism in the U.S.S.R.

Finally, the task of the five-year plan was to create all the necessary technical and economic prerequisites for increasing to the utmost the defensive capacity of the country, enabling it to organize determined resistance to any attempt at military intervention from abroad, to any attempt at military attack from abroad.

What are the results of the five-year plan in four years in the sphere of industry?

We did not have an iron and steel industry, the basis for the industrialization of the country. Now we have one.

We did not have a tractor industry. Now we have one.

We did not have an automobile industry. Now we have one.

We did not have a machine-tool industry. Now we have one.

We did not have a big and modern chemical industry. Now we have one.

We did not have a real and big industry for the production of modern agricultural machinery. Now we have one.

We did not have an aircraft industry. Now we have one.

In output of electric power we were last on the list. Now we rank among the first.

In output of oil products and coal we were last on the list. Now we rank among the first.

And as a result of all this the capitalist elements have been completely and irrevocably ousted from industry, and socialist industry has become the sole form of industry in the U.S.S.R.

Let us pass to the question of the results of the five-year plan in four years in the sphere of agriculture. The Party has succeeded in the course of some three years in organizing more than 200,000 collective farms and about 5,000 state farms devoted to grain growing and livestock raising, and at the same time it has succeeded during four years in expanding the crop area by 21 million hectares. The Party has succeeded in getting more than 60 per cent of the peasant farms to unite into collective farms, embracing more than 70 per cent of all the land cultivated by peasants; this means that we have fulfilled the five-year plan three times over. The Party has succeeded in converting the U.S.S.R. from a country of small-peasant farming into a country of the largest-scale agriculture in the world. Do not all these facts testify to the superiority of the Soviet system of agriculture over the capitalist system?

Finally, as a result of all this the Soviet Union has been converted from a weak country, unprepared for defense, into a country mighty in defense, a country prepared for every contingency, a country capable of producing on a mass scale all modern means of defense and of equipping its army with them in the event of an attack from abroad.

For Further Reflection

■ What were the fundamental aims and achievements of the First Five-Year Plan? What benefits, if any, did the peoples of the Soviet Union derive from this economic experiment in a planned economy?

Source: J. V. Stalin. "The Results of the First Five-Year Plan. Report Delivered at the Joint Plenum of the Central Committee and the Central Control Commission of the C.P.S.U.(B.), January 7, 1933." From J. V. Stalin, *Problems of Leninism.* Peking: Foreign Languages Press, 1976, pp. 578–630.

thinking about TRADITIONS

Challenges to the Liberal Order

In the years following the Great War, new political ideologies emerged in European societies. What were those new ideologies, and how did they overturn traditional ideals of political democracy and capitalism?

widespread popularity in many European countries, it rarely threatened the political order and, with the exception of Italy and Germany, never overthrew a parliamentary system. Political and economic frustrations made fertile ground for fascist appeals outside Europe, and potential fascist movements sprang up during the 1930s in Japan, China, and South Africa; in Latin American societies such as Brazil and Argentina; and in several Arab lands. Nevertheless, that potential for fascism never reproduced the major characteristics of European fascism, and fascism remained basically a European phenomenon of the era between the two world wars.

Defining Fascism During the 1920s and 1930s, fascism attracted millions of followers and proved especially attractive to middle classes and rural populations. These groups became radicalized by economic and social crises and were especially fearful of class conflict and the perceived threat from the political left. Fascism also proved attractive to nationalists of all classes, who denounced their governments for failing to realize the glorious objectives for which they had fought during the Great War. Asserting that society faced a profound crisis, fascists sought to create a new national community, which they defined either as a nation-state or as a unique ethnic or racial group. As part of their quest, fascist movements commonly dedicated themselves to the revival of allegedly lost national traditions and, hence, differed widely. Nevertheless, most fascist movements shared certain common features, such as the veneration of the state, a devotion to a strong leader, and an emphasis on ultranationalism, ethnocentrism, and militarism.

Fascist ideology consistently invoked the primacy of the state, which stood at the center of the nation's life and history and which demanded the subordination of the individual to the service of the state. Strong and often charismatic leaders, such as Benito Mussolini in Italy or Adolf Hitler in Germany, embodied the state and claimed indisputable authority. Consequently, fascists were hostile to liberal democracy, its devotion to individualism, and its institutions, which they viewed as weak and decadent. Fascism was also extremely hostile to class-based visions of the future promoted by socialism and communism. Fascist movements emphasized chauvinism (a belligerent form of nationalism) and xenophobia (a fear of foreign people), which they frequently linked to an exaggerated ethnocentrism. Some fascist leaders, accordingly, viewed

national boundaries as artificial restraints limiting their union with ethnic or racial comrades living in other states. The typical fascist state embraced *militarism,* a belief in the rigors and virtues of military life as an individual and national ideal. In practice, militarism meant that fascist regimes maintained large and expensive military establishments, tried to organize much of public life along military lines, and generally showed a fondness for uniforms, parades, and monumental architecture.

Italian Fascism

The first fascist movement grew up in Italy after the Great War. Conditions conducive to the rise of fascism included a widespread disillusionment with uninspired political leadership and ineffective government, extensive economic turmoil and social discontent, and a growing fear of socialism. In addition, there was vast disappointment over Italy's skimpy territorial spoils from the peace settlement after the Great War.

Italian dictator Benito Mussolini strikes a dramatic pose on horseback in 1940. Such images of Mussolini and Adolf Hitler (see page 807) testify to the importance that the fascist leaders placed on propaganda.

A 1924 painting of Hitler as a knight in shining armor, as the standard-bearer for National Socialism, became the state-sanctioned Hitler portrait for 1938; reproductions in poster and postcard form proved very popular.

war. In 1922, Mussolini and his followers decided the time was ripe for a fascist seizure of power, and on 28 October, they staged a march on Rome. While Mussolini stayed safely in Milan awaiting the outcome of events, thousands of his blackshirted troops converged on Rome. Rather than calling on the military to oppose the fascist threat, King Victor Emmanuel III hastily asked Mussolini on 29 October to become prime minister and form a new government. Mussolini inaugurated a fascist regime in 1922.

The Fascist State Between 1925 and 1931, Italy's fascists consolidated their power through a series of laws that provided the legal basis for the nation's transformation into a one-party dictatorship. In 1926 Mussolini seized total power as dictator and subsequently ruled Italy as *Il Duce* ("the leader"). The regime moved quickly to eliminate all other political parties, curb freedom of the press, and outlaw free speech and association. A Special Tribunal for the Defense of the State, supervised by military officers, silenced political dissent. Marked as antifascist subversives, thousands of Italians found themselves imprisoned or exiled on remote islands, and some faced capital punishment. Allying himself and his movement with business and landlord interests, *Il Duce* also crushed labor unions and prohibited strikes. In an effort to harmonize the interests of workers, employers, and the state, the regime tried to establish a corporatist order. This order was based on the vague fascist concept of corporatism, which viewed society as an organic entity through which the different interests in society came under the control of the state. Thus, in theory, a National Council of Corporations settled labor disputes and supervised wage settlements; but, in reality, this scheme was little more than a propaganda effort. In 1932, on the tenth anniversary of the fascist seizure of

Benito Mussolini The guiding force behind Italian fascism was Benito Mussolini, a former socialist and, from 1912 to 1914, editor of Italy's leading socialist daily *Avanti!* ("Forward!"). In 1914 he founded his own newspaper, *Il Popolo d'Italia* ("The People of Italy"), which encouraged Italian entry into the Great War. Mussolini was convinced that the war represented a turning point for the nation. The soldiers returning from the front, he argued, would spearhead the thorough transformation of Italian society and create a new type of state. After the Great War, the one-time socialist advanced a political program that emphasized virulent nationalism, demanded repression of socialists, and called for a strong political leader. In 1919 he established the *Fasci Italiani di Combattimento* (Italian Combat Veteran League).

Mussolini's movement gained widespread support after 1920, and by 1921 his league managed to elect thirty-five fascists to the Italian parliament. Much of the newly found public support resulted from the effective use of violence against socialists by fascist armed squads known as Blackshirts. The Italian socialist party had organized militant strikes throughout Italy's northern industrial cities, causing considerable chaos. By early 1921 Italy was in a state of incipient civil power, Mussolini felt confident enough to announce "that the twentieth century will be a century of fascism, the century of Italian power."

Racism and anti-Semitism were never prominent components of Italian fascism, but in 1938 the government suddenly issued anti-Semitic laws that labeled Jews unpatriotic, excluded them from government employment, and prohibited all marriages between Jews and so-called Aryans. This development may have been occasioned by Mussolini's newfound friendship with fellow dictator Adolf Hitler. In 1936 Mussolini told his followers that from now on, world history would revolve around a Rome-Berlin Axis. In May 1939 the leaders of fascist Italy and Nazi Germany formalized their political, military, and ideological alliance by signing a ten-year Pact of Steel. This Pact of Steel illustrated the strong links between the Italian and German variants of fascism.

German National Socialism

Hitler and the Nazi Party After his postwar political awakening, Adolf Hitler came into contact with an obscure political party sympathetic to his ideas. In 1921 he became chairman of the party now known as the National Socialist German Workers' Party. National Socialism (the Nazi movement) made its first major appearance in 1923 when party members and Hitler attempted to overthrow the democratic Weimar Republic that had replaced the German empire in 1919. The revolt quickly fizzled under the gunfire of police units; Hitler was jailed, and the Nazi movement and its leader descended into obscurity. When Hitler emerged from prison in 1924, he resolved to use new tactics. Recognizing the futility of armed insurrection, he reorganized his movement and launched it on a "path of legality." Hitler and his followers were determined to gain power legally through the ballot box and, once successful, to discard the very instrument of their success.

The Struggle for Power National Socialism made rapid gains after 1929 because it had broad appeal. Hitler attracted disillusioned people who felt alienated from society and frightened by the specter of socialist revolution. A growing number of people blamed the young German democracy for Germany's misfortunes: a humiliating peace treaty—the Treaty of Versailles—that identified Germany as responsible for the Great War and assigned reparation payments to the Allies; the hyperinflation of the early 1920s that wiped out the savings of the middle class; the suffering brought on by the Great Depression; and the seemingly unending and bitter infighting among the nation's major political parties. Adolf Hitler promised an end to all those misfortunes by creating a new order that would lead to greatness for Germany. By stressing racial doctrines, particularly anti-Semitism, the Nazis added a unique and frightening twist to their ideology. Although the Nazis avoided class divisions by recruiting followers from all strata of society, National Socialism in the main appealed to the members of the lower-middle classes: ruined shopkeepers and artisans, impoverished farmers, discharged white-collar workers, and disenchanted students.

The impact of the Great Depression and political infighting led to bloody street battles, shaking the foundations of Germany's fragile young democracy. The leaders of the nation's democratic and liberal parties groped for solutions to mounting unemployment but were hindered by lack of consensus and the public's loss of faith in the democratic system. The electorate became radicalized. Fewer and fewer Germans were willing to defend a parliamentary system they considered ineffective and corrupt. Between 1930 and 1932 the Nazi party became the largest party in parliament, and the reactionary and feeble president, Paul von Hindenburg (1847–1934), decided to offer Hitler the chancellorship. Promising to gain a majority in the next elections, Hitler lost little time in transforming the dying republic into a single-party dictatorship. He promised a German *Reich,* or empire, that would endure for a thousand years.

Consolidation of Power Under the guise of a state of national emergency, the Nazis used all available means to impose their rule. They began by eliminating all working-class and liberal opposition. The Nazis suppressed the German communist and socialist parties and abrogated virtually all constitutional and civil rights. Subsequently, Hitler and his government outlawed all other political parties, made it a crime to create a new party, and made the National Socialist Party the only legal party. Between 1933 and 1935 the regime replaced Germany's federal structure with a highly centralized state that eliminated the autonomy previously exercised by state and municipal governments. The National Socialist state then guided the destruction of trade unions and the elimination of collective bargaining, subsequently prohibiting strikes and lockouts. The Nazis also purged the judiciary and the civil service, took control of all police forces, and removed enemies of the regime—both real and imagined—through incarceration or murder.

The Racial State Once securely in power, the Nazi regime translated racist ideology, especially the notions of racial superiority and racial purity, into practice. The leaders of the Third Reich pursued the creation of a race-based national community by introducing eugenic measures designed to improve both the quantity and the quality of the German "race." Implicit in this racial remodeling was the conviction that there was no room for the "racially inferior" or for "biological outsiders."

Women and Race Alarmed by declining birthrates, the Nazis launched a campaign to increase births of "racially valuable" children. This battle against the empty cradle meshed agreeably with Nazi ideology, which relegated women primarily to the role of wife and mother. Through tax credits, special child allowances, and marriage loans,

"Mother and Child" was the slogan on this poster, idealizing and encouraging motherhood. The background conveys the Nazi predilection for the wholesome country life, a dream that clashed with the urban reality of German society.

man families were unwilling to change their reproductive preferences for fewer children.

Nazi Eugenics The quantity of offspring was not the only concern of the new rulers, who were obsessed with quality. Starting in 1933, the regime initiated a compulsory sterilization program for men and women whom the regime had identified as having "hereditarily determined" sicknesses, including schizophrenia, feeblemindedness, manic depression, hereditary blindness, hereditary deafness, chronic alcoholism, and serious physical deformities. Between 1934 and 1939 more than thirty thousand men and women underwent compulsory sterilization. Beginning in 1935 the government also sanctioned abortions—otherwise illegal in Germany—of the "hereditary ill" and "racial aliens." The mania for racial health culminated in a state-sponsored euthanasia program that was responsible for the murder of approximately two hundred thousand women, men, and children. Between 1939 and 1945 the Nazis systematically killed—by gassing, lethal injections, or starvation—those people judged useless to society, especially the physically and mentally handicapped. Nazi eugenics measures served as a precursor to the wholesale extermination of peoples classified as racial inferiors, such as gypsies and Jews.

Anti-Semitism Anti-Semitism, or prejudice against Jews, was a key element in the designs to achieve a new racial order and became the hallmark of National Socialist rule. Immediately after coming to power in 1933, the Nazis initiated systematic measures to suppress Germany's Jewish population. Although Nazi anti-Semitism was based on biological racial theories dating to the nineteenth century, government

the authorities tried to encourage marriage and, they hoped, procreation among young people. Legal experts rewrote divorce laws so that a husband could get a divorce decree solely on the ground that he considered his wife sterile. At the same time, the regime outlawed abortions, closed birth control centers, restricted birth control devices, and made it difficult to obtain information about family planning. The Nazis also became enamored with a relatively inexpensive form of propaganda: pronatalist (to increase births) propaganda. They set in motion a veritable cult of motherhood. Annually on 12 August—the birth date of Hitler's mother—women who bore many children received the Honor Cross of the German Mother in three classes: bronze for those with more than four children, silver for those with more than six, and gold for those with more than eight. By August 1939 three million women carried this prestigious award, which many Germans cynically called the "rabbit decoration." In the long term, however, any efforts by the Nazis to increase the fecundity of German women failed, and the birthrate remained below replacement level. Ger-

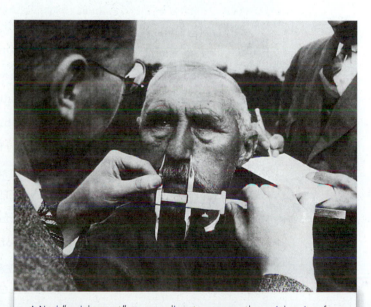

A Nazi "racial expert" uses a caliper to measure the racial purity of a German.

authorities used religious descent to determine who was a Jew. A flood of discriminatory laws and directives designed to humiliate, impoverish, and segregate Jews from the rest of society followed. In 1935 the notorious Nuremberg Laws deprived German Jews of their citizenship and prohibited marriage and sexual intercourse between Jews and other Germans. The Nazi party, in cooperation with government agencies, banks, and businesses, took steps to eliminate Jews from economic life and expropriate their wealth. Jewish civil servants lost their jobs, and Jewish lawyers and doctors lost their gentile, or non-Jewish, clients. Party authorities also supervised the liquidation of Jewish-owned businesses or argued for their purchase—at much less than their true value—by companies owned or operated by gentiles.

The official goal of the Nazi regime was Jewish emigration. Throughout the 1930s thousands of Jews left Germany, depriving the nation of many of its leading intellectuals, scientists, and artists. The exodus gained urgency after what came to be known as *Kristallnacht* ("the night of broken glass"). During the night of 9–10 November 1938, the Nazis arranged for the destruction of thousands of Jewish stores, the burning of most synagogues, and the murder of more than one hundred Jews throughout Germany and Austria. This *pogrom* (Yiddish for "devastation") was a signal that the position of Jews in Hitler's Reich was about to deteriorate dramatically. Although they had difficulty finding refuge, approximately 250,000 Jews left Germany by 1938. Those staying behind, especially the poor and the elderly, contemplated an uncertain destiny.

in perspective

In the decades after the Great War, European intellectuals questioned and challenged established traditions. While scientists and social thinkers conceived new theories that reshaped human knowledge and perceptions, artists forged a contemporary aesthetic. In an age of global interdependence, the U.S. stock market crash of 1929 ushered in a period of prolonged economic contraction and social misery that engulfed much of the world. As most of the industrialized world reeled under the impact of the Depression, the leadership of the Soviet Union embarked on a state-sponsored program of rapid industrialization. Though causing widespread human suffering, a series of five-year plans transformed the Soviet Union into a major industrial and military power.

Italians under the leadership of Mussolini rebuilt their state through fascist policies and imperial expansion. In Germany the effects of the Great Depression paved the way for the establishment of the Nazi state, which was based on the principle of racial inequality. Although many peoples suffered under the racist regime, Jews were the principal victims. Adolf Hitler's mission in life, envisioned in the wake of the Great War, was coming to a spectacular conclusion that culminated in another world war. That war brought both the fulfillment and the destruction of the goals and dreams he had crafted in an age of anxiety. ●

CHRONOLOGY	
1905	Einstein publishes special theory of relativity
1907	Picasso paints *Les Demoiselles d'Avignon*
1918–1920	Civil war in Russia
1919	Mussolini launches fascist movement in Italy
1919	Walter Gropius founds the Bauhaus
1921–1928	Lenin's New Economic Policy
1927	Heisenberg establishes the uncertainty principle
1928–1932	First Soviet Five-Year Plan
1929	U.S. stock market crash
1929	Beginning of Great Depression
1929	Hemingway and Remarque publish antiwar novels
1933–1945	Hitler rules Germany
1935–1938	Stalin's Great Purge in the Soviet Union
1939	Steinbeck publishes *The Grapes of Wrath*

For Further Reading

Malcolm Bradbury and James McFarlane, eds. *Modernism, 1890–1930.* Atlantic Highlands, N.J., 1978. A comprehensive survey of the new trends in literature.

Michael Burleigh. *The Third Reich: A New History.* New York, 2000. A new treatment of the Nazi dictatorship that stresses the tacit consent of the German people.

Peter Conrad. *Modern Times, Modern Places.* New York, 1999. Evocative appraisal of twentieth-century art and thought.

Sarah Davies and James Harris, eds. *Stalin: A New History.* New York, 2005. Reassessment of the Soviet leader based on newly available sources.

Richard Evans. *The Coming of the Third Reich.* New York, 2004. The first of a three-volume series, this work chronicles the Nazi movement's rise to power.

————. *The Third Reich in Power, 1933–1939.* New York, 2005. The second work in a three-volume series, this book starts with the Nazis' assumption of power, and ends at the beginning of World War II in Europe.

Sheila Fitzpatrick. *The Russian Revolution, 1917–1932.* 2nd ed. New York, 1984. This work stands out for the author's ability to make complex processes accessible to the general reader and still instruct the specialist.

George Gamow. *Thirty Years That Shook Physics.* Garden City, N.Y., 1966. A leading physicist engagingly tells the story of modern physics.

Peter Gay. *Freud: A Life for Our Time.* New York, 1988. A balanced biography of one of the most influential social thinkers of the twentieth century.

George Heard Hamilton. *Painting and Sculpture in Europe, 1880–1940.* 6th ed. New Haven, 1993. A classic that presents a discerning overview of the subject.

Ian Kershaw. *Hitler: 1889–1936: Hubris.* New York, 1999.

————. *Hitler: 1936–1945: Nemesis.* New York, 2000. One of the foremost historians of the Nazi era pens the definitive biography of Adolf Hitler.

Charles Kindleberger. *The World in Depression, 1929–1939.* London, 1973. A sophisticated analysis that focuses on developments in the United States and Europe.

A. J. H. Latham. *The Depression and the Developing World, 1914–1939.* London, 1981. One of the few works that looks beyond the industrialized world to give a global perspective on the subject.

Michael Mann. *Fascists.* New York, 2004. Comparative analysis of fascist movements in interwar Europe.

Colleen McDannell. *Picturing Faith: Photography and the Great Depression.* New Haven, 2004. Examination of depression-era photographs as evidence of the importance of religion in American life.

Robert Paxton. *The Anatomy of Fascism.* New York, 2004. A groundbreaking and fascinating history of fascism.

Nikolaus Pevsner. *Pioneers of Modern Design: From William Morris to Walter Gropius.* Rev. ed. New York, 1964. This work chronicles the rise of the international style in architecture.

Richard Pipes. *The Russian Revolution.* New York, 1990. When the Communist Party collapsed in 1991, this sweeping study was quickly translated into Russian and became a national bestseller.

Eli Zaretsky. *Secrets of the Soul: A Social and Cultural History of Psychoanalysis.* New York, 2004. Flawed but useful history of the broad social impacts of Freud's theories.

Nationalism and Political Identities in Asia, Africa, and Latin America

chapter 35

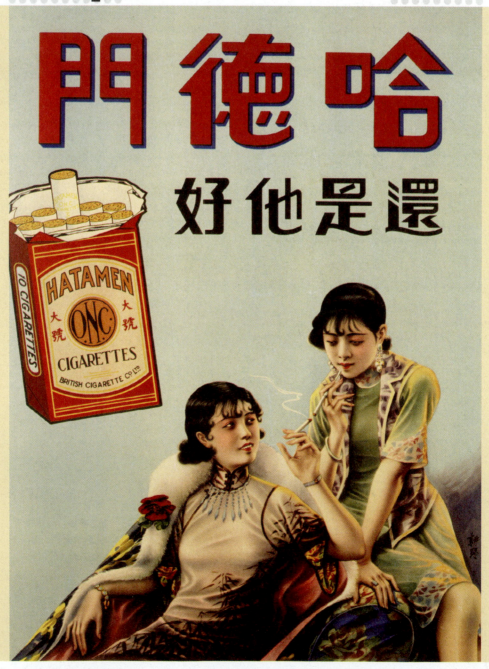

In this cigarette advertisement from 1935, Chinese women are shown challenging traditions. They are "new women," affected by the radical changes in identity and behavior taking place after the Great War and during the Great Depression.

PART

EYEWITNESS:

Shanfei Becomes a New and Revolutionary Young Woman in China

Shanfei lived in politically exciting times. The daughter of a wealthy landowning man of the Chinese gentry, she grew up with luxuries and opportunities unknown to most girls. Her father allowed her to attend school, and her mother clothed her in beautiful silk dresses. Shanfei, however, matured into a woman who rejected the rich trappings of her youth. Her formative years were marked by political ferment and the unsettling cultural changes that engulfed the globe in the wake of the Great War. The rise of nationalism and communism in China after the revolution of 1911 and the Russian revolution in 1917 guided the transformation of Shanfei—from a girl ruled by tradition and privilege, she became an active revolutionary dedicated to the cause of women and communism.

With the exception of Shanfei's father, the members of her family in Hunan province took in the new spirit of the first decades of the twentieth century. Her brothers returned from school with strange and compelling ideas, including some that challenged the subordinate position of women in China. Shanfei's mother, to all appearances a woman who accepted her subservience to her husband, proved instrumental to Shanfei's departure from the common destiny of Chinese girls. She listened quietly to her sons as they discussed new views, and then she applied them to her daughter. She used every means at her disposal to persuade her husband to educate their daughter. She wept, begged, and cajoled. He relented but still insisted that Shanfei receive an old-fashioned education and submit to foot binding and childhood betrothal.

When Shanfei was eleven years old, her father suddenly died, and his death emboldened her mother. She ripped the bandages off Shanfei's feet and sent her to a modern school far from home. In the lively atmosphere of her school, Shanfei bloomed into an activist. At sixteen she incited a student strike against the administration of her school, transferred to a more modern school, and became famous as a leader in the student movement. She went to school with men and broke tradition in her personal and political life. In 1926 Shanfei abandoned her studies to join the Communist Youth, and she gave up her fiancé for a free marriage to the man she loved: a peasant leader in the communist movement.

The twists of fate that altered the destiny of Shanfei had parallels throughout the colonial world after 1914. Two major events, the Great War and the Great Depression, defined much of the turmoil of those years. Disillusion and radical upheaval marked areas as distinct as Asia, Africa, and Latin America. As peoples around the world struggled to come to terms with the aftermath of war, an unprecedented economic contraction gripped the international economy. The Great Depression complicated peoples' struggles for national sovereignty and financial solvency, especially in Asia, where Japan's militarist leaders sought to build national strength through imperial expansion. Latin American states worked to alter the economic domination of its "good neighbor" to the north while African peoples suffered a contraction in living standards along with the economically weakened imperial industrialists.

European empires still appeared to dominate global relations, but the Great War had opened fissures within the European and U.S. spheres of influence. Beneath colonial surfaces, nationalist and communist ferment brewed. Nationalist and anti-imperial movements gathered strength, and in the postwar years resistance to foreign rule and a desire for national unity were stronger than ever. This situation was especially true in India and China, where various visions of national identity competed, but it also pertained to those in Africa and Latin America who struggled against the domination of imperial powers. While peoples in Africa worked to become independent of outright imperial control, those in Latin America had to fight off the more indirect economic effects of postindependence colonialism, usually termed *neocolonialism.* The roots of all of these developments lay in the global storm of a world war that shook the foundations of established traditions, which crumbled in Shanfei's home in Hunan as much as in the Kikuyu highlands and Mexico City.

ASIAN PATHS TO AUTONOMY

The Paris peace settlement had barely altered the prewar colonial holdings of Europeans, yet indirectly the Great War affected relations between Asian peoples and the imperial powers. In the decades following the Great War, nationalism developed into a powerful political force in Asia, especially in India and China, where growing numbers of people were influenced by the self-determination concept that was one of the legacies of the Paris Peace Conference. Achieving the twin ideals of independence from foreign powers and national unity became a dream of intellectuals and a goal of new political leaders. Even as foreign control was being rejected, Asian leaders availed themselves of European ideologies such as nationalism and socialism, but in their search for new identities untainted by the dependent past, Asians either transformed or adapted those ideologies to fit indigenous traditions. In that sense, peoples in India and China followed in the footsteps of Japan, which had already adapted European and U.S. economic strategies to its advantage. Still dissatisfied with its status, Japan used militarism and imperial expansion in the interwar years to enhance its national identity.

Indian, Chinese, and Japanese societies underwent a prolonged period of disorder and struggle until a new order emerged. In India the quest for national identity focused on gaining independence from British rule, a pursuit that was complicated by sectarian differences between Hindus and Muslims. The Chinese path to national identity was fraught with foreign and civil war as two principal groups—the

Nationalist and Communist Parties—contended for power. Deeply divided by ideologies, both parties opposed foreign domination, rejected the old Confucian order, and sought a unified Chinese state. Japanese militarists made China's quest for national unity more difficult, because Japan struggled to overcome its domestic problems through conquests that focused on China.

India's Quest for Home Rule

By the beginning of the twentieth century, Indian nationalism threatened the British empire's hold on India. The construction of a vast railway network across India to facilitate the export of raw materials contributed to the idea of national unity by bringing the people of the subcontinent within easy reach of one another. Moreover, because it was impossible for a small group of foreigners to control and administer such a vast country, the British had created an elite of educated Indian administrators to help in this task. A European system of education familiarized the local middle-class intelligentsia with the political and social values of European society. Those values, however—democracy, individual freedom, and equality—were the antithesis of empire, and they promoted nationalist movements.

Indian National Congress Of all the associations dedicated to the struggle against British rule, the greatest and most influential was the Indian National Congress, founded in 1885. This organization, which enlisted the support of

many prominent Hindus and Muslims, at first stressed collaboration with the British to bring self-rule to India, but after the Great War the congress pursued that goal in opposition to the British. The formation of the Muslim League, established in 1906 with the encouragement of the British government, added a new current into the movement for national liberation. Both organizations were dedicated to achieving independence for India, but members of the Muslim League increasingly worried that Hindu oppression and continued subjugation of India's substantial Muslim minority might replace British rule.

During the Great War, large numbers of Indians—Hindus and Muslims—rallied to the British cause, and nationalist movements remained inactive. But as the war led to scarcities of goods and food, social discontent increasingly focused on the British colonizer. Indian nationalists also drew encouragement from ideas emanating from Washington, D.C., and St. Petersburg. They read Woodrow Wilson's Fourteen Points, which called for national self-determination, and Lenin's appeal for a united struggle by proletarians and colonized peoples. The British government responded to the upsurge of nationalist activity that came in the wake of the peace settlement with a series of repressive measures that precipitated a wave of violence and disorder throughout the Indian subcontinent.

Mohandas K. Gandhi

Into this turmoil stepped Mohandas Karamchand Gandhi (1869–1948), one of the most remarkable and charismatic leaders of the twentieth century. Gandhi grew up in a prosperous and pious Hindu household, married at thirteen, and left his hometown in 1888 to study law in London. In 1893 he went to South Africa to accept a position with an Indian firm, and there he quickly became involved in organizing the local Indian community against a system of racial segregation that made Indians second-class citizens. During the twenty-five years he spent in South Africa, Gandhi embraced a moral philosophy of *ahimsa* (tolerance and nonviolence) and developed the technique of passive resistance that he called *satyagraha* ("truth and firmness"). His belief in the virtue of simple living led him to renounce material possessions, dress in the garb of a simple Indian peasant, and become a vegetarian. He renounced sex—testing his willpower by chastely sleeping with various comely young women—and extolled the virtues of a daily saltwater enema. He also spent an hour each morning in careful study of the Bhagavad Gita (Sanskrit for "The Lord's Song"), one of the most sacred writings of Hinduism, which he regarded as a spiritual dictionary.

Returning to India in 1915, Gandhi became active in Indian politics. He succeeded in transforming the Indian National Congress from an elitist body of anglicized gentlemen into a mass organization that became an effective instrument of Indian nationalism. Although the reform program of the congress appeared remote from the needs of common people, Gandhi spoke in a language that they could understand. His unique mixture of spiritual intensity and political activism appealed to a broad section of the Indian population, and in the eyes of many he quickly achieved the stature of a political and spiritual leader, their Mahatma, or "great soul." Although he was a member of the merchant caste, Gandhi was determined to eradicate the injustices of the caste system. He fought especially hard to improve the status of the lowest classes of society, the casteless Untouchables, whom he called *harijans* ("children of God").

Under Gandhi's leadership the congress launched two mass movements: the Non-Cooperation Movement of 1920–1922 and the Civil Disobedience Movement of 1930. Convinced that economic self-sufficiency was a prerequisite for self-government, Gandhi called on the Indian people to boycott British goods and return to wearing rough homespun cotton clothing. He disagreed with those who wanted India to industrialize, advocating instead manual labor and the revival of rural cottage industries. Gandhi furthermore admonished his people to boycott institutions operated by the British in India, such as schools, offices, and courts. Despite Gandhi's cautions against the use of force, violence often accompanied the protest movement. The British retaliated with arrests. That the British authorities could react brutally was shown in 1919 in the city of Amritsar in Punjab, where colonial troops freely used their rifles to disperse an unarmed crowd, killing 379 demonstrators.

The India Act

When repressive measures failed to quell the movement for self-rule, the British offered a political compromise. After years of hesitation and deliberation, the British parliament enacted the Government of India Act, which gave India the institutions of a self-governing state. The legislation allowed for the establishment of autonomous legislative bodies in the provinces of British India, the creation of a bicameral (two-chambered) national legislature, and the formation of an executive arm under the control of the British government. On the urging of Gandhi, the majority of Indians approved the measure, which went into effect in 1937.

The India Act proved unworkable, however, because India's six hundred nominally sovereign princes refused to cooperate and because Muslims feared that Hindus would dominate the national legislature. Muslims had reason for concern because they already faced economic control by Hindus, a fact underlined during the Great Depression, which had a severe impact on India. On top of Indians suffering the typical devastations associated with agricultural economies during depression, they had to cope with added hurdles erected by an imperial government that did not respond with energetic efforts to mitigate the effects of the economic crisis. Moreover, the Great Depression exacerbated conflict between Muslims and Hindus, as Muslims constituted the majority of indebted tenant farmers, who found themselves increasingly unable to pay rents and debts. Their landlords were mainly Hindus. Muslims felt keenly what they perceived as economic exploitation by Hindus, and their recognition of this economic discrimination bolstered calls for a separate Muslim state. Muhammad Ali Jinnah (1876–1948), an eloquent and brilliant lawyer who headed the Muslim League, warned that a unified India represented nothing less than a threat to the Muslim faith and its Indian community. In place of one India, he proposed two states, one of which would be the "land of the pure," or Pakistan. Jinnah's proposal reflected an uncomfortable reality that society in India was split by hostility between Hindus and Muslims, making national unification an illusory goal.

China's Search for Order

As Shanfei's life story suggested, during the first half of the twentieth century China was in a state of almost continual revolutionary upheaval. The conflict's origins dated from the nineteenth century, when the Chinese empire came under relentless pressure from imperialist powers that rushed in to fill the vacuum created by China's internal political disintegration (see chapter 31). As revolutionary and nationalist uprisings gained widespread support, a revolution in 1911 forced the Xuantong emperor, still a child (also known as Puyi), to abdicate. The Qing empire fell with relative ease. Dr. Sun Yatsen (1866–1925), a leading opponent of the old regime, proclaimed a Chinese republic in 1912 and briefly assumed the office of president. The dynasty was dead, but there remained the problems of how to bury it and what to put in its place.

The Republic
The revolution of 1911 did not establish a stable government. Indeed, the republic soon plunged into a state of political anarchy and economic disintegration marked by the rule of warlords, who were disaffected generals from the old imperial Chinese army, and their troops. While the central government in Beijing ran the post office and a few other services, the warlords established themselves as provincial or regional rulers. Because the warlords were responsible for the neglect of irrigation projects crucial to the survival of farmers, for the revival of the opium trade, which they protected, and for the decline of crucial economic investments, they contributed to the deterioration of Chinese society. They never founded a new dynasty, nor did they create the semblance of a stable central state. Yet warlords were just one symbol of the disintegration of the political order. The fragmented relationship between native authority and foreign powers was another. Since the nineteenth century, a collection of treaties, known in China as the unequal treaties, had guided Chinese relations with foreign countries. Those treaties had established a network of foreign control over the Chinese economy that effectively prevented economic development. The continued sway of unequal treaties and other concessions permitted foreigners to intervene in Chinese society. Foreigners did not control the state, but through their privileges they impaired its sovereignty.

Chinese Nationalism
After the Great War, nationalist sentiment developed rapidly in China. Youths and intellectuals, who in the previous decade had looked to Europe and the United States for models and ideals for the reform of China, eagerly anticipated the results of the 1919 Peace Conference in Paris. They expected the U.S. government to support the termination of the treaty system and the restoration of full Chinese sovereignty. Those hopes were shattered, however, when the peacemakers approved increasing Japanese interference in China. That decision gave rise to the May Fourth Movement. Spearheaded by students and intellectuals in China's urban areas, the movement galvanized the country, and all classes of Chinese protested against foreign, especially Japanese, interference. In speeches, newspapers, and novels, the movement's leaders pledged themselves to rid China of imperialism and reestablish national unity. Student leaders such as Shanfei rallied their comrades to the cause.

Disillusioned by the cynical self-interest of the United States and the European powers, some Chinese became interested in Marxist thought as modified by Lenin (see chapter 33) and the social and economic experiments under way in the Soviet Union. The anti-imperialist rhetoric of the Soviet leadership struck a responsive chord, and in 1921 the Chinese Communist Party (CCP) was organized in Shanghai. Among its early members was Mao Zedong (1893–1976), a former teacher and librarian who viewed a Marxist-inspired social revolution as the cure for China's problems. Mao's political radicalism extended to the issue of women's equality, which he and other communists championed. As Shanfei's personal experience suggested, Chinese communists believed in divorce, opposed arranged marriages, and campaigned against the practice of foot binding.

Sun Yatsen
The most prominent nationalist leader at the time, Sun Yatsen, did not share the communists' enthusiasm for a dictatorship of the proletariat and the triumph of communism. Sun's basic ideology, summarized in

thinking about TRADITIONS

Chinese Revolutions
In the period before, during, and after the Great War, Chinese political thinkers and leaders questioned contemporary Chinese political and cultural practices. How did Chinese nationalism and communism promote challenges to long-standing Chinese political and cultural traditions, such as those pertaining to peasants and women?

sources from the past

"Self-Rule Is My Birthright"

Bal Gangadhar Tilak (1856–1920) was a fiery Indian nationalist who galvanized public support for India's independence movement. Although he was a great Sanskrit scholar and a very successful journalist, people best remember Tilak as a political activist who sought a Hindu revival and independence from Great Britain. His slogan, "Swaraj (Self-Rule) is my birthright," inspired millions of Indians. Whereas the British labeled him the "Father of Indian Unrest," Mohandas K. Gandhi more generously called him the "Maker of Modern India." What follows is an excerpt from Tilak's address to the Indian National Congress in 1907, calling for a boycott of British goods and resistance to British rule.

One fact is that this alien government has ruined the country. In the beginning, all of us were taken by surprise. We were almost dazed. We thought that everything that the rulers did was for our good and that this English Government has descended from the clouds to save us from the invasions of Tamerlane and Chingis Khan, and, as they say, not only from foreign invasions but from internecine warfare. We felt happy for a time, but it soon came to light that the peace which was established in this country did this . . . —that we were prevented from going at each other's throats, so that a foreigner might go at the throat of us all. Pax Britannica has been established in this country in order that a foreign Government may exploit the country. That this is the effect of this Pax Britannica is being gradually realized in these days. It was an unhappy circumstance that it was not realized sooner. . . . English education, growing poverty, and better familiarity with our rulers, opened our eyes. . . . Your industries are ruined utterly, ruined by foreign rule; your wealth is going out of the country and you are reduced to the lowest level which no human being can occupy. In this state of things, is there any other remedy by which you can help yourself? The remedy is not petitioning but boycott. We say prepare your forces, organize your power, and then go to work so that they cannot refuse you what you demand. . . . Every Englishman knows that they are a mere handful in this country and it is the business of every one of them to befool you in believing that you are weak and they are strong. This is politics. We have been deceived by such policy so long. What the new party wants you to do is realize the fact that your future rests entirely in your own hands. . . . We shall not give them assistance to collect revenue and keep peace. We shall not assist them in fighting beyond the frontiers or outside India with Indian blood and money. We shall not assist them in carrying on the administration of justice. We shall have our own courts, and when time comes we shall not pay taxes. Can you do that by your united efforts? If you can, you are free from to-morrow. . . .

For Further Reflection

■ What does Tilak suggest the British duped Indians into believing, and how would an Indian boycott let the British know that Indians would no longer be fooled?

Source: Bal Gangadhar Tilak. *Bal Gangadhar Tilak: His Writings and Speeches.* Madras: Ganesh and Co., 1923, pp. 56–65.

---

his *Three Principles of the People,* called for elimination of special privileges for foreigners, national reunification, economic development, and a democratic republican government based on universal suffrage. To realize those goals, he was determined to bring the entire country under the control of his Nationalist People's Party, or *Guomindang.* In 1923, members of the small CCP began to augment the ranks of the Guomindang and by 1926 made up one-third of the Guomindang's membership. Both organizations availed themselves of the assistance offered by the Soviet Union. Under the doctrine of Lenin's democratic centralism—stressing centralized party control by a highly disciplined group of professional revolutionaries—Soviet advisors helped reorganize the Guomindang and the CCP into effective political organizations. In the process, the Soviets bestowed on China the basis of a new political system.

Civil War After the death of Sun Yatsen in 1925, the leadership of the Guomindang fell to Jiang Jieshi (Chiang Kai-shek, 1887–1975), a young general who had been trained in Japan and the Soviet Union. In contrast to the communists, he did not hold a vision for social revolution that involved the masses of China. Before long, Jiang Jieshi launched a political and military offensive, known as the Northern Expedition, that aimed to unify the nation and bring China under Guomindang rule. Toward the end of his successful campaign, in 1927, Jiang Jieshi brutally and unexpectedly turned against his former communist allies, bringing the alliance of convenience between the Guomindang and the CCP to a bloody end. In the following year, nationalist forces occupied Beijing, set up a central government in Nanjing, and declared the Guomindang the official government of a unified and sovereign Chinese state. Meanwhile, the badly mauled communists

MAP 35.1

The struggle for control in China, 1927–1936.
Compare the continental territories controlled by Japan and the Guomindang in 1934.

How would the size of Japan's territories in Manchuria and Korea influence Chinese abilities to challenge Japanese expansion?

retreated to a remote area of southeastern China, where they tried to reconstitute and reorganize their forces.

The nationalist government had to deal with many concerns, but Chinese leaders evaded one major global crisis—the Great Depression. China's large agrarian economy and small industrial sector were connected only marginally to the world economy. Foreign trade in such items as tea and silk, which did decline, made up only a small part of China's economy, which was otherwise dominated by its large domestic

markets. Although the new government in China generally avoided having to contend with global economic devastation, it did have to confront three major problems during the 1930s. First, the nationalists actually controlled only part of China, leaving the remainder of the country in the hands of warlords. Second, by the early 1930s communist revolution was still a major threat. Third, the Guomindang faced increasing Japanese aggression. In dealing with those problems, Jiang Jieshi gave priority to eliminating the CCP and its Red Army.

Adversaries in the struggle for power in China: at left, Jiang Jieshi (Chiang Kai-shek); at right, Mao Zedong.

No longer able to ward off the relentless attacks of nationalist forces, the communists took flight in October 1934 to avoid annihilation. Bursting through a military blockade around their bases in Jiangxi province in southeastern China, some eighty-five thousand troops and auxiliary personnel of the Red Army began the legendary Long March, an epic journey of 10,000 kilometers (6,215 miles). After traveling across difficult terrain and fighting for survival against hunger, disease, and Guomindang forces, the marchers arrived in a remote area of Shaanxi Province in northwestern China in October 1935 and established headquarters at Yan'an. Although thousands had died in this forced retreat, the Long March inspired many Chinese to join the Communist Party. During the Long March, Mao Zedong emerged as the leader and the principal theoretician of the Chinese communist movement. He came up with a Chinese form of Marxist-Leninism, or Maoism, an ideology grounded in the conviction that peasants rather than urban proletarians were the foundation for a successful revolution. Village power, Mao believed, was critical in a country where most people were peasants.

Imperial and Imperialist Japan

After the Great War, Japan achieved great power status and appeared to accept the international status quo that the major powers fashioned in the aftermath of war. After joining the League of Nations as one of the "big five" powers, the Japanese government entered into a series of international agreements that sought to improve relations among countries with conflicting interests in Asia and the Pacific. As a signatory to several Washington Conference treaties in 1922, Japan agreed to limit naval development, pledged to evacuate Shandong Province of China, and guaranteed China's territorial integrity. In 1928 the Japanese government signed the Kellogg-Briand Pact, which renounced war as an instrument of national policy. Concerns about earlier Japanese territorial ambitions, highlighted by the Twenty-one Demands on China in 1915, receded from the minds of the international community.

Japan's limited involvement in the Great War gave a dual boost to its economy. Japanese businesses profited from selling munitions and other goods to the Allies throughout the war, and they gained a bigger foothold in Asia as the war led Europe's trading nations to neglect Asian markets. Economic prosperity was short-lived, however, as the postwar economy of Japan faced serious challenges. Rapid inflation and labor unrest appeared by 1918, followed by a series of recessions that culminated in a giant economic slump caused by the Great Depression. Like the economies of other industrial nations tied into the global economy, Japan's economy experienced plummeting industrial production, huge job layoffs, declining trade, and financial chaos. Economic contraction set the stage for social unrest and radical politics.

Public demands for sweeping political and social reforms, including a broadening of the franchise, protection for labor unions, and welfare legislation, figured prominently in Japanese domestic politics throughout the 1920s. Yet conservatives blocked any major advances beyond the suffrage law of 1925, which established universal male suffrage. By the early 1930s an increasingly frustrated public blamed its government for the nation's continuing economic problems and became more disenchanted with leading politicians tainted by bribery scandals and corrupt connections to business conglomerates. Right-wing political groups called for an end to party rule, and xenophobic nationalists dedicated themselves to the preservation of a unique Japanese culture and the eradication of Western influences. A campaign of assassinations, targeting political and business leaders, culminated in the murder of Prime Minister Inukai Tsuyoshi (1855–1932).

Politicians who supported Japan's role in the international industrial-capitalist system faced increasing opposition from those who were inclined toward a militarist vision of a self-sufficient Japan that would dominate east Asia. The hardships of the depression undermined support for the internationalist position, and the militarists were able to benefit from Japanese martial traditions and their own unwillingness to be constrained by international cooperation. China's unification, aided by international attempts to reinstate its sovereignty, threatened Japan's economic interests in Manchuria. Moreover, political instability, the result of nationalists and communists vying for power, made China an inviting target. Manchuria had historically been Chinese territory, but by the twentieth century it was a sphere of influence where Japan maintained the Manchurian Railroad (built in 1906), retained transit rights, and stationed troops. In 1931 Japan's military forces in Manchuria acted to assert control over the region.

The Mukden Incident On the night of 18 September 1931, Japanese troops used explosives to blow up a few feet of rail on the Japanese-built South Manchuria Railway north of Mukden. They accused the Chinese of attacking their railroad. This "Mukden incident" became the pretext for war

> *"The persistence of colonialism led to the development of African nationalism and the birth of embryonic nationalist movements."*

between Japanese and Chinese troops. Although the civilian government in Japan tried to halt this military incursion, by 1932 Japanese troops controlled all of Manchuria, thereby ensuring Japan preeminence and protecting its long-term economic and industrial development of the region. The Japanese established a puppet state called Manchukuo, but in reality Japan had absorbed Manchuria into its empire, challenged the international peace system, and begun a war. In response to the Manchurian invasion, the Guomindang (Nationalist Party) leader Jiang Jieshi appealed to the League of Nations to halt Japanese aggression. After a lengthy investigation, the league called for the withdrawal of Japanese forces and for the restoration of Chinese sovereignty. The Japanese responded by leaving the league, and, although China gained the moral high ground in international eyes, nothing was done to stop the aggression. This reaction set the pattern for future responses to the actions of expansionist nations such as Japan. Embarking on conquests in east Asia, Japanese militarists found a sure means to promoting a new militant Japanese national identity. They also helped provoke a new global conflagration.

The Great War and the Great Depression made signal contributions to the ongoing nationalist and political upheav-

als taking place throughout Asia. New ideologies and old conflicts intersected to complicate the processes of independence and national unification in India and China. The global economic crisis led to some lessening of European imperial influence, while it prompted an industrialized Japan to exert its imperial will on the Asian sphere. Only the aftermath of another world war brought any resolution to the turmoil within and among Asian nations.

AFRICA UNDER COLONIAL DOMINATION

The Great War and the Great Depression similarly complicated quests for national independence and unity in Africa. The colonial ties that bound African colonies to European powers ensured that Africans became participants in the Great War, willing or not. European states transmitted their respective animosities and their military conflicts to African soil and drew on their colonies for the recruitment of soldiers and carriers. The forced recruitment of military personnel led some Africans to raise arms against their colonial overlords, but Europeans generally prevailed in putting down those uprisings. African contributions to the Great War and the wartime rhetoric of self-determination espoused by U.S. President Woodrow Wilson led some Africans to anticipate a different postwar world. The peacemakers in Paris, however, ignored African pleas for social and political reform.

Rather than retreating, colonialism consolidated its hold on the African continent. In the decades following the peace settlement of 1919, the European powers focused on the economic exploitation of their colonies. The imposition of a rapacious form of capitalism destroyed the self-sufficiency of many African economies and turned the resulting colonial economies into extensions of those of the colonizing powers. As a result, African economic life became enmeshed in the global economy. The persistence of colonialism led to the development of African nationalism and the birth of embryonic nationalist movements. During the decades following the Great War, African intellectuals searched for new national identities and looked forward to the construction of nations devoid of European domination and exploitation.

Africa and the Great War

The Great War had a profound impact on Africa. The conflict of 1914–1918 affected Africans because many belligerents were colonial powers who ruled over the greater part of Africa. Except for Spanish-controlled territories, which remained neutral, every African colony took sides in the war. In practice this meant that the German colonial administration faced the combined colonial forces of Great Britain, France, Belgium, Italy, and Portugal. Even the last remaining independent states on the continent—Liberia and Ethiopia—did not avoid involvement. Whereas Lij Iyasu (reigned 1913–1916), the uncrowned, pro-Muslim boy emperor of Ethiopia, aligned his nation with Turkey until he was overthrown by

A Senegalese regiment of the French Colonial Infantry on parade in Africa during the Great War. Over a million African soldiers participated in military campaigns in Africa.

pro-Christian nobles in 1916, Liberia joined the Allies in 1917 when the United States entered the war.

War in Africa Although Germany had been a latecomer in the race for overseas colonies, German imperialists had managed to carve out a rudimentary colonial empire in Africa that included Togo, Cameroon, German South-West Africa, and German East Africa. Thus, one immediate consequence of war for Africans in 1914 was that the Allies invaded those German colonies. Specific strategic interests among the Allies varied. British officers and soldiers, trying to maintain naval supremacy, attempted to put German port facilities and communications systems out of action. The British also anticipated that victory in the German colonies would bring victors' spoils after the war. France's objective was to recover territory in Cameroon that it had ceded to Germany in 1911. The Germans, in contrast, simply tried to hold on to what they had. Outnumbered ten to one, the Germans could not hope to win the war in Africa. Yet, by resorting to guerrilla tactics, some fifteen thousand German troops tied sixty thousand Allied forces down and postponed defeat until the last days of the war.

More than one million African soldiers participated directly in military campaigns, in which they witnessed firsthand the spectacle of white people fighting one another. Colonial "masters" sent them to fight on African soil, in the lands of southwest Asia, and on the western front in Europe. The colonial powers also encouraged their African subjects in uniforms to

kill the enemy "white man," whose life until now had been sacrosanct because of his skin color. Even more men, as well as women and children, served as carriers to support armies in areas where supplies could not be hauled by conventional methods such as road, rail, or pack animal. The colonial powers raised recruits for fighting and carrier services in three ways: on a purely voluntary basis; in levies supplied by African chiefs that consisted of volunteer and impressed personnel; and through formal conscription. In French colonies, military service became compulsory for all males between the ages of twenty and twenty-eight, and by the end of the war more than 480,000 colonial troops had served in the French army. The British also raised recruits in their African colonies. In 1915 a compulsory service order made all men aged eighteen to twenty-five liable for military service. In the Congo, the Belgians impressed more than half a million porters. Ultimately, more than 150,000 African soldiers and carriers lost their lives, and many more suffered injury or became disabled.

thinking about ENCOUNTERS

Colonial Legacies of the Great War
During the Great War, Europeans relied on the military service and conscripted labor of many in their colonial empires. How did African participation in the Great War, for example, alter African expectations for their political future?

Challenges to European Authority While the world's attention was focused on the slaughter taking place in European lands between 1914 and 1918, Africans mounted bold challenges to European colonial authority. As the war dragged on, European commercial and administrative personnel began to leave the colonies in large numbers, whether for combat in Europe or for enlistment in locally based units for campaigns in Africa. That spread an already thin European presence even thinner, a fact not missed by colonial subjects. Africans took the opportunity to stage armed uprisings and other forms of protest. When they could least afford trouble, colonial regimes had no choice but to divert scarce military resources to meet those challenges.

The cause of widespread revolts varied. In some cases, as in Libya, revolts simply represented continued resistance to European rule. In other cases, the departure of European personnel, which seemed to signal a weakening of power, encouraged those who had previously only contemplated revolt. In yet other instances, pan-Islamic opposition to the war manifested itself in uprisings. The British had nervous moments, for example, when the Sufi brotherhood, based in Libya and still busy battling Italian occupation there, responded to a Turkish call for holy war and invaded western Egypt. The Mumbo cult in Kenya targeted Europeans and their Christian religion, declaring that "all Europeans are our enemies, but the time is shortly coming when they will disappear from our country." The major inspiration for most revolts, however, stemmed from the resentment and hatred engendered by the compulsory conscription of soldiers and carriers. No matter the cause, colonial authorities responded ruthlessly and succeeded in putting down all the revolts.

The Colonial Economy

The decades following the Great War witnessed a thorough transformation of African economic life. Colonial powers pursued two key economic objectives in Africa: they wanted to make sure that the colonized paid for the institutions—bureaucracies, judiciary, police, and military forces—that kept them in subjugation; and they developed export-oriented economies characterized by the exchange of unprocessed raw materials or minimally processed cash crops for manufactured goods from abroad. In pursuit of those goals, colonial authorities imposed economic structures that altered, subordinated, or destroyed previously self-sufficient African economies. In their place came colonial economies, tightly integrated into and dependent on a European-dominated global economy. The Great Depression of the 1930s exposed the vulnerability of dependent colonial economies. As international markets for primary products shrank under the impact of the depression, European companies that controlled the export of African products suffered accordingly. Trade volume often fell by half, and commodity prices dropped even more sharply.

Infrastructure Africa's economic integration required investment in infrastructures. Thus, during the early twentieth century, the new colonial economy first became visible in the form of port facilities, roads, railways, and telegraph

This poster, produced by the Empire Marketing Board, presented an idealized image of the dominant European role in forwarding African economic progress.

EAST·AFRICAN TRANSPORT~NEW STYLE

wires. Efficient transportation and communication networks not only facilitated conquest and rule but also linked the agricultural or mineral wealth of a colony to the outside world. Although Europeans later claimed that they had given Africa its first modern infrastructure, Europeans and their businesses were usually its main beneficiaries. It was Africans who paid for the infrastructure with their labor and taxes, yet Europeans never considered the needs of local African economies.

Farming and Mining Colonial taxation was an important tool designed to drive Africans into the labor market. To earn the money to pay the taxes levied on land, houses, livestock, and people themselves, African farmers had to become cash crop farmers or seek wage labor on plantations and in mines. Cash crop farming embraced the largest proportion of Africans. In most colonies, farmers who kept their land specialized in one or two crops, generally destined for export to the country governing them. African farmers grew a variety of cash crops for the international marketplace, among them peanuts from Senegal and northern Nigeria, cotton from Uganda, cocoa from the Gold Coast, rubber from the Congo, and palm oil from the Ivory Coast and the Niger delta. In areas with extensive white settlement, such as in Kenya, Rhodesia, and South Africa, settler agriculture was most prominent. Production of agricultural commodities intended for overseas markets remained in the hands of white settlers, whose governments saw to it that they received large and productive areas of land. In British-controlled Kenya, for example, four thousand white farmers seized the Kikuyu highlands, which comprised seven million acres of the colony's richest land. In South Africa, the government reserved 88 percent of all land for whites, who made up just 20 percent of the total population.

Colonial mining enterprises relying on African labor loomed large in parts of central and southern Africa. Engaged in the extraction of mineral wealth such as copper, gold, and diamonds, these enterprises recruited men from rural areas and paid them minimal wages. The recruitment practices set in motion a vast pattern of labor migration that persisted throughout the twentieth century. The absence of male labor and the payment of minimal wages had the effect of impoverishing the rural areas. In many cases, the wives left behind could not grow enough food to feed their children and elderly relatives.

Labor Practices Where taxation failed to create a malleable native labor force, colonial officials resorted to outright forced labor. Indeed, forms of forced labor and barely disguised variants of slavery were prominent features of the colonial economy. A white settler in Kenya candidly expressed the view held by many colonial administrators: "We have stolen his land. Now we must steal his limbs. Compulsory labor is the corollary to our occupation of the country." Much of the labor abuse originated with concessionary companies, which were authorized by their governments to exploit a region's resources with the help of their own system of taxation and labor recruitment. Frequently, the conduct of such companies with respect to labor practices was downright brutal. For example, the construction of railways and roads often depended on forced labor regimes. When the French undertook the construction of the Congo-Ocean railway from Brazzaville to the port at Point-Noir, they rounded up some ten thousand workers annually. Within a few years, between fifteen and twenty thousand African laborers had perished from starvation, disease, and maltreatment.

African Nationalism

In the decades following the Great War, European powers consolidated their political control over the partitioned continent and imposed economies designed to exploit Africa's natural and labor resources. Many Africans were disappointed that their contributions to the war went unrewarded. In place of anticipated social reforms or some degree of greater political participation came an extension and consolidation of the colonial system. Nevertheless, ideas concerning self-determination, articulated by U.S. President Woodrow Wilson during the war, and the notion of the accountability of colonial powers that had been sown during the war gained adherents among a group of African nationalists. Those ideas influenced the growth of African nationalism and the development of incipient nationalist movements. An emerging class of native urban intellectuals, frequently educated in Europe, became especially involved in the formation of ideologies that promised freedom from colonialism and promoted new national identities.

Africa's New Elite Colonialism prompted the emergence of a novel African social class, sometimes called the "new elite." This elite derived its status and place in society from employment and education. The upper echelons of Africa's elite class contained high-ranking civil servants, physicians, lawyers, and writers, most of whom had studied abroad either in western Europe or sometimes in the United States. A case in point was Jomo Kenyatta (1895–1978), who spent almost fifteen years in Europe, during which time he attended various schools and universities, including the London School of Economics. An immensely articulate nationalist, Kenyatta later led Kenya to independence from the British. Even those who had not gone abroad had familiarized themselves with the writings of European authors. Below them in status stood teachers, clerks, and interpreters who had obtained a European-derived primary or secondary education. Although some individuals were self-employed, such as lawyers and doctors, most of them held jobs with colonial governments, with foreign companies, or with Christian missions. In short, these were the Africans who spoke and understood the language of the colonizer, moved with ease in the world of the colonizer, and outwardly adopted the cultural norms of the colonizer such as

sources from the past

Africa for Africans

Marcus Garvey (1887–1940) is best remembered as a pivotal figure in black nationalism, one who inspired nationalist movements as well as many African leaders. A powerful orator, Garvey preached the greatness of the African heritage and called on European colonial powers to leave Africa. Convinced that blacks in the diaspora could never secure their rights as minorities, this "Black Moses" rejected the idea of integration and instead championed a "Back to Africa" movement. According to Garvey, a Jamaican who garnered notoriety during his time in the United States, only in ancestral Africa would it be possible to establish an autonomous black state that featured its own unique culture.

George Washington was not God Almighty. He was a man like any Negro in this building, and if he and his associates were able to make a free America, we too can make a free Africa. Hampden, Gladstone, Pitt and Disraeli were not the representatives of God in the person of Jesus Christ. They were but men, but in their time they worked for the expansion of the British Empire, and today they boast of a British Empire upon which "the sun never sets." As Pitt and Gladstone were able to work for the expansion of the British Empire, so you and I can work for the expansion of a great African Empire. Voltaire and Mirabeau were not Jesus Christs, they were but men like ourselves. They worked and overturned the French Monarchy. They worked for the Democracy which France now enjoys, and if they were able to do that, we are able to work for a democracy in Africa. Lenin and Trotsky were not Jesus Christs, but they were able to overthrow the despotism of Russia, and today they have given to the world a Social Republic, the first of its kind. If Lenin and Trotsky were able to do that for Russia, you and I can do that for Africa. Therefore, let no man, let no power on earth, turn you from this sacred cause of liberty. I prefer to die at this moment rather than not to work for the freedom of Africa. If liberty is good for certain sets of humanity it is good for all. Black men, Colored men, Negroes have as much right to be free as any other race that God Almighty ever created, and we desire freedom that is unfettered, freedom that is unlimited, freedom that will give us a chance and opportunity to rise to the fullest of our ambition and that we cannot get in countries where other men rule and dominate.

We have reached the time when every minute, every second must count for something done, something achieved in the cause of Africa. . . . It falls to our lot to tear off the shackles that bind Mother Africa. Can you do it? You did it in the Revolutionary War. You did it in the Civil War; You did it at the Battles of the Marne and Verdun; You did it in Mesopotamia. You can do it marching up the battle heights of Africa. Let the world know that 400,000,000 Negroes are prepared to die or live as free men. Despise us as much as you care. Ignore us as much as you care. We are coming 400,000,000 strong. We are coming with our woes behind us, with the memory of suffering behind us—woes and suffering of three hundred years—they shall be our inspiration. My bulwark of strength in the conflict of freedom in Africa, will be the three hundred years of persecution and hardship left behind in this Western Hemisphere.

For Further Reflection

■ In his speech, how does Marcus Garvey convey the significance of Africa for both Africans and those involved in the black diaspora?

Source: Amy Jacques Garvey, compiler. *Philosophy and Opinions of Marcus Garvey or Africa for Africans.* London: Frank Cass and Co., 1967, pp. 73–74.

---

wearing European-style clothes or adopting European names. It was within the ranks of this new elite that ideas concerning African identity and nationhood germinated.

Because colonialism had introduced Africans to European ideas and ideologies, African nationalists frequently embraced the European concept of the nation as a means of forging unity among disparate African groups. As they saw it, the nation as articulated by European thinkers and statesmen provided the best model for mobilizing their resources and organizing their societies, and it offered the best chance to mount effective resistance to colonialism. Although the concept of the nation proved a useful general framework for African nationalists, there remained differences as to what constituted a nation or a people's national identity.

Forms of Nationalism   Some nationalists in search of a national identity looked to the precolonial past for inspiration. There they found identities based on ethnicity, religion, and languages, and they believed that any future nation must reconstitute institutions crucial to those identities, such as distinctively African forms of spiritual and political authority. Race had provided colonial powers with one rationale for conquest and exploitation; hence it was not surprising that some nationalists used the concept of an African race as a founda-

A European colonialist takes advantage of African labor and is "Traveling in Hammock," as this 1912 photograph's title suggests.

tion for identity, solidarity, and nation building. Race figured as an important concept in another important strain of African nationalism, which originated in the western hemisphere among the descendants of slaves. Typically it was U.S. blacks and Afro-Caribbean intellectuals who thought of themselves as members of a single race and who promoted the unification of all people of African descent into a single African state. Representatives of this Pan-Africanism were the black U.S. activist and intellectual W. E. B. DuBois (1868–1963) and the Jamaican nationalist leader Marcus Garvey (1887–1940), who preached black pride and called on blacks living in the African diaspora to go "Back to Africa." Still other nationalists discarded the concept of a unique racial identity altogether and looked rather for an African identity rooted in geography. This approach commonly translated into a desire to build the nation on the basis of borders that defined existing colonial states. Collectively these ideas influenced the development of nationalist movements during the 1930s and 1940s, but it took another world war before these ideas translated into demands for independence from colonialism.

LATIN AMERICAN STRUGGLES WITH NEOCOLONIALISM

The postcolonial history of Latin American states in the early twentieth century offered clues about what the future might hold for those areas in Asia and Africa still chafing under colonial dominion but seeking independence. Having gained their independence in the nineteenth century, most

sovereign nations in Latin America thereafter struggled to achieve political and economic stability in the midst of interference from foreign powers. The era of the Great War and the Great Depression proved crucial to solidifying and exposing to view the neocolonial structures that guided affairs in Latin America. Generally seen as an indirect and more subtle form of imperial control, neocolonialism usually took shape as foreign economic domination but did not exclude more typically imperial actions such as military intervention and political interference. In Central and South America, as well as in Mexico and the Caribbean, this new imperial influence came not from former colonial rulers in Spain and Portugal but, rather, from wealthy, industrial-capitalist powerhouses such as Great Britain and especially the United States. Neocolonialism impinged on the independent political and economic development of Latin American states, but it did not prevent nationalist leaders from devising strategies to combat the newfound imperialism.

The Impact of the Great War and the Great Depression

Reorientation of Political and Nationalist Ideals

The Great War and the Russian revolution, along with the ongoing Mexican revolution, spread radical ideas and the promise of new political possibilities throughout Latin America. The disparate ideals emerging from this time of political ferment found receptive audiences in Latin America before but especially during the global economic crisis of the Great Depression. Marxism, Vladimir Lenin's theories on

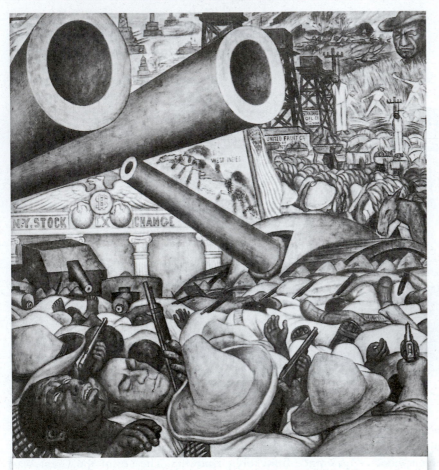

Diego Rivera's *Imperialism* was one in a series of paintings on the United States and offered a visual critique of U.S. neocolonialism in Latin America.

lutions inimical to ideals of the United States, university students hailed the Mexican and Russian revolutions and in the 1920s began to demand reforms. Students wanted more representation within the educational system, and their political activism resulted in the long-term politicization of the student bodies at Latin American universities. Universities thereafter became training grounds for future political leaders, including Fidel Castro (1926–), and the ideas explored within an academic setting—from Marxism to anti-imperialism—exerted great influence on those budding politicians.

The currency of radicalism also expressed itself in the formation of political parties that either openly espoused communism or otherwise adopted rebellious agendas for change. Peruvians, for example, created a number of radical new political parties, many of which had connections to a self-educated young Marxist intellectual, José Carlos Mariátegui (1895–1930). Mariátegui felt particular concern for the poor and for the Indians, who constituted approximately 50 percent of Peru's population. He castigated Peru's leaders in journals and newspapers for not helping the downtrodden, and he suffered exile to Europe as a result. He came back from Europe a dedicated Marxist and in 1928 established the Socialist Party of Peru. Mariátegui continued to write and rally in support of laborers, and he was in the midst of helping to create the Peruvian Communist Party when he died from cancer in 1930.

The same agitation that filled José Carlos Mariátegui affected others in Peru and led in the 1920s and 1930s to violence and strikes. The *Alianza Popular Revolucionaria Americana* (Popular American Revolutionary Alliance, or APRA) gave another voice to those critical of Peru's ruling system. This party's followers, known as *Apristas,* advocated indigenous rights and anti-imperialism among other causes. *Aprismo* offered a radical but noncommunist alternative to Peruvians, and it stemmed from the ideas of Victor Raúl Haya de la Torre (1895–1979). Haya de la Torre began his political activism as a student protester and as a supporter of a workers' movement. Exiled like Mariátegui, Haya de la Torre nonetheless imparted his eclectic views to APRA, including both staunch anti-imperialism and a plan for capitalist development that had peasants and workers cooperating with the middle class. The more traditional power of the military and landed elites in Peru managed to contain these rebellious movements, but the cultural and political popularity of radicalism and its intellectual proponents persisted.

capitalism and imperialism, and a growing concern for the impoverished Indian masses as well as exploited peasants and workers in Latin American societies informed the outlooks of many disgruntled intellectuals and artists. Although those revolutionary doctrines did not achieve full-scale adoption by Latin American states during the interwar era, their increasing popularity and perceived viability as political options suggested the alternatives open to nations in the future. The Enlightenment-derived liberalism that had shaped independence movements and the political systems of many postindependence nations no longer served as the only form of political legitimacy.

University Protests and Communist Parties

The Great War had propelled the United States into a position of world economic leadership. The peoples of Latin America came to experience most intensely this new U.S. economic power, and it was probably no coincidence that the capitalism embraced by the United States came under attack. One of the first institutions in Latin America to witness this rebelliousness was the university. Taking their inspiration from two revo-

Diego Rivera and Radical Artistic Visions

The ideological transformations apparent in Latin America be-

came stunningly and publicly visible in the murals painted by famed Mexican artist Diego Rivera (1886–1957). Artistically trained in Mexico in his youth, Rivera went to study in Europe in 1907 and did not return to Mexico until 1921. Influenced by the art of both Renaissance artists and cubists, Rivera also experienced the turmoil and shifting political sensibilities taking place during the Great War and its aftermath. He blended his artistic and political visions in vast murals that he intended for viewing and appreciation by the masses. He believed that art should be on display for working people. Along with other Mexican muralists, such as David Alfaro Siqueiros (1896–1974) and José Clemente Orozco (1883–1949), Rivera shaped the politicized art of Mexico for decades.

Diego Rivera celebrated indigenous Mexican art and pre-Columbian folk traditions, and he incorporated radical political ideas in his style and approach to mural painting. The government commissioned him in the late 1920s and 1930s to create large frescoes for public buildings, and Rivera artistically transcribed the history of Mexico, replete with its social ills, on the walls of such structures as the National Palace and the Ministry of Education in Mexico City. An activist in the Mexican Communist Party, he taught briefly in Moscow in the late 1920s. In the early 1930s the Detroit Institute of Arts commissioned him to paint murals for a U.S. audience, and this migration of his art to the United States soon caused a controversy.

In 1933 Rivera received a request to paint murals for the RCA building in Rockefeller Center in New York City. He included in one panel a portrait of Vladimir Lenin, which outraged those who had commissioned the work. His mural was destroyed. Rivera in turn undertook a series of twenty-one paintings on United States history titled *Portrait of America*. He labeled one of the most pointed and critical paintings *Imperialism,* which visualized and advertised the economic interference and political repressiveness engendered by U.S. neocolonialism in Latin America. Rivera depicted massive guns and tanks extending over the New York Stock Exchange. In the foreground and at the edges of the Stock Exchange are a variety of Latin American victims of this monied-military oppression, including Central Americans laboring for the United Fruit Company and others toiling for the Standard Oil Company. Overlooking all of this in the upper-right corner is Augusto César Sandino (1893–1934), the martyred nationalist hero who opposed U.S. intervention in Nicaragua. Rivera made visible the impact of U.S. imperialism on Latin American societies, and by doing so he helped spread political activism in the Americas.

The Evolution of Economic Imperialism

United States Economic Domination Latin American states were no strangers to foreign economic domination in the nineteenth and early twentieth centuries. Their export-oriented economies had long been tied to global finances and had long been subject to controls imposed by foreign investors, largely those from Great Britain and the United States. The major evolution in economic neocolonialism during this period concerned the growing predominance of the United States in the economic affairs of Latin American nations. The Great War sealed this transition to U.S. supremacy, and U.S. investments in Latin America soared in the 1920s. Between 1924 and 1929, U.S. banks and businesses more than doubled their financial interests in Latin America as investments grew from $1.5 billion to $3.5 billion. Much of that money went toward the takeover of businesses extracting vital minerals, such as copper-mining firms in Chile and oil-drilling concerns in Venezuela.

Dollar Diplomacy That U.S. neocolonialism was meant to be largely economic became evident in the policies of President William Howard Taft (1857–1931). In his final address to Congress in 1912, Taft argued that the United States should substitute "dollars for bullets" in its foreign policy. He wanted businesses to develop foreign markets through peaceful commerce and believed that expensive military intervention should be avoided as much as possible. Likewise, by replacing European investments with U.S. investments, the United States would face fewer tests of the Monroe Doctrine or its 1904 Roosevelt corollary, which justified direct intervention in Latin American nations deemed unstable by the United States. This new vision of U.S. expansion abroad, dubbed "dollar diplomacy" by critics, encapsulated the gist of what those in Latin America perceived as "Yankee imperialism."

Economic Depression and Experimentation The economic crisis of the Great Depression demonstrated the extent to which Latin America had become integrated in the world economy. With some exceptions, exports had continued in the interwar period to help nations achieve basic solvency and even enough economic expansion to institute social reforms. The Great Depression, however, halted fifty years of economic growth in Latin America and illustrated the region's susceptibility to global economic crises. The increasing U.S. capital investments for nascent industries and other financial concerns during the 1920s could not be maintained during this catastrophic economic downturn. Most Latin American states, because they exported agricultural products or raw materials, were further vulnerable to the effects of the depression. The prices of sugar from the Caribbean, coffee from Brazil and Colombia, wheat and beef from Argentina, tin from Bolivia, nitrates from Chile, and many other products fell sharply after 1929. Attempts by producers to raise prices by holding supplies off the market—Brazilians, for example, set fire to coffee beans or used them in the construction of highways—failed, and throughout Latin America unemployment rates increased rapidly. The drastic decline in the price of the region's exports and the drying-up of foreign capital prompted Latin American governments to raise tariffs on foreign products and impose various other restrictions on foreign trade. Those same conditions also

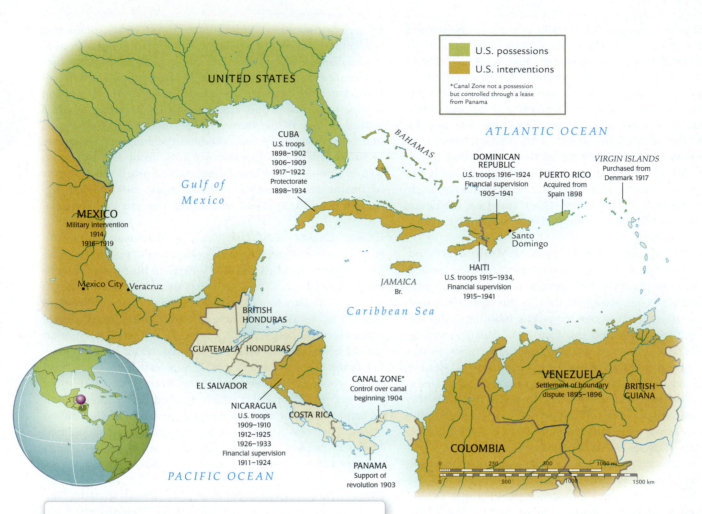

MAP 35.2
The United States in Latin America, 1895–1941.
Note the number of Latin American states where U.S. troops intervened in local politics.

On what basis did U.S. policymakers justify those interventions?

encouraged domestic manufacturing, which made important gains in many Latin American nations.

Although the weaknesses of export-oriented economies and industrial development financed by foreigners became evident during the Great Depression, the international crisis also allowed Latin American nations to take alternative paths to economic development. Economic policy stressing internal economic development was most visible in Brazil, where dictator-president (1930–1945, 1950–1954) Getúlio Dornelles Vargas (1883–1954) turned his nation into an *estado novo* (new state). Ruling with the backing of the military but without the support of the landowning elite, Vargas and his government during the 1930s and 1940s embarked on a program of industrialization that created new enterprises. Key among them was the iron and steel industry. The Vargas regime also implemented protectionist policies that shielded domes-

tic production from foreign competition, which pleased both industrialists and urban workers. Social welfare initiatives accompanied industrial development, protecting workers with health and safety regulations, minimum wages, limits on working hours, unemployment compensation, and retirement benefits. The Great Depression contributed in many ways to the evolution of both economic neocolonialism and economic experimentation within Latin American states.

Conflicts with a "Good Neighbor"

The "Good Neighbor Policy"   The pressures of the Great Depression and the instability of global politics led to a reassessment of U.S. foreign policy in Latin America during the late 1920s and 1930s. U.S. leaders realized the costliness and the ineffectiveness of their previous direct interventions in Latin America, especially when committing U.S. Marines as peacekeeping forces. To extricate U.S. military forces and rely more fully on dollar diplomacy, policymakers instituted certain innovations that nonetheless called into question any true change of heart among U.S. neocolonialists. They approved "sweetheart treaties" that guaranteed U.S. financial control in the Caribbean economies of Haiti and the Dominican Republic, for example, and the U.S. Marines provided training for indigenous police forces to keep the peace and maintain law and order. These national guards tended to be less expensive than maintaining forces of U.S. Marines, and the guards' leaders usually worked to keep cordial relations with the United States. This revamped U.S. approach to relations with Latin America became known as the "Good Neighbor Policy," and it was most closely associated with the administration of Franklin D. Roosevelt (1882–1945). Although Roosevelt appeared more well-intentioned in his exercise of the policy, events in Nicaragua before and during the beginning of his administration highlighted the limits of U.S. neighborliness.

Nicaragua and the *Guarda Nacional* U.S. financial interests had long influenced the economy of Nicaragua, and those substantial investments—whether in the transportation industry or in bananas—served to justify U.S. intervention when revolts or civil wars broke out. The mid- and late 1920s again witnessed the outbreak of civil war in Nicaragua and the repeated insertion of the Marines to restore order. Leading the opposition to Nicaraguan conservatives and the occupation of Nicaragua by U.S. Marines was Augusto César Sandino, a nationalist and liberal general who refused to accept any peace settlement that left Marines on Nicaraguan soil.

As part of a plan to remove U.S. forces, the United States established and trained the *Guarda Nacional,* or National Guard, in Nicaragua. The U.S.-supervised elections of 1932 brought Juan Batista Sacasa (president, 1932–1936) into power, and U.S. troops departed, having positioned the brutal but trusted Anastacio Somoza Garcia (1896–1956) as commander of the Guard. Even though conflicts between Sandino's forces and Somoza's Guard persisted, Sandino explored options with Sacasa and Somoza for ending the rebellion given the departure of the Marines. Officers from the National Guard murdered Sandino in 1934, and Somoza soon after fulfilled his ambitions and became president of his country. Somoza endeavored successfully to maintain the loyalty of the National Guard and to prove himself a good neighbor to the United States. He visited Washington, D.C., in 1939 and renamed the Nicaraguan capital city's main thoroughfare after Roosevelt. He also began to collect what became the largest fortune in Nicaragua's history and to establish a political dynasty that ruled the nation for decades to come. In the meantime, Sandino gained heroic status as a martyr who died in part because he fought the good neighbor to the north.

Cárdenas' Mexico However flawed, the Good Neighbor Policy evolved under Roosevelt into a more conciliatory U.S. approach to Latin American relations. The interventionist corollary to the Monroe Doctrine enunciated previously by President Theodore Roosevelt (1859–1919) was formally renounced in December 1933, when Secretary of State Cordell Hull attended the Seventh International Conference of American

A 1920s photograph of Nicaraguan patriot leader Augusto César Sandino. Sandino opposed the presence of the United States in Nicaragua and fought to expel U.S. Marines in his country. He was murdered by officers from the U.S.-friendly National Guard in 1934.

States in Montevideo, Uruguay. Hull signed the "Convention on the Rights and Duties of States," which held that "no state has the right to intervene in the internal or external affairs of another." That proposition faced a severe challenge in March 1938 when Mexican president Lázaro Cárdenas (1895–1970) nationalized the oil industry, much of which was controlled by foreign investors from the United States and Great Britain.

Given the history of tempestuous relations between the United States and Mexico, including multiple U.S. military incursions into Mexico during the revolution, there was little panies, and his nationalization of the oil industry proved popular with the Mexican people.

Neighborly Cultural Exchanges

Although the nationalization crisis in Mexico ended in a fashion that suggested the strength of the Good Neighbor Policy, a good deal of the impetus for that policy came from economic and political concerns associated with the Great Depression and the deterioration of international relations in the 1930s. The United States wanted to cultivate Latin American markets for its exports, and it wanted to distance itself from the militarist behavior of Asian and European imperial powers. The U.S. government knew it needed to improve relations with Latin America, if only to secure those nations' support in the increasingly likely event of another global war. Widespread Mexican migration to the United States during and after the Great War suggested the attractiveness of the United States for at least some Latin Americans. Filling the migration void left by Europeans prevented from coming to the United States by the war and by the U.S. immigration restriction laws of the 1920s, Mexican men, women, and children entered the United States in the hundreds of thousands to engage in agricultural and industrial work. The migrants suffered the animosity of some U.S. citizens, who considered them "cheap Mexican labor," but the political power of agribusinesses prevented the government from instituting legal restrictions on Mexican migration. Federal and local officials managed, however, to deport thousands of Mexicans during the Great Depression.

This Hollywood publicity photo of Carmen Miranda features the type of lively costuming that made her a colorful favorite in both the United States and Latin America.

Trying to contribute to the repairing of relations and the promoting of more positive images of Latin American and U.S. relations, Hollywood adopted a Latin American singing and dancing sensation, Carmen Miranda (1909–1955). Born in Portugal but raised from childhood in Brazil, Miranda found fame on a Rio de Janeiro radio station and recorded hundreds of hit songs. A Broadway producer lured her to the United States, but she gained her greatest visibility in such films as *Down Argentine Way* (1940) and many others produced during World War II. Carmen Miranda appeared as an exotic Latin American woman, usually clothed in sexy, colorful costumes that featured amazing headdresses adorned with the

chance for a peaceful resolution to this provocative move on the part of Cárdenas. The reluctance of U.S. and British oil companies to adhere to an arbitration decree granting concessions to Mexican oil workers prompted him to this drastic act. His radical persuasions also drove Cárdenas to this extreme, as did his intent to implement some of the progressive provisions of the Constitution of 1917. Despite calls for a strong U.S. and British response, Roosevelt and his administration officials resisted the demands of big businesses and instead called for a cool, calm response and negotiations to end the conflict. This plan prevailed, and the foreign oil companies ultimately had to accept only $24 million in compensation rather than the $260 million that they initially demanded. Cárdenas cleverly based the compensation price on the tax value claimed by the oil com-

Chiquita Banana, an advertising icon used to promote a good image of the United Fruit Company, was a replica in fruit of the singing and acting sensation Carmen Miranda.

fruits grown in Latin America—such as bananas. She softened representations of Latin Americans for audiences in the United States, providing a less threatening counterpoint to laboring migrants or women guerrilla fighters in Mexico's revolution. She also became a source of pride for Brazilians, who reveled in her Hollywood success. Hollywood's espousal of Roosevelt's Good Neighbor Policy proved a success.

Equally successful as a marketing device, although one that illustrated the continued limitations of the Good Neighbor Policy, was the United Fruit Company's appropriation of Carmen Miranda's image for the selling of the bananas that symbolized U.S. economic control of regions throughout Central America and the Caribbean. The United Fruit Company owned 160,000 acres of land in the Caribbean by 1913, and already by 1918 U.S. consumers bought fully 90 percent of Nicaragua's bananas. Not content with such market control, the United Fruit Company's advertising executives in 1944 crafted "Chiquita Banana," a female banana look-alike of Carmen Miranda. In singing radio commercials, Chiquita Banana taught U.S. consumers about the storage and various uses of bananas ("I'm Chiquita Banana / And I've come to say / Bananas have to ripen / In a certain way"). This singing banana promoted the sales of United Fruit Company bananas, and for consumers in the United States, it gave the prototypical neocolonial company in Latin America

a softer, less threatening image—one that challenged, for example, the more ideologically raw representation in Diego Rivera's *Imperialism*.

in**perspective**

In the decades after the Great War, and in the midst of the Great Depression, intellectuals and political activists in Asia, Africa, and Latin America challenged the ideological and economic underpinnings of empire and neocolonialism. Often embracing the ideas and theories that disseminated around the globe as a result of the war, including self-determination, socialism, communism, and anti-imperialism, radicals and nationalists revised understandings of political identity in the colonial and neocolonial worlds.

Japanese and U.S. imperial practices incited military and civil discord within their respective spheres, while European colonial rulers continued to limit, often brutally, the freedom of peoples in India and Africa. Like Shanfei, young intellectuals and older political leaders alike emerged transformed in these years. Their efforts to inspire nationalism and to achieve economic and political autonomy came to fruition later—after another world war had come and gone. ●

CHRONOLOGY	
1912	Taft establishes dollar diplomacy as U.S. foreign policy
1914–1918	2.5 million African troops and carriers serve in the Great War
1919	May Fourth Movement in China
1920	Non-Cooperation Movement in India
1921	Rivera returns to Mexico to paint
1928	Socialist Party of Peru is founded
1929	Beginning of Great Depression
1930	Civil Disobedience Movement in India
1930s–1940s	Vargas's *Estado Novo* in Brazil
1931	Japanese invasion of Manchuria
1933	Roosevelt begins practice of the Good Neighbor Policy
1934	Long March by Chinese Communists
1934	Sandino is murdered in Nicaragua
1935	Government of India Act
1938	Cárdenas nationalizes oil industry in Mexico

For Further Reading

A. Adu Boahen, ed. *Africa under Colonial Domination, 1880–1935.* Berkeley, 1985. Part of the ambitious UNESCO General History of Africa (vol. 7), this work reflects how different Africans view their history.

Judith Brown. *Modern India: The Origins of Asian Democracy.* 2nd ed. Oxford, 1994. This survey is a good introduction to the past two hundred years of Indian history.

Victor Bulmer-Thomas, John H. Coatsworth, and Robert Cortés Conde, eds. *The Cambridge Economic History of Latin America.* Vol. 2: *The Long Twentieth Century.* Cambridge, 2006. Scholarly collection of essays that outlines the region's main economic trends and developments.

Ian Buruma. *Inventing Japan, 1853–1964.* New York, 2003. A respected journalist compresses a century of complex history into a short and elegant book.

Prasenjit Duara. *Sovereignty and Authenticity: Manchukuo and the East Asian Modern.* Lanham, Md., 2003. Using the Japanese puppet state of Manchukuo as a focal point, this is a technical and highly demanding but impressive study of imperialism, nationalism, and modernity.

Cynthia Enloe. *Bananas, Beaches & Bases: Making Feminist Sense of International Politics.* Berkeley, 1989. A gendered analysis of U.S. and other foreign policies through such categories as tourism and diplomats' spouses.

William Gould. *Hindu Nationalism and the Language of Politics in Late Colonial India.* New York, 2004. Political history of India on the eve of independence.

Robert E. Hannigan. *The New World Power: American Foreign Policy, 1898–1917.* Philadelphia, 2002. A detailed account of U.S. foreign relations that links class, race, and gender influences to policymakers.

Lawrence James. *Raj: The Making and Unmaking of British India.* New York, 1998. A sweeping, narrative account of the Raj and British influence in the Indian subcontinent.

Robert W. July. *A History of the African People.* 5th ed. Long Grove, Ill., 1997. A critically acclaimed survey that explores themes that cut across time and place.

Patrick Marnham. *Dreaming with His Eyes Wide Open: A Life of Diego Rivera.* Berkeley, 2000. An engaging and well-received biography, which includes an appendix with reprints of Rivera's major mural paintings.

Jim Masselos. *Indian Nationalism: A History.* 3rd ed. Columbia, 1998. A keen work that remains the standard, most readable introduction to Indian leaders and movements.

Michael C. Meyer, William L. Sherman, and Susan M. Deeds. *The Course of Mexican History.* 6th ed. Oxford, 1999. An updated survey of Mexican history from pre-Columbian to modern times.

Roland Oliver and Anthony Atmore. *Africa since 1800.* 4th ed. Cambridge, 1994. An updated version of a well-regarded survey.

Anthony Read and David Fisher. *The Proudest Day: India's Long Road to Independence.* New York, 1998. Written for the general reader, this is a compelling and colorful account of India's road to freedom.

Elizabeth Schmidt. *Mobilizing the Masses: Gender, Ethnicity, and Class in the Nationalist Movement in Guinea, 1939–1958.* Portsmouth, N.H., 2005. Details the emergence of lesser-known but powerful subaltern anticolonial networks that preceded formal nationalist organizations in French West Africa.

Vera Schwarcz. *The Chinese Enlightenment: Intellectuals and the Legacy of May Fourth Movement of 1919.* Berkeley, 1986. A gracefully written, thoughtful work.

Steve Striffler and Mark Moberg, eds. *Banana Wars: Power, Production, and History in the Americas.* Durham, 2003. Interdisciplinary analysis of the transformative impact of the banana industry on global trade and the consequences for Latin American societies and economies.

Odd Arne Westad. *Decisive Encounters: The Chinese Civil War, 1946–1950.* Stanford, 2003. An engagingly written work that introduces the reader to the salient political and military events that led to the eventual defeat of the Guomindang.

New Conflagrations: World War II and the Cold War

chapter 36

A Japanese child crouches and cries in the rubble of Hiroshima in the aftermath of the atomic bombing, expressing the profound sadness of war and its devastating weapons.

PART 7

EYEWITNESS:
Victor Tolley finds Tea and Sympathy in Nagasaki

On 6 August 1945, as he listened to the armed services radio on Saipan (a U.S.-controlled island in the north Pacific), U.S. marine Victor Tolley heard the news: the president of the United States announced that a "terrible new weapon" had been deployed against the city of Hiroshima, Japan. Tolley and the other marines rejoiced, realizing that the terrible new weapon—the atomic bomb—might end the war and relieve them of the burden of invading Japan. A few days later Tolley heard that the city of Nagasaki had also been hit with an atomic bomb. He remembered the ominous remarks that accompanied the news of this atomic destruction: radio announcers suggested it might be decades before the cities would be inhabitable.

Imagine Tolley's astonishment when a few weeks later, after the Japanese surrender, he and his buddies were assigned to the U.S. occupation forces in Nagasaki. Assured by a superior officer that Nagasaki was "very safe," Tolley lived there for three months, during which he became very familiar with the devastation wrought by the atomic bomb. On his first day in Nagasaki, Tolley investigated the city. As he noted, "It was just like walking into a tomb. There was total silence. You could smell this death all around ya. There was a terrible odor."

Tolley also became acquainted with some of the Japanese survivors in Nagasaki, which proved to be an eye-opening experience. After seeing "young children with sores and burns all over," Tolley, having become separated from his unit, encountered another young child. He and the boy communicated despite the language barrier between them. Tolley showed the child pictures of his wife and two daughters. The Japanese boy excitedly took Tolley home to meet his surviving family, his father and his pregnant sister. Tolley recalled,

This little kid ran upstairs and brought his father down. A very nice Japanese gentleman. He could speak English. He bowed and said, "We would be honored if you would come upstairs and have some tea with us." I went upstairs in this strange Japanese house. I noticed on the mantel a picture of a young Japanese soldier. I asked him, "Is this your son?" He said, "That is my daughter's husband. We don't know if he's alive. We haven't heard." The minute he said that, it dawned on me that they suffered the same as we did. They lost sons and daughters and relatives, and they hurt too.

Before his chance meeting with this Japanese family, Tolley had felt nothing except contempt for the Japanese. He pointed out, "We were trained to kill them. They're our enemy. Look what they did in Pearl Harbor. They asked for it and now we're gonna give it to 'em. That's how I felt until I met this young boy and his family." But after coming face-to-face with his enemies, Tolley saw only their common humanity, their suffering, and their hurt. The lesson he learned was that "these people didn't want to fight us."

The civility that reemerged at the end of the war was little evident during the war years. The war began and ended with Japan. In 1931 Japan invaded Manchuria, thereby ending the post–Great War peace, and the United States concluded hostilities by dropping atomic bombs on Hiroshima and Nagasaki. Between 1931 and 1945 the conflict expanded well beyond east Asia. By 1941 World War II was a truly global war. Hostilities spread from east Asia and the Pacific to Europe, north Africa, and the Atlantic, and large and small nations from North America, Asia, Europe, Africa, and Australia came into close contact for the duration of the war. Beyond its immense geographic scope, World War II exceeded even the Great War (1914–1918) in demonstrating the willingness of societies to make enormous sacrifices in lives and other resources to achieve complete victory. At least sixty million people perished in the war, and civilian deaths likely outnumbered military casualties. In this total war, contacts with enemies, occupiers, and liberators affected populations around the world. World War II redefined gender roles and relations between colonial peoples and their masters, as women contributed to their nations' war efforts and as colonial peoples exploited the war's weakening of imperial nations.

The atomic age and cold war that began as World War II ended complicated the task of postwar recovery. The cold war, over time, illustrated how deep the rift between the United States of America and the Union of Soviet Socialist Republics (USSR) had grown since 1945, and signaled a major realignment in international relations and the global balance of power. The cold war was a strategic struggle that developed after World War II between the United States and its allies on the one hand and the USSR and its allied communist countries on the other. It was this clash between the forces of democratic capitalism and communism, each armed with increasingly powerful nuclear weapons, that gave rise to a new set of global relationships, shaping the foreign policies, economic systems, and political institutions of nations throughout the world. The hostility between these new adversaries resulted in a divided world. First Europe, and Germany in particular, split into separate blocs and states. Then the cold war became global in scale as the superpowers came into conflict in nations as far afield as Korea and Cuba. Over the course of four decades, the cold war evolved from mutual hostility to peaceful coexistence and détente, finally coming to a close near the end of the twentieth century.

ORIGINS OF WORLD WAR II

In 1941 two major alliances squared off against each other. Japan, Germany, and Italy, along with their conquered territories, formed the Axis powers, the name of the alignment between Nazi Germany and Fascist Italy that had been formed in October 1936. The term was used later to include Germany's other allies in World War II, especially Japan. The Allied powers included France and its empire; Great Britain and its empire and Commonwealth allies (such as Canada, Australia, and New Zealand); the Soviet Union; China; and the United States and its allies in Latin America. The construction of these global alliances took place over the course of the 1930s and early 1940s.

Driven in part by a desire to revise the peace settlements that followed the Great War and affected by the economic distress of the worldwide depression, Japan, Italy, and Germany engaged in a campaign of territorial expansion that ultimately broke apart the structure of international cooperation that had kept the world from violence in the 1920s. These *revisionist powers,* so called because they revised, or overthrew, the terms of the post–Great War peace, confronted nations that were committed to the international system and to the avoidance of another world war. To expand their global influence, the revisionist nations remilitarized and conquered territories they deemed central to their needs and to the spread of their imperial control. The Allies acquiesced to the revisionist powers' early aggressive actions,

a landing area for armies bound for Nanjing. By December 1937 Shanghai and Nanjing had fallen, and during the following six months Japanese forces won repeated victories.

The Rape of Nanjing China became the first nation to experience the horrors of World War II: brutal warfare against civilians and repressive occupation. During the invasion of China, Japanese forces used methods of warfare that led to mass death and suffering on a new, almost unimaginable, level. Chinese civilians were among the first to feel the effects of aerial bombing of urban centers; the people of Shanghai died by the tens of thousands when Japanese bombers attacked the city to soften Chinese resistance. What became known as the Rape of Nanjing demonstrated the horror of the war as the residents of Nanjing became victims of Japanese troops inflamed by war passion and a sense of racial superiority. Over the course of two months, Japanese soldiers raped seven thousand women, murdered hundreds of thousands of unarmed soldiers and civilians, and burned one-third of the homes in Nanjing. Four hundred thousand Chinese lost their lives as Japanese soldiers used them for bayonet practice and machine-gunned them into open pits.

Chinese Resistance Despite Japanese military successes and the subsequent Japanese occupation of Chinese lands, Chinese resistance persisted throughout the war. Japanese aggression aroused feelings of nationalism among the Chinese that continued to grow as the war wore on. By September 1937 nationalists and communists had agreed on a "united front" policy against the Japanese, uniting themselves into standing armies of some 1.7 million soldiers. Although Chinese forces failed to defeat the Japanese, who retained naval and air superiority, they tied down half the Japanese army, 750,000 soldiers, by 1941.

Throughout the war, the coalition of nationalists and communists threatened to fall apart. Although neither side was willing to risk open civil war, the two groups engaged in numerous military clashes as their forces competed for both control of enemy territory and political control within China. Those clashes rendered Chinese resistance less effective, and while both sides continued the war against Japan, each fought ultimately for its own advantage. The nationalists suffered major casualties in their battles with Japanese forces, but they kept the Guomindang government alive by moving inland to Chongqing. Meanwhile, the communists carried on guerrilla operations against the Japanese invaders. Lacking air force and artillery, communist guerrillas staged hit-and-run operations from their mountain bases, sabotaged bridges and railroads, and harassed Japanese troops. The guerrillas did not defeat the Japanese, but they captured the loyalty of many Chinese peasants through their resistance to the Japanese and their moderate policies of land reform. At the end of the war, the communists were poised to lead China.

Japanese soldiers execute Chinese prisoners. In the Japanese invasion of China, four hundred thousand Chinese died when the Japanese used them for bayonet practice or executed them.

but after they had been attacked, in the late 1930s and early 1940s, the Allies engaged the Axis powers in a total war.

Japan's War in China

The global conflict opened with Japan's attacks on China in the 1930s: the conquest of Manchuria between 1931 and 1932 was the first step in the revisionist process of expansionism and aggression. Within Japan a battle continued between supporters and opponents of the aggressive policies adopted in Manchuria, but during the course of the 1930s the militarist position dominated, and for the most part civilians lost control of the government and the military. In 1933, after the League of Nations condemned its actions in Manchuria, Japan withdrew from the league and followed an ultranationalist and promilitary policy.

Seeing territorial control as essential to its survival, Japan launched a full-scale invasion of China in 1937. A battle between Chinese and Japanese troops at the Marco Polo Bridge in Beijing in July 1937 was the opening move in Japan's undeclared war against China. Japanese troops took Beijing and then moved south toward Shanghai and Nanjing, the capital of China. Japanese naval and air forces bombed Shanghai, killing thousands of civilians, and secured it as

Japanese soldiers in 1938 engaged in strenuous physical education and kept fit in order to fight the Chinese.

The Japanese invasion of China met with intense international opposition, but by that time Japan had chosen another path—and it was an auspicious time to further its attack on the international system. Other world powers, distracted by depression and military aggression in Europe, could offer little in the way of an effective response to Japanese actions. The government of Japan aligned itself with the other revisionist nations, Germany and Italy, by signing the Tripartite Pact, a ten-year military and economic pact, in September 1940. Japan also cleared the way for further empire building in Asia and the Pacific basin by concluding a neutrality pact with the Soviet Union in April 1941, thereby precluding hostilities on any other front, especially in Manchuria. Japan did not face determined opposition to its expansion until December 1941, when conflict with the United States created a much broader field of action for Japan and its growing empire.

Italian and German Aggression

Italy's expansionism helped destabilize the post–Great War peace and spread World War II to the European continent. Italians suffered tremendously in World War I. Six hundred thousand Italian soldiers died, and the national economy never recovered sufficiently for Italy to function as an equal to other European military and economic powers. Many Italians expected far greater recompense and respect than they received at the conclusion of the Great War. Rather than being treated as a real partner in victory by Britain and France, Italy found itself shut out of the divisions of the territorial spoils of war.

Italy Benito Mussolini promised to bring glory to Italy through the acquisition of territories that it had been denied after the Great War. Italy's conquest of Ethiopia in 1935 and 1936, when added to the previously annexed Libya, created an overseas empire. Italy also intervened in the Spanish Civil War (1936–1939) on the side of General Francisco Franco (1892–1975), whose militarists overthrew the republican government, and annexed Albania in 1939. (Mussolini viewed Albania as a bridgehead for expansion into the Balkans.) The invasion and conquest of Ethiopia in particular infuriated other nations; but, as with Japan's invasion of Manchuria, the League of Nations offered little effective opposition.

What angered nonrevisionists about Italy's conquest of Ethiopia was not just the broken peace. The excessive use of force against the Ethiopians also rankled. Mussolini sent an army of 250,000 soldiers armed with tanks, poison gas, artillery, and aircraft to conquer the Ethiopians, who were entirely unprepared for the assault. The mechanized troops mowed them down. Italy lost 2,000 soldiers while 275,000 Ethiopians lost their lives. Despite its victories in Ethiopia, Italy's prospects for world glory never appeared quite as bright as Japan's, especially since few Italians wanted to go to war. Throughout the interwar years, Italy played a diplomatic game that kept European nations guessing as to its future intentions, but by 1938 it was firmly on the side of the Axis.

Germany Japan and Italy were the first nations to challenge the post–World War I settlements through territorial conquest, but it was Germany that systematically undid the Treaty of Versailles and the fragile peace of the interwar years. Most Germans and their political leaders deeply resented the harsh terms imposed on their nation in 1919, but even the governments of other European nations eventually recognized the extreme nature of the Versailles treaty's terms and turned a blind eye to the revisionist actions of Adolf Hitler (1889–1945) and his government. Hitler came to power in 1933, riding a wave of public discontent with Germany's postwar position of powerlessness and the suffering caused by the Great Depression. Hitler referred to the signing of the 1918 armistice as the "November crime" and blamed it on those he viewed as Germany's internal enemies: Jews, communists, and liberals of all sorts. Neighboring European states—Poland, France, Czechoslovakia, Yugoslavia, Hungary, and Austria—also shared in the blame. Hitler's scheme for ridding Germany of its enemies and reasserting its power was remilitarization—which was legally denied to Germany under the Versailles treaty. Germany's dictator abandoned the peaceful efforts of his predecessors to ease the provisions of the treaty and proceeded unilaterally to destroy it step-by-step. Hitler's aggressive foreign policy helped relieve the German public's feeling of war shame

Ethiopian soldiers train with outmoded equipment that proves no match for Italian forces. At the end of the Great War, Italy, under Benito Mussolini, sought to redress perceived wrongs that denied it territorial gain by conquering Ethiopia with an army of a quarter-million soldiers.

and depression trauma. After withdrawing Germany from the League of Nations in 1933, his government carried out an ambitious plan to strengthen the German armed forces. Hitler reinstated universal military service in 1935, and in the following year his troops entered the previously demilitarized Rhineland that bordered France. Germany joined with Italy in the Spanish Civil War, during which Hitler's troops, especially the air force, honed their skills. In 1938 Hitler began the campaign of expansion that ultimately led to the outbreak of World War II in Europe.

Germany's forced *Anschluss* ("union") with Austria took place in March 1938. Hitler justified this annexation as an attempt to reintegrate all Germans into a single homeland. Europe's major powers, France and Britain, did nothing in response, thereby enhancing Hitler's reputation in the German military and deepening his already deep contempt for the democracies. Soon thereafter, using the same rationale, the Nazis attempted to gain control of the Sudetenland, the western portion of Czechoslovakia. This region was inhabited largely by ethnic Germans, whom Hitler conveniently regarded as persecuted minorities. Although the Czech government was willing to make concessions to the Sudeten Germans, Hitler in September 1938 demanded the immediate cession of the Sudetenland to the German Reich. Against the desires of the Czechoslovak government, the leaders of France and Britain accommodated Hitler and allowed Germany to annex the Sudetenland. Neither the French nor the British were willing to risk a military confrontation with Germany to defend Czechoslovakian territory.

Peace for Our Time At the Munich Conference held in September 1938, European politicians consolidated the policy that came to be known throughout the 1930s as *appeasement*. Attended by representatives of Italy, France, Great Britain, and Germany, the meeting revealed how most nations outside the revisionist sphere had decided to deal with territorial expansion by aggressive nations, especially Germany. In conceding demands to Hitler, or "appeasing" him, the British and French governments extracted a promise that Hitler would cease further efforts to expand German territorial claims. Their goal was to keep peace in Europe, even if it meant making major concessions. Because of public opposition to war, the governments of France and Britain approved the Munich accord. Britain's prime minister, Neville Chamberlain (1869–1940), arrived home from Munich to announce that the meeting had achieved "peace for our time." Unprepared for war and distressed by the depression, nations sympathetic to Britain and France also embraced peace as an admirable goal in the face of aggression by the revisionist nations.

Hitler, however, refused to be bound by the Munich agreement, and in the next year German troops occupied most of Czechoslovakia. As Hitler next threatened Poland, it became clear that the policy of appeasement was a practical and moral failure, which caused Britain and France to abandon it by guaranteeing the security of Poland. By that time Joseph Stalin (1879–1953) was convinced that British and French leaders were conspiring to deflect German aggression toward the Soviet Union. Despite deep ideological differences that divided communists from Nazis, Stalin accordingly sought an accommodation with the Nazi regime. In August 1939 the foreign ministers of the Soviet Union and Germany signed the Russian-German Treaty of Nonaggression, an agreement that shocked and outraged the world. By the terms of the pact, the two nations agreed not to attack each other, and they promised neutrality in the event that either of them went to war with a third party. Additionally, a secret protocol divided eastern Europe into German and Soviet spheres of influence. The protocol provided for German control over western Poland while granting the Soviet Union a free hand in eastern Poland, eastern Romania, Finland, Estonia, Latvia, and Lithuania. Hitler was ready to conquer Europe.

TOTAL WAR: THE WORLD UNDER FIRE

Two months after the United States became embroiled in World War II, President Franklin Roosevelt (1882–1945) delivered one of his famous radio broadcasts, known as fireside chats. In it he explained the nature of the war: "This war is a new kind of war," he said. "It is warfare in terms of every continent, every island, every sea, every air lane." There was little exaggeration in FDR's analysis. Before World War II was over, almost every nation had participated in it. Battles raged across the vast Pacific and Atlantic oceans, across Europe and northern Africa, and throughout much of Asia. Virtually every weapon known to humanity was thrown into the war. More than the Great War, this was a conflict where entire societies engaged in warfare and mobilized every available material and human resource.

The war between Japan and China had already stretched over eight years when European nations stormed into battle. Between 1939 and 1941, nations inside and outside Europe were drawn into the conflict. They included the French and British colonies in Africa, India, and the British Dominion allies: Canada, Australia, and New Zealand. Germany's stunning military successes in 1939 and 1940 focused attention on Europe, but after the Soviet Union and the United States entered the war in 1941, the conflict took on global proportions. Almost every nation in the world had gone to war by 1945.

Blitzkrieg: Germany Conquers Europe

During World War II it became common for aggressor nations to avoid overt declarations of war. Instead, the new armed forces relied on surprise, stealth, and swiftness for their conquests. Germany demonstrated the advantages of that strategy in Poland. German forces, banking on their air force's ability to soften resistance and on their *Panzer* ("armored") columns' unmatched mobility and speed, moved into Poland unannounced on 1 September 1939. Within a month they subdued its western expanses while the Soviets took the eastern sections in accordance with the Nazi-Soviet pact. The Germans stunned the world, especially Britain and France, with their *Blitzkrieg* ("lightning war") and sudden victory.

While the forces of Britain and France coalesced to defend Europe without facing much direct action with Nazi forces, the battle of the Atlantic already raged. This sea confrontation between German *Unterseeboote* ("U-boats,"

German dive-bombers like this one dominated the early air war in World War II and played a significant role in Blitzkrieg.

or submarines) and British ship convoys carrying food and war matériel proved decisive in the European theater of war. The battle of the Atlantic could easily have gone either way—to the German U-boats attempting to cut off Britain's vital imports or to the convoys devised by the British navy to protect its ships from submarine attacks. Although British intelligence cracked Germany's secret code to the great advantage of the Allies, advance knowledge of the location of submarines was still not always available. Moreover, the U-boats began traveling in wolf packs to negate the effectiveness of convoys protected by aircraft and destroyers.

The Fall of France As the sea battle continued, Germany prepared to break through European defenses. In April 1940 the Germans occupied Denmark and Norway, then launched a full-scale attack on western Europe. Their offensive against Belgium, France, and the Netherlands began in May, and again the Allies were jolted by Blitzkrieg tactics. Belgium and the Netherlands fell first, and the French signed an armistice in June. The fall of France convinced Italy's Benito Mussolini that the Germans were winning the war, and it was time to enter the conflict and reap any potential benefits his partnership with the Germans might offer.

Before the battle of France, Hitler had boasted to his staff, "Gentlemen, you are about to witness the most famous

victory in history!" Given France's rapid fall, Hitler was not far wrong. Field Marshal Erwin Rommel put it more colorfully: "The war has become practically a lightning Tour de France!" In a moment of exquisite triumph, Hitler had the French sign their armistice in the very railroad car in which the Germans had signed the armistice in 1918. Trying to rescue some Allied troops before the fall of France, the British engineered a retreat at Dunkirk, but it could not hide the bleak failure of the Allied troops. Britain now stood alone against the German forces.

The Battle of Britain The Germans therefore launched the Battle of Britain, led by its air force, the *Luftwaffe*. They hoped to defeat Britain almost solely through air attacks. "The Blitz," as the British called this air war, rained bombs on heavily populated metropolitan areas, especially London, and killed more than forty thousand British civilians. The Royal Air Force staved off defeat, however, forcing Hitler to abandon plans to invade Britain. By the summer of 1941, Hitler's conquests included the Balkans, and the battlefront extended to north Africa, where the British fought both the Italians and the Germans. The swastika-bedecked Nazi flag now waved from the streets of Paris to the Acropolis in Athens, and Hitler had succeeded beyond his dreams in his quest to reverse the outcome of World War I.

The German Invasion of the Soviet Union

Flush with victory in the spring of 1941, Hitler turned his sights on the Soviet Union. This land was the ultimate German target, from which Jews, Slavs, and Bolsheviks could be expelled or exterminated to create more *Lebensraum* ("living space") for resettled Germans. Believing firmly in the bankruptcy of the Soviet system, Hitler said of Operation Barbarossa, the code name for the June invasion of the Soviet Union, "You only have to kick in the door, and the whole rotten structure will come crashing down."

Operation Barbarossa On 22 June 1941, Adolf Hitler ordered his armed forces to invade the Soviet Union. For the campaign against the Soviet Union, the German military assembled the largest and most powerful invasion force in history, attacking with 3.6 million soldiers, thirty-seven hundred tanks, and twenty-five hundred planes. The governments of Hungary, Finland, and Romania declared war on the Soviet Union and augmented the German invasion force with their own military contingents totaling about thirty divisions. The invasion, along a front of 3,000 kilometers (1,900 miles), took Stalin by surprise and caught the Red Army off guard. By December 1941 the Germans had captured the Russian heartland, Leningrad had come under siege, and German troops had reached the gates of Moscow. Germany seemed assured of victory.

However, German Blitzkrieg tactics that had earlier proved so effective in Poland and western Europe failed the Germans in the vast expanses of Russia. Hitler and his military leaders underestimated Soviet personnel reserves and industrial capacity. Within a matter of weeks, the 150 German divisions faced 360 divisions of the Red Army. Also, in the early stages of the war Stalin ordered Soviet industry to relocate to areas away from the front. About 80 percent of firms manufacturing war matériel moved to the Ural Mountains between August and October 1941. As a result, the capacity of Soviet industry outstripped that of German industry. The Soviets also received crucial equipment from their allies, notably trucks from the United States. By the time the German forces reached the outskirts of Moscow, fierce Soviet resistance had produced eight hundred thousand German casualties.

The arrival of winter—the most severe in decades—helped Soviet military efforts and prevented the Germans from capturing Moscow. So sure of an early victory were the Germans that they did not bother to supply their troops with winter clothing and boots. One hundred thousand soldiers suffered frostbite, and two thousand of them underwent amputation. The Red Army, in contrast, prepared for winter and

Adolf Hitler proudly walks through conquered Paris in 1940, with the Eiffel Tower as a backdrop.

The devastation caused by German bombardments is visible in the wreckage of a London neighborhood in 1944.

found further comfort as the United States manufactured thirteen million pairs of felt-lined winter boots. By early December, Soviet counterattacks along the entire front stopped German advances.

German forces regrouped and inflicted heavy losses on the Red Army during the spring. The Germans briefly regained the military initiative, and by June 1942 German armies raced toward the oil fields of the Caucasus and the city of Stalingrad. As the Germans came on Stalingrad in September, Soviet fortunes of war reached their nadir. At this point the Russians dug in. "Not a step back," Stalin ordered, and he called on his troops to fight a "patriotic" war for Russia. Behind those exhortations lay a desperate attempt to stall the Germans with a bloody street-by-street defense of Stalingrad until the Red Army could regroup for a counterattack.

Battles in Asia and the Pacific

Before 1941 the United States was inching toward greater involvement in the war. After Japan invaded China in 1937, Roosevelt called for a quarantine on aggressors, but his plea fell mostly on deaf ears. However, as war broke out in Europe and tensions with Japan increased, the United States took action. In 1939 it instituted a cash-and-carry policy of supplying the British, in which the British paid cash and carried the materials on their ships. More significant was the lend-lease program initiated in 1941, in which

the United States "lent" destroyers and other war goods to the British in return for the lease of naval bases. The program later extended such aid to the Soviets, the Chinese, and many others.

Pearl Harbor German victories over the Dutch and the French in 1940 and Great Britain's precarious military position in Europe and in Asia encouraged the Japanese to project their influence into southeast Asia. Particularly attractive were the Dutch East Indies (now Indonesia) and British-controlled Malaya, regions rich in raw materials such as tin, rubber, and petroleum. In September of 1940, moving with the blessings of the German-backed Vichy government of France, Japanese forces began to occupy French Indochina (now Vietnam, Laos, and Cambodia). The government of the United States responded to that situation by freezing Japanese assets in the United States and by imposing a complete embargo on oil. Great Britain, the Commonwealth of Nations, and the independent colonial government of the Dutch East Indies supported the U.S. oil embargo. Economic pressure, however, did not persuade the Japanese to accede to U.S. demands, which included the renunciation of the Tripartite Pact and the withdrawal of Japanese forces from China and southeast Asia. To Japanese militarists, given the equally unappetizing alternatives of succumbing to U.S. demands or engaging the United States in war, war seemed the lesser of two evils. In October 1941, defense

Flames consumed U.S. battleships in Pearl Harbor after the Japanese attack on 7 December 1941.

PART 7

minister general Tojo Hideki (1884–1948) assumed the office of prime minister, and he and his cabinet set in motion plans for war against Great Britain and the United States.

The Japanese hoped to destroy American naval capacity in the Pacific with an attack at Pearl Harbor and to clear the way for the conquest of southeast Asia and the creation of a defensive Japanese perimeter that would thwart the Allies' ability to strike at Japan's homeland. On 7 December 1941, "a date which will live in infamy," as Franklin Roosevelt concluded, Japanese pilots took off from six aircraft carriers to attack Hawai`i. More than 350 Japanese bombers, fighters, and torpedo planes struck in two waves, sinking or disabling eighteen ships and destroying more than two hundred. Except for the U.S. aircraft carriers, which were out of the harbor at the time, American naval power in the Pacific was devastated.

On 11 December 1941, though not compelled to do so by treaty, Hitler and Mussolini declared war on the United States. That move provided the United States with the only reason it needed to declare war on Germany and Italy. The United States, Great Britain, and the Soviet Union came together in a coalition that linked two vast and interconnected theaters of war, the European and Asian-Pacific theaters, and ensured the defeat of Germany and Japan. Adolf Hit-

ler's gleeful reaction to the outbreak of war between Japan and the United States proved mistaken: "Now it is impossible for us to lose the war: We now have an ally who has never been vanquished in three thousand years." More accurate was Winston Churchill (1874–1965), prime minister of Britain, who expressed a vast sense of relief and a more accurate assessment of the situation when he said, "So we had won after all!"

Japanese Victories After Pearl Harbor the Japanese swept on to one victory after another. The Japanese coordinated their strike against Pearl Harbor with simultaneous attacks against the Philippines, Guam, Wake Island, Midway Island, Hong Kong, Thailand, and British Malaya. For the next year the Japanese military maintained the initiative in southeast Asia and the Pacific, capturing Borneo, Burma, the Dutch East Indies, and several Aleutian Islands off Alaska. Australia and New Zealand were now in striking distance. The Japanese navy emerged almost unscathed from these campaigns. The humiliating surrender of British-held Singapore in February 1942 dealt a blow to British prestige and shattered any myths of European military invincibility.

Singapore was a symbol of European power in Asia. The slogan under which Japan pursued expansion in Asia was

After the Pearl Harbor attack, Americans expressed great hostility toward the Japanese nationals and Japanese Americans living in the United States, primarily on the west coast. In 1942 President Franklin Roosevelt authorized the forcible removal of approximately 120,000 Japanese and Japanese Americans to relocation or internment camps. This photograph from Seattle in March 1942 shows both the gloom and the patriotism of those on a train bound for a camp; the family is flashing the World War II "V for victory" sign while a boy holds the American flag.

"Asia for Asians," implying that the Japanese would lead Asian peoples to independence from the despised European imperialists and the international order they dominated. In this struggle for Asian independence, Japan required the region's resources and therefore sought to build a "Greater East Asia Co-Prosperity Sphere." The appeal to Asian independence at first struck a responsive chord, but conquest and brutal occupation made it soon obvious to most Asians that the real agenda was "Asia for the Japanese." Proponents of the Greater East Asia Co-Prosperity Sphere advocated Japan's expansion in Asia and the Pacific while cloaking their territorial and economic designs with the idealism of Asian nationalism.

Defeat of the Axis Powers

The entry of the Soviet Union and the United States into the war in 1941 was decisive, because personnel reserves and industrial capacity were the keys to the Allied victories in the European and Asia-Pacific theaters. Despite the brutal exploitation of conquered territories, neither German nor Japanese war production matched that of the Allies, who outproduced their enemies at every turn. The U.S. automotive industry alone, for instance, produced more than four million armored, combat, and supply vehicles of all kinds during the war. Not until the United States joined the struggle in 1942 did the tide in the battle in the Atlantic turn in

favor of the Allies. Although German submarines sank a total of 2,452 Allied merchant ships and 175 Allied warships in the course of six years, U.S. naval shipyards simply built more "Liberty Ships" than the Germans could sink. By the end of 1943, sonar, aircraft patrols, and escort aircraft from carriers finished the U-boat as a strategic threat.

Allied Victory in Europe By 1943, German forces in Russia lost the momentum and faced bleak prospects as the Soviets retook territory. Moscow never fell, and the battle for Stalingrad, which ended in February 1943, marked the first large-scale victory for Soviet forces. Desperate German counteroffensives failed repeatedly, and the Red Army, drawing on enormous personnel and material reserves, pushed the German invaders out of Russian territory. By 1944 the Soviets had advanced into Romania, Hungary, and Poland, reaching the suburbs of Berlin in April 1945. At that point, the Soviets had inflicted more than six million casualties on the German enemy—twice the number of the original German invasion force. The Red Army had broken the back of the German war machine.

With the Eastern front disintegrating under the Soviet onslaught, British and U.S. forces attacked the Germans from north Africa and then through Italy. In August 1944 the Allies forced Italy to withdraw from the Axis and to

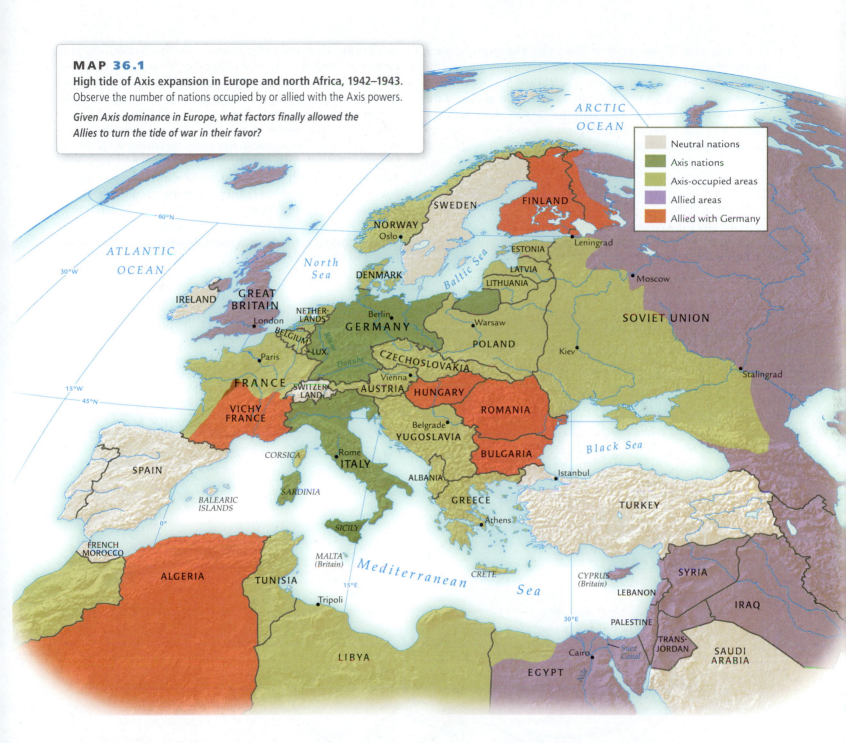

MAP 36.1

High tide of Axis expansion in Europe and north Africa, 1942–1943.
Observe the number of nations occupied by or allied with the Axis powers.

Given Axis dominance in Europe, what factors finally allowed the Allies to turn the tide of war in their favor?

Legend:
- Neutral nations
- Axis nations
- Axis-occupied areas
- Allied areas
- Allied with Germany

join them. In the meantime, the Germans also prepared for an Allied offensive in the west, where the British and U.S. forces opened a front in France. On D-Day, 6 June 1944, British and U.S. troops landed on the French coast of Normandy. Although the fighting was deadly for all sides, the Germans were overwhelmed. With the two fronts collapsing around them and round-the-clock strategic bombing by the United States and Britain leveling German cities, German resistance faded. Since early 1943, Britain's Royal Air Force had committed itself to area bombing in which centers of cities became the targets of nighttime raids. U.S. planes attacked industrial targets in daytime. The British firebombing raid on Dresden in February 1945 literally cooked German men, women, and children in their bomb shelters: 135,000 people died in the firestorm. A brutal street-by-street battle in Berlin between Germans and Russians, along with a British and U.S. sweep through western Germany, forced Germany's unconditional surrender on 8 May 1945. A week earlier, on 30 April, as fighting flared right outside his Berlin bunker, Hitler committed suicide, as did many of his Nazi compatriots. He therefore did not live to see the Soviet red flag flying over the Berlin *Reichstag,* Germany's parliament building.

Turning the Tide in the Pacific The turning point in the Pacific war came in a naval engagement near the Midway Islands on 4 June 1942. The United States prevailed there partly because U.S. aircraft carriers had survived the attack on Pearl Harbor. Although the United States had few carriers, it did have a secret weapon: a code-breaking operation known as *Magic,* which enabled a cryptographer monitoring Japanese radio frequencies to discover the plan to attack Midway. On the morning of 4 June, thirty-six carrier-launched dive-bombers attacked the Japanese fleet, sinking three Japanese carriers in one five-minute strike and a fourth one later in the day. This victory changed the character of the war in the Pacific. Although there was no immediate shift in Japanese fortunes, the Allies took the offensive. They adopted an island-hopping strategy, capturing islands from which they could make direct air assaults on Japan. Deadly, tenacious fighting characterized these battles in which the United States and its allies gradually retook islands in the Marianas and the Philippines and then, early in 1945, moved toward areas more threatening to Japan: Iwo Jima and Okinawa.

MAP 36.2

World War II in Asia and the Pacific.

Compare the geographic conditions of the Asian-Pacific theater with those of the European theater.

What kinds of resources were necessary to win in the Asian-Pacific theater as opposed to the European theater?

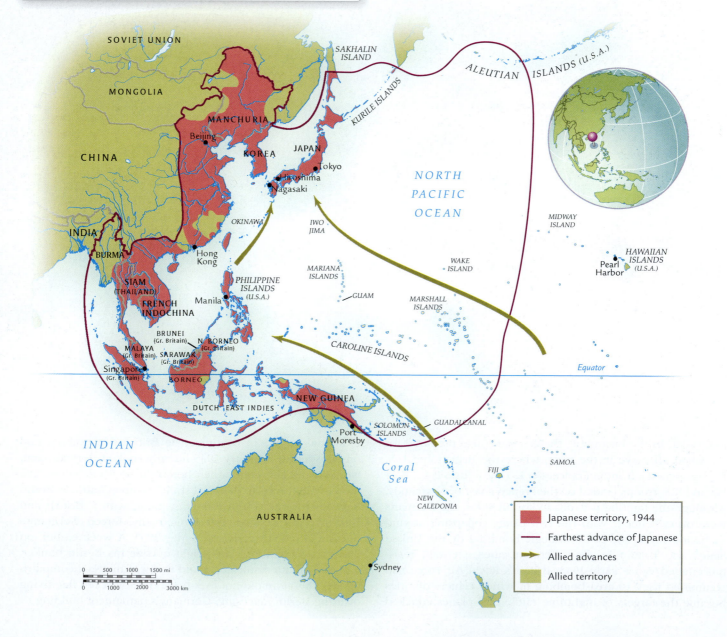

Legend:
- Japanese territory, 1944
- Farthest advance of Japanese
- Allied advances
- Allied territory

sources from the past

A Hiroshima Maiden's Tale

Yamaoka Michiko, at fifteen years of age, worked as an operator at a telephone exchange in Hiroshima and attended girls' high school. Many young women had been mobilized for work during World War II, and they viewed even civilian work on telephone exchanges as a means of helping to protect Japan during wartime. On the morning of 6 August 1945, when the first U.S. atomic bomb used in battle devastated Hiroshima, Yamaoka Michiko had just started off for work.

That morning I left the house at about seven forty-five. I heard that the B-29s [U.S. bomber planes] had already gone home. Mom told me, "Watch out, the B-29s might come again." My house was one point three kilometers from the hypocenter [the exact point of the atomic bomb's impact in Hiroshima]. My place of work was five hundred meters from the hypocenter. I walked toward the hypocenter. . . . I heard the faint sound of planes. . . . The planes were tricky. Sometimes they only pretended to leave. I could still hear the very faint sound of planes. . . . I thought, how strange, so I put my right hand above my eyes and looked up to see if I could spot them. The sun was dazzling. That was the moment.

There was no sound. I felt something strong. It was terribly intense. I felt colors. It wasn't heat. You can't really say it was yellow, and it wasn't blue. At that moment I thought I would be the only one who would die. I said to myself, "Goodbye, Mom."

They say temperatures of seven thousand degrees centigrade hit me. You can't really say it washed over me. It's hard to describe. I simply fainted. I remember my body floating in the air. That was probably the blast, but I don't know how far I was blown. When I came to my senses, my surroundings were silent. There was no wind. I saw a threadlike light, so I felt I must be alive. I was under stones. I couldn't move my body. I heard voices crying, "Help! Water!" It was then I realized I wasn't the only one. . . .

"Fire! Run away! Help! Hurry up!" They weren't voices but moans of agony and despair. "I have to get help and shout," I thought. The person who rescued me was Mom, although she herself had been buried under our collapsed house. Mom knew the route I'd been taking. She came, calling out to me. I heard her voice and cried for help. Our surroundings were already starting to burn. Fires burst out from just the light itself. It didn't really drop. It just flashed. . . .

My clothes were burnt and so was my skin. I was in rags. I had braided my hair, but now it was like a lion's mane. There were people, barely breathing, trying to push their intestines back in. People with their legs wrenched off. Without heads. Or with faces burned and swollen out of shape. The scene I saw was a living hell.

Mom didn't say anything when she saw my face and I didn't feel any pain. She just squeezed my hand and told me to run. She was going to rescue my aunt. Large numbers of people were moving away from the flames. My eyes were still able to see, so I made my way toward the mountain, where there was no fire, toward Hijiyama. On this flight I saw a friend of mine from the phone exchange. She'd been inside her house and wasn't burned. I called her name, but she didn't respond. My face was so swollen she couldn't tell who I was. Finally, she recognized my voice. She said, "Miss Yamaoka, you look like a monster!" That's the first time I heard that word. I looked at my hands and saw my own skin was hanging down and the red flesh exposed. I didn't realize my face was swollen up because I was unable to see it. . . .

I spent the next year bedridden. All my hair fell out. When we went to relatives' houses later they wouldn't even let me in because they feared they'd catch the disease. There was neither treatment nor assistance for me. . . . It was just my Mom and me. Keloids [thick scar tissue] covered my face, my neck. I couldn't even move my neck. One eye was hanging down. I was unable to control my drooling because my lip had been burned off. . . .

The Japanese government just told us we weren't the only victims of the war. There was no support or treatment. It was probably harder for my Mom. Once she told me she tried to choke me to death. If a girl had terrible scars, a face you couldn't be born with, I understand that even a mother could want to kill her child. People threw stones at me and called me Monster. That was before I had my many operations.

For Further Reflection

■ What did Yamaoka Michiko's psychological and physical reaction to the atomic bombing of Hiroshima suggest about the nature of these new weapons? Why did friends and relatives treat her as if she were a "monster"?

Source: Yamaoka Michiko. "Eight Hundred Meters from the Hypocenter." In Haruko Taya Cook and Theodore F. Cook, *Japan at War: An Oral History.* New York: The New Press, 1992, pp. 384–87.

A photograph titled "Planes over Tokyo Bay," taken from the U.S.S. *Missouri*, visually captured a sense of U.S. power and victory on V-J Day, 1945.

Iwo Jima and Okinawa The fighting on Iwo Jima and Okinawa was savage. Innovative U.S. amphibious tactics were matched by the vigor and sacrifice of Japanese soldiers and pilots. On Okinawa the Japanese introduced the *kamikaze*—pilots who "volunteered" to fly planes with just enough fuel to reach an Allied ship and dive-bomb into it. In the two-month battle, the Japanese flew nineteen hundred kamikaze missions, sinking dozens of ships and killing more than five thousand U.S. soldiers. The kamikaze, and the defense mounted by Japanese forces and the 110,000 Okinawan civilians who died refusing to surrender, convinced many people in the United States that the Japanese would never capitulate.

Japanese Surrender The fall of Saipan in July 1944 and the subsequent conquest of Iwo Jima and Okinawa brought the Japanese homeland within easy reach of U.S. strategic bombers. Because high-altitude strikes in daylight failed to do much damage to industrial sites, military planners changed tactics. The release of napalm firebombs during low-altitude sorties at night met with devastating success. The firebombing of Tokyo in March 1945 destroyed 25 percent of the city's buildings, annihilated approximately one hundred thousand people, and made more than a million homeless. The final blows came on 6 and 9 August 1945, when the United States used its revolutionary new weapon, the atomic bomb, against the cities of Hiroshima and Nagasaki. The atomic bombs either instantaneously vaporized or slowly killed by radiation poisoning upward of two hundred thousand people.

The Soviet Union declared war on Japan on 8 August 1945, and this new threat, combined with the devastation caused by the bombs, persuaded Emperor Hirohito (1901–1989) to surrender unconditionally. The Japanese surrendered on 15 August, and the war was officially over on 2 September 1945. When Victor Tolley sipped his conciliatory cup of tea with a Nagasaki family, the images of ashen Hiroshima and firebombed Tokyo lingered as reminders of how World War II brought the war directly home to millions of civilians.

LIFE DURING WARTIME

The widespread bombing of civilian populations during World War II, from its beginning in China to its end in Hiroshima and Nagasaki, meant that there was no safe home front during the war. So too did the arrival of often brutal occupation forces in the wake of Japanese and German conquests in Asia and Europe. Strategic bombing slaughtered men, women, and children around the world, and occupation troops forced civilians to labor and die in work and extermination camps. In this total war, civilian death tolls far exceeded military casualties. Beside the record of the war's brutality can be placed testimony to the endurance of the human spirit personified in the contributions of resistance groups battling occupying forces, in the mobilized women, and in the survivors of bombings or concentration camps.

Occupation, Collaboration, and Resistance

Axis bombardments and invasion were followed by occupation, but the administration imposed on conquered territories by Japanese and German forces varied in character. In territories such as Manchukuo, Japanese-controlled China, Burma, and the Philippines, Japanese authorities installed puppet governments that served as agents of Japanese rule. Thailand remained an independent state after it aligned itself with Japan, for which it was rewarded with grants of territory from bordering Laos and Burma. Other conquered territories either were considered too unstable or unreliable for self-rule or were deemed strategically too important to be left alone. Thus territories such as Indochina (Laos, Cambodia, and Vietnam), Malaya, the Dutch East Indies, Hong Kong, Singapore, Borneo, and New Guinea came under direct military control.

In Europe, Hitler's racist ideology played a large role in determining how occupied territories were administered. As a rule, Hitler intended that most areas of western and northern Europe—populated by racially valuable people, according to him—would become part of a Greater Germanic Empire. Accordingly, Denmark retained its elected government and monarchy under German supervision. In Norway and Holland, whose governments had gone into exile, the

kamikaze (KAH-mih-kah-zee)

Germans left the civilian administration intact. Though northern France and the Atlantic coast came under military rule, the Vichy government remained the civilian authority in the unoccupied southeastern part of the country. Named for its locale in central France, the Vichy government provided a prominent place for those French willing to collaborate with German rule. The Germans had varying levels of involvement in eastern European and Balkan countries, but most conquered territories came under direct military rule as a prelude for harsh occupation, economic exploitation, and German settlement.

Exploitation Japanese and German authorities administered their respective empires for economic gain and proceeded to exploit the resources of the lands under their control for their own benefit regardless of the consequences for the conquered peoples. The occupiers pillaged all forms of economic wealth that could fuel the German and Japanese war machines. The most notorious form of economic exploitation involved the use of slave labor. As the demands of total war stimulated an insatiable appetite for workers, Japanese and German occupation authorities availed themselves of prisoners of war (POWs) and local populations to help meet labor shortages. By August 1944, more than seven million foreign workers labored inside the Third Reich. In China alone, the Japanese military mobilized more than ten million civilians and prisoners of war for forced labor. These slave laborers worked under horrific conditions and received little in the way of sustenance. Reaction to Japanese and German occupation varied from willing collaboration and acquiescence to open resistance.

Atrocities The treatment of POWs by German and Japanese authorities spoke to the horrors of the war as well. The death rate among soldiers in Japanese captivity averaged almost 30 percent, and the mortality rate among Chinese POWs was even higher. The racial ideologies of Hitler's regime were reflected in the treatment meted out to Soviet prisoners of war in particular. By February 1942, 2 million out of the 3.3 million Soviet soldiers in German custody had died from starvation, exposure, disease, or shootings.

Beyond the callous mistreatment of POWs, both German and Japanese authorities engaged in painful and often deadly medical experiments on thousands of unwilling subjects. In China, special Japanese military units, including the most infamous Unit 731, conducted cruel experiments on civilians and POWS. Victims, for example, became the subject of vivisection (defined as surgery conducted on a living organism) or amputation without anesthesia. Tens of thousands of Chinese became victims of germ warfare experiments, dying of bubonic plague, cholera, anthrax, and other diseases. German physicians carried out similarly unethical medical experiments in concentration camps. Experimentation ranged from high-altitude and hypothermia investigations by air force medical personnel, designed to facilitate the survival of German military personnel, to bone-grafting surgeries without anesthesia and exposing victims to phosgene and mustard gas to test possible antidotes. German doctors also directed painful serological experiments to determine how different "races" withstood various contagious diseases.

Collaboration The majority of people resented occupation forces but usually went on with life as much as possible. That response was especially true in many parts of Japanese-occupied lands in Asia, where local populations found little to resent in the change from one colonial administration to another. In Asia and Europe, moreover, local notables often joined the governments sponsored by the conquerors because collaboration offered them the means to gain power. In many instances, bureaucrats and police forces collaborated because they thought it was better that natives rule than Germans or Japanese. Businesspeople and companies often collaborated because they prospered financially from foreign rule. Still other people became collaborators and assisted occupation authorities by turning in friends and neighbors to get revenge for past grievances. In western Europe, anticommunism motivated Belgians, French, Danish, Dutch, and Norwegians to join units of Hitler's elite military formations, the Waffen SS, creating in the process a multinational army tens of thousands strong. In China several Guomindang generals went over to the Japanese, and local landowners and merchants in some regions of China set up substantial trade networks between the occupiers and the occupied.

Resistance Occupation and exploitation created an environment for resistance that took various forms. The most dramatic forms of resistance were campaigns of sabotage, armed assaults on occupation forces, and assassinations. Resistance fighters as diverse as Filipino guerrillas and Soviet partisans harassed and disrupted the military and economic activities of the occupiers by blowing up ammunition dumps, destroying communication and transportation facilities, and sabotaging industrial plants. More quietly, other resisters gathered intelligence, hid and protected refugees, or passed on clandestine newspapers. Resistance also comprised simple acts of defiance such as scribbling anti-German graffiti or walking out of bars and restaurants when Japanese soldiers entered. In the Netherlands, people associated the royal House of Orange with national independence and defiantly saluted traffic lights when they turned orange.

German and Japanese citizens faced different decisions about resistance than conquered peoples did. They had no antiforeign axe to grind, and any form of noncompliance constituted an act of treason that might assist the enemy and lead to defeat. Moreover, many institutions that might have formed the core of resistance in Japan and Germany, such as political parties, labor unions, or churches, were weak or had been destroyed. As a result, there was little or no opposition to the state and its policies in Japan, and in

Germany resistance remained generally sparse and ineffective. The most spectacular act of resistance against the Nazi regime came from a group of officers and civilians who tried to kill Adolf Hitler on 20 July 1944. The plot failed when their bomb explosion killed several bystanders but inflicted only minor injuries on Hitler.

Attempts to eradicate resistance movements in many instances merely fanned the flames of rebellion because of the indiscriminate reprisals against civilians. Despite the deadly retaliation meted out to people who resisted occupation, widespread resistance movements grew throughout the war. Life in resistance movements was tenuous at best and entailed great hardship—changing identities, hiding out, and risking capture and death. Nevertheless, the resisters kept alive their nations' hopes for liberation.

The Holocaust

By the end of World War II, the Nazi regime and its accomplices had physically annihilated millions of Jews, Slavs, Gypsies, homosexuals, Jehovah's Witnesses, communists, and others targeted as undesirables. Jews were the primary target of Hitler's racially motivated genocidal policies, and the resulting Holocaust epitomized the tragedy of conquest and occupation in World War II. The Holocaust, the near destruction of European Jews by Germany, was a human disaster on a scale previously unknown.

The murder of European Jews was preceded by a long history of vilification and persecution of Jews. For centuries Jewish communities had been singled out by Christian society as a "problem," and by the time the Nazi regime assumed power in 1933, anti-Semitism had contributed signifi-

Titled "Abyss of Human Horror," this photograph shows a survivor of the concentration camp at Nordhausen, Germany, on its liberation by Allies in 1945.

cantly to the widespread tolerance for anti-Jewish measures. Marked as outsiders, Jews found few defenders in their societies. Nazi determination to destroy the Jewish population and Europeans' passive acceptance of anti-Semitism laid the groundwork for genocide. In most war-torn European countries, the social and political forces that might have been expected to rally to the defense of Jews did not materialize.

Initially, the regime encouraged Jewish emigration. Although tens of thousands of Jews availed themselves of the opportunity to escape from Germany and Austria, many more were unable to do so. Most nations outside the Nazi orbit limited the migration of Jewish refugees, especially if the refugees were impoverished, as most of them were because Nazi authorities had previously appropriated their wealth. This situation worsened as German armies overran Europe, bringing an ever-larger number of Jews under Nazi control. At that point Nazi "racial experts" toyed with the idea of deporting Jews to Nisko, a proposed reservation in eastern Poland, or to the island of Madagascar, near Africa. Those ideas proved to be impractical and threatening. The concentration of Jews in one area led to the dangerous possibility of the creation of a separate Jewish state, hardly a solution to the so-called Jewish problem in the Nazi view.

The Final Solution The German occupation of Poland in 1939 and invasion of the Soviet Union in the summer of 1941 gave Hitler an opportunity to solve what he considered the problem of Jews in Germany and throughout Europe. When German armies invaded the Soviet Union in June 1941, the Nazis also dispatched three thousand troops in mobile detachments known as SS *Einsatzgruppen* ("action squads") to kill entire populations of Jews and Roma (or Gypsies) and many non-Jewish Slavs in the newly occupied territories. The action squads undertook mass shootings in ditches and ravines that became mass graves. By the spring of 1943, the special units had killed over one million Jews, and tens of thousands of Soviet citizens and Roma.

Sometime during 1941 the Nazi leadership committed to the "final solution" of the Jewish question, a solution that entailed the attempted murder of every Jew living in Europe. At the Wannsee Conference on 20 January 1942, fifteen leading Nazi bureaucrats gathered to discuss and coordinate the implementation of the final solution. They agreed to evacuate all Jews from Europe to camps in eastern Poland, where they would be worked to death or exterminated. Soon German forces—aided by collaborating authorities in foreign countries—rounded up Jews and deported them to specially constructed concentration camps in occupied Poland. The victims from nearby Polish ghettos and distant assembly points all across Europe traveled to their destinations by train. On the way the sick and the elderly often perished in overcrowded freight cars. The Jewish victims packed into these suffocating railway cars never knew their destinations, but rumors of mass deportations and mass deaths nonetheless spread among Jews remaining at

sources from the past

"We Will Never Speak about It in Public"

On 4 October 1943, Heinrich Himmler, leader of the SS and chief of the German police, gave a three-hour speech to an assembly of SS generals in the city of Posen (Poznan), in what is now Poland. In the following excerpt, Himmler justified Nazi anti-Jewish policies that culminated in mass murder. The speech, recorded on tape and in handwritten notes, was entered into evidence at the Nuremberg war crimes trials in 1945.

I also want to speak to you here, in complete frankness, of a really grave chapter. Amongst ourselves, for once, it shall be said quite openly, but all the same we will never speak about it in public. . . .

I am referring here to the evacuation of the Jews, the extermination of the Jewish people. This is one of the things that is easily said: "The Jewish people are going to be exterminated," that's what every Party member says, "sure, it's in our program, elimination of the Jews, extermination—it'll be done." And then they all come along, the 80 million worthy Germans, and each one has his one decent Jew. Of course, the others are swine, but this one, he is a first-rate Jew. Of all those who talk like that, not one has seen it happen, not one has had to go through with it. Most of you men know what it is like to see 100 corpses side by side, or 500 or 1,000. To have stood fast through this and except for cases of human weakness to have stayed decent, that has made us hard. This is an unwritten and never-to-be-written page of glory in our history. . . .

The wealth they possessed we took from them. I gave a strict order, which has been carried out by SS *Obergrup-penfuehrer* Pohl, that this wealth will of course be turned over to the Reich in its entirety. We have taken none of it for ourselves. Individuals who have erred will be punished in accordance with the order given by me at the start, threatening that anyone who takes as much as a single Mark of this money is a dead man. A number of SS men, they are not very many, committed this offense, and they shall die. There will be no mercy. We had the moral right, we had the duty towards our people, to destroy this people that wanted to destroy us. But we do not have the right to enrich ourselves by so much as a fur, as a watch, by one Mark or a cigarette or anything else. We do not want, in the end, because we destroyed a bacillus, to be infected by this bacillus and to die. I will never stand by and watch while even a small rotten spot develops or takes hold. Wherever it may form we will together burn it away. All in all, however, we can say that we have carried out this most difficult of tasks in a spirit of love for our people. And we have suffered no harm to our inner being, our soul, our character. . . .

For Further Reflection

■ Himmler argued that SS officers and soldiers "stayed decent" while overseeing the extermination of the Jews; why then does he focus so much attention on punishing those who took money from the dead Jews?

Source: International Military Tribunal. *Trial of the Major War Criminal,* Nuremberg, Germany, 1948; volume 29, Document 1919-PS. Translation Copyright 2002 Yad Vashem.

large and among the Allied government leaders, who were apparently apathetic to the fate of Jews.

In camps such as Kulmhof (Chelmno), Belzec, Majdanek, Sobibòr, Treblinka, and Auschwitz, the final solution took on an organized and technologically sophisticated character. Here, the killers introduced gassing as the most efficient means for mass extermination, though other means of destruction were always retained, such as electrocution, phenol injections, flamethrowers, hand grenades, and machine guns. The largest of the camps was Auschwitz, where at least one million Jews perished. Nazi camp personnel subjected victims from all corners of Europe to industrial work, starvation, medical experiments, and outright extermination. The German commandant of Auschwitz explained proudly how his camp became the most efficient at killing Jews: by using the fast-acting crystallized prussic acid Zyklon B as the gassing agent, by enlarging the size of the gas chambers, and by lulling victims into thinking they were going through a delousing process. At Auschwitz and elsewhere, the Germans also constructed large crematories to incinerate the bodies of gassed Jews and hide the evidence of their crimes. This systematic murder of Jews constituted what war crime tribunals later termed a "crime against humanity."

Jewish Resistance The murder of European Jewry was carried out with the help of the latest technology and with the utmost efficiency. For most of the victims, the will to resist was sapped by prolonged starvation, disease, and mistreatment. Nevertheless, there was fierce Jewish resistance throughout the war. Thousands of Jews joined anti-Nazi partisan groups and resistance movements while others led rebellions in concentration camps or participated in ghetto uprisings from Minsk to Krakow. The best-known uprising took place in the Warsaw ghetto in the spring of

MAP 36.3

The Holocaust in Europe, 1933–1945.
Observe the geographic locations of the concentration and extermi-nation camps.

Why were there more concentration camps in Germany and more extermination camps in Poland?

1943. Lacking adequate weapons, sixty thousand Jews who remained in the ghetto that had once held four hundred thousand rose against their tormentors. It took German se-curity forces using tanks and flamethrowers three weeks to crush the uprising. Approximately 5.7 million Jews perished in the Holocaust.

Women and the War

Observing the extent to which British women mobilized for war, the U.S. ambassador to London noted, "This war, more than any other war in history, is a woman's war." A poster en-couraging U.S. women to join the WAVES (Women Appointed for Volunteer Emergency Service in the navy) mirrored the thought: "It's A Woman's War Too!" While hundreds of thou-

sands of women in Great Britain and the United States joined the armed forces or entered war industries, women around the world were affected by the war in a variety of ways. Some nations, including Great Britain and the United States, barred women from engaging in combat or carrying weapons, but Soviet and Chinese women took up arms, as did women in resistance groups. In fact, women often excelled at resis-tance work because they were women: they were less sus-pect in the eyes of occupying security forces and less subject to searches. Nazi forces did not discriminate, though, when rounding up Jews for transport and extermination: Jewish women and girls died alongside Jewish men and boys.

Women's Roles Women who joined military services or took jobs on factory assembly lines gained an indepen-dence and confidence previously denied them, but so too did women who were forced to act as heads of household in the absence of husbands killed or away at war, captured as prisoners of war, or languishing in labor camps. Women's roles changed during the war, often in dramatic ways, but those new roles were temporary. After the war, women war-

This famous 1942 poster of an idealized woman war worker in the United States featured the archetypal "Rosie the Riveter" and coined the motto for women meeting the challenges of the war: "We Can Do It!"

designed to snag Nazi aircraft from the skies, drove ambulances and transport vehicles, and labored in the fields to produce foodstuffs. More than 500,000 women joined British military services, and approximately 350,000 women did the same in the United States.

Comfort Women Women's experiences in war were not always ennobling or empowering. The Japanese army forcibly recruited, conscripted, and dragooned as many as two hundred thousand women age fourteen to twenty to serve in military brothels, called "comfort houses" or "consolation centers." The army presented the women to the troops as a gift from the emperor, and the women came from Japanese colonies such as Korea, Taiwan, and Manchuria and from occupied territories in the Philippines and elsewhere in southeast Asia. The majority of the women came from Korea and China.

Once forced into this imperial prostitution service, the "comfort women" catered to between twenty and thirty men each day. Stationed in war zones, the women often confronted the same risks as soldiers, and many became casualties of war. Others were killed by Japanese soldiers, especially if they tried to escape or contracted venereal diseases. At the end of the war, soldiers massacred large numbers of comfort women to cover up the operation. The impetus behind the establishment of comfort houses for Japanese soldiers came from the horrors of Nanjing, where the mass rape of Chinese women had taken place. In trying to avoid such atrocities, the Japanese army created another horror of war. Comfort women who survived the war experienced deep shame and hid their past or faced shunning by their families. They found little comfort or peace after the war.

THE COLD WAR

The end of World War II produced moving images of peace, such as Soviet and U.S. soldiers clasping hands in camaraderie at the Elbe River, celebrating their victory over the Germans. But by the time Germany surrendered in the spring of 1945, the wartime alliance between the Soviet Union, the United States, and Great Britain was disintegrating. The one-time partners increasingly sacrificed cooperation for their own national interests. Within two years the alliance forged by mutual danger gave way to a cold war between two principal rivals. It was a contest in which neither side gave way; yet, in the end, a direct clash of arms was always avoided, hence the term *cold war*.

The cold war became a confrontation for global influence principally between the United States and the Soviet Union. It was a tense encounter between rival political and economic systems—between liberal democracy and capitalism on the one hand and international communism and one-party rule on the other. The

riors and workers were expected to return home and assume their traditional roles as wives and mothers. In the meantime, though, women made the most of their opportunities. In Britain, women served as noncombatant pilots, wrestled with the huge balloons and their tethering lines

thinking about TRADITIONS

The "Home" Front
Many observers during World War II acknowledged the significant role women played in the war effort. Traditionally bound to the home, women worked both on the home front and in the armed forces to support their nations' fight. In what ways did women transform their roles during the war? What sorts of jobs symbolized those changes?

British women handle a balloon used for defense in the Battle of Britain.

geopolitical and ideological rivalry between the Soviet Union and the United States and their respective allies lasted almost five decades and affected every corner of the world. The cold war was responsible for the formation of military and political alliances, the creation of client states, and an arms race of unprecedented scope. It engendered diplomatic crises, spawned military conflicts, and at times brought the world to the brink of nuclear annihilation. Among the first manifestations of the cold war was the division of the European continent into competing political, military, and economic blocs—one dependent on the United States and the other subservient to the USSR—separated by what Winston Churchill in 1946 called an "iron curtain."

Origins of the Cold War

The United Nations
Despite their many differences, the Allies were among the nations that agreed to the creation of the United Nations (UN) in October 1945, a supranational organization dedicated to keeping world peace and security. The commitment to establish a new international organization derived from Allied cooperation during the war. Unlike its predecessor, the League of Nations (1920), which failed in its basic mission to prevent another world war, the United Nations created a powerful Security Council responsible for maintaining international peace. Recognizing that peace could be maintained only if the great powers were in agreement, the UN founders made certain that the Security Council consists of five permanent members and six rotating elected members. The United States, the Soviet Union, Great Britain, France, and China—the members of the full Allied alliance in World War II—are the five permanent powers, and their unanimous vote is required on all substantive matters. The decisions of the Security Council are binding on all members.

Despite this initial cooperation, the wartime unity of the former Allies began to crack. Even before the defeat of Germany, the Allies had expressed differences over the future of Poland and eastern European nations liberated and subsequently occupied by the Soviet Red Army. On the surface, all sides agreed at the wartime conference at Yalta to "the earliest possible establishment through free elections of governments responsive to the will of the people." A determined Joseph Stalin, however, insisted on "friendly" governments that were controlled by the Soviet Union in order to safeguard against any future threat from Germany. From the American and British perspectives, Stalin's intentions signaled the permanent Soviet domination of eastern Europe and the threat of Soviet-influenced communist parties coming to power in the democracies of western Europe. Their worst fears were realized in 1946 and 1947, when the Soviets helped bring communist governments to power in Romania, Bulgaria, Hungary, and Poland. Communists had previously gained control in Albania and Yugoslavia in 1944 and 1945.

Truman Doctrine The enunciation of the Truman Doctrine on 12 March 1947 crystallized the new U.S. perception of a world divided between "free" (democratic) and "enslaved" (communist) peoples. Articulated partly in response to crises in Greece and Turkey, where communist movements seemed to threaten democracy and U.S. strategic interests, the Truman Doctrine starkly drew the battle lines of the cold war. As President Harry Truman (1884–1972) explained to the U.S. Congress: "At the present moment in world history nearly every nation must choose between alternative ways of life. I believe that it must be the policy of the United States to support free peoples who are resisting attempted subjugation by armed minorities or by outside pressures." The United States then committed itself to an interventionist foreign policy, dedicated to the "containment" of communism, which meant preventing any further expansion of Soviet influence.

Marshall Plan As an economic adjunct to the Truman Doctrine, the U.S. government developed a plan to help shore up the destroyed infrastructures of western Europe. The European Recovery Program, commonly called the

MAP 36.4

Occupied Germany, 1945–1949.

Locate the city of Berlin in Soviet-controlled territory.

How was it possible for the British, American, and French to maintain their zones of control in Berlin, given such geographic distance from western Germany?

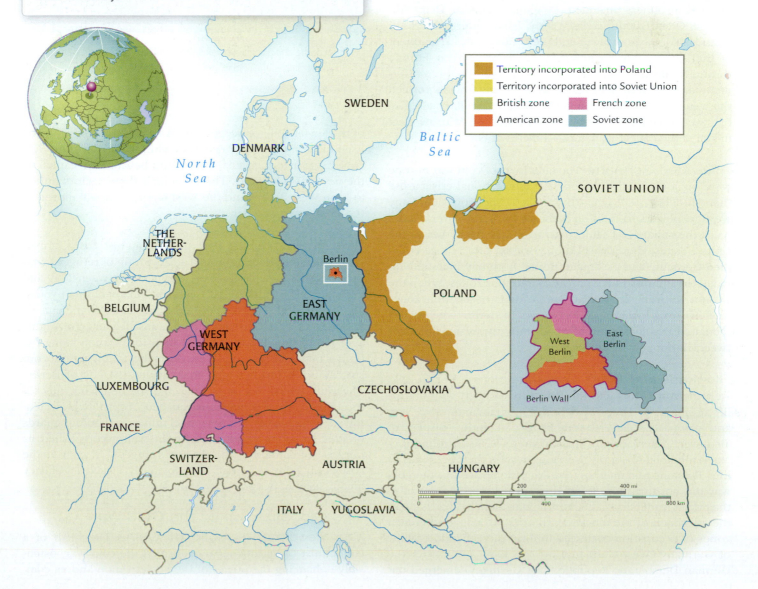

Marshall Plan after U.S. Secretary of State George C. Marshall (1880–1959), proposed to rebuild European economies through cooperation and capitalism, forestalling communist or Soviet influence in the devastated nations of Europe. Proposed in 1947 and funded in 1948, the Marshall Plan provided more than $13 billion to reconstruct western Europe. Although initially included in the nations invited to participate in the Marshall Plan, the Soviet Union resisted what it saw as capitalist imperialism and countered with a plan for its own satellite nations. The Soviet Union established the Council for Mutual Economic Assistance (COMECON) in 1949, offering increased trade within the Soviet Union and eastern Europe as an alternative to the Marshall Plan.

Military Alliances The creation of the U.S.-sponsored North Atlantic Treaty Organization (NATO) and the Soviet-controlled Warsaw Pact signaled the militarization of the cold war. In 1949 the United States established NATO as a regional military alliance against Soviet aggression. The original members included Belgium, Canada, Denmark, France, Great Britain, Iceland, Italy, Luxembourg, the Netherlands, Norway, Portugal, and the United States. The intent of the alliance was to maintain peace in postwar Europe through collective defense. When NATO admitted West Germany and allowed it to rearm in 1955, the Soviets formed the Warsaw Pact as a countermeasure. A military alliance of seven communist European nations, the Warsaw Pact matched the collective defense policies of NATO.

A Divided Germany The fault lines of cold war Europe were most visible in Germany. An international crisis arose there in 1948–1949 when the Soviet Union pressured the western powers to relinquish their jurisdiction over Berlin. After the collapse of Hitler's Third Reich, the forces of the United States, the Soviet Union, Britain, and France occupied Germany and its capital, Berlin, both of which they divided for administrative purposes into four zones. When the western powers decided to merge their occupation zones in Germany—including their sectors in Berlin—the Soviets retaliated by blockading all road, rail, and water links between Berlin and western Germany.

Blockade and Airlift In the first serious test of the cold war, the Americans and the British responded with an airlift designed to keep West Berlin's inhabitants alive, fed, and warm. For eleven months, in a daunting display of airpower, American and British aircrews flew around-the-clock missions to supply West Berlin with the necessities of life. Tensions remained high during the airlift, but the cold war did not turn hot. Stymied by British and U.S. resolve, the Soviet leadership called off the blockade in May 1949. In the aftermath of the blockade, the U.S., British, and French zones of occupation coalesced to form the Federal Republic of Germany (West Germany) in May 1949. In October the German Democratic Republic (East Germany) emerged out

Barbed wire and a concrete wall in front of the Brandenburg Gate in Berlin symbolized the cold war division of Europe.

of the Soviet zone of occupation. A similar process repeated itself in Berlin, which was deep within the Soviet zone. The Soviet sector formed East Berlin and became the capital of the new East Germany. The remaining three sectors united to form West Berlin, and the West German capital moved to the small town of Bonn.

The Berlin Wall By 1961 the communist East German state was hemorrhaging from a steady drain of refugees who preferred life in capitalist West Germany. Between 1949 and 1961 nearly 3.5 million East Germans—many of them young and highly skilled—left their homeland, much to the embarrassment of East Germany's communist leaders. In August 1961 the communists reinforced their fortification along the border between East and West Germany, following the construction of a fortified wall that divided the city of Berlin. The wall, which began as a layer of barbed wire, quickly turned into a barrier several layers deep, replete with watchtowers, searchlights, antipersonnel mines, and border guards ordered to shoot to kill. The Berlin Wall accomplished its purpose of stemming the flow of refugees, though at the cost of shaming a regime that obviously lacked legitimacy among its own people.

The Globalization of the Cold War

The People's Republic of China The birth of a communist China further transformed the cold war, ostensibly enhancing the power of the Soviet Union and its communist allies. With the defeat of Japan in 1945, the civil war in China had resumed. By mid-1948 the strategic balance favored the communists, who inflicted heavy military defeats on the nationalists throughout 1948 and 1949, forcing the national government under Jiang Jieshi (Chiang Kai-shek) to seek refuge on the island of Taiwan. In the meantime, Mao Zedong, the chairman of the Chinese Communist Party (CCP), proclaimed the establishment of the People's Republic of China on 1 October 1949. This declaration brought to an end the long period of imperialist intrusion in China and spawned a close relationship between the world's largest and most powerful socialist states.

Fraternal Cooperation   Moscow and Beijing drew closer during the early years of the cold war. This relationship was hardly astonishing, because the leaders of both communist states felt threatened by a common enemy, the United States, which sought to establish anticommunist bastions throughout Asia. Most disconcerting to Soviet and Chinese leaders was the American-sponsored rehabilitation of their former enemy, Japan, and the forming of client states in South Korea and Taiwan. The Chinese-Soviet partnership matured during the early 1950s and took on a distinct form when Beijing recognized Moscow's undisputed authority in world communism in exchange for Russian military equipment and economic aid.

Confrontations in Korea   In conjunction with the communist victory in China, the unforeseen outbreak of hostilities on the Korean peninsula in the summer of 1950 shifted the focus of the cold war from Europe to east Asia. At the end of World War II, the leaders of the Soviet Union and the United States had partitioned Korea along the thirty-eighth parallel of latitude into a northern Soviet zone and a southern U.S. zone. Because the superpowers were unable to agree on a framework for the reunification of the country, in 1948 they consented to the establishment of two separate Korean states: in the south, the Republic of Korea, with Seoul as its capital, and in the north, the People's Democratic Republic of Korea, with Pyongyang as its capital. After arming their respective clients, each of which claimed sovereignty over the entire country, U.S. and Soviet troops withdrew.

On the early morning of 25 June 1950, the unstable political situation in Korea came to a head. Determined to unify Korea by force, the Pyongyang regime ordered more than one hundred thousand troops across the thirty-eighth parallel in a surprise attack, quickly pushing back South Korean defenders and capturing Seoul on 27 June. Convinced that the USSR had sanctioned the invasion, the United States persuaded the United Nations to adopt a resolution to repel the aggressor. Armed with a UN mandate and supported by small armed forces from twenty countries, the U.S. military went into action, and within months had pushed the North Koreans back to the thirty-eighth parallel. However, sens-

ing an opportunity to unify Korea under a pro-U.S. government, they pushed on into North Korea and within a few weeks had occupied Pyongyang. Subsequent U.S. advances toward the Yalu River on the Chinese border resulted in Chinese intervention in the Korean conflict. A combined force of Chinese and North Koreans pushed U.S. forces and their allies back into the south, and the war settled into a protracted stalemate near the original border at the thirty-eighth parallel. After two more years of fighting that raised the number of deaths to three million—mostly Korean civilians—both sides finally agreed to a cease-fire in July 1953. The failure to conclude a peace treaty ensured that the Korean peninsula would remain in a state of suspended strife that constantly threatened to engulf the region in a new round of hostilities.

Beyond the human casualties and physical damage it wrought, the Korean conflict also encouraged the globalization of the U.S. strategy of containment. Viewing the North Korean offensive as part of a larger communist conspiracy to conquer the world, the U.S. government extended military protection and economic aid to the noncommunist governments of Asia. It also entered into security agreements that culminated in the creation of the Southeast Asian Treaty Organization (SEATO), an Asian counterpart of NATO. By 1954 U.S. President Dwight D. Eisenhower (1890–1969), who had contemplated using nuclear weapons in Korea, asserted the famous "domino theory." This strategic theory rationalized worldwide U.S. intervention on the assumption that if one country became communist, neighboring ones would collapse to communism the way a row of dominoes falls sequentially until none remains standing. Subsequent U.S. administrations extended the policy of containment to areas beyond the nation's vital interests and applied it to local or imagined communist threats in Central and South America, Africa, and Asia.

Cracks in the Soviet-Chinese Alliance   Despite the assumptions of U.S. leaders, there was no one monolithic communist force in global politics, as was demonstrated by the divisions between Chinese and Soviet communists that appeared over time. The Chinese had embarked on a crash program of industrialization, and the Soviet Union rendered valuable assistance in the form of economic aid and technical advisors. By the mid-1950s the Soviet Union was China's principal trading partner, annually purchasing roughly half of all Chinese exports. Before long, however, cracks appeared in the Soviet-Chinese alliance. From the Chinese perspective, Soviet aid programs were far too modest and had too many strings attached. By the end of 1964, the rift between the Soviet Union and the People's Republic of China became embarrassingly public, with both sides engaging in name-calling. In addition, both nations openly competed for influence in Africa and Asia, especially in the nations that had recently gained independence. The fact that the People's Republic had conducted successful nuclear tests in 1964 enhanced its prestige. An unanticipated outcome of

The visceral beauty of nuclear explosions, such as this one in the Marshall Islands in 1954, masked the terror and the tensions that beset the Soviet Union, the United States, and the rest of the world during the cold war.

the Chinese-Soviet split was that many countries gained an opportunity to pursue a more independent course by playing capitalists against communists and by playing Soviet communists against Chinese communists.

The Nuclear Arms Race A central feature of the cold war world was a costly arms race and the terrifying proliferation of nuclear weapons. The Soviet Union had broken the U.S. monopoly on atomic weaponry by testing its own atomic bomb in 1949, but because the United States was determined to retain military superiority and because the Soviet Union was equally determined to reach parity with the United States, both sides amassed enormous arsenals of nuclear weapons and developed a multitude of systems for deploying those weapons. In the 1960s and beyond, the superpowers acquired so many nuclear weapons that they reached the capacity for mutually assured destruction, or MAD. This balance of terror, while often frightening, tended to restrain the contestants and stabilize their relationship, with one important exception.

Cuba: Nuclear Flashpoint Ironically, the cold war confrontation that came closest to unleashing nuclear war took place not at the expected flashpoints in Europe or Asia but on the island of Cuba. In 1959 a revolutionary movement headed by Fidel Castro Ruz (1926–) overthrew the autocratic

Fulgencio Batista y Zaldivar (1901–1973), whose regime had gone to great lengths to maintain the country's traditionally subservient relationship with the United States, especially with the U.S. sugar companies that controlled Cuba's economy. Fidel Castro's new regime gladly accepted a Soviet offer of massive economic aid—including an agreement to purchase half of Cuba's sugar production—and arms shipments. In return for the Soviet largesse, Castro declared his support for the USSR's foreign policy. In December 1961 he confirmed the U.S. government's worst suspicions when he publicly announced: "I have been a Marxist-Leninist all along, and will remain one until I die."

Bay of Pigs Invasion Cuba's alignment with the Soviet Union spurred the U.S. government to action. Newly elected president John F. Kennedy (1917–1963) authorized a clandestine invasion of Cuba to overthrow Castro and his supporters. In April 1961 a force of fifteen hundred anti-Castro Cubans trained, armed, and transported by the Central Intelligence Agency (CIA) landed on Cuba at a place called the Bay of Pigs. The arrival of the invasion force failed to incite a hoped-for internal uprising, and when the promised American air support failed to appear, the invasion quickly fizzled. Within three days, Castro's military had either captured or killed the entire invasion force. The Bay of Pigs fiasco diminished U.S. prestige, especially in Latin America. It also, contrary

This propaganda poster celebrated the leadership of Fidel Castro during his rise to revolutionary power in Cuba.

thinking about ENCOUNTERS

Cold War in Cuba

The very definition of the cold war meant that the two superpowers, the United States and the Soviet Union, avoided direct military confrontations and struggled instead on a largely ideological plane. Why did this "cold" version of war turn potentially so hot in Cuba in 1962? What made this superpower contest in Cuba so frightening?

to U.S. purposes, actually strengthened Castro's position in Cuba and encouraged him to accept the deployment of Soviet nuclear missiles in Cuba as a deterrent to any future invasion.

On 26 October 1962 the United States learned that Soviet technicians were assembling launch sites for medium-range nuclear missiles on Cuba. The deployment of nuclear missiles that could reach targets in the United States within minutes represented an unacceptable threat to U.S. national security. Thus President John F. Kennedy issued an ultimatum, calling on the Soviet leadership to withdraw all missiles from Cuba and stop the arrival of additional nuclear armaments. To back up his demand, Kennedy imposed an air and naval quarantine on the island nation. The superpowers seemed poised for nuclear confrontation, and for two weeks the world's peoples held their collective breath. After two weeks, finally realizing the imminent possibility of nuclear war, the Soviet government yielded to the U.S. demands. In return, Soviet Premier Nikita Khrushchev (1894–1971) extracted an open pledge from Kennedy to refrain from attempting to overthrow Castro's regime and a secret deal to remove U.S. missiles from Turkey. The world trembled during this crisis, awaiting the apocalypse that potentially lurked behind any superpower encounter.

Dissent, Intervention, and Rapprochement

De-Stalinization Even before the Cuban missile crisis, developments within the Soviet Union caused serious changes in eastern Europe. Within three years of Joseph Stalin's death in 1953, several communist leaders startled the world when they openly attacked Stalin and questioned his methods of rule. The most vigorous denunciations came from Stalin's successor, Soviet Premier Nikita Khrushchev, who embarked on a policy of de-Stalinization, that is, the end of the rule of terror and the partial liberalization of Soviet society. Government officials removed portraits of Stalin from public places, renamed institutions and localities bearing his name, and commissioned historians to rewrite textbooks to deflate Stalin's reputation. The de-Stalinization period, which lasted from 1956 to 1964, also brought a "thaw" in government control and resulted in the release of millions of political prison-

ers. With respect to foreign policy, Khrushchev emphasized the possibility of "peaceful coexistence" between different social systems and the achievement of communism by peaceful means. This change in Soviet doctrine reflected the recognition that a nuclear war was more likely to lead to mutual annihilation than to victory.

Soviet Intervention The new political climate in the Soviet Union tempted communist leaders elsewhere to experiment with domestic reforms and seek a degree of independence from Soviet domination. Eastern European states also tried to become their own masters, or at least to gain a measure of autonomy from the Soviet Union. The nations of the Soviet bloc did not fare well in those endeavors. The most serious challenge to Soviet control came in 1956 from nationalist-minded communists in Hungary. When the communist regime in Hungary embraced the process of de-Stalinization, large numbers of Hungarian citizens demanded democracy and the breaking of ties to Moscow and the Warsaw Pact. Soviet leaders viewed those moves as a serious threat to their security system. In the late autumn of 1956, Soviet tanks entered Budapest and crushed the Hungarian uprising.

Twelve years after the Hungarian tragedy, Soviets again intervened in eastern Europe, this time in Czechoslovakia. In 1968 the Communist Party leader, Alexander Dubček (1921–1992), launched a "democratic socialist revolution." He supported a liberal movement known as the "Prague Spring" and promised his fellow citizens "socialism with a human face." The Czechs' move toward liberal communism aroused fear in the Soviet Union because such ideas could lead to the unraveling of Soviet control in eastern Europe. Intervention by the Soviet army brought an end to the Prague Spring. Khrushchev's successor, Leonid Ilyich Brezhnev (1906–1982), justified the invasion of Czechoslovakia by the Doctrine of Limited Sovereignty. This policy, more commonly called the "Brezhnev doctrine," reserved the right to invade any socialist country that was deemed to be threatened by internal or external elements "hostile to socialism." The destruction of the dramatic reform movement in Czechoslovakia served to reassert Soviet control over its satellite nations in eastern Europe and led to tightened controls within the Soviet Union.

Détente Amid those complications of the cold war and the challenges issuing from allies and enemies alike, Soviet and U.S. leaders began adjusting to the reality of an unmanageable world—a reality they could no longer ignore. By the late 1960s the leaders of the Soviet Union and the United States agreed on a policy of *détente,* or a reduction in hostility, trying to cool the costly arms race and slow their competition in developing countries. Although détente did not resolve the deep-seated antagonism between the superpowers, it did signal the relaxation of cold war tensions and prompted a new spirit of cooperation. The spirit of détente was most visible in negotiations designed to reduce the threat posed by strategic nuclear weapons. The two cold war antagonists cooperated despite the tensions caused by the U.S. incursion into Vietnam, Soviet involvement in Angola and other African states, and continued Soviet repression of dissidents in eastern Europe. Likewise symbolic of this rapprochement between democratic and communist nations were the state visits in 1972 to China and the Soviet Union made by U.S. President Richard Nixon (1913–1994). Nixon had entered politics in 1946 on the basis of his service in World War II and his staunch belief in anticommunism, and his trips to the two global centers of communism suggested a possible beginning to the end of World War II and cold war divisions.

in perspective

At the end of World War II, it was possible for a U.S. marine to enjoy the hospitality of a Japanese family in Nagasaki, but not for Soviet and U.S. troops to continue embracing in camaraderie. World War II was a total global war that forced violent encounters between peoples and radically altered the political shape of the world. Beginning with Japan and China in 1931, this global conflagration spread to Europe and its empires and to the Pacific Ocean and the rest of Asia. Men, women, and children throughout the world became intimate with war as victims of civilian bombing campaigns, as soldiers and war workers, and as slave laborers and comfort women. When the Allies defeated the Axis powers in 1945, destroying the German and Japanese empires, the world had to rebuild as another war began. The end of the war saw the breakup of the alliance that had defeated Germany and Japan, and within a short time the United States and the Soviet Union and their respective allies squared off against each other in a cold war, a rivalry waged primarily on political, economic, and propaganda fronts. A longer-lasting realignment in world politics came about after World War II as colonial nations gained independence through the process of decolonization. ●

CHRONOLOGY	
1937	Invasion of China by Japan
1937	The Rape of Nanjing
1939	Nazi-Soviet Pact
1939	Invasion of Poland by Germany
1940	Fall of France, Battle of Britain
1941	German invasion of the Soviet Union
1941	Attack on Pearl Harbor by Japan
1942	U.S. victory at Midway
1943	Soviet victory at Stalingrad
1944	D-Day, Allied invasion at Normandy
1945	Capture of Berlin by Soviet forces
1945	Atomic bombing of Hiroshima and Nagasaki
1945	Establishment of United Nations
1947	Truman Doctrine
1948	Marshall Plan
1949	Division of Berlin and Germany
1949	Establishment of the People's Republic of China
1950–1953	Korean War
1961	Construction of Berlin Wall
1962	Cuban missile crisis

For Further Reading

Gar Alperovitz. *Atomic Diplomacy: Hiroshima and Potsdam.* Rev. ed. New York, 1985. The classic account of the atomic origins of the cold war.

Christopher Bayly and Tim Harper. *Forgotten Armies: The Fall of British Asia, 1941–1945.* Cambridge, 2005. Broad study of the impact of World War II on Britain's Asian empire.

Herbert P. Bix. *Hirohito and the Making of Modern Japan.* New York, 2001. A groundbreaking, unvarnished biography that details the strong and decisive role the emperor played in wartime operations during World War II.

Christopher R. Browning with contributions by Jürgen Matthäuss. *The Origins of the Final Solution: The Evolution of Nazi Jewish Policy, September 1939–March 1942.* Lincoln, Neb., and Jerusalem, 2004. Standard work on the evolution of Nazi anti-Jewish policies from persecution to mass murder.

Ian Buruma. *The Wages of Guilt: Memories of War in Germany and Japan.* New York, 1995. A moving account of how societies deal with the war crimes of World War II.

Winston Churchill. *The Second World War.* 6 vols. New York, 1948–60. An in-depth account of the war from one of the major players.

Dwight Eisenhower. *Crusade in Europe.* New York, 1948. An account of the European war from the military point of view of the supreme Allied commander.

John Lewis Gaddis. *The Cold War: A New History.* New York, 2005. A fresh and concise history of the cold war by the dean of cold war historians.

Tsuyoshi Hasegawa. *Racing the Enemy: Stalin, Truman, and the Surrender of Japan.* Cambridge, Mass., 2005. Impressive international history of the end of World War II in the Pacific that argues the Soviet threat was the decisive factor in Japan's surrender, not Truman's use of nuclear weapons.

Brian Masaru Hayashi. *Democratizing the Enemy: The Japanese American Internment.* Princeton, 2004. Important account of the experience of Japanese Americans in World War II.

Margaret Higgonet, Jane Jenson, Sonya Michel, and Margaret Weitz, eds. *Behind the Lines: Gender and the Two World Wars.* New Haven, 1987. A penetrating series of articles on women in both world wars, focusing generally on U.S. and European experiences.

Raul Hilberg. *The Destruction of the European Jews.* New York, 1967. One of the most important works on the Holocaust.

Akira Iriye. *The Cold War in Asia: A Historical Interpretation.* Englewood Cliffs, N.J., 1974. A leading diplomatic historian provides an excellent introduction to the subject.

———. *The Origins of the Second World War in Asia and the Pacific.* New York, 1987. An examination of the Asian and Pacific origins of the war by one of the field's leading scholars.

John Keegan. *The Second World War.* New York, 1989. An exhaustive military history.

Williamson Murray and Alan R. Millet. *A War to Be Won: Fighting in the Second World War, 1937–1945.* Cambridge, Mass., 2000. A fine single-volume history focusing on military operations.

Martin Sherwin. *A World Destroyed: The Atomic Bomb and the Grand Alliance.* New York, 1975. A classic study of how the bomb influenced the end of the war.

You-Li Sun. *China and the Origins of the Pacific War, 1931–1941.* New York, 1993. An account of the origins of the war in which China takes center stage.

William Taubman. *Stalin's American Policy: From Entente to Détente to Cold War.* New York, 1982. An important work that focuses on the Soviet perspective of the cold war.

Studs Terkel. *"The Good War": An Oral History of World War II.* New York, 1984. A valuable collection of oral histories on the war from a U.S. perspective.

Gerhard L. Weinberg. *Visions of Victory: The Hopes of Eight World War II Leaders.* Cambridge, 2005. A close examination of eight political leaders and their visions for the postwar world.

The End of Empire

chapter37

This saintly image of Mohandas K. Gandhi captures his spiritual significance to the independence movement in India both before and after his death.

PART

EYEWITNESS:
Mohandas Gandhi's Saintly Last Words

"Hé Ram" were the last words that escaped his lips after three bullets savagely ripped through his frail body. Roughly translated, he uttered, "O! God," and then died. It had begun as a day much like any other in the life of Mohandas K. Gandhi (1869–1948), or "Bapuji" as he was fondly called—a dear father of the country of India. On 30 January 1948, a few months after India gained its independence from Great Britain, he awakened at Birla House in Delhi at an early hour, 3:00 A.M., to continue his work hammering out solutions to the problems that plagued his land. That morning, he labored on a draft of a new constitution for the Indian National Congress, stressing as usual his major concerns for his newly independent and strife-ridden nation: that villages be empowered, that discrimination based on the caste system be abolished, that religious intolerance and violence between Hindus and Muslims cease. Still distraught over the partitioning of his land into a Hindu India and Muslim Pakistan, he had weakened himself after independence through fasts and hunger strikes staged as *satyagraha,* or "truth and firmness," protests against the killings of Hindus and Muslims and the mistreatment of Pakistan. He weighed a mere 107 pounds that day.

Alternating between working, talking with visitors, and napping, Gandhi finally took a meal at 4:30 P.M. He nibbled on raw and cooked vegetables and oranges, and drank goat's milk and a special brew made with aloe juice, lemons, ginger, and strained butter. A little over half an hour later, he made his way to the evening prayer meeting he was to lead. A bit late, the skies already darkening, he took a shortcut across the emerald green, finely trimmed lawns of Birla House to reach the dais where he would speak. As he approached the dais, he stopped to press his palms together, offering the traditional Hindu greeting to the crowd waiting at the meeting. At that moment, out of the crowd stepped a large and impatient man who suddenly pulled a Beretta pistol from his pants pocket and fired the three shots that ended the life of the man many credited with Indian independence, the man seen as the very soul and conscience of India. The force of the shots crumpled Gandhi's thin body, his chest and abdomen riddled by bullets. As he slumped to the ground, his glasses fell from his face, his sandals slipped from his feet, and large crimson blood stains spread starkly over his white homespun shawl. After he whispered "Hé Ram," his breathing stilled.

Two days before he was assassinated by the Hindu extremist Nathuram Godse, Gandhi prophetically said, "If I am to die by the bullet of a mad man, I must do so smiling. There must be no anger within me. God must be in my heart and on my lips." Gandhi died as he had wanted, and as he lived, without anger and with God on his lips. His assassination, however, stood in bleak contrast to the nonviolence embraced by Gandhi throughout his life. Gandhi could have been forgiven some anger given the apparent failure of his nonviolence doctrine in the days after independence—a failure made publicly evident in communal killings after partition and personally evident in his violent death. Not all Hindus agreed with Gandhi's rejection of violence and avowal of religious tolerance for Muslims. Before he was executed by hanging in 1949, his assassin Godse declared Gandhi a "curse for India, a force for evil."

Gandhi's murder suggested the troubles and traumas faced by nations and peoples adjusting to independence from colonial rule, but his martyrdom also enshrined his principles of nonviolence and religious tolerance in Indian life after independence. Gandhi's death discredited Hindu extremism and halted communal violence, for a time. He became a more mythic hero in India, a new national symbol to be invoked in times of trouble and violence. His life and death spoke to the promise and perils of independence and its aftermath. Despite the hazards of life in a world without empires, peoples in the colonial world fought tenaciously for independence and then for national unity after World War II.

The expansion of European power since 1500 is one of the principal themes of world history. For over four centuries, European colonies and empires dominated large parts of the planet. Beginning in the early twentieth century, however, a series of developments undermined Europe's global hegemony. The catalyst for change was the Great War (World War I), which sapped the strength and the prestige of the major colonial powers such as Great Britain and France. The Great Depression further undermined the strength of the imperialist nations, and by the end of World War II the same nations were so exhausted, so economically debilitated, and so demoralized that any realistic attempt to assert or reassert control over colonies was simply out of the question. Europe's palsied condition was not lost on leaders of independence movements in Asia and Africa, and they lost little time in taking advantage of Europe's unparalleled weakness. Many intellectual and political leaders of independence movements (Gandhi, Nehru, Nkrumah, and Ho Chi Minh) had been educated in Europe and the United States, where they had been exposed to ideals of freedom, self-determination, and national sovereignty. In the decades after 1945, peoples in the colonial world fought tenaciously for independence and then for national unity, and by 1990, nationalist movements had swept away colonial rule and given birth to over ninety new nations.

This process of decolonization was aided by several factors. It became increasingly apparent that there was a significant growth of democratic and anti-imperialist sentiments within imperial countries themselves, and political leaders could no longer count on a war-weary public to make serious sacrifices to maintain overseas colonies. The short-lived Japanese empire contributed to colonial revolutions throughout Asia, where European military prestige had been severely and permanently damaged after the Japanese defeated the British in Burma and Malaya, the French in Indochina, the Dutch in Indonesia, and the United States in the Philippines. With the emergence of the two postwar superpowers, the United States and the Soviet Union, both of which opposed European colonialism, the stage was set for a drastic overturning of colonial rule. The end of empire was one of the most important outcomes of World War II.

Peoples in the former colonial world labored to build national identities, balancing their traditions against demands for development. Such difficulties were true for nations in areas of the world where independence came long ago and in areas where peoples achieved independence from colonial or imperial rule recently. Despite all the complications of decolonization and its aftermath, colonial peoples in Asia and Africa fought for freedom and then for security. The desire of nations to seek peace and stability after independence seemed reasonable, especially because independence often led to numerous problems. Freedom did not remain elusive for the nations of Asia, Africa, and Latin America, but peace often did—a fact Gandhi acknowledged in the days after Indian independence and on the day of his death.

INDEPENDENCE IN ASIA

In the wake of World War II, the power of Asian nationalism was irrepressible. New nations emerged throughout Asia, from India and Pakistan in south Asia to diverse Arab nations in southwest Asia and to Vietnam, Cambodia, and Laos in southeast Asia. These lands encountered different conditions in their quests for independence and freedom from imperial control, but everywhere Asian nationalists rallied their people against colonialism and imperialism. Whether fighting against colonial powers, which established formal political and territorial control, or against imperial powers, which often exercised a more informal and indirect control, Asians were successful. The result of their efforts, measured in years or decades, was independence and the end of empire in Asia.

India's Partitioned Independence

In the 1930s Great Britain had granted numerous reforms in response to the tireless campaign of Mohandas K. Gandhi and the Congress Party, as well as Muhammad Ali Jinnah and the Muslim League. The gradual trend toward Indian self-rule, as in the India Act of 1935, faced challenges in the form of increasing calls for independent yet separate Hindu and Muslim states. World War II, however, interrupted the drive for any sort of self-rule.

The Coming of Self-Rule Under the leadership of Winston Churchill, who despised Gandhi and vowed never "to preside over the liquidation of the British empire," measures for home rule were suspended, and India was ordered to support the war effort. British recalcitrance about Indian independence evaporated after the war, however. The British people voted Churchill out of office. His conservative government was replaced with a Labour government more inclined to dismantle the empire. The economic devastation of the war made it unrealistic for Britain to continue bearing the financial burden of empire in India.

The issue of Muslim separatism grew in importance as the probability of Indian independence became more pronounced, and Muslims increasingly feared their minority status in a free India dominated by Hindus. Muhammad Ali Jinnah (1876–1948), leader of the Muslim League, felt no qualms about frankly expressing Muslim concerns and desires for a separate Muslim state, even as Congress Party leaders such as Jawaharlal Nehru (1889–1964) and Gandhi urged all Indians to act and feel as one nation, undivided

Jawaharlal Nehru (left) and Mohandas K. Gandhi, Hindu leaders of India's independence movement. Gandhi's nonviolent resistance powerfully contributed to the end of the British rule of India. Nehru promoted a strategy of nonalignment for the newly independent nation.

by what came to be known as communalism—emphasizing religious over national identity. In August 1946, in the midst of negotiations with the British to reach terms regarding independence, the Muslim League called for a Day of Direct Action, even though the league's leaders recognized that Muslim demonstrations might lead to rioting and fighting between Muslims and Hindus. Some six thousand people died in the Great Calcutta Killing that resulted, further fueling communal feeling and adding weight to Jinnah's claim: "The only solution to India's problem is Pakistan."

Partition and Violence

Partition and Violence The idea of partition, the division of India into separate Hindu and Muslim states, violated the stated ideals of men such as Gandhi and Nehru, who sickened at the prospect and only reluctantly came to accept the notion of a divided and independent India. Gandhi nonetheless condemned the division of his homeland as a "vivisection," using a term that refers to the cutting up of a living body. He avoided the celebrations on 15 August 1947 that accompanied independence for India and Pakistan, glumly prophesying that "rivers of blood" would flow in the wake of partition. His vision came true as the terms of partition were announced and hundreds of thousands of Muslim and Hindu refugees migrated either to Muslim Pakistan (divided between parts of Bengal in the east and Punjab in the west) or to Hindu India. By mid-1948 an estimated ten million refugees made the torturous journey to one state or the other, and between half a million and one million people died in the violence that accompanied those massive human migrations. The hostility between migrating Hindus and Muslims spilled over into the enmity between the two states, complicating efforts to build their independent nations.

Though mired in violence, Indian independence became a reality with momentous consequences for the process of decolonization. India was the jewel in the crown of the British empire, and its breakaway marked a significant turning point. Just as Gandhi's nonviolent resistance to British rule inspired nationalists around the globe before and after World War II, independence in India and Pakistan further encouraged anti-imperial movements throughout Asia and Africa. Another way in which Indian independence inspired nations and set a pattern for grappling with decolonization in the midst of a cold war was through Nehru's promotion of a nonalignment strategy. Nehru proved instrumental in fashioning a compelling position for newly independent nations caught in the cold war and in the superpower tug-of-war contests for the loyalties of new nations. He became one of the impassioned defenders of nonalignment, especially at the Bandung Conference, where he was one of the most visible participants.

Nonalignment

Nonalignment Leaders of new African and Asian countries first discussed nonalignment at the Bandung Conference. In April 1955, leaders from twenty-three Asian and six African nations met in Bandung, Indonesia, partly to find a "third path," an alternative to choosing either the United States or the Soviet Union. Besides neutrality in the cold war, the Bandung Conference stressed the struggle against colonialism and racism, and Indonesian president Achmad Sukarno (1901–1970) proudly proclaimed Bandung "the first international conference of coloured peoples in the history of mankind." Bandung was the precursor of the broader Nonaligned Movement, which held occasional meetings so that its members could discuss matters of common interest, particularly their relations with the United States and the Soviet Union. The movement's primary goal was to maintain formal neutrality. However, the Nonaligned Movement suffered from a chronic lack of unity among its members and ultimately failed to present a genuinely united front. Although theoretically nonaligned with either cold war superpower, many member states had close ties to one or the other, and that situation caused dissension within the movement.

Nationalist Struggles in Vietnam

In contrast to India, Vietnam over time had more difficulty in keeping its nationalist struggle for independence separate from the complications of the cold war. In its fight for independence, Vietnam became deeply enmeshed in the cold war, but immediately after World War II the Vietnamese first engaged in a battle to free themselves from French colonial control. Vietnam's nationalist communist leader, Ho Chi Minh (1890–1969), had exploited wartime conditions to advance the cause of Vietnamese independence.

Fighting the French

Fighting the French After the Japanese conquest of Vietnam, which effectively ended French rule, Ho helped oust the Japanese from Vietnam in the waning days of World War II. He then issued the Vietnamese Declaration of Independence, which was modeled on the U.S. declaration. However, the French, humiliated by their country's easy defeat and occupation by the Germans, sought to reclaim their world-power status through their imperial possessions. Armed with British and U.S. weapons, the French recaptured Saigon and much of southern Vietnam in 1945. Faced with the hostility of the northern nationalist communists, organized as the Viet Minh, the French retook the north brutally, bombing Hanoi and Haiphong and killing

thinking about TRADITIONS

Independence and Nonviolence

Mohandas Gandhi embodied the modern principle of nonviolence, which had a deep and long history of acceptance in Indian society. What happened to this traditional belief as India gained its independence from Great Britain?

sources from the past

Muhammad Ali Jinnah on the Need for a Muslim Pakistan

Muhammad Ali Jinnah (1876–1948) served as the most visible and articulate leader of India's Muslims during the first half of the twentieth century. Like Mohandas K. Gandhi, he initially promoted cooperation and unity among Muslims and Hindus in order to achieve freedom from British rule. He came to feel strongly, however, that Muslims in an independent but Hindu-controlled India would only suffer from the discrimination they already faced from the Hindu majority. In the following speech to the Muslim League in 1940, Jinnah formulated some of the reasons why Muslims indeed deserved and already constituted their own nation.

It is extremely difficult to appreciate why our Hindu friends fail to understand the real nature of Islam and Hinduism. They are not religions in the strict sense of the word, but are, in fact, different and distinct social orders, and it is a dream that the Hindus and Muslims can ever evolve a common nationality, and this misconception of one Indian nation has gone far beyond the limits and is the cause of most of your troubles and will lead India to destruction if we fail to revise our notions in time. The Hindus and Muslims belong to two different religious philosophies, social customs, literatures. They neither intermarry nor interdine together and, indeed, they belong to two different civilizations which are based mainly on conflicting ideas and conceptions. Their aspects on life and of life are different. It is quite clear that Hindus and Mussalmans [Muslims] derive their inspiration from different sources of history. They have different epics, different heroes, and different episodes. Very often the hero of one is the foe of the other and, likewise, their victories and defeats overlap. To yoke together two such nations under a single state, one as a numerical minority and the other as a majority, must lead to growing discontent. . . .

[W]e know that the history of the last twelve hundred years has failed to achieve unity and has witnessed, during the ages, India always divided into Hindu India and Muslim India. The present artificial unity of India dates back only to the British conquest and is maintained by the British bayonet, but termination of the British regime, which is implicit in the recent declaration of His Majesty's government, will be the herald of the entire break-up with worse disaster than has ever taken place during the last one thousand years under Muslims. Surely that is not the legacy which Britain would bequeath to India after one hundred fifty years of her rule, nor would Hindu and Muslim India risk such a sure catastrophe. Muslim India cannot accept any constitution which must necessarily result in a Hindu majority government. Hindus and Muslims brought together under a democratic system forced upon the minorities can only mean Hindu raj [rule]. . . .

Mussalmans are a nation according to any definition of a nation, and they must have their homelands, their territory, and their state. We wish to live in peace and harmony with our neighbors as a free and independent people. We wish our people to develop to the fullest our spiritual, cultural, economic, social, and political life in a way that we think best and in consonance with our own ideals and according to the genius of our people. Honesty demands and the vital interests of millions of our people impose a sacred duty upon us to find an honorable and peaceful solution, which would be just and fair to all.

For Further Reflection

■ How does Jinnah employ the idea of "difference" to justify his calls for a separate Muslim state in an independent India?

Source: Muhammad Ali Jinnah, "Hindus and Muslims: Two Separate Nations," from *Sources of Indian Tradition*, 2nd ed., vol. 2, edited by Stephen Hay. New York, 1988, pp. 228–31.

at least ten thousand civilians. By 1947 the French appeared to have secured their power, especially in the cities, but that security proved to be temporary. Much like the Chinese communists in their battles against the Japanese and then against the nationalists in the postwar years, the Vietnamese resistance forces, led by Ho Chi Minh and General Vo Nguyen Giap (1912–), took to the countryside and mounted a campaign of guerrilla warfare. The Vietnamese communists grew increasingly influential in the anti-imperial war, especially after 1949 when communist China sent aid and arms to the Viet Minh. Thus strengthened, they defeated the French at their fortress in Dienbienphu in 1954. The French had to sue for peace at the conference table.

The Geneva Conference and Partial Independence The peace conference, held in Geneva in 1954, determined that Vietnam should be temporarily divided at the seventeenth parallel; North Vietnam would be controlled by Ho Chi Minh and the communist forces, whereas South Vietnam would remain in the hands of noncommunists. The communist affiliation of Ho and his comrades, along with the globalization of the cold war that accompanied the Korean

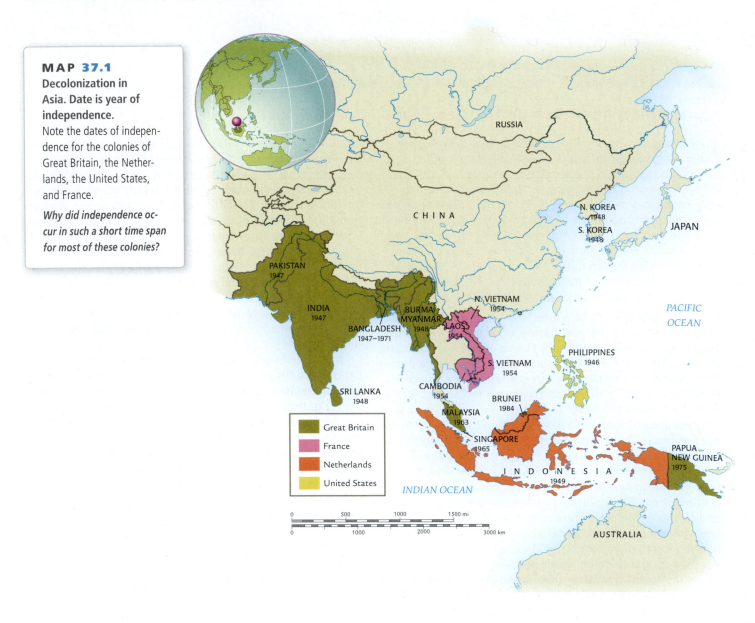

MAP 37.1

Decolonization in Asia. Date is year of independence.

Note the dates of independence for the colonies of Great Britain, the Netherlands, the United States, and France.

Why did independence occur in such a short time span for most of these colonies?

War, persuaded the United States to lend its support first to the French war effort and then to the government of South Vietnam. U.S. president Dwight Eisenhower applied the domino theory to Vietnam. Violating the terms of the Geneva Agreements, which required elections that would likely have brought Ho to power, South Vietnam's leaders, with U.S. support, avoided elections and sought to build a government that would prevent the spread of communism in South Vietnam and elsewhere in Asia. Ngo Dinh Diem (1901–1963), the first president of the Republic of (South) Vietnam, and other South Vietnamese leaders did not garner popular support with the people, however, and growing discontent sparked the spread of guerrilla war in the south.

In 1960, Vietnamese nationalists formed the National Liberation Front (NLF) to fight for freedom from South Vietnamese rule. Although Vietnamese from the south made up the majority in this organization, it received direction, aid, weapons, and ultimately troops from the north also. In turn, the government in the north received economic and military assistance from the Soviet Union and China, and a cold war stalemate ensued.

Vietnam's "American War" Given the lack of popular support for Diem and U.S.-style democratic reforms, the nationalist communist attacks against the South Vietnamese government met with continued success. In 1965 President Lyndon Johnson (1908–1973) embarked on a course of action that exponentially increased U.S. involvement in Vietnam. He ordered a bombing campaign against North Vietnam and sent U.S. ground troops to augment the South Vietnamese army. Yet, even with the overwhelming firepower and military personnel, the best the United States and South Vietnam could achieve against the Viet Cong was a draw. North Vietnam found a stalemate quite acceptable. Vietnamese forces fought for freedom from outside interference of any sort and could show patience while making progress toward independence.

Vietnamese Victory Their patience was rewarded as opposition to the war grew in the United States. Recognizing his country's distaste for the Vietnam War, presidential candidate Richard Nixon pledged in 1968 to end the war. After his election, he implemented his strategy of turning the war over to the South Vietnamese—termed *Vietnamization*—by escalating the conflict. Nixon extended the war into Cambodia through bombing and invasion in 1969 and 1970, and he resumed the heavy bombing of North Vietnam. He also opened diplomatic channels to the Soviet Union and China, hoping to get them to pressure North Vietnam into a negotiated end to the war. U.S. troops gradually withdrew from the conflict, and in January 1973 the "American War," as the Vietnamese termed it, ended with the negotiated Paris Peace Accords. War itself did not end, as forces from North Vietnam and the NLF continued their struggle to conquer South Vietnam and unite the nation. They achieved their goals with the military defeat of South Vietnam in 1975 and with national reunification in 1976.

Arab National States and the Problem of Palestine

With the exception of Palestine, the Arab states of southwest Asia had little difficulty freeing themselves from the colonial powers of France and Britain by the end of World War II. Before the war, Arab states agitated for concessions under the mandate system, which limited Arab nationalist aspirations after the Great War. In fact, Egypt had almost complete autonomy from British rule, an autonomy limited by British military control of the strategic Suez Canal and the oil-rich Persian Gulf.

Arab Independence After the war, although Syria, Iraq, Lebanon, and Jordan gained complete independence, significant vestiges of imperial rule impeded Arab sovereignty. The battle to rid southwest Asia of those remnants of imperialism took some twists and turns as the superpowers interfered in the region, drawn by its vast reserves of oil, the lifeblood of the cold war's military-industrial complexes. Throughout, one ambiguous legacy of imperialism—Palestine—absorbed much of the region's energies and emotions.

Palestine Great Britain served as the mandate power in Palestine after the Great War and, before and during its mandate, made conflicting promises to the Palestinian Arabs and to the Jews migrating to Palestine to establish a secure homeland where they could avoid persecution. With the Balfour

Ho Chi Minh, leader of North Vietnam from 1945 to 1969 and one of southeast Asia's most influential communist leaders.

Declaration of 1917, the British government committed itself to the support of a homeland for Jews in Palestine, a commitment engendered in part by the vibrant Zionist movement that had been growing in Europe since the 1890s. Zionists were dedicated to combating the violent anti-Semitism prevailing in central and eastern Europe by establishing a national Jewish state. The Zionist dream of returning to Palestine, considered the site of the original Jewish homeland, received a boost from the Balfour Declaration and from the Allies' support for it at the Paris Peace Conference in 1919. Thus the British were compelled to allow Jewish migration to Palestine under their mandate, but they also had to allay the fears of those in possession of the land—the Palestinian Arabs. The British therefore limited the migration and settlement of Jews and promised to protect the Arabs' political and economic rights.

At the end of World War II, a battle brewed. As Arab states around Palestine gained their freedom from imperial rule, they developed a pan-Arab nationalism sparked by support for their fellow Arabs in Palestine and opposition to the possibility of a Jewish state there. The Holocaust, along with the British policy of limiting Jewish migration to Palestine after the war, intensified the Jewish commitment to build a state capable of defending the world's remaining Jews—and the tens of thousands of Palestinian Jews who had fought in the British army during the war were seen as potential defenders of the new state.

The Creation of Israel The British could not adjudicate the competing claims of the Arabs and the Jews in Palestine. While the Arabs insisted on complete independence under Arab rule, in 1945 the Jews embarked on a course of violent resistance to the British to compel recognition of Jewish demands for self-rule and open immigration. The British gave up in 1947, stating that they intended to withdraw from Palestine and turn over the region to the newly created United Nations. Delegates to the UN General Assembly debated the idea of dividing Palestine into two states, one Arab and the other Jewish. The United States and the Soviet Union lent their support to that notion, and in November 1947 the General Assembly announced a proposal for the division of Palestine into two distinct states. Arabs inside and outside Palestine found that solution unacceptable, and in late 1947 civil war broke out. Arab and Jewish troops battled each other as the British completed their withdrawal from Palestine, and in May 1948 the Jews in Palestine proclaimed the creation of the independent state of Israel.

Israel's proclamation of statehood provoked a series of military conflicts between Israeli and various Arab forces spanning five decades, most notably in 1948–49, 1956, 1967, 1973, and 1982. As a result of those wars, Israel substantially increased the size of its territory beyond the area granted to it by the original UN partition, and hundreds of thousands of Palestinians became refugees outside the state of Israel. Because Arabs and Israelis failed to reach a comprehensive and permanent peace agreement, hostilities continued. Beginning in 1987 a popular mass movement known as the *intifada* initiated a series of demonstrations, strikes, and riots against Israeli rule in the Gaza Strip and other occupied territories. Violence continued well into the twenty-first century, and the future of the occupied territories remains undetermined.

Egypt and Arab Nationalism Egyptian military leaders, under the direction of Gamal Abdel Nasser (1918–1970), committed themselves to opposing Israel and taking com-

mand of the Arab world. Forsaking constitutional government and democratic principles, they began a political revolution and campaign of state reform through militarism, suppressing the ideological and religious opposition organized by communists and the Muslim Brotherhood. In July 1952 Nasser and other officers staged a bloodless coup that ended the monarchy of Egypt's King Farouk. After a series of complicated intrigues, Nasser named himself prime minister in 1954 and took control of the government. He then labored assiduously to develop Egypt economically and militarily and make it the fountainhead of pan-Arab nationalism.

In his efforts to strengthen Egypt, Nasser adopted an internationalist position akin to Nehru's nonalignment policy in India. Nasser's neutralism, like Nehru's, was based on the belief that cold war power politics were a new form of imperialism. Nasser condemned states that joined with foreign powers in military alliances, such as the Baghdad Pact, a British- and U.S.-inspired alliance that included Turkey, Iraq, and Iran. Nevertheless, he saw in the new cold

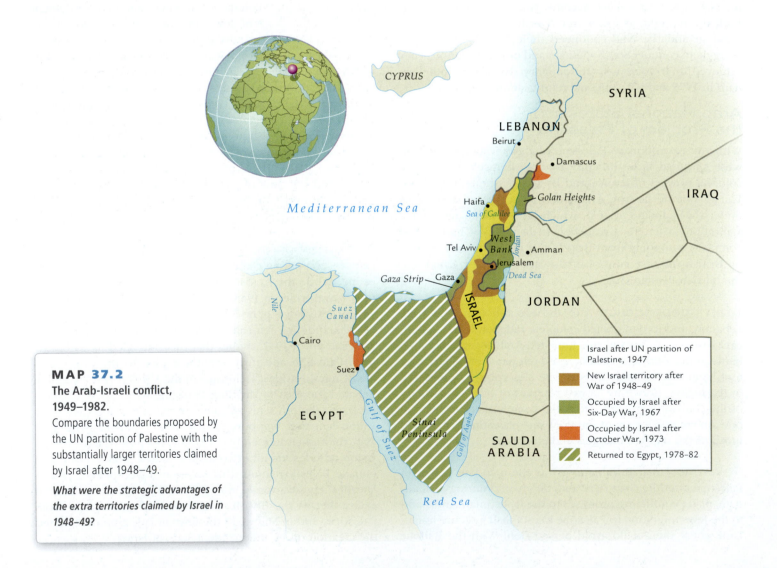

MAP 37.2

The Arab-Israeli conflict, 1949–1982.

Compare the boundaries proposed by the UN partition of Palestine with the substantially larger territories claimed by Israel after 1948–49.

What were the strategic advantages of the extra territories claimed by Israel in 1948–49?

Israel after UN partition of Palestine, 1947

New Israel territory after War of 1948–49

Occupied by Israel after Six-Day War, 1967

Occupied by Israel after October War, 1973

Returned to Egypt, 1978–82

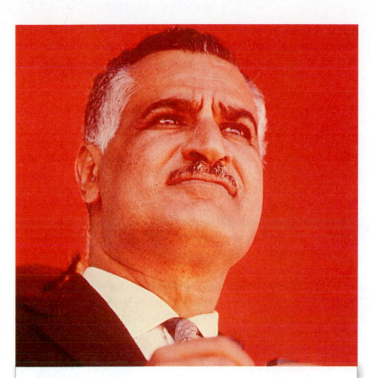

Gamal Abdel Nasser was president of Egypt from 1954 until his death in 1970. He successfully demonstrated how newly independent nations could avoid alignment with the cold war powers. Nasser also sought to rid Egypt and the Arab world of lingering imperialist influences. In particular, he sought the destruction of the state of Israel.

to wrest control of the canal away from him. Their military campaign was successful, but they failed miserably on the diplomatic level and tore at the fabric of the cold war world system. They had not consulted with the United States, which strongly condemned the attack and forced them to withdraw. The Soviet Union also objected forcefully, thereby gaining a reputation for being a staunch supporter of Arab nationalism. Nasser gained tremendous prestige, and Egypt solidified its position as leader of the charge against imperial holdovers in southwest Asia and north Africa.

Despite Nasser's successes, he did not manage to rid the region of Israel, which was growing stronger with each passing year. More wars were fought in the decades to come, and peace between the Arab states and Israel seemed not only elusive but at times impossible. Although the partition that took place in Palestine appeared to lend itself to manipulation by the superpowers, the region of southwest Asia confused, complicated, and undermined elements of bipolarism. The strategic importance of oil dictated that both superpowers vie for favor in the Arab states, and while the United States became a firm ally of Israel, the Soviet Union also supported Israel's right to exist. The Suez crisis further tangled cold war power politics because it divided the United States and its allies in western Europe. Southwest Asia proved successful at ousting almost all imperial control and at challenging the bipolar worldview.

DECOLONIZATION IN AFRICA

Agitation for independence in sub-Saharan Africa took many forms—some peaceful and some violent—and decolonization occurred at different paces in different nations. Complicating the decolonization process were internal divisions in African societies, which undermined attempts to forge national or pan-African identities. Tribal, ethnic, religious, and linguistic divides within and between state boundaries, all of which colonial rulers had exploited, posed a challenge to African leaders, particularly once independence came and the imperial outsider departed. In colonies where imperial rule had the support of European settlers, as in Algeria or Kenya, for example, decolonization became mired in violence. In many instances, African nations symbolized and sealed their severance from imperial control by adopting new names that shunned the memory of European rule and drew from the glory of Africa's past empires. Ghana set the pattern, and the map of Africa soon featured similar references to precolonial African places such as Zambia, Malawi, and Zimbabwe.

war world, opportunities that could be exploited for the advancement of Egypt, and he used his political savvy to extract pledges of economic and military assistance from the United States and the Soviet Union. Nasser demonstrated how newly independent nations could evade becoming trapped in either ideological camp and could force the superpowers to compete for influence.

Nasser also dedicated himself to ridding Egypt and the Arab world of imperial interference, which included destroying the state of Israel. He gave aid to the Algerians in their war against the French. Nasser did not neglect the remaining imperial presence in Egypt: he abolished British military rights to the Suez Canal in 1954. Through such actions and through his country's antipathy toward Israel, he laid claim to pan-Arab leadership throughout southwest Asia and north Africa.

The Suez Crisis Nasser sealed his reputation during the Suez crisis, which left him in a dominant position in the Arab world. The crisis erupted in 1956, when Nasser decided to nationalize the Suez Canal and use the money collected from the canal to finance construction of a massive dam of the Nile River at Aswan. When he did not bow to international pressure to provide multinational control of the vital Suez Canal, British, French, and Israeli forces combined

Forcing the French out of North Africa

In Africa as in southeast Asia, the French resisted decolonization. In Algeria the French fought a bloody war that began in 1954, the year France suffered its defeat at Dienbienphu. Somewhat ironically, while it focused its efforts on Algeria in the 1950s and 1960s, France allowed all its other territories in Africa to gain independence. In 1956 France granted

This 1960 photograph served as the identity-card portrait for an Algerian woman. During the war for Algerian independence, colonial French authorities forced such documentation, which included having women violate Muslim practices of remaining veiled in public.

independence to its colonies in Morocco and Tunisia, and thirteen French colonies in west and equatorial Africa won their independence in 1960, a year that came to be known as "the year of Africa."

France in Africa

France's concessions to its other African colonies illustrated its determination to control Algeria at all costs. The French people expressed differing opinions on the Algerian conflict, being less determined than their government leaders. French settlers demanded that the government in Paris defend their cause in north Africa. Two million French settled or were born there by the mid-1940s. The end of World War II, however, marked the beginning of a revitalized nationalist movement in Algeria, fueled by desire for independence from France and freedom from domination by white settlers. The event that touched off the Algerian revolt came in May 1945. French colonial police in the town of Sétif fired shots into an otherwise peaceful demonstration in support of Algerian and Arab nationalism. Algerian rioting and French repression of the disturbances took place in the wake of the incident. In the resulting melee more than eight thousand Algerian Muslims died, along with approximately one hundred French.

War in Algeria

The Algerian war of liberation began in 1954 under the command of the Front de Libération Natio-

nale (FLN, or National Liberation Front). The FLN adopted tactics similar to those of nationalist liberation groups in Asia, relying on bases in outlying mountainous areas and resorting to guerrilla warfare. The French did not realize the seriousness of the challenge they faced until 1955, when the FLN moved into more urbanized areas. France sent thousands of troops to Algeria to put down the revolution, and by 1958 it had committed half a million soldiers to the war. The war became ugly: Algerians serving with the French had to kill fellow Algerians or be killed by them; Algerian civilians became trapped in the crossfire of war, often accused of and killed for aiding FLN guerrillas; thousands of French soldiers died. By the war's end in 1962, when the Algerians gained independence from France, hundreds of thousands of Algerians had died.

Frantz Fanon

One ideological legacy for Africa stemmed from Algeria's war of independence. Frantz Fanon (1925–1961) gained fame as an Algerian revolutionary and as an influential proponent of national liberation for colonial peoples through violent revolution. Born in Martinique in the West Indies, Fanon studied psychiatry and medicine in France, went to Algeria to head a hospital's psychiatric department, and then participated in Algeria's battle to free itself from French rule. Fanon furthered his fame and provided ideological support for African nationalism and revolution in his writings. In works such as *The Wretched of the Earth* (1961), he urged the use of violence against colonial oppressors as a means of overcoming the racist degradation experienced by peoples in developing or colonial nations outside the Soviet-U.S. sphere. Fanon died shortly before Algerians achieved independence, but his ideas influenced the independence struggles ongoing in Africa.

Black African Nationalism and Independence

Before and during World War II, nationalism flourished in sub-Saharan Africa. African nationalists celebrated their blackness and Africanness in contrast to their European colonial rulers. Drawing from the pan-African movements that emerged in the United States and the Caribbean, African intellectuals, especially in French-controlled west Africa, established a movement to promote *Négritude* ("Blackness"). Reviving Africa's great traditions and cultures, poets and writers expressed a widely shared pride in Africa.

Growth of African Nationalism

This celebration of African culture was accompanied by grassroots protests against European imperialism. A new urban African elite slowly created the sorts of associations needed to hold demonstrations and fight for independence. Especially widespread, if sporadic, were workers' strikes against oppressive labor practices and the low wages paid by colonial overlords in areas such as the Gold Coast and Northern Rhodesia. Some independent Christian churches also provided

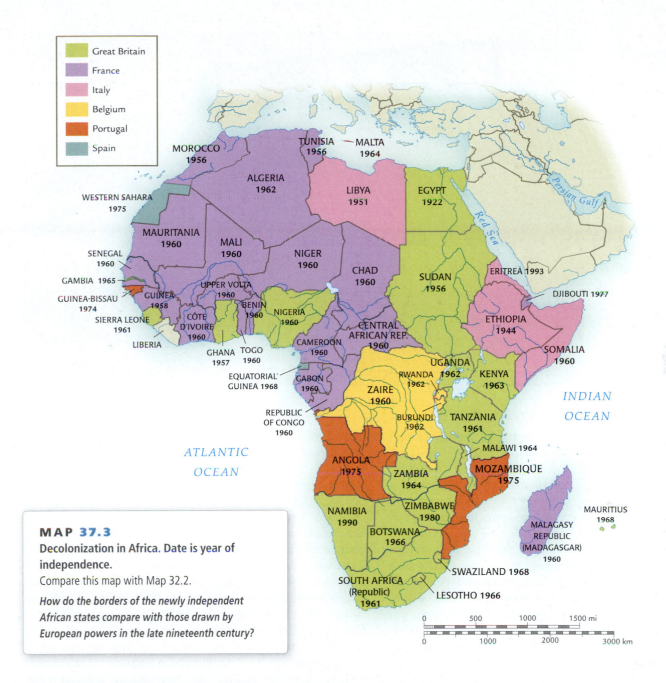

MAP 37.3

Decolonization in Africa. Date is year of independence.

Compare this map with Map 32.2.

How do the borders of the newly independent African states compare with those drawn by European powers in the late nineteenth century?

avenues for anticolonial agitation, as prophets such as Simon Kimbangu in the Belgian Congo promised his churchgoers that God would deliver them from imperial control. In the years after World War II, African poets associated with the *Négritude* movement continued to express their attachment to Africanness and encourage Africans to turn away from European culture and colonial rule.

African Independence The dreams and hopes of African nationalists frequently had to be placed on hold in the early years after World War II. Often assuming that black Africans were incapable of self-government, imperial powers planned for a slow transition to independence. The

presence of white settlers in certain African colonies also complicated the process of decolonization. The politics of the cold war allowed imperial powers to justify oppressive actions in the name of rooting out a subversive communist presence. Despite the delays, however, sub-Saharan states slowly but surely won their independence as each newly independent nation inspired and often aided other lands to win their freedom.

Freedom and Conflict in Sub-Saharan Africa

Ghana was the first sub-Saharan country to achieve independence from colonial rule. Located in west Africa, its

Roadside portraits of Queen Elizabeth II and Kwame Nkrumah in Accra. The British monarch made a postindependence visit to Ghana in November 1961.

people had been engaged in direct sea trade with Europe since the fifteenth century. Trading originally centered on gold but then shifted to the lucrative slave trade in the seventeenth century. By the time Ghana became part of the British empire as a Crown colony in 1874, its economy had developed into an important center for growing and exporting cacao.

Ghana's success in achieving its freedom from British rule in 1957 served as a hallmark in Africa's end of empire. Under the leadership of Kwame Nkrumah (1909–1972), political parties and strategies for mass action took shape. Although the British subjected Nkrumah and other nationalists to jail terms and repressive control, gradually they allowed reforms and negotiated the transfer of power in their Gold Coast colony.

Ghana After it became independent in 1957, Ghana emboldened and inspired other African nationalist movements. More than thirty other African countries followed Ghana's example and declared their own independence within the next decade. Nkrumah, as a leader of the first sub-Saharan African nation to gain independence from colonial rule, became a persuasive spokesperson for pan-African unity. His ideas and his stature as an African leader symbolized the changing times in Africa. In preparation for the 1961 visit of Britain's Queen Elizabeth II (1926–), the people of Ghana erected huge side-by-side posters of the queen and their leader, Nkrumah. Those roadside portraits offered a stunning vision of newfound equality and distinctiveness. Ex-colonial rulers, dressed in royal regalia, faced off against new Afri-

can leaders, clothed in traditional African fabrics, the once-dominating white faces matched by the proud black faces.

Anticolonial Rebellion in Kenya The process of attaining independence did not always prove as nonviolent as in Ghana. The battle that took place in the British colony of Kenya in east Africa demonstrated the complexity and difficulty of African decolonization. The situation in Kenya turned tense and violent in a clash between powerful white settlers and nationalists, especially the Kikuyu, one of Kenya's largest ethnic groups. Beginning in 1947, Kikuyu rebels embarked on an intermittently violent campaign against Europeans and alleged traitorous Africans. The settlers who controlled the colonial government in Nairobi refused to see the uprisings as a legitimate expression of discontent with colonial rule. Rather, they branded the Kikuyu tribes as radicals bent on a racial struggle for primacy. As one settler put it, "Why the hell can't we fight these apes and worry about the survivors later?" Members of the militant nationalist movements were labeled by the British government as Mau Mau subversives or communists.

In reality, Kikuyu radicalism and violence had much more to do with nationalist opposition to British colonial rule, especially land policies in Kenya. Kikuyu resentment of the British stemmed from their treatment in the 1930s and 1940s, when white settlers pushed them off the most fertile highland farm areas and reduced them to the status of wage slaves or relegated them to overcrowded "tribal reserves." Resistance began in the early 1940s with labor strikes and violent direct action campaigns designed to force or frighten

sources from the past

Kwame Nkrumah on African Unity

As the leader of the first African nation to gain independence, Kwame Nkrumah (1909–1972) became a respected spokesperson for African unity as a strategy for dealing with decolonization during the cold war. In his book I Speak of Freedom: A Statement of African Ideology *(1961), Nkrumah made an eloquent case for an African solution for the problems of African independence during a global cold war.*

It is clear that we must find an African solution to our problems, and that this can only be found in African unity. Divided we are weak; united, Africa could become one of the greatest forces for good in the world.

Never before have a people had within their grasp so great an opportunity for developing a continent endowed with so much wealth. Individually, the independent states of Africa, some of them potentially rich, others poor, can do little for their people. Together, by mutual help, they can achieve much. But the economic development of the continent must be planned and pursued as a whole. A loose confederation designed only for economic cooperation would not provide the necessary unity of purpose. Only a strong political union can bring about full and effective development of our natural resources for the benefit of our people.

The political situation in Africa today is heartening and at the same time disturbing. It is heartening to see so many new flags hoisted in place of the old; it is disturbing to see so many countries of varying sizes and at different levels of development, weak and, in some cases, almost helpless. If this terrible state of fragmentation is allowed to continue it may well be disastrous for us all.

Critics of African unity often refer to the wide differences in culture, language and ideas in various parts of Africa. This is true, but the essential fact remains that we are all Africans, and have a common interest in the independence of Africa. The difficulties presented by questions of language, culture and different political systems are not insuperable. If the need for political union is agreed by us all, then the will to create it is born; and where there's a will there's a way.

The greatest contribution that Africa can make to the peace of the world is to avoid all the dangers inherent in disunity, by creating a political union which will also by its success, stand as an example to a divided world. A union of African states will project more effectively the African personality. It will command respect from a world that has regard only for size and influence.

We have to prove that greatness is not to be measured in stockpiles of atom bombs. I believe strongly and sincerely that with the deep-rooted wisdom and dignity, the innate respect for human lives, the intense humanity that is our heritage, the African race, united under one federal government, will emerge not as just another world bloc to flaunt its wealth and strength, but as a Great Power whose greatness is indestructible because it is not built on fear, envy and suspicion, nor won at the expense of others, but founded on hope, trust, friendship and directed to the good of all mankind.

For Further Reflection

■ How does Nkrumah's call for African unity rather than fragmentation reflect the tensions between decolonization and the ongoing cold war?

Source: Kwame Nkrumah. *I Speak of Freedom: A Statement of African Ideology.* New York: Frederick A. Praeger, 1961, pp. x–xii.

---

the white settlers off their lands. In the 1950s, attacks on white settlers and black collaborators escalated, and in 1952 the British established a state of emergency to crush the anticolonial guerrilla movement through detention and counterinsurgency programs. Unable or unwilling to distinguish violent activism from nonviolent agitation, the British moved to suppress all nationalist groups and jailed Kenya nationalist leaders, including Jomo Kenyatta (1895–1978) in 1953. Amid growing resistance to colonial rule, the British mounted major military offenses against rebel forces, supporting their army troops with artillery, bombers, and jet fighters. By 1956 the British had effectively crushed all military resistance in a conflict that claimed the lives of twelve thousand Africans and one hundred Europeans.

Despite military defeat, Kikuyu fighters broke British resolve in Kenya and gained increasing international recognition of African grievances. The British resisted the radical white supremacism and political domineering of the settlers in Kenya and instead responded to calls for Kenya independence. In 1959 the British lifted the state of emergency, and as political parties formed, nationalist leaders like Kenyatta reemerged to lead those parties. By December 1963 Kenya had negotiated its independence.

Internal Colonialism in South Africa

As elsewhere in Africa, the presence of large numbers of white settlers in South Africa long delayed the arrival of black freedom. South Africa's black population, though a majority, remained

These Kikuyu children were photographed in 1952 in a British government prison camp, where rebel nationalists and their families were detained.

dispossessed and disfranchised. Anticolonial agitation thus was significantly different in South Africa than in the rest of sub-Saharan Africa: it was a struggle against internal colonialism, against an oppressive white regime that denied basic human and civil rights to tens of millions of South Africans.

Apartheid The ability of whites to resist majority rule had its roots in the South African economy, the strongest on the continent. That strength had two sources: extraction of minerals and industrial development, which received a huge boost during World War II. The growth of the industrial sector opened many jobs to blacks, creating the possibility of a change in their status. Along with black activism and calls for serious political reform after World War II, these changes struck fear into the hearts of white South Africans. In 1948 the Afrikaner National Party, which was dedicated to quashing any move toward black independence, came to power. Under the National Party the government instituted a harsh new set of laws designed to control the restive black population; these new laws constituted the system known as apartheid, or "separateness."

The system of apartheid asserted white supremacy and institutionalized the racial segregation established in the years before 1948. The government designated approximately 87 percent of South Africa's territory for white residents. Remaining areas were designated as homelands for black and colored citizens. Nonwhites were classified according to a variety of ethnic identifications—colored or mixed-race peoples, Indians, and "Bantu," which in turn was subdivided into numerous distinct tribal affiliations (for example, Zulu, Xhosa, Sotho). As other imperial powers had done in Africa, white South Africans divided the black and colored population in the hope of preventing the rise of unified liberation movements. The apartheid system, complex and varied in its composition, evolved into a system designed to keep blacks in a position of political, social, and economic subordination.

Dispossessed peoples all found in apartheid an impetus for resistance to white rule. The African National Congress (ANC), formed in 1912, gained new young leaders such as Nelson Mandela (1918–), who inspired direct action campaigns to protest apartheid. In 1955 the ANC published its Freedom Charter, which proclaimed the ideal of multiracial democratic rule for South Africa. Because its goals directly challenged white rule, the ANC and all black activists in South Africa faced severe repression. The government declared all its opponents communists and escalated its actions against black activists. Protests increased in 1960, the so-called year of Africa, and on 21 March 1960 white police gunned down black demonstrators in Sharpeville, near Johannesburg. Sixty-nine blacks died and almost two hundred were wounded. Sharpeville instituted a new era of radical activism.

When the white regime banned black organizations such as the ANC and jailed their adherents, international opposition to white South African rule grew. Newly freed nations in Asia and Africa called for UN sanctions against South Africa, and in 1961 South Africa declared itself a republic, withdrawing from the British Commonwealth. Some leaders of the ANC saw the necessity of armed resistance, but in 1963 government forces captured the leaders of ANC's military unit, including Nelson Mandela. The court sentenced them to life in prison, and Mandela and others became symbols of oppressive white rule. Protests against the system persisted in the 1970s and 1980s, spurred especially by student activism and a new black-consciousness movement. The combined effects of widespread black agitation and a powerful international anti-apartheid boycott eventually led to reform and a growing recognition that, if it was to survive, South Africa had to change.

The End of Apartheid When F. W. de Klerk (1936–) became president of South Africa in 1989, he and the National Party began to dismantle the apartheid system. De Klerk released Mandela from jail in 1990, legalized the ANC, and worked with Mandela and the ANC to negotiate the end of white minority rule. Collaborating and cooperating, the National Party, the ANC, and other African political groups created a new constitution and in April 1994 held elections that were open to people of all races. The ANC won overwhelmingly, and Mandela became the first black president of South Africa. In 1963, at the trial that ended in his jail sentence, Mandela proclaimed, "I have cherished the ideal of a democratic and free society in which all persons live

Whites telephone kiosk. The South African system of apartheid institutionalized racial segregation.

together in harmony and with equal opportunities. It is an ideal which I hope to live for and to achieve. But if needs be, it is an ideal for which I am prepared to die." Mandela lived to see his ideal fulfilled. In 1994, as president, he proclaimed his nation "free at last."

AFTER INDEPENDENCE: LONG-TERM STRUGGLES IN THE POSTCOLONIAL ERA

Political and economic stability proved elusive after independence, particularly in those developing nations struggling to build political and economic systems free from the domination of more powerful nations. The legacies of imperialism, either direct or indirect, hindered the creation of democratic institutions in many parts of the world—in recently decolo-

nized nations, such as those of Africa, and in some of the earliest lands to gain independence, such as those of Latin America. Continued interference by the former colonial powers, by the superpowers, or by more developed nations impeded progress, as did local elites with ties to the colonial powers. The result was an unstable succession of governments based on an authoritarian one-party system or on harsh military rule. South Africa and India, however, transformed themselves into functioning democracies despite deep racial and religious divides. In Asia and the Islamic world, some governments kept order by relying on tightly centralized rule, as in China, or on religion, as in Iran after the 1979 revolution. Few developing or newly industrialized countries, however, escaped the disruption of war or revolution that also characterized the postcolonial era.

Communism and Democracy in Asia

Except for Japan and India, the developing nations in south, southeast, and east Asia adopted some form of authoritarian or militarist political system, and many of them followed a communist or socialist path of political development. Under Mao Zedong (1893–1976), China served as a guide and inspiration for those countries seeking a means of political development distinct from the ways of their previous colonial masters.

Mao's China Mao reunified China for the first time since the collapse of the Qing dynasty, transforming European communist ideology into a distinctly Chinese communism. After 1949 he embarked on programs designed to accelerate development in China. The economic and social transformation of Chinese society centered on rapid industrialization and the collectivization of agriculture (making landownership collective, not individual). Emulating earlier Soviet experiments, the Chinese introduced their first Five-Year Plan in 1955. Designed to speed up economic development, the Five-Year Plan emphasized improvements in infrastructure and the expansion of heavy industry at the expense of consumer goods. A series of agrarian laws promoted an unprecedented transfer of wealth among the population, virtually eliminating economic inequality at the village level. After confiscating the landholdings of rich peasants and landlords, the government redistributed the land so that virtually every peasant had at least a small plot of land. After the government took over the grain market and prohibited farmers from marketing their crops, though, collective farms replaced private farming. Health care and primary education anchored to collectives permitted the extension of social services to larger segments of the population. In the wake of economic reforms came social reforms, many of which challenged and often eliminated Chinese family traditions. Supporting equal rights for women, Chinese authorities introduced marriage laws that eliminated practices such as child or forced marriages, gave women equal access to divorce, and legalized abortion. Foot binding, a symbol of women's subjugation, also became a practice of the past.

A 1966 poster shows Mao Zedong inspiring the people to launch the Great Proletarian Cultural Revolution.

Continuing China's push for development were the Great Leap Forward (1958–1961) and the Great Proletarian Cultural Revolution (1966–1976). These were far-reaching policies that contrarily hampered the very political and economic development that Mao sought.

Mao envisioned his Great Leap Forward as a way to overtake the industrial production of more developed nations, and to that end he worked to collectivize all land and to manage all business and industrial enterprises collectively. Private ownership was abolished, and farming and industry became largely rural and communal. The Great Leap Forward—or "Giant Step Backward" as some have dubbed it—failed. Most disastrous was its impact on agricultural production in China: the peasants, recalcitrant and exhausted, did not meet quotas, and a series of bad harvests also contributed to one of the deadliest famines in history. Rather than face reality, Mao blamed the sparrows for the bad harvests, accusing these counterrevolutionaries of eating too much grain. He ordered tens of millions of peasants to kill the feathered menaces, leaving insects free to consume what was left of the crops. Between 1959 and 1962 as many as

twenty million Chinese may have died of starvation and malnutrition in this crisis.

The Cultural Revolution In 1966 Mao tried again to mobilize the Chinese and reignite the revolutionary spirit with the inauguration of the Great Proletarian Cultural Revolution. Designed to root out the revisionism Mao perceived in Chinese life, especially among Communist Party leaders and others in positions of authority, the Cultural Revolution subjected millions of people to humiliation, persecution, and death. The elite—intellectuals, teachers, professionals, managers, and anyone associated with foreign or bourgeois values—constituted the major targets of the Red Guards, youthful zealots empowered to cleanse Chinese society of opponents to Mao's rule. Victims were beaten and killed, jailed, or sent to corrective labor camps or to toil in the countryside. The Cultural Revolution, which cost China years of stable development and gutted its educational system, did not die

The student democracy movement in Tiananmen Square, Beijing, June 1989. Many Chinese students had been encouraged by the government to study abroad. Their exposure to democratic societies prompted protests for change at home that were violently suppressed.

down until after Mao's death in 1976. It fell to one of Mao's political heirs, Deng Xiaoping, to heal the nation.

Deng's Revolution

Although he was a colleague of Mao, Deng Xiaoping (1904–1997) suffered the same fate as millions of other Chinese during the Cultural Revolution: he had to recant criticisms of Mao, identify himself as a petit-bourgeois intellectual, and labor in a tractor-repair factory. When a radical faction failed to maintain the Cultural Revolution after Mao's death, China began its recovery from the turmoil. Deng came to power in 1981, and the 1980s are often referred to as the years of "Deng's Revolution." Deng moderated Mao's commitment to Chinese self-sufficiency and isolation and engineered China's entry into the international financial and trading system, a move that was facilitated by the normalization of relations between China and the United States in the 1970s.

Tiananmen Square

To push the economic development of China, Deng opened the nation to the influences that were so suspect under Mao—foreign, capitalist values. His actions included sending tens of thousands of Chinese students to foreign universities to rebuild the professional, intellectual, and managerial elite needed for modern development. Those students were exposed to the democratic societies of western Europe and the United States. When they staged pro-democracy demonstrations in Beijing's Tiananmen Square in 1989, Deng, whose experiences in the Cultural Revolution made him wary of zealous revolutionary movements, approved a bloody crackdown. Not surprisingly, Deng faced hostile world opinion after crushing the student movement. The issue facing China as it entered the global economy was how (or whether) to reap economic benefits without compromising its identity and its authoritarian political system. This issue gained added weight as Hong Kong, under British administration since the 1840s and in the throes of its own democracy movement, reverted to Chinese control in 1997. Chinese leaders in the twenty-first century have managed to maintain both centralized political control over China and impressive economic growth and development. The evidence of China's increasing global power and prominence became especially visible during the 2008 summer Olympics in Beijing.

Indira Gandhi delivers a speech in 1972. Gandhi led India into the "green revolution," which sought to increase agricultural production to help feed the country's eight hundred million people. The campaign's mixed results, among other reasons, led to her temporarily losing power in 1977 before regaining it in 1980.

Indian Democracy

The flourishing of democracy in India stands in stark contrast to the political trends in many other developing nations. Whereas other nations turned to dictators, military rule, or authoritarian systems, India maintained its political stability and its democratic system after gaining independence in 1947. Even when faced with the crises that shook other developing nations—ethnic and religious conflict, wars, poverty, and overpopulation—India remained committed to free elections and a critical press. Its first postindependence prime minister, Jawaharlal Nehru, guided his nation to democratic rule.

In 1966 Indira Gandhi (1917–1984), Nehru's daughter (and no relation to Mohandas K. Gandhi), became leader of the Congress Party. She served as prime minister of India from 1966 to 1977 and from 1980 to 1984, and under her leadership India embarked on the "green revolution" that increased agricultural yields for India's eight hundred million people. Although the new agricultural policies aided wealthier farmers, the masses of peasant farmers fell deeper into poverty. Beyond the poverty that drove Indians to demonstrations of dissatisfaction with Gandhi's government, India was beset by other troubles—overpopulation and continuing sectarian conflicts.

Those problems prompted Indira Gandhi to take stringent action to maintain control. To quell growing opposition to her government, she declared a national emergency (1975–1977) that suspended democratic processes. She used her powers under the emergency to forward one of India's most needed social reforms, birth control. But rather than persuading or tempting Indians to control the size of their families (offering gifts of money for those who got vasectomies, for example), the government engaged in repressive birth control policies, including involuntary sterilization. A record eight million sterilization operations were performed in 1976 and 1977. The riots that ensued, and the fear of castration among men who might be forced to undergo vasectomies, added to Gandhi's woes.

When Indira Gandhi allowed elections to be held in 1977, Indians voted against her because of her abrogation of democratic principles and her harsh birth control policies. She returned to power in 1980, however, and again faced great difficulty keeping the state of India together in the face of religious, ethnic, and secessionist movements. One such movement was an uprising by Sikhs who wanted greater autonomy in the Punjab region. The Sikhs, representing perhaps 2 percent of India's population, practiced a religion that was an offshoot of Hinduism, and they had a separate identity—symbolized by their distinctive long hair and headdresses—and a history of militarism and self-rule. Unable or unwilling to compromise in view of the large number of groups agitating for a similar degree of autonomy, Indira Gandhi ordered the army to attack the sacred Golden Temple in Amritsar, which harbored armed Sikh extremists. In retaliation, two of her Sikh bodyguards—hired for their martial skills—assassinated her a few months later in 1984.

Indira Gandhi's son Rajiv Gandhi (1944–1991) took over the leadership of India in 1985 and offered reconciliation to the Sikhs. He was assassinated by a terrorist in 1991 while attempting to win back the office he lost in 1989. Despite those setbacks, however, Nehru's heirs maintained democracy in India and continued to work on the problems plaguing Indian development—overpopulation, poverty, and sectarian division. The legacy of Mohandas K. Gandhi lived on in the form of brutal assassinations and continued quests for peace and religious tolerance.

Islamic Resurgence in Southwest Asia and North Africa

The geographic convergence of the Arab and Muslim worlds in southwest Asia and north Africa encouraged the development of Arab nationalism in states of those regions that gained independence in the year after World War II. Whether in Libya, Algeria, or Egypt in north Africa or in Syria, Saudi Arabia, or Iraq in southwest Asia, visions of Arab nationalism, linked to the religious force of Islam, dazzled nations that wished to fend off European and U.S. influence. In north Africa, Egypt's Gamal Abdel Nasser provided the leadership for this Arab nationalism, and Arab-Muslim opposition to the state of Israel held the dream together.

The hopes attached to pan-Arab unity did not materialize. Although Arab lands shared a common language and religion, divisions were frequent and alliances shifted over time. The cold war split the Arab-Muslim world; some states allied themselves with the United States, and others allied with the Soviet Union. Some countries also shifted between the two, as Egypt did when it left the Soviet orbit for the U.S. sphere in 1976. Governments in these nations included military dictatorships, monarchies, and Islamist revolutionary regimes. Religious divisions also complicated the attainment of Arab unity, because Sunni and Shia Muslims followed divergent theologies and foreign policies.

Islamism In the 1970s, Muslims in many countries began to seek, sometimes violently, the revival of Islamic

thinking about ENCOUNTERS

Islamism and the World
Given the multiple encounters between Muslims, Europeans, Americans, and Israelis in the decades after World War II, Muslims turned away from the peoples and ways of life outside the Islamic sphere. How did that rejection of the non-Muslim world manifest itself?

values in the political and social sphere. Leading Islamic thinkers called for the rigorous enforcement of the *sharia* (Islamic law), emphasized pan-Islamic unity, and urged the elimination of non-Muslim economic, political, or cultural influences in the Muslim world. In the view of many proponents, the Muslim world had been slipping into a state of decline, brought about by the abandonment of Islamic traditions. Many Muslims had become skeptical about European and American models of economic development and political and cultural norms, which they blamed for economic and political failure as well as for secularization and its attendant breakdown of traditional social and religious values. Disillusionment and even anger with European and American societies, and especially with the United States, became widespread. The solution to the problems faced by Muslim societies lay, according to Islamists, in the revival of Islamic identity, values, and power. The vast majority of Islamic activists have sought to bring about change through peaceful means, but an extremist minority has claimed a mandate from God that calls for violent transformations. Convinced that the Muslim world is under siege, extremists used the concept of *jihad*—the right and duty to defend Islam and the Islamic community from unjust attack—to rationalize and legitimize terrorism and revolution.

The Iranian Revolution The Arab-Muslim world was divided on a number of issues, but the revolution that took place in Iran in 1979 demonstrated the power of Islam as a means of staving off secular foreign influences. Islamist influences penetrated Iran during the lengthy regime of Shah Mohammed Reza Pahlavi (1919–1980), whom the CIA helped bring to power in 1953. The vast sums of money that poured in from Iran's oil industry helped finance industrialization, and the United States provided the military equipment that enabled Iran to become a bastion of anti-communism in the region. In the late 1970s, however, opposition to the shah's government coalesced. Shia Muslims despised the shah's secular regime, Iranian small businesses detested the influence of U.S. corporations on the economy, and leftist politicians rejected the shah's repressive policies. The shah fled the country in early 1979 as the revolution gained force, and power was captured by the Islamist movement under the direction of Ayatollah Ruhollah Khomeini (1900–1989).

The revolution took on a strongly anti-U.S. cast, partly because the shah was allowed to travel to the United States for medical treatment. In retaliation, Shia militants captured sixty-nine hostages at the U.S. embassy in Tehran, fifty-five of whom remained captives until 1981. In the meantime, Iranian leaders shut U.S. military bases and confiscated U.S.-owned economic ventures. This Islamic power play against a developed nation such as the United States inspired other Muslims to undertake terrorist actions. The resurgent Islam of Iran did not lead to a new era of solidarity, however. Iranian Islam was the minority sect of Shia Islam, and one of Iran's neighbors, Iraq, attempted to take advantage of the revolution to invade Iran.

By the late 1970s Iraq had built a formidable military machine, largely owing to oil revenues and the efforts of Saddam Hussein (1937–2006), who became president of Iraq in 1979. Hussein launched his attack on Iran in 1980, believing that victory would be swift and perhaps hoping to become the new leader of a revived pan-Arab nationalism. (Iran is Muslim in religion, but not ethnically Arab, as are Iraq, Kuwait, and Saudi Arabia.) Although they were initially successful, Iraqi troops faced a determined counterattack by Iranian forces, and the conflict became a war of attrition that did not end until 1988.

The Iran-Iraq War The Iran-Iraq War killed as many as one million soldiers. In Iran the human devastation is still visible, if not openly acknowledged, in a nation that permits little dissent from Islamist orthodoxy. Young people are showing signs of a growing discontent caused by the war and by the rigors of a revolution that also killed thousands. Signs of recovery and a relaxation of Islamist strictness appeared in Iran in the late 1990s, but the destruction from war also remained visible. Islamism has reemerged in twenty-first-century Iran and has aroused some international concern, particularly for the United States. A conservative supreme leader, the Ayatollah Khamenei (1939–), and a conservative president, Mahmoud Ahmadinejad (1956–), represented this trend. Ahmadinejad took office in 2005 and touted Iran's nuclear program and his antipathy to the state of Israel, which had the effect of increasing his status in the Islamic world while intensifying tensions with the United States.

Iraqis continued on a militant course. Two years after the end of the Iran-Iraq War, Hussein's troops invaded Kuwait (1990) and incited the Gulf War (1991). The result was a decisive military defeat for Iraq, at the hands of an international coalition led by the United States, and further hardships for the Iraqi people.

Colonial Legacies in Sub-Saharan Africa

The optimism that accompanied decolonization in sub-Saharan Africa faded as the prospects for political stability gave way to civil wars and territorial disputes. This condition largely reflected the impact of colonialism. As European powers departed their decolonized lands, they left behind territories whose borders were artificial conveniences that did not correspond to any indigenous economic or ethnic divisions. Historically hostile communities found themselves jammed into a single "national" state. In other instances, populations found themselves in newly independent states whose borders were unacceptable to neighboring states. As a result, decolonization was frequently accompanied or followed by civil wars and border disputes that resisted resolution.

Iranians show their devotion to the Ayatollah Khomeini at his funeral in 1989.

The Organization of African Unity (OAU), created in 1963 by thirty-two member states, recognized some of those problems and attempted to prevent conflicts that could lead to intervention by former colonial powers. The artificial boundaries of African states, though acknowledged as problematic, were nonetheless held inviolable by the OAU to prevent disputes over boundaries. International law too treated postcolonial borders as inviolable. The OAU also promoted pan-African unity, at least in the faction headed by Kwame Nkrumah, as another way for African states to resist interference and domination by foreign powers. But although national borders have increasingly held, unity has not. African nations have been unable to avoid internal conflicts. Nkrumah, the former president of Ghana, is a case in point: he was overthrown in 1966, and Ghanaians tore down the statues and photographs that celebrated his leadership. Thus in Ghana, as in many other sub-Saharan states, politics evolved into dictatorial one-party rule, with party leaders forgoing multiparty elections in the name of ending political divisiveness. Several African nations fell prey to military rule in a large number of unsettling coups.

As political institutions foundered, the grinding poverty in which many African peoples lived increased tensions and made the absence of adequate administration and welfare programs more glaring. Poverty also prevented nations from accumulating the capital that could have contributed to a sound political and economic infrastructure. Africa's economic prospects after decolonization were not always so bleak, however. The continent is rich in mineral resources, raw materials, and agricultural products, and the postwar period saw a growing demand for Africa's commodity exports. Because many newly independent nations lacked the capital, the technology, and the foreign markets to exploit their natural wealth, they developed or maintained financial links with ex–colonial powers to finance economic development. After the 1970s many nations faced similar crises: falling commodity prices, rising import costs, and huge foreign debts. Africa's burdens were complicated by droughts, famines, and agricultural production that could not keep pace with population growth. Leaders of African nations were among the strongest supporters of the New International Economic Order that was called for by a coalition of developing nations. These states sought a more just allocation of global wealth, especially by guaranteeing prices and markets for commodities. Nevertheless, African states have continued to attempt wider integration into the global economy, despite the dependency that this move often entails.

Politics and Economics in Latin America

The uneasy aftermath of independence visible throughout Asia and Africa also affected states on the other side of the world—states that gained their freedom from colonial rule more than a century before postwar decolonization. Nations in Central and South America along with Mexico grappled with the conservative legacies of Spanish and Portuguese colonialism, particularly the political and economic power of the landowning elite of European descent. Latin America moreover had to deal with neocolonialism, because the United States not only intervened militarily when its interests were threatened but also influenced economies through investment and full or part ownership of enterprises such as the oil industry. In the nineteenth century Latin American states may have looked to the United States as a model of liberal democracy, but by the twentieth century U.S. interference provoked negative reactions. That condition was true after World War I, and it remained true during and after World War II.

Mexico Only President Lázaro Cárdenas (in office 1934–1940) had substantially invoked and applied the reforms guaranteed to Mexicans by the Constitution of 1917. The constitution's provisions regarding the state's right to redistribute land after confiscation and compensation, as well as its claim to government ownership of the subsoil and its products, found a champion in Cárdenas. He brought land reform and redistribution to a peak in Mexico, returning forty-five million acres to peasants, and he wrested away control of the oil industry from foreign investors. Cárdenas's nationalization of Mexico's oil industry allowed for the creation of the *Petróleos Mexicanos* (PEMEX), a national oil company in control of Mexico's petroleum products. The revenues generated by PEMEX contributed to what has been called "El Milagro Mexicano," or the Mexican economic miracle, a period of prosperity that lasted for decades. Conservative governments thereafter, controlled by the one-party rule of the Institutional Revolutionary Party (PRI), often acted harshly and experimented with various economic strategies that decreased or increased Mexico's reliance on foreign markets and capital. The PRI came under attack in the 1990s as Mexican peasants in the Chiapas district protested their political oppression. Cuauhtemoc Cárdenas, the son of Lázaro Cárdenas, took on the leadership of an opposition party, the Democratic Revolutionary Party (PRD), and this shift to democratic political competition and multiparty elections has continued into the twenty-first century.

Argentina Mexico served as one model for political development in Latin America, and Argentina seemed to be another candidate for leadership in South America. It had a reasonably expansive economy based on cattle raising and agriculture, a booming urban life, the beginnings of an industrial base, and a growing middle class in a population composed mostly of migrants from Europe. Given its geographic position far to the south, Argentina remained relatively independent of U.S. control and became a leader in the Latin American struggle against U.S. and European economic and political intervention in the region. A gradual shift to free elections and a sharing of political power beyond that exercised by the landowning elite also emerged. Given the military's central role in its politics, however, Argentina be-

In this 1950 photo taken in Buenos Aires, Eva Perón waves to adoring *descamisados,* or shirtless ones, to whose poverty she ceaselessly ministered. Although many thought of Eva Perón as a "saint," others viewed her own extravagant lifestyle as a sign of her opportunism.

came a model of a less positive form of political organization: the often brutal and deadly sway of military rulers.

Juan Perón During World War II, nationalistic military leaders gained power in Argentina and established a government controlled by the army. In 1946 Juan Perón (1895–1974), a former colonel in the army, was elected president. Although he was a nationalistic militarist, his regime garnered immense popularity among large segments of the Argentine population, partly because he appealed to the more downtrodden Argentines. He promoted a nationalistic populism, calling for industrialization, support of the working class, and protection of the economy from foreign control.

Evita However opportunistic Perón may have been, his popularity with the masses was real. His wife, Eva Perón (1919–1952), helped to foster that popularity, as Argentinians warmly embraced their "Evita" (little Eva). She rose from the ranks of the desperately poor. An illegitimate child who migrated to Buenos Aires at the age of fifteen, she found work as a radio soap-opera actress. She met Perón in 1944, and they were married shortly thereafter. Reigning in the Casa Rosada (the Pink House) as Argentina's first lady from 1946 to 1952, Eva Perón transformed herself into a stunningly beautiful political leader, radiant with dyed gold-blonde hair and clothed in classic designer fashions. While pushing for her husband's political reforms, she also tirelessly ministered to the needs of the poor, often the same *descamisados,* or "shirtless ones," who formed the core of her husband's supporters. Endless lines of people came to see her in her offices at the labor ministry—asking for dentures, wedding clothes, medical care, and the like. Eva Perón accommodated those demands and more: she bathed lice-ridden children in her own home, kissed lepers, and created the Eva Perón Foundation to institutionalize and extend such charitable endeavors. When she died of uterine cancer at the age of thirty-three, the nation mourned the tragic passing of a woman who came to be elevated to the status of "Santa Evita."

Some saw Eva Perón not as a saint but as a grasping social climber and a fascist sympathizer and saw her husband as a political opportunist, but after Juan Perón's ouster from office in 1955, support for the Perónist party remained strong. However, with the exception of a brief return to power by Perón in the mid-1970s, brutal military dictators held sway for the next three decades. Military rule took a sinister turn in the late 1970s and early 1980s when dictators approved the creation of death squads that fought a "dirty war" against suspected subversives. Between six thousand and twenty-three thousand people disappeared between 1976 and 1983. Calls for a return to democratic politics increased in the aftermath of the dirty war, demands that were intensified by economic disasters and the growth of the poor classes.

Guatemala and Nicaragua The political models and options open to states in Latin America were rather diverse, even though cold war issues complicated some political choices made after World War II. The establishment of communist and socialist regimes in Central and South America—or the instigation of programs and policies that hinted of progressive liberalism or anti-Americanism—regularly provoked a response from the United States. The United States did not need the impetus of a communist threat to justify its intervention in Latin America, because the northern neighbor had upheld the right to make southern incursions since the enunciation of the Monroe Doctrine in 1823. Moreover, one hundred years later, Latin America had become the site of fully 40 percent of U.S. foreign investments. Nonetheless, cold war imperatives shaped many U.S. actions in Latin America in the postwar years, especially in the Central American nations of Guatemala and Nicaragua.

Democratically elected president of Guatemala in 1951, Jacobo Arbenz Guzmán (1913–1971) publicly announced in 1953 a government seizure of hundreds of thousands of acres of uncultivated land owned by the United Fruit Company, a private enterprise controlled mainly by U.S. investors. Foreign companies such as the United Fruit Company dominated Guatemala's economy and its major export crop of bananas. President Arbenz was attempting to reassert Guatemala's control over its economy and its lands—for redistribution to the peasants. He offered monetary compensation to the company, based on the land's declared value for tax payments, but both the company and the United States government found that amount insufficient. U.S. officials also believed Arbenz's policies to be communist inspired, and they feared a spread of such radical doctrines throughout Central America.

President Dwight Eisenhower therefore empowered the CIA to engineer the overthrow of Arbenz's government. The United States sent arms to Guatemala's neighbors, Nicaragua and Honduras, to shore up their defenses against communism, and the CIA trained noncommunist Guatemalans under Colonel Carlos Castillo Armas (1914–1957) to attack and weaken the Arbenz government. With a continued supply of U.S. weapons and air support, Castillo Armas and his troops forced the fall of Arbenz in 1954. Castillo Armas established a military government, returned land to the United Fruit Company, and ruthlessly suppressed opponents with methods that included torture and murder. After his assassination in 1957, Guatemalans plunged into a civil war that did not end until the 1990s.

Anastacio Somoza Garcia (1896–1956) served as president of Nicaragua in 1954, just as the CIA was helping Guatemalan rebels overthrow what many believed was a communist-inspired government. During that time, Somoza demonstrated himself to be a staunch anticommunist U.S. ally. He had funneled weapons to Guatemalan rebels opposing Arbenz, and he outlawed the communist party in Nicaragua during the cold war. Somoza first grasped power in the 1930s, when members of his Nicaraguan National Guard killed nationalist Augusto Cesar Sandino (1893–1934), who had led a guerrilla movement aimed at ending U.S. interference in Nicaragua. After murdering Sandino, Somoza and his sons, Luis Somoza Debayle (d. 1967) and Anastacio Somoza Debayle (1928–1980), controlled Nicaraguan politics for more than forty years, aided by U.S. financial and military support.

The brutality, corruption, and pro-U.S. policies of the Somoza family—which extended to allowing the United States to use Nicaragua as a staging place during the Bay of Pigs attack on Cuba in 1961—alienated other Latin American nations as well as Nicaraguans. In the early 1960s, a few Nica-raguans created the Sandinista Front for National Liberation, in honor of the murdered Augusto Sandino. The Sandinistas, as they became known, launched guerrilla operations aimed at overthrowing the Somozas, and they finally took power in 1979. Although the administration of U.S. president Jimmy Carter (1924–) recognized the Sandinistas, the fervent anti-communist president Ronald Reagan (1911–2004), who came to the presidency in 1981, abandoned and reversed Carter's policies. Because Reagan believed that the Sandinistas were abetting communist rebels elsewhere in Central America, such as in El Salvador, he halted aid to Nicaragua and instituted an economic boycott of the country. By 1983 Reagan offered increasing support—monetary and military—to the Contras, a CIA-trained counterrevolutionary group dedicated to overthrowing the Sandinistas and engaging over time in such activities as the bombing of oil facilities and the mining of harbors.

In the face of U.S. efforts to destabilize Sandinista rule in Nicaragua, Central American leaders decided to take action themselves on their region's troubles. President Oscar Arias Sánchez (1940–) of Costa Rica became especially influential in promoting a negotiated end to the Contra war in Nicaragua. A 1989 agreement provided for the presence of a UN peacekeeping force, for monitored elections, and for the disarming of the Contras. Elections in the following decade brought new political parties to the forefront, and the Sandinistas worked to form coalition governments with opposition parties. Sandinista power was weakened but not eliminated despite the overwhelming interference of the United States, and democratic politics and a normalization of relations with the United States emerged in Nicaragua in the late twentieth century.

Nicaragua's experiences after World War II suggested clearly the political complications associated with continued U.S. interference in Latin America. The economic and political conditions in South and Central America nonetheless made experiments with revolutionary doctrines and Marxist programs attractive to many of the region's peoples. These interested people included members of normally conservative institutions such as the Catholic Church; numerous priests in Latin America embraced what was called "liberation theology," a mixture of Catholicism and Marxism meant to combat the misery and repression of the masses through revolutionary salvation. Brutal regimes ordered the assassinations of hundreds of priests preaching this message of liberation, including Archbishop Oscar Romero in El Salvador in 1980.

Liberation for Nations and Women Revolutionary ideologies and political activism also provided opportunities for Latin American women to agitate for both national and women's liberation. Nicaraguan women established the Association of Women Concerned about National Crisis in 1977 and fought as part of the FSLN to rid their nation of Somoza's rule. In 1979 they renamed the organization the Luisa Amanda Espinoza Association of Nicaraguan Women

(AMNLAE) to honor the first woman who died in the battle against Somoza. The group's slogan—"No revolution without women's emancipation: no emancipation without revolution"—suggested the dual goals of Nicaraguan women. By the mid-1980s, AMNLAE had over eighty thousand members. Despite facing problems typical to women's movements trying to navigate between national and personal needs, AMNLAE has been credited with forwarding women's participation in the public and political spheres, an impressive accomplishment in a region where women's suffrage had often been delayed. Although women in Ecuador attained voting rights in 1929, women in Nicaragua could not vote until 1955; Paraguay's women waited for suffrage rights until 1961, when that nation became the last in Latin America to incorporate women into the political process.

The Search for Economic Equity The late twentieth century witnessed a revival of democratic politics in Latin America, but economic problems continued to limit the possibility of widespread change or the achievement of economic and social equity. In many Latin American nations, the landowning elites who gained power during the colonial era were able to maintain their dominant position, which resulted in societies that remained divided between the few rich, usually backed by the United States, and the masses of the poor. It was difficult to structure such societies without either keeping the elite in power or promoting revolution on behalf of the poor, and the task of fashioning workable state and economic systems was made even more troublesome given the frequency of foreign interference, both military and economic. Despite the difficulties, the mid-twentieth century offered economic promise. During World War II, many Latin American nations took advantage of world market needs and pursued greater industrial development. Profits flowed into these countries during and after the war, and nations in the region experienced sustained economic growth through expanded export trade and diversification of foreign markets. Exports included manufactured goods and traditional export commodities such as minerals and foodstuffs such as sugar, fruits, and coffee.

Dependency Theory Latin American nations realized the need to reorient their economies away from exports and toward internal development, but the attempts to do so fell short. One influential Argentine economist, Raul Prebisch (1901–1985), who worked for the United Nations Commission for Latin America, explained Latin America's economic problems in global terms. Prebisch crafted the "dependency" theory of economic development, pointing out that developed industrial nations—such as those in North America and Eu-

rope—dominated the international economy and profited at the expense of less developed and industrialized nations burdened with the export-oriented, unbalanced economies that were a legacy of colonialism. To break the unequal relationship between what Prebisch termed the "center" and the "periphery," developing nations on the periphery of international trade needed to protect and diversify domestic trade and to use strategies of import-substituting industrialization to promote further industrial and economic growth.

Prebisch's theories about the economic ills of the developing world, though influential at the time, have since declined in currency. Latin American economies have shown resilience in the late twentieth and early twenty-first centuries, and Latin American nations have maintained links to global markets and money. Their economies appeared strong enough to limit the effects of their export-oriented systems and their use of foreign investment monies, and further economic growth should aid in the search for a social and economic equity that have been elusive in Latin America from colonial times.

in**perspective**

In the years immediately before and after World War II, a few nations controlled the political and economic destiny of much of the world. The imperial and colonial encounters between European elites and indigenous peoples defined much of the recent history of the world before the mid-twentieth century. The decades following 1945 witnessed the stunning reversal of that state of affairs, as European empires fell and dozens of newly independent nations emerged. Decolonization changed the world's political, economic, and social landscape in often radical ways, and the peoples of these newly free countries thereafter labored to reshape their national identities and to build workable political and economic systems. The effervescence of liberty and independence at times gave way to a more sober reality in the days, years, and decades after liberation. Religious and ethnic conflict, political instability, economic challenges, and neoimperialism dampened spirits and interfered with the ability of nations to achieve peace and stability. Nothing, however, could ever truly diminish the historic significance of what transpired in the colonial world after World War II. The global balance of power had been irrevocably altered by this attainment of worldwide independence and pointed to the emergence of a new kind of world order: one without borders. ●

CHRONOLOGY	
1947	Partition of India
1948	Creation of Israel
1948–1989	Apartheid in South Africa
1954	Overthrow of Arbenz in Guatemala
1954	French defeat at Dienbienphu
1954–1962	Algerian war of liberation
1955	Bandung Conference
1956	Suez crisis
1957	Ghana gains independence
1958–1961	Great Leap Forward in China
1963	Founding of Organization of African Unity
1973	Arab-Israeli War
1976	Reunification of Vietnam
1979	Revolution in Iran
1979	Sandinistas in power in Nicaragua
1980–1988	Iran-Iraq War
1990–1991	Gulf War
1997	Transfer of British Hong Kong to People's Republic of China

For Further Reading

David Anderson. *Histories of the Hanged: The Dirty War in Kenya and the End of Empire.* New York, 2005. History of Kenya's Kikuyu insurrection as a consequence of British colonial violence and land appropriation.

Franz Ansprenger. *The Dissolution of the Colonial Empires.* New York, 1989. A discerning and thorough treatment of the dismantling of European empires and colonies.

Mark Borthwick, ed. *Pacific Century: The Emergence of Modern Pacific Asia.* Boulder, 1992. An excellent source for an overview of southeast and east Asia.

Greg Campbell. *Blood Diamonds: Tracing the Deadly Path of the World's Most Precious Stones.* New York, 2002. A look at the dark side of the Sierra Leone–centered diamond trade.

M. E. Chamberlain. *Decolonization: The Fall of European Empires.* Oxford, 1985. A brief but competent summary of the demise of empires.

Gloria Chuku. *Igbo Women and Economic Transformation in Southeastern Nigeria, 1900–1960.* New York, 2004. Study of the impact of colonial policies on gender relations in postcolonial Nigeria from economic and political perspectives.

Nancy L. Clark and William H. Worger. *South Africa: The Rise and Fall of Apartheid.* New York, 2004. A survey of the history of the apartheid regime from 1948 to its collapse in the 1990s.

Michael J. Cohen. *Palestine and the Great Powers 1945–48.* 2nd ed. Princeton, 1992. An evenhanded assessment of the role played by the great powers in the partition of Palestine and the creation of Israel.

Basil Davidson. *The Black Man's Burden: Africa and the Curse of the Nation State.* New York, 1992. A critical postindependence account that emphasizes the shortcomings of nationalism and the national state.

Prasenjit Duara, ed. *Decolonization (Rewriting Histories).* New York, 2004. The perspective of the colonized is privileged through a selection of writings by leaders of the colonizing countries.

Carlene J. Edie. *Politics in Africa: A New Beginning?* New York, 2002. Examines the domestic and external pressures that have transformed postcolonial African states and societies.

Caroline Elkins. *Imperial Reckoning: The Untold Story of Britain's Gulag in Kenya.* New York, 2004. Powerful study of British atrocities in late colonial Kenya.

Robert Hardgrave Jr. and Stanley A. Hardgrave. *India: Government and Politics in a Developing Nation.* 4th ed. San Diego, 1986. A work that centers on Indian postindependence politics.

Sunil Khilani. *The Idea of India.* New York, 1988. A lively and incisive analysis of the many meanings of India.

Phyllis M. Martin and Patrick O'Meara, eds. *Africa.* 3rd ed. Bloomington, 1995. An insightful collection of articles addressing the cultural, social, economic, and political development of Africa.

Mark Mathabane. *Kaffir Boys: The True Story of a Black Youth's Coming of Age in Apartheid South Africa.* New York, 1986. A gripping real-life story.

Robert A. Mortimer. *The Third World Coalition in International Politics.* New York, 1980. Surveys the political evolution of the nonaligned world.

Timothy H. Parsons. *The 1964 Army Mutinies and the Making of Modern East Africa.* Westport, Conn., 2003. Detailed analysis of soldiers' anticolonial protests in Tanganyika, Uganda, and Kenya.

Thomas E. Skidmore and Peter H. Smith. *Modern Latin America.* New York, 1992. Excellent overview covering the region from the 1880s to the 1980s and supported by an extensive bibliography.

Thomas W. Walker. *Nicaragua: Living in the Shadow of the Eagle.* 4th ed. Boulder, 2003. Best and most comprehensive treatment of the nation in the past two decades.

PART 7

chapter 38

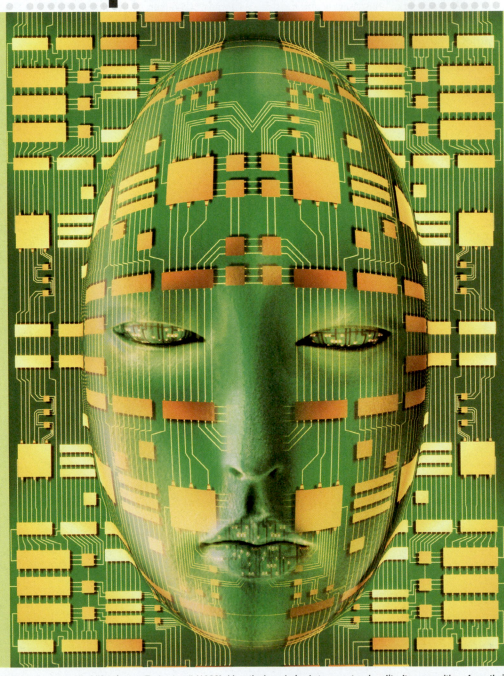

This stunning digitally crafted photograph, called "Omnipotent Technology" (1999), blurs the boundaries between art and reality. Its composition of an ethnically fluid face from computer chips and hardware suggests how global identity has morphed and how computers have breached borders between humans and machines.

EYEWITNESS:
Kristina Matschat and a Falling Wall

On 9 November 1989, Kristina Matschat felt excitement and tension in the night air of Berlin. She had joined thousands of other East Germans at Checkpoint Charlie, one of the most famous crossing points in the Berlin Wall. Anticipating that some momentous event was soon to occur at the wall, that the wall might come down that night, she also shivered in fear at the proximity of the *Volkspolizei* ("people's police")—the same officers who since 1961 gunned down East Germans attempting to scale the wall and escape to freedom in West Berlin. She wore running shoes in case she needed to sprint away if shooting broke out or tanks rumbled through East Berlin to prevent the destruction of the wall.

She remembered that "everybody was full of fear—but also full of hope." Bitter memories flooded her consciousness as she recalled not being allowed to study what she wanted in school, not being able to speak freely of her discontent in case her friends were government spies, and not being able to locate disgruntled colleagues whom the government had condemned as "unwanted elements." Her hope overcame her fears, though, as she chanted with her fellow compatriots, "Tear the wall down! Open the gates!" She could see that on the other side of the wall massive crowds of West Berliners had gathered to join their demonstration. Thrilled by this open protest against the most salient symbol of the cold war, she was nonetheless psychologically unprepared for victory when it came. Just before midnight East German soldiers suddenly began not only opening gates in the Wall but also gently helping East Germans cross to the West, often for the first time in their lives. Her near disbelief at the swift downfall of Berlin's decades-old barricade registered in the word she heard shouted over and over again by those passing through the wall: *Wahnsinn* ("craziness").

Kristina Matschat remained at the wall until 3:00 or 4:00 A.M., celebrating with the hundreds of thousands of other Berliners who now mingled, drinking champagne and dancing on top of the wall. While celebrating the fall of the barbed wire and mortar structure, she became aware of the significance of a world without borders: "Suddenly we were seeing the West for the first time, the forbidden Berlin we had only seen on TV or heard about from friends. When we came home at dawn, I felt free for the first time in my life. I had never been happier." The fall of the Berlin Wall brought down one of the world's most notorious borders and symbolized the breaching of all sorts of boundaries in the contemporary world.

Along with decolonization, the fall of the Berlin Wall, and the end of the cold war, many other forces were at work to create a new, more open, world. One pronounced feature of this world was an increased level of economic interaction between countries and a tighter economic integration of the world. The forces driving the world economy in this direction, often referred to as *globalization,* included advances in communication technology, an enormous expansion of international trade, and the emergence of new global enterprises as well as governments and international organizations that favored market-oriented economics.

Although certain formal national borders changed only after decolonization and the end of the cold war, cultural and technological developments since World War II had steadily broken down the distances between countries and peoples. Cultural integration resulted from the never-ending stream of ideas, information, and values spreading from one society to another. Consumer goods, popular culture, television, computers, and the Internet all spread outward from advanced capitalist and industrialized nations, particularly Europe and the United States, and other societies had to come to terms with this breakdown of cultural and technological barriers. Cultural traditions from Europe and the United States were challenged as often as they were accepted, as most of the world's peoples attempted to blend foreign traditions with their own.

The world's peoples themselves underwent changes in a world with fewer barriers. Women struggled to close the divide between the sexes, at times fighting for equal economic, social, and political rights and at other times abiding by gender expectations while waiting for new opportunities to improve their condition. As populations grew at often alarming rates, women spent much of their time at the traditional female task of child rearing, but both women and men embarked on migrations when their societies could no longer adequately support their growing populations. They moved to the cities or to other nations either to escape suffering or to seek new fortunes.

The populations moving around the globe revealed the diminishing significance of national boundary lines, but they also posed problems that could not be solved by any one state acting alone. International organizations such as the United Nations acknowledged that global problems needed global solutions, underscoring anew the tenuousness of borders in the contemporary world. The global troubles posed by epidemic diseases, labor servitude, terrorism, and human rights also crossed national boundaries and prompted international cooperation. Not everyone experienced the ecstasy Kristina Matschat felt at the Berlin Wall when that most restrictive border disappeared, but global interconnectedness made it more difficult to maintain boundaries among the peoples and countries of the world.

THE END OF THE COLD WAR

Between 1989 and 1991, the Soviet system in Europe collapsed with indecent haste. This was partly encouraged by U.S. President Ronald Reagan (in office 1981–1989), who reinvigorated cold war animosities, zeroing in on communism and the USSR, which he called "the evil empire." Beyond adopting this rhetorical fervor, Reagan advocated enormous military spending. Reagan's cold war rhetoric and budgets challenged détente and the Soviet ability to match U.S. spending, but internal changes in the Soviet Union and eastern Europe worked most effectively to end communism and the cold war. Whether forced by internal dissent or by the horrendous military and economic costs of the cold war, the superpowers soon backed down from their traditional polarizing division of the world. The result was the collapse of the cold war world, whose disintegration began in eastern Europe and the Soviet Union. Between 1989 and 1990, through a series of mostly nonviolent revolutions, the peoples of eastern and central Europe regained their independence, instituted democratic forms of government, and adopted market-based economies.

The downfall of communist regimes in Europe was the direct consequence of interrelated economic and political developments. The economic weakness of the communist regimes in eastern and central Europe and the Soviet Union became so apparent as to require reforms. The policies espoused by a new Soviet leader, Mikhail S. Gorbachev (1931–), who came to power in 1985, represented an effort to address this economic deterioration, but they also unleashed a tidal wave of revolution that brought down communist governments. As communism unraveled throughout eastern and

At a U.S./U.S.S.R. summit in 1985, a Soviet flag served as a dramatic backdrop and counterpoint to U.S. President Ronald Reagan's speech.

central Europe, Gorbachev desperately tried to save the Soviet Union from disintegration by restructuring the economy and liberalizing society. Caught between the rising tide of radical reforms and the opposition of entrenched interests, however, there was little he could do except watch as events unfolded beyond his control. By the time the Soviet Union collapsed in 1991, the Soviet vision of socialism had ceased to inspire either fear or emulation. The cold war system of states and alliances became irrelevant to international relations.

Revolutions in Eastern and Central Europe

The inability to connect communism with nationalism left communist regimes vulnerable throughout eastern and central Europe. Those regimes were born in Moscow, transplanted by the Soviet army, and shored up by tanks and bayonets. To most eastern and central Europeans, the Soviet-imposed governments lacked legitimacy from the beginning, and despite the efforts of local communist leaders, the regimes never became firmly established. The Polish intellectual Leszek Kolakowski echoed the sentiments of many when he bitterly complained in 1971 that "the dead and by now also grotesque creature called Marxist-Leninism still hangs at the necks of the rulers like a hopeless tumor."

Despite economic stagnation, an accelerated arms race with the United States that further strained the Soviet economy, and obvious signs of discontent, the rulers of eastern and central Europe were too reluctant to confront the challenge and restructure their ailing systems. It remained for Gorbachev to unleash the forces that resulted in the disappearance of the Soviet empire in Europe. By the time Gorbachev visited East Berlin in 1989 on the fortieth anniversary of the founding of the German Democratic Republic, he had committed himself to a restructuring of the Soviet Union and to unilateral withdrawal from the cold war. In public interviews he surprised his grim-faced hosts with the announcement that the Brezhnev Doctrine was no longer in force and that from then on each country would be responsible for its own destiny. As one observer put it, the "Sinatra doctrine" ("I did it my way") replaced the Brezhnev Doctrine. The new Soviet orientation led in rapid succession to the collapse or overthrow of regimes in Poland, Bulgaria, Hungary, Czechoslovakia, Romania, and East Germany.

Poland, Bulgaria, and Hungary   The end of communism came first in Poland, where Solidarity—a combined trade union and nationalist movement—put pressure on the crumbling rule of the Communist Party. The Polish government legalized the previously banned Solidarity movement and agreed to multiparty elections in 1989 and 1990. The voters favored Solidarity candidates, and Lech Walesa (1943–), the movement's leader, became president of Poland. In Bulgaria popular unrest forced Todor Zhivkov (1911–1998), eastern Europe's longest-surviving communist dictator, to resign in November 1989. Two months later a national assembly began dismantling the communist state. Hungarians tore down the Soviet-style political system during 1988 and 1989. In 1990 they held free elections and launched their nation on the rocky path toward democracy and a market economy.

Velvet and Violent Revolutions   The disintegration of communism continued elsewhere in eastern Europe. In Czechoslovakia a "velvet revolution" swept communists out of office and restored democracy by 1990. The term *velvet revolution* derived from the fact that aside from the initial suppression of mass demonstrations, little violence was associated with the transfer of power in societies formerly ruled by an iron fist. The communist leadership stood by and watched events take their course. In 1993, disagreements over the time frame for shifting to a market economy led to a "velvet divorce," breaking Czechoslovakia into two new

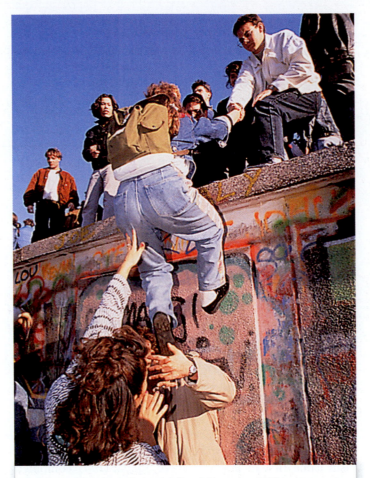

Berliners climb the wall after it fell on 9 November 1989.

The Collapse of the Soviet Union

The desire to concentrate attention and resources on urgent matters at home motivated Gorbachev's decision to disengage his nation from the cold war and its military and diplomatic extensions. When he came to power in 1985, Gorbachev was keenly aware of the need for economic reform and the liberalization of Soviet society, although he never intended to abolish the existing political and economic system. Yet it proved impossible to fix parts of the system without undermining the whole.

Gorbachev's Reforms Gorbachev's reform efforts focused on the ailing economy. Antiquated industrial plants, obsolete technologies, and inefficient government control of production resulted in shoddy and outmoded products. The diversion of crucial resources to the military made it impossible to produce enough consumer goods—regardless of their quality. The failure of state and collective farms to feed the population compelled the Soviet government to import grains from the United States, Canada, and elsewhere. By 1990 the government imposed rationing to cope with the scarcity of essential consumer goods and food. Economic stagnation in turn contributed to the decline of the Soviet standard of living. Ominous statistics documented the disintegration of the state-sponsored health care system: infant mortality increased while life expectancy decreased. Funding of the educational system dropped precipitously, and pollution threatened to engulf the entire country. Demoralization affected ever larger numbers of Soviet citizens as divorce rates climbed, corruption intensified, and alcoholism became more widespread.

Perestroika and Glasnost Under the slogan of *uskorenie,* or "acceleration," Gorbachev tried to shock the economy out of its coma. Yet the old methods of boosting production and productivity through bureaucratic exhortation and harassment paid few dividends; in fact, they called attention to the drawbacks of centralized economic control. Gorbachev then contemplated different kinds of reform, using the term *perestroika,* or "restructuring," to describe his efforts to decentralize the economy. To make perestroika work, the Soviet leader linked it to *glasnost,* a term that referred to the opening of Soviet society to public criticism and admission of past mistakes.

Perestroika proved more difficult to implement than Gorbachev imagined, and glasnost unleashed a torrent of criticism that shook the Soviet state to its foundations. When Gorbachev pushed economic decentralization, the profit motive and the cost-accounting methods he instituted engendered the hostility of those whose privileged positions depended on the old system. Many of Gorbachev's comrades and certain factions of the military objected to perestroika and worked to undermine or destroy it. Glasnost also turned out to be a two-edged sword, since it opened the door to public criticism of party leaders and Soviet institu-

nations, the Czech Republic and Slovakia. In Romania, by contrast, the regime of dictator Nicolae Ceaușescu (1918–1989) refused to acknowledge the necessity of reform. In 1989 *Securitate,* a brutal secret police force, savagely repressed demonstrations, setting off a national uprising that ended within four days and left Ceaușescu and his wife dead.

Fall of the Berlin Wall East Germany had long been a staunchly communist Soviet satellite. Its aging leader, Erich Honecker (1912–1994), openly objected to Gorbachev's ideas and clung to Stalinist policies. When he showed genuine bewilderment at the fact that East German citizens fled the country by the thousands through openings in the iron curtain in Hungary and Czechoslovakia, his party removed him from power. It was too late for anything other than radical changes, and when the East German regime decided to open the Berlin Wall to intra-German traffic on 9 November 1989, the end of the German Democratic Republic was in sight. The end to a divided Berlin was also in sight, literally, as thousands of east and west Berliners tore down the Berlin Wall in the last weeks of 1989. In 1990 the two Germanies, originally divided by the cold war, formed a united nation.

tions in a way unimaginable a short time earlier. While discontent with Soviet life burst into the open, long-repressed ethnic and nationalist sentiments bubbled to the surface, posing a threat to the multiethnic Soviet state. Only half of the 285 million Soviet citizens were Russian. The other half included numerous ethnic minorities, most of whom never fully reconciled themselves to Soviet dominance.

The pressures on the Soviet system were exacerbated by an ill-considered and costly Soviet military intervention in 1979 to save a Marxist regime in Afghanistan. For nine years well-equipped Soviet forces fought a brutal, unsuccessful campaign against *Afghan mujahideen,* or Islamic warriors, who gradually gained control of most of the countryside. Weapons and money from the United States, Saudi Arabia, Iran, Pakistan, and China sustained the mujahideen in their struggle. The Central Intelligence Agency of the United States

supplied the decisive weapons in the war: ground-to-air Stinger missiles, which could be used to shoot down heavily armored Soviet helicopters, and thousands of mules to haul supplies from Pakistan. In 1986 the Kremlin decided to pull its troops out of the costly, unpopular, and unwinnable war. A cease-fire negotiated by the United Nations in 1988 led to a full Soviet withdrawal in 1989.

Collapse   By the summer of 1990, Gorbachev's reforms had spent themselves. As industrial and agricultural production continued their downward slide against a backdrop of skyrocketing inflation, the Soviet economy disintegrated. Inspired by the end of the Soviet empire in eastern and central Europe, many minorities now contemplated secession from the Soviet Union. The Baltic peoples—Estonians, Latvians, and Lithuanians—were first into the fray, declaring their independence in August 1991. In the following months the remaining twelve republics of the Soviet Union followed suit. The largest and most prominent of the Soviet republics, the Russian Soviet Federated Socialist Republic, and its recently elected president, Boris N. Yeltsin (1931–2007), led the drive for independence. Soviet leaders vacillated between threats of repression and promises of better

MAP 38.1

The collapse of the Soviet Union and European communist regimes, 1991.

Note the number of states suddenly created by the breakup of the Soviet Union.

How would this affect the ability of each to survive, both economically and politically?

treatment, but neither option could stop the movement for independence.

Although the pace of reform was neither quick nor thorough enough for some, others convinced themselves that they had gone too far. While Gorbachev was vacationing in the Crimea in August 1991, a group of conspirators—including discontented party functionaries, disillusioned KGB (secret police) officials, and dissatisfied military officers—decided to seize power. Gorbachev's former friend and ally, the flamboyant Boris Yeltsin, crushed the coup with the help of loyal Red Army units. Gorbachev emerged unscathed from house arrest, but his political career had ended. He watched from the sidelines as Yeltsin dismantled the Communist Party and pushed the country toward market-oriented economic reforms. As the Soviet system disintegrated, several of its constituent regions moved toward independence. On 25 December 1991 the Soviet flag fluttered for the last time atop the Kremlin, and by the last day of that year the Union of Soviet Socialist Republics ceased to exist.

Toward an Uncertain Future In many ways, the cold war provided comfort to the world—however cold that comfort seemed at the time. World War II left most of the major imperialist, fascist, and militarist nations in shambles, and the United States and the Soviet Union stepped into what could have been an uncomfortable vacuum in global leadership. Perilous and controlling it may have been, but the cold war that resulted from the ideological contest between the superpowers had ordered and defined the world for almost fifty years. The cold war also shaped how the nations and peoples of the world perceived themselves—as good capitalists fighting evil communists, as progressive socialists battling regressive capitalists, or as nonaligned peoples striving to follow their own paths. Although those perceptions placed constraints on the choices open to them, particularly given the control exerted by the United States and the USSR at the peak of their power, the choices nonetheless were familiar. At the end of the cold war, those easy choices disappeared. The end of the cold war suggested the possibility of a radical shift in power relations, a global realignment that marked a new era of world history devoid of the categories embraced during the cold war.

THE GLOBAL ECONOMY

The global economy came into public view after the spectacular collapse of communism in 1990. Economists pointed to a new economic order characterized by the expansion of trade between countries, the growth of foreign investments, the unfettered movement of capital, the privatization of former state enterprises, a wave of deregulation that undermined the control that national governments once exercised over economic activity, and the emergence of a new breed of corporations. Supporting the new global economy were technological developments in communications; semi-conductors, fiber-optic cables, and satellites have virtually eliminated geographic distances, causing an ever-faster integration of the market economy. The forces driving the world economy toward increased economic integration have been responsible for a process termed *globalization*.

Economic Globalization

Globalization is a widely used term that can be defined in a number of ways. There is general agreement, however, that in an economic context, globalization refers to the reduction and removal of barriers between national borders to facilitate the flow of goods, capital, services, and labor. Global economic interaction and integration is not a new phenomenon. Ancient Rome and China, for example, controlled and economically integrated vast regions of the ancient world. In more recent centuries, the nations of western Europe—through their global outreach and encounters with far-flung societies—created worldwide empires in which goods and people moved with relative ease. The more recent phenomenon of globalization, however, has been different and unprecedented in both scope and speed, and it has the potential to transform the social and political as well as the economic contours of the world.

Free Trade International trade proved to be a key driving force behind economic globalization. Trade across long distances especially has figured prominently in the shaping of human history, and for at least the past five hundred years it has served as an integrating force. Of more recent origin is the phrase *free trade,* meaning freedom from state-imposed limits and constraints on trade across borders. The issue of free trade engendered a debate about the extent to which free trade enhances the prosperity of a society. In the aftermath of World War II, leaders from industrialized nations, especially from the United States, took a decisive stand on the issue.

GATT and WTO U.S. politicians and business leaders wanted to establish an international trading system that suited their interests, and they pushed for the elimination of restrictive trading practices that stood in the way of free trade. The main vehicle for the promotion of unrestricted global trade was the General Agreement on Tariffs and Trade (GATT), which was signed by the representatives of 23 noncommunist nations in 1947. In 1994, the member nations of GATT signed an agreement to establish the World Trade Organization (WTO), which took over the activities of GATT in 1995. The WTO has developed into a forum for settling international trade disputes, with the power to enforce its decisions. The WTO has 153 member nations, which account for 97 percent of all world trade.

Global Corporations The emergence of a new breed of corporation played another key role in the development of the new economic order. Global corporations have in-

This image of a "Balanced World Economy" (1996) artistically expresses the precariousness of economic globalization.

Global corporations have become the symbols of the new economy. They also have begun to transform the political and social landscape of many societies. During the past fifty-five years, major corporations throughout the developed world have been operating under the constraints of a social compact with their employees and communities. Through a combination of collective bargaining agreements, tax laws, and environmental regulations, these companies had to contribute to the welfare of their respective home communities. Highly mobile global corporations that are no longer bound to any particular location have managed, however, to escape those obligations and break the social compact. Competing with companies around the world, the global corporation has moved jobs from high-wage facilities to foreign locations where wages are low and environmental laws are weak or nonexistent.

Economic Growth in Asia

Globalization and the speeding up of worldwide economic integration also benefited from economic developments in east and southeast Asia, where the economies of Japan, China, and the so-called Asian tigers underwent dramatic economic growth. This Asian "economic miracle" was largely a result of economic globalization.

Japan U.S. policies jump-started Japan's economic revival after its defeat in 1945, and by 1949 the Japanese economy had already attained its prewar level of productivity. Just as western European countries had benefited from the Marshall Plan, so Japan benefited from direct U.S. financial aid ($2 billion), investment, and the timely abandonment of war reparations. In addition, there were no restrictions on the entry of Japanese products into the U.S. market. The United States, in its role as Japan's military protector, contributed to long-term economic growth as well. Because a 1952 mutual defense treaty stipulated that Japan could never spend more than 1 percent of its gross national product on defense, Japan's postwar leaders channeled the nation's savings into economic development.

At first sight, Japan's economy was ill equipped for intensive economic growth. Japan had lost its overseas empire and was hampered by a large population and a lack of natural resources. Japan's economic planners sidestepped many of those disadvantages by promoting an economic policy that emphasized export-oriented growth supported by low wages. The large and mostly compliant workforce, willing to endure working conditions and wages considered intolerable by organized labor in western Europe and the United States, gave Japanese employers a competitive edge over international rivals. Although Japanese industries had to pay for the import of most raw materials, the low cost of Japanese labor ensured the production of goods that were cheap enough to compete on the basis of price.

Initially, the Japanese economy churned out labor-intensive manufactured goods such as textiles, iron, and

creasingly replaced the more traditional international or multinational forms of corporate enterprises. International companies were born out of the desire to extend business activities across borders in pursuit of specific activities such as importation, exportation, and the extraction of raw materials. International companies evolved into multinationals, which conducted their business in several countries but had to operate within the confines of specific laws and customs of a given society. During the past twenty-five years, the transformation of the corporate landscape has resulted in the birth of some fifty thousand global corporations. In contrast to the multinational, the typical global corporation relies on a small headquarters staff while dispersing all other corporate functions across the globe in search of the lowest possible operating costs. Global corporations treat the world as a single market and act as if the nation-state no longer exists. Many multinational corporations, such as General Motors, Siemens AG, and Nestlé, have transformed themselves into global enterprises, both benefiting from and contributing to the ongoing process of globalization.

steel slated for export to markets with high labor costs, particularly the United States. During the 1960s Japanese companies used their profits to switch to more capital-intensive manufacturing and produced radios, television sets, motorcycles, and automobiles. In the 1970s Japanese corporations took advantage of a highly trained and educated workforce and shifted their economic resources toward technology-intensive products such as random access memory chips, liquid crystal displays, and CD-ROM drives. By that time the label "Made in Japan," once associated with cheap manufactured goods, signified state-of-the-art products of the highest quality. Japan's economic achievements gave its banks, corporations, and government an increasingly prominent voice in global affairs. By the 1980s Japan seemed poised to overtake the United States as the world's largest economy. In the 1990s, however, it became clear that postwar growth rates were not sustainable, and the Japanese economy sputtered into a recession that has continued into the twenty-first century. Nevertheless, the Japanese success story served as an inspiration for other Asian countries.

The Little Tigers The earliest and most successful imitators of the Japanese model for economic development were Hong Kong, Singapore, South Korea, and Taiwan. Their remarkable and rapid growth rates earned them the sobriquet of the "four little tigers," and by the 1980s these newly industrializing countries had become major economic powers. Like Japan, all four countries suffered from a shortage of capital, lacked natural resources, and had to cope with overpopulation. But like Japan a generation earlier, they transformed apparent disadvantages into advantages through a program of export-driven industrialization. By the 1990s the four little tigers were no longer simply imitators of Japan but had become serious competitors. As soon as new Japanese products had carved out market niches, corporations based in the four little tigers moved in and undercut the original item with cheaper versions. Before long, Indonesia, Thailand, and Malaysia joined the original tigers in their quest for economic development and prosperity.

Perils of the New Economy For the supporters of the new global economy, the spectacular economic development of so many Asian societies was proof that globalization could deliver on the promise of unprecedented prosperity. By the late 1990s, however, critics could point to the perils of the new global economy as many of the Asian tigers went from boom to bust economies.

At the center of this bust was a financial crisis that came to a head in 1997. In the preceding twenty years, the developing Asian economies had started to embrace the market, opening their borders to imports and courting foreign investments. After years of generous lending and growing national debts, the international investment community suddenly lost confidence in the booming economies and withdrew support. The crisis began in Thailand in mid-1997,

when investments that once easily poured into the country now left it equally quickly, causing the value of the baht (Thai national currency) to plummet. In quick succession, the Thai stock market lost 75 percent of its value, and the country found itself in the grip of a depression. For no obvious reason, the financial panic—and with it economic contraction—then moved to Malaysia, Indonesia, the Philippines, and South Korea. In each instance, the rise and fall of the individual economies resulted from their integration in the new global economy, which rewarded and punished its new participants with equal ease.

BRICs Contrary to all expectations, the nations hit so hard by the financial crisis recovered quickly. Their recovery was matched by other emerging economies, often identified as BRICs because they include the fast-growing and developing economies of Brazil, Russia, India, and China. (South Korea and Mexico are usually classified as developed economies.) In the aftermath of the cold war, the governments composing the BRICs initiated political and economic reforms that embraced capitalism and allowed their countries to join the world economy. To make these nations more competitive, their leaders have simultaneously emphasized education, domestic entrepreneurship, foreign investment, and domestic consumption. Predictions point to China and India becoming the dominant global suppliers of manufactured goods and services, with Brazil and Russia becoming similarly dominant suppliers of raw materials. Among these emerging economies, China already figures as an economic titan.

The Rise of China China's leaders launched economic reforms in the late 1970s that reversed some earlier policies and opened Chinese markets to the outside world, encouraged foreign investment, and imported foreign technology. With the economy growing dramatically, the government in 1992 signaled the creation of a socialist market economy. In effect, the planned economic system of the past gave way to a market economy, where demand for goods and services determined production and pricing, and where the role of the government was limited to providing a stable but competitive environment. Besides acting as a major exporter, China benefited from its large pool of cheap labor and its enormous domestic markets have made the Chinese economy the destination of choice for foreign investment capital. In December 2001 China became a member of the World Trade Organization and moved to global economic superpower status.

Emerging nations scour the earth for raw materials, are responsible for a steep rise in world energy demand and consumption, and cause an alarming increase in emissions of greenhouse gases and air pollution. The once-poor world is not only getting richer but also increasingly making its weight felt in international organizations on everything from trade issues to membership in the United Nations Security Council. What all this means is that the rich developed countries no longer dominate the global economy the way they did during the nineteenth and twentieth centuries. This shift is not as astonishing as it first seems, as some of today's emerging economies are simply regaining their former preeminence. Until the late nineteenth century, for example, China and India were the world's biggest economies.

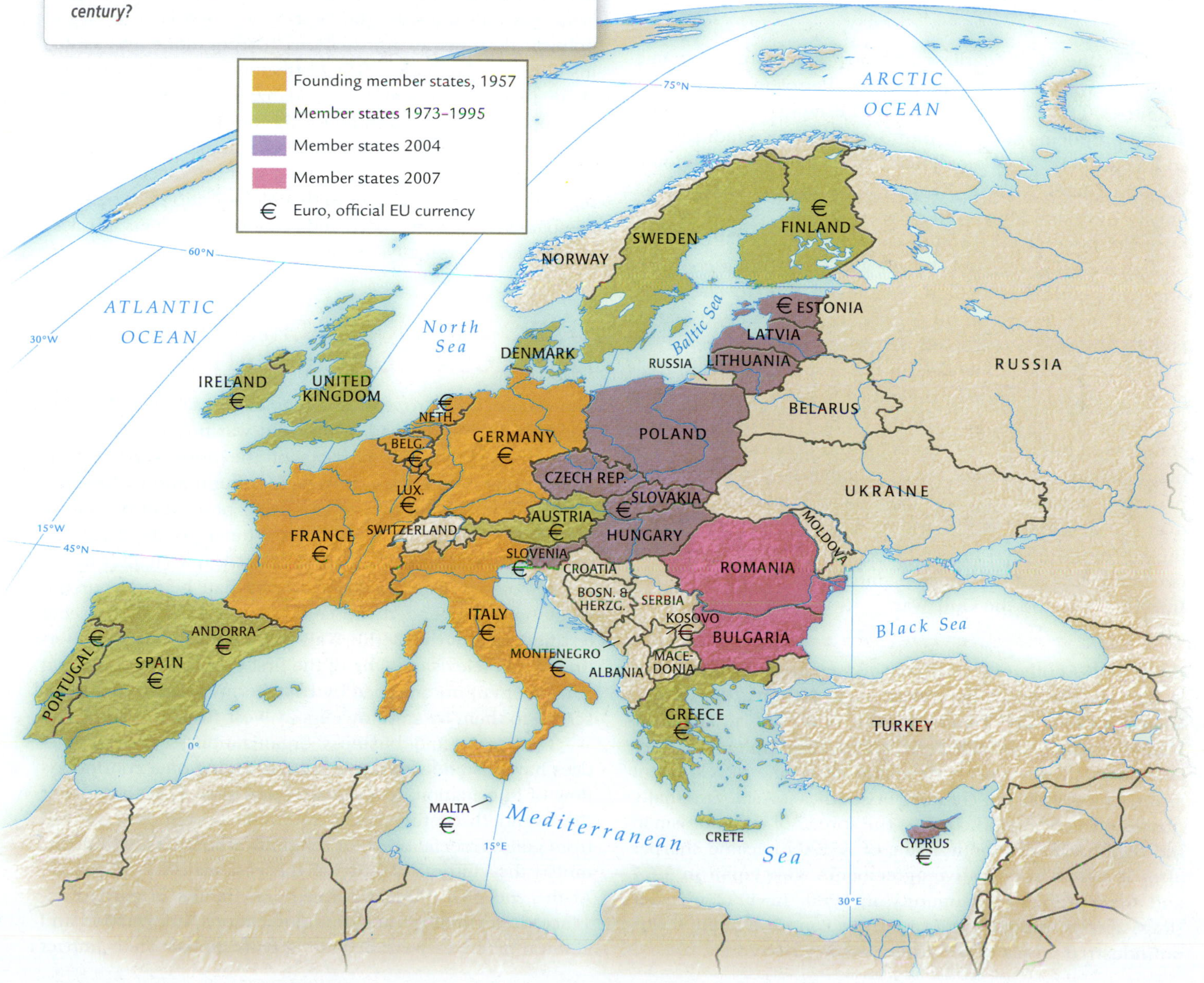

Trading Blocs

Accepting free trade and open markets meant acknowledging global economic interdependence; no single economic power could fully control global trade and commerce. In the rapidly changing global economy, groups of nations have therefore entered into economic alliances designed to achieve advantages and greater strength for their partners in the competitive global economy.

European Union The most famous and most strongly integrated regional bloc is the European Union, which is characterized by a common market and free trade. In March 1957, representatives of six nations—France, West Germany, Italy, the Netherlands, Belgium, and Luxembourg—took

MAP 38.2

European Union membership, 2007.

In 2007 the European Union celebrated the fiftieth anniversary of its founding as a supranational and intergovernmental organization that encompasses twenty-seven member states.

What major challenge faced the European Union in the twenty-first century?

Legend:
- Founding member states, 1957
- Member states 1973–1995
- Member states 2004
- Member states 2007
- € Euro, official EU currency

a significant step in this direction by signing the Treaty of Rome. This treaty established the European Economic Community—renamed the European Community in 1967. At the heart of this new community of nations lay the dismantling of tariffs and other barriers to free trade among member nations. Subsequent treaties creating political institutions such as the Council of Ministers and the European Parliament facilitated the long-range goal of European political integration. The development of a supranational organization dedicated to increasing European economic and political integration culminated in the Maastricht Treaty of 1993, which established the European Union. Twenty-seven European nations have submerged much of their national sovereignty in the European Union, and since 1999 sixteen members have adopted a common currency. In the future, this tight economic integration is expected to lead to a European Political Union.

OPEC One of the earliest and most successful economic alliances was the Organization of Petroleum Exporting Countries (OPEC), a producer cartel established in 1960 by the oil-producing states of Iran, Iraq, Kuwait, Saudi Arabia, and Venezuela, and later joined by Qatar, Libya, Indonesia, Abu Dhabi, Algeria, Nigeria, Ecuador, and Gabon. The mostly Arab and Muslim member states of OPEC sought to raise the price of oil through cooperation, but OPEC demonstrated during the Arab-Israeli War of 1973 that cooperation had political as well as economic potential. The cartel ordered an embargo on oil shipments to the United States, Israel's ally, and quadrupled the price of oil between 1973 and 1975. The huge increase in the cost of petroleum triggered a global economic downturn, as did a curtailment of oil exports in the later 1970s. OPEC's policies therefore contributed to the global recession and debt crisis that hurt many developing nations, but its members—also developing nations—demonstrated how the alliance could exert control over the developed world and its financial system. OPEC's influence diminished in the 1980s and 1990s as a result of overproduction and dissension among its members over the Iran-Iraq War and the Gulf War.

ASEAN Another well-established economic partnership is the Association of Southeast Asian Nations, or ASEAN. Established in 1967 by the foreign ministers of Thailand, Malaysia, Singapore, Indonesia, and the Philippines, its principal objectives were to accelerate economic development and promote political stability in southeast Asia. Originally conceived as a bulwark against the spread of communism in the region, the economic focus of ASEAN became sharper after it signed cooperative agreements with Japan in 1977 and the European Community in 1980. In 1992 member states agreed to establish a free-trade zone and to cut tariffs on industrial goods over a fifteen-year period.

Globalization and Its Critics The global economy is still very much a work in progress, and it is not clear what the long-term effects will be on the economies and societies it touches. To its supporters, the global economy delivers markets that operate with maximum efficiency, speedily directing goods and services wherever there is demand for them and always expecting the highest returns possible. Proponents of globalization also argue that the new economy is the only way to bring prosperity—the kind previously enjoyed only by industrialized nations—to the developing world. To its critics—nongovernmental organizations ranging from labor unions to tribal-rights activists—the global economy is an untamed juggernaut that is neither inevitable nor desirable, a force that rewards the few and impoverishes the many. The specific charges leveled by antiglobalization groups and coalitions are many. They assert that globalization diminishes the sovereignty of local and national governments and transfers the power to shape economic and political destinies to transnational corporations and global institutions such as the WTO. Detractors of globalization also claim that the hallmark of globalization—rapid economic development—is responsible for the destruction of the environment, the widening gap between rich and poor societies, and the worldwide homogenization of local, diverse, and indigenous cultures. It is certain that globalization has been accompanied by serious social and economic problems. It is less certain, however, if anyone can succeed in taming its power.

CROSS-CULTURAL EXCHANGES AND GLOBAL COMMUNICATIONS

The demise of European colonial empires, the fall of the Berlin Wall, and the end of the cold war brought down the most obvious political barriers of the post–World War II world. Long before then, however, cultural and technological developments had started a similar process of breaching boundaries. By showcasing the consumer goods of capitalist societies and spreading news of each new chapter in the fall of communism, television in fact had helped spur the revolutions that ended the cold war. As Kristina Matschat testified, before the Berlin Wall fell she had seen West Berlin only on television. One of the first products of the global consumer culture imbibed by East Germans was Coca-Cola, served to them by store owners in West Berlin.

Like trade and business organizations, cultural practices have also become globalized, thriving on a continuous flow of information, ideas, tastes, and values. At the turn of the twentieth century, local traditions—commonly derived from gender, social class, or religious affiliation—still determined the cultural identity of the vast majority of people. At the end of the twentieth century, thanks in part to advances in technology and communications, information and cultural practices were becoming truly global. Their impact

was summarized in a jingle popularized by the Walt Disney corporation during the 1964–1965 World's Fair in New York City: "It's a small world after all."

Consumption and Cultural Interaction

New communications media have tied the world together and have promoted a global cultural integration whose hallmark is consumption. Beginning in the eighteenth century, industrialization and the subsequent rise in per capita income gave birth to a type of society in which the consumption of goods and services satisfied wants and desires rather than needs or necessities. Although the desire to consume is hardly novel, the modern consumer culture means more than simple consumption. It implies that consumers want more than they need and that the items they consume take on symbolic value. Consumption, in other words, has become a means of self-expression as well as a source for personal identity and social differentiation. The peculiar shape of this consumer culture resulted from two seemingly contradictory trends: a tendency toward homogenization of cultural products and heightened awareness of local tastes and values. Critics sometimes refer to the homogenizing aspect of global culture as the "Americanization" or "McDonaldization" of the world.

Those terms suggest that the consumer culture that developed in the United States during the mid-twentieth century has been exported throughout the world, principally through advertising. Thus it is no accident that young people clad in blue jeans and T-shirts sing the same Usher or Eminem lyrics in San Francisco, Sarajevo, and Beijing. Still, nothing symbolizes the global marketing of U.S. mass culture more than the spread of its food and beverage products. While Pepsi and Coca-Cola fight battles over the few places on earth that their beverages have not yet dominated, fast-food restaurants such as Burger King, McDonald's, and Pizza Hut sell their standardized foods throughout the world. The closing of many bistros and cafés in France, for instance, is the result of more French people opting for fashionable fast food instead of taking the time for more traditional and lengthy lunches. So successful has the global spread of U.S. mass culture been that it seems to threaten local or indigenous cultures everywhere.

The export of U.S. products and services is not the sole determinant of global cultural practices, however. Because the contemporary consumer culture stresses minute differences between products and encourages consumers to make purchase decisions based on brand names designed to evoke particular tastes, fashion, or lifestyle, it also fosters differentiation. Indeed, global marketing often emphasizes the local or indigenous value of a product. Genuinely Australian products, such as Drizabone wet-weather gear and Foster's Lager, have become international commodities precisely because they are Australian in origin. Likewise, young upwardly mobile consumers continue to prefer Rolex watches from Switzerland, Armani clothes from Italy, miniature electronics from Japan, and Perrier mineral water from France.

Pan-American Culture The experiences in the Americas demonstrate that U.S. patterns of cultural consumption have not simply dominated the globe without competition or critical evaluation. For example, as she was dying, the Argentine political and cultural icon Eva Perón is reputed to have said, "I will return and I will be millions." Her prophecy has come true in the images of her that continually appear around the world, especially in the Americas. In Buenos Aires, city housing projects are named after her, a new Argentine film about her life played in 1996, and her face appears on souvenir T-shirts sold in the streets. In an Argentine supper club, the show's cast members sing "Don't Cry for Me, Argentina" as their grand finale, and audiences rise to their feet applauding. The song is from the musical *Evita* by Sir Andrew Lloyd Webber and Tim Rice, which was first performed in London and subsequently became a hit on Broadway (1979). While Argentine performers sing a Euro-American song, their Evita has become an icon in the United States and Europe, not only in the musical, but also in the 1996 film *Evita* starring Madonna.

Although Latin American critics often decry the spell cast by North American popular culture on Latin American audiences, Evita-mania has indicated that the sharing or imposing of cultural practices is a two-way phenomenon. A trend in Latin America is Music Television (MTV) Latino, perceived by many critics as another case of foreign cultural intrusion, whereby Latin video deejays speak "Spanglish" or "Chequenos" ("check us out"), mixing Spanish and English. Yet, whereas Latin Americans once had called for protection against such alien influence, by the 1990s many had relaxed their guard. They see evidence of increased cultural sharing among Latin societies, noting that MTV and cable television have come to serve as a means of communication and unity by making the nations of Latin America more aware of one another. While the sheer dominance and size of the U.S. entertainment-technology industry keeps cultural sharing lopsided, cultural dominance is

thinking about ENCOUNTERS

Coca-Cola and MTV

The process of globalization as it relates to culture has often been reduced to the notion of the Americanization of the globe—or to the idea of a "McWorld," given the spread of McDonald's restaurants around the world. Were cultural exchanges so one-sided? How did the globalization of culture reveal a more complicated sharing of images, ideas, and products?

also limited by those societies' ability to blend and absorb a variety of foreign and indigenous practices.

The Age of Access

Throughout history, technological advances such as in shipbuilding provided the means to dissolve boundaries between localities and peoples and thus allowed cultural transmission to take place. Today virtually instantaneous electronic communications have dissolved time and space. Contemporary observers have labeled our era "the age of access." Communication by radio, telephone, television, fax machine, and networked computers has spawned a global village that has swept away the social, economic, and political isolation of the past. However, because it takes capital to purchase the necessary equipment, maintain and upgrade it, and train people to use it, many societies find it difficult to plug into the global village. The existing gulf between the connected and the unconnected has the potential therefore to become one border in a world without borders.

Preeminence of the English Language
This new world of global interconnectedness is not without its detractors. Critics have charged, for instance, that mass media are a vehicle for cultural imperialism because most electronic media and the messages they carry emanate from advanced capitalist societies. A specific consequence is that English is becoming the primary language of global communications systems, effectively restricting vernacular languages to a niche status.

The Internet reinforces the contemporary fact that English has become the universal tongue of the twenty-first century. As a result of British colonialism, subjugated peoples the world over had been compelled to learn English and become at least bilingual, speaking their own languages along with those of the colonizer. In more recent times, many peoples have voluntarily adopted the language of a politically and economically preeminent English-speaking society, especially the United States. In this fashion, English has almost become a universal language, enjoying acceptance in scientific, diplomatic, and commercial circles. However understandable, English-language dominance on the Internet rankles some users. Xia Hong, a manager for an Internet access provider in Shanghai, articulates this concern:

> There's no question about it: the Internet is an information colony. From the moment you go online, you're confronted with English hegemony. It's not merely a matter of making the Net convenient for users in non-English-speaking countries. People have to face the fact that English speakers are not the whole world. What's the big deal about them, anyway? Our ideal is to create an exclusively Chinese-language network. It will be a Net that has Chinese characteristics, one that is an information superhighway for the masses.

Such sentiments apparently reflect the thinking of Chinese political leaders, for authorities are going to great lengths to ensure that China and its communications sys-

A citizen of Kuwait lugs a television through streets filled with European and U.S. consumer products. From tennis shoes to automobiles to English-language signs, cultural interpenetration is occurring around the globe.

tem do not become a spiritual colony of capitalist powers such as the United States. Accordingly, officials of China's Public Security Bureau—an agency that concerns itself with crimes ranging from murder to cultural espionage—are trying to contain the influence of the Internet by erecting around China a so-called "firewall" or *fanghuo qiang* (a direct translation from the English). The more prevailing and popular phrase for it is *wangguan* (literally, "net wall"), a name that invokes many centuries of Chinese efforts to repulse foreign invaders. However, because the original Great Wall had limited success, the fate of its digital successor remains an open question.

Adaptations of Technology Some societies have managed to adapt European and U.S. technology to meet their needs while opposing cultural interference. Television, for example, has been used to promote state building around the world, since most television industries are state controlled. In Zaire, for example, the first television picture residents saw each day was of Mobutu Sese Seko. He especially liked to materialize in segments that pictured him walking on clouds—a miraculous vision of his unearthly power. The revolution in electronic communications has been rigidly controlled in other societies—including Vietnam and Iraq—where authorities limit access to foreign servers on the Internet. They thus harness the power of technology for their own purposes while avoiding cultural interference.

GLOBAL PROBLEMS

By the end of the twentieth century, many traditional areas of state responsibility—whether pertaining to population policies, health concerns, or environmental issues—needed to be coordinated on an intergovernmental level. Global problems demanded global solutions, and together they compelled the governments of individual states to surrender some of their sovereignty to larger international organizations such as the United Nations. Issues concerning labor servitude, poverty, epidemic diseases, terrorism, and human rights demanded attention and action on a scale greater than the nation-state.

Population Pressures and Climate Change

The past hundred years or so have been accompanied by vast population increases. As the result of advances in agriculture, industry, science, medicine, and social organization, the world experienced a fivefold population increase over a period of three hundred years: from 500 million people in 1650 to 2.5 billion in 1950. After World War II the widespread and successful use of vaccines, antibiotics, and insecticides, along with improvements in water supplies and increased agricultural yields, caused a dramatic decline in worldwide death rates. The rapid decline in mortality among people who also maintained high levels of fertility led to explosive population growth in many areas of Asia and Africa. In some developing nations, population growth now exceeds 3.1 percent, a rate that ensures the doubling of the population within twenty-three years. In 2005 roughly 6.5 billion people shared the planet, and the population division of the United Nations has estimated that the earth's population will stabilize around 9 billion in 2050. In the meantime, 75 million people are joining the world's total population each year, and unless fertility declines to replacement levels—that is, two children per woman—the world's population will grow forever.

More optimistic voices, however, have pointed out that the odds of a population explosion and its dreaded consequences are exaggerated and are in fact receding. In part this decline is the result of the AIDS crisis, which is taking a heavy demographic toll in societies where fertility rates are high. More important, fertility rates have been falling fast in the past two decades, both in rich and in poor societies.

TABLE 38.1	Population (in Millions) for Major Areas of the World, 1900–2050				
Major Area	**1900**	**1950**	**1975**	**2005**	**2050**
Africa	133	224	416	906	1937
Asia	947	1396	2395	3905	5217
Europe	408	547	676	728	653
Latin America	74	167	322	561	783
North America	82	172	243	331	438
Oceania	6	13	21	33	48
World (total)	1650	2519	4074	6465	9076

Source: *World Population Prospects: The 2004 Revision. Highlights*. New York: United Nations, 2005.

The same optimists also argue that despite rapid population growth, wages have risen and the cost of everything extracted or grown from the earth has declined. Equally significant is the fact that food production has more than kept pace with the growing population.

The Planet's Carrying Capacity

A large population changes the earth and its environment, raising an important question: How many people can the earth support? The exact carrying capacity of the planet is, of course, a matter of debate, but by many measures the earth seems to strain already to support the current population. Scientists and concerned citizens have become increasingly convinced that human society cannot infinitely expand beyond the physical limits of the earth and its resources. Beginning in 1967 a group of international economists and scientists—dubbed the Club of Rome—attempted to specify the limits of both economic and population growth in relation to the capacity of the planet to support humanity. Praised by some observers as the conscience of the world and decried by others as being excessively negative, the club issued a report in 1972 with the subtitle "The Limits to Growth." Because the world's physical resources are in finite supply, the Club of Rome concluded, any transgression of those limits would be calamitous. Two decades later, fifteen hundred scientists, including ninety-nine Nobel laureates and representatives from a dozen of the world's most prestigious academies, signed a document titled "Warning to Humanity" (1992). The report sounded a clear alarm, stating that "human beings and the natural world are on a collision course . . . [that] may so alter the living world that it will be unable to sustain life in the manner that we know."

The prophets of doom are not without their detractors, who have eagerly pointed out that the predictions of the Club of Rome and similar ones by other organizations and by concerned governments have not been borne out by the facts. For example, the Club of Rome predicted that the global reserves of oil, natural gas, silver, tin, uranium, aluminum, copper, lead, and zinc were approaching exhaustion and that prices

Smokestacks in Siberia releasing carbon dioxide emissions into the atmosphere. Most scientists argue that emissions such as these, along with other hydrocarbon emissions and methane, contribute to global warming, the increases of world temperatures that are having a negative impact on the world's economy and natural environment.

would rise steeply. In every case but tin, reserves have actually grown since 1972. Eight years later the prices for virtually all minerals—excepting only zinc and manganese—had dropped and continue to do so. The Club of Rome's inaccurate predictions have not diminished its dystopian confidence. In a more recent and widely acclaimed work, *Beyond the Limits* (1999), the Club of Rome, while acknowledging that its earlier predictions had been too pessimistic, persisted in being equally pessimistic about the future.

Climate Change The problem is not simply one of depleting nonrenewable resources or expanding populations. The prodigious growth of the human population is at the root of many environmental problems. As people are born, pollution levels increase, more habitats and animal and plant species disappear, and more natural resources are consumed. In recent decades one environmental issue has taken center stage: climate change. In the context of environmental debates and policymaking, climate change usually refers to a human-induced climate change known as global warming.

Global warming is the phenomenon of increasing average air temperature near the surface of the earth over the past two centuries. On the basis of detailed observations, scientists have concluded that the influence of human activities since the beginning of industrialization have altered the earth's climate. More specifically, most scientists are convinced that most of the observed temperature increases since the middle of the twentieth century are caused by increasing concentrations of greenhouse gases, which prevent solar heat from escaping from the earth's atmosphere. Like the glass panes in a greenhouse, hydrocarbon emissions from automobiles, and methane emitted from the stool of farm animals, trap heat within the atmosphere, leading to a rise in global temperatures. Climate model projections indicate that the global surface temperature is likely to rise a further 1.1°C–6.4°C (2.0°F–11.5°F). An average rise of global temperature by more than 2°C (3.6°F), however, would cause significant economic and ecological damage.

A vigorous debate is in progress over the extent and seriousness of rising surface temperatures, their consequences for the environment, and the necessity to limit further warming. In the ancient Japanese capital of Kyoto, at a conference dedicated to climate change, the delegates from 187 nations agreed in 1997 to cut greenhouse emissions blamed for global warming. The Kyoto protocol went into force in 2005 and imposed targets for carbon emission reductions on developed countries until 2012. The protocol did not require developing countries—some of them major polluters, such as India and China—to reduce their emissions. The world's second largest polluter after China, the United States, did not sign the protocol because it required nothing of developing countries. Since Kyoto, global carbon-dioxide emissions have risen by a third.

International efforts in dealing with climate change have been hampered by a split between developed and developing countries; only the former committed themselves to cutting emissions. Developing countries made no such promise and insisted that the rich world bear the costs of reducing emissions. In 2009, delegates from 193 countries gathered in Copenhagen, Denmark, to renew the Kyoto protocol beyond 2012, with tougher limits on emissions. They struggled to find a way to a new protocol that would include commitments from developing countries. The Copenhagen conference ended without a new protocol or binding extensions to the Kyoto agreements. The only positive outcome was that developing as well as developed countries agreed to an international monitoring of any emissions reductions they promised to pursue.

Population Control For decades the issue of population control was highly politicized. Political leaders in developing countries, for example, charged representatives of industrialized countries with racism when they raised concerns regarding overpopulation. Industrialized nations were also accused of trying to safeguard their outrageous consumption patterns of the world's nonrenewable resources. Some leaders, such as Mexico's Luis Echeverría, went so far as to promote pronatalist measures (to increase births), urging his fellow citizens to have numerous children. The problems caused by rapid population growth eventually persuaded many governments to take action to control fertility. By that time, the old pervasive notion that a large population is a source of national power had given way to the idea that the best way to promote the health and well-being of a population is to control its growth.

As death rates declined persistently throughout the world during the latter part of the twentieth century, reducing birthrates became a central concern of many governments, and to date some eighty countries have adopted birth control programs. The United Nations and two of its specialized agencies, the World Health Organization and the UN Fund for Population Activities, have aided many countries in organizing and promoting family-planning programs. However, the availability and promotion of contraceptives does not guarantee effective control of fertility. Whereas China has, however stringently, significantly reduced its population growth rate and some Latin American societies also have a decline in their birthrates, people in other societies have resisted efforts to reduce birthrates. In some instances, resistance stems from both religious and political motives. In India, for example, the Hindu emphasis on fertility has impeded birth control efforts. Thus global attempts to prevent excessive population growth have had mixed results.

Economic Inequities and Labor Servitude

The unequal distribution of resources and income, and the resulting poverty, have materialized as key concerns of the contemporary world. Several hundred million people, especially in the developing areas of eastern Europe, Africa, Latin America, and Asia, struggle daily for sufficient food,

sources from the past

Climate Change: An Inconvenient Truth

Premiering in 2006, An Inconvenient Truth *is a documentary film, directed by Davis Guggenheim, about the campaign waged by former United States vice president Al Gore (1948–) to educate the public about the severity of the climate crisis and especially global warming. Gore discusses the scientific opinion on climate change, as well as the present and future effects of global warming, and stresses that climate change "is really not a political issue, so much as a moral one." The selection below is taken from the introduction to the book by the same title, released in conjunction with the film, which elaborates upon the same overall message. Gore and the Intergovernmental Panel on Climate Change were jointly awarded the Nobel Peace Prize in 2007, and the film won an Academy Award the same year.*

Some experiences are so intense while they are happening that time seems to stop altogether. When it begins again and our lives resume their normal course, those intense experiences remain vivid, refusing to stay in the past, remaining always and forever with us.

Seventeen years ago my youngest child was badly—almost fatally—injured. This is a story I have told before, but its meaning for me continues to change and to deepen.

That is also true of the story I have tried to tell for many years about the global environment. It was during that interlude 17 years ago when I started writing my first book, *Earth in the Balance.* It was because of my son's accident and the way it abruptly interrupted the flow of my days and hours that I began to rethink everything, especially what my priorities had been. Thankfully, my son has long since recovered completely. But it was during that traumatic period that I made at least two enduring changes: I vowed always to put my family first, and I also vowed to make the climate crisis the top priority of my professional life.

Unfortunately, in the intervening years, time has not stood still for the global environment. The pace of destruction has worsened and the urgent need for a response has grown more acute.

The fundamental outline of the climate crisis story is much the same now as it was then. The relationship between human civilization and the Earth has been utterly transformed by a combination of factors, including the population explosion, the technological revolution, and a willingness to ignore the future consequences of our present actions. The underlying reality is that we are colliding with the planet's ecological system, and its most vulnerable components are crumbling as a result.

I have learned much more about this issue over the years. I have read and listened to the world's leading scientists, who have offered increasingly dire warnings. I have watched with growing concern as the crisis gathers strength even more rapidly than anyone expected.

In every corner of the globe—on land and in water, in melting ice and disappearing snow, during heat waves and droughts, in the eyes of hurricanes and the tears of refugees—the world is witnessing mounting and undeniable evidence that nature's cycles are profoundly changing.

I have learned that, beyond death and taxes, there is at least one absolutely indisputable fact: Not only does human-caused global warming exist, but it is also growing more and more dangerous, and at a pace that has now made it a planetary emergency.

This digitized photograph offers a stunning image of global warming through its depiction of the earth afire.

For Further Reflection

■ Al Gore suggests in this passage that his concern for the global environment coincided with the trauma of his six-year-old son's near-deadly accident. (He was hit by a car while crossing a street.) Why do you think the personal and the political, or the local and the global, intersected for Gore? How does Gore's thinking compare with Aung San Suu Kyi's thoughts in the other selection for Sources from the Past in this chapter?

Source: Al Gore. *An Inconvenient Truth: The Planetary Emergency of Global Warming and What We Can Do About It* (New York: Rodale Books, 2006), p. 8.

A poster advertising China's one-child family rule.

clean water, adequate shelter, and other basic necessities. Poverty is a lack of basic human necessities, and its effects are as wide-ranging as they are devastating. Malnutrition among the poor has led to starvation and death. As one of the most persistent effects of poverty, malnutrition is also responsible for stunted growth, poor mental development, and high rates of infection. Typically, vitamin and mineral deficiencies accompany malnutrition, causing mental disorders, organ damage, and vision failure among poor children and adults. Because of inadequate shelter, lack of safe running water, and the absence of sewage facilities, the poor have been exposed disproportionally to bacteria and viruses carried by other people, insects, and rodents. Poverty has correlated strongly with higher-than-average infant mortality rates and lower-than-average life expectancies.

The Causes of Poverty The division between rich and poor has been a defining characteristic of all complex societies. Although relative poverty levels within a given society remain a major concern, it is the continuing division between rich and poor societies that has attracted the attention of the international community. A worldwide shortage of natural resources as well as the uneven distribution of resources have figured as major causes of poverty and have divided nations into the haves and have-nots. Excessively high population densities and environmental degradation have caused the depletion of available resources, leading to shortages of food, water, and shelter and ultimately to poverty. The other major cause of poverty, the unequal distribution of resources in the world economy, resulted from five hundred years of colonialism, defined by the appropriation of labor and natural resources. Pervasive poverty characterizes many former colonies and dependencies. All of these developing societies have tried to raise income levels and eliminate poverty through diversified economic development, but only a few, such as South Korea, Singapore, Malaysia, and Indonesia, have accomplished their aims. In the meantime, economic globalization has generated unprecedented wealth for developed nations, creating an even deeper divide between rich and poor countries.

Labor Servitude Poor economic conditions have been closely associated with forms of servitude similar to slavery. Although legal slavery ceased to exist when Saudi Arabia and Angola abolished slavery officially in the 1960s, forced and bonded labor practices continue to affect millions of poor people in the developing world. Of particular concern is child-labor servitude. According to the International Labor Organization, a specialized agency of the United Nations, more than 250 million children between ages five and fourteen work around the world, many in conditions that are inherently harmful to their physical health and emotional well-being. Child-labor servitude is most pronounced in south and southeast Asia, affecting an estimated 50 million children in India alone. Most child labor occurs in agriculture, domestic service, family businesses, and the sex trade, making it difficult to enforce existing prohibitions and laws against those practices. Many children are born into a life of bonded labor because their parents have worked in debt bondage, a condition whereby impoverished persons work for very low wages, borrow money from their employer, and pledge their labor as security.

Trafficking A growing and related global problem that touches societies on every continent is the trafficking of persons. In this insidious form of modern slavery, one to two million human beings annually are bought and sold across international and within national boundaries. Trafficking has appeared in many forms. In Russia and the Ukraine, for example, traffickers lure victims with the promise of well-paying jobs abroad. Once the victims arrive in the countries of their destination, they become captives of ruthless traffickers who force them into bonded labor, domestic servitude, or the commercial sex industry through threats and physical brutality—including rape, torture and starvation, incarceration, and death. Most of the victims of trafficking are girls and women, which is a reflection of the low social and economic status of women in many countries. In south Asia, for instance, it is common for poverty-stricken parents or other relatives to sell young women to traffickers for the sex trade or forced labor. The trafficking industry is one of the fastest growing and most lucrative criminal enterprises in the world, generating billions of dollars annually in profits.

Global Diseases

Since the dawn of history, disease has played a significant role in the development of human communities. Its impact has been as dramatic as it has been destructive. For example, the most devastating impact of the Columbian exchange (see chapter 22) came in the wake of diseases that Europeans introduced into the Americas following the voyages of Christopher Columbus and others. The introduction of diseases to populations that lacked any form of immunity killed perhaps as many as 90 percent of native Americans in the span of 150 years. More recently, an influenza pandemic that swept the globe in 1918 and 1919 killed between twenty and forty million people, far more than died as the result of the Great War that had just ended. Since then, medical experts, public health officials, and scientists scored major victories in their fight against diseases, eradicating smallpox and diphtheria, for example. Buoyed by those successes, the United Nations in 1978 called for the elimination of all infectious diseases by the year 2000. That goal was unrealistic and, in the meantime, ancient diseases once thought under control, such as malaria and tuberculosis, are on the rise again. Equally ominous, public health officials have identified new lethal diseases such as HIV/AIDS.

HIV/AIDS The most serious epidemic threat comes from acquired immunodeficiency syndrome (AIDS). This fatal disorder of the immune system is caused by the human immunodeficiency virus (HIV), which slowly attacks and destroys the immune system, leaving the infected individual vulnerable to diseases that eventually cause death. AIDS is the last stage of HIV infection, during which time these diseases arise. The HIV infection is spread through sexual contact with an infected person, contact with contaminated blood, and transmission from mother to child during pregnancy and, after birth, through breast feeding. Factors contributing to the spread of AIDS include poverty, ignorance, the prohibitive cost of drugs, and sexual promiscuity.

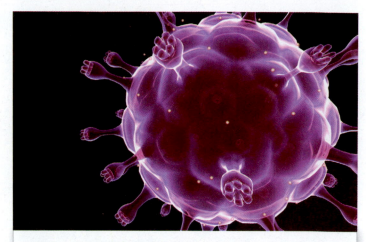

This is a microscopic vision of the human immunodeficiency virus (HIV).

Medical experts identified AIDS for the first time in 1981 among homosexual men and intravenous drug users in New York and San Francisco. Subsequently, evidence for an epidemic appeared among heterosexual men, women, and children in sub-Saharan Africa, and rather quickly AIDS developed into a worldwide epidemic that affected virtually every nation. At the end of 2008, the number of people living with HIV/AIDS was 33.4 million, and over 25 million AIDS deaths had occurred since the beginning of the epidemic.

AIDS in Africa The AIDS epidemic is a serious public health threat throughout the world, but the disease has struck the developing world hardest, especially sub-Saharan Africa. Statistics paint a grim picture. Of the 33.4 million people identified with HIV/AIDS worldwide, 22.4 million of them currently live in sub-Saharan Africa. If current trends persist, AIDS deaths and the loss of future population from the demise of women in childbearing ages will lead to a 70-million drop in population by 2010. Between 2005 and 2010, the life expectancy in the region is expected to decline from fifty-nine years to forty-five. Africa is also home to 80 percent of the children who are living with HIV/AIDS worldwide. AIDS has touched children in two ways: as a disease infecting children and as a disease that leaves them orphans. Thus far the epidemic has orphaned over 14 million children in sub-Saharan Africa, and unless this pattern is reversed Africa will have 40 million AIDS orphans, most of whom will grow up with little or no social nurturing.

The AIDS epidemic threatens to overwhelm the social and economic fabric of African societies, rolling back decades of progress toward a healthier and more prosperous future. The health infrastructure of some African nations cannot cope with the impact of the AIDS epidemic. Although sophisticated palliative treatments—not cures—are available, only the wealthy can afford them. Most Afri-

Adults and children estimated to be living with HIV/AIDS as of December 2008

WESTERN EUROPE
850,000

EASTERN EUROPE and CENTRAL ASIA
1.5 Million

EAST ASIA
850,000

NORTH AMERICA
1.4 Million

NORTH AFRICA and MIDDLE EAST
310,000

SOUTH and SOUTHEAST ASIA
3.8 Million

CARIBBEAN
240,000

SUB-SAHARAN AFRICA
22.4 Million

LATIN AMERICA
2 Million

OCEANIA
50,000

Note: Some numbers do not add up due to rounding.

Source: UNAIDS. *AIDS epidemic update 2009*, December 2009.

Total: 33.4 Million

MAP 38.3

Global estimates of HIV/AIDS.

HIV infection in humans is one of the most destructive pandemics in recorded history. The virus has infected nearly 60 million people and has claimed 25 million lives since scientists first identified it in 1981. Slow progress has been made since then; for example, the life expectancy of people with HIV has increased dramatically with the advent of antiretroviral therapies. Still, the epidemic continues to spread at disturbingly high levels. The annual number of HIV/AIDS-related deaths has gone down slightly since 2004 but still exceeds 2 million, and the number of new annual infections remains high—2.7 million in 2008, of which 430,000 were children under age fifteen. Moreover, the number of people living with HIV continues to increase, rising 20 percent since 2000.

What regions of the world have been most affected by HIV/AIDS?

---

cans are desperately poor. As the AIDS epidemic deepens, it leaves an economically weakened continent in its wake. Families who must care for a member who is ill with AIDS often deplete financial resources that would otherwise be used to cover necessities or to invest in children's futures. When AIDS claims the lives of people in their most productive years, grieving orphans and elders must contend with the sudden loss of financial support, communities must bear the burden of caring for those left behind, and countries must draw on a diminishing number of trained and talented workers.

There are signs that HIV incidence may stabilize in sub-Saharan Africa. So many people in the sexually active population have been affected that only a small pool of people is still able to acquire the infection. In addition, successful prevention programs in a small number of countries, notably in Uganda, have reduced infection rates and contributed to a regional downturn of the epidemic.

The good news from Africa is tainted by bad news from Asia. Although infection rates in Asia remain low, health officials fear that the disease will spread faster as it traverses India, the world's second most populous nation. There is fear that the infection rate will escalate during the next decade, causing the epidemic in India to dwarf the problems seen in Africa. Although no vaccine has yet emerged to prevent or cure HIV infection, some advances have been made. When scientists first identified AIDS, there was no treatment for the disease. Existing antiviral drugs at best delayed the inevitable and at worst failed completely. By 1995, though, researchers succeeded in developing a new class of drugs known as protease inhibitors and, in combination with some of the older drugs, they produced what is now known as highly active antiretroviral therapy, or HAART. In most cases, HAART can prolong life indefinitely. The high cost of these sophisticated drugs initially prevented poor people from sharing in their benefits, but this too is changing. By 2007 over one million people in sub-Saharan Africa routinely received anti-AIDS drugs, and optimistic estimates suggest that, soon, effective AIDS drugs will be available to all who might benefit from them.

Global Terrorism

Terrorism has become a persistent feature of the globalized world. Although not a recent phenomenon, since it has been practiced throughout history, terrorism attained its greatest impact in a world distinguished by rapid technological advances in transportation, communications, and weapons development. Heightened media awareness, especially the ubiquity of worldwide television coverage, has exposed the grievances and demands of terrorists to millions of viewers, but it has also transformed the practice of terrorism. Acts of terror therefore punctuated the era following World War II, as individuals and groups the world over attempted to destabilize or overthrow political systems within or outside the borders of their countries. Terrorism figured prominently in anticolonial conflicts in Algeria and Vietnam; in struggles over a homeland between national groups such as

Israelis and Palestinians; in clashes between religious denominations such as Protestants and Catholics in Northern Ireland; and between revolutionary forces and established regimes in lands such as Indonesia, Iran, and Nicaragua.

Defining Terrorism   No universally agreed-on definition of terrorism exists, but experts agree that a key feature of terrorism is the deliberate and systematic use of violence against civilians, with the aim of advancing political, religious, or ideological causes. Terrorists use violent means—from hijackings and hostage-taking to assassinations and mass murder—to magnify their influence and power. In contrast to the populations and institutions they fight, terrorists and their organizations are limited in size and resources. Despite their ability to destabilize societies, terrorist organizations have rarely if ever realized their stated goals. In fact, terrorist tactics have more commonly discredited otherwise potentially worthy and commendable causes. During the last decades of the twentieth century and the first decade of the twenty-first century, terrorism increasingly assumed a global character because sustained terror campaigns require sophisticated financial support networks, a reliable and sustained supply of weapons technology, and places of

This smoky image of New York City's skyline on 12 September 2001 reveals the void and the airborne debris left by the collapse of the World Trade Center's two towers.

sanctuary. Aside from regional initiatives such as those emanating from the European Union, however, the international community did not respond to the threat of global terrorism in a coherent or unified manner. The thorny issues of what constitutes terrorism and how to respond to it gained renewed attention, however, as a result of the terror attacks against the United States in September 2001.

11 September On the morning of the second Tuesday in September, New York City and Washington, D.C., became the targets of a coordinated terrorist attack that was unprecedented in scope, sophistication, and destructiveness. Hijackers seized four passenger jetliners and used them as guided missiles. Two of the planes crashed into the World Trade Center towers, causing the collapse of the two towers, the ancillary destruction of adjacent skyscrapers, and thousands of deaths. Before the morning was over, another plane crashed into the Pentagon, the nerve center of the U.S. military in Washington, D.C., and the fourth jet crashed into a field outside Pittsburgh, Pennsylvania. Intended for another Washington, D.C., landmark, the fourth jet was thwarted in its mission when passengers stormed the hijackers. As millions around the world watched events unfold on television, the U.S. government launched an intensive investigation and identified the Islamic militant Osama bin Laden (1957–) as the mastermind behind the attacks. Officials also accused bin Laden of directing previous attacks on U.S. interests in Africa and southwest Asia. Before the dust of the collapsed World Trade towers had settled, U.S. President George W. Bush (1946–) declared war on Osama bin Laden and global terrorism itself.

Osama bin Laden headed *al-Qaeda* ("the base"), the core of a global terrorist network. He became a popular figure in the U.S.-backed effort to aid mujahideen (Islamic warriors) who fought Soviet forces in Afghanistan. By the end of the Persian Gulf War (1990–1991), however, he began to regard the United States and its allies with unqualified hatred. The stationing of U.S. troops on the holy soil of Saudi Arabia, the bombing of Iraq, and supporting Israeli oppression of Palestinians, bin Laden claimed, were tantamount to a declaration of war against God. Convinced that he was carrying out God's will, bin Laden in 1998 publicly called on every Muslim to kill Americans and their allies "wherever he finds them and whenever he can." Viewed by many as the personification of evil, yet admired by some for his convictions and aims, Osama bin Laden has moved to the forefront of Islamist violence.

War in Afghanistan and Iraq Another related radical manifestation of Islam's resurgence was the creation of the Islamic State of Afghanistan in 1996 by the Taliban movement. The Taliban emerged out of the disorder and devastation of the Afghan-Soviet war (1979–1988) and the later civil war. Promoting itself as a new force for unity and determined to create an Islamic state according to its own

austere interpretation of Islam, the Taliban proclaimed its followers the liberators who brought peace to Afghanistan. In that pursuit of the purest Muslim state on earth, Taliban intolerance figured prominently, and Islamist strictures quickly alienated people both inside and outside Afghanistan. Dominated by Pashtuns—the majority ethnic group of Afghanistan—the Taliban under its leading *mullah* (male religious leader), Mohammed Omar, fought a series of holy wars against other ethnic and Muslim groups, such as Afghanistan's Shia minority. At the same time, the Taliban provided sanctuary and training grounds for Islamist fighters in southwest and central Asia, most notably for Osama bin Laden and al-Qaeda.

The Taliban espoused a strict brand of Islam that barred women from education and the workplace. As all forms of European and American dress became taboo, women had to be completely veiled in *burkas,* and men had to eschew neckties and grow full, untrimmed beards. The stringent form of Taliban-promoted Islam also called for a ban on television, movie theaters, photographs, and most styles of music. Some of those rules had little to do with pure Islam, but a religious police, the Ministry of the Promotion of Virtue and Prevention of Vice, enforced them with an extremely harsh code of justice. The United Nations and most governments in the world withheld recognition of the Taliban as Afghanistan's legitimate government. De jure recognition came instead to a Taliban opposition force, the Northern Alliance, composed of the country's smaller religious and ethnic groups, mainly Tajiks, Uzbeks, and Hazaras. The Northern Alliance became a crucial ally of the United States in its mission to find and punish those responsible for the 11 September attacks.

When the United States government announced its war against global terrorism it also pointedly targeted "those harboring terrorists," that is, governments and states that supported and provided sanctuary for terrorists. The refusal of the Taliban government to surrender Osama bin Laden prompted the United States and its allies on 7 October 2001 to begin military operations against Taliban military positions and terrorist training camps. The U.S. military and its international allies generally limited their operations to intelligence missions and massive air strikes, fighting the war on the ground through Afghan proxies, most notably the forces of the Northern Alliance. By November, U.S.-led bombardments permitted Northern Alliance troops to capture Kabul and other key Afghan cities. The United States' coalition hampered both the Taliban and al-Qaeda, but conflicts continued. The war against terrorism beyond Afghanistan also promised to be a long-term struggle necessitating a great deal of international cooperation.

Another international action against terrorism came in March 2003, when President Bush coordinated what he termed "Operation Iraqi Freedom." A multinational coalition force some three hundred thousand strong, largely made up of U.S. and British troops but also including those from

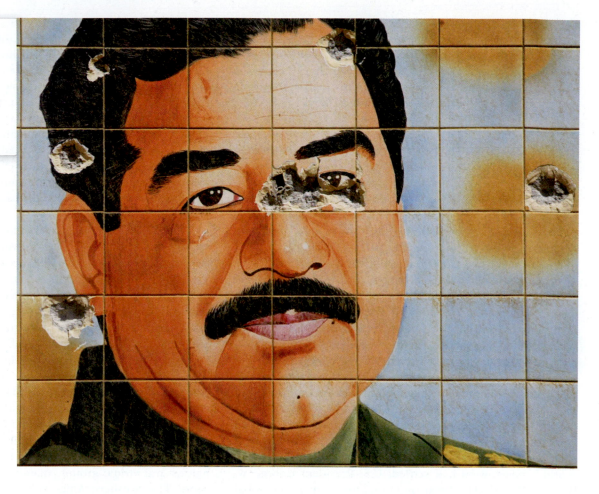

A photographer captured the ruin of Saddam Hussein in this image of a tiled mural pitted and pocked by the destruction in Baghdad as a result of Operation Iraqi Freedom.

approximately two dozen other nations, carried out an invasion of Iraq designed to wage further war on terrorism by ousting the regime of Saddam Hussein and creating a democratic state. One special target was Hussein's suspected stockpile of chemical and biological weapons, otherwise termed "weapons of mass destruction," devastating implements of war that could presumably be employed by global terrorists to wreak destruction on a scale even greater than that of 11 September 2001. Hussein himself made another special target, although he eluded capture for months. Coalition forces managed to establish their military supremacy in Iraq, but they did not uncover any such cache of weapons nor did they immediately control Hussein. President Bush declared an end to major battle operations on 1 May 2003, and coalition forces since that time struggled in their efforts to occupy and stabilize Iraq. Hussein was finally caught in December 2003 and executed in 2006, but deadly resistance in Iraq persisted.

The costs of the Iraq War climbed in terms of both casualties and expenditures. Tens of thousands of Iraqi military personnel and civilians have died, as have over 4,700 coalition soldiers by mid-2010. The United States has spent approximately $4 billion per month to maintain troops in Iraq. While President Bush sustained the United States' willing-

ness to pay such a price, some critics in the United States and around the globe balked at the president's aggressive approach to the war on terrorism. Dubbed by some the "Bush Doctrine of Deterrence," his preemptive strike against Iraq—which had not overtly committed a terrorist act or been proven to harbor terrorists—set a troubling precedent in U.S. foreign policy. Moreover, the increased presence of foreign military personnel in Iraq may only serve to intensify the sort of Islamist fervor already fanned by Osama bin Laden. U.S. President Barack Obama (1961–), elected in 2008, has shifted the war on terror away from Iraq and toward Afghanistan and bin Laden.

Coping with Global Problems: International Organizations

Although the world's nations and peoples are becoming increasingly interdependent, governments still operate on the basis of the territorially delimited state. Because global economic and cultural interdependence demands that political activity focus on cross-societal concerns and solutions, nations are under pressure to surrender portions of their sovereignty. Moreover, as national borders become less important in the face of new economic and cultural connections, the effectiveness of national governments has declined. The wide-

spread recognition that the national state is ill equipped to handle problems of a global magnitude has led to an increase in the number of organizations dedicated to solving global problems through international coordination and action. Often categorized as nongovernmental international organizations and governmental international organizations, these institutions are important because they have the potential to tackle problems that do not respect territorial boundaries and are beyond the reach of national governments.

Nongovernmental Organizations Contemporary efforts at global cooperation have antecedents in the past. A prototypical nongovernmental organization (NGO) is the Red Cross, an international humanitarian agency. Founded on the initiative of the Swiss philanthropist Jean Henri Dunant (1828–1910), this agency was originally dedicated to alleviating the sufferings of wounded soldiers, prisoners of war, and civilians in time of war. In 1864 the representatives of twelve nations signed the first Geneva Convention, which laid down the rules for the treatment of the wounded and the protection of medical personnel and hospitals. The convention adopted the red cross as a symbol of neutral aid. (Most Muslim countries use a red crescent.) Later protocols—signed by most nations—revised and amended the original principles enunciated in the first Geneva Convention to include protection for noncombatants as well. The Red Cross ultimately extended its mission to peacetime, rendering medical aid and other help for victims of natural disasters such as floods, earthquakes, and famines.

The United Nations The premier international governmental organization is the United Nations, which superseded the League of Nations (1920–1946). This association of sovereign nations attempts to find solutions to global problems and to deal with virtually any matter of concern to humanity. Unlike a national parliament, the UN does not legislate. Yet, in its meeting rooms and corridors, representatives of the vast majority of the world's countries have a voice and a vote in shaping the international community of nations.

Under its charter a principal purpose of the UN is "to maintain international peace and security." Cynics are quick to point to the UN's apparent inability to achieve that goal, citing as evidence the eight-year war between Iraq and Iran, the civil war in Somalia, and the many years of bloodshed in Afghanistan. However flawed its role as an international peacemaker and a forum for conflict resolution, the UN has compiled an enviable record with respect to another role defined in its charter, namely, "to achieve international cooperation in solving international problems of an economic, social, cultural, or humanitarian character." Quietly and without attracting attention from the news media, the specialized agencies of the UN have achieved numerous successes. For example, in 1980 the World Health Organization proclaimed the worldwide eradication of smallpox as a result of its thirteen-year global program. On other fronts,

UN efforts resulted in more than a 50 percent decrease in both infant and child mortality rates in developing countries between 1960 and 2002. The organization's efforts also promoted an increase in female literacy, especially in Africa, where for the first time in history the majority of women—50.8 percent in 2000—were deemed to be literate. The UN as well worked to provide access to safe water for over one billion people living in rural areas.

Human Rights Governmental and nongovernmental organizations have focused much of their attention on the protection of human rights, the notion that all persons are entitled to some basic rights, especially rights that protect an individual against state conduct prohibited by international law or custom. The concept of human rights originated with Greco-Roman natural law doctrines and subsequently evolved into specific efforts to protect the rights of humanity such as the abolition of slavery and the implementation of universal suffrage. Universal recognition and acceptance of the concept of human rights came in the aftermath of World War II, especially with the exposure of crimes that the Nazi regime unleashed on its own citizens and all those that had come under Nazi control during the war. The Nuremberg war crimes trials, designed to bring Nazi leaders to justice, challenged the notion of unlimited national sovereignty and created the concept of "crimes against humanity," which warranted international judgment and punishment. In the charter establishing the United Nations in 1945, fifty member nations pledged to achieve "universal respect for, and observance of, human rights, and fundamental freedoms." In 1948, the National Assembly of the UN adopted the Universal Declaration of Human Rights, which contributed to the codification of international human rights laws. The declaration singled out specific human rights violations such as extrajudicial or summary executions, arbitrary arrest and torture, and slavery or involuntary servitude as well as discrimination on racial, sexual, or religious grounds. The concern for human rights is shared by nongovernmental organizations such as Amnesty International and the Human Rights Watch, which bring the pressure of world public opinion to bear on offending governments. By the late 1980s, human rights had emerged as one of the principal themes of global politics.

Given the present level of global interaction, international coordination to solve global problems is a necessity. However, collaboration within and between international organizations has often been inadequate. Meetings, talks, and consultations have frequently deteriorated into arguments. At the height of the cold war, this situation hampered progress in finding solutions to crucial problems. Contentious issues have sometimes paralyzed the UN and its affiliated organizations, because societies at different stages of economic development have pursued sometimes conflicting social and political goals. Cultural diversity continues to make it difficult for people to speak a common language. Despite the shortcomings of international organizations, however, for the present they represent the closest thing humanity has to a global system of governance that can help the world's peoples meet the challenges of international problems.

CROSSING BOUNDARIES

Human populations also underwent radical transformations. Peoples throughout the world challenged gender definitions and embarked on large-scale migrations. Women in Europe, the United States, China, and the Soviet Union gained greater equality with men, partly by advocating women's liberation and a nonbiological or culturally defined understanding of gender. Elsewhere, women continued to follow their societies' dictates for acceptable female behavior, although extraordinary circumstances propelled some women to prominence even in countries that resisted the feminist revolution. Both women and men also experienced either forced or voluntary migrations and in the process helped to create an increasingly borderless world.

Women's Traditions and Feminist Challenges

The status of women began changing after World War II. Women gained more economic, political, social, and sexual rights in highly industrialized states than in developing nations, but nowhere have they achieved full equality with men. Although women have increasingly challenged cultural norms requiring their subordination to men and confinement in the family, attainment of basic rights for

women has been slow. Agitation for gender equality is often linked to women's access to employment, and the industrialized nations have the largest percentage of working women. Women constitute 40 to 50 percent of the workforce in industrial societies, compared with only 20 percent in developing countries. In Islamic societies, 10 percent or less of the workforce is composed of women. In all countries, women work primarily in low-paying jobs designated as female—that is, teaching, service, and clerical jobs. Forty percent of all farmers are women, many at the subsistence level. Rural African women, for example, do most of the continent's subsistence farming and produce more than 70 percent of Africa's food. Whether they are industrial, service, or agricultural workers, women earn less than men earn for the same work and are generally kept out of the highest-paid professional careers.

Feminism and Equal Rights The discrimination that women faced in the workplace was a major stimulus for the feminist movement in industrialized nations. Women in most of those nations had gained the right to vote after the Great War, but they found that political rights did not guarantee economic or sexual equality. After World War II, when more and more women went to work, women started to protest job discrimination, pay differentials between women and men, and their lack of legal equality. In the 1960s those complaints expanded into a feminist movement that criticized all aspects of gender inequality. In the United States, for example, the civil rights movement that

Women belonging to the U.S. feminist group the National Organization for Women (NOW) march for equal rights in Washington, D.C., in 1992. Although American and European women have experienced many gains with respect to achieving full equality with men, they remain less powerful in many areas. Pressures against equality for women remain strong in many developing areas of the world.

Education offers hope for the future of Muslim and Arab women.

demanded equality for African-Americans influenced the women's movement and provided a training ground for many women activists.

Women started to expose the ways in which a biologically determined understanding of gender led to their oppression. In addition to demanding equality in the workplace, women demanded full control over their bodies and their reproductive systems. Access to birth control and abortion became as essential to women's liberation as economic equality and independence. Only with birth control measures would women be able to determine whether or when to have children and thus avoid the notion that "biology is destiny." The U.S. Civil Rights Act of 1964 prohibited discrimination on the basis of both race and sex, and the introduction of the birth control pill in the 1960s and legal protection of abortion in the 1970s provided a measure of sexual freedom. The gender equality that an Equal Rights Amendment would have secured never materialized, however, because the amendment failed to achieve ratification before the 1982 deadline.

Gender Equality in China Some socialist or communist societies transformed their legal systems to ensure basic equality. Legally, the position of women most closely matched that of men in communist or formerly communist countries such as the Soviet Union, Cuba, and China. "Women hold up half the sky," Mao Zedong had declared, and that eloquent acknowledgment of women's role translated into a commitment to fairness. The communist dedication to women's rights led to improvement in the legal status of Chinese women once the communists gained power in China. In 1950, communist leaders passed a marriage law that declared a "new democratic marriage system, which is based on free choice of partners, on monogamy, on equal rights for both sexes, and on protection of the lawful interests of women and children." The law abolished patriarchal practices such as child betrothal and upheld equal rights for men and women in the areas of work, property ownership, and inheritance.

Critics argue that despite such laws China's women have never gained true equality. Certainly, few women have gained high status in the Communist Party's leadership. And although most women in China have full-time jobs outside the home, they do not receive wages equal to those of men. They do most of the work at home as well. Nevertheless, they are able to enter most professions, although most Chinese women engage in menial work. Long-standing

Confucian values continue to degrade the status of women, especially in rural areas. Parents almost universally prefer boys over girls. One unintended consequence of China's population policies, which limits couples to one child, is the mysterious statistical disappearance of a large number of baby girls. Demographers estimate that annually more than one-half million female births go unrecorded in government statistics. Although no one can with certainty account for the "missing" girls, some population experts speculate that a continued strong preference for male children causes parents to send baby girls away for adoption or to be raised secretly or, in some cases, to single them out for infanticide.

Domesticity and Abuse Although girls and women in industrial and communist nations are guaranteed basic if not fully equal legal rights and are educated in roughly the same numbers as boys and men, women in other areas of the world have long been denied access to education. Expected to stay at home, girls and women have high illiteracy rates in these societies. In Arab and Muslim lands, women are twice as likely as men to be illiterate, and in some places nine of ten women are illiterate. This situation is beginning to change. Fifty years ago most women in these societies were illiterate, but in the past twenty-five years girls have begun to catch up with boys in education.

The same cannot be said for girls and women in India, despite some real advances made during the late twentieth century. By 2001 female literacy had reached 54 percent, and yet women remained largely confined to the home. Labor force participation remained low. Less than one-quarter of women of all ages were engaged in work, while the birthrate remained high even with the greater availability of birth control measures. This condition has ensured a life of domesticity for many Indian women. The issue that has most dramatically illustrated the perilous status of women in south Asia, though, is the prevalence of dowry deaths. What makes the birth of girl children in India so burdensome is the custom of paying dowries (gifts of money or goods) to the husband and his family upon a woman's marriage, a requirement that is difficult for many Indian families to meet. If the husband and his family perceive the dowry as inadequate, if the husband wants a new wife without returning his first wife's dowry, or even if the wife has simply annoyed the husband or her in-laws, the wife is doused with kerosene and set on fire—so that her death can be explained as a cooking accident. In 1995 the government of India reported six thousand dowry deaths, though unofficial estimates put the number closer to twenty-five thousand.

This form of domestic abuse has not been restricted to India and Hindu women, but has spread through south Asia. In Pakistan more than five hundred husbands set fire to their wives between 1994 and 1997. The motives for burnings go beyond dowry, because husbands have set fire to wives who overcooked or oversalted the men's food. The victims themselves, some of whom survive, voice perhaps the saddest aspect of this treatment: resignation to their fate. One Pakistani survivor noted, "It's my fate. From childhood, I have seen nothing but suffering." These attitudes may be changing, though, as Indian and Pakistani women activists challenge these practices and establish shelters for women threatened with burning.

Women Leaders Around the world most women have the right to vote. They do not, however, exert political power commensurate with their numbers. Some women have nonetheless attained high political offices or impressive leadership positions. The same south Asia that revealed so many continued barriers to women's rights on a day-to-day basis also elevated numerous women to positions of power, breaking down other political barriers. Indira Gandhi (1917–1984) and Benazir Bhuto (1953–2007) led India and Pakistan as effective politicians, having been raised by fathers who themselves were prominent in politics. In 1994 Chandrika Bandaranaike Kumaratunga (1945–) became the first female president of Sri Lanka. Both her parents had previously served as prime ministers; her mother, Sirimavo Bandaranaike (1916–2000), became the first elected woman prime minister in 1960. As president, Kumaratunga appointed her mother to serve a third term as prime minister.

In Myanmar (formerly Burma), Aung San Suu Kyi (1945–) has emerged as a leader, also deriving her political authority from her father, Aung San, assassinated in 1947. Assuming the leadership of the democracy movement after her return from exile in 1988, Suu Kyi called for a nonviolent revolution against Myanmar's "fascist government." The government placed her under house arrest from 1989 to 1995, during which time she created a new political institution, the "gateside meeting," speaking to her followers from behind the gates of her home. In the 1990 elections Suu Kyi and her party won a landslide victory, but they were not allowed to come to power. Awarded the Nobel Peace Prize for her efforts in 1991, she could not accept the award personally because she was still under house arrest. She remained in detention or under house arrest for much of the next two decades.

thinking about TRADITIONS

Female Freedom and Subjugation

Despite the major transformations in the lives of women after World War II, the practice of limiting the freedom of women persisted in many areas of the world. Why was the feminism evident in Europe and the Americas less effective and applicable elsewhere? How did women in Asia and Africa experience both freedom and subjugation?

Opposition leader and Nobel Prize winner Aung San Suu Kyi at a gateside meeting in Rangoon, Myanmar. The government of Myanmar placed Suu Kyi under house arrest as a leader of a democracy movement, thus restricting her meetings with followers to the gates of her home.

Women demonstrated their leadership abilities in a variety of ways. They became highly visible political figures, as in south Asia, or they more anonymously joined organizations or participated in activities designed to further the cause of women's rights. The United Nations launched a Decade for Women program in 1975, and since then global conferences on the status of women have been held regularly, attracting large crowds. Even in Iran, where the Islamic revolution severely limited opportunities for women, internal forces could radically transform the image and role of women. Today revolutionary patrols walk the streets of Tehran making sure that women conform to the society's rule of dress and behavior, but during the war with Iraq, Iranian women became revolutionaries, picking up guns and receiving weapons training. They protected their national borders while defying gender boundaries.

Migration

Migration, the movement of people from one place to another, is as old as humanity and has shaped the formation and identity of societies throughout the world. The massive influx of outsiders has transformed the ethnic, linguistic, and cultural composition of indigenous populations. With the advent of industrialization during the eighteenth century, population experts distinguished between two types of migration: internal migration and external or international migration. Internal migration describes the flow of people from rural to urban areas within one society, whereas external migration describes the movement of people across long distances and international borders. Both types of migration result from push factors, pull factors, or a combination of the two. Lack of resources such as land or adequate food supplies, population pressure, religious or political persecution, or discriminatory practices aimed at ethnic minorities push people to move. Conversely, opportunities for better employment, the availability of arable land, or better services such as health care and education pull people to move. In the most general sense, migration is caused by differences, and because differences among societies are widening, the potential for migration has increased.

Internal Migration The largest human migrations today are rural-urban flows. During the last half of the twentieth century, these internal migrations led to rapid urbanization in much of the world. Today the most highly urbanized societies are those of western and northern Europe, Australia, New Zealand, and temperate South America and North America. In these societies the proportion of people living in urban areas exceeds 75 percent; in some countries, such as Belgium, it exceeds 97 percent. (A more recent phenomenon visible in developed countries is a reverse migration, from the city to the country.) The societies of tropical Latin America are in an intermediate stage of urbanization, with 50 to 65 percent of the population living in cities. In many countries in Africa and Asia, the process of urbanization has just begun. Although most people still reside in rural areas, the rate of urbanization is very high.

Urbanization Urbanization has proved to be a difficult and challenging transformation for rural folk who have chosen or been forced to adjust to a new way of life. In Latin America, Africa, and south Asia, large numbers of people have migrated to metropolitan areas in search of relief from rural poverty. Once in the cities, though, they often find

sources from the past

Politics and Family: The Hope of and for Girl Children

Since the late 1980s, Aung San Suu Kyi (1945–), the girl child of the assassinated Burmese independence leader Aung San, has remained a beacon of democratic hope for the nation now known as Myanmar. Leader of the political opposition to a military-ruled government, she has been arrested, jailed, and placed under house arrest during most of her residence in the country. Despite that, she managed to win the Nobel Peace Prize in 1991, and she has likewise managed to communicate her political messages and hopes. In the following passage, from one of many letters written to a Japanese newspaper in 1996, Suu Kyi discusses the meaning of the birth of her friends' first grandchild, a girl, and meditates on the political future of Myanmar's children through health care and education. She in fact committed her Nobel Peace Prize money, equal to US $1.3 million, to a trust in support of these causes for her people.

A couple of weeks ago some friends of mine became grandparents for the first time when their daughter gave birth to a little girl. The husband accepted his new status as a grandfather with customary joviality, while the wife, too young-looking and pretty to get into the conventional idea of a cosily aged grandmother, found it a somewhat startling experience. . . . I was told the paternal grandfather was especially pleased because the baby had been born in the Burmese month of *Pyatho*—an auspicious time for the birth of a girl child.

In societies where the birth of a girl is considered a disaster, the atmosphere of excitement and pride surrounding my friends' granddaughter would have caused astonishment. In Burma there is no prejudice against girl babies. In fact, there is a general belief that daughters are more dutiful and loving than sons and many Burmese parents welcome the birth of a daughter as an assurance that they will have somebody to take care of them in their old age. . . .

Babies, I have read somewhere, are specially constructed to present an appealingly vulnerable appearance aimed at arousing tender, protective instincts: only then can tough adults be induced to act as willing slaves to demanding little beings utterly incapable of doing anything for themselves. It is claimed that there is something about the natural smell of a baby's skin that invites cuddles and kisses. Certainly I like both the shape and smell of babies, but I wonder whether their attraction does not lie in something more than merely physical attributes. Is it not the thought of a life stretching out like a shining clean slate on which might one day be written the most beautiful prose and poetry of existence that engenders such joy in the hearts of the parents and grandparents of a newly born child? The birth of a baby is an occasion for weaving hopeful dreams about the future.

However, in some families parents are not able to indulge in long dreams over their children. The infant mortality rate in Burma is 94 per 1000 live births, the fourth highest among the nations of the East Asia and Pacific Region. The mortality rate for those under the age of five too is the fourth highest in the region, 147 per 1000. And the maternal mortality rate is the third highest in the region at the official rate of 123 per 100,000 live births. (United Nations agencies surmise that the actual maternal mortality rate is in fact higher, 140 or more per 100,000.)

The reasons for these high mortality rates are malnutrition, lack of access to safe water and sanitation, lack of access to health services, and lack of caring capacity, which includes programmes for childhood development, primary education, and health education. Yet government expenditure in both sectors, as a proportion of the budget, has been falling steadily. . . .

Some of the best indicators of a country developing along the right lines are healthy mothers giving birth to healthy children who are assured of good care and a sound education that will enable them to face the challenges of a changing world. Our dreams for the future of the children of Burma have to be woven firmly around a commitment to better health care and better education.

For Further Reflection

■ How did Aung San Suu Kyi make the leap from personal observations about her friends' granddaughter to political issues central to the future of Burma/Myanmar? Can you make similar connections back in time to Suu Kyi's birth and its symbolic meaning for the country?

Source: Aung San Suu Kyi, *Letters from Burma* (New York: Penguin, 1996), pp. 55–57, as cited in Kevin Reilly, ed., *Worlds of History: A Comparative Reader,* vol. 2, 2nd ed. Boston: Bedford/St. Martin's, 2004, pp. 512–13.

Seeking relief from rural poverty, large numbers of people throughout the developing world have migrated to urban areas ill equipped to meet their needs and have had to settle in slums such as this one in Rio de Janeiro.

themselves equally destitute. Life is bleak in the slums outside Mumbai; in the shantytowns around Kinshasa or Nairobi; and in the *barriadas, barrios,* and *villas miserias* of Lima, Mexico City, and Buenos Aires. More than ten million people cram the environs of cities such as Calcutta, Cairo, and Mexico City, straining those cities' resources. The few services originally available to the slum dwellers—potable water, electricity, and medical care—have diminished with the continuous influx of new people. Among the unemployed or underemployed, disease runs rampant, and many suffer from malnutrition.

External Migration A combination of voluntary and forced international migrations has transformed the human landscape, especially during the past five hundred years. Between the sixteenth and the twentieth centuries, more than sixty million European migrants, for example, colonized the Americas, Australia, Oceania, and the northern half of Asia.

Between 1820 and 1980, in the course of the Atlantic migration, thirty-seven million migrants of European descent made their home in the United States. Slave migrations supplemented those voluntary movements of people. Between the sixteenth and the nineteenth centuries, slave traders consigned about twelve million Africans to the Americas, though many died in the appalling conditions of the Atlantic voyages.

During World War II the Nazi regime initiated the largest mass expulsions of the twentieth century, deporting eight million people to forced-labor sites and extermination camps. Following the war, the Soviet regime expelled ten million ethnic Germans from eastern and central Europe and transported them back to Germany. The largest migrations in the second half of the twentieth century have consisted of refugees fleeing war. For example, the 1947 partition of the Indian subcontinent into two independent states resulted in the exchange of six million Hindus from Pakistan and seven million Muslims from India. More recently, three million to four million refugees fled war-torn Afghanistan during the 1980s. According to UN estimates, at the end of 2003 there were some ten million refugees who lived outside their countries of origin and who could not return because of fear of persecution.

Afghan refugees fled to Iran in 1986, joining the ranks of the hundreds of thousands of forced displaced persons in the contemporary world.

Many of these migrants left their home countries because they wanted to escape the ravages of war, but economic inequities between societies have caused most international migration. That is, people leave their country of birth in search of better jobs and more readily available health care, educational opportunities, and other services provided by the new society. Thus most contemporary mass migrations involve movement from developing countries to developed ones. Since 1960 some 13 million "guest workers" from southern Europe, Turkey, and northern Africa have taken up permanent residence in western Europe, and more than 10 million permanent migrants—mostly from Mexico—have entered the United States. Foreigners currently make up more than half the working population in the oil-producing countries of southwest Asia. Approximately 130 million people currently live outside their country of citizenship, collectively constituting a "nation of migrants" equivalent in size to Japan, the world's eighth most populous nation.

Migrant Communities International mass migrations have accelerated and broadened the scope of cross-cultural interaction. After their arrival on foreign shores, migrants established cultural and ethnic communities that maintained their social customs and native languages. The sounds of foreign languages as well as the presence of ethnic foods, arts, and music have transformed especially large cities into multicultural environments. Although the arrival of migrants has enriched societies in many ways, it has also sparked resentment and conflict. People in host countries often believe that foreigners and their ways of life undermine national identity, especially if defined by language and other cultural characteristics. Beyond that, many citizens of host societies view migrants, who are often willing to work for low wages and not join labor unions, as competitors for jobs. When unemployment rates climb, there is a tendency to look for scapegoats, and all too frequently the blame falls on migrants. In many countries, governments have come under pressure to restrict immigration or even expel foreign residents. Moreover, xenophobia, or an unreasonable fear of foreigners, has sometimes produced violence and racial tension, as when skinheads (shaved-head youths) in England assaulted members of ethnic minority groups or when neo-Nazis in Germany bombed the community centers of Turkish workers. Thus, while migrants are reshaping the world outside their home countries, international mass migration poses challenges both to the migrants themselves and to the host society.

Transient Migrants A more recent and transient form of migration is tourism. Although travelers have established cultural links between societies since the beginning of recorded history, travel for a long time took place mainly in connection with military conquest, religious pilgrimage, trade, or diplomacy. If more people did not take to travel, it was because most had little incentive to leave their homes, especially when transport was slow, expensive, and inconvenient. So risky was travel that most people regarded travelers as either very courageous or very foolish. Industrial society gave birth to mass tourism by providing both safer and faster transport and by institutionalizing two modern features of social life—leisure and travel.

In the early and mid-1800s, it became fashionable in Europe for the affluent to vacation, often for extended periods, and then later in the century working people began to copy the fashions of the wealthy. Working-class families took to the road during holidays to escape the grimy drudgery of the industrial city and, in the process, created working-class pleasure zones such as seaside resorts in Britain, Coney Island in the United States, or Varna at the Black Sea. People journeyed for pleasure and engaged in activities they normally did not do, such as breathing fresh air, wearing oddly colorful clothes, or taking long walks for no reason at all. By the twentieth century, leisure travel took on added symbolic value when travelers could show off the special clothes required for their journeys, such as ski apparel or bikinis. Others established that they had traveled through changes in their physical appearance, which could include varying degrees of sunburn or a leg encased in plaster. After World War II, companies created the packaged tour, which enabled millions of tourists to swarm across the world. Today middle-class tourists, new age travelers, and ecotourists—often weighted down by duty-free goods—busily crisscross the entire planet in their search for rarely visited sites.

Effects of Mass Tourism Travel and tourism have become the largest industry on the planet. The industry is sustained by growing personal wealth, which continues to produce more tourists, and by cheaper and more efficient transport, especially the jet plane. According to World Travel and Tourism Council estimates, the total economic value of goods and services attributable to tourism in 2010 was $5.7 trillion, or 9.2 percent of the gross global product. The tourism business also provided work for approximately 255 million people. The attraction of an industry that generates wealth and jobs relatively quickly—and often with minimal investment compared with establishing a manufacturing industry, for example—has served as a powerful incentive for both governments and businesses in the developed and the developing worlds to further promote tourism. On the downside, tourism most often creates low-paying jobs, and most of the profits flow to the developed world, where the majority of tourism businesses are located. The travel boom has also sparked concerns connected to the cultural impact of mass tourism. Tourism has acted as a globalizing influence, sometimes initiating dramatic and irreversible changes within the cultural traditions of host communities. Large numbers of visitors have the tendency to transform local cultural traditions into commodities, which are then consumed like any other commodity. Religious rituals, ethnic rites, and festivals are reduced and sanitized to conform to tourist expectations, resulting in a "reconstructed ethnicity."

in perspective

The decades following World War II were largely dominated by cold war politics and by nations seeking their independence from colonial rule. Borders created by the cold war world and European empires dissolved and reshaped the world's landscape. Another barrier-crushing development that became visible at the end of the century was economic globalization, a process responsible for the unprecedented integration of the global economy. A growing share of the world's societies embraced market-oriented economies and thus hitched their fortunes to the vagaries of the global marketplace.

Globalization pointed to the new relevance of international organizations and to the increasing irrelevance of national boundaries; it signified the arrival of a world without borders. Technological and cultural developments likewise combined to break down barriers and create a global village that connected diverse peoples. Although many societies resisted cultural influences from Europe and the United States, the prevalence of communications technology and cultural diffusion made interactions and encounters inevitable. Women's efforts to achieve greater equality with men also collided with cultural traditions; and, although many barriers to women's liberation remain, others have fallen. The global movement of human populations crisscrossed boundaries, both internal and external, and contributed to global problems that could be solved only through international cooperation. In the borderless world of contemporary times, nothing less is acceptable. ●

CHRONOLOGY	
1947	Establishment of GATT
1948	UN adopts Universal Declaration of Human Rights
1950	World population at 2.5 billion
1960	Introduction of birth control pill
1960	Creation of OPEC
1967	Establishment of ASEAN
1967	Birth of European Community
1981	Identification of AIDS
1982	Defeat of Equal Rights Amendment in U.S.
1989	Fall of Berlin Wall
1991	Collapse of the Soviet Union
1992	Beginning of socialist market economy in China
1995	WTO supersedes GATT
2000	World population at 6 billion
2001	China joins WTO
2001	Terrorist attacks against the United States
2003	Operation Iraqi Freedom

For Further Reading

Peter Baldwin. *Disease and Democracy: The Industrialized World Faces AIDS.* Berkeley, 2005. Probing comparative history of the public health policies implemented by Western democracies to contain domestic AIDS epidemics in the 1980s and 1990s.

Jagdish Bhagwati. *In Defense of Globalization.* New York, 2004. A convincing rebuttal to popular fallacies about global economic integration.

Joel E. Cohen. *How Many People Can the Earth Support?* New York, 1997. An author who treads where few demographers dare to go.

Tim Flannery. *The Weather Makers: How Man Is Changing the Climate and What It Means for Life on Earth.* New York, 2006. A passionate and clear account that looks at the connection between human-made climate change and global warming.

Thomas L. Friedman. *The Lexus and Olive Tree.* New York, 1999. A readable overview that does justice to the complexities of globalization.

Kevin J. Gaston and John I. Spicer. *Biodiversity: An Introduction.* 2nd ed. Oxford, 2004. A simple and concise overview of biodiversity—what it is and why it is important.

Karl Gerth. *China Made: Consumer Culture and the Creation of the Nation.* Cambridge, Mass., 2003. Links notions of nationalism and consumerism in twentieth-century China.

Andrei Grachev. *Gorbachev's Gamble: Soviet Foreign Policy and the End of the Cold War.* Boston, 2008. A penetrating account of the end of the cold war, as seen from the Soviet side.

Francis Harris, ed. *Global Environmental Issues.* New York, 2004. A clear, nontechnical introduction to a broad range of environmental issues.

Margaret Jean Hay and Sharon Stichter. *African Women South of the Sahara.* Boston, 1984. An analysis of social and economic change and how it affected African women in the twentieth century.

Michael J. Hogan, ed. *The End of the Cold War: Its Meaning and Implications.* Cambridge and New York, 1997. A thoughtful collection of essays by leading academics about the end of the cold war.

Nikki R. Keddie and Beth Baron, eds. *Women in Middle Eastern History: Shifting Boundaries in Sex and Gender.* New Haven, 1992. A sensitive selection of articles by the leading scholars in the field.

Naomi Klein. *No Space, No Choice, No Jobs, No Logo: Taking Aim at the Brand Bullies.* New York, 2000. Part cultural analysis and part political manifesto, this work makes an angry case against multinational corporations.

Joanna Liddle and Rama Doshi. *Daughters of Independence: Gender, Caste, and Class in India.* New Delhi, 1986. A work on the contemporary women's movement that covers the Indian caste system, British colonial rule, and class structure.

J. R. McNeill. *Something New under the Sun: An Environmental History of the Twentieth-Century World.* New York, 2000. A brilliant but dark tale of the past century's interaction between humans and the environment.

Julian L. Simon. *Population Matters: People, Resources, Environment, and Immigration.* New Brunswick, N.J. 1990. Broad and general treatment of demographic, environmental, and economic problems.

Joseph Stiglitz. *Globalization and Its Discontents.* New York, 2002. A former chief economist at the World Bank and 2002 Nobel Prize winner takes aim at the institutions that govern globalization, especially the IMF.

Wang Gungwu, ed. *Global History and Migrations.* Boulder, 1997. A fine collection of essays on topics that range from the Atlantic slave trade to diasporas and their relationship to the nation-state.

Martin Wolf. *Why Globalization Works.* 2nd ed. New Haven, 2005. A sophisticated defense of the global market economy and free trade.

State of the World
A World Destroyed / A World Reborn

The global history of the twentieth century catalogued staggering numbers of human deaths and massive amounts of material destruction. It was, to date, the world's most violent century, and that violence announced itself in assassinations of figures as diverse as the Austro-Hungarian Archduke Francis Ferdinand and the nationalist Indian hero Mohandas Gandhi. Those assassinations also symbolized the forces responsible for destroying the world as it had existed at the turn of the century: world wars of unprecedented scope and horror and the final dismantling of colonial empires in a process of decolonization that was at once liberating and sobering for those seeking national independence. Tens of millions of soldiers and civilians on both sides of mighty European and global alliances died often horrid deaths, from weapons as mundane as guns to those as bewilderingly new and appallingly destructive as the atomic bombs that demolished Hiroshima and Nagasaki. The imperial and industrial power amassed by European and North American states dissipated as a result of the human and economic cost of world wars and the relatively short-lived cold war that followed those wars. That power also diminished as colonial peoples in Asia and Africa fought for their freedom and independence and thus destroyed as surely as the world wars had the global domination of imperial nations.

The geopolitical alliances that had shaped wars and divided peoples from the time of the Great War through the cold war evaporated one by one, leaving in their wake a seemingly borderless world of both promise and peril. No longer contained by European imperial hegemony, newly independent nations from India to Ghana, from Indonesia to Vietnam, contributed to the rebirth of a world free of empire. The tearing down of literal barriers between people, such as the Berlin Wall, was matched by the fall of figurative barriers between peoples as ushered in by the process of globalization. The disintegration of the world as it existed at the beginning of this era of contemporary global realignments led to a new sort of integration at the end of the century and into the twenty-first century, led by technological and economic forces that broke through national boundaries and connected the world's peoples through a complex web of communications, transportation, and economic interconnectedness. Resisted by some, and criticized by many, globalization has nonetheless remade the world and undermined old divisions, underscoring in its own way the commonality of human experience.

Destruction and disaster have not disappeared in the twenty-first century, and indeed, vast natural disasters have devastated societies and reminded humans of their vulnerability to the forces of nature—a vulnerability that ties twenty-first-century humans to their earliest ancestors. The devastating Indian Ocean earthquake and tsunami in 2004 and the Haitian earthquake of 2010 have suggested anew that fragility of human existence. What is different about these natural disasters is the new globalized world, wherein intricate networks of communications and transportation can be used to support and help those humans in desperate need, wherein the world's common humanity can be reasserted and reaffirmed, and wherein massive destruction can be countered to some extent by a human cooperation little witnessed at the beginning of this era of contemporary global realignments.

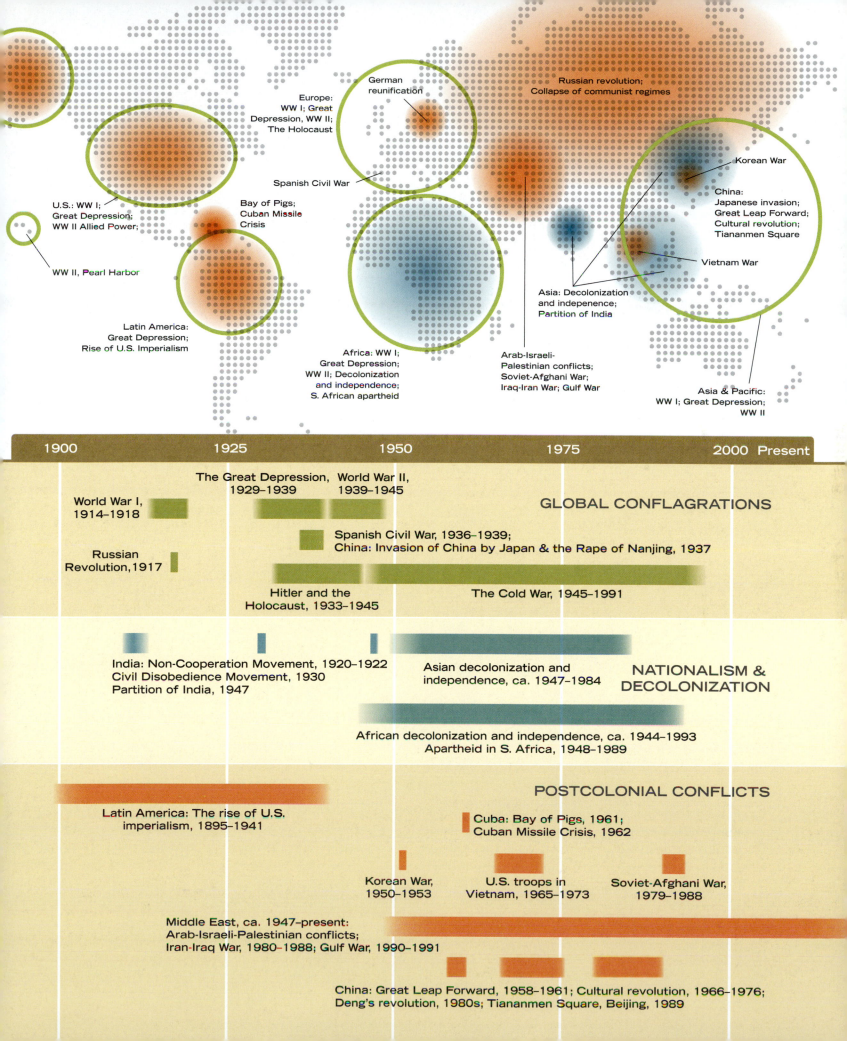

German reunification

Europe:
WW I; Great
Depression, WW II;
The Holocaust

Russian revolution;
Collapse of communist regimes

Korean War

Spanish Civil War

China:
Japanese invasion;
Great Leap Forward;
Cultural revolution;
Tiananmen Square

U.S.: WW I;
Great Depression;
WW II Allied Power;

Bay of Pigs;
Cuban Missile
Crisis

Vietnam War

WW II, Pearl Harbor

Asia: Decolonization
and indepence;
Partition of India

Latin America:
Great Depression;
Rise of U.S. Imperialism

Africa: WW I;
Great Depression;
WW II; Decolonization
and independence;
S. African apartheid

Arab-Israeli-
Palestinian conflicts;
Soviet-Afghani War;
Iraq-Iran War; Gulf War

Asia & Pacific:
WW I; Great Depression;
WW II

1900	1925	1950	1975	2000 Present

The Great Depression,
1929–1939

World War II,
1939–1945

World War I,
1914–1918

GLOBAL CONFLAGRATIONS

Spanish Civil War, 1936–1939;
China: Invasion of China by Japan & the Rape of Nanjing, 1937

Russian
Revolution, 1917

Hitler and the
Holocaust, 1933–1945

The Cold War, 1945–1991

India: Non-Cooperation Movement, 1920–1922
Civil Disobedience Movement, 1930
Partition of India, 1947

Asian decolonization and
independence, ca. 1947–1984

NATIONALISM &
DECOLONIZATION

African decolonization and independence, ca. 1944–1993
Apartheid in S. Africa, 1948–1989

POSTCOLONIAL CONFLICTS

Latin America: The rise of U.S.
imperialism, 1895–1941

Cuba: Bay of Pigs, 1961;
Cuban Missile Crisis, 1962

Korean War,
1950–1953

U.S. troops in
Vietnam, 1965–1973

Soviet-Afghani War,
1979–1988

Middle East, ca. 1947–present:
Arab-Israeli-Palestinian conflicts;
Iran-Iraq War, 1980–1988; Gulf War, 1990–1991

China: Great Leap Forward, 1958–1961; Cultural revolution, 1966–1976;
Deng's revolution, 1980s; Tiananmen Square, Beijing, 1989

glossary & pronunciation key

AH *a* sound, as in *car, father*
IH short *i* sound, as in *fit, his, mirror*
OO long *o* sound, as in *ooze, tool, crew*
UH short *u* sound, as in *up, cut, color*
A short *a* sound, as in *asp, fat, parrot*
EE long *e* sound, as in *even, meet, money*
OH long *o* sound, as in *open, go, tone*
EH short *e* sound, as in *ten, elf, berry*
AY long *a* sound, as in *ape, date, play*
EYE long *i* sound, as in *ice, high, bite*
OW diphthong *o* sound, as in *cow, how, bow*
AW diphthong *a* sound, as in *awful, paw, law*

Note on emphasis: Syllables in capital letters receive the accent. If there is no syllable in capitals, then all syllables get equal accent.

Abbasid (ah-BAH-sihd) Cosmopolitan Arabic dynasty (750–1258) that replaced the Umayyads; founded by Abu al-Abbas and reached its peak under Harun al-Rashid.

Abolitionism Antislavery movement.

Absolutism Political philosophy that stressed the divine right theory of kingship: the French king Louis XIV was the classic example.

Abu Bakr (ah-BOO BAHK-uhr) First caliph after the death of Muhammad.

Achaemenid empire (ah-KEE-muh-nid) First great Persian empire (558–330 B.C.E.), which began under Cyrus and reached its peak under Darius.

Aeschylus (ES-kuh-luhs) Greek tragedian, author of the *Oresteia*.

Age grades Bantu institution in which individuals of roughly the same age carried out communal tasks appropriate for that age.

Ahimsa (uh-HIM-suh) Jain term for the principle of nonviolence to other living things or their souls.

Ahura Mazda (uh-HOORE-uh MAHZ-duh) Main god of Zoroastrianism who represented truth and goodness and was perceived to be in an eternal struggle with the malign spirit Angra Mainyu.

Al-Andalus (al-ANN-duh-luhs) Islamic Spain.

Ali'i nui Hawaiian class of high chiefs.

Allah (AH-lah) God of the monotheistic religion of Islam.

Amon-Re (AH-muhn RAY) Egyptian god, combination of the sun god Re and the air god Amon.

Angkor (AHN-kohr) Southeast Asian Khmer kingdom (889–1432) that was centered on the temple cities of Angkor Thom and Angkor Wat.

Anti-Semitism Term coined in the late nineteenth century that was associated with a prejudice against Jews and the political, social, and economic actions taken against them.

Antonianism African syncretic religion, founded by Dona Beatriz, that taught that Jesus Christ was a black African man and that heaven was for Africans.

Apartheid (ah-PAHR-teyed) South African system of "separateness" that was implemented in 1948 and that maintained the black majority in a position of political, social, and economic subordination.

Appeasement British and French policy in the 1930s that tried to maintain peace in Europe in the face of German aggression by making concessions.

Arianism Early Christian heresy that centered on teaching of Arius (250–336 C.E.) and contained the belief that Jesus was a mortal human being and not coeternal with God; Arianism was the focus of Council of Nicaea.

Artha Hindu concept for the pursuit of economic well-being and honest prosperity.

Arthashastra (AR-thah-sha-strah) Ancient Indian political treatise from the time of Chandragupta Maurya; its authorship was traditionally ascribed to Kautalya, and it stressed that war was inevitable.

Aryans (AIR-ee-anns) Indo-European migrants who settled in India after 1500 B.C.E.; their union with indigenous Dravidians formed the basis of Hinduism.

Association of Southeast Asian Nations (ASEAN.) Regional organization established in 1967 by Thailand, Malaysia, Singapore, Indonesia, and the Philippines; the organization was designed to promote economic progress and political stability; it later became a free-trade zone.

Assyrians (uh-SEAR-ee-uhns) Southwest Asian people who built an empire that reached its height during the eighth and seventh centuries B.C.E.; it was known for a powerful army and a well-structured state.

Astrolabe Navigational instrument for determining latitude.

Aten Monotheistic god of Egyptian pharaoh Akhenaten (r. 1353–1335 B.C.E.) and a very early example of monotheism.

Audiencias Spanish courts in Latin America.

Australopithecus (ah-strah-loh-PITH-uh-kuhs) "Southern ape," oldest known ancestor of humans; it lived from around four million down to around one million years ago, and it could walk on hind legs, freeing up hands for use of simple tools.

Austronesians People who as early as 2000 B.C.E. began to explore and settle islands of the Pacific Ocean basin.

Avesta Book that contains the holy writings of Zoroastrianism.

Axum African kingdom centered in Ethiopia that became an early and lasting center of Coptic Christianity.

Aztec empire Central American empire constructed by the Mexica and expanded greatly during the fifteenth century during the reigns of Itzcoatl and Motecuzoma I.

Balfour Declaration British declaration from 1917 that supported the creation of a Jewish homeland in Palestine.

Bantu (BAN-too) African peoples who originally lived in the area of present-day Nigeria; around 2000 B.C.E. they began a centuries-long migration that took them to most of sub-Saharan Africa; the Bantu were very influential, especially linguistically.

Bedouins (BEHD-oh-ihnz) Nomadic Arabic tribespeople.

Benefice Grant from a lord to a vassal, usually consisting of land, which supported the vassal and signified the relationship between the two.

Berlin Conference Meeting organized by German chancellor Otto von Bismarck in 1884–1885 that provided the justification for European colonization of Africa.

Bezant Byzantine gold coin that served as the standard currency of the Mediterranean basin from the sixth through the twelfth century.

Bhagavad Gita (BUH-guh-vahd GEE-tuh) "Song of the Lord," an Indian short poetic work drawn from the lengthy *Mahabharata* that was finished around 400 C.E. and that expressed basic Hindu concepts such as karma and dharma.

Bhakti (BAHK-tee) Indian movement that attempted to transcend the differences between Hinduism and Islam.

Black Hand Pre–World War I secret Serbian society; one of its members, Gavrilo Princip, assassinated Austrian archduke Francis Ferdinand and provided the spark for the outbreak of the Great War.

Blitzkrieg German style of rapid attack through the use of armor and air power that was used in Poland, Norway, Denmark, Belgium, the Netherlands, and France in 1939–1940.

Bodhisattvas (BOH-dih-SAT-vuhs) Buddhist concept regarding individuals who had reached enlightenment but who stayed in this world to help people.

Bolshevik (BOHL-shih-vehk) Russian communist party headed by Lenin.

Bourgeoisie Middle class in modern industrial society.

Brahmins (BRAH-minz) Hindu caste of priests.

Brezhnev Doctrine Policy developed by Leonid Brezhnev (1906–1982) that claimed for the Soviet Union the right to invade any socialist country faced with internal or external enemies; the doc-trine was best expressed in Soviet invasion of Czechoslovakia.

Buddha (BOO-duh) The "enlightened one," the term applied to Siddhartha Gautama after his discoveries that would form the foundation of Buddhism.

Buddhism (BOO-diz'm) Religion, based on Four Noble Truths, associated with Siddhartha Gautama (563–483 B.C.E.), or the Buddha; its adherents desired to eliminate all distracting passion and reach nirvana.

Bunraku (boon-RAH-koo) Japanese puppet theater.

Byzantine Empire (BIHZ-ann-teen) Long-lasting empire centered at Constantinople; it grew out of the end of the Roman empire, carried the legacy of Roman greatness, and was the only classical society to survive into the early modern age; it reached its early peak during the reign of Justinian (483–565).

Caesaropapism Concept relating to the mixing of political and religious authority, as with the Roman emperors, that was central to the church-versus-state controversy in medieval Europe.

Cahokia (kuh-HOH-kee-uh) Large structure in modern Illinois that was constructed by the mound-building peoples; it was the third largest structure in the Americas before the arrival of the Europeans.

Caliph (KAL-ihf) "Deputy," Islamic leader after the death of Muhammad.

Capetian (cah-PEE-shuhn) Early French dynasty that started with Hugh Capet.

Capitalism An economic system with origins in early modern Europe in which private parties make their goods and services available on a free market.

Capitulation Highly unfavorable trading agreements that the Ottoman Turks signed with the Europeans in the nineteenth century that symbolized the decline of the Ottomans.

Carolingians Germanic dynasty that was named after its most famous member, Charlemagne.

Carthage Northern African kingdom, main rival to early Roman expansion, that was defeated by Rome in the Punic Wars.

Çatal Hüyük Important Neolithic settlement in Anatolia (7250–6150 B.C.E.).

Cathars Medieval heretics, also known as the Albigensians, who considered the material world evil; their followers renounced wealth and marriage and promoted an ascetic existence.

Catholic Reformation Sixteenth-century Catholic attempt to cure internal ills and confront Protestantism; it was inspired by the reforms of the Council of Trent and the actions of the Jesuits.

Caudillos (KAW-dee-ohs) Latin American term for nineteenth-century local military leaders.

Central Powers World War I term for the alliance of Germany, Austria-Hungary, and the Ottoman empire.

Chaghatai One of Chinggis Khan's sons, whose descendants ruled central Asia through the Chaghatai khanate.

Chan Buddhism (CHAHN BOO-diz'm) Influential branch of Buddhism in China, with an emphasis on intuition and sudden flashes of insight instead of textual study.

Chanchan (chahn-chahn) Capital of the pre-Incan, South American Chimu society that supported a large population of fifty thousand.

Chavín cult Mysterious but very popular South American religion (1000–300 B.C.E.).

Chimu Pre-Incan South American society that fell to Incas in the fifteenth century.

Chinampas Agricultural gardens used by Mexica (Aztecs) in which fertile muck from lake bottoms was dredged and built up into small plots.

Chivalry European medieval code of conduct for knights based on loyalty and honor.

Chola Southern Indian Hindu kingdom (850–1267), a tightly centralized state that dominated sea trade.

Chucuito Pre-Incan South American society that rose in the twelfth century and fell to the Incas in the fifteenth century.

City-state Urban areas that controlled surrounding agricultural regions and that were often loosely connected in a broader political structure with other city-states.

Cohong Specially licensed Chinese firms that were under strict government regulation.

Collectivization Process beginning in the late 1920s by which Stalin forced the Russian peasants off their own land and onto huge collective farms run by the state; millions died in the process.

COMECON The Council for Mutual Economic Assistance, which offered increased trade within the Soviet Union and eastern Europe; it was the Soviet alternative to the United States' Marshall Plan.

Communalism A term, usually associated with India, that placed an emphasis on religious rather than national identity.

Communism Philosophy and movement that began in middle of the nineteenth century with the work of Karl Marx; it has the same general goals as socialism, but it includes the belief that violent revolution is necessary to destroy the bourgeois world and institute a new world run by and for the proletariat.

Confucianism (kuhn-FYOO-shuhn-iz'm) Philosophy, based on the teachings of the Chinese philosopher Kong Fuzi (551–479 B.C.E.), or Confucius, that emphasizes order, the role of the gentleman, obligation to society, and reciprocity.

Congress of Vienna Gathering of European diplomats in Vienna, Austria, from October 1814 to June 1815. The representatives of the "great powers" that defeated Napoleon—Britain, Austria, Prussia, and Russia—dominated the proceedings, which aimed to restore the prerevolutionary political and social order.

Conquistadores (kohn-KEE-stah-dohr-ayz) Spanish adventurers such as Cortés and Pizarro who conquered Central and South America in the sixteenth century.

Constitutionalism Movement in England in the seventeenth century that placed power in Parliament's hands as part of a constitutional monarchy and that increasingly limited the power of the monarch; the movement was highlighted by the English Civil War and the Glorious Revolution.

Containment Concept associated with the United States and specifically with the Truman Doctrine during the cold war that revolved around the notion that the United States would contain the spread of communism.

Corporation A concept that reached mature form in 1860s in England and France; it involved private business owned by thousands of individual and institutional investors who financed the business through the purchase of stocks.

Corpus iuris civilis (KOR-puhs yoor-uhs sih-VEE-lihs) *Body of the Civil Law,* the Byzantine emperor Justinian's attempt to codify all Roman law.

Criollos (kree-OH-lohs) Creoles, people born in the Americas of Spanish or Portuguese ancestry.

Cross staff Device that sailors used to determine latitude by measuring the angle of the sun or the pole star above the horizon.

Cuneiform Written language of the Sumerians, probably the first written script in the world.

Daimyo (DEYEM-yoh) Powerful territorial lords in early modern Japan.

Dao Key element in Chinese philosophy that means the "way of nature" or the "way of the cosmos."

Daodejing (DOW-DAY-JIHNG) Book that is the fundamental work of Daoism.

Daoism (DOW-i'zm) Chinese philosophy with origins in the Zhou dynasty; it is associated with legendary philosopher Laozi, and it called for a policy of noncompetition.

Dar al-Islam The "house of Islam," a term for the Islamic world.

Declaration of Independence Drafted by Thomas Jefferson in 1776; the document expressed the ideas of John Locke and the Enlightenment, represented the idealism of the American rebels, and influenced other revolutions.

Declaration of the Rights of Man and the Citizen Document from the French Revolution (1789) that was influenced by the American Declaration of Independence and in turn influenced other revolutionary movements.

Decolonization Process by which former colonies achieved their independence, as with the newly emerging African nations in the 1950s and 1960s.

Deism (DEE-iz'm) An Enlightenment view that accepted the existence of a god but denied the supernatural aspects of Christianity; in deism, the universe was an orderly realm maintained by rational and natural laws.

Descamisados "Shirtless ones," Argentine poor who supported Juan and Eva Perón.

Détente A reduction in cold war tension between the United States and the Soviet Union from 1969 to 1975.

Devshirme Ottoman requirement that the Christians in the Balkans provide young boys to be slaves of the sultan.

Dharma (DAHR-muh) Hindu concept of obedience to religious and moral laws and order; also, the basic doctrine of Buddhism.

Dhimmi (dihm-mee) Islamic concept of a protected people that was symbolic of Islamic toleration during the Mughal and Ottoman empires.

Dhow Indian, Persian, and Arab ships, one hundred to four hundred tons, that sailed and traded throughout the Indian Ocean basin.

Diaspora People who have settled far from their original homeland but who still share some measure of ethnic identity.

Dionysus Greek god of wine, also known as Bacchus; Greek plays were performed in his honor.

Dravidians Peoples who produced the brilliant Harappan society in India, 3000–1500 B.C.E.

Dreadnoughts A class of British battleships whose heavy armaments made all other battleships obsolete overnight.

Duma Russian parliament, established after the Revolution of 1905.

Dutch learning European knowledge that reached Tokugawa Japan.

East India Company British joint-stock company that grew to be a state within a state in India; it possessed its own armed forces.

Eight-legged essay Eight-part essays that an aspiring Chinese civil servant had to compose, mainly based on a knowledge of Confucius and the Zhou classics.

Encomienda (ehn-KOH-mee-ehn-dah) System that gave the Spanish settlers *(encomenderos)* the right to compel the indigenous peoples of the Americas to work in the mines or fields.

Engenho Brazilian sugar mill; the term also came to symbolize the entire complex world relating to the production of sugar.

Enlightenment Eighteenth-century philosophical movement that began in France; its emphasis was on the preeminence of reason rather than faith or tradition; it spread concepts from the Scientific Revolution.

Epicureans (ehp-ih-kyoo-REE-uhns) Hellenistic philosophers who taught that pleasure—as in quiet satisfaction—was the greatest good.

Equal-field system Chinese system during the Tang dynasty in which the goal was to ensure an equitable distribution of land.

Essenes Jewish sect that looked for the arrival of a savior; they were similar in some of their core beliefs to the early Christians.

Etruscans (ih-TRUHS-kuhns) Northern Italian society that initially dominated the Romans; the Etruscans helped convey Greek concepts to the expanding Romans.

Eunuchs (YOO-nihks) Castrated males, originally in charge of the harem, who grew to play major roles in government; eunuchs were common in China and other societies.

European Community (EC) Organization of European states established in 1957; it was originally called the European Economic Community and was renamed the EC in 1967; it promoted economic growth and integration as the basis for a politically united Europe.

European Union Established by the Maastricht Treaty in 1993, a supranational organization for even greater European economic and political integration.

Fascism Political ideology and mass movement that was prominent in many parts of Europe between 1919 and 1945; it sought to regenerate the social, political, and cultural life of societies, especially in contrast to liberal democracy and socialism; fascism began with Mussolini in Italy, and it reached its peak with Hitler in Germany.

Five Pillars The foundation of Islam: (1) profession of faith, (2) prayer, (3) fasting during Ramadan, (4) almsgiving, and (5) pilgrimage, or hajj.

Five-year plans First implemented by Stalin in the Soviet Union in 1928; five-year plans were a staple of communist regimes in which every aspect of production was determined in advance for a five-year period; five-year plans were opposite of the free market concept.

Four Noble Truths The foundation of Buddhist thought: (1) life is pain, (2) pain is caused by desire, (3) elimination of desire will bring an end to pain, (4) living a life based on the Noble Eightfold Path will eliminate desire.

Front de Libération Nationale (FLN) The Algerian organization that fought a bloody guerrilla war for freedom against France.

Fulani (foo-LAH-nee) Sub-Saharan African people who, beginning in the seventeenth century, waged a series of wars designed to impose their own strict interpretation of Islam.

Gathas (GATH-uhs) Zoroastrian hymns believed to be compositions by Zarathustra.

Gauchos (GOW-chohz) Argentine cowboys, highly romanticized figures.

General Agreement on Tariffs and Trade (GATT) Free-trade agreement first signed in 1947; by 1994 it had grown to 123 members and formed the World Trade Organization (WTO).

Ghana (GAH-nuh) Kingdom in west Africa during the fifth through the thirteenth century whose rulers eventually converted to Islam; its power and wealth was based on dominating trans-Saharan trade.

Ghazi (GAH-zee) Islamic religious warrior.

Ghaznavids Turkish tribe under Mahmud of Ghazni who moved into northern India in the eleventh century and began a period of greater Islamic influence in India.

Gilgamesh Legendary king of the Mesopotamian city-state of Uruk (ca. 3000 B.C.E.), subject of the *Epic of Gilgamesh,* world's oldest complete epic literary masterpiece.

Glasnost (GLAHS-nohst) Russian term meaning "openness" introduced by Mikhail Gorbachev in 1985 to describe the process of opening Soviet society to dissidents and public criticism.

Globalization The breaking down of traditional boundaries in the face of increasingly global financial and cultural trends.

Global warming The emission of greenhouse gases, which prevents solar heat from escaping the earth's atmosphere and leads to the gradual heating of the earth's environment.

Golden Horde Mongol tribe that controlled Russia from the thirteenth to the fifteenth century.

Greater East Asia Co-Prosperity Sphere Japanese plan for consolidating east and southeast Asia under their control during World War II.

Great Game Nineteenth-century competition between Great Britain and Russia for the control of central Asia.

Great Zimbabwe Large sub-Saharan African kingdom in the fifteenth century.

Greenpeace An environmental organization founded in 1970 and dedicated to the preservation of earth's natural resources.

Guomindang (GWOH-mihn-dahng) Chinese nationalist party founded by Sun Yatsen (1866–1925) and later led by Jiang Jieshi; it has been centered in Taiwan since the end of the Chinese civil war.

Gupta (GOOP-tah) Indian dynasty (320–550 C.E.) that briefly reunited India after the collapse of the earlier Mauryan dynasty.

Hacienda (HAH-see-ehn-dah) Large Latin American estates.

Hagia Sophia (HAH-yah SOH-fee-uh) Massive Christian church constructed by the Byzantine emperor Justinian and later converted into a mosque.

Hajj (HAHJ) Pilgrimage to Mecca.

Hammurabi's Code (hahm-uh-RAH-beez) Sophisticated law code associated with the Babylonian king Hammurabi (r. 1792–1750 B.C.E.).

Harappan (hah-RAP-puhn) Early brilliant Indian society centered in Harappa and Mohenjo-daro.

Harijans "Children of God," Gandhi's term for the Untouchables.

Hebrews Semitic-speaking nomadic tribe influential for monotheistic belief in Yahweh.

Heian (HAY-ahn) Japanese period (794–1185), a brilliant cultural era notable for the world's first novel, Murasaki Shikibu's *The Tale of Genji.*

Hellenistic Era Phase in Greek history (328–146 B.C.E.), from the conquest of Greece by Philip of Macedon until Greece's fall to the Romans; this era was a more cosmopolitan age facilitated by the conquests of Alexander the Great.

Hieroglyphics (heye-ruh-GLIPH-iks) Ancient Egyptian written language.

Hijra Muhammad's migration from Mecca to Medina in 622, which is the beginning point of the Islamic calendar and is considered to mark the beginning of the Islamic faith.

Hinayana (HEE-nah-yah-nuh) Branch of Buddhism known as the "lesser vehicle," also known as Theravada Buddhism; its beliefs include strict, individual path to enlightenment, and it is popular in south and southeast Asia.

Hinduism Main religion of India, a combination of Dravidian and Aryan concepts; Hinduism's goal is to reach spiritual purity and union with the great world spirit; its important concepts include dharma, karma, and samsara.

Holocaust German attempt in World War II to exterminate the Jews of Europe.

Home front Term made popular in World War I and World War II for the civilian "front" that was symbolic of the greater demands of total war.

Hominid (HAWM-ih-nihd) A creature belonging to the family Hominidae, which includes human and humanlike species.

Homo erectus (HOH-MOH ee-REHK-tuhs) "Upright-walking human," which existed from two million to two hundred thousand years ago; *Homo erectus* used cleavers and hand axes and learned how to control fire.

Homo sapiens (HOH-MOH SAY-pee-uhns) "Consciously thinking human," which first appeared around two hundred fifty thousand years ago and used sophisticated tools.

Huitzilopochtli (wee-tsee-loh-pockt-lee) Sun god and patron deity of the Aztecs.

Hundred Days of Reform Chinese reforms of 1898 led by Kang Youwei and Liang Qichao in their desire to turn China into a modern industrial power.

Hyksos (HICK-sohs) Invaders who seized the Nile delta and helped bring an end to the Egyptian Middle Kingdom.

Iconoclasts (eye-KAHN-oh-klasts) Supporters of the movement, begun by the Byzantine Emperor Leo III (r. 717–741), to destroy religious icons because their veneration was considered sinful.

Ilkhanate (EEL-kahn-ate) Mongol state that ruled Persia after abolition of the Abbasid empire in the thirteenth century.

Imperialism Term associated with the expansion of European powers and their conquest and colonization of African and Asian societies, mainly from the sixteenth through the nineteenth century.

Inca empire Powerful South American empire that would reach its peak in the fifteenth century during the reigns of Pachacuti Inca and Topa Inca.

Indentured labor Labor source for plantations; wealthy planters would pay the laboring poor to sell a portion of their working lives, usually seven years, in exchange for passage.

Indo-Europeans Tribal groups from southern Russia who, over a period of millennia, embarked on a series of migrations from India through western Europe; their greatest legacy was the broad distribution of Indo-European languages throughout Eurasia.

Indra Early Indian god associated with the Aryans; Indra was the king of the gods and was associated with warfare and thunderbolts.

Intifada Palestinian mass movement against Israeli rule in the Gaza Strip and other occupied territories.

Investiture (ihn-VEHST-tih-tyoor) One aspect of the medieval European church-versus-state controversy, the granting of church offices by a lay leader.

Iroquois (EAR-uh-kwoi) Eastern American Indian confederation made up of the Mohawk, Oneida, Onondaga, Cayuga, and Seneca tribes.

Islam Monotheistic religion announced by the prophet Muhammad (570–632); influenced by Judaism and Christianity, Muhammad was considered the final prophet because the earlier religions had not seen the entire picture; the Quran is the holy book of Islam.

Jainism (JEYEN-iz'm) Indian religion associated with the teacher Vardhamana Mahavira (ca. 540–468 B.C.E.) in which every physical object possessed a soul; Jains believe in complete nonviolence to all living beings.

Jati Indian word for a Hindu subcaste.

Jizya (JIHZ-yuh) Tax in Islamic empires that was imposed on non-Muslims.

Joint-stock companies Early forerunner of the modern corporation; individuals who invested in a trading or exploring venture could make huge profits while limiting their risk.

Ka'ba (KAH-buh) Main shrine in Mecca, goal of Muslims embarking on the hajj.

Kabuki (kah-BOO-kee) Japanese theater in which actors were free to improvise and embellish the words.

Kama Hindu concept of the enjoyment of physical and sexual pleasure.

Kamikaze (KAH-mih-kah-zee) A Japanese term meaning "divine wind" that is related to the storms that destroyed Mongol invasion fleets; the term is symbolic of Japanese isolation and was later taken by suicide pilots in World War II.

Kanun (KAH-noon) Laws issued by the Ottoman Süleyman the Magnificent, also known as Süleyman Kanuni, "the Lawgiver."

Kapu Hawaiian concept of something being taboo.

Karma (KAHR-mah) Hindu concept that the sum of good and bad in a person's life will determine his or her status in the next life.

Khoikhoi South African people referred to pejoratively as the Hottentots by Europeans.

Kongo Central African state that began trading with the Portuguese around 1500; although their kings, such as King Affonso I (r. 1506–1543), converted to Christianity, they nevertheless suffered from the slave trade.

Koumbi-Saleh Important trading city along the trans-Saharan trade route from the eleventh to the thirteenth century.

Kshatriayas (KSHAHT-ree-uhs) Hindu caste of warriors and aristocrats.

Kulaks Land-owning Russian peasants who benefited under Lenin's New Economic Policy and suffered under Stalin's forced collectivization.

Kush Nubian African kingdom that conquered and controlled Egypt from 750 to 664 B.C.E.

Lamaist Buddhism (LAH-muh-ihst BOO-diz'm) Branch of Buddhism that was similar to shamanism in its acceptance of magic and supernatural powers.

La Reforma Political reform movement of Mexican president Benito Juárez (1806–1872) that called for limiting the power of the military and the Catholic church in Mexican society.

Latifundia (LAT-ih-FOON-dee-uh) Huge state-run and slave-worked farms in ancient Rome.

League of Nations Forerunner of the United Nations, the dream of American president Woodrow Wilson, although its potential was severely limited by the refusal of the United States to join.

Lebensraum (LAY-behnz-rowm) German term meaning "living space"; the term is associated with Hitler and his goal of carving out territory in the east for an expanding Germany.

Legalism Chinese philosophy from the Zhou dynasty that called for harsh suppression of the common people.

Levée en masse (leh-VAY on MASS) A term signifying universal conscription during the radical phase of the French revolution.

Lex talionis (lehks tah-lee-oh-nihs) "Law of retaliation," laws in which offenders suffered punishments similar to their crimes; the most famous example is Hammurabi's Laws.

Li (LEE) Confucian concept, a sense of propriety.

Linear A Minoan written script.

Linear B Early Mycenaean written script, adapted from the Minoan Linear A.

Luddites Early-nineteenth-century artisans who were opposed to new machinery and industrialization.

Machismo (mah-CHEEZ-moh) Latin American social ethic that honored male strength, courage, aggressiveness, assertiveness, and cunning.

Madrasas (MAH-drahs-uhs) Islamic institutions of higher education that originated in the tenth century.

Magyars (MAH-jahrs) Hungarian invaders who raided towns in Germany, Italy, and France in the ninth and tenth centuries.

Mahabharata (mah-hah-BAH-rah-tah) Massive ancient Indian epic that was developed orally for centuries; it tells of an epic civil war between two family branches.

Mahayana (mah-huh-YAH-nah) The "greater vehicle," a more metaphysical and more popular northern branch of Buddhism.

Majapahit (MAH-ja-PAHT) Southeast Asian kingdom (1293–1520) centered on the island of Java.

Mali (MAH-lee) West African kingdom founded in the thirteenth century by Sundiata; it reached its peak during the reign of Mansa Musa.

Manchus Manchurians who conquered China, putting an end to the Ming dynasty and founding the Qing dynasty (1644–1911).

Mandate of Heaven Chinese belief that the emperors ruled through the mandate, or approval, of heaven contingent on their ability to look after the welfare of the population.

Mandate system System that developed in the wake of World War I when the former colonies ended up mandates under European control, a thinly veiled attempt at continuing imperialism.

Manichaeism (man-ih-KEE-iz'm) Religion founded by the prophet Mani in the third century C.E., a syncretic version of Zoroastrian, Christian, and Buddhist elements.

Manor Large estates of the nobles during the European middle ages, home for the majority of the peasants.

Maori (mow-ree) Indigenous people of New Zealand.

Marae Polynesian temple structure.

Marathon Battlefield scene of the Athenian victory over the Persians in 490 B.C.E.

Maroons Runaway African slaves.

Marshall Plan U.S. plan, officially called the European Recovery Program, that offered financial and other economic aid to all European states that had suffered from World War II, including Soviet bloc states.

Mauryan empire Indian dynasty (321–185 B.C.E.) founded by Chandragupta Maurya and reaching its peak under Ashoka.

Maya (Mye-uh) Brilliant Central American society (300–1100) known for math, astronomy, and a sophisticated written language.

May Fourth Movement Chinese movement that began 4 May 1919 with a desire to eliminate imperialist influences and promote national unity.

Medes (meeds) Indo-European branch that settled in northern Persia and eventually fell to another branch, the Persians, in the sixth century B.C.E.

Meiji Restoration (MAY-jee) Restoration of imperial rule under Emperor Meiji in 1868 by a coalition led by Fukuzawa Yukichi and Ito Hirobumi; the restoration enacted western reforms to strengthen Japan.

Melaka (may-LAH-kah) Southeast Asian kingdom that was predominantly Islamic.

Mesopotamia Term meaning "between the rivers," in this case the Tigris and Euphrates; Sumer and Akkad are two of the earliest societies.

Mestizo (mehs-TEE-zoh) Latin American term for children of Spanish and native parentage.

Métis (may-TEE) Canadian term for individuals of mixed European and indigenous ancestry.

Millet An autonomous, self-governing community in the Ottoman empire.

Ming Chinese dynasty (1368–1644) founded by Hongwu and known for its cultural brilliance.

Minoan (mih-NOH-uhn) Society located on the island of Crete (ca. 2000–1100 B.C.E.) that influenced the early Mycenaeans.

Missi dominici (mihs-see doh-mee-nee-chee) "Envoys of the lord ruler," the noble and church emissaries sent out by Charlemagne.

Mithraism (MITH-rah-iz'm) Mystery religion based on worship of the sun god Mithras; it became popular among the Romans because of its promise of salvation.

Mochica (moh-CHEE-kuh) Pre-Incan South American society (300–700) known for their brilliant ceramics.

Moksha Hindu concept of the salvation of the soul.

Monotheism (MAW-noh-thee-iz'm) Belief in only one god, a rare concept in the ancient world.

Monroe Doctrine American doctrine issued in 1823 during the presidency of James Monroe that warned Europeans to keep their hands off Latin America and that expressed growing American imperialistic views regarding Latin America.

Mughals (MOO-guhls) Islamic dynasty that ruled India from the sixteenth through the eighteenth century; the construction of the Taj Mahal is representative of their splendor; with the exception of the enlightened reign of Akbar, the increasing conflict between Hindus and Muslims was another of their legacies.

Muhammad (muh-HAH-mehd) Prophet of Islam (570–632).

Muslim A follower of Islam.

Mycenaean (meye-seh-NEE-uhn) Early Greek society on the Peloponnese (1600–1100 B.C.E.) that was influenced by the Minoans; the Mycenaeans' conflict with Troy is immortalized in Homer's *Odyssey*.

Nara era Japanese period (710–794), centered on the city of Nara, that was the highest point of Chinese influence.

National Policy Nineteenth-century Canadian policy designed to attract migrants, protect industries through tariffs, and build national transportation systems.

NATO The North Atlantic Treaty Organization, which was established by the United States in 1949 as a regional military alliance against Soviet expansionism.

Ndongo (n'DAWN-goh) Angolan kingdom that reached its peak during the reign of Queen Nzinga (r. 1623–1663).

Neandertal (nee-ANN-duhr-tawl) Early humans (100,000 to 35,000 years ago) who were prevalent during the Paleolithic period.

Negritude (NEH-grih-tood) "Blackness," a term coined by early African nationalists as a means of celebrating the heritage of black peoples around the world.

Neo-Confucianism (nee-oh-kuhn-FYOO-shuhn-iz'm) Philosophy that attempted to merge certain basic elements of Confucian and Buddhist thought; most important of the early Neo-Confucianists was the Chinese thinker Zhu Xi (1130–1200).

Neolithic New Stone Age (10,000–4000 B.C.E.), which was marked by the discovery and mastery of agriculture.

Nestorian (neh-STOHR-ee-uhn) Early branch of Christianity, named after the fifth-century Greek theologian Nestorius, that emphasized the human nature of Jesus Christ.

New Economic Policy (NEP) Plan implemented by Lenin that called for minor free-market reforms.

Nirvana (nuhr-VAH-nuh) Buddhist concept of a state of spiritual perfection and enlightenment in which distracting passions are eliminated.

Noble Eightfold Path Final truth of the Buddhist Four Noble Truths that called for leading a life of balance and constant contemplation.

North American Free Trade Agreement (NAFTA) Regional accord established in 1993 between the United States, Canada, and Mexico; it formed world's second largest free-trade zone.

Nubia (NOO-bee-uh) Area south of Egypt; the kingdom of Kush in Nubia invaded and dominated Egypt from 750 to 664 B.C.E.

Oceania Term referring to the Pacific Ocean basin and its lands.

Olmecs Early Mesoamerican society (1200–100 B.C.E.) that centered on sites at San Lorenzo, La Venta, and Tres Zapotes and that influenced later Maya.

Oracle bones Chinese Shang dynasty (1766–1122 B.C.E.) means of foretelling the future.

Organization of African Unity (OAU) An organization started in 1963 by thirty-two newly independent African states and designed to prevent conflict that would lead to intervention by former colonial powers.

Organization of Petroleum Exporting Countries (OPEC) An organization begun in 1960 by oil-producing states originally for purely economic reasons but that later had more political influence.

Osiris Ancient Egyptian god that represented the forces of nature.

Ottoman empire Powerful Turkish empire that lasted from the conquest of Constantinople (Istanbul) in 1453 until 1918 and reached its peak during the reign of Süleyman the Magnificent (r. 1520–1566).

Paleolithic Old Stone Age, a long period of human development before the development of agriculture.

Palestinian Liberation Organization (PLO) Organization created in 1964 under the leadership of Yasser Arafat to champion Palestinian rights.

Paris Peace Accords Agreement reached in 1973 that marked the end of the United States' role in the Vietnam War.

Parsis (pahr-SEES) Indian Zoroastrians.

Parthians Persian dynasty (247 B.C.E.–224 C.E.) that reached its peak under Mithradates I.

Pater familias (PAH-tur fuh-MEE-lee-ahs) Roman term for the "father of the family," a theoretical implication that gave the male head of the family almost unlimited authority.

Patriarch (PAY-tree-ahrk) Leader of the Greek Orthodox church, which in 1054 officially split with the Pope and the Roman Catholic church.

Patricians Roman aristocrats and wealthy classes.

Pax Romana (pahks roh-MAH-nah) "Roman Peace," a term that relates to the period of political stability, cultural brilliance, and economic prosperity beginning with unification under Augustus and lasting through the first two centuries C.E.

Peninsulares (pehn-IHN-soo-LAH-rayz) Latin American officials from Spain or Portugal.

Perestroika (PAYR-eh-stroy-kuh) "Restructuring," a Russian term associated with Gorbachev's effort to reorganize the Soviet state.

Pharaohs (FARE-ohs) Egyptian kings considered to be gods on earth.

Plebians (plih-BEE-uhns) Roman common people.

Polis (POH-lihs) Greek term for the city-state.

Popol Vuh (paw-pawl vuh) Mayan creation epic.

Prehistory The period before the invention of writing.

Proletariat Urban working class in a modern industrial society.

Protestant Reformation Sixteenth-century European movement during which Luther, Calvin, Zwingli, and others broke away from the Catholic church.

Ptolemaic (TAWL-oh-may-ihk) Term used to signify both the Egyptian kingdom

founded by Alexander the Great's general Ptolemy and the thought of the philosopher Ptolemy of Alexandria (second century C.E.), who used mathematical formulas in an attempt to prove Aristotle's geocentric theory of the universe.

Putting-out system Method of getting around guild control by delivering unfinished materials to rural households for completion.

Qadi Islamic judge.

Qanat (kah-NAHT) Persian underground canal.

Qi (chee) Chinese concept of the basic material that makes up the body and the universe.

Qin (chihn) Chinese dynasty (221–207 B.C.E.) that was founded by Qin Shihuangdi and was marked by the first unification of China and the early construction of defensive walls.

Qing (chihng) Chinese dynasty (1644–1911) that reached its peak during the reigns of Kangxi and Qianlong.

Qizilbash (gih-ZIHL-bahsh) Term meaning "red heads," Turkish tribes that were important allies of Shah Ismail in the formation of the Safavid empire.

Quetzalcoatl (keht-zahl-koh-AHT'l) Aztec god, the "feathered serpent," who was borrowed originally from the Toltecs; Quetzalcoatl was believed to have been defeated by another god and exiled, and he promised to return.

Quinto (KEEN-toh) The one-fifth of Mexican and Peruvian silver production that was reserved for the Spanish monarchy.

Quipu (KEE-poo) Incan mnemonic aid comprised of different-colored strings and knots that served to record events in the absence of a written text.

Quran (koo-RAHN) Islamic holy book that is believed to contain the divine revelations of Allah as presented to Muhammad.

Ramayana (rah-mah-yah-nah) Ancient Indian masterpiece about the hero Rama that symbolized the victory of *dharma* (order) over *adharma* (chaos).

Rape of Nanjing Japanese conquest and destruction of the Chinese city of Nanjing in the 1930s.

Realpolitik (ray-AHL-poh-lih-teek) The Prussian Otto von Bismarck's "politics of reality," the belief that only the willingness to use force would actually bring about change.

Reconquista (ray-kohn-KEE-stah) Crusade, ending in 1492, to drive the Islamic forces out of Spain.

Reconstruction System implemented in the American South (1867–1877) that was designed to bring the Confederate states back into the union and also extend civil rights to freed slaves.

Romanov (ROH-mah-nahv) Russian dynasty (1610–1917) founded by Mikhail Romanov and ending with Nicholas II.

Rubaiyat (ROO-bee-aht) "Quatrains," famous poetry of Omar Khayyam that was later translated by Edward Fitzgerald.

Safavid (SAH-fah-vihd) Later Persian empire (1501–1722) that was founded by Shah Ismail and that became a center for Shiism; the empire reached its peak under Shah Abbas the Great and was centered on the capital of Isfahan.

Sakk Letters of credit that were common in the medieval Islamic banking world.

Saljuqs (sahl-JYOOKS) Turkish tribe that gained control over the Abbasid empire and fought with the Byzantine empire.

Samsara (sahm-SAH-ruh) Hindu term for the concept of transmigration, that is, the soul passing into a new incarnation.

Samurai (SAM-uhr-eye) A Japanese warrior.

Sasanids (suh-SAH-nids) Later powerful Persian dynasty (224–651) that would reach its peak under Shapur I and later fall to Arabic expansion.

Sati (SUH-TEE) Also known as *suttee,* Indian practice of a widow throwing herself on the funeral pyre of her husband.

Satraps (SAY-traps) Persian administrators, usually members of the royal family, who governed a satrapy.

Satyagraha (SAH-tyah-GRAH-hah) "Truth and firmness," a term associated with Gandhi's policy of passive resistance.

Scholasticism Medieval attempt of thinkers such as St. Thomas Aquinas to merge the beliefs of Christianity with the logical rigor of Greek philosophy.

Scientific racism Nineteenth-century attempt to justify racism by scientific means; an example would be Gobineau's *Essay on the Inequality of the Human Races.*

Seleucids (sih-LOO-sihds) Persian empire (323–83 B.C.E.) founded by Seleucus after the death of Alexander the Great.

Self-determination Belief popular in World War I and after that every people should have the right to determine their own political destiny; the belief was often cited but ignored by the Great Powers.

Self-Strengthening Movement Chinese attempt (1860–1895) to blend Chinese cultural traditions with European industrial technology.

Semitic (suh-miht-ihk) A term that relates to the Semites, ancient nomadic herders who spoke Semitic languages; examples of Semites were the Akkadians, Hebrews, Aramaics, and Phoenicians, who often interacted with the more settled societies of Mesopotamia and Egypt.

Sepoys Indian troops who served the British.

Serfs Peasants who, though not chattel slaves, were tied to the land and who owed obligation to the lords on whose land they worked.

Shamanism (SHAH-mah-niz'm) Belief in shamans or religious specialists who possessed supernatural powers and who communicated with the gods and the spirits of nature.

Shari'a (shah-REE-ah) The Islamic holy law, drawn up by theologians from the Quran and accounts of Muhammad's life.

Shia (SHEE-ah) Islamic minority in opposition to the Sunni majority; their belief is that leadership should reside in the line descended from Ali.

Shintoism (SHIHN-toh-iz'm) Indigenous Japanese religion that emphasizes purity, clan loyalty, and the divinity of the emperor.

Shiva (SHEE-vuh) Hindu god associated with both fertility and destruction.

Shogun (SHOH-gun) Japanese military leader who ruled in place of the emperor.

Shudras (SHOO-druhs) Hindu caste of landless peasants and serfs.

Siddhartha Gautama (sih-DHAR-tuh GOW-tau-mah) Indian *kshatriya* who achieved enlightenment and became known as the Buddha, the founder of Buddhism.

Sikhs (SIHKS) Adherents of an Indian syncretic faith that contains elements of Hinduism and Islam.

Silk roads Ancient trade routes that extended from the Mediterranean in the west to China in the east.

Social Darwinism Nineteenth-century philosophy, championed by thinkers such as Herbert Spencer, that attempted to apply Darwinian "survival of the fittest" to the social and political realm; adherents saw the elimination of weaker nations as part of a natural process and used the philosophy to justify war.

Socialism Political and economic theory of social organization based on the collective ownership of the means of production; its origins were in the early nineteenth century, and it differs from communism by a desire for slow or moderate change compared with the communist call for revolution.

Solidarity Polish trade union and nationalist movement in the 1980s that was headed by Lech Walesa.

Song (SOHNG) Chinese dynasty (960–1279) that was marked by an increasingly urbanized and cosmopolitan society.

Soviets Russian elected councils that originated as strike committees during the 1905 St. Petersburg disorders; they represented a form of local self-government that went on to become the primary unit of government in the Union of Soviet Socialist Republics. The term was also used during the cold war to designate the Soviet Union.

Spanish Inquisition Institution organized in 1478 by Fernando and Isabel of Spain to detect heresy and the secret practice of Judaism or Islam.

Srivijaya (sree-VIH-juh-yuh) Southeast Asian kingdom (670–1025), based on the island of Sumatra, that used a powerful navy to dominate trade.

Stateless societies Term relating to societies such as those of sub-Saharan Africa after the Bantu migrations that featured decentralized rule through family and kinship groups instead of strongly centralized hierarchies.

Stoics (STOH-ihks) Hellenistic philosophers who encouraged their followers to lead active, virtuous lives and to aid others.

Strabo (STRAH-boh) Greek geographer (first century C.E.).

Strategic Arms Limitations Talk (SALT) Agreement in 1972 between the United States and the Soviet Union.

Stupas (STOO-pahs) Buddhist shrines.

Sufis (SOO-fees) Islamic mystics who placed more emphasis on emotion and devotion than on strict adherence to rules.

Sui (SWAY) Chinese dynasty (589–618) that constructed the Grand Canal, reunified China, and allowed for the splendor of the Tang dynasty that followed.

Süleyman (SOO-lee-mahn) Ottoman Turkish ruler Süleyman the Magnificent (r. 1520–1566), who was the most powerful and wealthy ruler of the sixteenth century.

Sumerians (soo-MEHR-ee-uhns) Earliest Mesopotamian society.

Sundiata (soon-JAH-tuh) Founder of the Mali empire (r. 1230–1255), also the inspiration for the *Sundiata,* an African literary and mythological work.

Sunni (SOON-nee) "Traditionalists," the most popular branch of Islam; Sunnis believe in the legitimacy of the early caliphs, compared with the Shiite belief that only a descendant of Ali can lead.

Suu Kyi, Aung San (SOO KEY, AWNG SAHN) Opposition leader (1945–) in Myanmar; she was elected leader in 1990 but she was not allowed to come to power; she was a Nobel Peace Prize recipient in 1991.

Swahili (swah-HEE-lee) East African city-state society that dominated the coast from Mogadishu to Kilwa and was active in trade.

Taino (TEYE-noh) A Caribbean tribe who were the first indigenous peoples from the Americas to come into contact with Christopher Columbus.

Taiping rebellion (TEYE-pihng) Rebellion (1850–1864) in Qing China led by Hong Xiuquan, during which twenty to thirty million were killed; the rebellion was symbolic of the decline of China during the nineteenth century.

Taliban Strict Islamic organization that ruled Afghanistan from 1996 to 2002.

Tang Taizong (TAHNG TEYE-zohng) Chinese emperor (r. 627–649) of the Tang dynasty (618–907).

Tanzimat "Reorganization" era (1839–1876), an attempt to reorganize the Ottoman empire on Enlightenment and constitutional forms.

Temüjin (TEM-oo-chin) Mongol conqueror (ca. 1167–1227) who later took the name Chinggis Khan, "universal ruler."

Tenochtitlan (the-NOCH-tee-tlahn) Capital of the Aztec empire, later Mexico City.

Teotihuacan (tay-uh-tee-wah-KAHN) Central American society (200 B.C.E.– 750 C.E.); its Pyramid of the Sun was the largest structure in Mesoamerica.

Teutonic Knights Crusading European order that was active in the Baltic region.

Third Rome Concept that a new power would rise up to carry the legacy of Roman greatness after the decline of the Second Rome, Constantinople; Moscow was referred to as the Third Rome during the fifteenth century.

Three Principles of the People Philosophy of Chinese Guomindang leader Sun Yatsen (1866–1925) that emphasized nationalism, democracy, and people's livelihood.

Tian (TEE-ehn) Chinese term for heaven.

Tikal (tee-KAHL) Maya political center from the fourth through the ninth century.

Timur-i lang (tee-MOOR-yee LAHNG) "Timur the Lame," known in English as Tamerlane (ca. 1336–1405), who conquered an empire ranging from the Black Sea to Samarkand.

Tokugawa (TOH-koo-GAH-wah) Last shogunate in Japanese history (1600–1867); it was founded by Tokugawa Ieyasu who was notable for unifying Japan.

Toltecs Central American society (950–1150) that was centered on the city of Tula.

Trail of Tears Forced relocation of the Cherokee from the eastern woodlands to Oklahoma (1837–1838); it was symbolic of U.S. expansion and destruction of indigenous Indian societies.

Triangular trade Trade between Europe, Africa, and the Americas that featured finished products from Europe, slaves from Africa, and American products bound for Europe.

Triple Alliance Pre–World War I alliance of Germany, Austria-Hungary, and Italy.

Triple Entente (ahn-TAHNT) Pre–World War I alliance of England, France, and Russia.

Truman Doctrine U.S. policy instituted in 1947 by President Harry Truman in which the United States would follow an interventionist foreign policy to contain communism.

Tsar (ZAHR) Old Russian term for king that is derived from the term *caesar.*

Twelver Shiism (SHEE'i'zm) Branch of Islam that stressed that there were twelve perfect religious leaders after Muhammad and that the twelfth went into hiding and would return someday; Shah Ismail spread this variety through the Safavid empire.

Uighurs (WEE-goors) Turkish tribe.

Ukiyo Japanese word for the "floating worlds," a Buddhist term for the insignificance of the world that came to

represent the urban centers in Tokugawa Japan.

Ulaanbaatar (OO-lahn-bah-tahr) Mongolian city.

Ulama Islamic officials, scholars who shaped public policy in accordance with the Quran and the *sharia.*

Umayyad (oo-MEYE-ahd) Arabic dynasty (661–750), with its capital at Damascus, that was marked by a tremendous period of expansion to Spain in the west and India in the east.

Umma (UM-mah) Islamic term for the "community of the faithful."

United Nations (UN) Successor to the League of Nations, an association of sovereign nations that attempts to find solutions to global problems.

Upanishads (oo-PAHN-ee-shahds) Indian reflections and dialogues (800–400 B.C.E.) that reflected basic Hindu concepts.

Urdu (OOR-doo) A language that is predominant in Pakistan.

Uruk (OO-rook) Ancient Mesopotamian city from the fourth millennium B.C.E. that was allegedly the home of the fabled Gilgamesh.

Vaishyas (VEYES-yuhs) Hindu caste of cultivators, artisans, and merchants.

Vaqueros (vah-KEHR-ohs) Latin American cowboys, similar to the Argentine gaucho.

Varna (VAHR-nuh) Hindu word for caste.

Varuna (vuh-ROO-nuh) Early Aryan god who watched over the behavior of mortals and preserved the cosmic order.

Vedas (VAY-duhs) "Wisdom," early collections of prayers and hymns that provide information about the Indo-European Aryans who migrated into India around 1500 B.C.E.; *Rig Veda* is the most important collection.

Velvet revolution A term that describes the nonviolent transfer of power in Czechoslovakia during the collapse of Soviet rule.

Venta, La (VEHN-tuh, lah) Early Olmec center (800–400 B.C.E.).

Venus figurines Small Paleolithic statues of women with exaggerated sexual features.

Vernacular (ver-NA-kyoo-lar) The language of the people; Martin Luther translated the Bible from the Latin of the Catholic church into the vernacular German.

Versailles (vehr-SEYE) Palace of French King Louis XIV.

Viet Minh North Vietnamese nationalist communists under Ho Chi Minh.

Vietnamization President Richard Nixon's strategy of turning the Vietnam War over to the South Vietnamese.

Vijayanagar (vee-juh-yah-NAH-gahr) Southern Indian kingdom (1336–1565) that later fell to the Mughals.

Vikings A group that raided the British Isles from their home at Vik in southern Norway.

Vishnu (VIHSH-noo) Hindu god, preserver of the world, who was often incarnated as Krishna.

Vodou (voh-DOW) Syncretic religion practiced by African slaves in Haiti.

Volksgeist (FOHLKS-geyest) "People's spirit," a term that was coined by the German philosopher Herder; a nation's volksgeist would not come to maturity unless people studied their own unique culture and traditions.

Volta do mar (VOHL-tah doh MAHR) "Return through the sea," a fifteenth-century Portuguese sea route that took advantage of the prevailing winds and currents.

Voltaire (vohl-TAIR) Pen name of French philosophe François-Marie Arouet (1694–1778), author of *Candide*.

Waldensians Twelfth-century religious reformers who criticized the Roman Catholic church and who proposed that the laity had the right to preach and administer sacraments; they were declared heretics.

Walesa, Lech (WAH-lehn-sah, LEHK) Leader of the Polish Solidarity movement.

Wanli (wahn-LEE) Chinese Ming emperor (r. 1572–1620) whose refusal to meet with officials hurried the decline of the Ming dynasty.

War Communism The Bolshevik policy of nationalizing industry and seizing private land during the civil war.

Warsaw Pact Warsaw Treaty Organization, a military alliance formed by Soviet bloc nations in 1955 in response to rearmament of West Germany and its inclusion in NATO.

Wind wheels Prevailing wind patterns in the Atlantic and Pacific Oceans north and south of the equator; their discovery made sailing much safer and quicker.

Witte, Sergei (VIHT-tee, SAYR-gay) Late-nineteenth-century Russian minister of finance who pushed for industrialization.

World Health Organization (WHO) United Nations organization designed to deal with global health issues.

World Trade Organization (WTO) An organization that was established in 1995 with more than 120 nations and whose goal is to loosen barriers to free trade.

Wuwei (woo-WAY) Daoist concept of a disengagement from the affairs of the world.

Xia (shyah) Early Chinese dynasty (2200–1766 B.C.E.).

Xianyang (SHYAHN-YAHNG) Capital city of the Qin empire.

Xiao (SHAYOH) Confucian concept of respect for one's parents and ancestors.

Xinjiang (shin-jyahng) Western Chinese province.

Xuanzang (SHWEN-ZAHNG) Seventh-century Chinese monk who made a famous trip to India to collect Buddhist texts.

Yahweh (YAH-way) God of the monotheistic religion of Judaism that influenced later Christianity and Islam.

Yangshao (YAHNG-show) Early Chinese society (2500–2200 B.C.E.).

Yangzi (YAHNG-zuh) River in central China.

Yongle (YAWNG-leh) Chinese Ming emperor (r. 1403–1424) who pushed for foreign exploration and promoted cultural achievements such as the *Yongle Encyclopedia*.

Young Turks Nineteenth-century Turkish reformers who pushed for changes within the Ottoman empire, such as universal suffrage and freedom of religion.

Yu (yoo) Legendary founder of the Xia dynasty (ca. 2200 B.C.E.).

Yuan (yoo-AHN) Chinese dynasty (1279–1368) that was founded by the Mongol ruler Khubilai Khan.

Yucatan (yoo-kuh-TAN) Peninsula in Central America, home of the Maya.

Yurts (yuhrts) Tents used by nomadic Turkish and Mongol tribes.

Zaibatsu (zeye-BAHT-soo) Japanese term for "wealthy cliques," which are similar to American trusts and cartels but usually organized around one family.

Zambos (ZAHM-bohs) Latin American term for individuals born of indigenous and African parents.

Zamudio, Adela (ZAH-moo-dee-oh, ah-DEH-lah) Nineteenth-century Bolivian poet, author of "To Be Born a Man."

Zarathustra (zar-uh-THOO-struh) Persian prophet (ca. sixth century B.C.E.) who founded Zoroastrianism.

Zemstvos (ZEHMST-voh) District assemblies elected by Russians in the nineteenth century.

Zen Buddhism Japanese version of Chinese Chan Buddhism, with an emphasis on intuition and sudden flashes of insight instead of textual study.

Zhou (JOH) Chinese dynasty (1122–256 B.C.E.) that was the foundation of Chinese thought formed during this period: Confucianism, Daoism, Zhou Classics.

Zhu Xi (ZHOO-SHEE) Neo-Confucian Chinese philosopher (1130–1200).

Ziggurats (ZIG-uh-rahts) Mesopotamian temples.

Zimbabwe (zihm-BAHB-way) Former colony of Southern Rhodesia that gained independence in 1980.

Zoroastrianism (zohr-oh-ASS-tree-ahn-iz'm) Persian religion based on the teaching of the sixth-century-B.C.E. prophet Zarathustra; its emphasis on the duality of good and evil and on the role of individuals in determining their own fate would influence later religions.